Social Inequality

Patterns and Processes

Sixth Edition

Martin N. Marger

Mc
Graw
Hill

Connect
Learn
Succeed™

*The **McGraw·Hill** Companies*

Connect
Learn
Succeed™

SOCIAL INEQUALITY: PATTERNS AND PROCESSES, SIXTH EDITION

Published by McGraw-Hill, a business unit of The McGraw-Hill Companies, Inc., 1221 Avenue of the Americas, New York, NY 10020. Copyright © 2014 by Martin N. Marger. All rights reserved. Printed in the United States of America. Previous editions © 2011, 2008, 2005, and 2002. No part of this publication may be reproduced or distributed in any form or by any means, or stored in a database or retrieval system, without the prior written consent of The McGraw-Hill Companies, Inc., including, but not limited to, in any network or other electronic storage or transmission, or broadcast for distance learning.

Some ancillaries, including electronic and print components, may not be available to customers outside the United States.

This book is printed on acid-free paper

5 6 7 8 9 0 CD/CD 25 24 23 22 21 20

ISBN 978-0-07-802693-5
MHID 0-07-8026938

Senior Vice President, Products & Markets: *Kurt L. Strand*
Vice President, General Manager, Products & Markets: *Michael Ryan*
Vice President, Content Production & Technology Services: *Kimberly Meriwether David*
Executive Director of Development: *Lisa Pinto*
Managing Director: *Gina Boedeker*
Brand Manager: *Courtney Austermehle*
Marketing Specialist: *Alexandra Schultz*
Managing Development Editor: *Sara Jaeger*
Editorial Coordinator: *Adina Lonn*
Director, Content Production: *Terri Schiesl*
Buyer: *Nichole Birkenholz*
Project Manager: *Judi David*
Media Project Manager: *Sridevi Palani*
Cover Designer: *Studio Montage, St. Louis, MO.*
Cover Image: *John Foxx/Getty Images*
Typeface: *10/12 Palatino*
Compositor: *Aptara®, Inc.*
Printer: *R.R. Donnelly*

All credits appearing on page or at the end of the book are considered to be an extension of the copyright page.

Library of Congress Cataloging-in-Publication Data

Marger, Martin.
    Social inequality : patterns and processes / Martin N. Marger, Michigan State University.
    — Sixth edition.
        pages cm
    Includes bibliographical references and index.
    ISBN-13: 978-0-07-802693-5 (alk. paper)
    ISBN-10: 0-07-802693-8 (alk. paper)
    1. Equality. 2. Social classes. 3. Social structure. 4. Marginality, Social. I. Title.
HM821.M37 2013
305—dc23   2012051477

The Internet addresses listed in the text were accurate at the time of publication. The inclusion of a website does not indicate an endorsement by the authors or McGraw-Hill, and McGraw-Hill does not guarantee the accuracy of the information presented at these sites.

www.mhhe.com

 Contents

Chapter 9:   Public Policy and the Class System   255

 # Preface

The pervasive and seemingly inevitable condition of social inequality has been observed and commented upon repeatedly by philosophers, historians, and, in recent decades, social scientists. In the early years of the twenty-first century, inequality within and between societies remains ubiquitous and starkly apparent. Nothing on the horizon, furthermore, portends a serious reduction in—let alone an end to—this inexorable state, either in the developing world or in the postindustrial world. In the latter, despite the creation of affluence about which earlier generations could only fantasize, the maldistribution of wealth between the haves and the have-nots is as severe and steadfast as it was in any previous era. The level of inequality in American society has become especially evident. There, sociologists and economists point to the almost unprecedented gap between rich and poor, a veritable chasm that continues to expand at an alarming rate. Meanwhile, the middle classes find themselves struggling merely to maintain their tenuous status from year to year.

This book is intended to serve as an introduction to the patterns and processes of social inequality in its major forms—class, racial/ethnic, gender, political—in the United States and other contemporary societies. Its objective is also to help the reader develop an awareness of how inequality impinges on virtually all facets of individual and group life. It is designed primarily for an undergraduate student audience and assumes little prior exposure to the social sciences. A more general readership also may find its contents informative and enlightening.

Inequality, in its sundry forms, has long been a staple of sociological inquiry but has held an important place in other social science disciplines as well. In recent years its prominent status among the traditional concerns of social scientists has been raised higher. In the United States, issues of *economic* inequality not only have been standard points of sociological discourse but have become an increasingly salient element of political debate. *Racial/ethnic* inequality has always served as a focal point of American sociology, but it has grown even more compelling with the emergence of several ongoing societal trends: a persistent economic gap between Euro-American groups and racial/ethnic minorities, a public dialogue that has arisen in response to efforts to deal with that gap, and the influx of new immigrants, who have created a more pluralistic ethnic mélange. *Gender* issues are a fundamental component of the social inequality mix, and in recent years particular attention has been paid to the manner in which they intersect with class and ethnic issues. The *political* dimension underlies all other forms of social inequality, and the ability of citizens to hold leaders accountable and to affect public policies is an abiding concern not only in the United States but in all contemporary societies, including those where democratic institutions ordinarily prevail.

In my years of teaching courses in social stratification, race and ethnic relations, and political sociology, I have discovered that most texts either narrowly focus on one or another form of inequality or analytically conflate those forms, making it difficult to distinguish them. Although the major dimensions of inequality are obviously interwoven, they do not fall neatly together in a coherent package, either for individuals or for whole societies. Accordingly, I have treated different forms of inequality in self-standing chapters, although the interrelationships among them are discussed throughout. I do consider the class dimension to be most basic, however, and it is there that the book is primarily focused. In the discussions of racial/ethnic, gender, and political inequalities, emphasis is placed on how they relate to and overlap with class inequalities.

Perhaps no other area of inquiry in the social sciences better lends itself to an interdisciplinary approach than social inequality. Although sociology usually has taken the lead, economics, political science, and anthropology all focus in various ways on this universal phenomenon. As social scientists have acknowledged the interweaving and overlapping nature of the major dimensions of social inequality, university courses in this field have become more integrative and comprehensive. I have tried to design this book to conform to such an interdisciplinary and inclusive perspective.

I also believe that students can acquire a more profound understanding of the patterns and processes of social inequality in their own country through comparative analysis. American university students commonly enter social science courses with an inflated view of the United States vis-à-vis the rest of the world; unfortunately, they often leave with that view unchanged. One of the objectives of this book, therefore, is to inform readers of how the nature of social inequality in the United States is both distinct from and similar to social inequality in other contemporary societies. Although most chapters emphasize conditions in American society, each contains discussions of U.S. inequality in a cross-national context, drawing illustrations and data from other comparable societies.

Chapter 1 sets the tone of the book, exploring the unique ways in which sociologists deal with issues of inequality and establishing a lexicon of key terms and concepts. It also explains the extant forms of inequality in modern societies and provides a preview of succeeding chapters.

Chapter 2 examines theories of social inequality, particularly those that seek to explain social class. It should be noted that much theoretical discussion is contained in other chapters that deal with particular issues, such as poverty, the elite structure, and mobility, or with racial/ethnic, gender, and political dimensions of inequality. The purpose of this chapter is to examine class theories in a more general context.

Chapter 3 describes the American class system, presenting a bird's-eye view of the class hierarchy and an examination of the distribution of income and wealth. Chapters 4, 5, and 6 deal with the three major class divisions—the rich, the classes in the middle, and the poor—emphasizing socioeconomic issues and patterns. Chapter 4 also discusses the power elite and the ways in which power relates to wealth. Chapter 7 begins with a description of the major systems of stratification, explaining the provision for mobility in each, and then looks at the forms, extent, and issues of social mobility in the United States.

Chapter 8 is devoted to ideology and the legitimation process. The basic objective is to explore the functions of ideology in solidifying and sustaining social inequality. The features of the prevailing American ideology are discussed, along with the role of major institutions in communicating that ideology. This chapter explains the persistence of social inequality, not primarily as a result of coercion but through other, less blatant and obvious means. In my view, the role of ideology is central in explaining how difficult it is to alter well-established patterns of inequality when they are rationalized by key institutions and become an accepted part of the social landscape.

Chapter 9 examines the ways in which government affects the distribution of wealth and power. An underlying assumption of this chapter is that public policies play a fundamental role in determining the shape and depth of inequality in all modern societies. Much of the discussion centers on how the U.S. welfare state differs from those of other postindustrial societies.

Chapter 10 deals with issues of racial/ethnic inequality. Over the years, I have discovered a disturbing lack of awareness on the part of U.S. students, as well as the general public, of the most elemental features of the American racial/ethnic system, particularly the demographics of specific groups and categories, as well as a basic understanding of the misused and often confusing concepts of race and ethnicity. These topics are therefore covered as a prerequisite to the main topic of the chapter, racial/ethnic stratification.

Chapter 11 focuses on the gender dimension of inequality. With the enormously wide range of issues that today constitute gender studies, coverage of gender as part of a comprehensive introduction to social inequality must be selective. Among gender issues, it is changes in the occupational role of women, in my view, that have rendered the most far-reaching societal effects during the last several decades. Much of this chapter, therefore, concerns patterns and processes of gender inequality in the workplace, though other institutional areas are discussed, including politics and the family.

Chapter 12 examines political inequality. The first part of the chapter covers the more prominent theories and debates about the U.S. power structure and the role of political elites. The second part deals with the role of masses, exploring how and to what degree they can effectively influence the political system and, through it, the structure of inequality.

Although I did not set out deliberately to frame these chapters thematically, as I wove together the various topics, a leitmotif seemed to emerge: the discordant societal currents of *liberty* and *equity*. In all societies, various forms of social inequality, the efforts and policies that address them, and the theories that seek to explain them appear to revolve around the clash of those two overarching values. This ideological confrontation is particularly evident in the United States, where the sanctity of individual freedom within capitalism conflicts with notions of democracy and equality. This is an age-old philosophical battle, of course, not limited to the contemporary world or to capitalist democracies. As the nineteenth-century essayist Walter Bagehot put it, "There is no method by which men can be both free and equal."

Changes to the Sixth Edition

This, the sixth edition, has been revised in a number of significant ways. The core content and organization of previous editions, however, have been left intact and the book's approach is unchanged. One noticeable structural change is the blending of what in earlier editions had been two self-standing chapters: *racial/ethnic differentiation* and *racial/ethnic stratification*. A number of reviewers and past adopters had suggested that combining these two chapters was more topically logical and, after much thought, I agreed. The most important issues of the former chapter on differentiation—the concepts of race and ethnicity and the use of racial and ethnic categories in American society—now serve as an introduction to racial/ethnic stratification, which is Chapter 10's major focus.

Many new or recent empirical and theoretical works, produced by both scholars and investigative journalists, are cited in virtually every chapter. The most current statistical data, gathered from both government agencies and research institutes, as well as survey data from national and international survey research organizations, form the basis of the book's more than eighty tables and figures, many of them entirely new. Many new comparative data and discussions have been introduced throughout the book, giving readers additional opportunities to look at U.S. inequality in an international context. Specific sections of several chapters have been expanded or rewritten extensively to reflect societal and global changes that have occurred since publication of the fifth edition. These include:

- An entirely new section on Pierre Bourdieu's contribution to theoretical issues of social inequality (Chapter 2).
- New tables and figures showing the unceasing expansion of the income and wealth gaps (Chapters, 3, 4, 5, 6, and 9).
- Expanded discussion of the continued decline of the middle classes, a process that began in the 1980s and has yet to be reversed (Chapters 3, 5, 7, and 9).
- New illustrations of the impact of the Great Recession on the class system, including changes in the labor force and their effects on workers and on those living on the edge of poverty or having dropped into the ranks of the poor (Chapters 5 and 6).
- Discussion of the declining trend of upward mobility in the U.S., in comparison to other postindustrial societies, as well as new graphics showing the role of education as a sorting mechanism (Chapter 7).
- Expanded explanation and new figures illustrating the impact of public policy in shaping and stabilizing the class, racial/ethnic, and gender hierarchies (Chapters 9, 10, and 11).
- Updated discussion of political partisanship and competing approaches to the U.S. political economy (Chapters 9 and 12).
- New figures highlighting the changing ethnic makeup of American society and the socioeconomic disparities among racial/ethnic groups (Chapter 10).
- New tables showing changing patterns of gender segregation in the workforce, as well as the persistence of a gender wage gap (Chapter 11).
- Amplified discussion and current examples of the growing influence of money in politics and the power of dominant economic interests in the political process (Chapter 12).
- Discussion of the emergence of incipient social movements, on both the political left and right, revolving about issues of income and wealth inequalities and the role of government in the distributive process (Chapter 12).

The Nobel Prize-winning economist Joseph Stiglitz has written that "The simple story of America is this: the rich are getting richer, the richest of the rich are getting still richer, the poor are becoming poorer and more numerous, and the middle class is being hollowed out" (2012:7). These are patterns whose onset dates not from a year or even a decade ago; unfailing data reveal that they have been advancing continuously for the past forty years. Until the near-collapse of the American economy in 2008, however, the response of political leaders and the media to expanding socioeconomic inequality seemed muted, if it was acknowledged at all. Sociologists and economists studied and discussed it routinely, but their findings did not often reach a wider audience, confined, as they were, mainly to university classrooms and academic journals. In the few years since the previous edition of *Social Inequality: Patterns and Processes* was published, that situation has changed radically. Indeed, perhaps nothing is more significant regarding the study of social inequality than the fact that its core issues have been elevated to prominence in the public discourse. It would not be an exaggeration to proclaim that we have witnessed the emergence of the most intense social awareness of differences in income and wealth since the Great Depression of the 1930s. References to "class warfare," "redistribution," "the ninety-nine percent," "the shrinking middle," "tax fairness," and a host of other inequality-related catch phrases are now regularly heard in heated debates at all levels of government and in the media. And, the increasingly wide economic disparities, intertwined with racial/ethnic and gender differences, that characterize American society have become basic focal points of the bitter partisan polarization that has so dominated U.S. politics in the past decade. In a real sense, then, the critical relevance of the topics that are dealt with in *Social Inequality: Patterns and Processes* has never been greater.

Accompanying Test Bank

A comprehensive Test Bank is available for instructor download on the password-protected sixth edition website at www.mhhe.com/marger6e.

Acknowledgments

As with past editions, I greatly appreciate the support of the editorial and production staff at McGraw-Hill: Gina Boedeker, Sara Jaeger, Judi David, Alexandra Schultz, Courtney Austermehle, Nicole Bridge, and Adina Lonn. Thanks also to copyeditor Beth Bulger and to project manager Sumit Makarh. Also to be acknowledged are the reviewers for this edition who contributed helpful insights and suggestions: Jennifer Johnson, Virginia Commonwealth University; Daniel Egan, University of Massachusetts-Lowell, Karen Sternheimer, University of Southern California, and Donna Goyer, CSU-San Marcos.

About the Author

Martin N. Marger has written widely in the fields of race and ethnic relations, social inequality, and political sociology. He is the author of *Race and Ethnic Relations: American and Global Perspectives*, now in its ninth edition, and *Elites and Masses: An Introduction to Political Sociology*, and coeditor, with the late Marvin Olsen, of *Power in Modern Societies*. His articles have appeared in many sociological and political science journals.

1

An Introduction to the Study of Social Inequality

[F]or centuries and over almost the whole of the globe, it has been a basic assumption in societies of any size or complexity that some men are born to power and luxury, others to toil and poverty.
PHILIP MASON

Equality would be a heaven, if we could attain it.
ANTHONY TROLLOPE

In the Los Angeles community of North Beverly Park, houses are so large and elaborate that calling them private residences seems almost ludicrous. Many resemble small hotels, with 20,000, 30,000, and even 40,000 square feet. Gyms, home theaters, elegant swimming pools, fountains, and massive underground garages are standard. Of the few homes on the market, the asking price of the most expensive is $50 million; the cheapest is $14 million. Among the residents are some of the most familiar names in the entertainment and sports worlds: Eddie Murphy, Barry Bonds, Sylvester Stallone, Rod Stewart, Reba McEntire. Many business tycoons, such as the billionaire Viacom chairman Sumner Redstone, also call North Beverly Park home. Secured by gatehouses, constantly patrolled by guards, and filled with security cameras, North Beverly Park has assured its residents that few outsiders will ever penetrate their gated paradise (Groves, 2008; Waxman, 2006).

No more than a few miles away is a district that, compared to North Beverly Park, can only be described as a netherworld. It is America's largest encampment of homeless people, an area on the south edge of downtown Los Angeles known as "The Bottoms." Some residents—perhaps 4,000—literally live on the streets in tents, tarps, blankets, and cardboard boxes. Others—estimated to number 10,000—who have found a more secure place to sleep are crammed into dingy, rat-infested residential hotels and shelters. Portable toilets have been placed on some corners to keep people from defecating on the street, but the stench from human waste and rotting trash—"toxic enough to buckle your legs," as one journalist describes it—is everywhere (Lopez, 2005). "Hard to look at," writes another journalist after exploring the district, "the streets are harder to smell" (Nieves, 2006).

At the other end of the country, a contrast in opulence and poverty is equally stark. Among Miami's many wealthy areas, Fisher Island is perhaps its most exclusive, situated off the mainland and accessible only by yacht, helicopter, or ferry. No luxury is lacking for its 1,500 residents, most of whom occupy condos as second or third homes, whose average net worth is $10 million (Sampson, 2010; Swartz, 2007).

Only minutes from Fisher Island across Biscayne Bay are neighborhoods that are among the most impoverished in the United States. In the Overtown section, for example, more than half of its 3,000 mostly African American families live below the poverty line. Some of Overtown's residents work on Fisher Island as maids, dishwashers, and groundskeepers for little more than minimum wage.

The disparity between North Beverly Park and the Bottoms and between Fisher Island and Overtown is as grim and disquieting as can be seen anywhere in the contemporary world. These communities demonstrate social inequality in the extreme. But one needn't think of Los Angeles or Miami as exceptional; virtually all American cities or towns reflect a similar, if perhaps less dramatic, disparity of living conditions. And, as we will see, the enormous gap between rich and poor—more accurately between the rich and everyone else—continues to grow wider.

In this, however, the United States is far from unique. Although there are relative differences among them, in all societies today there is a significant disparity between those at the top of the social hierarchy and those at the bottom. Moreover, the gap between whole nations, rich and poor, is also great and in most cases shows little sign of closing. Table 1-1 shows that the annual per capita gross national income in the United States is $48,000, compared to less than $2,000 in many Asian and most sub-Saharan African countries. Consider that the average American has an income almost sixty-three times greater than that of the average Bangladeshi.

How can we explain these inequalities? Are inequalities within and between human societies natural and inevitable? Is equality ever more than a chimera, an ideal that can never be realized? Social scientists have been wrestling with those questions since the nineteenth century. This book is about social inequality: its origins, its scope, the ways in which it is sustained, and the ways in which humans seek to reduce it.

No sphere of inquiry is more fundamental in any social science, whether it be sociology, economics, or political science. Each of these disciplines deals most basically with human inequalities, specifically, differences in income and wealth, differences in social standing and prestige, and differences in power. In one way or another, all questions and issues in the various social science disciplines ultimately involve, directly or indirectly, matters of inequality. Indeed, we would not be stretching the matter to declare quite simply that inequality is the transcendent issue of all social

Table 1-1 ▪ Per Capita Gross National Income (GNI) of Selected Countries, 2011 (U.S. Dollars)

Country	GNI
Norway	$88,890
Sweden	53,230
Netherlands	49,730
United States	48,450
Canada	45,560
Japan	45,180
France	42,420
Italy	35,330
Israel	28,930
Korea, Rep.	20,870
Czech Republic	18,520
Poland	12,480
Brazil	10,720
Turkey	10,410
Russian Federation	10,400
Mexico	9,240
South Africa	6,960
Colombia	6,110
Jamaica	4,980
China	4,930
Egypt	2,600
India	1,410
Nigeria	1,200
Bangladesh	770
Liberia	240

Source: The World Bank: Per Capita Gross National Income of Selected Countries. World Development Indicators 2012. Reprinted by permission.

science. As the sociologist Orlando Patterson has put it, "The basic problem of social science . . . is—or should be—to explain how inequality came into the world and how it is maintained" (1978:36).

Major Issues in the Study of Social Inequality

Our concern is with different types of social inequality. This entails the exploration of many specific questions and issues. We can summarize our investigation of inequality, however, by posing a few very basic and broadly conceived questions, which form the essential structure of the chapters that follow.

Key Questions

1. *What is social inequality?* In pursuing this question, we will look at how sociologists and other social scientists conceive of social inequality and how they go about studying this phenomenon. Social inequality, as explained, has been one of the central concerns of sociology from its very beginnings. We will then look at the various forms of inequality and the dimensions of society in which inequality is most evident and deep-seated. We will also see how social inequality is *structured,* that is, built into the culture and institutions of the society and not the result of chance or entirely of individual actions.

2. *Why is there social inequality? Is inequality inevitable in all societies? And what, if any, functions does inequality serve?* These are interrelated questions that compel us to investigate different theories that sociologists have developed. As one of the most primary, if not the most basic, issues of sociology, inequality is a phenomenon that the major sociological theorists have dealt with extensively. Karl Marx and Max Weber, two of the most prolific and influential, have left a gigantic legacy of thought on issues of social inequality, and much of our attention will focus on their theories.

3. *What is the nature of economic inequality today in American society and in other societies like it?* One of this book's central objectives is to present a picture of the actual condition of social inequality in the United States and in other advanced capitalist societies of the contemporary world. Differences in economic standing constitute only one dimension of inequality, but it is, arguably, the most significant and consequential. The essential query here is "who gets what?" As we will see, in the United States and other modern societies like it, income and wealth are distributed in a highly inequitable manner, with enormous differences among those who receive a huge proportion, those who receive some, and those who receive little or none.

4. *What is "power" and who are the powerful in society?* As we will see, differences in power underlie all forms of inequality. Thus, power is implicit in all of our queries. Our concern is institutional, or societal, power, where actions and decisions affect much or perhaps all of the society. Such power lies within the major economic and political institutions, like the federal government and giant corporations. In the United States and other democratic societies, it is assumed that individuals, regardless of their social station, can have some say over how they are governed and can influence those who shape public life. We will investigate whether this belief has much basis in reality or whether the few always exert power over the many.

5. *What is the nature of racial and ethnic inequality?* In modern multiethnic societies, like the United States and Canada, people's ethnic and racial identities have much social significance and weigh heavily in determining their opportunities for acquiring the society's valued resources, such as jobs, housing, and education. We will analyze the concepts of "race" and "ethnicity," examine inequality among various American racial and ethnic groups, and look at how race and ethnicity have an impact on other forms of inequality.

6. *What is gender inequality?* In addition to inequalities based on economic wealth and race and ethnicity, gender is a factor in how people are treated. Quite simply, as we will see, in no society do men and women receive the same rewards. Why this is so is an essential question with which we will deal. We will also look at the actual nature of inequality between men and women in various areas of social, economic, and political life in the United States and similar societies and will examine how those patterns are changing.

7. *How is social inequality sustained and, conversely, how do societies move toward greater social equality?* Social inequality is evident in all societies; some groups and individuals always get more of the society's valued resources than do others. Moreover, the patterns of distribution are structured and thus remain firm for long periods of time. Powerful groups and individuals, through their actions and decisions, are able to sustain the system of inequality, but we will discover that people's beliefs about the system and how it works—ideology—also help uphold it. Prevailing patterns of inequality, however, are often challenged by those who receive less and believe they are entitled to more; hence, efforts arise to equalize the distribution of valued resources. In the United States, as in all modern societies, government plays a central role in stabilizing the system of inequality but also in providing the tools for change. This, we will see, is a result of different public policies.

A Comparative Approach

In exploring these essential questions, our focus will fall mostly on the United States. Keep in mind, however, that although American institutions and events are often the focal point of the rest of the world, the United States is not the *world*; it is one society among many, increasingly linked to others in global institutions and structures. This necessitates a more international perspective and requires that we incorporate comparisons with other societies on matters of social inequality. Are the patterns and dimensions of social inequality in American society radically different from those of other contemporary societies? Or are there similarities and common features?

Ironically, a comparative approach not only exposes us to the nature of inequality in other societies but also provides us with a sharper insight into inequality in the United States. It has often been observed that we cannot truly understand our own society without some knowledge of others. Comparing ourselves with others forces us to adopt a perspective that often yields not only new understandings but also curious and intriguing surprises.

Examining Inequality in a Sociological Mode

Before we can begin to explore social inequality, we need to become aware of how sociologists analyze social phenomena and how their perspective differs from other ways of interpreting the social world. Approaching social inequality by using the sociological mode will yield a more accurate and reliable picture than can be obtained by relying on conventional or popular modes of inquiry and sources of information. We can conceptualize the difference between these two modes as encompassing a few components.

The Sociological Mode

Going beyond the Obvious   To begin with, sociology questions ideas that are often accepted as "true," or simply "common sense." The basic assumption of sociology, as sociologist Peter Berger has so poignantly put it, is "Things are not what they seem" (1963:23). The basic objective of sociology, therefore, is to explain how society really works, not how it seems to work or how we think it ought to work. Simply stated, sociologists seek to explain what *is*, not what *appears* to be or what *should* be.

To illustrate, let's consider how people formulate their views of economic inequality. For middle-class Americans, a superficial view of poverty or wealth might lead to the conclusion that both the poor and the rich are few in number. Middle-class people are not likely to maintain much contact with either the rich or the poor. The United States, therefore, would seem to be, from this perspective, a thoroughly middle-class society. Relying on one's personal experience is a common and logical way of substantiating a belief and might be employed as a way to begin one's investigation. One might question the assertion of economists and sociologists that there are vast differences in income and wealth in American society because one rarely sees any poor people or, conversely, any extremely wealthy people.

To explore this issue sociologically, however, would require that we go beyond our own very limited social worlds. We may have seen few poor or rich people because our daily interactions are confined to a constricted social sphere, limited to our personal experience. How much time do any of us spend among people who are fundamentally different from ourselves in social class? Probably not a great deal. Those with whom we go to school, work, and interact closely are generally people whose levels of income and wealth (that is, their social class) are similar to our own. What most people know of society therefore derives mostly from their particular niche of society. Hence, they tend to generalize from their own social experiences. Movie director Martin Scorsese tells of growing up in New York's Little Italy in the 1950s, watching television shows like *Leave It to Beaver* and *Father Knows Best*. The families in those shows depicted a suburban way of life that was completely alien to Scorsese and those in his neighborhood. "They existed on some other planet. We couldn't understand those people. . . . We'd ask ourselves, Who are these people? Why are they speaking to us? What do they want us to think? *That's* not America. *This* is America. Little Italy is America" (Lyman, 1998:B14).

Obviously, basing one's beliefs on only a limited range of interactions is apt to lead to a distorted and inaccurate picture. Therefore, we need to extend our range of thought and perspective to encompass other social groups in what are, comparatively speaking, other social worlds. Sociology forces us to do this. To begin to understand inequality from a sociological perspective, then, requires more than reliance on one's personal experience.

Turning to journalistic accounts—television news, newspapers, books—takes us one step beyond personal experience, but these, too, are not always reliable sources of information. Increasingly, all mass media, whether electronic or print, aim to entertain, not necessarily inform, the viewer or reader. Most TV news programs and newspaper articles are designed to present a simplified, easy-to-understand story line that can be conveyed quickly and that poses a minimal intellectual challenge. There are always elements of validity in these chronicles, but they are usually oversimplified pictures that do not take into account the complexities that ordinarily are involved. If daily journalism "often works best with black and white," as one journalist (Scott, 2008) has put it, sociology works mostly with gray. Moreover, the presentation of numerous news items and stories in rapid-order succession, as is characteristic of the modern media, does not enable us to carefully absorb and process this information, considering different points and perspectives. Sociologists, by contrast, study social issues, such as inequality, in a more rigorous fashion, looking at every possible angle and nuance. It is a much slower, deliberate process and one that, in the end, is more frustrating, for it does not always yield a clear-cut conclusion.

Looking through the Lens of Sociology   Few political issues of our time do not concern inequality in some fashion or another. Wages, jobs, welfare, taxes, social security, health care, affirmative action, criminal justice, education—all of these are most essentially issues of inequality, concerning who will get what portion of the society's wealth, prestige, and power. They are the major issues that politicians debate, that commentators speak and write about, and that citizens ponder. Inequality, then, is not a social phenomenon that can be explored without evoking strong opinions and, at times, burning emotions. We would be less than human if we did not maintain some views and preferences on these matters. But the approach taken by politicians, commentators, or citizens in addressing issues of inequality is ordinarily not the same as the approach taken by sociologists. How do they differ?

Politicians and commentators consider issues of inequality within a value-laden framework. This means that their views are shaped essentially by their beliefs and opinions about what constitutes the "good society" and about how people, as members of society, should behave. Should the poor receive more or less welfare? Should taxes be raised or reduced? Should special preference in employment and educational access be given to racial minorities and women? On such issues, politicians base their actions on views that reflect their political philosophies or that seem expedient to win elections. Similarly, commentators are paid to interpret these issues according to their views. Their objective is to persuade us or, at minimum, to present an argument that is convincing enough to make us think about an issue and to think about it with a view the commentator feels is correct.

All of us, of course, including sociologists, have opinions and perhaps strong feelings about these issues. But using the sociological approach compels us to hold those opinions and attitudes in abeyance as we go about the business of examining forms and processes of social inequality. This approach, ordinarily referred to as *objectivity,* is a cardinal principle of all rational pursuits, whether in sociology or in any other human endeavor.

This does not mean, however, that as sociologists we need to divest ourselves of our values; indeed, we could not do this even if we wanted to. The ability to conceptualize values—ideas of right and wrong, good and bad, beautiful and ugly, and so on—is one of the principal features that distinguish humans as a species. All that is necessary is that we be prepared to accept what may be surprising and perhaps even displeasing to us if our findings do not support what we strongly believe or hold dear. It is analogous to sharpening our vision by wearing glasses with corrective lenses. Metaphorically, to observe social inequality using sociological lenses, then, gives us a view quite different from that which we would ordinarily maintain with the naked eye. It provides us with a truer vision.

Using the Tools of Sociology   How do you know what you believe is true? This may sound like a question designed to puzzle or to evoke a philosophical debate, but it addresses the root of the difference between the thinking of sociologists and laypersons on most basic issues of society, including inequality. To maintain, as was suggested above, that the gap between rich and poor is very wide and even expanding might be questioned by those who would like to believe that the United States is a more egalitarian society and that differences in wealth are exaggerated by those who want to bring about change. How can we be certain that the gap is in fact wide and getting wider?

The basis of sociologists' assertions is *empirical substantiation.* This means that they are subject to inspection and investigation. They are founded on data collected through research, which can be verified by others. This, too, is a fundamental principle of the scientific approach, with which all of us are familiar, having been exposed to it in almost all of our schooling.

In the case of the rich-poor gap, the sociological approach would entail a careful examination of income and wealth data gathered by various social scientists and organizations. Sociologists might pore intensively over statistics gathered by census takers and other agencies, looking for patterns among the mass of numbers, or they might collect data on their own by questioning people through surveys and in-depth interviews. In investigating issues of social inequality, journalists and even laypersons might, of course, also employ these techniques, and to that extent, they are operating in a sociological mode. Usually, though, only sociologists and other social scientists are prepared to invest time, energy, and other resources into such study. This reflects their professional training and demonstrates the slow pace at which sociological investigation takes place. Journalists need answers quickly; they have deadlines to meet. Laypersons do not have the time or inclination to engage in tedious and time-consuming research. Sociological inquiry, however, is deliberate and laborious, requiring huge investments of time and energy, which, incidentally, do not always yield useful results.

Seeing Probabilities, Not Certainties   Not only does the sociological mode require us to set aside our values and to invest much time and effort that may not guarantee rewards, it is apt to create frustrations. To employ the sociological approach is to invoke a principle of *skepticism*. In science, no belief is absolute. Sociologists and other social scientists, therefore, must be prepared to question not only the conventional wisdom, what "everyone knows to be true," but even their own findings and conclusions. Social science, like physical or biological science, seeks discovery of "truth." But truth, in any scientific field, is ephemeral—that is, it is short-lived and thus subject to change and reformulation. We might say that, in science, there is no truth with a capital T. There are no final answers.

This is especially the case in sociology, where the subjects under scrutiny are humans, not physical elements or even lower animal species, and where predictability and generalization are therefore far more difficult to produce. Sociologists repeatedly discover, much to their chagrin, that humans are not always rational and that models and theories that appear solid on paper turn out to be applicable only in selective cases. Economists, too, often build models of economic processes based on the assumption that people will act rationally in the market—that is, they will seek out the most profitable alternatives in their consumer choices and other financial decisions. These models do not always hold up, however, because people's spending patterns are not based entirely on purely rational factors. Consumers may purchase one brand of cereal over another not because the quality is superior or the cost is lower but because they like the shape or because it is endorsed by their favorite basketball player. Advertisers know very well that price and quality are not the only bases of consumer decisions, and they commonly play on those irrational tendencies.

Hence, in sociology we must be content to deal with *probabilities*, not certainties. But this in itself should not detract from the value of the sociological approach. We cannot predict the behavior of any single individual or event. But we can make predictions about aggregate behavior, that is, about collectivities of people and events. In studying human physiology, for example, no one would question the assertion that men are generally taller than women, despite the fact that some men are shorter than some women. Similarly, in studying inequality and its various aspects, we would not be off base if, for example, we were to assert that upper-class Americans generally support Republicans and working-class Americans generally support Democrats, despite the fact that some rich people support Democratic candidates and some workers support Republicans. Again, we must think in terms of probabilities, not airtight certainties. When we are aware of what people of particular social categories (women, Catholics, urban residents, Mexican Americans, teenagers, farmers, welfare recipients, bowlers, etc.)

usually do, and we have observed this behavior repeatedly and over long periods of time (observing "aggregate regularities"), we are then able to make reasonable generalizations about people in those categories.

As an example, consider occupation. As we will see, occupation is a key element of social class, and knowing this single feature enables us to predict with some accuracy many other characteristics of a person's social identity and behavior. If you meet a woman and learn that she is a physician, can you not make a good estimate of her income? What kind of house and neighborhood she lives in? Even what kind of leisure activities she prefers? You could assess all of these things, not necessarily with 100 percent accuracy, but with a high degree of probability.

Thinking in terms of probabilities rather than certainties, however, can bring about discomfort and frustration. All of us want to think that our beliefs and views are valid and free of ambiguity. Operating on the basis of faith is a way of avoiding such uncertainty. In sociology, however, uncertainty is unavoidable. Sociologists, like scientists of all fields, are naturally skeptical. But skepticism in science is a virtue and not to be resisted. To question what is "tried and true" is, in fact, what sociology, or any science, is about. Here we need to reiterate Berger's principle of sociological thinking, that "things are not what they seem." Sociologists are often accused of telling us in high-blown fashion what we already know. But in fact sociologists more often tell us that what we know is not always true. Sociologists may have few unassailable answers to problems and issues of inequality, or any other social phenomenon, but they can inform us of and lead us to the paths of inquiry we need to travel in seeking answers.

This book may challenge many orthodox ideas about social inequality in its various forms. Its intent is to expose you to different views and to stimulate new ways of thinking about the distribution of income, wealth, and power; about the impact of class, ethnicity, and gender on that distribution; and about the role of major groups and institutions in creating, sustaining, and perhaps changing those patterns. Sociology is, in many ways, an inherently iconoclastic discipline: It calls into question venerable and often unchallenged beliefs and ideas. As such, it can sometimes seem hypercritical of dominant institutions and social structures. This is especially the case in the study of social inequality. But if the use of sociological knowledge is to provide some of the intellectual bricks and mortar in building a more informed society, we need to consider the English novelist and poet Thomas Hardy's reminder: "If way to the better there be, it exacts a full look at the worst."

Objectives of Inquiry

In examining inequality in societies, sociologists pursue questions that involve description, explanation, and prescription.

Description   At times, sociologists simply try to describe the characteristics of a particular social phenomenon or group. Regarding social inequality, some questions they might pose, for example, are these: How much of the society's wealth is owned by what percentage of the population, and how much of the society's total income is earned by what share of all American families? Have those of the upper class reached the top of the social ladder through their work efforts or through inheritance? How do patterns of inequality change over time? Do the wealthy stay wealthy? And what are the chances that those born into poverty will be able to achieve a higher social position? These are all questions whose answers involve descriptions of "what is."

In describing inequality—or any social issue—sociologists rely on rigorous empirical data, use precise terminology, and frame their descriptions in theories. Journalists and others examining inequality may often operate similarly, but ordinarily they do not dig as deeply, nor are they as precise and rigorous in their procedures of gathering information.

Explanation   At the explanatory level, efforts are made to explain various aspects of social inequality. The objective is to go beyond merely describing the extent and nature of inequality and try to account for it. This calls for "why" questions. Why is inequality evident in all societies? Why are the poor poor and the rich rich? Why do patterns of inequality remain stable over many generations? Why do Euro-Americans enjoy higher status in American society than members of racial and ethnic minorities? Why do men, rather than women, seem to hold the majority of power positions in all societies?

Here, sociologists use the scientific method or, at minimum, subscribe to the scientific spirit. They perform empirically based studies and, in order to make their explanations more generalizable, try to place their findings into theoretical schemes. Journalists and commentators may emulate this process in some fashion, but their analyses are usually more speculative in nature. Moreover, rarely are their explanations guided by theory, as sociologists' are.

Prescription   In pursuing prescriptive questions, the concern is with strategies of change. The prescriptive approach essentially involves policy applications of sociological knowledge. This level of inquiry addresses issues of what should be done to bring about social change. Although it is the role of the sociologist to describe and explain the structures and patterns of social inequality, it is decision makers in both public and private realms who may implement sociological findings in changing those structures and patterns. Any attempt to determine what "should be done" involves the application of the political beliefs and preferences of those making the proposal. Social scientists may offer their views on policy issues, but in the end, social prescriptions are actually applied by policymakers. Should taxes be raised or cut? Should welfare be reformed? Should affirmative action continue to give special preference to some over others? How one weighs such issues and reaches decisions on them may involve sociological insight, but those decisions should not be confused with description and explanation.

Individuals and Social Forces

Americans are firmly committed to the notion that people are shaped mainly by their individual actions. Indeed, as will be shown in Chapter 8, this is the essence of the American ideology. Social inequality, therefore, is most commonly interpreted as a product of individual differences. Most people, if queried about why some individuals have achieved great wealth and fame while others are penniless and forgotten, why some are esteemed and others held in disrepute, why some have achieved great political power while others merely follow or observe the actions of others, would respond that these differences are the result of personal effort and ability. Achievement, in other words, makes for inequality.

Sociology, however, compels us to look not simply at how individuals act but at the social forces that shape their actions. People's fates are determined by structural factors, in addition to individual effort. Structural factors are those social institutions, organizations, and groups in which we act and are acted upon. Take, for example, occupation. We might assume that people reach particular positions in their places of work on the basis of their individual achievements, and in the same way, we might conclude that those who lose their jobs do so because they have insufficient ambition or skills. Their job fate, in short, is a product solely of their personal actions. This, of course, can readily be seen as a fatuous explanation. It is true that people are often hired and fired on the basis of their individual skills and performance. But people are hired and fired for any number of reasons that have nothing to do with their personal characteristics or abilities. If your favorite uncle lost his job, would you conclude that he "simply didn't try hard enough" or that "he lacked what it takes"? Probably you would look for an explanation that goes beyond your uncle's individual efforts. Did his company replace his job with a machine? Did the company need to eliminate jobs because of continued low profitability? Did the company move his plant abroad, where the cost of labor is considerably cheaper? Here we can begin to see that larger forces, part of what sociologists call social structure, set limits and impose constraints on people, regardless of their individual abilities and attitudes.

Inequality, then, is the result not merely of people's personal actions. It is determined by structural forces of the society and even global structural forces. Political leaders make decisions regarding tax policy, educational loans, welfare, tariffs, and countless other issues, all of which have an impact in some manner on the economic and social fate of individuals. Similarly, corporate executives have much power in shaping the labor market as well as the consumer market. Moreover, we live in a time in which we are subject to the dynamics of markets not only in the United States but in the world as a whole. Giant transnational corporations make decisions about how many jobs will be created, where they will be located, and how much workers will be paid. And it is on such decisions—about which individual workers have virtually no say—that people's economic fate hinges. At this level—the structural level—individual effort and achievement have no consequence.

C. Wright Mills, an influential American sociologist writing in the 1950s, referred to the "sociological imagination" as the ability to recognize the difference between "troubles" and "issues." Personal troubles, Mills explained, are mostly personal in origin whereas public issues are social in origin. Thus, one person unemployed is a "trouble" that might be explained in terms of that person's character, skills, or ambition. But the unemployment of 8 or 9 percent of fully able workers in the United States is an "issue" that can be explained only as part of the workings of the society's economic and political institutions. Using the sociological imagination enables us to understand our place on the larger social stage as more than simply the product of our personal drama acted out on our personal stage, that is, our limited social environment.

This is not to deny the significance of individual differences in talent, ambition, and effort in creating social inequality. Those are undeniably factors of great importance. But they come into play only within the context of a much wider societal—and global—structure that is far outside the realm of the individual.

Some Basic Terms and Concepts in the Study of Inequality

Precision in the use of terms is one attribute of social science analysis that separates it from casual explanations of social issues or from the reporting of journalists. The following section examines some concepts and terminology that will arise repeatedly throughout this book.

Social Differentiation

All societies are diverse in some regards. Biology imposes some of this diversity. Males and females obviously differ, as do people of various ages and physical characteristics. All but the most technologically primitive societies, however, also exhibit diversity on certain social bases. Not all people perform the same economic functions, for example, and therefore a set of diverse occupational roles is evident. Distinguishing individuals on the basis of their occupations creates an occupational order. We might think of this as the horizontal dimension of social structure. Let us suppose that society X has a simple occupational order, made up of six specific roles: doctor, teacher, soldier, toolmaker, farmer, and laborer. Arranging those who fill these six occupations horizontally simply demonstrates that people in this society perform six different tasks (Figure 1-1a). It tells us nothing about how people in each of these occupations are rewarded (who gets more of the society's wealth and who gets less) or how much prestige is attached to each occupational position. It implies not necessarily a rank order, only an order of differentiation. However, differentiation does establish the basis for inequality and stratification.

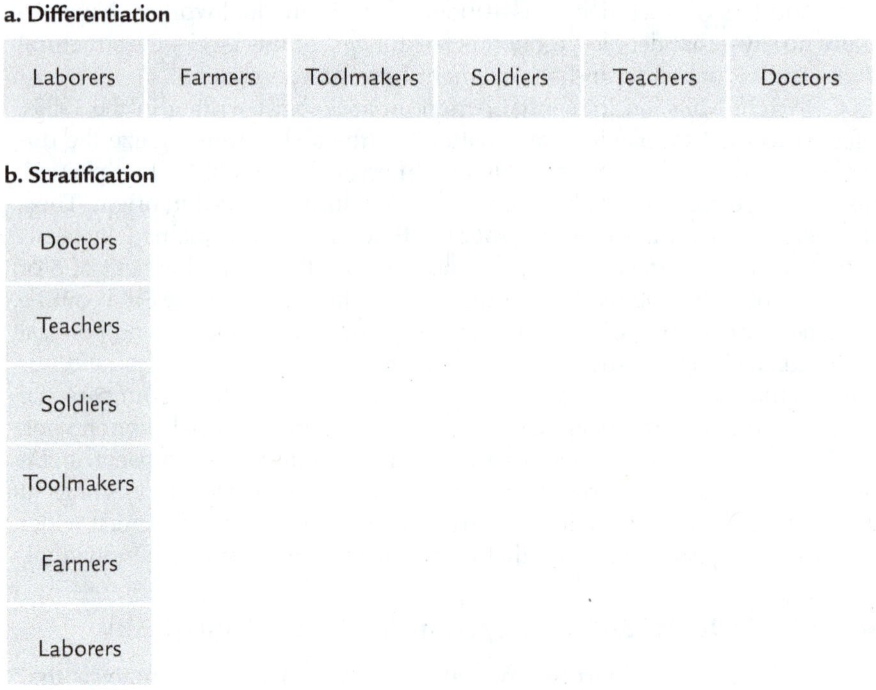

a. Differentiation

| Laborers | Farmers | Toolmakers | Soldiers | Teachers | Doctors |

b. Stratification

Doctors

Teachers

Soldiers

Toolmakers

Farmers

Laborers

Figure 1-1 ▪ Social Differentiation and Stratification, by Occupation.

Social Stratification

If societies were divided only along horizontal lines, there would be little social conflict, for although people might be assigned to different groupings and perhaps even be segregated, there would not necessarily be invidious differences among them. That is, there would be no basis for envy or feelings of injustice so long as no differential rewards were accorded the different groupings. Clearly, however, in all societies people receive different shares of what is valued and scarce, that is, what is desirable and what members of the society strive for. These can be referred to as **social resources.** People are, in other words, differently rewarded.

This unequal distribution of the society's resources creates a system of stratification. Stratification, as sociologists use the term, is akin to the geological concept. Geologists describe the different layers of subsoil—strata—as having different properties. Digging beneath the ground at a particular location, we might find a layer of soil, then rock, shale, water, perhaps even oil. The sociological meaning of stratification is essentially the same as the geological meaning, except it is human groups that are arranged in a vertical order.

If we take the graphic depiction of the occupational order of society X and tip it on its side, we then have a hierarchy of occupations (Figure 1-1b). Now we can see that doctors are at the top of the structure, laborers at the bottom, and the others between them in relative order. This is no longer simply diversity or differentiation, but stratification. **Social stratification,** then, is the ranking of persons and groups on the basis of various social, and sometimes physical, characteristics. It is the vertical dimension of social structure. Concentrations of people with roughly similar amounts of societal resources form points on this hierarchy, and this rank order ordinarily remains fixed from generation to generation. That is, the divisions persist over time.

Stratification Dimensions   Sociologists, following Max Weber, have usually explained social stratification as comprising three dimensions: wealth, prestige, and power. Individuals rank differently on each dimension, depending on their accumulation of social resources or rewards.[1]

Wealth refers to economic resources. In capitalist societies, these comprise people's market capacity, that is, their ability to purchase the material things that they want and need. People receive different amounts of income and other sources of wealth and thus enjoy more or less of the society's benefits. Economic inequalities are a function primarily of people's occupations. Lawyers generally earn more than truck drivers, who earn more than dishwashers, and so on.

Prestige, or status, is the deference that people are given by others. It is, essentially, social esteem. Important positions in the society's major institutions usually carry with them a great deal of prestige, and people who occupy those positions are therefore treated with much respect and deference. The president of the United States, for example, would never be referred to by his first name by anyone but his family and closest friends. Social custom would dictate that others address him as "Mr. President" or, at minimum, "Sir." We need not look at such an extreme case, however, to understand prestige. A worker would interact with his manager quite differently than with a co-worker; he would accord his manager greater deference.

In modern societies, status derives, for the most part, from one's occupation. Doctors have more status than teachers, who, in turn, have more than factory workers, and so on. Other important bases of status, in addition to occupation, are age and ethnicity. The latter is particularly critical in multiethnic societies.

Power underlies all forms of inequality. As a social resource, power refers to people's authority in groups and organizations. Some have the power, as a result of their positions, to command others, to get them to do things, as Weber described, even against their will. The more important and broadly based the position, the greater the scope of one's power. The president of the United States has greater political power, as a result of his position, than a state governor, who, in turn, has greater power than a county sheriff. In the corporate world, the chief executive officer has greater power in the company than a regional manager, who, in turn, has greater power than a local salesperson. These power differentials are evident in all spheres of social life but are particularly critical in economic and political realms.

---

[1]Weber's theory will be discussed in more detail in the next chapter.

Inequalities in wealth, prestige, and power are usually closely related. Thus, those who have a disproportionate share of economic resources will likely be accorded a similar degree of prestige and will have comparable power. This consistency across the three dimensions of inequality, however, is not always evident. Teachers, for example, are accorded more occupational prestige than their salaries would seem to warrant.

In sum, not only are people differentiated in their social roles, they are rewarded unequally as well. Some get more of the society's scarce and valued items than others. Some are treated with more esteem than others. And some have more power than others. Subsequently, people are grouped on the basis of how much of the society's rewards they receive, and these groups, or strata, are arranged in a rank order, or *hierarchy*. Those at the top receive the most of what there is to get, and those at the bottom the least.

Stratification Forms

All societies rank their members on the basis of some characteristics. In societies with low levels of technological development, those typical of the premodern world, stratification systems are quite simple, with only a few bases of differentiation and an equally few bases of ranking. Usually sex and age are the only two sources of social difference. Each man of a particular age plays a role similar to that of other men of that age, and the same is true of women. Moreover, there are minimal differences in rewards. This is because almost all that is produced is used immediately to provide the basic needs (food, clothing, shelter, and so on) to all members of the society. There is little in the way of a surplus to be divided and thus no basis for competition. Hence, everyone is rewarded pretty much the same.

Modern societies, with high levels of technological development, are far more complex, and as a result, there are numerous bases of differentiation. Think, for example, of the thousands of occupations that make up the labor force of an industrial society. And, with high levels of production, there is a huge surplus for which people are in competition. This creates the conditions for stratification. Thus, there are many social hierarchies, each based on some social characteristic. The most important, however, are hierarchies of class, race and ethnicity, and gender. In each case, people receive unequal shares of the society's wealth, are afforded differential status, and are able to exert different degrees of power over others.

Class   Social class is a concept that has been the focus of much sociological debate and theorizing. Essentially, however, it refers to groupings of people with approximately similar incomes and occupations. Class hierarchies are characteristic of all modern societies, and they are enormously consequential. Much of our analysis of social inequality, therefore, will focus on them.

Race and Ethnicity   In societies composed of a variety of racial and ethnic groups, such as the United States and Canada, people's race and/or ethnicity become the basis of categorization and, subsequently, of inequality. In no multiethnic society are these racial and ethnic divisions of no consequence. On the contrary, in almost all cases, race or ethnicity becomes a major differentiating characteristic and distinct racial/ethnic hierarchies are formed.

Gender In no society do men and women perform identical functions, but, more important, in none do they rank equally and, thus, in none are they treated equally. A gender hierarchy is part of all societies regardless of their level of technological development or the complexity of their social structure.

Age All societies differentiate people on the basis of age, and they subsequently rank them as well. People of different age groups are expected to play particular roles and are given more or less of the society's power, wealth, and prestige. Children are not expected to do what adults do, and they don't have the same powers as adults; at the other end of the life cycle, the elderly have certain privileges that younger people do not have, but they also may be divested of other powers and privileges.

Structured Inequality

Societies may comprise any number of hierarchies based on various social characteristics (income, occupation, ethnicity, gender, age, and so on), but in all cases, this system of inequality is **structured.** This means that stratification is not random, with groups and individuals occupying different positions by chance; rather, social institutions such as government, the economy, and education operate to assure the position of various groups. Those who comprise the upper class do not lose their high position from one year or even one generation to another. The rich remain rich; the poor, for the most part, remain poor; and those in the middle tend to remain in the middle. Likewise, ethnic minorities do not lose their minority status and receive the same treatment as dominant group members without great struggle over long periods of time. The same is true of the relationship of men and women. Moreover, the system of stratification in all societies is legitimized by an ideology that justifies inequality. The pattern of stratification in a society therefore remains in place for many generations.

Life Chances and Inequality of Opportunity

Social resources, as noted earlier, are those things that people strive for, things material and nonmaterial that are valued and scarce. The uneven distribution of social resources produces **inequality of condition**—variations in people's actual living standards or life conditions. This is not the same as **inequality of opportunity,** however, which means differences in people's chances of acquiring social resources. Weber referred to the opportunities that people have to acquire

social resources as **life chances.** Among the most basic life chances in modern societies are education, physical and mental health, residence, and justice.

To illustrate life chances and the creation of inequality of opportunity, consider two children. One is born into a family in which the father is a medical doctor and the mother an attorney. We can predict with a good deal of certainty that this child will be exposed to opportunities that will almost automatically assure her social success as she proceeds through life. As a result of her parents' high-status occupations and the correspondingly high income they earn, she will enjoy the opportunity to acquire a superior education; the best in health care; and, if needed, the best in legal aid. These, in turn, will assure that she, like her parents, will most likely work in a high-paying and rewarding occupation. Compare her life chances with those of a child born into a family in which the parents (or, more likely, parent) are high school dropouts and possess hardly any occupational skills. Just as the probabilities of social success for the child from the more well-to-do family are extremely high, for this second child, the probabilities of social failure are equally high.[2]

---

[2]Here is a good example of the idea of probabilities. We could not predict social success or failure for any particular child. One from a well-to-do-family might fail miserably in life, just as one from a poor family might overcome all the handicaps imposed by poverty. But the probability of either of these occurrences is not great.

All of our life chances are determined by our position, or as children, the position of our parents, in the various stratification hierarchies, particularly the class hierarchy. Take health, for example. We might assume on the face of it that health is mainly a product of genetic inheritance. To a great extent that is the case. We have no say in whether we will be born with healthy bodies or with genetic defects that may handicap us. Some of us will need to wear corrective lenses all our lives, whereas others will enjoy 20/20 vision. Statistics indicate, however, that those in the lower classes have higher rates of illness and lower life expectancy than those higher in social class. Differences in health care may explain some of this, but medical sociologists suggest that environmental and psychosocial conditions probably play a larger role (Williams, 1990; Charlson et al., 1993). Poor people live and work in more toxic, hazardous, and nonhygienic environments. More stressful family and work conditions may also lead to unhealthy lifestyle characteristics, like excessive use of tobacco and alcohol or poor nutrition. Although it is not yet fully understood, the relationship between health and social class has been apparent for generations (Carpiano et al., 2008; Mullaby et al., 2004; Williams and Lardner, 2005; Syme and Berkman, 1997).

The same is true of another basic life chance, justice. Again, we might assume that all people in the United States or societies like it, where there are constitutions and other legal protective mechanisms, are equal before the law; that justice, therefore, is "blind," distributed with no undue preference to any group or individual. If we conducted a census of prisons, however, we would find that they are filled mostly with people from the lower social classes. Is this because the poor commit most crimes? The answer is both yes and no. Crime knows no class bounds; middle- and upper-class people commit crimes just as people lower in the class hierarchy do. But the kinds of crimes committed by the poor are usually those that are defined as socially threatening and are pursued arduously by the police. They are the kinds of crimes with which the criminal justice system is designed to deal. Crimes committed by the nonpoor, in contrast, are most often less starkly menacing and more deceptive; therefore, they are not viewed as harshly or treated by the police and the courts as severely as crimes committed by the poor.

Even if there were no differences in the types of crime committed, the nonpoor are in a better position to defend themselves within the criminal justice system. Most simply, they can purchase more and better legal assistance. It is true, of course, that the nonpoor who are accused of crimes are not always acquitted and, if guilty, do not always receive lesser sentences than poor criminals, but their chances of winning favor in this way are increased enormously by their ability to pay for better quality justice.

Life chances are acquired, then, as a result of factors that are only partially in the control of individuals. Obviously, our class position at birth is ascribed; over this we can exercise no control. People's initial class position and, therefore, the dimensions of their opportunities and future prospects are essentially an "accident of birth." Certainly, people may subsequently enhance their life chances through individual effort, but those of lower social origins will need to overcome many socially imposed handicaps to do so. Again, it is important to think in terms of probabilities. Obviously some born into wretched social environments are able to escape and go on to a significantly higher social standing. But we cannot use the experiences of these relative few as examples of typical patterns followed by the many, since most do not escape. Tongue-in-cheek, people might be advised that if they want to assure themselves a comfortable and secure future, they should choose their family carefully!

Although inequality of condition is not the same as inequality of opportunity, the two are closely interdependent. Debate on public policies regarding issues of inequality often revolves around the question of whether people should be afforded greater equality of opportunity or equality of condition.

Stability in Systems of Inequality

Social hierarchies are ordered. They are arranged in a systematic way and do not change radically over long periods of time. How is this order and stability of inequality, in class, race/ethnicity, and gender, maintained?

The Society's Culture   A society's cultural norms and values may support inequality. This is particularly the case in capitalist societies. The basic objective of behavior within a capitalist system is to maximize personal interests, that is, to acquire as much as one can even at the expense of others. Competition within the market is the central operating principle of a capitalist economy. This automatically produces inequality; it can be no other way. Competition yields winners and losers. Capitalism, then, encourages, indeed requires, inequality.

In capitalist societies, ownership of property is sanctified. Private property is, in other words, a fundamental societal value. Children learn early on to respect others' property and to protect their own. Elaborate bodies of law spell out the rights of property, and crimes against property are enforced rigorously.

Inequality in noneconomic realms is also supported by the society's culture. Consider education. Students are expected to compete against each other for grades. This competition and the resultant inequality is such a basic part of Americans' perception of the educational environment and so ingrained that most students would recoil at the thought of a collective classroom effort, one that would reward high grades to everyone regardless of their individual contribution.

Individual and Organizational Power   Inequality is stabilized through the efforts of powerful individuals and organizations. Power, as earlier explained, is the foundation of all forms of inequality. Differentials in power, therefore, create and sustain inequality in other forms. Those who possess power are not apt to voluntarily relinquish it.

Effective power in modern societies is wielded by individuals, but they act within the context of organizations and institutions. In the United States and advanced capitalist societies like it, power is essentially an interplay of government and business. The consequences of the actions of business and government leaders affect all people; the far-reaching issues of inequality—jobs, prices, public services, education, and so on—are settled by them. Thus, it is in large measure through the decisions of leaders within these institutions that the distribution of wealth, prestige, and power is both upheld and changed.

Ideology and Legitimation It is not only through cultural expectations and the power of groups and individuals that stratification systems are stabilized. For a system of inequality to endure, people must come to see differences in power and wealth as natural and even socially beneficial. When this is accomplished, social inequality acquires legitimacy, and ruling groups need not resort to coercion to maintain their power and privilege. Such long-range stability and popular acceptance require the development of an effective ideology and its communication through socialization. This process is referred to as *legitimation*.

An *ideology* is a set of beliefs and values that explains and justifies a society's system of power and privilege, that is, structured inequality. Although a number of competing ideologies may be evident, a dominant ideology emerges that explains and justifies the status quo. This becomes the prevailing or generally accepted belief system of the society. Chapter 8 discusses the dominant ideology in American society; for the moment we can describe it simply as comprising the belief that people are responsible for their fate and that their social position is essentially a product of their personal efforts and talents. The American ideology is, in a word, *individualism*. The opportunity structure is presumed to be open, and as a result, equality of opportunity provides everyone with an equal chance of rising to the top. Positions are awarded on the basis of merit, and thus people themselves earn their ultimate fate in the social hierarchies. The system of inequality, then, is fair and just. To the extent that people subscribe to these beliefs, they are disinclined to question, let alone challenge, the prevailing system of inequality. Obviously, this is a far more effective means of sustaining a hierarchical order than is the coercive power of a ruling class or an authoritarian leadership.

Change in Systems of Inequality

Although patterns of social inequality are structured and endure for very long periods of time, they are not static. Individuals do change their place on the stratification hierarchies, and even entire social categories may change their rank.

Individual Mobility The ability of individuals to change their position in a social hierarchy is referred to as *mobility*. Generally, individual mobility is limited to one's economic class. In societies with class systems, such as the United States, theoretically there are no impediments to movement up or down. Thus, one born into poverty may advance upward without limit, just as one born into wealth may experience a free fall into the ranks of the poor.

Neither of these cases is typical. Here we need to reapply the idea of structural factors. Although one's individual mobility may be theoretically unlimited, in fact numerous obstacles hinder people's movement. To move up the occupational ladder, for example, requires that good jobs be available. Thus, individual occupational mobility is very much dependent not simply on one's personal achievement but on the state of the labor market.

Also, the social position of a person's family of birth will influence that person's mobility chances more than his or her individual efforts will. The resources accumulated by parents are inherited by their children, and the prevailing patterns of inequality are thereby perpetuated from one generation to the next.

Nonetheless, individual mobility is not uncommon, especially in societies like the United States, where the economic and political systems place few formal or official impediments before people. Also, despite the overarching importance of structural factors—and of luck—we should not think that personal efforts are of no consequence in people's quest for higher social positions. In fact, there is a great deal of individual mobility in American society, though most people who move do so only in small steps, not in great leaps. Rags-to-riches stories are rare (and riches-to-rags stories are even rarer).

Group Mobility   Although stratification systems are stable for long periods, they are not immune to change. In fact, social hierarchies are at times challenged successfully by lower-ranked groups. American workers in the late nineteenth century, for example, launched a movement that led to the creation of trade unions that forced employers to recognize their rights and modify the conditions of work. Again in the 1930s, a workers' movement produced a greatly expanded system of labor unions that effectively challenged the power of industrialists.

Ethnic and gender hierarchies are also successfully challenged at times by lower-ranking groups. The civil rights movement, beginning in the 1950s, led to a fundamental change in the social and economic status of African Americans. Similarly, the women's movement of the 1960s and 1970s yielded basic changes in the status of women. In these cases, a group's hierarchical position vis-à-vis others changed, and the extent of inequality among them was modified.

These institutional challenges are usually supported by corresponding changes in ideologies. Workers' movements were undergirded by the belief that workers had certain basic rights in the workplace that employers could not violate. The so-called muckrakers of the late nineteenth and early twentieth centuries described conditions of capitalism that led to a greater awareness of injustices and the need for institutional reforms. People's ideas of what was a "just" and "fair" work environment began to change, creating public support for workers' rights. Similarly, changes in the perception of racial and ethnic minorities accompanied the demands of African Americans for equal rights. Until the 1930s, few in American society, including social scientists, questioned the assumption that black people were intellectually and morally inferior to white people. As that belief was effectively challenged, greater impetus was given to the demands for black rights, and public support was strengthened.

Equity versus Liberty

Capitalist democracies, like the United States, constantly struggle with the conflicting forces of equity and liberty. On the one hand, they honor the principle of democracy, which dictates adherence to **equity**—that is, distribution of the society's rewards in a just manner. If all citizens see themselves as part of a unified nation, they are thereby required to engage in some collective acts, such as paying taxes, in order to bring about a fairer apportionment of resources than would occur if they acted only on the basis of personal interest. Collective interests, in other words, tend to take precedence over individual interests.

On the other hand, as capitalist societies, they are committed to the principle of **liberty**—that is, freedom to pursue one's interests as one desires and to reap the benefits of one's efforts. Such personal freedom naturally produces inequality; in a competitive, free-market system, some are bound to get more than others. Where liberty prevails, individual interests are expected to take precedence over collective, or societal, interests.

Reconciling the opposing influences of liberty and equity is a major focus of political philosophers who have wrestled with the notion of **distributive justice**. As a normative issue, the question is not "who gets what?" but "who *should* get what?" What, in other words, is a just, fair distribution of the society's valued items? Libertarian thinkers, on one side, maintain that social arrangements should be constructed with the idea that protecting individual interests is paramount. Robert Nozick (1974) has been a major philosophical influence on this side of the debate. Nozick holds that a fair distribution is accomplished if all persons are entitled to what they receive. What is most important, in this view, is not the resultant pattern of distribution but the process by which the society's valued goods are apportioned. It is individuals who engage in voluntary exchanges, and if they are entitled to what they have, the distribution is just.

Egalitarian thinkers, on the other side, hold that there is a wider collective interest that must be met in the distribution of the society's valued resources. John Rawls's theory of justice is a widely cited defense of this position. Rawls acknowledges that personal liberties should be maximized and accepts the idea that individuals will get more or less, but maintains that "social and economic inequalities . . . are just only if they result in compensating benefits for everyone, and in particular for the least advantaged members of society" (1971:14–15). That is, there are inequalities, but ideally they are arranged in such a way that they contribute to the benefit of the least advantaged.

Economists Gar Alperovitz and Lew Daly advance the equity position even further by proposing a "knowledge inheritance" model. Society as a whole, they argue, rather than any particular individual (let alone elites) is the beneficiary of inherited knowledge created by past generations. Those who are "successful," in this view, have done nothing to "earn" the knowledge that, more than anything, enabled them to accumulate their wealth. In this view, a redistribution of the society's resources is fully justified. As they explain,

> It is certainly true that private wealth creation depends fundamentally on publicly supported education and research, and on public creation and maintenance of an orderly market. It depends even more fundamentally, however, on the fact that all current economic production is overwhelmingly dependent on a long, long prior history of socially created science, technology, and other knowledge. There is every reason to reward individuals for the specific contributions they make. There is no reason to hand over to them excessively large shares of that which comes to us all as the gift of the past. (2008:140–141)

Some have pointed out that liberty and equity are not really alternatives but are woven together at different points and levels. "Liberty is among the possible *fields of application* of equality," notes the philosopher Amartya Sen, "and equality is among the possible *patterns* of distribution of liberty" (1995:22–23). Thus, the issue of equality cannot be avoided even for libertarian thinkers any more than issues of liberty and personal freedom can be ignored by egalitarians (Patterson, 1978).

Although our objective is to describe how and why the society's valued resources are apportioned as they *are* rather than how we think they *should be* apportioned, it is important to keep in mind that the distribution of wealth, power, and prestige always hinges on a delicate balance between these two forces. At certain times equity outweighs liberty, and at other times liberty takes precedence. The latter has certainly been the case in the United States throughout most of its history, but it has been exceedingly prevalent in the last thirty years. In western European societies and Canada, by contrast, equity has more often seemed to outweigh liberty. The conflict between the forces of equity and liberty is a theme that will resurface at various points in the chapters that follow.

Summary

The major issues in the study of social inequality concern what forms it takes, why it exists, how it is sustained, and whether it is inevitable in all societies. Key questions involve the nature of economic inequality, inequalities in power, racial and ethnic inequality, and gender inequality. Studying social inequality in American society requires comparisons with other societies, looking at how the United States is both different and similar.

Using the sociological mode in examining inequality entails going beyond the obvious, that is, questioning ideas that are often accepted as conventional wisdom. The sociological approach also compels us to set aside our values and examine issues objectively. Using sociological tools requires the use of empirical substantiation, subjecting assertions to inspection and investigation. To employ the sociological approach in looking at inequality is to invoke a principle of skepticism, questioning not only commonly held ideas but also scientific findings. Predictability and generalization are more difficult to produce in sociology than in the hard sciences, forcing us to be content with probabilities, not certainties.

In looking at social inequality, sociologists work at three different levels of analysis. At the descriptive level, they describe the actual nature and extent of inequality: what share of the society's resources is acquired by which groups. At the explanatory level, efforts are made to explain why various forms of social inequality exist and why the processes that produce inequality occur. At the prescriptive level, policy applications of sociological knowledge are made. This level of inquiry addresses issues of what should be done to bring about social change.

Sociology compels us to look not only at how individuals act but at the social forces that shape their actions. Inequality is thus seen as the result not only of people's personal actions but of the way social institutions are structured and function, over which people have little control.

Social differentiation refers to the diversity of a society's groups; social stratification, by contrast, refers to the division of society into a hierarchical order of groups. In all societies, people receive different shares of wealth, prestige, and power. The major forms of stratification in modern societies are social class, race/ethnicity, gender, and age.

Differences in social resources produce inequality of condition, that is, differences in people's actual living standards or life conditions. Life chances, such as education, health, and justice, are opportunities that people have to acquire resources. Differences in life chances produce inequality of opportunity.

Systems of inequality, arrangements of "who gets what," remain stable for long periods of time. A society's cultural norms and values ordinarily support inequality. This is especially so in a capitalist society. Inequality is stabilized as well through the efforts of powerful individuals and organizations that seek to protect their privilege and power through the development and communication of an ideology that explains and justifies the structure of inequality.

Individuals do change their positions on the social hierarchy, a process called social mobility. Individual mobility is not uncommon in the United States and other advanced industrial societies, though the distance moved is ordinarily slight. Groups also may change their position in the structure of stratification by successfully challenging powerful institutions and prevailing beliefs and ideologies.

In democratic capitalist societies, liberty and equity are conflicting objectives. As a result, the distribution of the society's rewards is always contingent on the shifting balance between the two.

2

Theories of Class and Social Inequality

The history of all previous societies has been the history of class struggles.
KARL MARX

"Property" and "lack of property" are . . . the basic categories of all class situations.
MAX WEBER

Describing the "who" and "what" of inequality will be the concern of most of the following chapters. As explained earlier, however, social scientists are not content to merely describe a social phenomenon; they seek to explain *why* it exists. This chapter explores the major theoretical traditions that have been most influential in shaping modern sociological thought on issues of social inequality.

If you were asked to give your view of why some people are rich while others are poor, or why some dutifully accept their place in society whereas others rebel, or why women and men often differ so noticeably in their occupational roles, you would probably not hesitate to respond. Your answers would be based on your intuition, your past observations, what you have read and heard from various sources, and perhaps what you have learned through formal education. This is not unlike what social scientists do in beginning their search for explanations. Where they differ from lay-persons, however, is in erecting a framework within which to organize their observations, insights, and data. This framework is a theory. Some theories are quite specific, whereas others are more encompassing and less formalized. The latter are theoretical perspectives, sometimes called models or paradigms, that comprise a set of general assumptions concerning various aspects of society.

All theories of class and social inequality focus on two basic issues: (1) *Why is there inequality in societies?* and (2) *Is inequality inevitable,* part of the human condition? Other issues (for example, Is inequality necessary? or Who benefits from inequality?) stem from these fundamental questions.

Much of this chapter is devoted to the theories of Karl Marx and Max Weber because of their influence and importance. The strength of their theories is attested by their endurance. Many of the basic notions that Marx and Weber presented in the nineteenth and early twentieth centuries remain vibrant and continue to be applied and debated by contemporary social scientists. Following an exploration of Marx's and Weber's ideas regarding social inequality, a few theories with more contemporary roots are presented.

It is important to consider at the outset that even though they may seem hopelessly at odds, different theoretical views of social inequality are not necessarily "either-ors." It is not a question of which theory is correct and which is incorrect. Theoretical explanations may overlap one another in some ways, and each may simply focus more sharply on one or more specific aspects of inequality.

Marx's Theory of Social Inequality

To call Marx one of the founding fathers of modern social science, as many have, would not be overstating his significance. Though he lived and wrote in the middle and latter nineteenth century, his theories remain relevant and form part of the foundation not only of contemporary sociology but also of the other social sciences. So sweeping was the range of his thought that few areas of social life were untouched by his analysis. As a result, Marx would be hard to categorize in the context of modern-day academic disciplines. Sociology, political science, and economics can each claim a Marxian tradition. Indeed, it has often been remarked that all social science since Marx's time has, in one form or another, involved a response to his ideas. This is surely true in the case of stratification and inequality. Others before Marx had dealt with issues of social class, but Marx gave these issues a primary place in social analysis and offered related ideas and concepts that today remain basic points of inquiry in studying social inequality.

It is not possible in just a few pages to attempt a detailed examination of Marx's contribution to the study of social inequality. Many scholars have devoted their entire careers to such a task and have compiled literally thousands of volumes containing analyses, critiques, defenses, and refutations of his works. In fact, one of the difficulties in any study of Marx is this extremely wide range of interpretations. French sociologist Raymond Aron reminded us that "if only there were not so many millions of Marxists, there would be no question at all about what Marx's leading ideas are or what is central to his thought" (1968:145). We might take comfort in knowing that the dilemma is not new in our era. The many different interpretations and applications of his work, even in his own time, prompted Marx to declare that he was "not a Marxist" (Lewis, 1972:9).

One factor that has contributed to the proliferation of interpretations of Marx is the rather unsystematic manner in which his writings were presented. Friedrich Engels, a wealthy factory owner, was a close working associate of Marx and organized much of Marx's work, in the process supplementing it with ideas of his own. Furthermore, Marx's extremely broad scope of social analysis has undoubtedly helped to open the door to conflicting views of his thought.

As well as an explanation of inequality in societies, Marx's work encompassed a sweeping theory of sociohistorical change, a full explanation of the capitalist economic system, and a Utopian vision. Each of these units of thought is, of course, essentially interrelated and cannot be considered independently. Furthermore, within the context of the Marxian perspective—Marx saw societies as *total*—one cannot isolate any single aspect of society. The specific elements can be understood only in relation to the whole. What is of paramount importance to the study of inequality, however, is how Marx's analysis addresses the two key theoretical issues: Why is there inequality? and Is inequality inevitable?

The Economic Foundation

Fundamental to the Marxian theory of inequality is the pivotal role of a society's economic institutional structure. The predominance of economic institutions is so overwhelming, in Marx's estimation, that they are the determinants of the entire system of society. He saw the dynamics of society originating in economic, or productive, activity—securing food, shelter, and all the other necessities: "Life involves before everything else eating and drinking, a habitation, clothing, and many other things. The first historical act is thus the production of the means to satisfy these needs, the production of material life itself" (Marx in Tucker, 1972:120).

It is out of this economic reality, the process by which people fulfill their material needs, that a society's culture arises—its various structures of law, religion, education, and politics and the belief systems attached to these structures. In short, the manner in which people organize to produce their needs and the relations that develop out of those activities determine all other aspects of social life.

This system of production by which people provide for their material existence is the society's economic foundation or, as Marx put it, the **mode of production.** As the economic foundation changes, so do people's ideas, but it is fundamental that the former impel the latter. In a famous passage Marx explained this process:

> The mode of production of material life conditions the social, political and intellectual life process in general. It is not the consciousness of men that determines their being, but, on the contrary, their social being that determines their consciousness. (Marx and Engels, 1968:182)

The idea of economic reality, how people solve the problem of survival, is, then, the basic starting point for understanding the nature of power and inequality in societies.

The primacy of the economic mode cannot be overemphasized. For Marx, the central fact of all human history is the necessity for societies, in every epoch, to provide the necessary goods and materials for sustenance. How do people in society organize in order to provide these things? That is the fundamental question with which any societal analysis must begin. To understand social inequality, then, one must look not to the dominant philosophy of a historical period but to the dominant economic form. It is this *historical materialism* that is the cornerstone of Marxian thought.

Economic Base and Superstructure   Whatever form the economic base, or substructure, takes requires a whole superstructure of noneconomic activity and thought. This superstructure of noneconomic institutions—the family, religion, education, the state—necessarily reflects the foundation on which it is raised. The economic activity of an agrarian society, for example, is centered on the land. What the society produces for survival derives primarily from the soil, and most people will engage in occupations that relate to agriculture: farming, maintaining agricultural tools, and so on. To complement this mode of production, a set of noneconomic institutions will develop that helps sustain an agrarian economic system. The family will be large in order to provide as many hands as possible to work the land; religious rites will coincide with planting and harvesting times; the legal system will be concerned primarily with the ownership rights and inheritance of land; and the political system will be designed to protect the economic and social interests of those who own the land and the tools with which it is worked.

All of these institutions are shaped to fit the needs of an agrarian society; they would not accommodate an industrial mode of production. As a society's economic base changes, therefore, the form and content of its non-economic institutions must also change. Marx thus explains societal change as the result of changes in the mode of production:

> In acquiring new productive forces men change their mode of production, and in changing their mode of production, their manner of gaining a living, they change all their social relations. The windmill gives you society with the feudal lord, the steammill, society with the industrial capitalist. (1920:119)

The Class Division

Marx's answer to the first key theoretical question—Why is there inequality?—follows from the core place of economic activity in a society: Inequality arises as a result of control of productive resources, those things that are necessary to supply the society's economic needs. Marx referred to these as the **means of production.** And the division of the society is relatively simple: One element of the population owns these basic resources, whereas the other owns no productive property and can offer only human labor in exchange for material needs. Thus, the latter is forced to work for the former. Although the workers are responsible for the production of economic wealth through their labor, it is the owning class that garners the bulk of the society's wealth.

A social class, for Marx, comprises those who stand in a common position with regard to the productive process. There are, then, essentially two classes in all societies: the owners of the means of production and the workers. All types of societies at different stages of human development and with different productive systems give rise to these two opposing classes, whether masters and slaves in slave societies or lords and serfs in feudal societies. In capitalist societies, these two classes are the **bourgeoisie,** or **capitalist class,** and the **proletariat,** or industrial working class.

The Hegemony of the Capitalist Class   This two-part division of society into owners and workers produces gross inequality. Capitalists, the dominant class, receive the bulk of societal rewards, and workers get very little. The capitalist class is able to maintain its power as a result of the possession of three key assets: the means of production, control of the state, and control of ideas and values.

First, workers must submit to the rules established by the capitalists, because, in the end, they have no other choice. Without control of the means of production, they must sell their labor to the capitalists and must accept what the capitalists will pay. Workers do not get the full value of what they produce through their labor; they get only what the capitalist is prepared to pay them: enough to keep them alive and to make certain that they will return to work the next day. The remainder is taken by the capitalist as profit. Under these conditions, there is little likelihood that workers can save enough to eventually possess productive property and become capitalists themselves. Thus, Marx felt that any basic changes in the class structure could be realized only by a revolutionary movement that would divest the bourgeoisie of its control of the means of production.

Second, the capitalist class is a **ruling class** in the sense that it controls the state, that is, government. Marx's view of the state is neatly summarized in *The Communist Manifesto:* "The executive of the modern State is but a committee for managing the common affairs of the whole bourgeoisie" (Marx in Tucker, 1972:337). Thus, even if capitalists themselves may not be in key governing positions, they are represented by those who act in their interests. Political institutions and the actions of political leaders are outgrowths of the class structure and therefore function to protect the property and privileges of the bourgeoisie. Instead of Who governs the society? the more telling question is, Who owns and controls the means of production? Answering that question is tantamount to identifying those who dominate the state, that is, those who govern.

Third, control of ideas and values by the bourgeoisie is perhaps as important as control of the means of production and the state in assuring compliance with the social order of capitalist society. Marx asserted that "the ideas of the ruling class are in every epoch the ruling ideas: i.e., the class which is the ruling *material* force of society, is at the same time its ruling *intellectual* force" (Marx in Tucker, 1972:136). In this view, the rules and values of the sociopolitical system are created, disseminated, and enforced by the dominant class and are ultimately accepted by the society as a whole.

The institutions of education, religion, and the state aid in socializing people to the dominant values. They are merely reflections of ruling-class interests. And by controlling the means of communication (the press and, in modern societies, electronic media), the capitalist class is able to stifle opposing ideas effectively. Lacking class consciousness—that is, being unaware of their own class interests—members of the proletariat regard the ideas of the ruling class as "natural." The prevailing sociopolitical system is thus seen as just, fair, and working in the interests of all social classes, not simply the capitalists. Engels referred to this as **false consciousness.**

It is important to understand that Marx saw the breakdown of society into two opposing classes as a structural phenomenon. The class system is just that: a *system*. The personal identities of the capitalists or the workers are of no relevance. Whether they are good people or bad, kind and generous, or nasty and stingy is of no consequence. All are part of a system. In their role in this system, capitalists are obliged to exploit workers. To give their workers a share of their profits or to pay workers more in wages would only undercut their position vis-à-vis other capitalists and eventually force them out of business. They therefore have no choice but to pay their workers as little as necessary. To see capitalists as avaricious is to miss the point: They are simply doing what they are expected to do as capitalists. Workers likewise have no choice but to continue to work for less than their fair share of the product; it is the only way they can keep themselves and their families alive. So capitalists and workers come and go. A few workers may even eventually amass enough resources to become capitalists themselves. But this does not change the nature of the system. New capitalists will act like capitalists and exploit their workers. That is the system's logic.

Class Conflict and Societal Change

Marx believed that classes become political groups in that individuals eventually recognize their common socioeconomic interests and are prepared to engage in struggle to protect and enhance them. It is this power struggle between opposing classes that produces social change. Class conflict, Marx explained, is a certainty in societies as long as private ownership of property is sanctioned, thereby enabling one class to control the productive process, the distribution of wealth, and the communication of ideas. But class conflict generates social change, eventually giving rise to a new mode of production and thereby creating a new ruling class. Thus the feudal system, with its ruling class of nobles and lords who owned the land, replaced the slave system. In the same way, feudalism gave way to capitalism, bringing to power a new ruling class of capitalist owners. In each case, irreversible historical and economic forces led to the change and to the ascendance of a new dominant class.

By this logic, then, capitalism will give way to a more advanced form of social and economic organization as the relations of capitalist society are no longer capable of supporting new productive forces. Just as capitalism replaced feudalism, the demise of capitalism and its replacement by a socialist productive system in which the means of production are collectively rather than privately owned would be an unavoidable future development, Marx felt. The momentum behind the passing of capitalism and the emergence of socialism is the conflict between capitalists and workers. Once the workers become conscious of their true class interests, they are transformed into a political group, a *klasse für sich* (literally, a "class for itself"), as Marx described it, prepared to engage in revolutionary confrontation with the bourgeoisie. And just as irresistible historical and economic forces previously favored the capitalist class in its conflict with the landowning class, they now favor the working class.

As to the nature of the revolutionary struggle, Marx was not certain. Advancing industrialization and increasing worker exploitation, he felt, would eventually propel such a movement. But the organizational details of the revolution were left to practitioners such as Lenin to clarify and carry out, well after the deaths of Marx in 1883 and Engels in 1895.

The nature of post-capitalist society was also left largely to speculation, and it is here that Marx was more a visionary than a social scientist. The broad outlines of post-capitalism, however, were well-formulated thoughts. Following the revolution, two stages were envisioned, ultimately climaxing in a classless society. The first phase, *socialism,* was seen as an indeterminate transitional period in which the workers would control the means of production. By this fact alone, power relations would be radically changed, bringing worker exploitation to an end. The state would necessarily still be present, but it would now be a proletarian state, which Marx called the *dictatorship of the proletariat.* The details of this workers' government were not made clear by either Marx or Engels, but, as noted, Lenin fashioned its actual working order, at least in the Soviet Union.

It is only with the total abolition of social classes that the final stage of post-capitalism—communism—would emerge. The classless society is manifestly Utopian, characterized by the complete socialization of the productive system, the end of all economic exploitation, and the appearance of individuals no longer impelled by acquisitive and individualistic values. It is at this point that the well-known dictum "from each according to his abilities, to each according to his needs" is fulfilled. With these conditions in place, the state withers away, since there are no more class interests to protect and no need to impose social controls.

In the end, then, Marx was optimistic about the possibilities for the elimination of inequality. Regarding the second key theoretical question, whether social inequality is inevitable, Marx answers a qualified "no." Although it would certainly be a long-term affair, the creation of a classless—and thus equitable—society was possible.

We should keep in mind that capitalism, to Marx, was a very beneficial productive system when compared with previous ones. It had created the technology and material abundance that made it possible for people to enter into a social condition in which poverty, both material and psychological, would no longer exist. But to make that condition a reality required the organization of society into a socialist productive system. Capitalism had had its place; indeed, it had been a necessary step in societal development. But its utility, Marx felt, was ended by the middle of the nineteenth century.

Marxian Theory in Summary

The essence of the Marxian theory of stratification and inequality can be distilled into a few simple premises.

- Reality consists of the constant production of basic life needs—food, clothing, shelter. Through work, people in society realize themselves, and it is around this productive process that history unfolds.

- Societies in different stages of social and technological development create different productive systems. Economic institutions (that is, the productive system) shape the general nature of beliefs and practices in all other areas of social life.

- In all societies, a class division evolves. Those who own or control the society's productive resources (the *means of production*) are inevitably in conflict with those who do not. In this conflict, the owning class controls key economic, political, and ideological institutions, all of which therefore reflect and protect its interests.

- Class struggle is a contest between these two primary and opposing classes, and it is here that the dynamic forces of society lie. Class struggle is the generator of societal change.

- All productive systems, with their attendant classes, give way to more advanced systems. This will occur with capitalism, too, as it gives way to socialism, wherein workers will control the means of production. Eventually, a communist society will emerge in which there will be no classes and thus no exploitation.

One might ask, Of what relevance is a theory constructed in the mid-nineteenth century to conditions and issues of our time? Many specific Marxian propositions are clearly not germane to contemporary societies. Others, however, have had lasting impact and remain meaningful.

The Failure of Marx's Vision

Although parts of it are pertinent to the whole course of human social development, Marx's analysis is concerned primarily with the structure and dynamics of capitalist industrial societies. It is in such societies that

Marx foresaw the occurrence of the workers' revolution. Obviously this has failed to materialize, especially in the West, where Marx believed the social and economic conditions were conducive to such a movement. Why did the Marxian vision not take shape?

To begin with, class struggle in advanced capitalist societies did not become more acute, as Marx predicted. Instead, the working classes of those societies seemed to settle for an accommodation with the capitalist system. As industrial capitalism thrived, the fundamental objective of workers became a more sizable share of the capitalist product, not a change in the productive system itself. Labor unions, for example, became less political organizations than groups designed to operate on behalf of workers within the accepted rules of union-management relations. Particularly in the United States, unions became forces of stabilization, not of radical change. Marx had seen workers' organizations as mobilizing agents, designed to instill consciousness and alter the prevailing power structure, rather than simply as bargaining agents that would represent labor's interests vis-à-vis the capitalist class. Rather than destroy capitalism, workers have sought to gain a bigger share of the product.

Further invalidation of Marxian theory is shown in the changing class structure itself. Serious class conflict was averted in advanced capitalist societies because the polarization of classes did not progress as Marx felt it would; rather, the very opposite occurred—an increasingly complex and diverse class structure. The Marxian formula called for a growing contraposition of the two major classes, capitalists and workers. The former would become smaller and more concentrated, and the latter would swell in size, gradually absorbing more and more of the marginal capitalists, mainly small entrepreneurs. Instead, the middle class grew, dimming the split between the two extremes. Moreover, as will be seen in Chapter 5, automation and the emergence of a global labor market continue to eliminate traditional working-class occupations. Accompanying the decline in blue-collar occupations has been the growth of the professional-managerial and service sectors, the largest elements of the workforce of postindustrial societies. The place of these classes was not well defined or overly important in Marx's analysis. As will be discussed later in this section, some contemporary Marxist theorists have tried to deal with this issue by constructing a more complex model of the class system.

Another change in the class structure concerns the place of the capitalist class. Today it is difficult to clearly discern a "capitalist" class in the Marxian sense, that is, those who actually own the means of production. Stock ownership, though still very concentrated, is far more dispersed than in past times. Many workers, therefore, own stock in the companies for which they work or hold retirement funds that are invested in the stock market. Moreover, effective power in giant corporations lies with a professional managerial class, who may not necessarily be among the major owners of the corporations they manage. It is true, of course, that the top-ranking executives do typically own large amounts of stock in their companies.

In addition to the increasing complexity of the class system, the workers' material state did not deteriorate but improved markedly from the degrading conditions typical of Marx's time. These improvements were the result of various social forces and institutions, chief among them the intervention of the state in dealing with the vacillations of a capitalist economy and the formation of strong labor unions. Neither of these developments seemed possible to Marx. As a result, class conflict in the United States and other advanced capitalist societies did not intensify.

The Marxian idea seems to have failed as well in those societies that did experience a so-called socialist revolution. Paradoxically, socialist revolutions of the twentieth century occurred in societies in which the economic and social conditions required for the kind of movement Marx forecast were least present. Russia in 1917, China in 1948, and Cuba in 1959 were societies in which capitalist development was not great. However, it is unlikely that the socialist systems of these societies, as they took shape, ever represented Marxism in anything but ideology. In many ways, they were aberrations of the Marxian legacy and must be seen as unique social orders. On few of their essential problems did Marx's theory shed any light (Harrington, 1973). Indeed, the political, economic, and social policies of those regimes could have been the same had Marx never lived.

Finally, Marx's assertion that class is the most fundamental and consequential form of social division has been shown to be questionable in societies with diverse racial and ethnic populations. Marx assumed that people everywhere will identify with others who have similar class interests and that such self-conscious class units would eventually come together as a potent political force. But in the United States and other ethnically diverse societies, class identity and action have seemed to take a backseat to racial and ethnic identity and political action. Racial and ethnic conflict has been more severe and frequent in the United States than has been class conflict, and ethnic identities have proved themselves far more effective as a source of collective action than have class interests. Most internal conflicts in all countries today revolve not around issues of class inequality but around ethnic nationalism and the desire of ethnic groups to maintain their cultural and political autonomy. Gender divisions, too, have been extremely potent in affecting life chances and the distribution of society's wealth, power, and prestige, irrespective of class differences.

Enduring Points of Marx's Theory

Though the details of Marx's model of inequality and his vision of the future are certainly refutable in light of modern history, his theoretical contribution is, in a more general sense, of lasting and fundamental significance.

First, and perhaps most important, Marx proffered the idea of social class as the key ingredient in the process of societal conflict and change. Starting with Marx, class became a basic idea of social science that would henceforth enter into any and all societal analyses. Moreover, Marx established a perspective that linked economics and politics, **political economy,** that forces us to recognize the meshing of these two basic institutions in modern societies and the manner in which they operate to create and sustain the class system.

Second, the Marxian perspective demonstrates the way in which our social and political worlds are ideologically created. As will be shown in Chapter 8, we are attuned to a certain way of thinking about and seeing society. This is a highly one-sided process, however. The prevailing modes of social, political, and economic thought are not "natural" in the sense that they produce themselves without input from the social environment. Most simply, we *learn* to perceive our world in a particular way. And our learning is confined to that which we are offered by the society's socializing agents—the family, the state, the school, the media—all disseminators of the dominant ideology. Social and political behavior and attitudes we consider "normal" or "just" are, in fact, defined for us through this ideology. As Michael Harrington explained, the Marxian perspective "asserts that the common sense of any given society is a rationalization for that society, that vocabularies normally conceal as well as communicate, particularly when they speak of anything that has to do with power" (Harrington, 1976:192).

Our concepts regarding right and wrong, good and bad, then, do not simply come upon us. Rather, the ideas and values of the dominant class generally become those of the society as a whole, creating a legitimacy for the structure of power and contributing to its perpetuation. As sociologist Frank Parkin noted,

> Dominant values are in a sense a representation of the perceptions and interests of the relatively privileged; yet by virtue of the institutional backing they receive, such values often form the basis of moral judgements of underprivileged groups. In a way, dominant values tend to set the standards for what is considered to be objectively "right." (1971:83)

This being so, it should not surprise us that those who are seemingly oppressed by a socioeconomic system often are among its staunchest defenders.

Revising Marx

Neo-Marxist theorists have acknowledged the very different forms and conditions of modern capitalism from Marx's time and thus the need to revise Marxian theory in order to make it more relevant to contemporary issues. In doing so, however, they have retained the essence of the Marxian perspective.

A theoretical point of particular focus concerns the emergence of an extraordinarily more complex workforce, calling for a more elaborate model of the class structure than the two-part Marxian scheme. Although Marx did forecast an increasingly complex division of labor as capitalism evolved, he could not foresee the extent of that complexity (Grimes, 1991). A related point with which modern Marxist theorists have dealt is the changed role of capitalists and workers in the productive system. Erik Olin Wright's work has most clearly addressed these issues.

Although accepting the basic Marxian class scheme, Wright delineates classes not on the basis of property ownership but on the basis of control of economic resources. In capitalist society, people may control financial capital, the physical means of production (such as factories), or labor (authority over workers). Major capitalists—the bourgeoisie—control all three, whereas the working class controls none. Members of a third class, the petty bourgeoisie (independent, self-employed producers), have economic ownership and possession of the means of production but, since they employ no one, lack authority over workers (Wright, 1978). Thus, Wright accepts the fundamental Marxian idea of the division of capitalist society into opposing classes based on their relation to the means of production.

Wright recognizes, however, that many work situations do not fall neatly into this capitalist–worker–self-employed scheme. He suggests that in between these three classes are those who can control some, though not all, aspects of production. Wright calls these *contradictory class locations* (1978). For example, there are some who, in their class positions, exploit labor (à la capitalists) but who themselves are exploited (à la workers). Corporate managers occupy such a position. On the one hand, they are salaried workers themselves, but on the other, they have much control over the workers whom they supervise. Professionals such as doctors, lawyers, and teachers may also be in such a contradictory class location. They have little or no control over the means of production but have much influence on the nature of their work as well as on that of employees who work at their direction (e.g., nurses, secretaries, and aides).

In later works (1985, 1997), Wright further refined this model so as to include several additional class categories. In this more complex scheme, one's class location is based not only on control of financial resources, control of the means of production, and control of labor but also on the possession of assets, including property, skills, and organizational position. This generates additional contradictory class locations.

Wright's theory, then, provides for changes in the class order of advanced capitalist societies while still retaining the basic Marxian notion that one's class is defined in relation to one's place in the society's productive system. His revised model, of course, does not speak to all the problems of applying traditional Marxian theory to contemporary capitalism, but it illustrates how neo-Marxist theorists have tried to adapt the theory to modern conditions. It also demonstrates how Marxists continue to be confounded in their efforts to sort out and systematically arrange the property and power relations of modern capitalist societies.

All social scientists today recognize the utility of at least some aspects of Marx's analysis. But obviously some are more strongly committed to this approach than others. Among those who do lean more favorably toward this approach, however, Marx is not interpreted in an absolute or mechanical fashion. Instead, Marxian ideas are accepted primarily as a method for helping to understand society rather than as a definitive explanation. C. Wright Mills referred to this group of scholars as "plain Marxists" who "are generally agreed that Marx's work bears the trademarks of the nineteenth-century society, but that his general model and his ways of thinking are central to their own intellectual history and remain relevant to their attempts to grasp present-day social worlds" (1962:98). Only among the dogmatic, or "vulgar," Marxists, then, should we expect to find attempts to apply Marxian ideas in a literal sense to societies of the present age.

In analyzing social inequality, Marx's theory is seminal. It is composed of original ideas, providing the seeds from which further thinking about inequality grew. Just as Darwin's and Einstein's ideas changed the way people thought about certain areas of biology or about physics, respectively, so the ideas of Marx propelled social thinking in new directions. Others who followed him took his ideas and built upon them. It is the general thrust of the theory rather than its specific elements that remains most relevant to the study of inequality today.

Weber: The Inevitability of Inequality

Max Weber, a German sociologist whose writing spanned the latter years of the nineteenth century and the early decades of the twentieth, is considered, along with Marx, to be one of the most important contributors to sociological theory. Although not a contemporary of Marx, Weber was certainly influenced by Marx's ideas, as were most social thinkers of that time. Indeed, it has been said that all theorists who followed Marx engaged in a "dialogue with Marx's ghost." In some ways, Weber's approach to stratification and inequality is built upon Marx's analysis, but Weber went beyond the Marxian model, modifying and elaborating on it. Thus, Weber did not dispute Marx as much as he augmented his theory and made it more complete.

Whereas Marx's view of stratification—that classes are founded on economic criteria—was essentially unidimensional, Weber suggested a more elaborate, multidimensional model. People's class positions are based not simply on their relation to the means of production but also on a number of interdependent variables. In addition to a hierarchy based on economic factors, Weber denoted hierarchies based on status and on political power. Let's look at these three distinct dimensions of social inequality—class, status, and party.

Class

Weber's notion of class is, to some degree, similar to Marx's: A class comprises those who stand in a similar position with regard to their opportunities to acquire the society's economic rewards (i.e., life chances). Weber, however, saw a greater variety of factors that are important in class formation, such as skills and credentials. Marx, remember, conceptualized class essentially as one's place in the productive system: worker or owner. But Weber pointed out, for example, that although a doctor and a custodian may both be hospital workers, not owners, they are in distinctly different class positions. Moreover, even within the bourgeoisie there are distinctions. A landlord who acquires his income from rent or a stockowner who receives dividends is not the same as an entrepreneur who operates a small business. Each, Weber pointed out, will possess different life chances.

Weber's notion of class, then, is more complete than Marx's. Some people may possess greater life chances than others as a result of their ownership of property, as Marx suggested, but others may possess greater life chances as a result of skills or expertise in a profession, enabling them to command high salaries even if they do not own productive property. Occupation rather than ownership or nonownership of property is, therefore, the basis of the formation of classes. People with common occupations, earning approximately similar incomes, constitute a class.

Status

There is more to stratification, however, than occupation or income, Weber explained. **Status** refers to differences in prestige that derive from a particular lifestyle, not from purely economic factors. The status dimension, therefore, consists of groups that display a particular lifestyle and that are aware of differences between themselves and other status groups. Weber explains the difference between class and status:

> With some over-simplification, one might . . . say that "classes" are stratified according to their relations to the production and acquisition of goods; whereas "status groups" that are stratified according to the principles of their *consumption* of goods are represented by special "styles of life." (Gerth and Mills, 1946:193)

The concept of status, or prestige, is extremely important in analyzing social inequality because it elucidates the complexity of modern stratification systems. To illustrate, consider two individuals, a truck driver and a schoolteacher. In looking at their approximate incomes, we find that they are not too different. Moreover, neither is a self-employed worker. In terms of economic position, then, they earn pretty much the same and are both nonowners. But would we really consider the truck driver and the teacher to be part of the same social class? We probably wouldn't—because of differences in status, or prestige. Teaching is more prestigious than driving a truck. Also, to become a teacher requires extensive formal training, usually a college degree. Truck drivers ordinarily learn on the job, and few possess college degrees. This automatically differentiates the two people, even though they are basically the same in terms of purely economic factors. (In fact, some truck drivers outearn some teachers.) Those who hold college degrees are held in higher esteem socially than those who are only high school graduates.

Not only are the truck driver and the teacher differentiated in terms of prestige, they also consume differently. That is, they enjoy noticeably different lifestyles. Their preferences in music, entertainment, fashion, food, housing, cars, and numerous other aspects of social life will probably differ radically. Whereas the teacher may enjoy going to art museums in his or her leisure time, for example, the truck driver might prefer hunting and fishing. When looking for a restaurant, the teacher might prefer nouvelle cuisine, whereas the truck driver may prefer a steak house. Because of the differences in how they live and spend their incomes, they can no more be considered part of the same social class than could a banker and a factory worker, despite their common economic standing.

These sharply different lifestyles make for the formation of what Weber called **status communities,** each made up of people who have similar cultural and social interests and common consumer patterns. As in the case of the teacher and the truck driver, people usually associate with others who have the same cultural tastes, live in neighborhoods made up of people like themselves, and probably marry partners of similar status. Status communities may become tightly closed, as is the case, for example, of the old rich. They may also be founded on social characteristics other than lifestyle. In multiethnic societies, for example, people's social prestige is to a great degree based on their ethnicity.

Weber pointed out that status and class are by no means unrelated. To enjoy a particular lifestyle necessitates a certain economic standing. Any style of life, therefore, will be based for the most part on occupation and income. Ordinarily, then, those who enjoy similar status will occupy a similar economic position. There are exceptions to that relationship, however, as the teacher and truck driver illustrate.

Delineating a status dimension of stratification is important, for inequality is not necessarily founded primarily on economic factors in all societies. Consider the Indian caste system (to be discussed in Chapter 7) in which inequality is based almost exclusively on one's status, with wealth playing no role. In modern, class-stratified societies, status may decline in significance but is nonetheless critical in many cases. Ethnic minorities and women, for example, commonly have been treated differently on the basis of their ethnic and gender status, regardless of their economic position.

Party

Weber's third dimension, *party,* denotes political rank—one's standing in a collectivity or organization whose "action is oriented toward the acquisition of social 'power,' that is to say, toward influencing a communal action" (Gerth and Mills, 1946:194). Such organizations may represent either class interests or status group interests or perhaps both. In addition to formal political organizations like parties, examples in modern societies include labor unions, consumer groups, business and professional associations, and ethnic organizations—in short, any group designed for or capable of involvement in political action. In modern societies, it is the state that people and groups try to influence, for it is the state that decides most public issues.

Differentiating a political dimension enables us to see that some may be very powerful yet not necessarily be part of the top class or status group. Many politicians, even at the national level, for example, are quite ordinary people in terms of class and status. Some who enter politics are small business owners or local lawyers or professionals, people who would hardly be considered (or consider themselves) part of the elite.

Weber on Power

Weber responded to Marx in another way, by questioning the basis of ruling-class power that Marx had so vividly described. Whereas Marx saw the power of a ruling class as deriving from its economic ascendance and control of resources, Weber saw the fact of modern social organization as the most significant force compelling the formation of ruling groups. Weber's explanation stressed the nature of bureaucracy and how this uniquely modern organizational form created elite power.

Weber defined power as "the possibility of imposing one's will upon the behavior of other persons" (Weber, 1954:323). Power, Weber explained, is at the base of all forms of inequality—class, status, and party—and is a primary element of all types of human interaction. Although the relationship between power and wealth is undeniable, in modern societies it is *organizational* power that is most critical. Power, then, stems not simply from the extent of one's income and wealth but, more important, from one's organizational position.

Bureaucracy With the modernization of society, government leaders and executives of large business firms become more and more dependent on organizations made up of specialists and experts to advise them and ultimately carry out critical decisions. This type of social organization takes the form of **bureaucracy.** A bureaucratic organization enables vast numbers of people playing specialized roles to blend into cohesive, well-functioning units. It is, in a sense, a social machine whose purpose is to instill efficiency, speed, and precision into organized human effort. "The decisive reason for the advance of bureaucratic organization," Weber noted, "has always been its purely technical superiority over any other form of organization" (Gerth and Mills, 1946:214). Indeed, it seems unlikely that the complex political, economic, and educational institutions of modern societies could be arranged in any other way.

Authority In modern bureaucratic organizations there are clear distinctions of power. Think of the power hierarchy in the U.S. federal government. Within the executive branch, for example, the president has more power than the attorney general, who in turn has more power than an FBI officer. But this is true of any social organization. In a school, teachers have more power than students, but both have less power than the school's principal. Whether within government, businesses, schools, churches, or any type of social organization, some people have more power than others. Weber described this kind of organizational power as **authority.** By virtue of their position in the organization, they have the capacity to impose their will over others. Societal power, therefore, emanates not from ownership of the means of production (à la Marx) but from the control of administration. Executives and managers of huge corporations, for example, exert great power not through ownership but as a result of their control of corporate resources and the authority of their positions. The same is true of government leaders.

Weber saw the historical development of societies as a movement toward rational forms of organization, that is, groups organized not on the basis of the authority of personalities and traditions but on the basis of specific functions to perform or objectives to meet. Weber called this **legal-rational authority** and distinguished it from two forms of authority based on nonrational criteria. In **traditional** systems of authority, people obey out of a sense of tradition. In a monarchy, for example, the monarch inherits the throne and is recognized as the leader because "it has always been that way." In **charismatic authority,** people obey certain individuals who assume and maintain their positions on the sheer strength of personal appeal. In such cases, leaders acquire and retain their positions as a result of their ability to capture the allegiance of large numbers of people. Loyalty and compliance are given not to a rational system or even to custom but to a particular personality. Lenin, Hitler, Mao, Gandhi, and Castro are figures of modern history whose authority derived in large measure from their charisma.

As societies move toward legal-rational authority, greater and greater power is concentrated in bureaucratic organizations, which maintain control over vast human, material, and intellectual resources. Political and corporate bureaucracies exercise dominance even over elected officials in democratic societies or self-appointed leaders in autocratic systems. In turn, control over bureaucracies constitutes an immense power resource.

Weber's Contribution to Inequality Theory

Both the Marxian and the Weberian models of stratification are valuable, and they are necessary to fully understand structured inequality in societies. The basic difference between them, however, is that with Weber's multidimensional model, stratification can be seen as emanating from several sources, not simply one's place in the productive system. This is particularly important to racial and ethnic stratification and to stratification based on gender. In those cases, people are ranked on the basis of their ethnic group membership and their gender in addition to their economic position. Although there is generally a close correlation between these different dimensions of stratification, they do not always coincide.

Unlike Marx, who envisioned the possibility of a future society in which inequality was not a basic characteristic, Weber saw modern societies heading down a path of greater rationality and bureaucratization and, thus, more inequality and alienation. Even if socialism were to triumph, Weber felt, it would be a system characterized by bureaucracy, with its imposition of hierarchy and authority. It would thus be little different from capitalism in its depersonalizing effects on people. The result, then, would be an unavoidable subordination of the many to the dictates of the few (Giddens, 1975). Like Marx, Weber explained social inequality as rooted in power; but unlike Marx, Weber did not envision its eventual demise.

Dahrendorf: Neo-Weberian

Almost all contemporary sociologists have drawn upon the ideas of both Marx and Weber in their conceptualizations of class and their formulations of the class systems of modern societies. Ralf Dahrendorf (1959) has proffered a theory that is essentially Weberian, though it also rests in part on what are Marxian notions. As a result, Dahrendorf may be considered both a neo-Marxian theorist as well as a neo-Weberian (Grimes, 1991).

Dahrendorf recognizes the Marxian division of society into two opposing and conflicting classes, one superordinate, one subordinate. But he rejects the idea that these classes are in conflict as a result of ownership or nonownership of property. Instead, it is different degrees of *authority* that make for class divisions and conflict.

In all spheres of social life—the economy, politics, education, the media, religion—modern societies are dominated by large, impersonal organizations. And all of these organizations have authority structures in which there are some people (a few) who have the right to issue authoritative commands, and other people (the majority) who must abide by those commands. Like Weber, Dahrendorf sees the inevitability of bureaucracy and a structure of authority in such organizations. Dahrendorf adopts a Weberian notion to refer to these organizations: *imperatively coordinated associations.* It is differences in organizational authority, Dahrendorf contends, that lead to different interests and around which classes form. Hence, authority, not relationship to the means of production, is the most important basis of class and class conflict in modern societies, a view basically in line with Weber's theory.

Dahrendorf posits that the Marxian assumption that classes are based on ownership or nonownership of productive property is no longer meaningful in the context of contemporary capitalist societies. Large, bureaucratically organized corporations dominate the economy, and it is a professional managerial class that exerts essential control over the resources of those corporations. Hence, the question of who owns the means of production, so fundamental to the Marxian theory, is irrelevant. Corporate managers make decisions regarding the assets of these firms and direct the firms' workers, though the managers themselves may not necessarily be among the owners. What is most critical, therefore, is authoritative power: Who controls the decision-making apparatus of organizations? That, in Dahrendorf's view, is the basis of class division in modern societies.

Bourdieu: Forms of Capital

Pierre Bourdieu is a contemporary French sociologist whose theories are clearly linked to both Marx and Weber, but whose focus is less on describing the shape of stratification per se and more on explaining how that structure of inequality is formed and sustained from one generation to the next. Recall from Chapter 1 that systems of social inequality are structured and thus not easily challenged and changed. Bourdieu provides an explanation of the process by which inequality is reproduced, that is, how power and privilege in a society are transmitted, legitimized, and perpetuated.

Bourdieu explains that there are several forms of capital that are attached to different societal areas (institutional "fields," as he refers to them), but economic, cultural, and social capital are the more general forms. Social classes, therefore, comprise people with different amounts of these three distinct forms of capital. These forms of capital are key to understanding the dynamics of class inequality.

Economic capital is simple enough to conceptualize. This is what we ordinarily think of as income and wealth. In modern societies these are the monetary resources that families and individuals possess. This is not essentially different from Marx's or Weber's understanding of economic capital.

Cultural capital is related to what Weber referred to as "status," that is, the norms and values and specific cultural tastes—the lifestyles—that are characteristic of various classes and subclasses, the latter of which Bourdieu refers to as "class fractions." But, as Bourdieu explains, it is the culture of the dominant class that clearly holds sway in the society as a whole. Here Bourdieu focuses on specific aspects of culture, not simply the general notion of culture as a society's way of life. It is the dominant class that controls the major means of cultural production and transmission.

It is through the socialization process, specifically within the family and, later, in the school, that individuals acquire different esthetic preferences. Although differences in tastes for music, art, food, and fashion may seem of little consequence, Bourdieu explains that these are, in fact, critical in separating one class from another. A colleague and biographer of Bourdieu explains it this way: "The aesthetic sense exhibited by different groups, and the lifestyles associated with them, define themselves in opposition to one another. Taste is first and foremost the distaste of the tastes of others" (Wacquant, 2008:271). Members of different classes usually feel an aversion to or discomfort with the cultural tastes and lifestyles of other classes. Upper- or upper-middle-class people, for example, may characterize working-class fashion or lifestyles as "crude" or "boorish," and make jokes about their lack of sophistication, and, similarly, working-class people may see those above them in the class hierarchy as snobbish or boring or lacking "common sense." These characterizations help to sustain and enforce class divisions. Above all, it is the cultural preferences of the dominant class that come to be defined as the "correct" culture, that to which others are expected to aspire.

Bourdieu focuses much attention on how, at the individual level, people are socialized to accept the cultural ways determined mostly by the dominant class. He stresses the importance of education in shaping and communicating (and thus controlling) culture. In modern societies, those with more and better educations are most apt to attain success. Education, then, is a key determinant of one's social class. But the educational experience is hardly the same for children of different classes. Indeed, much of students' academic success or lack thereof is determined even before they enter formal schooling and is greatly influenced by the ability of the family to begin to impart aspects of culture (cultural capital) that will benefit the child in the formal educational system. Obviously the resources of middle- and upper-class families provide advantages that working-class and lower-class children lack; these, in turn, usually assure success in school and, later, in the quest for good jobs and other key life chances. Schools perpetuate the dominance of upper-class culture by teaching its content and rewarding those who learn it. Those who come away from the socialization process with high amounts of cultural capital understand how to behave in various social contexts and circumstances and are thus able to take advantage of opportunities that those lower in the class hierarchy will rarely encounter.

Social capital, as Bourdieu explains it, comprises the key social relationships and networks within which individuals function in their daily lives. Most simply, we can think of it as social "connections." And, through these social connections one is able to enhance his or her stock of cultural and economic capital. As we will see in Chapter 7, social connections can play a critical role in determining the extent to which people may move up the social hierarchy and, by the same token, spell doom for those who lack such connections and therefore are not afforded similar opportunities for upward mobility.

These three forms of capital are interwoven and are, in many ways, interdependent. Having established a friendship at university, for example, may lead to a lucrative job opportunity upon graduation, thus enhancing one's economic capital. And, in turn, these may enable one to travel or to participate in activities that will further one's stock of cultural capital. It is through the distribution and use of these forms of capital that social classes take shape and through which individuals either change or remain stationary in their class position.

In advanced societies that do not discourage mobility, there is, of course, a leveling effect of mass education and the opportunities that it provides. Thus, although, as we will see, the upper class and power elite do, in fact, perpetuate their wealth and power over long periods, a few from lower social classes are able to penetrate the higher rungs of the social hierarchy. Bourdieu's theory, however, is compelling in its explanation of how systems of inequality are reproduced. As he explains it, capital "is what makes the games of society—not least, the economic game—something other than simple games of chance offering at every moment the possibility of a miracle" (1968:241). As we will see in Chapter 7, despite the spread of educational opportunities in the United States and other postindustrial societies, class systems do not seem to change radically; nor have levels of individual mobility risen to a significant degree. Those from families with high amounts of economic, cultural, and social capital—that is, those of the upper middle and upper classes—automatically enter the quest for wealth, power, and prestige with resources that essentially assure their advantage over those lower in the social hierarchy. Thus is the class system reproduced from one generation to the next.

Functionalism and Conflict Theory

In the 1950s a new theoretical approach emerged in the study of social inequality. It gave rise to a sharp debate among sociologists regarding the origins, inevitability, and social functions of inequality. The essential argument revolved around whether stratification was necessary in society. The two sides represented two general schools of thought in sociology: those who see the primary characteristic of societies as *order* and those who see it as *conflict*.

Order theorists, whose tradition is most heavily influenced by the early-twentieth-century French sociologist Émile Durkheim, view society as a relatively balanced system made up of differently functioning but interrelated parts. In this view, society is held together and social order maintained through a consensus of values among its groups and through the imperatives of functional interdependence. People generally agree on the basic rules of society, recognizing that only by abiding by such rules can they collectively survive.

In contrast, conflict theorists, beginning with Marx, see societies as held together not by functional needs and broad agreements among groups but by the power of dominant classes and ruling elites who impose their will on the majority. Stability and order are maintained through coercion, not consensus. People abide by the rules of society because they are coerced into doing so, not because they recognize some common survival purpose. Whereas order theorists stress the manner in which societies maintain cohesion and balance, conflict theorists emphasize the disintegrative aspects of societies and the manner in which they change.

Human societies are, of course, neither wholly ordered nor wholly in conflict; rather, societies have "two faces," as Dahrendorf puts it: conflict and consensus (Dahrendorf, 1959). Nonetheless, sociologists have favored one or the other of these broad theoretical perspectives in their analyses.

Let's examine how these two approaches deal with the key issues of stratification and inequality; namely, Why is there inequality? and Is inequality inevitable?

Functional Theory: The Need for Inequality

In line with the order perspective, functional theorists begin with the assumption that all societies are made up of different and necessary roles that must be filled in order for the society to function. Society, in this view, is comparable to the human body, made up of various organs that must be working for the body to be in balance. A person cannot function as well with one lung as with two and, without at least one, cannot live at all. Roles in society, as in the body, must be filled. Some people must farm if the society is to eat; some people must work in factories if the society is to manufacture cars and refrigerators; some must teach if the society is to train its young; some must govern if there is to be order; and so on.

In this functional scheme, some roles are more vital than others; that is, some entail more important societal functions and require more expertise and training. In modern societies, for example, it would be hard to argue that medical doctors are not more critical to the society's well-being than are sanitation workers. Moreover, some positions require more extensive skills and training than others. Consider the time and effort involved in training a doctor, as opposed to a sanitation worker. Doctors must go through rigorous schooling that is costly in terms of time, energy, and money. It might require as much as six or seven years of training beyond a bachelor's degree before one qualifies to practice medicine. Sanitation workers, by contrast, can be trained to do their jobs in a matter of minutes.

So what we have is a situation in which certain positions, presumably more crucial and more challenging, must be filled. The question is, how are they to be filled and by whom? Obviously, they must be occupied by the most qualified people, that is, the smartest and most talented. How do societies assure that these "best and brightest" people will, in fact, fill the most crucial roles? How, for example, do societies persuade people to endure the hardships and sacrifices needed to train to be a doctor? The answer, according to these theorists, is to promise them more of the society's rewards. Kingsley Davis and Wilbert Moore, in an article that first articulated the functionalist theory, summarized this position: "Social inequality is . . . an unconsciously evolved device by which societies insure that the most important positions are conscientiously filled by the most qualified persons" (1945:243). In modern societies, this means paying them more than others. Inequality, then, is needed to induce the most qualified persons to fill the most important positions and, once the positions are filled, to ensure that they will continue to perform their duties in those positions.

Inequality, in this view, is inevitable. In no society can all roles be of equal importance. In addition, not all persons will be qualified to fill the more important positions. The functionalist theory not only posits that inequality is a built-in feature of all societies but argues that it is beneficial. All members of a society need the most qualified people to fill the most important positions. Hence, it is in everyone's interest to reward them with a greater share of the society's wealth.

Conflict Theory: The Dysfunctions of Inequality

At first glance, the functionalists' argument seems convincing. How else to explain why doctors earn perhaps ten or fifteen times more than sanitation workers? Although the theory may explain such obvious cases, conflict theorists point out that it is flawed in numerous ways.

To begin with, if the functionalist assumption regarding the integrative nature of society is true—that various roles must be played for the society to function adequately—then aren't all roles critical? In 1965, sanitation workers in New York City went on strike. After several weeks, the heaping mounds of garbage piled on the city's streets posed so serious a threat to public health that the mayor requested the state governor to call up the National Guard to begin collecting the trash. Even sanitation workers, it was discovered, play a crucial social role.

How are the "most important" positions in society really identified? Although doctors versus sanitation workers may be an extreme case, can we say that teachers are less important than doctors? Judging from the average income of teachers, one would have to conclude that they are considerably less important. If we accept the logic of the functionalist position—that people are rewarded according to the relative importance of their social role—we would also have to conclude that rock musicians earning hundreds of thousands of dollars for each performance or professional basketball players, whose average annual salary is $5 million, are even more important than doctors. Indeed, one could reverse the argument of the functionalists and offer the view that, logically, societies would pay more to people doing the more odious and unappreciated tasks—like collecting garbage—to induce them to play those roles.

What, then, makes it possible for some positions to emerge as presumably more important and thus more deserving? "Power" is the conflict theorists' answer. Those who are given the most rewards, it is argued, are able to apply the greater power resources they possess. Doctors can command high salaries because they can threaten to deny people their services. How long would society tolerate a doctors' strike? Moreover, doctors have the persuasive power to convince the society that their positions are in fact more important and thus merit more in rewards than many other positions. The American Medical Association (AMA), for example, is politically very influential and can sway public opinion with its views of medicine and public health. In a sense, doctors and other highly paid workers, in the conflict theorists' view, have convinced the rest of society that their positions are more important and thus warrant disproportionately high incomes.

Conflict theorists argue that there are no assurances that the most qualified individuals will actually occupy key societal roles.[1] Assuming that the most important positions can be identified, how do societies discover the most capable people to fill them? If the society were one in which equality of opportunity were truly a reality, we could conclude that the only determining factors are people's skills and talents. But people start out in considerably different circumstances—for example, one child's father is a corporate executive earning several hundred thousand dollars a year; another child's father is an hourly paid factory worker. Both children dream of being doctors. Which one is more likely to realize that dream? The answer is obvious and has little to do with their innate talents, intelligence, or ambitions. Those from more well-to-do families are not necessarily the best and brightest, but they are given the opportunities, the "stage," so to speak, in which to pursue and fully develop their aspirations. The system by which the "most capable" are chosen to fill the most important positions is rigged in favor of those closer to the top of the social hierarchy.

Another criticism offered by the conflict theorists concerns what seems to be the need to use material rewards to induce the presumably more qualified to fill the society's important positions. The assumption of the functionalist argument is that only when people are promised a greater financial reward can they be induced to undergo the training and sacrifices needed to qualify for those positions. But this discounts the other rewards that people often acquire from their work, like prestige or self-gratification (Tumin, 1953). Many doctors, for example, will explain that high earnings are not the sole reason they were attracted to their profession. Perhaps they were genuinely interested in medicine or enjoyed the prestige that doctors are afforded or altruistically felt the need to work in a profession that helps people. These individuals might have studied medicine even if there had been no generous monetary rewards for doing so. Most college professors must train for years beyond their bachelor's degrees to attain Ph.D.'s, but in many cases they end up earning no more than factory workers. Why, then, do they undergo the rigor and hardship? Most professors would answer that they enjoy intellectual pursuits, desire the contemplative and independent lifestyle of scholars, and would not think of doing anything else, even if they were offered more lucrative opportunities.

Finally, conflict theorists ask whether the extreme differences in the distribution of rewards are really necessary, even if we accept the functionalists' basic argument (that some positions are more important and must be rewarded accordingly). Perhaps it is justifiable that doctors earn more than sanitation workers. But *how much* more is justifiable? Again, it is power, not societal need, that is the determining factor in explaining this discrepancy.

---

[1]In recent years, many high-ranking corporate executives have been rewarded with generous bonuses and retirement packages despite their dismal managerial performance, often resulting in their company's decline or even demise.

Inequality, in this view, is neither inevitable nor functional but stems from the ability of the powerful to protect their privileges and to coerce the rest of society into accepting the stratification system.

In sum, the essence of this sociological debate is simply this: The unequal distribution of power, wealth, and prestige is the result of either (a) the need to induce those with necessary skills and talents to fill the most important societal positions by rewarding them unequally, or (b) the power of those at the top of the social hierarchy, who use their power and privilege to prevent others from securing a greater share of society's rewards.

Each of the arguments made by the conflict side was met with counter-arguments by the functionalists, but the debate has never really been resolved. It is of some note, however, that on one point the two theories were never in disagreement: the universality of stratification. Tumin, in his famous response to the functionalists, acknowledged that "The fact of social inequality in human society is marked by its ubiquity and its antiquity. Every known society, past and present, distributes its scarce and demanded goods and services unequally" (1953:387). It is in their explanations of how and why that inequality arose and whether it is inevitable that the two sides have disagreed.

Lenski's Synthesis

Gerhard Lenski's theory of stratification and inequality is an attempt at a synthesis of the functional and conflict theoretical perspectives. Lenski holds that the distribution of societal rewards is based on the seemingly contradictory principles of both need and power. His theory suggests that inequality can be explained in terms of both.

The Distribution of Power, Privilege, and Prestige   Lenski begins by postulating that most human action is motivated either by self-interest or by the interests of one's group. Furthermore, most of what people strive for is in short supply. These conditions assure that there will be social conflict. Paradoxically, however, for people to attain their basically selfish goals requires cooperation. Thus, despite the predominance of self-interest, people in society will cooperate to the extent that they must in order to survive and to meet their objectives. From this, Lenski posits what he calls the first law of distribution: "Men will share the product of their labors to the extent required to insure the survival and continued productivity of those others whose actions are necessary or beneficial to themselves" (1966:44). This recognizes the functionalist tenet that societies are basically cooperative units.

Problems begin to arise, however, once societies are capable of producing a surplus, that is, more than is needed for survival. Who will get what share of this surplus? Although an element of altruism may enter into the formula, for the most part it is through power struggles that the distribution is decided.

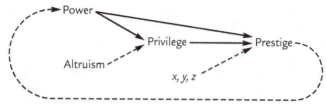

Figure 2-1 ■ The Relationship of Power, Privilege, and Prestige
Source: Gerhard Emmanuel Lenski, Jr., *Power and Privilege: A Theory of Social Stratification.*
Copyright © 1984 by the University of North Carolina Press. Used by permission of the publisher.

Hence, the second law of distribution: "Power will determine the distribution of nearly all of the surplus possessed by a society" (Lenski, 1966:44). Lenski refers to possession or control of part of this surplus as *privilege*. What follows is a third axiom: "Privilege is largely a function of power, and to a very limited degree, a function of altruism" (45). The third element of the distributive system, prestige, is essentially a product of both power and privilege.

Lenski's model (Figure 2–1) shows that privilege stems mainly from power and, to a very limited degree, from altruism. Prestige, in turn, flows mainly from power and privilege, though other minor variables may enter the picture. The dashed line indicates that there is some feedback from prestige to power. It is power, however, that is the fount of social inequality in its various other forms, political, economic, and ethnic.

Comparative Social Inequality   Lenski's theory seeks to explain not only why there is inequality in human societies but also why it varies in degree from one society to another. The keys to understanding the latter are two variables: the levels of technology and of power.

Human societies have advanced through stages differentiated by level of technological development. Where technology is very primitive and unchanging, the degree of inequality is low. This is because little in the way of a surplus can be produced, and as a result, there is minimal conflict over who will get what and how much. Moreover, the society's survival depends on cooperation. Consider a hunting-and-gathering society. Here each member must contribute to the goal of securing food. And because all hands are needed, everyone receives a proportionate share. Goods and services in these societies are distributed on the basis of *need*.

Once technology advances to a higher level, more than enough to consume at once is produced and the society is faced with the question of surplus distribution. Internal struggles arise over how the surplus will be distributed, and it is at that point that power enters the picture. The most powerful are able to take a greater share, and consolidating their economic resources reinforces and sustains their societal power. Thus, in societies that are in the initial stages of technological and industrial development (essentially agrarian societies), there is a high level of inequality. A small upper class or elite controls most of the society's wealth and is able to impose its will on the rest of the population. So goods and services in these societies are distributed on the basis of *power*. Contemporary global conditions seem to give weight to this idea. It is in societies that are usually referred to as "developing" or "Third World" that we see the most extreme gaps between the wealthy and the poor. A few affluent families or individuals own and control the bulk of the society's resources, and the massive peasantry remains relatively powerless and poor.

Although we might expect an even greater level of inequality as industrialism begins to emerge, modern industrial societies do not demonstrate this. In fact, the very opposite seems to occur—extremes of inequality begin to decline. As Lenski explains, "The appearance of mature industrial societies marks the first significant reversal in the age-old evolutionary trend toward ever increasing inequality" (1966:308). In these societies, political inequality is reduced, and although the distribution of income remains markedly unequal, it is less so than in nonindustrial societies. Why does this occur when it would seem logical that even greater inequality would be the result of much increased productivity?

Lenski attributes a reduction in inequality to several factors. To begin with, industrial societies are much more complex than earlier societal forms, thus compelling those at the top of the hierarchy to rely more and more on lieutenants and underlings. Delegating authority to others makes for a diffusion of power and privilege. Second, by granting lower classes a share of the economic surplus, ruling groups can neutralize worker hostility and the economic losses that can be suffered from strikes and work slowdowns. Third, in a highly productive economy, elites are no longer interested solely in enriching themselves and so may be willing to share more with others. Finally, in modern industrial societies, democratic ideology takes hold, making it necessary for those with power to concede some of it to the masses in order to avoid serious challenges to their position.

Summary

Two key issues form the focus of theories of social inequality: Why is there inequality? and Is inequality inevitable in human societies?

Marx saw social inequality as a basic characteristic throughout human history. All societies break down into two opposing and conflicting classes: those who own the means of economic production and those who do not. The latter have no choice but to work for the former. Inequality, then, is a product of ownership of the means of production. Those who control the society's productive resources are a ruling class. Their dominance is not only economic but political and social as well.

Inequality is not part of the human condition, according to Marx, but in capitalist society it is fundamental. Only through a workers' revolution, in which ownership of the means of production changes hands, can the capitalist system of inequality end. Although no specific formula or time frame was offered, Marx saw the end of capitalism as inevitable, just as other productive systems had passed and were replaced. Capitalism will give way to socialism, in which workers will control the means of production. Only with the development of an entirely new human being, one divested of personalistic and material values, can true social equality emerge in a communist society.

Weber saw modern forms of social inequality as emerging from the complexity of modern societies, and saw the power of ruling classes stemming from control of organizations, not ownership of property. Weber was more pessimistic than Marx, believing that so long as societies were large and complex, none could avoid the need to be bureaucratically organized, and that those bureaucracies would be controlled and directed by power elites.

The details of Marx's model of inequality, as well as his future vision, have not held up since the latter nineteenth century. But his theoretical contribution is seminal and remains, in a more general sense, of lasting significance. Neo-Marxian theorists have refined Marx's ideas to fit the conditions of modern societies. A theoretical debate more contemporary in origin is rooted in the order and conflict perspectives pioneered by Durkheim and Marx. Functionalists posit that inequality is not only inevitable but necessary, ensuring that the most capable individuals wind up occupying the most important societal positions. Conflict theorists reject that argument by asserting that inequality, rather than inevitable and functional, is mainly the result of powerful individuals' applying their resources to secure and sustain their places at the top of the hierarchy. Lenski has attempted to synthesize these two opposing views by suggesting that social inequality may, under different conditions, be both functional and conflict inducing. In technologically simple societies, humans will share because they must in order to survive. Once a surplus is produced, however, inequality sets in. In less economically developed societies, the surplus is distributed primarily on the basis of power. As societies industrialize, the level of inequality declines.

3

The American Class System

The rich and the middle class are now living in parallel universes, and the poor are almost invisible to both.
ROBERT REICH

Class is the great unmentionable in America.
ROBERT KUTTNER

Exploration of the major dimensions of inequality in the United States and other advanced industrial societies begins with studying class structure. Some argue that social class is the most consequential form of stratification, exceeding ethnicity, gender, and all others. Following a discussion of how social classes are conceptualized, this chapter presents a broad picture of the American class hierarchy, showing the socioeconomic characteristics of the different strata. Then it looks at the distribution of income and wealth, demonstrating through statistical data "who gets what." Finally, the chapter shows how patterns of inequality have changed during the last several decades.

Social Class: A Two-Dimensional Picture

Few people are unfamiliar with the idea of social class. Like race, ethnic group, and gender, class is a sociological concept that most of us make reference to from time to time. Early in life, we come to understand that this is one of the ways in which societies are divided. We are also apt to acquire some perception of our own social-class standing. But beyond this very general understanding, most Americans have only a vague notion of what social class entails or implies. To add to the confusion, sociologists themselves are often in disagreement about what social classes are and how they should be measured. To begin with, we need to understand that class can be seen in two dimensions—economic and behavioral.

Economic Class

As an economic concept, **social classes** can be understood most simply as groupings of people who share roughly similar incomes and wealth, similar occupations, and similar levels of education. These three aspects of class—

income and wealth, occupational prestige, and educational level—are closely intertwined and together create economic commonality. Income is, for most people, dependent on their occupation, which, in turn, is largely dependent on their education. Occasionally, of course, the three do not coincide. For instance, a truck driver with only a high school diploma may, through an extremely long and arduous schedule, earn over $100,000 a year, placing him among the society's highest income earners. Conversely, college professors with Ph.D.'s, obviously among the society's elite in terms of educational attainment, may sometimes earn less than unskilled workers. But cases such as these are not common. For the vast majority of people, income, occupation, and education coincide.

Sociologists often refer to a combination of these three social characteristics not as social class but as **socioeconomic status,** or simply SES. In a purely economic sense, classes are merely statistical units, and the lines of division between them can be drawn somewhat arbitrarily. Although this would seem to prompt an endless debate—where does one class begin and the other end?—there are roughly discernible divisions between economic classes, especially as they extend out from the center to the top and bottom poles of the class hierarchy.

Class as Lifestyle

There is a second dimension of social class that goes beyond a simple division of the society into socioeconomic units. Classes may be thought of as groupings in which people share not only similar occupations, incomes, and levels of education but also similar **lifestyles.** We recognize, for example, that upper-class people generally use different patterns of speech; maintain different tastes in music, fashion, and food; decorate their houses differently; and prefer different forms of leisure than do either middle-class or lower-class people. Social classes, then, are more than simply statistical units. They are real divisions of society that are manifested in people's behaviors.

This is not to imply that there is no correspondence between economic class and class as lifestyle. Indeed, as Max Weber so clearly pointed out, the two are very much interdependent. To maintain a particular lifestyle requires a certain income. One might prefer to drive a Mercedes, dine regularly on fine cuisine, and vacation on the French Riviera, but to support such an upscale standard of living would necessitate a commensurate income. Thus, people's lifestyles generally conform to their economic level. Moreover, those preferring to live a particular lifestyle probably will associate with people of similar tastes and preferences. Thus, what Weber referred to as status groups emerge among people with similar incomes, occupations, and educations. It is in this sense that classes become subcultures, in which similar patterns of behavior and beliefs are expressed. Beginning in early childhood, individuals learn class-based norms and values, and although these may change somewhat with social mobility, for most people they are quite enduring.

A story is told about a conversation between F. Scott Fitzgerald and Ernest Hemingway, two of America's great twentieth-century novelists. While sitting in a Paris cafe in the 1920s, Fitzgerald, whose novels often depicted life among the wealthy, is reputed to have remarked to Hemingway, "You know, Ernest, the rich are different from you and me." To which Hemingway replied, "Yes, Scott, they have more money." What Hemingway was referring to was the economic conception of classes—groupings of people with similar amounts of socioeconomic resources. Fitzgerald, however, was referring to classes as groupings of people who practice different lifestyles, or who constitute, in Weber's terms, status groups.

Popular Notions of the American Class Structure

Class Consciousness   Although most Americans have a vague awareness of class, their own as well as others, they have a low level of class consciousness—that is, an understanding of how social class has an impact on their lives and how the political, economic, and social interests of different classes conflict. Most Americans simply do not frame their perspective of politics and their social lives within class lines. In short, although they are implicitly aware of the fact that the United States is divided by class, they don't pay close attention to class divisions and the issues raised by those divisions, and they rarely think of themselves in class terms.

Americans, however, do pay close attention to other lines of social division, particularly race and ethnicity. Ethnicity remains an important part of most people's self-identification and many are aware of what they perceive as their ethnic interests. As a result, political issues in American society more often revolve around race and ethnicity than around social class.

Americans are also keenly aware of how ethnicity commonly impacts sharply on various spheres of social life. People may not consciously consider class differences in choosing a neighborhood in which to reside, for example, but they carefully consider its racial and ethnic makeup. Of course, people always implicitly choose their neighborhood on the basis of class, too, if for no other reason than that their income and occupation dictate that they live among those who are economically like themselves. This creates a society that is even more tightly segregated by social class than it is by race and ethnicity. Similarly, in dating and, ultimately, marriage, people ordinarily are implicitly aware of the social class of their partner even though they consider more consciously his or her race or ethnicity.

"America Is a Middle-Class Society"   Given their low level of class awareness, most Americans picture the U.S. class system in overly simplistic terms. The most popular conceptualization of the class hierarchy is a diamond-shaped structure with tiny upper and lower classes and a gigantic middle (Figure 3-1a). The fact that most people self-identify as somewhere in the middle seems to reflect this image. In social surveys conducted over the past

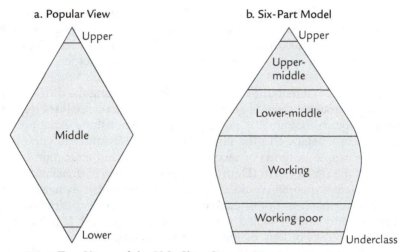

Figure 3-1 ▪ Two Views of the U.S. Class Structure

fifty years, almost all people, when asked to identify themselves in terms of class, consistently respond with "middle" or "working" class (Heath, 1998; Hout, 2008; Jackman and Jackman, 1983; Pew, 2008b; *Washington Post*, 2012).[1]

Another way of oversimplifying class divisions is to entirely dismiss the class structure, to thereby portray the United States as a "classless" society. Conservative politicians will often denounce any effort on the part of political opponents to point out sharp differences between the wealthy and other classes and will accuse these rivals of "exploiting the issue of class" or creating "class warfare." The idea is to deny that class divisions have any significance in the United States or even that classes exist at all.

The Reality of Class in the United States

The reality is that there are sharp differences in income and wealth, educational levels, and occupational status among the American population. These differences translate into a highly inequitable distribution of life chances and societal resources. They also produce strikingly different lifestyles.

The Six-Part American Class Structure

Dividing the population into class units is imprecise simply because there are no "natural" divisions, or breaking points, of the class hierarchy in terms of income and wealth, occupational status, and education. Any division of the

---

[1]The same view of people's class standing is evident in Canada and the UK, though the percentage calling themselves "working class" is considerably higher in the latter (see Robison, 2003).

society into a conceptualized hierarchy, therefore, is bound to be somewhat arbitrary. If, for example, one sociologist draws the line dividing middle and working classes at $40,000 annual income, another might draw it at $50,000. The boundaries of social classes are abstractions and thus do not lend themselves to precision.

Despite such inherent difficulties in clearly delineating the different units of the class hierarchy, there is general agreement among analysts regarding its basic shape. Although it is not possible to demonstrate exact points at which one class begins and the other ends, there are sufficient commonalities among people in terms of income, occupation, and education to draw a picture of the class system (Figure 3-1b). If those lines of division were not already apparent, people would be unable to distinguish themselves from others in terms of class. But of course they do make such distinctions. Both the very wealthy and the abject poor are easily recognized. It is the groups within the central portions of the hierarchy—the middle, or intermediate, classes—that are not so readily distinguished. Here, too, the divisions, though often hazy, are clear enough to be able to fill in the nuances of the American class hierarchy. Using the three major components of SES (income, occupation, and education), we may divide the hierarchy into six specific strata as depicted in Table 3-1.[2]

Table 3-1 is not intended to present a precise picture of the American class structure. The percentage of each class as part of the total class structure should be seen only as an approximation. Moreover, many families will not be consistent on all the indicators of social class. For example, the income of a family's major breadwinner may not reflect his or her level of education. Nonetheless, the table provides a bird's-eye view of the class system as a whole, the details of which will be discussed in Chapters 4, 5, and 6.

The Upper Class   At the top of the structure are those whose share of income and wealth far exceeds those in other classes. Of great significance is the fact that they generally derive the bulk of their income not from wages and salaries, as do most people, but from returns on investments, such as stocks and bonds, real estate, and other forms of property. This is why those at the top of the class hierarchy are sometimes referred to as the *capitalist* class. Some are corporate executives who have enormous ownership shares in their companies. Others have inherited wealth and may play no direct managerial role. Most are highly educated, often at the most prestigious prep schools, colleges, and universities. The upper class represents a very tiny percentage of the general class structure, no more than 1 percent.

Members of the capitalist class also enjoy maximum prestige and ordinarily occupy positions of great authority, giving them much societal power. Often it is difficult to distinguish between the capitalist class and those who

---

[2]This six-part depiction of the U.S. class structure draws heavily from the model suggested by Dennis Gilbert and Joseph A. Kahl (1993).

Table 3-1 ■ Model of the American Class Structure

Class	Percent of Families	Approximate Family Income Range	Major Source of Income	Typical Occupations	Level of Education
Upper or "capitalist"	<1	>$1,000,000	Assets	Investors, corporate executives	At least 4 years college
Upper-middle	18–20	$80,000–$1,000,000	Salaries	Upper-level managers; professionals; some business owners	At least 4 years college; postgraduate training for many
Lower-middle	25–30	$40,000–$80,000	Salaries and wages	Lower-level managers; semiprofessionals; small business owners; craftspersons	At least high school graduate; often some college
Working	25–30	$30,000–$45,000	Wages	Operatives; clerical, retail sales workers	High school graduate
Working poor	12–15	$15,000–$30,000	Wages	Lower-level service workers; unskilled operatives	Some high school
Underclass	9–12	<$15,000	Public assistance; underground economy	Unemployed	Some high school

comprise the higher range of the upper-middle class. Many of the truly wealthy may be professionals, such as doctors and lawyers, occupations typically held by the upper-middle class. Most important, however, is the fact that members of the capitalist class derive their income not primarily from their occupations, like the upper-middle class, but from their assets.

The Upper-Middle Class   Facetiously, it might be said that if the capitalist class "owns" the society, then those who constitute the upper-middle class "run" the society. While the upper-middle class is certainly distinguishable on the basis of income and wealth—well above average—these are the people whose skills and expertise are critical to the functioning of the society's major institutions: government, corporations, mass media, education, medicine, and so on. They are the executives and professionals who occupy the managerial and technical positions where critical, far-reaching societal decisions are made. Their occupations influence what we buy, eat, see on TV, and teach our children. Their decisions help set the agenda of government and determine the state of the economy.

More than any factor, education sets apart members of the upper-middle class from other classes and creates a common lifestyle. To be part of the upper-middle class is almost automatically to be college educated. The nature of upper-middle-class occupational positions makes higher education imperative. Managers must be trained in the skills of business and economics; doctors cannot expect to practice medicine or attorneys law without professional training. Similarly, engineers, scientists, and educators all require formal training at the highest levels.

Members of the upper-middle class derive their income not only from wages and salaries, which are high compared to other class groups, but also from investments. Moreover, the occupational positions of the upper-middle class rank high in terms of prestige, and members of this class are commonly among the most esteemed in the society. Studies have shown repeatedly that Americans accord greater prestige to people in professional positions (e.g., doctors, attorneys, and professors) and to top corporate managers than they do to those engaged in most other occupations. Obviously, these are also positions of significant authority and thus, as already noted, often carry with them substantial power to influence people's social and economic lives.

The upper-middle class has expanded more than any other during the last several decades as the occupational structure of the society has changed. In 1940 less than 15 percent of the workforce comprised managers, technicians, and professionals, but today 36 percent are part of these categories (U.S. Census Bureau, 1975, 2012a).

The Lower-Middle Class   The lower-middle class is probably the least clearly definable and most diverse among the various class strata. Occupationally, these are middle managers, semiprofessionals (e.g., nurses and technicians), craftspersons, and many service workers (such as nonretail salespersons), police and firefighters, and other government employees. Also part of the lower-middle class are proprietors of small businesses, the petty bourgeoisie, who employ only a few people and whose business assets are modest by comparison with large corporate firms.

Those in the lower-middle class can be expected to earn incomes close to the society's median. As to education, almost all are at least high school graduates and many have attended college, though the percentage of college graduates is far below that of the upper-middle class.

Although those of the lower-middle class may be esteemed, they do not enjoy the level of prestige of the upper-middle class nor do their positions afford them authority beyond their rather circumscribed social roles. Nonetheless, they share many of the attributes and values of the upper-middle class and aspire to upward mobility.

If there is a stratum that corresponds to the familiar description of "middle America," it is the lower-middle class. Conservative in their politics and in their social values, these are people who subscribe strongly to the basic beliefs of the American ideology, especially self-reliance.

The Working Class   Traditionally, the working class comprised those occupying manual laboring jobs. The term "blue collar" was attached to this stratum, denoting the physical nature of their work. The stereotypical blue-collar worker dressed in coveralls, carried a lunch bucket, and stopped at the corner bar for a beer on the way home from work. Today, the working class comprises a broad range of occupations, from skilled manual workers to retail sales clerks.

In the last few decades, the economies of modern industrial societies have changed from primarily production of goods to the provision of services. As that change has occurred, blue-collar jobs have declined and been replaced by service jobs. Many of these service jobs are only semiskilled, and the wages they pay are relatively low. As many traditional working-class jobs have been phased out, it is the occupants of these lower-skilled and lower-paying service jobs that today make up a growing part of the working class. The working class, then, comprises both blue- and white-collar workers. The jobs of both, however, are apt to be highly routinized, with little opportunity for creativity or innovation, and they entail little authority.

Occupations in this stratum usually require a high school diploma, but an increasing number of working-class people have completed some college, and a small, but growing, percentage are even college graduates. In line with these educational requirements, working-class incomes fall generally below the society's median. Although many among the working class may work for a salary, most are paid an hourly wage. Working-class people are thus able to maintain a standard of living that is adequate to provide the basic necessities of life but few of the amenities that the middle classes take for granted. Moreover, the expectations of upward mobility, so vital a part of the middle-class perspective, are much less evident. This is a result of the limited educational qualifications of working-class people as well as their more tenuous job security.

The upper-middle, lower-middle, and working classes are less distinct from each other than are those at the two extremes of the class hierarchy, the rich and the poor. Accordingly, they can be referred to as "classes in the middle," or the "intermediate classes." Certainly, there are vast and obvious differences between upper-middle-, lower-middle-, and working-class people. The point, however, is that the divisions among these middle classes are not discrete; rather, they blend into each other. Moreover, most of the social mobility that occurs in American society is experienced by people in these classes, moving from one stratum of the middle to another. Also, changes in the occupational structure of the society have been most evident within this intermediate segment of the class system, creating a picture that is mixed and in flux.

The Working Poor   Defining poverty is a highly debatable issue, as will be shown in Chapter 6. For now, the poor may be defined simply as those families that fall below the official U.S. government poverty line or are only slightly above it. Essentially, the poor can be broken down into two categories: the working poor and the abject poor, or underclass.

The working poor comprises those who are poor but are part of the working population. They may drift in and out of poverty as they experience unemployment periodically, or their wages may be so low that they are unable to rise above the poverty line. The jobs performed by the working poor are at the very bottom of the occupational hierarchy, those least desirable, least skilled, and requiring the least education. Correspondingly, these jobs pay the lowest wages, often the minimum wage, and have few or no benefits. Increasingly, people at this level work on a temporary or part-time basis, further contributing to their inability to rise above poverty, despite the fact that they may be employed. Many of the occupational handicaps faced by the working poor derive from their generally low educational level—few advance beyond high school, and many do not even finish high school.

The Underclass   A second element of the poor comprises those who are abjectly poor, that is, who remain chronically in poverty and who are, for the most part, dependent on government welfare of one kind or another. This component of the poor has been referred to as the underclass. To all intents and purposes, these are people outside the social and economic mainstream. They possess few skills that would enable them to function as part of the workforce, and many engage in petty crime or operate on the margins of the mainstream economy.[3] As sociologist Peter Saunders has described it, the underclass is permanently marginalized:

---

[3]The term *underclass* has been an issue of controversy in recent years. Some maintain that it is a pejorative term used to describe a group whose behaviors are disapproved by the nonpoor. Others, however, consider it simply a description of the socioeconomic position of those who experience long-term poverty. Here the term is used in the latter sense.

It seems surplus to economic requirements, and high rates of long-term unemployment make it difficult to argue that its members are essential to the efficient functioning of a capitalist economy, for there are many who will never find work again. (1990:120)

The underclass, though consisting of a variety of ethnic groups, is disproportionately African American and is confined primarily to inner-city areas. It has come to serve for the nonpoor as a kind of symbol of the social ills that afflict American society. And as sociologist Herbert Gans (1996) and others have suggested, the underclass is commonly seen as the "undeserving poor."

The Distribution of Income

For most people, their income is the single most significant determinant of their social class. Income is, most simply, monetary gain from any of a variety of sources. Most of it derives from wages and salaries, but dividends and interest payments are also forms of income. In order to begin to understand the structure of inequality in American society, it is necessary to look carefully at how income is distributed. The simple question is "Who gets what?"

Family Income   Income statistics are most commonly stated in terms of family or household, rather than personal or individual, income. As defined by the U.S. Census Bureau, **families** consist of two or more persons who live in the same housing unit and are related by marriage or blood, whereas **households** consist of both families as well as persons who live by themselves, with roommates, or with unmarried partners. A family's income, for example, might include the wages of two income earners, husband and wife, and perhaps even the wages of a child who is contributing to the total income. It would also include whatever interest and dividends the family members earned on their financial investments, such as savings accounts or stocks. A family income of, say, $65,000 might be broken down as follows:

Husband's wages	$40,000
Wife's wages	24,500
Dividends	500
TOTAL	$65,000

How is family or household income actually distributed in American society? Table 3-2 indicates that it is apportioned in a sharply unequal way: 13.7 percent of households earn less than $15,000. At the other end of the income hierarchy, 3.9 percent earn over $200,000.

Median Income   An important statistic in looking at income inequality is median family or household income. The median is a figure that indicates the midpoint of a distribution, where 50 percent fall above and 50 percent fall

Table 3-2 ▪ Percentage of Households by Income, 2010

Income	Percentage
Under $15,000	13.7
$15,000–$24,999	12.0
$25,000–$34,999	10.9
$35,000–$49,999	13.9
$50,000–$74,999	17.7
$75,000–$99,000	11.4
$100,000–$149,999	12.1
$150,000–$199,999	4.5
$200,000 or more	3.9

Source: U.S. Census Bureau, 2011a.

below. This is a more accurate indicator of a central point or "average" than is the mean, since the latter can be distorted by a few very extreme cases at either end. In the case of income distribution, the mean family income will be pushed up by the enormous incomes of a very small percentage of families at the top of the hierarchy. The median, however, gives the exact "middle" point. The median can then be used as a base point from which to observe deviations.

Figure 3-2 shows the median household income from 1967 to 2010 in constant dollars. Looking at changes in the median household income in current dollars would not tell us much about how this figure had changed over time, because the value of the dollar changes from year to year. It is therefore necessary to convert yearly figures into constant dollars, that is, the equivalent of the value of the dollar at the present time. Figure 3-2 shows that when measured in constant (2010) dollars, the actual increase in income has been quite modest. Indeed, annual income actually declined steadily after 2005.

Keep in mind that Figure 3-2 shows household income, not family income. The median family income for any year is higher than the comparable median household income because persons living alone—considered household units—usually earn less than family units. In 2010, while the median income for all households was $49,445, for family households only it was $61,554.

Income Quintiles   As a way of viewing the overall distribution of income, sociologists and economists commonly divide the population into income fifths, or quintiles, each with the same number of families. These income quintiles are arranged in the order of household or family income, from highest earners to lowest. The income received by all households in each of the quintiles is expressed as a percentage of total household income. Thus, there is the highest 20 percent of income earners, the second highest 20 percent, and so on. The best way to conceptualize this is to think of a pie

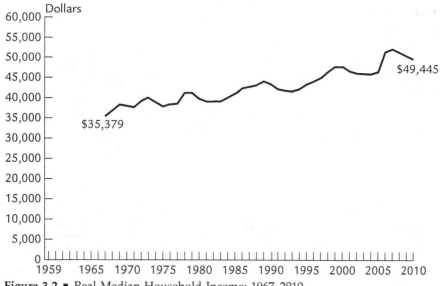

Figure 3-2 ■ Real Median Household Income: 1967–2010
Note: The data points are placed at the midpoints of the respective years. Median household income data are not available before 1967.
Source: U.S. Census Bureau, 2011a.

divided into five pieces. If income were distributed equally, with all households earning the same, each piece (or 20 percent) would receive 20 percent of the society's total income. To the extent that income is distributed unequally, the pieces of pie will be larger or smaller.

As Figure 3-3 shows, rather than proportionately divided, the income pie is immensely maldistributed. Table 3-3 provides some historical perspective on the distribution of income, showing its changes over the last several decades. To begin with, looking at any particular year, we can see that the richest 20 percent of households earned a highly disproportionate share of total income. In 2010, for example, the richest quintile earned half of all income. Also obvious is the enormous discrepancy between the richest and poorest quintiles. While the richest 20 percent of households earned 50 percent of total income, the poorest 20 percent earned just over 3 percent. The income of the top 20 percent, in other words, was almost fifteen times greater than that of the bottom 20 percent.

Concentrating on the discrepancy between the top and bottom fifths actually understates the extent of income inequality in the United States. Included in the top fifth are many households that are hardly among the very affluent. In 2010, for example, all households earning more than $100,000 were part of that top quintile. Thus, we need to move closer to the peak of the income hierarchy, that is, the richest 5 percent of households. As is seen in Table 3-3, in 2010, that top 5 percent earned more than 21 percent of all income. This was considerably more than the total income of the bottom two quintiles and almost as much as the poorest, second, and middle quintiles—60 percent of

Figure 3-3 ▪ The American
Income Pie
Source: U.S. Census Bureau, 2011a.

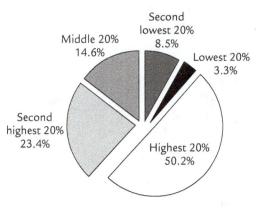

Table 3-3 ▪ Percentage of Income Received by Each Household Quintile

Category	1967	1974	1981	1989	1996	2005	2010
Top 5 Percent	*17.5*	*15.9*	*15.6*	*18.9*	*21.4*	*22.2*	*21.3*
Highest quintile	43.8	43.1	43.8	46.8	49.0	50.4	50.2
Fourth quintile	24.2	24.7	25.0	24.0	23.3	23.0	23.4
Middle quintile	17.3	17.1	16.8	15.8	15.1	14.6	14.6
Second quintile	10.8	10.6	10.2	9.5	9.0	8.6	8.5
Poorest quintile	4.0	4.4	4.2	3.8	3.7	3.4	3.3

Source: U.S. Census Bureau, 2009e, 2011a.

all households! Even this does not indicate the huge gap between those at the
top of the income hierarchy and the remainder of the society, since the bulk
of that 21 percent was earned by the top 1 percent and, even more specifically,
a fraction of that 1 percent. Consider that the top 0.1 percent receive in a day
and a half about what the bottom 90 percent receive in a year (Stiglitz, 2012).

The data in Table 3-3 do not reveal the impact of other dimensions of
inequality on the distribution of income. In American society, race and ethnicity relate closely to all measures of income. This means that those of a
particular racial or ethnic category will disproportionately fall at some point
on the income hierarchy. For example, African Americans and Hispanic
Americans collectively rank considerably below Euro-Americans in family
income, whereas Asian American family income, on average, is highest of
all. This does not mean that all African American and Hispanic American
families earn less than all Euro-American families. It means only that African
Americans are more likely to rank lower in the income hierarchy. (Remember the idea of "probability.") The same is true of women in comparison
with men. Chapters 10 and 11 look more closely at how ethnicity and gender influence income distribution. There are also regional disparities in
income. The median household income in Mississippi, for example, is little

Table 3-4 ▪ Median Income by Type of Household, 2010

Type of Household	Median Income
All households	$49,445
Family households	61,544
Married-couple families	72,751
Female householder, no husband present	32,031
Male householder, no wife present	49,718
Nonfamily households	29,730
Female householder	25,456
Male householder	35,627

Source: U.S. Census Bureau, 2011a.

more than half of what it is in Maryland. Even within particular states, there are often sharp contrasts from county to county and between rural and urban areas.

Family or household composition is especially critical in explaining variations in income inequality. This is shown clearly in Table 3-4. Married couple families in 2010 earned $73,000; female-headed families with no husband present earned not even half that amount.

The Distribution of Wealth

Having now looked at the distribution of income in American society, it should be apparent that the notion of the United States as a thoroughly middle-class society, in which there are no sharp class divisions, is largely fantasy. Income is distributed in a highly inequitable fashion and has been for many decades. Wealth is even more grossly maldistributed between those who have much, those who have some, and those who have little.

What Is "Wealth"? Wealth is not the same as income, and the distinction between them is important. Whereas income is monetary gain, wealth is the value of one's assets, or property. Economists have distinguished income and wealth by describing the former as a flow of money over time and the latter as a stock of things owned that have market value (Dowd, 1993; Atkinson, 1975; Inhaber and Carroll, 1992; Keister, 2000). Wealth is most commonly measured in terms of "net worth." In modern capitalist societies, wealth is ordinarily thought of as income-producing assets, not simply as one's material possessions (clothes, cars, etc.), though the latter are certainly assets. The major forms of wealth are stocks, bonds, and other financial instruments; cash; real estate; and business equity. Wealth, then, produces income in the form of dividends on investments or profits from business assets.

Inequalities in wealth are more consequential than inequalities in income because, as the old adage goes, "it takes money to make money."Although high income can lead to a comfortable standard of living, only through wealth can great riches be amassed. Usually, people use their wages—that is, their regular income—for living expenses. What they save from those wages and invest then becomes wealth. Few people, however, can ever save enough of their wages alone to amass a fortune. Even if they were to save regularly for their entire lifetime, it is unlikely that they would accumulate a sufficient amount to enter into the ranks of the truly wealthy, who earn their income primarily from their investments. But if wealth is acquired through investments, we have a kind of catch-22: Investments require wealth. As economist Lester Thurow has pointed out, "Once wealth is acquired, opportunities to make more money multiply, since accumulated wealth leads to income-earning opportunities that are not open to those without wealth" (1996:243). Moreover, as Thurow explains, there are limitations to what one can earn through wages since there are just so many hours that one can work. Wealth, however, is not limited in the same way; wealth generates wealth, and there is no constraining force, like time or energy, to inhibit the process.

Wealth is not only a source of income but also a kind of security for those who own it, who understand that even if their income is not forthcoming steadily, their assets will enable them to continue to live at a level to which they are accustomed. Thus, in times of economic crisis, such as the loss of one's job, a marital breakup, or a serious illness, wealth provides the means of consumption. "The very knowledge that wealth is at hand," notes economist Edward Wolff, "is a source of comfort for many families" (1995b:6).

Wealth more than income contributes to the perpetuation of the class hierarchy. This is because wealth can be passed down from generation to generation. Children usually inherit the wealth amassed by their parents, perhaps enhancing its amount further in their lifetimes and then handing it down to *their* children. Consider two college graduates entering their initial jobs: One knows that he will inherit $200,000 when his parents die; the other begins only with debts incurred from student loans that helped him pay his tuition. The first graduate can purchase some luxuries, like a new car, or rent an expensive apartment. More important, he can afford to take financial risks and perhaps invest some of the salary he will earn where it will yield dividends and thus quickly earn him more income. The second graduate, however, will have to budget carefully, will not be able to take chances with his money, and, unless his salary increases sharply in a short time, will have little left over to save after his bills are paid. It will be several years before he will be able to begin to save enough for any kind of substantial investment. By that time, his fellow graduate's investments will have put him many steps ahead in the competition for the society's rewards, not because of any superior effort or ambition but mainly because of the wealth his parents amassed. And once he marries and forms a family of his own, *his* children probably will be assured of some of the same advantages.

It is in this way that the rich stay rich and that the distribution of wealth does not change radically. Several years ago, the late Malcolm Forbes, publisher of *Forbes* magazine and one of the richest men in America, appeared on the *Late Show* with comedian David Letterman. In a serious moment, Letterman asked Forbes how he had acquired his fortune. With a perfectly straight face, Forbes replied, "My father died." Only if strict and formidable taxes on inheritance could be effected might we see a lessening of the continuation of wealth from one generation to the next. So long as the bulk of one's wealth can be passed on, the continuation of class inequality is virtually assured. Thus, the places on the class hierarchy of the rich, the poor, and those in the middle do not change much from one generation to the next. Entrance into the ranks of the wealthy occurs mainly through inheritance or, for the uncommon few, the ability to amass a fortune through extraordinary business success or through achievement in professional sports or the entertainment world.

Wealth in American Society: "The Rich and the Rest of Us"   Although income and wealth are not the same, there is an evident relationship between them. Not surprisingly, those who *earn* the most are *worth* the most. The top 20 percent of households in income have a median net worth twenty-two times greater than the middle quintile and 240 times those in the lowest quintile! The differences are actually much greater if only non-home wealth is included, since home equity is the major form of wealth for all but the very richest (Levine, 2012).

The breakdown of total wealth by household income, however, is actually an understatement of how much is owned by just a few. We can get a better idea of the extreme concentration of wealth by breaking down the top wealth quintile more specifically. As seen in Figure 3-4 and Table 3-5, the richest 10 percent of households in 2010 owned 75 percent of all wealth, but the super-rich—the top 1 percent—alone owned more than one-third. If we were to train a microscope on that richest 1 percent, however, we would see that within that tiny fraction, the majority of wealth is held by an even tinier fraction (Keister, 2000, 2005). Figure 3-5 reveals the extreme concentration of wealth in terms of dollars. The average net worth of the top 1 percent of households was almost $14 million. By contrast, the second to last quintile averaged $5,000 in wealth, while the poorest quintile had a *negative* net worth (that is, they were in debt) of $27,000. Table 3-5 also shows that during the past two decades wealth at the top (the richest 10 percent) increased, while wealth of the remaining 90 percent declined.

If we consider only financial assets—a concept of wealth that leaves out the value of owner-occupied housing—the concentration is even more astounding: As seen in Figure 3-4, the top 1 percent own more than 40 percent, and the top 10 percent own more than 80 percent of total financial wealth.

Table 3-5 ▪ Distribution of Wealth, 1989–2010 (percent)

		1989	1995	2001	2010
Top 1%	(The Super-Rich)	30.1%	34.6%	32.7%	34.5%
Next 9%	(The Rich)	37.1	33.2	37.1	40.0
Next 40%	(Everybody Else)	29.9	28.6	27.4	24.3
Bottom 50%		3.0	3.6	2.8	1.1

Source: Levine, 2012.

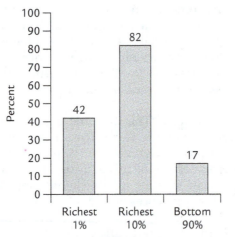

Figure 3-4 ▪ Distribution of Nonhome Wealth, 2009 (percent)
Source: From "The State of Working America's Wealth, 2011" by Sylvia A. Allegretto.
EPI Briefing Paper #29. Reprinted by permission of The Economic Policy Institute.

Looking at specific forms of wealth, we can further see how much is owned by so few. Take stock ownership, for example. Many like to extol the virtues of contemporary capitalism by exclaiming the great dispersion of stock ownership. No longer are corporations and banks owned solely by wealthy individuals or families, they point out, as stock ownership in these firms has become widespread among millions of ordinary people. The distortion in this assertion, however, is that among individually owned shares, the rich hold almost 90 percent. Most of the remainder of the stock-owning families own shares in retirement accounts.[4] The same pattern is evident for other forms of wealth: bonds, trusts, mutual funds, business equity, and nonhome real estate.

---

[4]Although the media pay much attention to rises and falls in stock market values and often give the impression that this is the major indicator of the state of the American economy, in fact only a minority of families are actually invested in the stock market, either directly or indirectly. Those who hold shares in a company own stock directly, while those who contribute to pension funds or mutual funds (which invest in the stock market) own them indirectly. Only 15 percent of households own stock directly and less than half of all households have stock holdings in *any* form (Bricker et al., 2012; Shierholz, 2012).

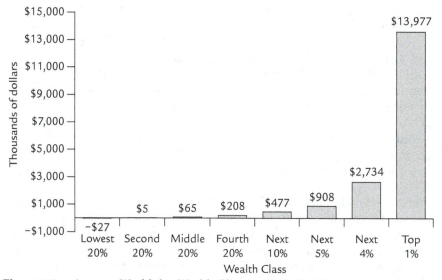

Figure 3-5 ▪ Average Wealth by Wealth Class in 2009 ($1,000)
Source: From "The State of Working America, 12 ed." by Lawrence Mishel et al. Reprinted by permission of The Economic Policy Institute.

In short, the top 10 percent of families own the majority of significant forms of wealth; most of the remaining 90 percent of families own little more than their homes and cars.

To understand the extreme inequality of wealth in America, we needn't look only at the difference between those at the very top, the super-rich, and those at the bottom, with little wealth or in debt. The differential is strikingly evident when comparing the top and the *middle*: The wealthiest 1 percent of households average 225 times the wealth of the median household (Allegretto, 2011). This is seen in Figure 3-5. Whereas the top 1 percent average almost $14 million in wealth, those in the middle quintile average $65,000. It is therefore hardly an exaggeration to refer to the distribution of wealth in America as "the rich and the rest of us."

Change and Continuity in Economic Inequality

Stratification systems are not static. This section examines how the American class structure has changed over the last few decades. Specifically, how has the distribution of income and wealth been modified? Have income and wealth been shared more equitably over the years, or has the tendency been in the opposite direction?

Trends in the Distribution of Income and Wealth

Extremes of income and wealth should not be surprising in the United States, where capitalism has been more unfettered and less regulated than in almost any other society. Throughout most of American history, however, various segments of the society—farmers, workers, women, immigrants, blacks—were enabled to share in relative prosperity. Although the process was slow and tortuous for most, these aggrieved groups were increasingly provided with the life chances, like education, to compete more fairly in the market system. In all these cases, the power of the state was used to rectify the inequality stemming from the excesses of capitalism left to its own forces. Despite periods of economic hardship, then, the capitalist economy, tempered by government, seemed to present opportunities for the advancement of each generation farther up the class hierarchy. This tendency reached a high point in the three decades following World War II.

The Post–World War II Boom   In the 1950s the United States embarked on a period of economic growth unprecedented in its history. Unburdened by war, the economy turned to the production of consumer goods—houses, automobiles, refrigerators, electronic goods, and the like. This stimulated job creation and higher wages, which, in turn, enabled families to enjoy a rising standard of living. Workers and management entered into an informal agreement in which both sides could realize advantages: Workers would remain loyal and support their companies in exchange for continued higher wages and benefits. The result was a significant expansion of the middle class. More and more people realized their piece of the American Dream—owning a home, sending their children to college, and earning enough to envision retirement with at least a modest degree of comfort.

Family income grew almost continuously from 1949 through 1973. Optimistically, Americans came to take for granted that this steady upward movement would continue indefinitely. Each generation, it was assumed, would exceed the economic level of the previous one. There was good reason for people to express such optimism. The growth in productivity gave a boost to family income in all social classes. Moreover, the gap between top and bottom, rich and poor, began to close. Looking again at Table 3-3, it can be seen that the income of the poorest quintile rose between the late 1960s and early 1970s at the same time that the income of the top quintile declined. Thus, the income pie, though still grossly maldistributed, was becoming less so. Economists have referred to this period as "the Great Prosperity" (Reich, 2010) or "the Great Compression" (Krugman, 2007).

The Post-1973 Era and Beyond   Changing conditions in the early 1970s, however, brought an abrupt end to what had seemed like a never-ending expansion of affluence. Economic growth began to decline, and as it did, the previously recorded wage and income gains ended. Median family income from 1973 on showed about as many year-to-year declines as increases (Danziger and Gottschalk, 1995). By the late 1970s, families, for the first time since the Great Depression of the 1930s, were on average worse off than families of a decade earlier. Median family income grew again during the 1980s, though at a rate far slower than in the 1960s, and then declined again in the early 1990s. By 1993, median family income was about the same as it had been twenty years earlier. For the first time in the post–World War II era, the middle class was not expanding but, on the contrary, seemed to be contracting. Those among the higher income groups continued to prosper, but those at the lower ends of the middle, particularly those among the working class, fared more poorly than at any time since the Great Depression.

As is seen in Table 3-3, the trend toward narrowing the gap between rich and poor now reversed itself: The richest 20 percent increased their share of total income, while the poorest 20 percent lost much of theirs. Whereas the richest quintile in 1981 received 43.8 percent of all income, by 2004 it received more than 50 percent. At the other end of the hierarchy, the poorest quintile received 4.2 percent of total income in 1981 but only 3.4 percent in 2004. Regardless of how it is measured, inequality in income and earnings increased between the mid-1970s and mid-1990s (Danziger and Gottschalk, 1995; Hacker et al., 2007; Massey, 2007; Ryscavage, 1999; Yellen, 1998).

In the first decade of the twenty-first century, the trend toward greater income inequality picked up more steam. But what appears to have occurred is a separation of the very top income earners from everyone else, including not only the poor but the middle classes as well. What became apparent during the 2000s is that most middle-class families were simply holding their ground and doing so primarily because more family members were working more hours.[5] In fact, when inflation is accounted for, the average real income of middle-class families, as well as that of low-income families, actually fell (Mishel et al., 2009; Shapiro and Friedman, 2006). Most of the benefits of the significant growth in productivity in the overall economy flowed to profits—earned by the wealthiest segment of the class structure—rather than to wages and salaries. The post-tax income of the top 1 percent of families was eight times higher than that of middle-income families in 1979, but twenty-one times higher by 2005; in the latter year, it was seventy times higher than the bottom fifth of families (Mishel et al., 2009).

In sum, the trend of income inequality since 1979 can be seen in Figure 3-6. The bottom quintile realized very little income growth, while the middle three quintiles gained only modestly. Clearly, those households constituting the top quintile were the big winners during those decades, but even more specifically, the biggest winners were those in the top 1 percent. Another way of demonstrating the growing income gap between those at the top and those in the lower segments of the class hierarchy during those years is to consider that in 1979 the top 5 percent of families earned on average about eleven times more than the earnings of the lowest 20 percent; by 2006, they earned over twenty-one times more (Mishel et al., 2009).

---

[5]Economist Heather Boushey (2011) explains that the typical middle class family today puts in nearly 570 more hours per year at work than it did in the late 1970s.

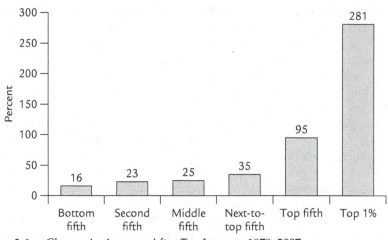

Figure 3-6 ▪ Change in Average After-Tax Income: 1979–2007
Source: Congressional Budget Office, 2011.

Growing Inequalities in Wealth   In recent times, trends in the distribution of wealth have paralleled those in income. Inequalities in wealth, however, are much greater, and the gap between the very wealthy and everyone else has grown enormously in the last three and a half decades. From the mid-1960s through the late 1970s, America experienced a decline in the maldistribution of wealth, just as income inequality declined during most of that period. This trend reversed itself sharply in the 1980s.

With increasing productivity, much new wealth was created in the 1980s. However, most of it went to those at the very top of the class hierarchy, with very little filtering downward. Between 1983 and 1989, the top 20 percent received virtually all (99 percent) of the total gain in marketable wealth. But even this figure does not reveal the extreme concentration of wealth expansion at the top. The richest 1 percent alone received 62 percent of all the new wealth. This pattern continued unabated throughout the 1990s and 2000s. Looking back at Table 3-5, we can see the increasing concentration of wealth from 1989 to 2010. In 1989, the richest 10 percent of families held two-thirds of the nation's wealth; by 2010 they held three-quarters, with the top 1 percent alone holding more than one-third.

The wealth gap that began to grow sharply in the 1980s accelerated during the 2000s, abetted by federal tax policies that disproportionately benefited those at the very top of the class structure. Between 1983 and 2004, the average wealth of the top 1 percent of households increased by $6 million or by 78 percent. During these years, while the top quintile of households saw their wealth increase by 82 percent, the middle quintile gained only 27 percent. But the lowest two quintiles—that is, 40 percent of households—*lost* almost 60 percent of their wealth, which fell to a meager average of $2,200 (Wolff, 2007). In sum, while the income gap, as we saw,

"The poor are getting poorer, but with the rich getting richer it all averages out in the long run."

Joseph Mirachi/The New Yorker Collection/www.cartoonbank.com

expanded sharply during the last three and a half decades, the wealth gap grew even more dramatically.

Economic and political analysts have shown that the rate and extent of the rise in wealth inequality during the last thirty-five years is almost unprecedented in American history. Not since the 1920s has there been a comparable upsurge of riches for those at the top (Barlett and Steele, 1992; Phillips, 1990, 2002; Wolff, 1995b, 2002). And never before has such a proliferation of millionaires and billionaires occurred in such a short time. As Kevin Phillips (1990) explains, by the late 1980s millionaires were almost commonplace. *Forbes* magazine, which each year publishes a list of the wealthiest people in the United States, reported in 1988 that the estimated number of billionaires in that year—fifty-one—was double the number from 1986. By 1992 the *Forbes* list of American billionaires had grown to seventy-one and by 2005 to more than four hundred (*Forbes,* 1988, 1992, 2006).

Looking Beyond

Looking at the class system overall, in the first decade of the new century, it seemed that, in a very real sense, the rich had gotten richer and the poor poorer, while most in the middle classes had struggled to keep pace or had seen their income and wealth actually decline. As the billionaire investor Warren Buffett described it, the average American had "been on a treadmill," while the very rich had "been on a space ship" (*New York Times,* 2007).

For most of the last quarter century, the American economy seemed to be functioning at its peak in terms of productivity. Yet this extraordinarily robust economy had had little effect on the distribution of income and wealth (Mishel, 2012a; Stiglitz, 2012; Stone et al., 2012). The income gap continued to grow as real wages stagnated, and, perhaps most important, wealth remained as concentrated as ever among the rich and the super rich. This period shows that economic growth does not assure a more equitable distribution of income and wealth. The problem of inequality, then, is a problem not of economic expansion and the production of wealth but of the way in which the society's economic resources are ultimately distributed.

Starting in 2007, the United States entered into its most severe economic downturn since the Great Depression of the 1930s. The seemingly unstoppable economic growth that had so characterized the previous decades now came to an abrupt halt. The financial system suffered an almost total meltdown, the housing market collapsed, and a sharp drop in consumer demand brought about a huge decline in the labor market, with unemployment reaching heights not seen for decades. More than 7 million jobs were lost in just one year between 2008 and 2009. No segment of the class system was immune to the negative impact of these developments. But, despite the fact that the economic pie seemed to be shrinking for all, this had virtually no impact on the distribution of income and wealth. Although the rich suffered losses to their fortunes, those below them were pushed into greater hardships. Employers at all levels slashed their workforces and imposed wage cuts on those whose jobs were saved. Adding to the financial straits of workers was the fact that the value of their homes and retirement packages plunged in value. The already precarious place of middle- and working-class families thus became even more uncertain.

As the economy began to recover, two developments seemed to take hold. First, virtually no measurable change occurred in the degree of income and wealth inequality that had grown so wide during the previous three decades. Although those at the top, like other Americans, saw their financial status decline, they quickly recouped their losses. In 2010, the first year of recovery, the top 1 percent garnered 93 percent of all income gains (Saez, 2012). A second development was more unusual and unexpected: a growing awareness on the part of Americans of the huge gap that separated the rich from all other classes. The notion of class conflict no longer remained confined to the writings of sociologists and economists but now became an issue of public discourse, prompting a rise in class consciousness. A national survey in 2012 showed that two-thirds of the American public believed there were strong conflicts between rich and poor, conflicts that now outranked other sources of group tension, like those between blacks and whites and between generational groups (Morin, 2012). The Occupy Wall Street movement helped to popularize the notion of the "99 percent" versus the "1 percent," and forced politicians to acknowledge the declining middle class. The issue of economic fairness now seemed to take political prominence to a degree not seen in decades.

In sum, at the outset of the twenty-first century, the American class structure appears to have evolved into a three-part configuration, with the rich taking the bulk of income and wealth, the poor receiving little, and those in the middle scrambling to maintain their standard of living. In the next three chapters we will look more closely at the factors that have contributed to these hardening patterns of income and wealth distribution. Briefly, however, much of the continued inequality of the last quarter century has been the result of economic restructuring, both in the United States and abroad. Those with critical occupational skills have fared comparatively well in the new economy, while those with few skills have lost out. Also, new industries have emerged, revolving around new technologies—especially computers and communications—creating in the process wide opportunities for the creation of instant fortunes and for those with capital to increase their wealth enormously. In addition to structural changes, government policies have been of great significance in the creation and maintenance of these unequal outcomes.

Economic Inequality: A Comparative Perspective

In no contemporary society are economic resources distributed equitably. In all, there are rich, poor, and those in the middle. What does differ among societies, however, is the relative gap between the classes, particularly between those at the top and those at the bottom. How does the United States compare to other countries in this regard? Is economic inequality more or less severe?[6]

Comparing the United States with developing countries yields a truly astounding picture. Whereas the income ratio of the richest 20 percent of families to the poorest 20 percent in the United States is about 15 to 1, it is, for example, 20 to 1 in Brazil, a country in the process of industrializing (World Bank, 2012). Huge portions of the Brazilian population live in severely depressed conditions, while a wealthy elite take a grossly disproportionate share of the society's wealth. In countries that are poorer and less developed than Brazil, the spread between the few rich and the many poor is sometimes even greater.[7]

But comparing the United States, the world's largest economy, to developing societies provides a comparison in only absolute, not relative, terms. It is hardly meaningful to contrast the level of inequality in Brazil, for example, to that in the United States, whose per capita income is more than five times larger. A more significant comparison would lie between the United States and other societies with comparable levels of economic development and resources,

---

[6]Keep in mind that making comparisons of the United States with other countries is risky since economic data do not always coincide precisely from one country to another. However, the data do provide for at least rough comparisons.

[7]Considering the world as a whole, the discrepancy between rich and poor is glaring. In 1993, the poorest 20 percent of the world's population received 1.4 percent of global income whereas the richest 20 percent received 85 percent, a ratio of 61 to 1 (UNDP, 1993). By 2005, the ratio had narrowed somewhat to 50 to 1. Placing the United States, one of the most affluent countries, side by side with some of the most impoverished yields a stunning comparison. In 1990, the average American was thirty-eight times richer than the average person in Tanzania. By 2005, the average American was sixty-one times richer (UNDP, 2005).

that is, other advanced industrial societies. When such comparisons are made, the United States is shown to be markedly more unequal in its distribution of income and wealth. Indeed, since the 1980s, the United States has had no peer in economic inequality. "The United States," writes economist Richard Freeman, "has now cemented its traditional position as the leader in inequality among advanced countries" (1999:3).

Comparative Income   Table 3-6 shows the concentration of income in the United States compared to other Western industrial societies using the Gini index (sometimes referred to as the Gini Coefficient). This is a statistical measure that indicates the difference between the actual distribution of income and a perfectly equal distribution. If the latter were the case, each 20 percent of the population would receive 20 percent of income. The Gini index ranges from 0 (perfect equality) to 100 (complete inequality); thus, the closer to 100, the greater the inequality of income.

Another way of comparing U.S. inequality with that of other societies is to look at workers' wages, the most important source of income for most people. As we have seen, wages during the past several decades have lagged far behind growth in economic productivity. Moreover, among advanced economies, the United States has the highest share of low-wage workers, who also have the fewest opportunities to move up in the occupational hierarchy (Gautié and Schmitt, 2009; Mishel et al., 2009). But American workers generally, not simply those at the bottom, are comparatively the least protected in terms not only of wages but also of non-wage benefits. When workers lose their jobs they have a meager and precarious social safety net to assist them.

Table 3-6 ▪ Gini Index for Selected Countries

Country	Gini Index
United States	38
Australia	34
Italy	34
United Kingdom	34
Japan	33
Canada	32
Korea	32
Germany	30
France	29
Netherlands	29
Sweden	26
Norway	25

Source: Data taken from Gini Index for Selected Countries, OECD 2011. "Society at a Glance" OECD Social Indicators. © OECD, 2011. Reprinted by permission.

In addition, most have little or no paid vacation and many do not even have paid (or unpaid) sick days. And, perhaps of greatest importance, the large majority of U.S. workers must depend on their job for health insurance. With a very low rate of unionization, most American workers work at the will of their employers, with little or no legal recourse to decisions made by those employers. Similar conditions of work are found in no other advanced economies (Freeman, 2007; Gautié and Schmitt, 2009; Ray et al., 2009; Schmitt, 2009).

A number of studies have also shown that there is a much larger income gap between managers and workers in the United States than in any other highly industrialized country. And that gap has grown enormously in the last several decades. In 1965, the typical CEO made 20 times more than the average worker; in 2011, the typical CEO made 231 times more. This means that a CEO earned in one workday more than the average worker earned in an entire year (Mishel et al., 2009; Mishel and Sabadish, 2012). Also, CEOs' wages are vastly higher in the United States than in other developed societies (Gordon and Dew-Becker, 2008; Mishel et al., 2009; Noah, 2012).

Comparative Wealth   The global distribution of wealth mirrors the U.S. distribution. The richest 10 percent of the world's population owns more than 85 percent of the world's wealth; the top 1 percent alone has 40 percent. By contrast, the bottom half of the world's population owns no more than 1 percent of global wealth. Moreover, not surprisingly, most of the world's wealth is concentrated in the highly developed countries, that is, nations of North America and Europe, and a few in Asia (Davies et al., 2008). Table 3-7 shows that fully half of the world's wealth is found in just two countries, the United States and Japan, despite the fact that they contain less than 10 percent of the world's population.

Data indicate, however, that wealth inequality in the United States is more extreme than in any other advanced industrial society. At the beginning of the twenty-first century, the United States, notes Kevin Phillips, "was not only the world's wealthiest nation and leading economic power, but also the Western industrial nation with the greatest percentage of the world's rich and the greatest gap between rich and poor" (2002:4). After making comparisons with other Western societies, Edward Wolff similarly concludes that "the U.S. continues to remain today the most unequal country in terms of wealth" (2002:36). The share of wealth held by the top 1 percent in Canada and Sweden, for example, is about half of what it is in the United States, and in Japan and France, the share is about two-thirds of the U.S. rate. In Table 3-7, notice the significantly higher Gini index for wealth in the United States compared to the other countries, each with more than 1 percent of global wealth.

Accounting for Differences   Many of the forces that drive the gap between the rich and the poor in the United States are also at work in other advanced industrial societies. Those societies have not been immune to the effects of economic restructuring, globalization, corporate downsizing, immigration,

Table 3-7 ▪ Share of Global Wealth Held by Selective Countries

Country	Population Share (percent)	Gini Index	World Wealth Share (percent)
United States	5.5	.801	32.6
Japan	2.7	.547	18.3
United Kingdom	1.2	.697	5.9
Germany	1.8	.667	5.7
Italy	1.0	.609	4.5
France	1.2	.730	4.1
China	22.8	.550	2.6
Spain	0.9	.570	2.2
Canada	0.6	.688	1.7
Netherlands	0.3	.650	1.4
Taiwan	0.4	.655	1.3
Brazil	2.8	.784	1.2
Mexico	1.5	.749	1.1
Korea	0.9	.579	1.1
Australia	0.4	.622	1.0

Source: Data taken from Gini Index for Selected Countries, OECD 2011. "Society at a Glance" OECD Social Indicators. © OECD, 2011. Reprinted by permission.

and changing demographics; all those factors will be discussed in the next few chapters. However, in most other affluent societies, inequality has been held in check to a much greater degree. As economist Richard Freeman pungently describes it, "If there were a gold medal for inequality, advanced country division, the United States would win hands down" (2007:43).

Much of the explanation for this difference lies in government policies. As we will see in Chapter 9, the United States is the society in which government plays the least influential role in moderating market forces and in which welfare policies designed to make more equitable the distribution of income and wealth are least developed. Labor unions are also more potent in other nations, helping to protect workers' wages and benefits.

Also, as we will see in Chapter 8, the overarching ideology of individualism has made Americans less inclined to look to government as a force to make income and wealth more equitable. Indeed, the very idea of making them more equitable generally is rejected.

Summary

Social classes can be conceived in two ways. As an economic concept, classes are groupings of people who share roughly similar incomes and wealth, occupations, and levels of education. Classes may also be thought of as groupings in which people share not only similar socioeconomic standing but similar lifestyles. The economic and behavioral dimensions of social class are closely interdependent.

Contrary to popular views, the United States is a society in which the class system is highly developed. There are marked differences in income and wealth, educational attainment, and occupational status among the American population. Specifically, the U.S. class system is a six-part structure, consisting of an upper (or capitalist) class, an upper-middle class, a lower-middle class, a working class, and a poverty population made up of two components: the working poor and the underclass.

Inequality in the distribution of income and wealth in the United States is very apparent. The richest 20 percent of families earn more than half of all income and own over 80 percent of all wealth. Inequalities in income and wealth have always characterized American society, but these inequalities expanded enormously throughout the 1980s. That trend was not reversed in the 1990s or 2000s; rather, the gap between those at the extreme top and the rest of the class hierarchy continued to widen.

Comparisons with other advanced industrial societies reveal a more inequitable distribution of income and wealth in the United States. Measured in various ways, the gap between rich and poor in the United States is wider than in any other society with comparable economic institutions and standards of living.

4

The Upper Class
and the Power Elite

If you can actually count your money then you are not really a rich man.
J. Paul Getty

*So far as men may do as they will with the property that they own or that they manage
for owners, they have power over other men.*
C. Wright Mills

As we have seen, most Americans identify themselves as part of the middle classes, and most people do in fact fall in the middle ranges of the class hierarchy. Nonetheless, there are certainly identifiable lower and upper classes. This chapter focuses on the latter—the upper class and the power elite—exploring their identities, the sources of their wealth and power, and the paths they follow to the top. It also considers the relationship between wealth and power. Certainly, the probabilities are great that the rich will be powerful and the powerful will be rich, but wealth and power are not the same and it is important to keep the two analytically separate. The upper class are those who hold great wealth, and the power elite are those who occupy positions of critical importance and whose decisions have a profound impact on the society.

The Upper Class

Where do we draw the line between the upper class and the rest of society? As with other parts of the class hierarchy, the division is largely arbitrary, but in purely financial terms, the separation of the rich from others is very clear.

Income

One way of separating those at the very top of the American class hierarchy from others is to use income as a guide. Traditionally $1 million has been a popular dividing line for identifying the rich. Although there has been a huge expansion in the last two decades of families earning $1 million or more, this still accounts for only a tiny portion of U.S. households, less than two-tenths

Source: Reprinted by permission of The Permissions Group, Inc. on behalf of TMS/MCT Reprints.

of 1 percent. In fact, less than 2 percent of all households have annual incomes of more than $250,000. So, despite its reduced significance, we can continue to use the $1 million income figure as a convenient cut-off point for identifying the rich (though, as we saw in Chapter 3, certainly not the "super-rich").

A key group among those whose incomes surpass $1 million are top-ranking corporate executives. The median income in 2011 for a chief executive officer (CEO) of one of the largest and most powerful American corporations was almost $10 million, including salary, bonuses, and other benefits, such as gains on stock options. For some among the corporate elite, earnings can only be described as stratospheric. Richard Fuld, for example, the long-time chief of Lehman Brothers, one of America's largest financial services firms, earned about $45 million in 2007, roughly $17,000 an hour. This, despite the disastrous performance of his company, which collapsed and disappeared in 2008, setting off the deepest U.S. financial crisis in seventy years. Fuld reportedly received almost one-half billion dollars in compensation between 1993 and 2007 (Kristof, 2008). In recent years, top investment bankers and traders have taken home even more. Compensation of the top fifty hedge and private equity fund managers in 2007 averaged $588 million each (Anderson et al., 2008). Clearly, in terms of income, corporate executives are in the highest class. "No matter how one cuts the figures," note economists James O'Toole and Edward Lawler, "even moderately well-paid CEOs of large corporations make about as much in a day as their average employee makes in a year" (2006:117).[1] Moreover, executive income has climbed considerably over the last several decades. Indeed, as economist Paul Krugman has pointed out, "there is simply no comparison between what executives got a generation ago and what they are paid today" (2002:63). Between 1989 and 2007, compensation for the average CEO grew 167 percent. As noted in Chapter 3, the altitudinous level of executive pay is a uniquely American phenomenon, with U.S. CEOs earning more than twice their foreign counterparts (Mishel et al., 2009; Noah, 2012; O'Toole and Lawler, 2006).

Some who are among the American rich may be considered the "celebrity rich"—entertainers and professional athletes whose names are easily recognized and who earn fabulously high incomes. Consider the earnings of a few prominent stars in a single year, 2012. Pop singers Rihanna, Lady Gaga, and Justin Bieber each made more than $50 million (which was only half of rapper Dr. Dre's $110 million). Talk show hosts David Letterman and Ellen DeGeneres earned $45 million and $53 million, respectively, and Oprah Winfrey brought in $165 million from a range of enterprises. Radio personalities Howard Stern ($95 million) and Rush Limbaugh ($69 million) were among the top-paid entertainers. In the sports world, the average NBA salary was $5 million, but a few stars, such as Kobe Bryant ($50 million) and LeBron James ($53 million), earned many times that amount through endorsements as well as their salaries. Tennis star Roger Federer ($52 million) and football quarterback Peyton Manning ($42 million) were high earners, as were golfers Tiger Woods ($58 million) and Phil Mickelson ($48 million). The earnings of some Hollywood personalities are equally impressive. Actors Jennifer Lopez ($52 million) and Tom Cruise ($75 million) were among the highest paid in 2012, while producer Steven Spielberg earned $130 million. All of these figures represent only earnings from salaries and endorsements and don't include the millions more that celebrities may derive from business investments.

Some people may be able to enrich themselves merely from having occupied a prominent position or from having a publicly recognizable name. Former political officials perhaps best exemplify this category. Several months after he left the presidency, Ronald Reagan was paid $2 million for two twenty-minute speeches in Japan (Wayne, 2004). Bill Clinton, as former president, was able to earn almost as much from one speaking engagement as his annual salary as president. In a single year, Rudy Giuliani, the former New York City mayor, earned $11 million for his talks, mostly before business groups, and in the same way, Sarah Palin, the former vice-presidential candidate, earned millions from her six-figure speaking fees. Noted authors, political commentators, and newscasters also commonly receive enormous fees

---

[1]More precisely, it would take more than 10 weeks for a minimum wage worker and almost one month for the average U.S. worker to earn what the median CEO earns in one hour.

from speaking engagements. The political pundit Sean Hannity, for example, charges $100,000 per engagement—and requires a private jet for his speaking dates (*Bloomberg Businessweek* 2012; Hindman, 2011; Kirkpatrick, 2007).

Wealth

Although high income is certainly a mark of great economic status, a key distinction of the rich from others is that most do not derive the bulk of their income from their occupations. While most families earn more than three-quarters of their income through wages, the richest 10 percent earn more than half of their income from their assets (Bricker et al., 2012).

The value of assets is perhaps the best indicator of the division between the rich and the remainder of the population. For this reason, the upper class has been referred to by some as the **capitalist class.** Industrialists and entre-preneurs own capital, that is, shares in companies, which typically grow in value over time and produce income in the form of dividends. Entertainers or athletes, by contrast, must continue to perform to maintain their flow of income. Their talent cannot be transferred to someone else, and their income-earning years may be few. To assure their lofty status and lifestyle, they must wisely invest the money they earn through their performances. As Andrew Hacker explains, although the rich are a sociologically diverse stratum, what is common among them is that "the dominant share of the group's income comes via their brokerage accounts" (1997:84).

To comprehend the rich in American society, therefore, we need to look more closely at wealth, that is, the ownership of assets, not simply income. It is primarily through assets—stocks and bonds, real estate, cash accounts and other financial instruments, and business investments—that the rich have acquired their high economic status. "As they have been for centu-ries," observes sociologist Lisa Keister, "the truly rich are still separated by their wealth rather than their income" (2000:83).

As noted in Chapter 3, a relative handful of individuals and families hold an enormously disproportionate share of the society's wealth. To reiterate a couple of compelling statistics, the richest 1 percent of American families own over one-third of all assets, and the richest 10 percent own three-quarters. It is important to also recall the relative stability of the unequal distribution of wealth in American society. Although wealth inequality has accelerated enor-mously in the last three decades, it has been a fundamental characteristic of the United States since the mid-nineteenth century (Dowd, 1993; Soltow, 1984; Williamson and Lindert, 1980).

At the very top of the wealth hierarchy, the assets of the richest people and families stagger the imagination. Consider that in 2009 each family in the richest 1 percent of the U.S. population had, on average, almost $14 million, which actually represented a decline from more than $19 million in 2007 (Allegretto, 2011)! And to reiterate an important point from Chapter 3, even within this very small number of families, the bulk of wealth is held by a much tinier number. "Even among the wealthy," notes Thurow, "wealth is very unequally distributed" (1999:200). To qualify as part of the top 1 percent, families had to have a net worth of at least $6 million, hardly qualifying most as part of the "richest of the rich."

One way to begin learning about the truly wealthy is to examine the annual issue of *Forbes* magazine that lists the four hundred richest Americans. Therein lies a trove of fascinating information about the rich: Predictably, most are men, in their fifties and sixties, and most are college graduates, though a few never even finished high school. What is most intriguing about this list, however, is that, with few exceptions, the names are unrecognizable to the general public. Those with truly great wealth are not entertainers, sports stars, or others whose names are household words, that is, the "celebrity rich."[2]

As to the actual wealth of the richest Americans, the numbers are quite astonishing. The aggregate net worth of the four hundred wealthiest Americans in 2012 was $1.7 trillion; every one of the four hundred had at least $1.1 billion, and their average net worth was $4.2 billion (*Forbes*, 2012b). The two richest people in the United States were Bill Gates, the founder of Microsoft, who was worth $66 billion, and Warren Buffet, whose $46 billion derived mainly from stock market investments. To put the wealth of the super-rich in relative perspective, economist Josh Bivens has compared the wealth of the Walton family, heirs of the Wal-Mart fortune, to the wealth of the median American family. In 2010, median household net worth was $77,300. The net worth of the Walton family was $89.5 billion. Thus, to equal the Walton's wealth would require the combined median wealth of 1.16 million American households. In absolute terms, the Walton family's wealth is equivalent to that of more than 40 percent of all American families (Bivens, 2012). Table 4-1 shows the twenty-five wealthiest Americans listed in the *Forbes* 400.

The Expansion of Wealth   The actual wealth of the rich can only be estimated since assets can be concealed and thus difficult to track. But it is very clear that during the last three decades the wealth of the rich has increased at a phenomenal pace. Households with net worth of over $1 million are still relatively few (about 6 percent) but their numbers have more than doubled since 1983 (Becerra et al., 2012; Wolff, 2010). To identify the super-rich in American society today one must think in terms of billions, not millions. To be placed on the *Forbes* list of the four hundred richest Americans in 1982

---

[2]The *Forbes* list, or any other similar to it, is, in the end, only an approximation of how much wealth the rich actually possess. Most of the truly wealthy do not reveal their assets to magazine reporters. Even if they did, as Inhaber and Carroll point out, "the financial affairs of the wealthiest are often so complicated and convoluted that reporters would have to have advanced degrees in finance or accounting to interpret them adequately. Few do" (1992:68). These figures, then, are estimates, a fact not disputed by *Forbes*.

Table 4-1 ▪ The Twenty-Five Wealthiest Americans

Rank	Name	Net Worth ($ bil)	Age	Source
1	Bill Gates	66.0	56	Microsoft
2	Warren Buffett	46.0	82	Berkshire Hathaway
3	Lawrence Ellison	41.0	68	Oracle
4	Charles Koch	31.0	76	manufacturing, energy
5	David Koch	31.0	72	manufacturing, energy
6	Christy Walton	27.9	57	Walmart
7	Jim Walton	26.8	64	Walmart
8	Alice Walton	26.3	62	Walmart
9	S. Robson Walton	26.1	68	Walmart
10	Michael Bloomberg	25.0	70	Bloomberg
11	Jeff Bezos	23.2	48	Amazon.com
12	Sheldon Adelson	20.5	79	casinos
13	Larry Page	20.3	39	Google
13	Sergey Brin	20.3	39	Google
15	George Soros	19.0	82	hedge funds
16	Forest Mars	17.0	81	candy
16	Jacqueline Mars	17.0	72	candy
16	John Mars	17.0	46	candy
19	Steve Ballmer	15.9	56	Microsoft
20	Paul Allen	15.0	59	Microsoft, investments
21	Carl Icahn	14.8	76	leveraged buyouts
22	Michael Dell	14.6	47	Dell
23	Phil Knight	13.1	74	Nike
24	Donald Bren	13.0	80	real estate
25	Len Blavatnik	12.5	55	diversified

Source: *Forbes*, 2012b.

required $75 million; today it requires more than $1 billion. Whereas today there are almost four hundred billionaires in America, in 1982 there had been only thirteen and in 1978 only one (*Forbes*, 1997, 2009, 2012b; Phillips, 1990). The wealth of these super-rich families has given rise to a tiny class that is removed not only from other classes but even from the everyday rich. There is really no precedent for the wealth of the super-rich. As political scientist Jacob Hacker and his colleagues have described them, they are "much richer than other Americans, than the affluent of other nations, and than American elites in historical perspective" (2007:7).

The Rich: Old and New

The rich are different, as F. Scott Fitzgerald put it, and it is not only that they have more money, as Ernest Hemingway retorted. More than other classes, the upper class, particularly those who comprise the "old rich," is distinguished by its singular and exclusive style of life. The lives of upper-class families revolve around select social clubs, prep schools, prestigious Ivy League universities, debutante balls, and other social and cultural institutions that promote an upper-class lifestyle. Their relative separation from the rest of the society and their close interrelations produce a class awareness that is missing among the other social classes. Even within the ranks of the wealthy, however, there are divisions, particularly between the "old rich," whose wealth is family-based and descended from several generations, and the "new rich," whose wealth has been earned more recently, usually in their own lifetimes.

The upper class is the social stratum least studied by sociologists, in large measure because it is so underexposed and relatively secluded. Few besides those who are actually part of the upper class have access to the institutions that are the foundation of upper-class life. As a result, we know far less about the rich than about the poor. This is particularly the case with many of the old rich, who prefer relative anonymity to celebrity.

Sociologist E. Digby Baltzell, himself a member of the upper class, presented one of the few intensive studies of the structure and formation of the American upper class. In his study, Baltzell (1958) pointed out a number of features of the upper-class subculture that distinguish it from the remainder of the population. Whereas the average American tends to stress the future and to de-emphasize the past as well as other forms of traditionalism, the upper classes "more or less revere the past, especially the past accomplishments of their ancestors" (52). Family life revolves around a complete set of activities:

> Even the most socially secure families . . . place a high value on belonging to the correct clubs and associations, and making an appearance at the fashionable balls, dancing assemblies, weddings, and funerals; and where their children are concerned, the right summer resorts, dancing classes, schools and colleges, and finally, their daughter's debut, are each and severally of vital importance. (54)

All these activities contribute to a sense of social cohesion and the formation of an upper-class community. As Baltzell noted, "More than at any other social class level . . . the upper class in America has many of the aspects of a caste" (69).

Although the difference between old and new wealth may no longer carry the kind of significance it once did, the inheritors of upper-class status may still look askance at the wealth and lifestyle of the newly enriched. Wealth, fame, and even political power are not, by themselves, always sufficient to gain entrance into the old upper class. One must be born to the "right" family and must possess the proper pedigree. Moreover, the source of one's wealth is ordinarily of critical importance. Some who have made their fortunes in their own lifetime through business success or in the entertainment or sports worlds may find that they still do not qualify to enter the social circles of the old upper class. The new rich also may spend their money ostentatiously, calling attention to their wealth, whereas the old upper class traditionally spend their money in a muted fashion.[3] It is ironic that members of the old upper class today are the progeny of those who were similarly looked upon by the old rich of their time as parvenus whose displays of wealth were seen as crude and vulgar.

Development of the Old Upper Class   The old-line families of great wealth in the United States emerged during the late nineteenth and early twentieth centuries through the formation of the great industrial empires of that age. The major entrepreneurs of the time—Rockefeller, Carnegie, Vanderbilt, Frick, Morgan, Ford, and others—acquired fortunes that became the basis of their family wealth (Allen, 1987). A few had established their wealth even earlier. The du Pont fortune, for example, stemmed from the production of gunpowder starting in the late eighteenth century, and the Astors's, from fur trading. These families became the old, established upper class, whose scions inherited their wealth with each succeeding generation. It was these families that formed the core of the American upper class and emerged as the closest the United States has come to an aristocracy.

During the Gilded Age, at the end of the nineteenth century, an upper-class lifestyle and class consciousness began to develop, with ostentatious displays of wealth by the new industrial millionaires. New York became the heart of this emergent upper-class society. Great mansions were built, along with opera houses and museums, that catered to the tastes of the nouveau riche. The *Social Register,* a book listing the families of this would-be aristocracy, was published in New York and other large cities. Having one's family name listed in the *Social Register* served as a kind of official recognition of upper-class status. Exclusive associations and institutions began to replace the family as important socializing agents and as meeting places for the upper class. Children were sent to New England boarding schools and then to Ivy League colleges, which were financially supported by the wealthy industrialists. Exclusive men's clubs and country clubs became places where business and social affairs of the rich were joined. All of these developments had the effect of creating a national upper class, linking families from various localities (Baltzell, 1958).

The New Rich   While the old established families of wealth are still evident, their position at the top of the class hierarchy has been challenged in

---

[3]The tendency for those of the old upper class to often look askance at the new is illustrated by the fact that entertainers Madonna and Cher, despite their wealth and fame, were refused permission to buy apartments in exclusive co-op buildings on Central Park East in New York City (Mason, 1996).

recent decades by newly enriched individuals and families who have acquired great wealth in their own lifetimes and done so through enterprises that they themselves either founded or nurtured. Political scientist Thomas Dye (2002) has referred to these mostly western and southern new rich as "cowboys" and contrasts them with the older established eastern "yankees." The differences between the two, Dye explains, lie in the sources of their wealth and in the recency of the cowboys' entrance into the top echelon. Whereas the old rich have a long line of money that extends back over several generations, the new rich are, if not self-made, people who have made their money in a rapid fashion in new industries, such as oil, aerospace, and discount merchandising, that have become predominant in the U.S. and global economies.

An even more recent element of the new rich attributes its wealth to the emergence of the knowledge and information industries. Computers and related technologies and telecommunications and other media are more typical sources of wealth of the most recent rich (Keister, 2005). Looking back at Table 4-1, we can see that almost one-third of the twenty-five wealthiest derived their fortunes from technology, computer software, or media. Many of the newly wealthy have benefited from the surging values of their companies' stock, which they acquired through stock options. The process by which the new rich have amassed their fortunes is comparable to the way in which fortunes were made in the past: Radical changes in technology—steel, railroads, electric power, for example, in past ages, computers in the present—create opportunities for great wealth to emerge. Thurow describes the process:

> New technologies mean change. Change means disequilibrium. Disequilibrium conditions create high-return, high-growth opportunities. The winners understand the new technologies, are lucky enough to be in the right place at the right time, and have the skills to take advantage of these new situations. They become rich. (1999:33)

A prime example of the new rich in the knowledge-based economy is H. Ross Perot, the Texas billionaire who ran for U.S. president in 1992 and 1996 as an independent candidate, funding most of the costs of the campaigns himself. Perot's family was not wealthy (his father was a horse trader), but he won an appointment to the U.S. Naval Academy. After four years of active military duty, he sold computers for IBM for a time and then decided to form his own software company, EDS (Electronic Data Systems). Through lucrative government contracts, EDS became the major subcontractor providing computer software for processing Medicare and Medicaid claims. Perot made other investments in oil, gas, and real estate that prospered greatly. In 1984, he sold EDS to General Motors for $2.5 billion.

It is also in the computer and telecommunications industries that the ability to capitalize on an idea in a rapid and spectacular fashion has been so evident. For example, Mark Andreessen, while an undergraduate at the

University of Illinois, conceived a software program, Netscape Navigator, that became a standard Internet tool. He became a multimillionaire at age twenty-four (Thomas, 1997). Another information technology success story is Mark Zuckerberg, founder of the social networking site Facebook. At age twenty, Zuckerberg left Harvard before graduating, secured an initial $500,000 investment to pursue his idea, and four years later was a member of the *Forbes* 400. His net worth in 2012 was $9.4 billion (*Forbes,* 2012b).

Many among the computer entrepreneurs of today exhibit a similar precipitous rise to great wealth. Perhaps the best case is Bill Gates, founder of Microsoft, the computer software giant. Gates's story is no poor-boy-makes-good epic. His mother was from a wealthy and prominent banking family, and his father was a senior partner in one of Seattle's most politically influential and prestigious law firms. In addition to the wealth acquired from his parents, a trust fund was left to him by his grandparents. After attending an exclusive prep school, Gates, a brilliant student, enrolled at Harvard, though he never graduated. In 1974, Gates and a friend, Paul Allen, were convinced that they were on the cutting edge of a computer revolution. Gates was nineteen at the time; Allen was twenty-one. They started a company, Microsoft, and the rest, of course, is history (Wallace and Erickson, 1992). So rapid and profound was Microsoft's success that in less than twenty years, Gates's net worth had made him the second-wealthiest person in America, soon to be the wealthiest. Allen also was made a billionaire as a result of their enterprise. Microsoft today thoroughly dominates the computer software industry, and dozens of people who invested in the company in its early years have become fabulously wealthy.

Much of the new wealth in American society today is highly volatile, given the fact that, increasingly, it derives from financial investments that are subject to extreme vacillations of boom and bust. As a result, the economic journalist Robert Frank explains, starting in the early 1980s, many of the elite wealthy became "more manic in their earnings and spending, and they were bi-products of a new system of financial incentives that rewarded extreme risk-taking, borrowing, speculation, and spending" (2011:15). He calls these new wealthy "the high-beta rich." Financial windfalls can make them fabulously rich, but their wealth is unstable and vulnerable. As Frank writes, many families among the high-beta rich lost much of their fortunes in the Great Recession of the late 2000s. Still, those among the top one percent were able to recover quickly, unlike middle- and working class families, whose losses were more devastating and long-term.

The Privileges of Wealth

There are unique privileges that attach to great wealth. Obviously, the rich can partake of whatever the society offers in the way of material things; it is in that sense that money can buy almost anything. Steve Hilbert, a corporate CEO, wanted to play basketball for Indiana University but wasn't good enough. So he built a $5.5 million replica of Indiana's arena, Assembly Hall, where, as he explains, "On Saturdays I hit the winning shot to beat everyone from UCLA to Michigan to whomever in my own fantasy [while] playing by myself" (quoted in Pappas, 1997). As a *Wall Street Journal* reporter, Robert Frank (2007) spent several years on a full-time assignment focusing on the activities of the contemporary American rich. Frank found that they are so far removed financially and culturally from the mainstream society that they have created a parallel country—he refers to it as "Richistan"—where there are virtually no limits to their lavish and excessive spending on astronomically expensive homes, cars, yachts, airplanes, jewelry, safaris, art, and countless other luxury items. The annual expenses of one super wealthy family included $1 million for cars, $3 million for air charters and private jet, $2 million for home entertaining, $300,000 for clothing, and $80,000 simply for massages. "At one home I visited," writes Frank, "the wife had so many dresses and suits in her 400-square-foot walk-in closet that she had it equipped with an elevated conveyor-belt system—the kind used in dry-cleaning factories—to store and retrieve her clothes" (131).

Sociologist Thorstein Veblen, writing at the turn of the last century, described the wealthy of that time in his classic work *The Theory of the Leisure Class* (1899). In it, he used the terms *conspicuous consumption* and *conspicuous leisure* to denote how people sought to demonstrate their wealth through styles and quantities of material goods and leisure activities. Such demonstrations of style and quantity are not relics of the past. Obviously, the need to flaunt one's wealth in an ostentatious and, as Veblen described it, wasteful way continues to drive much of the consumption behavior of the wealthy. The new rich ("Richistanis"), Frank observed, "like to flaunt their wealth. And never before have so many flaunted so much" (Frank, 2007:120).

The privileges of wealth reach beyond consumption, however. The rich are able to avoid many of the inconveniences and chores of everyday life that most of us must endure: shopping at the grocery store, going to the bank, driving to work, filling the car with gasoline, waiting to be seated at a restaurant, filling out forms, caring for one's children. "The ultimate perk of the ruling class," notes Eric Konigsberg, "is no longer merely money or power, but the ability to be free of hassles" (1993:22). The rich accomplish this by having others do these mundane things for them. Konigsberg describes how this works for a few of the rich and famous. Movie star Demi Moore, for example, "has six assistants: one for her clothes, one for her hair, one for makeup, a bodyguard, a nanny, and a general-purpose personal assistant, who has her own personal assistant, who is thinking of hiring one of her own" (22). But this does not even come close to the entourage of her (then) husband, actor Bruce Willis, who, on the set of a film he was shooting, required twenty-two assistants, "including four or five body-guards, a driver, a personal chef, a personal trainer, a masseuse and a hair and makeup stylist" (22). Not to be bothered by shopping, Saudi Prince

Bandar bin Sultan, while vacationing in Aspen, purchased one of every item in stock at the local Banana Republic (a retail clothing chain). As Konigsberg describes the event, the prince wasn't even in the store—he'd sent an assistant.

The rich and celebrated are also subject to different standards of conduct than others. Readers and viewers of supermarket and TV tabloids are fascinated by the various sexual exploits and love affairs of wealthy movie stars and entertainers, the kinds of behavior that they would look at scornfully if practiced among middle-class and, especially, poor people. These different standards often extend to the less ostentatious rich as well. Stock market tycoon Warren Buffett, currently America's second-wealthiest person, for many years remained married to his wife, whom he escorted to various public functions, while he lived happily with another woman, an arrangement approved by his wife. Buffett and his partner were finally married formally in 2006 (Lowenstein, 1995; Bailey and Dash, 2006).[4]

In addition to material privileges, wealth provides social esteem, or, as Max Weber referred to it, status. Moreover, wealth is ordinarily convertible into power in various social spheres. Most important, of course, is the fact that the life chances of the wealthy reach far beyond those of ordinary people. And those opportunities can be passed on to future generations of family members.

Inheritance, Effort, and Wealth

Several years ago, actor John Housman appeared in a TV commercial for Smith Barney, a Wall Street investment firm. In the commercial, Housman, looking the part of a stodgy banker, grumbled that "at Smith Barney we make money the old-fashioned way—we *earn* it!" How do people get to the top of the class system today? Do they do it "the old-fashioned way," or do they inherit it, acquiring wealth through little effort of their own? In getting to the top, does the idea of the "self-made millionaire" (or billionaire, as the case may be) have much validity in the United States early in the twenty-first century?

Studies of the sources of wealth of America's richest individuals and families often seem to diverge. Some find that there is a continual renewal of names and faces among the super wealthy, whereas others contend that inheritance remains critical. Among the *Forbes* 400 in 2000, 137 attributed their wealth to nothing more than inheritance. Many others on the list, of course, were the scions of successful entrepreneurial families of the past

---

[4]Buffett is no ordinary member of the wealthy elite. Despite his riches, he has lived modestly in a home in Omaha, Nebraska, that he purchased in 1959 for $31,500. In 2006 he announced that he was giving away about 85 percent of his fortune, most of it to the Bill and Melinda Gates foundation, whose goal is eliminating the world's fatal diseases. Gates himself has devoted much of his time and wealth in recent years to philanthropic activities.

that made the financial success of future family members all but a certainty. On the list of the twenty-five wealthiest in 2012 (Table 4-1), nine are there through inheritance (the Walton, Koch, and Mars heirs). In a major study of the effects of inheritance on wealth accumulation, economist John Brittain found that gifts and bequests, on average, accounted for half or more of the net worth of the very wealthy. He concluded that the transfers of wealth from one generation to the next were "a major force in the perpetuation of wealth inequality" (1978:22). Other studies underscore the importance of inheritance in the accumulation of wealth (Keister, 2000, 2005; McNamee and Miller, 1998; Oliver and Shapiro, 1995).

Some maintain that there is much more mobility at the top than is commonly assumed. Dye (2002) asserts that despite the inheritance of much wealth through family channels, such family-based wealth gradually dissipates over the generations. Moreover, the energy and business skills that originally built family fortunes are rarely demonstrated by later generations. Most important, according to Dye, is the fact that each generation produces a new crop of successful entrepreneurs who emerge as self-made tycoons. What is of major significance to Dye and to others who view wealth inequality in America in a similar fashion is not the degree of inequality itself, which has always been evident, but rather the opportunity to enter into the ranks of the rich and the super-rich. Some support for Dye's assertion is *Forbes*'s claim that more than half of the 400 richest Americans in 1997 were self-made, a claim repeated for the 2012 richest 400 (*Forbes*, 1997, 2012b).

What can be concluded from these seemingly conflicting accounts of how great wealth is acquired? Obviously, the surest (and most effortless) path to great wealth is simply to be born into it. This, in fact, characterizes the path followed by a large segment of the upper class. Moreover, as we will see in Chapter 7, even among those who earn their riches through their own enterprise and skill, family influences are apt to be hugely important, if not always acknowledged or recognized. Nonetheless, the confines of the super wealthy are never entirely closed and limited to inheritance. New technologies and marketing innovations (like computer technology) can yield windfall returns on investment, as can the ownership of businesses in growth industries, providing the basis for the acquisition of great wealth within one's lifetime. Moreover, many corporate managers have entered the world of the super-rich today as a result of their enormously high salaries rather than through inheritance (Krugman, 2007; Reich, 2007).

In any case, of course, those at the top of the wealth hierarchy will always number a relative few. Furthermore, however much circulation among the wealthy few occurs, there need be no effect on the inequality of wealth distribution. Indeed, as we have seen, despite the expansion of wealth in American society in recent decades, the distance between the wealthy and the rest of the society has widened enormously (Keister, 2005; Thurow, 1995). By the early 1990s, the share of wealth held by the top

1 percent of the population (40 percent) was essentially double what it had been in the mid-1970s. This degree of wealth concentration was comparable to what it had been in the late 1920s.

The Power Elite: Patterns and Theory

Phillips has written that "Whether five hundred years ago or now, power and wealth have rarely been far from one another" (2002:201). To examine the wealthy in American society (or any other, for that matter) is almost implicitly to examine the powerful as well. Societal power, broadly defined, is exercised by those in critical decision-making positions—together, the **power elite**—within various economic, political, and social organizations that have wide-ranging impact on the society. Chapter 12 will explore the various dimensions of societal power in more detail. In this section, we look at the social characteristics of the power elite and their relationship to the upper class.

In the United States, as in all modern societies, societal power is most essentially a synthesis of the actions of government and the economy. It is within those two institutional spheres that authority and influence are most crucial for the society as a whole and that societal resources are most highly concentrated. To examine the power elite therefore requires that we look at those in important decision-making governmental and corporate positions.

The Relationship between the Upper Class and the Power Elite

It would seem logical to assume that the wealthiest persons and families are also the most powerful. But consider whom you would select if you were asked to name the few most powerful people in the United States today. The president of the United States? The chief justice of the Supreme Court? The Speaker of the House? The chairman of the Federal Reserve Board? These are positions that immediately come to mind as "most powerful." They are, in fact, all positions of great power, but none of their incumbents is today among the truly wealthy.

There are others, outside the realm of politics, whose power is equally great but who are also not necessarily among the society's wealthiest persons. The top executives of any of a few dozen giant corporations; the editors of the *New York Times* and a few other major newspapers; and the producers of the major TV network news programs all hold positions that carry with them great societal power but that (with the exception, perhaps, of top corporate executives) are not generally at the pinnacle of the income and wealth hierarchies. Moreover, unlike the familiar figures of the political world, they are rarely known to the general public.

The most wealthy in society, then, are not necessarily also the most powerful. It is true nonetheless that the association between wealth and power is strong. Since wealth is the most important resource in a capitalist society, it can be converted into various forms of power. Wealth, power, and prestige generally move in a circular flow. As in the proverbial chicken-and-egg dilemma, it is often difficult to determine which is the initial component in the cycle, but once one is established, the others tend to follow (Lenski, 1966).

Money is the driving force behind the political system, and the wealthy do play a disproportionately major role in the electoral and policymaking processes. Nonetheless, as already explained, wealth and power are not the same, and the relationship between them is not always neat and uncomplicated. We need to examine, therefore, the extent to which the upper class is also a *ruling* class, that is, a group that exerts societal power commensurate with its economic position. Sociologists and political scientists have studied this issue intently. Let's look at some of their major theories and research findings.

Mills's "Power Elite"   More than any other social scientist, C. Wright Mills is responsible for generating the study of the structure of power in the United States. Writing in the 1950s, Mills was a maverick among sociologists of that time, disputing the generally accepted depiction of the American power structure as a plurality of various interest groups lacking social cohesion. He concluded instead that a relatively unified power elite, made up of top political, corporate, and military officials, made key societal decisions:

> By the power elite, we refer to those political, economic, and military circles which as an intricate set of overlapping cliques share decisions having at least national consequences. In so far as national events are decided, the power elite are those who decide them. (1956:18)

Mills investigated the power elite's sociological characteristics and found that its members were quite similar in general outlook, interests, and social background. They attended the same schools, exhibited similar career patterns, and were, for the most part, exposed to common socialization experiences. They were, as a result, a socially cohesive group.

Given their similar social background, the members of the power elite shared the same outlook regarding the society's needs. In addition, the overlapping interests and functions of their institutions caused them to come together in a working relationship, further strengthening their common social and psychological orientations. They thought and acted the same, Mills contended, because their social and career environments were the same. Within the power elite, it was the business leaders, in Mills's estimation, who wielded the greatest influence. And, by implication, the business elite was integrally tied to the upper class.

Domhoff's "Governing Class" Theory   For the past four decades, G. William Domhoff has researched the relationship between the American upper class and the power elite more extensively than any contemporary sociologist. Domhoff, far more directly than Mills, asserts the close ties between the upper class and the power elite. He concludes that the upper class is essentially a ruling class (Domhoff, 1967, 1979, 1983, 1998, 2010). Domhoff posits that there is a readily apparent relationship between those who own or control a disproportionate share of the society's wealth, those who exercise control over major corporations, and those who greatly influence the governmental elite. Significant societal wealth is found within the corporation, and those who dominate this key economic institution through ownership or management maintain maximum influence in the public policy–forming process. Domhoff (1967) calls this group a "governing class":

> A governing class is a social upper class which receives a disproportionate amount of a country's income, owns a disproportionate amount of a country's wealth, and contributes a disproportionate number of its members to the controlling institutions and key decision-making groups in that country. (142)

Domhoff's essential thesis is that top corporate owners and managers are the major power figures in American society. Their views dominate government, particularly at the federal level. His conclusion is that "a corporation-based capitalist class—manifesting itself most obviously as a social upper class—dominates the American government" (1993:171). The federal government, Domhoff concludes, "is dominated (which does not mean complete and total control) by a power elite rooted in the upper class and the corporate community" (177). He defines the power elite as "active, working members of the upper class and high-level employees in institutions controlled by members of the upper class, thereby making it the leadership group of the upper class" (172).

Domhoff (1998) emphasizes the social nature of the dominant corporate ownership and managerial class. The cohesiveness of this ruling group is largely a product of its members' common upper-class ties. "They belong to the same exclusive social clubs, frequent the same summer and winter resorts, and send their children to a relative handful of private schools. Members of the corporate community thereby become a *corporate rich* who create a nationwide *social upper class* through their social interaction" (2). Through these common points of social interaction, the upper class consolidates a consciousness of purpose and effectively controls the power process.

The corporate rich, Domhoff (1974, 1998, 2010) explains, sponsor a network of policy-formation groups and think tanks that strongly influence government policy. It is chiefly through elite men's clubs and through policy-planning organizations that the upper class formulates its policy preferences and communicates them to political decision makers. These clubs and organizations thus become major locations of upper-class interaction, not only for social purposes but for functional or working purposes as well.

Many of Domhoff's basic conclusions seem well founded. The social interaction of members of the corporate elite and top-ranking political officials is easily verified empirically. Domhoff has also shown that even though political leaders may not be found as frequently as corporate leaders on upper-class club rosters, their presence is felt in other ways. More important, he demonstrates upper-class participation in influential policy-formation groups as well as the overrepresentation of members of the upper class in significant political positions.

Dye's Institutional Model   Political scientist Thomas Dye has also closely observed the American power elite in recent decades. Although he conceptualizes the power elite in much the same terms as Mills and Domhoff, some of his conclusions are markedly different.

Dye defines the power elite as approximately six thousand individuals in seven thousand positions who "exercise formal authority over institutions that control roughly half of the nation's resources in industry, finance, insurance, mass media, foundations, education, law, and civic and cultural affairs" (2002:207). Though a tiny fraction of the total population, it is still a larger figure than that posited by Mills or Domhoff.

Unlike Domhoff and Mills, Dye does not subscribe to the notion of a close relationship between the wealthy and the powerful. He sees institutional wealth as more important than personal wealth and, thus, control of institutions as most critical. He points to people who are among the society's billionaires who wield little or no societal power: widows, retirees, and other inheritors, as well as independent entrepreneurs, none of whom has ever played a significant role in the corporate world. Dye also does not see the upper class as a key recruiting ground for top political leaders. The link between the corporate elite and the political elite, in Dye's opinion, is tenuous at best.

Also, in contrast to Mills and Domhoff, Dye discounts the significance of common social institutions among the wealthy, such as exclusive clubs and schools, as the basis of a dominant class. Although he does not deny the importance of prestigious private clubs, he maintains that members of such clubs are mainly from the corporate elite and do not interact with governmental leaders. As far as the exercise of power is concerned, the clubs, according to Dye, "merely help facilitate processes that occur anyway" (2002:149). Perhaps more important, even if there may be a strong presence of political and economic elites in upper-class organizations, what remains questionable is the extent to which their interaction within these organizations helps promote control of public policy. As political scientists Kenneth Prewitt and Alan Stone point out, "The overrepresentation of a social upper class no doubt gives some common tone and style to the elite circles, but it does not begin to explain what is politically critical about those circles" (1973:159).

Like Mills and Domhoff, Dye does see a concentration of economic power in American society among a relatively small group of corporate managers. He identifies an "inner group" within the power elite who combine their corporate power with influence among important foundations, universities, and cultural and civic organizations. He also sees this inner group as socially cohesive. They not only come together at corporate board meetings but attend similar cultural and civic events, foundation meetings, and university trustee and alumni gatherings and are members of the same exclusive social clubs (Dye, 2002).

Also like Mills and Domhoff, Dye sees members of this inner group as links between the corporate world and government. A basic assumption of Dye's model is that "the initial resources for research, study, planning, and formulation of national policy are derived from corporate and personal wealth" (2002:173–174). And it is within these policy-planning groups that leaders from various societal institutions are able to come together in shaping national policies.

Baltzell: The Conservative Elitist View   Further evidence of a strong overlap between the upper class and those who head the powerful institutions of American society is provided by E. Digby Baltzell (1958, 1964). Baltzell's conclusions regarding the interrelations between the upper class and the society's chief power wielders are similar to Domhoff's: Essentially, there exists a ruling class. But in contrast to Domhoff, Baltzell sees a ruling class as socially beneficial and its special privileges as justified.

Baltzell distinguishes three groups at the top of the social hierarchy. First, there is what he calls simply the "elite," made up of top functional leaders of various spheres of social activity. These are the important decision makers of the corporation, the government, education, the media, and so on. Second, there is an "upper class," composed of families of established wealth whose members are descendants of elite members of one or more generations ago and who make up a social upper class with a distinct style of life and primary group solidarity. When this class combines its wealth and status with functional power—that is, when its members are simultaneously elite members—there exists a ruling class, or what Baltzell calls an "establishment." This conceptualization of the power structure closely resembles Domhoff's.

Baltzell sees the need for a society to maintain a system of power that combines the traditional authority deriving from the past with the infusion of new groups into positions of functional power: "The most difficult and delicate problem faced by democratic societies is that of balancing the liberal need for the continuous circulation of individual elites with the conservative need for maintaining a continuity of family authority" (1964:72). Ideally, then, the establishment is made up of individuals whose power and prestige are inherited, but it remains open to the newly powerful, those recruited into the elite on the basis of talent and ability. This requires that members of the elite be accepted into the upper class regardless of ethnic origin or religion. Baltzell emphasizes that without the infusion of new blood from the elite, the upper class will degenerate into a group that neglects its leadership duties and concerns itself only with its rights to privilege. In a sense, Baltzell views the establishment as a "noble aristocracy," socialized into accepting its leadership role and conscious of its societal obligations.

Baltzell finds much overlapping of the upper class and the elite throughout American history. Those who have occupied positions of power in government, the corporation, and other societal institutions have been overwhelmingly representative of those of wealth and prestige. In recent decades, however, the upper class, Baltzell claims, has become more narrow in its social composition, excluding those of diverse ethnic and religious origins who have penetrated the society's functional elites.

Baltzell, then, does not see a close interrelationship of upper class and power elite in modern times. Although it did so in past eras, the upper class, he maintains, no longer constitutes or even necessarily controls the power elite. Those of non–upper-class origin are able to enter into top positions of power and may exercise their power independently of the upper class, which is increasingly concerned only with protecting its status and privilege, not with exercising power. Baltzell views this development apprehensively. A closed upper class creates the possibility that power will be wielded by those who lack socialization to upper-class values and who therefore have little understanding of their larger social responsibilities. Their legitimacy may thus become questionable and force them to resort to coercion and deception to govern effectively.

Social Class and the Power Elite

In considering who gets to the top of the power hierarchy, the American ideology suggests that there are no built-in impediments. With sufficient individual effort, the lowliest person can rise to the greatest heights. Anyone, therefore, can be the CEO of a major corporation or the owner of a broadcasting empire or even president of the United States.

In the latter decades of the nineteenth century, an American writer, Horatio Alger, Jr., authored a hundred novels that almost perfectly reflected the belief that hard work, thrift, and honesty lead to economic and social success. The leitmotif of each of Alger's books was the same: Even those of humble origins can make it to the top. Through adherence to the work ethic, along with a bit of luck, any adversity might be overcome. And in the Alger stories, the hero always conquers what seem to be overwhelming odds. Alger's novels were aimed primarily at a juvenile audience, particularly young boys who, he hoped, would use the stories as inspiration for living a good life. From Alger's novels came what has been called the **Horatio Alger myth,** essentially the idea that anyone, regardless of social standing, can reach the pinnacle of wealth and power with enough striving and perseverance. This has become a basic belief, held at least in the abstract, of Americans in explaining how people get to the top. To what extent does the idea of an essentially open system of elite recruitment hold true? The biographies of the past four American presidents are intriguing cases with which to explore this question.

Former President Bill Clinton would seem to validate in some part the Horatio Alger myth. Rising from seemingly ordinary beginnings, neither poor nor rich, Clinton displayed many of the characteristics of an inspired overachiever. He excelled academically as an undergraduate at Georgetown University and won a Rhodes scholarship to study at Oxford. He went on to Yale Law School, where he again earned outstanding grades. Clinton was determined to succeed in the political world and before his thirtieth birthday had been elected attorney general of Arkansas. By the age of thirty-two, he was elected Arkansas's governor, the youngest person ever to hold that office (Marannis, 1995). In 1992 he gained the Democratic Party's nomination for the presidency and subsequently won the election despite imposing political obstacles (Allen and Portis, 1992).

Barack Obama's ascension to the presidency is, in a number of ways, even more improbable than Clinton's. Like Clinton, Obama lacked a privileged class upbringing and was raised in a nontraditional family. But, like Clinton, he excelled academically in high school and college. Obama's mixed racial inheritance, of course, provided the most daunting obstacle to power not encountered by Clinton or any previous viable aspirant to the presidency. After attending Columbia University, Obama turned down more lucrative career opportunities and chose to work as a community organizer on Chicago's South Side for several years before entering Harvard Law School, where he was elected president of the Harvard Law Review. Following graduation he shunned a prestigious judicial clerkship and returned to Chicago to practice civil rights law. At age thirty-three he was elected to the Illinois House of Representatives, serving for eight years before winning an overwhelming election to the U.S. Senate; four years later he was the forty-fourth U.S. president.

Is Clinton's and Obama's rise to political power, however, typical of those who hold high office? The path followed by the forty-first and forty-third occupants of the White House, George H. W. Bush and his son George W. Bush, could not present a stronger contrast. Indeed, the Bushes' stories personify the upper-class, patrician model. The elder Bush's father was a U.S. senator who had been a partner in one of the largest Wall Street investment firms. Bush himself attended Phillips Andover, one of the most exclusive and prestigious prep schools, and then went on to Yale. Rather than joining his father's investment firm, Bush senior started as vice president of a Texas oil-drilling equipment company, of which his father was a director. With financing from his uncle, he formed several oil companies and while still in his thirties became a multimillionaire. Having succeeded in business, he then turned to the political world (Phillips, 2004). The junior Bush, like his father, attended exclusive private schools and Yale University. His subsequent business ventures were financed in large measure by friends and relatives and were largely unsuccessful until he parlayed a $600,000 investment in the Texas Rangers baseball club into a $14 million profit when he sold his share of ownership (Kristof and Bruni, 2000; Ratcliffe, 1998). Through the accident of birth, there was certainly a high probability, if not a guarantee, that the Bushes would take their place among the wealthy and powerful.

Which of these two types, then, typifies the quest for places in the power elite? The answer is a mixed picture. Although the linkage between wealth and power is usually very strong, there are nonetheless opportunities for those from less eminent origins who are determined and ambitious.

The Social-Class Origins of U.S. Elites

Examining the correlations between societal power and social variables such as class, ethnicity, gender, and age provides one means of determining the extent to which the society's power structure is open or closed. Do people of different social origins commonly enter powerful decision-making and influential groups, or do top leaders remain tightly knit in self-sustaining units? Chapters 10 and 11 examine the extent to which race, ethnicity, and gender affect entrance into positions of institutional power. The analysis in this section is limited to the significance of social class.

Almost all studies of top leaders of government and of the corporation conclude that the majority do not reflect the population as a whole in terms of social class. Specifically, they come from upper- or upper-middle-class families and have displayed such backgrounds since the founding of the nation.

Charles Beard, in a well-known historical study (1913), found that the members of the Constitutional Convention of 1787 were mostly the economic and social notables of their time. They were professional men, merchants, and landowners who, according to Beard, benefited economically from the adoption of the Constitution as it was written. The privileged status of these early political leaders is evident in their educational backgrounds. Philip Burch (1980) found that at a time when only a tiny element of the population attended college (about 0.2 percent), 87 percent of the major cabinet and diplomatic appointees of the George Washington and John Adams administrations had done so.

Studies of government leaders indicate that the predominance of those with privileged backgrounds has not been limited to the early eras of American history. Mills (1956) showed, for example, that the 513 men who occupied the top political offices of president, vice president, Speaker of the House, cabinet member, and Supreme Court justice between 1789 and 1953 were mainly from well-to-do professional or business families (see also Burch, 1980). Sociologist Lloyd Warner and his associates (Warner and Abegglen, 1963) studied eleven thousand top federal executives and found that well over half had fathers who were professionals, business owners, or executives; only 15 percent were the sons of laborers. A study of the Supreme Court showed that of the ninety-two men who served in that body up to 1959, only nine were not from families of economic importance, social prestige, and political influence (Schmidhauser, 1960). And a study of 180 members of the U.S. Senate who served between 1947 and 1957 concluded that, with few exceptions, they were selected from "near the top of the society's class system" (Matthews, 1973:44). A later study (Zweigenhaft, 1975) found no basic differences through the mid-1970s. For the past three decades, only a small number of members of Congress, both senators and representatives, have not come from high-status occupations, overwhelmingly in the business world or the legal profession (Amer and Manning, 2008; Marger, 1987). Moreover, with the inflated campaign funds that are now commonplace in national elections, the tendency for the wealthy to attain high elective positions has grown stronger. By the mid-1990s, over one-quarter of the Senate and at least fifty members of the House were estimated to be millionaires (Simpson, 1994).

As to the presidency, the notion that most men who have held the highest office have been of humble origins does not hold up under careful historical examination. In his study of the social origins of U.S. presidents, Edward Pessen (1984) reveals that most were born to families of unusually high social status and economic well-being, quite unlike the socioeconomic circumstances of most American families of their time. Pessen does see some change in recent decades in that presidents born into the upper class have become less common in favor of those born into the upper-middle class. The poor and the lower-middle class, however, continue to be bypassed. "Despite slight changes in the patterns of the presidents' social origins," Pessen concludes, "from one period in our history to another, the central fact, now as earlier, remains the almost total exclusion of men born to poor or modest stations" (72).

In short, throughout American history, top political leaders have been drawn from a narrow social base, not typical of the general populace. They have been and remain, as political scientist Donald Matthews put it sixty years ago, "far from common men in either their origins or their achievements" (1954:23–24).

If top-ranking political leaders generally display class origins higher than average, leaders of big business are even more clearly from privileged backgrounds. Knowing the class backgrounds of economic leaders is often a question of judgment, for we must rely mostly on what business executives themselves choose to reveal. Their perceptions of the extent of their upward mobility may exceed their actual experience. The image of the poor boy who has made it to the top—the Horatio Alger notion—is more publicly favorable than the image of an executive whose place at the top was never in doubt. Hence, business leaders may sometimes exaggerate the humbleness of their origins. Although this is also true of political leaders, their pasts are subject to much greater public exposure than is true of top officials in the business world; it is therefore more difficult to sustain a "born in a log cabin" image if that is not actually the case.

Despite these methodological difficulties, it is a basic conclusion of most studies of the corporate elite of the United States and other advanced capitalist societies that their members usually come from the top or near the top of the social hierarchy. One important study done in the 1960s

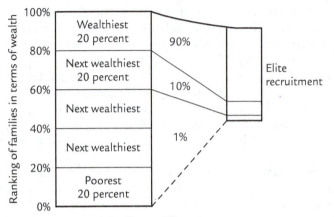

Figure 4-1 ▪ Class Origins of the Power Elite
Source: PREWITT, RULING ELITES, 1st, © 1973. Printed and Electronically reproduced by permission of Pearson Education, Inc., Upper Saddle River, New Jersey.

concluded that "whatever our national hopes, the business leaders of America are a select group, drawn for the most part from the upper-ranks" (Warner and Abegglen, 1963:14). Other studies have confirmed the upper- or upper-middle-class origins of the business elite since the emergence of the United States as an industrial society (Diamond, 1970; Newcomer, 1955; Keller, 1953; Lipset and Bendix, 1959).

Dye sees U.S. power elites as somewhat more varied in social-class background. He concludes that approximately 30 percent are of upper-class origins, having attended private prestigious prep schools and having parents who were high-ranking corporate, political, or other institutional officials. Thus, 70 percent appear to be middle class in family origin. On that basis Dye finds it illogical to conclude, as Domhoff and others have, that the upper class "dominates" the American power elite. Nonetheless, Dye recognizes that "even those who climbed the institutional ladder to high position generally started with the advantages of a middle-class upbringing" (2002:209). Moreover, half are graduates of prestigious private universities. Both Bill Clinton and Barack Obama, recall, despite their relatively commonplace beginnings, used attendance at elite Ivy League institutions as a launching pad for their upward climb.

It is quite apparent, then, that the top leaders of government and business in the United States are, in terms of social class, not typical of the general populace. Prewitt and Stone (1973) estimated that the wealthiest one-fifth of American families contributed about nine of every ten leaders of the political economy, and the next wealthiest fifth contributed most of the remainder (Figure 4-1). When elites of education, the military, and the media are combined with those of government and business, the same general pattern is evident. A later study drew a similar conclusion regarding the class origins of American elites. Most, the researchers concluded, "are the sons and daughters of upper-status white-collar workers" (Lerner et al., 1996:25).

Paths to Power

The Elite Recruitment Process

Although the historical patterns of elite recruitment seem to show that ascription is critical, cases such as Bill Clinton's, Barack Obama's, and a plethora of others who have risen in class and power indicate that there are opportunities for those who are not born into privilege. In the corporate world, entrance into the elite does not ordinarily occur without merit. This means that an individual cannot step into an executive position simply because his or her father was a high-ranking official of the company. To a lesser degree, the same is true in the political world. Government leaders must deal with a wide range of issues that often require specialized skills and expertise. The question, then, is how those born into lower social classes may be afforded the opportunities to acquire and subsequently display their skills and perhaps enter the power elite.

The Talent Pool   The elite recruitment process can be pictured as a system in which individuals are chosen from a potential talent pool. In this reservoir of possible leaders are the people with the skills, education, and other qualifications needed to fill elite positions. It is here that competition does exist, that the highest achievers do display their abilities, and that the best-qualified do generally succeed. Hence, what is most important is *entering this reservoir of qualified people* (Figure 4-2).

Many from sub-middle-class origins may have leadership potential, but unless they can gain entrance into the elite pool, their abilities will go unnoticed. Those of higher-class origins enter more easily into this competition because they have been afforded greater opportunities to secure the needed

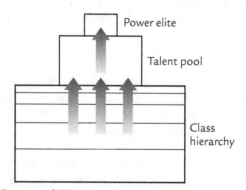

Figure 4-2 ■ The Process of Elite Recruitment

qualifications. They not only acquire college and professional degrees but often acquire them from the most prestigious institutions.

Social Connections   Following the acquisition of skills necessary to compete for elite places, one must then display them. There is, in a sense, a stage upon which potential elite members must audition their qualities. Having access to that stage means not only achieving the formal requirements for entering the talent pool (education above all) but also interacting within social circles where incumbent elites are likely to take notice of a talented individual. These are the social connections that come more naturally to those of higher-class families and that further filter out otherwise qualified persons from the competition. The familiar adage that "it's not what you know but who you know" is quite applicable to the process of elite recruitment.

Often, attendance at an elite university not only provides individuals with a prestigious degree but gives them an opportunity to nurture personal friendships and affiliations that will serve them well in the occupational world. To illustrate, assume that four individuals are born into the working class. They all have pretty much the same personal characteristics and are exposed to similar social environments. All are academically outstanding students. There are a few key differences among them, however. One is extraordinarily ambitious and talented; most think he will go far once he graduates from high school. A second has a very high IQ, and, like the first student, her teachers and peers expect her to go far. A third is very confident and assertive; he is known as someone who will not stop short of achieving whatever it is he attempts. The fourth has none of the extraordinary personal traits of the other three but has a good enough academic record and sufficient financial assistance to attend Harvard. The first three, for personal reasons, go on to a state university near their home community. Who among these four has the best chance of entering into the power elite? Remember the idea of probability in social science analysis. We cannot predict who among them will actually enter the elite, but the probability is greatest that the fourth student will do so. Harvard and other Ivy League schools are favorite recruiting grounds for top corporations and prestigious law firms, but in addition, at Harvard she will have formed personal relationships that will give her entree to networks of the powerful and influential.

The reservoir of qualified people is larger than the number of positions to be filled. Hence, knowing the "right" people and being able to connect with them becomes critical. In addition, of course, are other ascriptive factors—race and ethnicity, gender, even physical attractiveness—that further filter out candidates at this point in the selection process.

Self-Selection   In addition to formal qualifications and social connections, there are less obvious social-psychological factors that tend to further narrow the potential elite pool. These involve a subtle process of self-selection by which those of higher social standing assert themselves and by which those of lower social standing eliminate themselves from the competition for elite positions (Prewitt and Stone, 1973). For example, a young man or woman whose family has been active in politics, who has attended an elite university, and who has established a network of connections to the economic and political power establishments would not be starry-eyed in aspiring to a high position in the corporate or political world. Sociologist Dalton Conley has referred to this as an "envisioning" process, "the simple familiarity with and demystification of certain social roles that is afforded those in privileged positions" (2008:369). Consider again the case of the Bushes, described earlier.

By comparison, consider that a young person from a less prestigious family, who has no connections and has earned only a high school diploma or perhaps a college degree from a second-rate state university, would probably not visualize a future place for himself or herself at the top. As Prewitt and Stone explain, such an individual "has few models to emulate, no contacts to put him into the right channels, and little reason to think of himself as potentially wealthy or powerful" (1973:140). Thus, self-selection aids in filtering out those of lower social class from the pool of potential elites. Most eliminate themselves from the competition early in the game.

The Systemic Nature of Elite Recruitment

As should now be obvious, elite recruitment is mostly a process in which the cards are heavily stacked in favor of the society's affluent and highest-status groups. The structural forces of class, ethnicity, and gender, as well as the more subtle social-psychological forces of self-selection, tend to perpetuate the place of dominant groups in key power positions.

This need not be seen, however, as a conscious conspiracy on the part of a ruling class to preserve its power. Rather, the system of elite recruitment is largely self-directing. The fact that the social composition of elites tends to be consistent from one generation to another reflects the structural nature of societal power. Those who are upper- or upper-middle-class, white, Protestant, and male need not conspire to protect their favored social positions; they are automatically afforded easier access to the wealth, education, and social connections needed to qualify for power positions. And by the same token, a cumulation of disadvantages automatically works to the detriment of those of lower-class, working-class, and ethnic and gender minority groups. Recall the notion of the accident of birth and the way in which social resources are accumulated. Thus, top power-holders in almost all institutional spheres quite naturally continue to come predominantly from the same social groups.

Moreover, these repetitive patterns of elite recruitment come to be commonly expected, thereby further strengthening the hold of dominant social groups on top positions. Most people simply do not expect those of low-income or even working-class origins, for example, to head giant corporations, to be nominated for the presidency, or to be five-star generals. Social expectations of who should occupy power positions are reinforced by widely held negative stereotypes regarding the capabilities of sub-middle-class groups, helping to make their underrepresentation in power elites a self-fulfilling prophecy.

It should be remembered, however, that because the system is not tightly closed, some individuals of lower social origins do work their way into the elite. There is always room at the top for those few who overcome social handicaps; manage to enter the talent pool; and, once there, excel. President Obama's case illustrates this dramatically. Incumbent elites, in other words, are not able to totally frustrate the entrance of lower-status individuals into positions of power. As sociologists Seymour Martin Lipset and Reinhard Bendix note,

> No elite or ruling class controls the natural distribution of talent, intelligence, or other abilities, though it may monopolize the opportunities for education and training. As long as many of those with high abilities belong to the lower strata (and many contemporary studies suggest that this is so), there will be leaders who come from those strata. The chance for potential leaders to develop the skills which will take them up from the ranks may be small, but sooner or later some will break through. (1959:3)

The penetration of a few from lower social ranks, however, should not be mistaken as commonplace. On the contrary, such cases are clearly exceptional.[5] *The outstanding fact of elite recruitment in the United States is that leaders are chosen overwhelmingly from socially dominant groups and have been for many generations.* The entrance of the few from more humble backgrounds, however, reinforces the traditional belief that the process of elite recruitment accommodates all, regardless of class and status.

Power Elites in Other Societies

The predominance of those of higher social classes in elite positions is not unique to the United States. A similar pattern holds in virtually all other contemporary societies.

In the realm of government, leaders are rarely below the middle class in social origin, and the predominance of upper- and upper-middle-class men in top decision-making positions of the economy is especially evident. In Britain, for example, the corporate elite has been opened to a limited degree to a few from the middle ranks of the class structure, but not to those from working or lower middle classes (Coates, 1989). Similarly, in France, Germany, Italy, and Japan, most top executives and managers continue to come primarily from the upper and upper-middle classes and are

---

[5]It should also be obvious, of course, that those who are not qualified to run corporations or governments are not likely to be selected even if they are of privileged class and status origins.

educated at a few prestigious institutions (Bottomore and Brym, 1989; Scheuch, 2003). Moreover, those recruited from less privileged social backgrounds do not appreciably change the social attitudes and characteristics of the elite; rather they are co-opted into it and adopt similar behaviors and attitudes.

In Canada, too, studies of the 1960s and 1970s found that few business leaders came from sub-middle-class origins (Porter, 1965; Clement, 1975). Later research, however, shows that the Canadian business elite has become somewhat more open and is increasingly heterogeneous in terms of class and ethnicity (Ogmundson, 1999).

A Global Power Elite?   In a world in which the economies and governments of nations are increasingly drawn together, is it meaningful to consider the makeup of a "global power elite," one that transcends political boundaries? David Rothkopf (2008) posits that about six thousand people do in fact constitute such a collectivity. As he describes it, this supranational collectivity is uncannily similar in most regards to Mills's power elite: top government leaders, military leaders, and key corporate executives. In addition, Rothkopf sees a few extraordinarily influential artists, scientists, and academics (and even a few criminals) who complement these three key elements of the elite. The single largest component, however, is the leadership group of business and finance. What makes this coterie of leaders distinguishable from U.S. and other national power elites is that they are linked internationally, with common global interests.

Summary

In terms of income and wealth, the upper class in American society is far removed from other social classes. A relative handful of individuals and families earn multimillion-dollar salaries and, more important, possess wealth in even higher amounts. Moreover, the separation between the rich and the remainder of the U.S. population has widened during the last three decades. In a real sense, the rich have become richer.

The upper class of past generations consisted of families that acquired their wealth through the burgeoning heavy industries of the late nineteenth century. Most of today's new rich derive their wealth from the emergent knowledge/information industries of postindustrial society.

Although the upper class are those at the top of the class hierarchy in terms of income, wealth, and lifestyle, the power elite consists of those who occupy the society's most important institutional positions of authority. It is particularly in the corporate world and in government that these positions are found. Although the relationship between the upper class and the power elite is very strong, the two are not the same. Therefore, some individuals may be part of the upper class but not the power elite, and vice versa.

The recruitment process into the power elite is one in which those from privileged social backgrounds have great advantages. Even though the process is technically open and some persons of modest social origins do penetrate the elite, those from the upper and upper-middle classes tend to disproportionately occupy the major leadership positions of the corporation and government.

In all societies, correlations between certain social characteristics and power positions are quite evident. No matter how accessible the power structure may seem, the social backgrounds of leaders tend to remain relatively consistent for long periods of time. Those who hold leadership positions are generally replaced by individuals of similar social origins, and these repetitive patterns of replacement come to be commonly expected. However, the critical importance of ascribed characteristics, especially family of origin, do not rule out individual ability and effort as factors in elite recruitment. Individual talent and achievement do become important determinants in the selection of institutional leaders, but only after the competitive field has been thinned out.

5

The Middle Classes

Can you imagine an America without a strong middle class? If you can, would it still be America as we know it?
ELIZABETH WARREN

The general feeling in America is that you are middle class if you say so.
ALAN WOLFE

"America is a middle-class society." Countless chroniclers of American society have made that observation almost from its founding. The middle-class nature of the United States is both an objective fact and a subjective mood. As to the former, most people are neither at the top of the class hierarchy nor at the bottom. Two-thirds of American families have incomes between $25,000 and $150,000. While this certainly represents a broad range, it is a range whose components are clearly separated from the top 10 percent, who own most of the society's wealth, and the poor, who hover below or near the poverty line. In an economic sense, then, it is quite accurate to describe the United States as a society in which most people are "in the middle."

But the middle-class idea is also a state of mind; it is how people see themselves regardless of their actual economic position, and it is reflected in their attitudes and values. The level of class consciousness in the United States is markedly lower than in most other contemporary societies. National surveys for many decades have consistently shown that almost all Americans, when asked to classify themselves in the stratification system, almost reflexively answer "working class" or, more commonly, "middle class" (Heath, 1998; Pew Research Center, 2008b). Even those of very low or high income tend to identify as part of the great American middle. As one observer of the middle class has put it, "The widely perceived class *un*consciousness of the American people is a consequence of a class psychology characteristic not only of actual members of the middle class but of aspirants to that status, and overall, therefore, of the great majority of the nation" (Baritz, 1982:xii).

It is important to understand that there is no cohesive middle class, as such, but rather several classes that constitute neither the rich at the top nor the poor at the bottom. As described in Chapter 3, the classes in the middle consist of at least three specific categories: the upper-middle class, the lower-middle class, and the working class.

It seems logical to analyze these intermediate classes together for several reasons. First, despite the significant differences among the three in income, occupation, education, and lifestyle, they are all clearly set apart from those at the top and bottom of the American class hierarchy. The very affluent and the decision-making elite are, in both financial and lifestyle terms, far distant from other classes. And by the same token, those at the other end of the hierarchy, especially the underclass, are equally divorced from the mainstream. This leaves the "classes in the middle" or the "intermediate classes" as the bulk of the American population.

It is also the case that most of the mobility that occurs in the class system occurs within and between the units of this middle range. Rare are the rags-to-riches cases, with individuals moving from the bottom of the class system to the top. The most common forms of mobility are short-range, incremental moves that occur mostly within the working, lower-middle, and upper-middle classes.

Finally, the American economy has been restructured in the past three decades with the emergence of a global economic system. It is the classes in the middle that have been most seriously affected by that process.

Historical Development of the Middle Classes

Although the classes in the middle are seen as the backbone of American society and other economically developed societies, the emergence of these classes is a historically recent occurrence. Prior to the advent of industrial capitalism, agrarian societies consisted essentially of two classes: the landed aristocracy, who controlled most wealth, and the remainder of the populace, who worked the land as poor peasants, living in degraded and deprived conditions. As commercial activities and industrial production replaced agriculture as the major economic pursuits, a merchant class, or **bourgeoisie,** gradually replaced the landowners as the most powerful class, and their wealth increased commensurately.

Formation of the Middle Classes in the United States

Nowhere else in the Western world did the middle classes develop as thoroughly and as early as in the United States. Although colonial leaders did constitute an aristocratic elite of sorts, an American landed gentry never really existed.[1] There was no sharply divided system of aristocracy and peasantry,

---

[1]The antebellum southern planter class, however, displayed some of the characteristics of a landed aristocracy.

which had typified European societies. Hence, it was the classes in the middle, made up of independent farmers and entrepreneurs, that seemed to predominate almost from the outset. As the French politician and writer Alexis de Tocqueville observed in the 1830s, ". . . the social state of America is a very strange phenomenon. Men there are nearer equality in wealth and in mental endowments, or, in other words, more nearly equally powerful, than in any other country of the world or in any other age of recorded history" (1966:49).

From the beginning, farmers, who were the numerically dominant group until the end of the nineteenth century, owned their land. They were joined by small business owners—producers, tradesmen, merchants—who formed another part of the American middle. The most important fact linking farmers and merchants was their possession of property. As owners of their enterprises, they worked for themselves. Moreover, the ownership of property was widespread rather than characteristic of just a small portion of the society. The middle class that arose in the late eighteenth and early nineteenth centuries, then, was composed basically of entrepreneurs. This class of entrepreneurs epitomized the American ideology of individualism and free enterprise (Mills, 1951).

Industrialization and the Changing Class Structure

Growth of the Working Class The predominance of farmers and farm laborers as part of the workforce began to change as the society moved more fully toward industrialization. By the end of the nineteenth century, the shift toward an industrial workforce was clear and irreversible. Automation drove many farmworkers from the land, where their labor was no longer needed. Machines could do the work of men more efficiently and more cheaply. Moreover, the lure of better-paying jobs in factories in the urban areas was very strong, serving as an additional push of workers off the farms. In 1880, 20 man-hours were required to harvest an acre of wheat; by 1916, only 12.7 man-hours were needed; and by 1936, only 6.1 (Rifkin, 2004).[2]

As discussed in Chapter 2, Marx described capitalism as a system marked by a social division between those who owned the means of production—the factories and machines of the newly emergent industries—and the workers, whose labor produced the wealth of capitalism but who were dispossessed of power since they were not owners. Marx saw a continuing drop in the standard of living of industrial workers who, he felt, would be increasingly exploited by the capitalists. For many decades, the conditions of industrial Europe and the United States seemed to confirm Marx's dismal picture. The new industrial owners expanded their empires while their workers worked long hours under oppressive and often unsafe conditions. Steelworkers

---

[2]As Jeremy Rifkin explains, despite the fact that nearly half of all people on earth still farm, we are rapidly moving toward a world without farmers as technological changes in the production of food continue to advance. Consider that one farmworker in 1850 produced enough food to feed four people. Today, one farmer produces enough to feed seventy-eight people.

employed in the great Carnegie steel mills in western Pennsylvania, for example, labored twelve hours a day, seven days a week, constantly exposed to workplace hazards and debilitating injuries. For their toil, they earned about $10 a week, just above the poverty line of $500 a year. The annual earnings of Andrew Carnegie, by comparison, were the equivalent of the wages of almost four thousand steelworkers (*The American Experience,* 1997).

The New Middle Class   By the 1920s the United States had become a thoroughly industrialized society, and its workforce reflected that transformation. In addition, white-collar jobs, those in the service sector, began to grow with increasing speed. This contributed in great measure to the emergence of a large middle class in the mid-twentieth century. This new middle class was made up mainly of salaried white-collar workers working not for themselves but for employers, often as part of large, bureaucratic organizations. Marx had not anticipated the development of such a category of labor.

The emergence of a large white-collar sector of the labor force was brought about by the increasing concentration of the means of production into fewer and fewer large corporate enterprises. No longer were small, family-owned-and-operated firms the dominant form of business. Production and distribution became more complex and national in scope. As a result, smaller firms, with fewer resources, were unable to compete against large corporate enterprises, which were organized in bureaucracies with hundreds, perhaps thousands, of workers occupying highly specific work roles and led by a managerial elite.

Postindustrialism

Starting in the 1960s, a service economy began to emerge, in which most workers no longer labored in factories but instead provided services of one kind or another. The United States and other advanced industrial nations entered into what has been called postindustrialism (Bell, 1973). Unlike a traditional industrial society, **postindustrial society** is characterized by the production mainly of services and information rather than finished goods. This means that the majority of workers are white-collar rather than blue-collar, and many are professional, managerial, and technical workers. Postindustrial society is driven by knowledge, not so much of a practical kind, as was the case in industrial society, but of a theoretical or abstract nature. Thus, scientists, engineers, and academics play a critical role in maintaining the socioeconomic system.

As service workers became numerically dominant, industrial workers began to decline as a part of the labor force. In 1959, 40 percent of American workers were in the service sector and 60 percent were in manufacturing; by 1985, the ratio had reversed itself, with almost three-quarters in the service sector (Newman, 1999). This change was brought about by a shift in consumer patterns. Today, Americans spend more on services, including health care, education, and food service, than on manufactured goods, such as housing, appliances, and automobiles. In 1990, three times more was

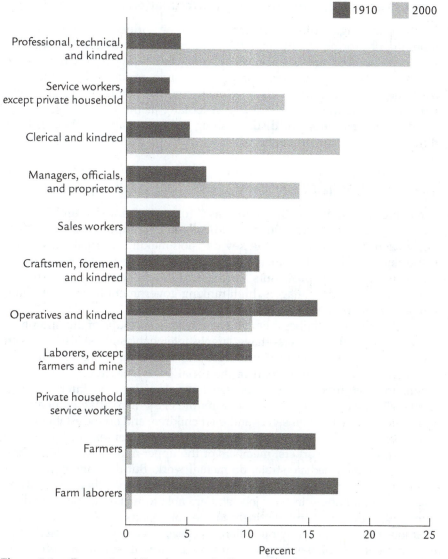

Figure 5-1 ▪ Proportional Employment in Occupational Categories, 1910 and 2000
Source: Wyatt and Hecker, 2006.

spent on health and medical care, for example, than was spent thirty years earlier (Farley, 1996). As personal services have become a greater proportion of consumer spending, a correspondingly greater need for service rather than production workers has developed.

The changed nature of the labor force during the last century can be seen in Figure 5-1. Note the radical decline of farmers and farmworkers and the equally sharp increase in professional and service workers.

The Classes in the Middle and the Occupational Structure

It is not an exaggeration to claim that nothing influences a person's life more than his or her occupation. Occupation not only determines the economic, power, and prestige aspects of social class but generally defines the parameters of a person's social life, cultural style, residential patterns, and consumer preferences. It is also the main cue that others use to view and make judgments about individuals. In looking at the three classes in the middle, perhaps the major distinguishing feature separating them is their different place in the occupational structure.

The Upper-Middle Class

Sometimes referred to as the "new class" (or as Barbara Ehrenreich (1989) refers to them, the "professional middle class"), the upper-middle class is made up of those who hold the key decision-making positions in various institutions. They are the doctors and lawyers, engineers, technicians and scientists, university professors, media editors and producers, corporate executives, financial managers, high-ranking government bureaucrats, and, at the lower end, schoolteachers.

As Ehrenreich describes them, the two major subgroups of this stratum—professionals and managers—have largely interchangeable skills and often move back and forth from one category to the other. Moreover, the two categories occupy the same part of the social landscape, living in the same neighborhoods, functioning in the same social circles, and intermarrying. Above all, among those of the upper-middle class there is an emphasis on formal education, for themselves and their children, and on the establishment of a stable career leading eventually to a comfortable retirement.

As **white-collar workers,** members of the upper-middle class, like many others in the intermediate strata, do mental work. But they are at a level of power and authority that clearly sets them apart from the other classes. They enjoy much autonomy in their jobs and are able to make independent decisions rather than respond routinely to the commands of others. Moreover, their jobs require, almost by definition, a college degree, which in itself gives them a higher social standing and presents them with substantial economic advantages.

Common occupational and educational experiences create a lifestyle and a set of consumer preferences that distinguish the upper-middle class from others. For example, professionals and managers at the upper end of this stratum typically own spacious suburban homes, drive upscale cars, and generally engage in trendy consumer behavior.

Politically, the upper-middle class is characteristically liberal on social issues such as abortion and civil rights but is generally conservative on economic issues of taxation and wages. Those of the upper-middle class are more politically active than are members of other classes. They vote more consistently and are more apt to participate in the electoral process in other ways as well, such as contributing money to political campaigns.

Studies have also shown that the upper-middle class is more active in voluntary associations (Skocpol, 1996; Smith, 1980). Moreover, much of the social life of upper-middle-class families is an outgrowth of their occupational lives, and the two are commonly combined. The country club or the dinner party often becomes a setting in which clients are entertained or colleagues are consulted.

The Lower-Middle Class

As one of the intermediate strata, the lower-middle class is the most difficult to define precisely since it is made up of so many disparate elements. It is a collection of occupational categories consisting mainly of small business owners and white-collar workers, including middle-level managers in the business world, paraprofessionals (e.g., nurses and legal workers), middle-level government bureaucrats, nonretail sales workers, secretaries and clerks, and medical technicians.

In terms of income, those in the lower-middle class span a broad range, according to specific occupation, but what is common to all is their relative lack of significant wealth. They are dependent primarily on their jobs for income and ordinarily do not own substantial assets aside from their homes.

Workers of the lower-middle class—with the exception of small business owners—exercise little power in their jobs. They ordinarily respond to the authority of managers and professionals of the upper-middle class.

Most within the lower-middle class have more than a high school education, but a college degree is not necessary to meet the qualifications of most of their occupations. Junior college or vocational training may therefore be the more common form of post-secondary schooling in this class. As with the upper-middle class, relatively common incomes and occupational statuses, along with common educational experiences, create a distinct lifestyle for the lower-middle class, along with corresponding consumer preferences.

Those of the lower-middle class are politically active, but not in the same way as the upper-middle class. Participation, though strong and common, does not usually extend much beyond voting. This is quite different from the political activism of the upper-middle class, who are participants at a higher level and who are more directly engaged in the political process.

The Working Class

What has traditionally characterized the working class more than anything else is the nature of its occupational role: **blue-collar work,** that is, work involving manual or physical labor. The skills of the working class, however, vary widely. At the top are skilled tradespeople and craft workers, such as carpenters, electricians, and plumbers. In the middle are those with mechanical skills, who, like most of the working class, work for an hourly wage. Tool-and-die makers, machinists, repair persons, and the like constitute this sector. At the bottom of the working class are those with few or no skills, who perform routine, perfunctory roles in factories or shops. These workers are usually referred to as operatives and constitute the largest element of the working class. Although the working class is still composed in large part of factory workers at different skill levels, starting around the 1960s, certain economic and technological forces began to emerge that led to a decline—which continues—of blue-collar occupations.

The educational level of the working class is limited by comparison with the lower-middle class and especially with the upper-middle class. Predictably, members of the working class possess little in the way of productive property, ordinarily owning only their homes and cars. Income, however, can vary among the different categories within the working class. Those at the top, the skilled tradespeople, may own their own businesses and thus exhibit some of the characteristics of the lower-middle class. Those at the bottom, the unskilled, may be one short step from the poverty class and may in fact drift in and out of the working-poor category.

The working-class subculture has been the subject of many studies, and the picture that emerges is one in which members marry younger (a result of the fact that education is usually curtailed earlier than among the upper- or lower-middle classes) and families are strongly patriarchal (Sennett and Cobb, 1973; Shostak, 1969). That traditional structure is breaking down, however, as working-class wives are now commonly part of the labor force, contributing their wages to family income. Indeed, like families in the other intermediate classes, working-class families today more often than not consist of two wage earners. As that has occurred, wives have asserted more family power (Rubin, 1994).

The consumer, housing, and leisure patterns of the working class are quite distinct from those of the other intermediate classes. Although these are often stereotyped and subject to a kind of upper-middle-class ridicule ("Joe Six-Pack," for example), there are identifiable features of the working class that may be said to constitute, roughly, a working-class lifestyle. As part of urban communities, working-class neighborhoods are clearly recognizable, made up of modest single-family dwellings or perhaps mobile homes. Leisure activities are also likely to differ noticeably. Whereas the upper-middle class and, increasingly, the lower-middle class may play golf or ski, the working class will more often bowl and hunt. Vacations among the working class are not likely to include foreign travel, as vacations frequently do for the upper- and even lower-middle classes, but more typically consist of road trips, perhaps in a recreational vehicle.

Work, for the working class, is separated from other spheres of life. Unlike the upper-middle class, where work and leisure are often combined, people "leave the job at work." Rather than realizing much personal fulfillment from one's occupation, as is typically the case among professionals and managers of the upper-middle class, working-class people, particularly the unskilled, ordinarily engage in boring and routine tasks, not those that present personal challenges.

In their politics, working-class people are a kind of mirror image of the upper-middle class: conservative on social issues but liberal on economic issues. Except among union members, however, they tend to be less politically active than either of the other two intermediate classes. Moreover, American working-class people are less politically active than their counterparts in almost all other contemporary industrial societies (Croteau, 1995). There is no major socialist or labor party in the United States catering primarily to working-class interests, as there is in most western European societies, as well as Canada and Japan. One explanation of this phenomenon is that American workers are no less committed than the classes above them to the idea of individual achievement. And as has been pointed out many times, workers generally have hopes of eventually establishing their own business and becoming their own boss. Thus, there is little sympathy among them for socialist ideas. There is no gainsaying the capitalist system among workers so long as most see themselves as future capitalists. We will discuss these ideas in greater detail in Chapter 8.

The Blurring of Traditional Occupational Categories   Today the blue-collar/white-collar distinction is no longer as meaningful as it once was, and as a result, the division between the lower-middle and working classes is, at times, hazy. It is not at all clear where the lower end of the lower-middle class begins to diverge from the higher end of the working class. Many white-collar jobs that in previous times would have been clearly distinguishable from blue-collar ones have been downgraded in skills and wages.

Some have referred to a "proletarianization" of white-collar workers, implying that there is no longer a significant difference between many blue- and white-collar jobs (Braverman, 1974; Glenn and Feldberg, 1977; Judis, 1994). White-collar jobs at the lower status levels have been deskilled, that is, reduced to repetitive, routine tasks that involve little brainpower. Consider a cashier in a fast-food restaurant or a department store. Little more is involved than taking the customer's payment, punching a few keys on a computer-connected cash register, and giving customers their receipts. Cashiers needn't even calculate the transaction since the cash register will do it for them. These routine tasks are not essentially different from unskilled blue-collar jobs, where workers perform a simple function repeatedly. Bank tellers are another illustration of deskilling—in handling commercial transactions today, they do little more than operate computer keyboards, entering a few items of information. Indeed, machines have brought bank tellers to the point of eventual extinction. Consider that their numbers dropped by forty-one thousand between 1985 and 1995 and that most of those who remained were converted to part-time positions. The first ATM (automatic teller machine) was installed at a bank in 1971; by 2000, almost 11 billion transactions were processed at four hundred thousand ATMs.

At the same time, the rise of a category of technicians has further blurred the distinction between white- and blue-collar workers. As Robert Reich (1994) describes them, "These workers often wear ties or dresses (as did their white-collar predecessors). But they also often work with their hands, use tools and monitor machinery (as did their blue-collar predecessors)." These are the people who design and test computer systems, repair copy machines, operate hospital equipment, and so on. In fact, as the nature of blue-collar jobs shifts toward the service sector, an increasing number of people with college experience are filling them. In 1973, only 12 percent of factory workers had some college training; by 2000, that figure had risen to 36 percent (Carnevale and Desrochers, 2002). In fact, many of the traditional blue-collar jobs done in the past by workers with only minimal education now require computer and other skills that call for at least some training beyond high school (Whoriskey, 2012).

As Herbert Gans (1988) has pointed out, even the lifestyle differences of the lower-middle and working classes are no longer sharply distinct:

> Working- and lower-middle-class people usually do not live in separate neighborhoods or speak and dress differently. The once sizable gulf in education, ways of raising children, furnishing dwellings, and spending leisure time have also declined. As long as note is taken of the remaining differences such as job security and working conditions, the two populations can often be described as middle Americans. (8)

The Changing U.S. Economy and the Classes in the Middle

In recent years the intermediate classes have been profoundly affected by what has been referred to as economic restructuring. Jobs, income, and wages have all been impacted by the advent of a global economy and by what has been called a third industrial revolution, in which occupations and the very nature of work itself are being transformed by new technologies. These changes have affected each of the intermediate classes in different ways. Those in the upper-middle class have generally prospered, while those in the working class and, to a lesser degree, the lower-middle class have been the losers. To better understand the current status of these classes, we need to briefly trace the major developments of the American economy and its workforce over the last few decades.

The Growth of the Middle Classes

The Great Depression During the 1930s, the United States, along with most other industrial societies, endured the most severe economic depression in its history. Capitalist economies had traditionally experienced periodic swings in which an era of prosperity was followed by recession, which, in turn, was followed by recovery. This pattern did not hold up in the 1930s, however, and the result was an inability to stimulate demand. Falling prices led to falling wages and extremely high unemployment. Some saw this as the beginning of the end of the capitalist system. Efforts of the Roosevelt administration to jump-start the economy through massive public spending programs did put many people back to work, but these measures were, in the end, not effective in ending the depression.

Not until the United States entered World War II did the economy finally recover from this most serious economic crisis. Starting in 1941, jobs became plentiful as the society prepared for the war effort. Factories that were converted into war production facilities needed workers. Plants that previously had made automobiles and kitchen appliances now produced tanks, jeeps, and airplanes. The recruitment of hundreds of thousands of men into the armed forces led to a labor shortage at home. This stimulated a migration of thousands from the rural South to northern industrial cities to work in the plants. Moreover, women were recruited into the industrial labor force, filling jobs that ordinarily had been occupied only by men. The image of "Rosie the Riveter" became a morale booster for the home front workforce.

The Postwar Years   Following the war, it was feared that the United States would once again be plunged into an economic depression. With the end of the conflict and the return of soldiers and sailors into the domestic workforce, images of an oversupply of labor resurfaced. What emerged instead, however, was a thriving economy that gave rise to a twenty-year period of great prosperity. The demand for consumer goods that had been denied people during the depression and the war stimulated the economy and led to a tremendous industrial expansion. Returning to civilian life, men and women married in record numbers, giving rise to the so-called baby boom. Those new families created a demand for new housing. The old housing stock of the central cities could no longer support the expanding population, which sought a more placid environment in which to raise families. This they found in the suburbs. The movement to the suburbs was boosted as well by the construction of a superhighway system in which expressways now enabled workers, whose jobs were still located mostly in the central cities, to commute back and forth.

Another factor that prevented a return to economic depression was the maintenance of a strong military. The army and navy had been disbanded after World War I, but at the end of World War II, the perceived threat of the Soviet Union and the onset of the Cold War provided the rationale for the continued support of a huge military establishment. The manufacture of weapons, therefore, became a mainstay of the American economy, providing jobs and income to thousands and generally providing a societywide economic stimulus.

American prosperity was also the result of the fact that the United States had emerged from the war as the only advanced society with its industrial infrastructure still in place. Americans at home had been unaffected by the fighting, unlike the Europeans and the Japanese, whose industrial bases were left in shambles. The United States, as a result, became an economic super-power unchallenged by any nation. It would be many years before Germany, Japan, and others would be able to present serious economic competition.

The upshot of this great economic boom was a substantial expansion of the middle classes. Rising productivity in the 1950s led to rising wages and higher family incomes (Danziger and Gottschalk, 1993; Kuttner, 2007; Levy, 1995, 1998; Reich, 2007, 2010). Many entered the middle class for the first time, gaining their piece of the American Dream: a secure and well-paying job, a relatively comfortable home in which to raise a family, and the avail-ability of an unprecedented variety of consumer goods. No image better reflected the American optimism of the 1950s than the television sitcom of that period *Ozzie and Harriet*. Here was the prototypical middle-class family: station wagon parked in the driveway of their suburban home, where their teenage boys were growing up in a world that promised nothing but con-tinued prosperity. That was the prospectus not only of the general public but also of economic and social forecasters. Economic expansion seemed unlim-ited, and Americans had every reason to believe that prosperity and eco-nomic supremacy in the world would continue not only for their generation but for their children and grandchildren as well.

The Post-1973 Period of Economic Restructuring   The unrelenting opti-mism of the 1950s and 1960s (the latter decade was one of great social turmoil, but economic prosperity for the middle classes did not abate) was halted by events and economic developments starting in the 1970s. The year 1973 is often used as a historic watershed. The OPEC oil embargo occurred in that year, and the American economy was forever changed afterward. The oil-producing nations, mostly of the Middle East, imposed for a time an embargo on oil shipments to the United States and subsequently placed limitations on the amount of oil for American export. Suddenly, the United States discovered that it was heavily dependent on outside sources for its economic well-being; no longer could it assume that its huge domestic market was unthreatened and its dominant place atop the world's economies unchallenged. In a sense, this marked the introduction to Americans of the global economy.

The Shrinking Middle

Starting in the mid-1970s, new socioeconomic patterns led to profound changes for the intermediate classes. Economists, sociologists, policymak-ers, and commentators began to speak of the U.S. stratification structure as "shrinking" in the middle. The basic idea is that those in the middle classes were being pushed up into the professional and managerial category, or they were being pulled down into the ranks of low-level service workers, many of whom were now part of the working poor. With some minor fluctuations, those overall trends have been unbroken for the past four decades. And, they continue to unfold ever more clearly at the present time.

This **middle-class squeeze,** or bifurcation, can be seen in the development of a two-tiered wage structure and in family income patterns.

Income and Wages   As pointed out in Chapter 3, inequality in American society is growing. The gap between those at the top and those at the bottom has been widening for the last three decades, and those in the middle have found it more difficult simply to keep pace. As some have described it, the United States is increasingly emerging as a two-tiered society: those who are doing well and are enriching themselves and those who are falling farther behind the successful people. Work itself is no longer a guarantee against poverty or downward mobility. Most of those who find themselves in a declining economic position are in fact employed.

Regardless of the definition applied or the unit measured—households, families, or individuals—the proportional size of the middle has been steadily decreasing (Duncan et al., 1993; Kacapyr, 1996; Mishel et al., 2009; Thurow, 1999). Looking at wages is one way to track the middle-class decline. While workers' wages increased consistently from the 1950s to around 1973, from that point forward they were stagnant except for those at the very highest earning level. The real (inflation-adjusted) average hourly wage for production and nonsupervisory workers (80 percent of the workforce) in 2007 was $17.42, compared to $16.88 in 1979; the real average weekly earnings had actually fallen to $590 in 2007, about $10 less than in 1979 and over $30 less than in 1973 (Mishel et al., 2009).

The stagnation of wages for most of the last forty years among the working class and part of the lower-middle class has created a growing fissure between them and the upper-middle class. Although the latter may also depend on their salaries for income, they are ordinarily able to supplement them with interest, dividends, capital gains, and other nonwage sources (Kacapyr, 1996).

Some of the gap between high- and low-wage workers is explained by education. Generally, the greater the level of education of the occupational group, the more wages have risen. Thus, workers at the high end of the labor force, professionals and managers, whose jobs require college degrees, have fared better than those with no college. By 2007, the real hourly wage of college-educated men was almost double that of high school graduates (Mishel et al., 2009). Since 1979, median family income for middle-income families declined more than 13 percent, but for professional-managerial families, it rose more than 7 percent (Williams and Boushey, 2010).

Not only has the wage gap widened, but merely keeping pace demands greater effort. Two-wage-earner families have become the norm, and thus family income, though hardly changed from 1973, is now most often the product of two workers. Indeed, Thurow has proclaimed that the "one-earner middle-class family is extinct" (1996:33). Many families in the middle have discovered that two incomes are essential merely to keep pace with the standard of living to which they have become accustomed. With both parents working, a new context for raising children has been created, placing additional pressures on families.

The curious side of income and wage polarization during the past four decades is that it occurred at the same time that most economic indicators were, by and large, positive: except for recessions in 1981 and 2001, productivity rose, corporate profits soared, and the stock market gained enormously. Furthermore, inflation was steadfastly under control, and unemployment was held in check. In brief, until the severe downturn beginning in 2007, the American economy, overall, appeared to be functioning well. None of this affected the precarious economic position of most workers, however. These developments demonstrated that a productive and growing economy does not necessarily translate into improved living standards for most families. A popular metaphor describing the effects of a growing economy is "a rising tide lifts all boats." From the late 1970s, however, only the yachts were rising; the other boats were trying hard to simply stay afloat.

The Decline of Middle-Income Jobs   Much of the explanation for the increasing bifurcation of income is attributable to the fact that the workforce is becoming more of a two-tiered structure—those whose jobs are in demand and who earn a good wage and those whose jobs are insecure and who earn a wage that often is not enough to support a family. What has occurred is an expansion of jobs at the top of the occupational hierarchy, particularly among professional, managerial, and technical workers, and at the bottom among service workers performing low-skill jobs that pay correspondingly low wages. Jobs in the middle of the occupational hierarchy have, as a result, declined.

During the 1980s and 1990s, the economy provided jobs for more and more people, including large numbers of women and immigrants who entered the workforce. In an analysis of census data, sociologist Reynolds Farley (1996) showed that many, perhaps most, of these new jobs were low-skill and low-paying but that there was also a rapid growth of new jobs at the high end of the wage scale. What had seemed to develop, then, was a growing gap between high-paid, high-skilled workers on the one hand and low-paid, low-skilled workers on the other (Rosenthal, 1995). The deep recession beginning in the late 2000s resulted in the massive loss of jobs at all levels, even among highly-skilled white-collar workers. But the bifurcated structure of the workforce remained basically unchanged.

This occupational bifurcation has been especially evident in the service sector, where over two-thirds of Americans now work. Service occupations are extremely varied, ranging from unskilled workers at the bottom, to clerical workers and salespersons in the middle, to highly trained professionals like doctors and lawyers at the top. Obviously, these jobs are considerably different in pay, skills, and prestige. In recent years, the most significant growth has occurred among the bottom portion of the service sector, those jobs requiring few skills, paying minimum wages, and offering little opportunity for upward mobility. The low end of the service sector includes such jobs as fast-food workers, kitchen workers, hospital workers such as orderlies and nurse's aides, nursing-home workers, maids, and child-care workers. However, significant growth has also occurred in the top portion of the service sector, including professionals and managers—hence the growing split between those at the top and those at the bottom, leaving a reduced middle.

The effects of a declining middle have hit well-paid blue-collar workers especially hard. Many have lost their jobs as a result of downsizing, mechanization, or globalization and now work precariously at jobs that pay a fraction of what they were previously earning. Many, of course, having lost their jobs, find themselves chronically under- or unemployed. This has been especially evident among older workers who cannot easily retrain or are simply passed over for younger workers entering the labor force who are prepared to work for a sharply lower wage. Take Craig Miller, a former sheet-metal worker for a large airline. When he was laid off and began to look for a job, he discovered that someone with his skills and educational level was unable to earn much more than minimum wage. He works behind the counter at a McDonald's, drives a school bus, and has started a small business changing furnace filters. His wife also works part-time. Between the two, they hold four different jobs, but their total income is less than half of what Craig had earned as a union sheet-metal worker. They had acquired a piece of the American Dream, which they now find slipping away. Craig's former work buddies have experienced a similar fall in income and status. One has taken a job as a school janitor. Another, unable to find other than a minimum wage job has been forced to move back home with his parents at age thirty-nine. He is no longer confident that he will ever marry and start a family of his own. "Women are just like me; they want security," he says. "What are they going to see in me?" (Johnson, 1994:A9). Cases such as these have proliferated enormously since the onset of the severe economic recession in 2007.

In addition, many workers today are temporary or part-time employees, hired or fired on the basis of seasonal or contingent needs where there is a built-in time limitation to the work (Greenhouse, 2009; Polivka, 1996). As the labor needs of employers change, the status of workers is thrown into jeopardy. Hence, the regularity of work is no longer assured. Retail sales personnel, for example, may be asked to work only those hours during which they are most needed. Employers commonly prefer to hire workers on a contingent basis so that they can adjust their wage costs to the utmost efficiency. This provisional nature of work has affected not only those workers nearer the bottom of the occupational hierarchy but also many at the higher end, even professionals. It is estimated that about 30 percent of all U.S. workers are now contingent workers—part-timers, temporaries, or subcontractors (U.S. GAO, 2006).

In short, the middle-class squeeze does not appear to be slowing down. The future of the classes in the middle will show a split along lines of skill, educational level, and wages. Low-skilled jobs in the service sector requiring little education or training and paying low wages continue to grow, while jobs at the higher end of the occupational hierarchy requiring at least a bachelor's degree and paying relatively well are also on the increase (Dohm and Shniper, 2007). Many among the latter, however, will find themselves pushed down in income and status.

With the economic downturn beginning in 2007, the job uncertainties that had traditionally been experienced by lower-status blue-collar and white-collar workers were brought home for the first time to many of those at the higher end of the middle classes. High-skilled workers in the auto industry were particularly hard hit as companies downsized, laying off thousands at all job levels. Chrysler offered its entire white-collar work-force a one-time buyout, an offer accepted by Doug Zupan, a thirty-five-year-old automotive designer with the company for six years. The father of three preschool-age children took the $50,000 payment when it became apparent that his job would soon be eliminated. Similarly, Craig Meyer, abruptly terminated as an automotive engineer, is surviving on unemployment, less than half of what he was earning at Chrysler, and his family is dipping into their savings for food and gas. Despite their skills, neither Zupan nor Meyer expect to work again in the automotive industry, and their employment futures are unpredictable (Vlasic and Bunkley, 2009).

Many older workers, accustomed to high wages and job security, have lost their places in the labor force and face the real possibility that they may never find employment again. They may lack the specific skills and qualifications needed for jobs different from those they had previously occupied and may be too old to make retraining practical. Moreover, they are less attractive to employers who are inclined to favor younger workers more easily trained, more technologically proficient, and less demanding. Consider Patricia Reid, age fifty-seven, a college graduate who worked for two decades at Boeing before losing her $80,000-a-year job. That was four years ago. Despite continued efforts, she has not had a single job offer since then. To help make ends meet she has taken to selling some of her jewelry and clothes online. "I have had nightmares about becoming a bag lady," she admits. Doing odd jobs and relying on her husband's declining earnings, she is still many years away from drawing her Social Security benefits (Rich, 2010).

Economic insecurity, then, not only threatens the traditional working class but is a concern of the lower-middle class and even, to some degree, the upper-middle class. Americans at all points within the intermediate classes are apprehensive about economic issues. Will their income enable them to maintain their lifestyle? How secure is their current job? What will be their occupational future?

Economic Restructuring and the Classes in the Middle

What accounts for the changes in the American economy that have led to shifting patterns among the intermediate classes in recent years? During the last four decades, the United States has been engaged in **economic restructuring**—the radical shift from what had been a manufacturing-based economy to a service-based economy, with its resultant effects on the labor force. These developments have been the result primarily of two major factors: the emergence of new technologies and the development of a global economy.

Technological Changes

Each historical period has produced innovations in production that have displaced workers. The development of mechanical forms of labor forced workers out of jobs that machines could perform more efficiently and cheaply. The notorious Luddite movement of the early nineteenth century in England, for example, was a response to the fears of workers that machines would replace them and thus divest them of their livelihood. The Luddites were bands of workingmen in England's industrial centers, especially textile manufacturing, who rebelled against the introduction of knitting machines, power looms, and wool-shearing machines (to which they attributed their low wages and high unemployment) by wrecking the machinery.

Today, it is workers in the manufacturing sector who have experienced the most serious decline as a result of new technologies. Increasingly, computers and robots do what workers once did. On automobile assembly lines, where workers once welded body parts together, robots now do the same tasks, only more efficiently. Since 1980, the number of automobiles made in North America has increased by 65 percent while the number of workers in the automobile industry has declined by 34 percent (O'Toole and Lawler, 2006). This trend has affected not only unskilled and semiskilled workers but also skilled production workers. Jeremy Rifkin bluntly claims that by the middle of the twenty-first century, "the blue-collar worker will have passed from history, a casualty of the Third Industrial Revolution and the relentless march toward ever greater technological efficiency" (2004:140).

Computers have changed the very nature of industrial production. Indeed, "computers," writes economist Sheila McConnell, "may be the most profound technology since steam power ignited the Industrial Revolution" (1996:3). In the past, large-scale industries made for low production costs. That is no longer the case. As a result of computer technology, the flow of materials, their quality, and changes in them can be managed more easily and efficiently. Moreover, manufacturers can deliver a larger variety of goods more quickly. Sales data can be gathered more rapidly and with less effort, making it possible to transmit such information to manufacturers, who can respond quickly with finished goods. Workers, too, can be managed more effectively (Garson, 1988). Unlike the impact of changing technologies of the past, which affected only specific industries, computers affect all industries and job categories.

During previous periods of mechanization and the development of new industries, old jobs that were destroyed were usually replaced by new jobs into which displaced workers could move. Thus, as blue-collar workers were phased out, the service sector usually absorbed them. Some, like Rifkin (2004), believe that the computer revolution, however, has rendered some workers permanently superfluous—that is, they have been displaced but there are no jobs for them to take in replacement, even in the service sector. Increasingly, technological advances have made obsolete many categories of jobs there, too. Voice-mail systems replace telephone operators and receptionists, electronic scanning machines replace cashiers and retail clerks, and so on. This has led to dramatic cuts in the workforce. Even professionals and artists are not immune to the impact of technological advances. Synthesizers, Rifkin notes, reduce musical sounds to digitized form, save them, and reproduce them in various combinations, thereby replacing live musicians.

Rifkin has posited that we are now at a point in the development of technology that may spell the end of work itself: "The road to a near-workerless economy is within sight" (2004:292). Whether this will open new opportunities and freedoms for people or lead to unemployment and depression is, in his estimation, contingent on how equitably the productivity gains of this new economy are distributed.

Others forecast a more positive future for the U.S. workforce. Technological innovations, they believe, will continue to create new jobs that will be filled by more highly educated working-class and middle-class people (Farrell et al., 1998; Reich, 2001). Many of those jobs, however, may be paid at a wage that is considered inadequate, thus widening the inequality gap (Reich, 2010).

Globalization

Perhaps the most important change that has occurred in the American economy during the last three decades is the globalization of production and distribution. In a real sense, the American economy is today part of a world economic system in which the economies of various politically independent countries are loosely tied together. This is what has been called the **global economy.** The emergence of the global economy has contributed in large measure to the changes now being experienced by the classes in the middle.

Development of a Global Economy   Although today we take for granted the global economy, in fact it is a relatively recent development. As recently as the first few decades of the twentieth century, the notion of a world economic system was unimaginable (Bloom and Brender, 1993). Several factors led to its rapid growth. One concerns technological changes in communications and transportation that have effectively reduced the geographic and social distance between countries. Travel from America to Europe, for example, that might have taken weeks by ship in the early part of the twentieth century now takes only hours. Reducing distance generates frequent contact among people and organizations. And it facilitates the delivery of goods to literally every corner of the globe. Items produced in Germany can be shipped for sale in Los Angeles as quickly and as easily as if they were produced in Chicago. Trade, then, has become increasingly internationalized.

The production process itself has been globalized. Although a Ford automobile may roll off the assembly line in Louisville, Kentucky, or Wayne, Michigan, its various parts are more likely to have been manufactured in any number of locations throughout the world. To call it an "American" car, therefore, is something of a misnomer; in fact, it is a "world" car, as are most others, regardless of where they are actually assembled. This decentralized global production process increasingly typifies many products. A computer assembled in the United States, for example, may be made up of components manufactured in China, Singapore, Mexico, Thailand, and Korea.

In the globalized production process, many large corporations no longer actually engage in the manufacture of their products. Instead, they become primarily marketing organizations that turn over their production activities to suppliers, many of whom are located abroad. This is a phenomenon referred to as "outsourcing." Levi Strauss & Co., for example, the most famous name in American jeans, closed six of its U.S. plants in 2002, shifting most of its production to cheaper overseas manufacturers and, in the process, eliminating 22 percent of its workforce. As the company's CEO explained the move, "There is no question that we must move away from owned-and-operated plants in the U.S. to remain competitive in our industry" (quoted in *Globe and Mail*, 2002).

Management, along with actual production, has been internationalized. Electronic communication systems, including telephones, computers, and interactive television, make it possible for organizations to conduct their business *from* anywhere *to* anywhere. As a result, vast resources in different parts of the world can be managed from a home base. At the Nike offices in Oregon, executives can instantaneously keep track of their supply of shoes in plants in Thailand or Indonesia. They can also keep account of what is occurring in those plants and can direct the plant managers without ever leaving their Oregon offices.

Most important, financial capital can be moved around the globe at the press of a key. People and organizations in one country invest in others. Capital may be moved almost at will wherever it can yield the greatest return on investment. International flows of capital thus continue to grow.

The result of all these technological changes is a world, as economist Lester Thurow has described it, in which "for the first time in human history, anything can be made anywhere and sold everywhere" (1996:115). American businesses and their workers consequently find themselves in competition with businesses and workers in other countries.

Transnational Corporations   The major units of the world economy are corporations whose operations span the globe. These are massive companies whose scale far exceeds that of other economic units. The wealth of corporations like General Electric or ExxonMobil exceeds the wealth of many nations of the world. These **transnational** (or multinational) **corporations** are spread out like octopus arms, with manufacturing and sales dispersed in numerous world locations. Most of the largest U.S. corporations operate as much abroad as they do in the United States. Consider some of the corporate names that we think of as "quintessentially American." Procter and Gamble—a company that provides products that most Americans use on a daily basis, from toothpaste to soap to toilet paper—today derives over half of its revenue from outside the United States as do other familiar business names like Intel, Apple, Caterpillar, GM, Ford, Otis Elevator, and Pfizer. Two-thirds of the sales of Coca-Cola, perhaps the most widely known of all American consumer goods, are made abroad, and the worldwide operations of McDonald's, another American corporate icon, far outdistance its U.S. domestic business (Gumbel, 2008). Even MTV has had regional production centers in Europe, Brazil, Japan, and India since 1987. These and hundreds of major corporations like them may fly the American flag in front of their world headquarters located in the United States, but they are "American" only in their origins. They are world firms.

American corporations are not alone in this globalizing trend. Japanese, German, French, British, Korean, and other transnational firms have become familiar global names. Honda, a Japanese company, manufactures cars in Ohio, which are then exported to and sold in Japan. Almost all electronic appliances bought by Americans, such as TVs, microwave ovens, and stereo equipment, are manufactured by Japanese or Korean firms whose factories are in East or Southeast Asian countries. Nestlé, a Swiss firm best known for chocolate, derives almost all of its revenue from outside Switzerland. Whether we buy gasoline from Shell (Dutch/British), mobile phones from Nokia (Finnish), aspirin from Bayer (German), HDTVs from SONY (Japanese), or shoes from Nike (American), we are participating in the global economy. The twenty-five leading transnational corporations are shown in Table 5-1.

In their international role, large corporations maintain few national loyalties. Their primary objective, as for all capitalist enterprises, is maximizing their return on investment. If that can be accomplished by producing in the United States, Mexico, China, or any other country, that is where it will be done. The global, not national, loyalties of transnational corporations were poignantly demonstrated in 1994 at the World Cup, the most important event in the sport of soccer, when it was held in the United States. Each country's best teams competed for several weeks in different venues. The various sports gear manufacturers all had "their" teams, that is, teams that were outfitted with the manufacturer's brand of shoes and uniforms. Outfitting professional and college sports teams with specific brands of equipment has, of course, become standard practice for these companies. Nike, an American-based company, has been one of the most aggressive in promoting its name in this manner. Few people in the world do not recognize the Nike "swoosh" logo, prominently displayed on sneakers, football jerseys, and the like. During the World Cup, Nike outfitted the Brazilian team. Adidas (a German firm)

Table 5-1 ■ The Twenty-five Leading Transnational Corporations

Rank	Company	Country	Industry	Sales ($ bil)	Profits ($ bil)	Assets ($ bil)
1	ExxonMobil	US	Oil & Gas	433.5	41.1	331.1
2	JP Morgan Chase	US	Banking	110.8	19.0	2,265.8
3	General Electric	US	Diverse	147.3	14.2	717.2
4	Royal Dutch Shell	Netherlands	Oil & Gas	470.2	30.9	340.5
5	ICBC	China	Banking	82.6	25.1	2,039.1
6	HSBC	UK	Banking	102.0	16.2	2,550.0
7	PetroChina	China	Oil & Gas	310.1	20.6	304.7
8	Berkshire Hathaway	US	Diversified Financial	143.7	10.3	392.6
9	Wells Fargo	US	Banking	87.6	15.9	1,313.9
10	PetroBras	Brazil	Oil & Gas	145.9	20.1	319.4
11	BP	UK	Oil & Gas	375.5	25.7	292.5
12	Chevron	US	Oil & Gas	236.3	26.9	209.5
13	China Construction Bank	China	Banking	68.7	20.5	1,637.8
14	Citigroup	US	Banking	102.6	11.1	1,873.9
15	Gazprom	Russia	Oil & Gas	117.6	31.7	302.6
16	Wal-Mart	US	Retailing	447.0	15.7	193.4
17	Volkswagen	Germany	Automobiles	221.9	21.5	328.7
18	Total	France	Oil & Gas	216.2	15.9	213.0
19	Agricultural Bank of China	China	Banking	62.4	14.4	1,563.9
20	BNP Paribas	France	Banking	119.0	7.9	2,539.1
21	Bank of China	China	Banking	60.8	15.8	1,583.7
22	Apple	US	Technology Hardware	127.8	33.0	138.7
23	Banco Santander	Spain	Banking	109.6	6.9	1,624.7
24	Sinopec-China Petroleum	China	Oil & Gas	391.4	11.6	179.8
25	Toyota	Japan	Automobiles	228.5	4.9	358.3

outfitted the American team. Phil Knight, CEO of Nike, talked of a natural evolution in the shoe and apparel industry as "dividing the world into their athletes and ours. And we glory ours." Knight was not referring to American

Source: Copyright © King Features Syndicate.

athletes versus other countries' athletes, however. He was talking of Nike-sponsored athletes versus those endorsing other brands. "When the U.S. played Brazil in the World Cup," he explained, "I rooted for Brazil because it was a Nike team. America was Adidas" (Lipsyte, 1996:B7).

Reich's Model   Economist Robert Reich, the former U.S. secretary of labor, has offered a model of how the U.S. workforce has been restructured as a result of the world economy. The model helps in explaining how the dynamics of globalization have impacted the American classes in the middle.

Reich suggests that traditional occupational classifications (white-collar, blue-collar, professional, managerial, etc.) no longer make sense in the context of the global economy. American workers (and workers in other countries as well) are today increasingly subdivided into three distinct categories: symbolic analysts, routine production workers, and routine personal service workers. Each has been affected differently by the emergence of an internationalized labor market.

Those whom Reich refers to as *symbolic analysts* are professional and managerial workers, who make up much of the upper-middle class. Reich calls them symbolic analysts because they are workers who "solve, identify, and broker problems by manipulating symbols" such as scientific formulas, legal arguments, and marketing strategies (Reich, 1992:178). They are highly trained and possess valued skills, making them adaptable to changing conditions. As a result, they are strongly competitive and can command high salaries in the international labor market. They have generally prospered in the global economy. Doctors, lawyers, engineers, publishers and editors, investment bankers, financial consultants, and top-level managers are typical occupations that fall into this category.[3] They make up about 30 percent of U.S. jobs (Dohm and Shniper, 2007).

Routine production workers are the traditional blue-collar workers, whose work consists of repetitive tasks and who are usually paid on an hourly basis. As noted earlier, many white-collar workers' jobs also have become increasingly routinized as a result of computerization. Obviously, the skill level of routine production workers is much lower than that of symbolic analysts, and their educational requirements are correspondingly reduced. Most important, routine production workers are in competition with similar workers worldwide and are therefore apt to be most negatively affected by the vagaries of the global economy. They constitute less than 20 percent of the American workforce, and their numbers continue to decline; thirty years ago they made up fully one-third of the labor force (Mishel et al., 2009). In the first decade of the twenty-first century, the United States lost millions of manufacturing jobs, few of which are likely to reappear (Dohm and Shniper, 2007; Goozner, 2004; O'Toole and Lawler, 2006).

Those whom Reich calls *routine personal service workers* are, like production workers, doing simple and repetitive tasks. They too are usually paid on an hourly basis, and their skill and educational level is low. The major difference between them and routine production workers is that they are not in competition with similar workers in other countries. Their jobs involve personal services, which cannot be supplied from abroad. In a sense, they are in competition against machines rather than against foreign workers. Restaurant workers, hospital workers, janitors and maids, secretaries, auto mechanics, and security personnel are among the typical occupations of this category. They constitute around 30 percent of the workforce, and their numbers are increasing rapidly. Routine personal service workers are disproportionately women and ethnic minorities and, in some areas, illegal immigrants. And unlike the wages of symbolic analysts, the wages of these workers have stagnated.

The split in the intermediate classes, then, can be seen as one in which the upper-middle class, consisting mostly of highly trained workers and professionals, drifts farther away from the other two sectors, whose economic status becomes increasingly tenuous and whose occupational prestige declines.

---

[3]In a later work, Reich refers to this category as "creative workers," whose creativity lies in "their insights into what can be done in a particular medium (software, finance, law, entertainment, music, physics, and so on), what can be done for a particular market, and how best to organize work in order to bring these two perspectives together" (2001:52).

The Decline of Labor Unions

The common end of all firms in a capitalist system—maximization of profit—is accomplished in large measure by lowering the costs of production. Labor is a critically important cost which business owners try to keep in check or drive down; workers seek to do the opposite. Where labor unions are strong, wages are driven upward. Unions put pressure on employers to keep wages high and improve the conditions of work. It is the threat of a strike that serves as the unions' weapon in this struggle. The 1950s and 1960s represented the apex of U.S. labor union strength. In the mid-1950s, about 40 percent of private sector workers and 5 percent of public sector workers were union members (Freeman, 1994). In 1970, unions still represented 31 percent of the workforce. By 1983, however, the percentage had declined to 20, and today less than 12 percent of workers are union members; among private sector workers, union members account for less than 7 percent (Bureau of Labor Statistics, 2012). This is the lowest rate of unionization among all countries of the developed world (Visser 2006).

Several factors account for the decline. Most important, unions lost their strength as the educational attainment of workers went up and manufacturing employment declined (Farley, 1996). As the American workforce shifted from manufacturing to service, it shifted from what had traditionally been the most heavily unionized sectors of the economy: automobiles, steel, and transportation. When those industries were at their peak after World War II, wages increased and inequality in income generally declined. With the turn toward service industries and the increasing movement of production abroad, the power of labor unions began to ebb. Although unions gained membership among some service workers, especially state and local government employees and health care workers, they lost far more in shrinking manufacturing industries.

More competitive markets, too, helped to reduce union power. With the domination of a few large corporations in various sectors of the economy ("oligopolies"), producers had been able to more readily accept union demands for wage increases, the cost of which could be passed on to consumers. With globalization and deregulation of various industries starting in the late 1970s, however, competition became more intense and companies in response began to reduce their workforces. "Unionized companies that failed to trim payrolls lost market share to unionized companies that did," explains Robert Reich. "And both lost consumers and investors to companies that were nonunionized from the start" (2007:83).

In addition to the loss of jobs in the manufacturing sector, antilabor policies and actions of the Reagan administration during the 1980s further weakened labor unions. In 1981, the Professional Air Traffic Controllers Organization (PATCO) attempted to strike in response to what it saw as inadequate working conditions and benefits. As government employees, the air traffic controllers had to bargain with the federal government. The Reagan administration not only rejected their demands but fired those controllers who went on strike, vowing not to rehire them. This action set the tone of labor relations in the 1980s (Ehrenreich, 1989).

A combination of high unemployment, automation, overseas production, and an unsympathetic federal administration reduced the threat of strikes, the traditional union weapon, as workers suffered job insecurity. Their major concern was simply holding on to their jobs rather than fighting for higher wages. As a result, they were disinclined to strike and more apt to accept concessions in their bargaining with companies. Whereas during the 1960s and 1970s work stoppages averaged almost three hundred per year, in the 1980s they averaged only eighty-three, and during the 1990s and 2000s, less than forty (U.S. Department of Labor, 2006b).

Some hold that the decline of American labor unions is a major factor which has contributed to the continued wage decline of the last three decades (Freeman and Katz, 1994; Mishel, 2012c; Noah, 2012; Western and Rosenfeld, 2011). During the years of high labor union membership, all workers benefited from union power, even those who were not organized. In order to avoid unionization, companies would often pay nonunion workers as much as their union counterparts or at least would keep wages competitively high.

It is of note that in other advanced industrial countries, the precipitous decline of union membership has not paralleled that of the United States. In Canada, the UK, and Germany, for example, union membership, despite decline, remains more than double that of the United States. This has translated into a greater voice for workers in matters of public policy and has been an important factor in explaining the much more generous social welfare policies of those countries, as well as tougher regulations governing plant closings and worker retraining (Alderson and Nielsen, 2002).

Downsizing, Outsourcing, and Offshoring

Downsizing is a popular term referring to the tendency for large corporations to cut their workforce, with the objective of becoming more efficient and profitable. In large measure, this has occurred in response to the global economy, in which American firms must now compete on a worldwide basis, no longer unaffected by economic trends in other countries. Lost jobs have been mostly in manufacturing, that is, typically blue-collar occupations. But downsizing has also affected the high-status jobs of upper-middle-class managers and professionals. In a global economy, downsizing is practiced by all companies, even those that are profitable (Thurow, 1999). Although replacement jobs are usually found for displaced workers, they are often not comparable in salary or prestige. For many, then, downsizing has meant downward social mobility. Managers or professionals with what had been secure and well-paying jobs may find themselves with jobs paying half of their former salary, with fewer benefits and virtually no security. Lower-middle- and upper-middle-class people have therefore begun to more fully comprehend the economic insecurity that has always plagued the poor and some elements of the working class (Newman, 1999). As noted earlier, this development became particularly acute in the economic downturn of the late 2000s, when millions of American workers, many of them in high-paying, high-status occupations, suddenly found themselves unemployed or in sharply downgraded jobs.

Much of the downsizing phenomenon is a result of the technological changes discussed earlier. U.S. Steel, the largest producer of steel in 1980, once employed 120,000 workers; by 1990 it employed only 20,000 but was producing about the same amount of steel (Rifkin, 2004). Similarly, in almost every other area of the workforce, companies can do as much or more with fewer workers. Between 1990 and 1995, ten of the largest corporations in the United States (including GM, Boeing, General Electric, IBM, and Sears) laid off almost 850,000 workers, 29 percent of their entire workforce, yet productivity rose dramatically among those ten (Koretz, 1997). Almost all of the largest industrial corporations in the United States made additional massive job reductions in the late 2000s. Globalization has also contributed to downsizing. By sending work abroad, transnational corporations cut their need for workers in the United States.

Labor Mobility and Outsourcing   The globalization of economic processes has led to a tremendous expansion of labor mobility. As noted above, the common end of all firms in a capitalist system—maximization of profit—is accomplished in large measure by lowering the costs of production. An important cost is labor, which is held in check by minimizing wages.

Today, labor costs are controlled by transnational corporations through the easy movement of capital. If a U.S.-based appliance manufacturer pays its workers an average of $15 an hour to produce refrigerators in Illinois but could produce the same refrigerators in Mexico where it pays workers an average of only $2 an hour, obviously, it will be in the company's interest to move its refrigerator production to Mexico (Greenhouse, 2009). Of course, other factors—such as workers' training and skill level, transportation costs, and the like—are involved in the decision about where to produce. Whirlpool makes washing machines in Ohio, where its workers are paid $23 an hour, including benefits. The company could pay $3 an hour in Mexico or $1 an hour in China, but shipping costs and the investment in building a factory make it unprofitable to move (Uchitelle, 2005). As noted above, however, the cost of labor is a critical factor in production and therefore provides a strong incentive for companies to transfer operations to other countries. In seeking out the cheapest cost of labor, firms naturally gravitate to low-wage areas, moving their facilities from location to location.[4] Consider that Apple pays its production workers in China making

---

[4]Whirlpool's CEO admits that if the Ohio factory did not already exist, "I'd probably put it in Mexico."

iPods an average of $1,540 a year, about 3 percent of what their U.S. counterparts would make (Noah, 2012). Obviously, then, most iPods are made in China. The upshot of this movement is that some workers win new jobs while others lose them.

As noted earlier, most large corporations today utilize outsourcing as a means of helping to reduce labor costs. Most simply, **outsourcing** is the subcontracting of various aspects of production to other, smaller, companies, thereby enabling corporations to reduce their workforce. Increasingly, these companies are located abroad, where wages are considerably cheaper than in the corporation's home country.

Offshoring   The impact of sending jobs overseas has been felt mostly by blue-collar workers, especially those in manufacturing jobs. Starting in the early 2000s, however, this trend became increasingly apparent among white-collar workers as well. Not only are jobs requiring limited skills being exported, thousands of well-paying high-tech jobs are being sent to countries such as India, Russia, Ireland, and China, where highly trained workers are able to perform tasks for a fraction of the salaries of U.S. workers (Greenhouse, 2009; Lohr, 2006; Miezkowski, 2003). This trend has been referred to as **offshoring.**

Virtually every type of work done in a large corporation—accounting, financial analysis, customer service, engineering, procurement, training, and research—can now be outsourced and managed to some degree offshore (Engardio, 2006; O'Toole and Lawler, 2006). Eli Lilly, one of the largest American pharmaceutical companies, for example, outsources 20 percent of its chemistry work to China for one-quarter of its U.S. cost. Similarly, a software engineer commanding a salary of $80,000 in the United States can be replaced by a counterpart in India earning $15,000 (Greenhouse, 2009). The financial services industry—banks, insurance firms, mortgage companies, brokerages—in particular has turned over much of its technical support to workers in foreign countries. A credit card holder in Chicago would probably be unaware that his question about a billing error might be answered by a company representative in Delhi, India, or that his life insurance application could be processed by a worker in Dublin, Ireland. Even medical services are now increasingly offshored. Faced with a shortage of radiologists, U.S. hospitals have found that they can send x-rays, CT scans, and MRIs over the Internet to radiologists in Australia, India, Israel, or Lebanon, who review them and e-mail the results within hours.

Demographic Factors

Immigration   In the last three decades, immigration to the United States has increased greatly. So great have the numbers been, in fact, that the flow has reached proportions resembling the classic period of immigration to America of the late nineteenth and early twentieth centuries. How have these newest immigrants had an impact on the labor market and, in particular, on the place of the working and middle classes?

Social scientists have debated the economic effects of immigration. Whereas some argue that immigrants constitute an added burden to an already swollen labor pool and drive down wages, others contend that the jobs they typically hold are those that native workers shun and, furthermore, that they create as many jobs as they take. Similarly, while some maintain that the new immigrants overburden the social welfare system, others hold that they pay in taxes more than they collect in benefits (Borjas, 2001; Camarota, 2007; Card, 2009; Congressional Budget Office, 2005; Lowenstein, 2006; Swain, 2007).

The newest immigration appears to favor some sectors of the economy and harm others. Most of the immigrants from Mexico (the largest single group) and the Caribbean are unskilled and take their place at the lowest occupational levels. They benefit employers in labor-intensive industries, such as fruit and vegetable harvesting, clothing manufacturing, or other work areas calling for cheap labor, but they depress the job opportunities of native low-status workers, especially African Americans (Mishel et al., 2005; Pear, 1997).

Not all the new immigrants come as unskilled workers, however. A large segment of some groups, particularly Asian Indians, Chinese, and Filipinos, are highly trained professionals and managers whose economic impact is far different from that of those who enter with few occupational resources. Many immigrant doctors, for example, staff large city hospitals, which would find it difficult to operate without them. The United States has also increasingly relied on immigrant engineers and other highly trained scientific workers (Muller, 1993; Burton and Wang, 1999). Consider that more than a third of U.S. residents holding Ph.D.'s in science and engineering are foreign-born (Wulf, 2005). Table 5-2 shows the broad range of jobs within the American workforce occupied by large numbers of immigrants. Notice that there are both high- and low-skilled occupational groups.

Table 5-2 ▪ Immigrants in U.S. Workforce

Occupation	Percentage
Medical scientists	45
Computer software engineers	27
Cooks	23
Janitors and building cleaners	20
Personal and home care aides	18
Nursing and home health aides	17
Postsecondary teachers	17
Registered nurses	11

Women in the Workforce   Women have entered the workforce in massive numbers during the last four decades, as a matter of both necessity and choice. Two income earners have become crucial in families trying to maintain a standard of living that most Americans have come to expect. Moreover, the rise of single-parent families has meant that women in such contexts must support their families through their work.

The entrance of women in the world of work in substantial numbers has affected not only women specifically but also the labor market as a whole. Women have often been prepared to accept lower wages than men, and this has contributed in some part to the failure of wages to rise in recent years.

Some claim that the entrance of large numbers of women into the labor force in the 1970s was, in itself, a contributing factor in wage declines. Walter Russell Mead, for example, notes that "when one woman went to work, the household income rose; but as millions of women went to work, labor became cheaper" (1998:34). Others such as Robert Reich, however, assert that Mead has it backward. Rather than women helping to bring down wages, it was low wages that prodded women into the workforce in order to maintain family incomes (1998).

The place of women in the labor force will be discussed in more detail in Chapter 11.

Public Policies and the Shrinking Middle

In addition to economic restructuring, globalization, and demographic trends, public policies have contributed significantly to the shrinking middle classes. As we saw in Chapter 3, government measures in the 1950s and 1960s—decades that marked the greatest expansion of the American middle classes—moved the class structure toward greater equality. That the share of income going to the top 20 percent of families declined in the 1950s and 1960s while the share going to the bottom 20 percent increased was due in large part to changes in tax policies and other government actions that benefited those at the lower end of the class hierarchy more than those at the top end. Many of those policies were reversed in the 1980s and 2000s, exacerbating the bifurcation that had been brought about as a result of economic restructuring in the global economy.

We will explore in more detail the impact of public policies on the class structure and on social inequality in general in Chapters 9 and 12. Here it is important to note, however, that increasingly, sociologists and economists have come to see changing government policies as the *major* factor in explaining the stunning increase in class inequality of the past three decades, particularly the shrinking middle. Revolutionary changes in technology and the advent of the global economy are undeniable forces that have altered the class system, but, in their view, it has been changes in the rules of the American capitalist political economy—the loosening of government controls on corporate power, an increasingly regressive tax system, the overwhelming influence of money in politics, the declining influence of labor unions—that has enabled the capitalist class to expand enormously its wealth and power while leaving middle-class families with more and more economic insecurity (Hacker, 2006; Hacker and Pierson, 2010; Krugman, 2007; Kuttner, 2007; Reich, 2007, 2010). Other advanced capitalist societies, they point out, have been subject to the same technological and economic changes, but have not produced the enormously widened gap between a super-rich few and the remainder of the class system, as has occurred in the United States.

The impact of public policies on the class system, particularly those in the middle, can be seen in comparison with Canada, a country as close as any to the United States not only geographically but culturally as well. The same technological and demographic developments and the same expansion of globalized markets that have affected the United States in the past several decades have been at work in Canada, but the effects on the class structure have not been the same. Although inequality, as in the United States, has increased in Canada, it has not done so at near the U.S. level, nor have the Canadian middle classes been as negatively impacted. The explanation for these differences, explains political scientist Jacob Hacker, is the effect of Canadian public policies, providing a more generous and substantial social safety net for those below the very top, a tax system that has not rewarded the wealthy at the expense of workers, and a stronger union movement aided by a more accommodating government. "Runaway inequality and its negative effects have been much more limited in Canada than in the United States," writes Hacker, "a striking contrast that has much less to do with market forces than it does with political realities that have made Canadian leaders more responsive to the concerns of less affluent citizens" (2009:26).

The Middle Classes: Lifestyles, Desires, and Debt

Today many among the intermediate classes find themselves unable to satisfy their material needs and teeter precariously on the brink of economic disaster, living from paycheck to paycheck. This is not difficult to explain for those among the working and even lower-middle classes. Moreover, many of these families have been severely impacted by the Great Recession, having suffered financial hardships, including loss of steady income, that were never anticipated. Curiously, it is apparent even among upper-middle-class families, who have continued to experience relative prosperity in recent years. How can this paradox be explained?

The New Consumerism

Economist Juliet Schor (1998, 1999, 2000) has written extensively on this issue and has offered several explanations. First, she describes a national culture of upscale spending, which she calls the "new consumerism." Increasingly, in this view, people acquire their consumer aspirations not just from their colleagues and peers but also from what they see on television and movies and in various forms of advertising. Rather than comparing their status and lifestyle with their neighbors and "keeping up with the Joneses," as in previous decades, "people are now more likely to compare themselves with, or aspire to the lifestyles of, those far above them in the economic hierarchy" (Schor, 1999:43). This higher standard is introduced primarily by the mass media, which expose people to upscale lifestyles. The new consumerism is also founded on the endless introduction of new products and on continually rising standards: "What we want grows into what we need, at a sometimes dizzying rate" (1998:6).

A puzzling aspect of the new consumerism is that it affects not, as might be expected, only the poor and those families with limited incomes but, as noted above, those that are solidly part of the lower- and, especially, upper-middle class. Schor explains that 27 percent of households making more than $100,000 and nearly 40 percent of those earning between $50,000 and $100,000 a year say they cannot afford to buy everything they really need. The important word here is *need*. As people earn more money, they compare their status not with others like themselves but with those who have even more. Hence, to try to keep up they are constrained to buy more, fueling the cycle of consumerism. Social essayist Roger Rosenblatt has written that "if one were to ask a couple making $40,000 per year before taxes and a couple making a pre-tax $200,000 what class they were in, both would answer (honestly and persuasively) not only that they belong to the middle class but also that they are just scraping by" (Rosenblatt, 1999:16). Economist Robert Frank (2000) has described this paradox as middle-income families "experiencing unprecedented levels of economic distress, largely because they are trying to keep up with a living standard they cannot afford" (64). Frank refers to a "spending cascade" in which "top-earners—the people who have fared the best in the current economy—initiate a process that leads to increased expenditures on down the line, even among those whose incomes have not risen" (2005:141).

Some hold that increasing levels of consumption are the product not of emulation of the wealthy and celebrated, but of the nature of the contemporary market system, which impels people to redefine themselves continually by changing experiences and lifestyles through their purchases (Holt, 2000; Thompson, 2000). In a related argument, Benjamin Barber suggests that ever-increasing consumption is systemic, driven by the appeals of advertisers and marketers whose intentions are not to satisfy true needs but to invent or create them. Moreover, contemporary consumerism is based on a child-like ethos, which he calls "infantilization." Producers and sellers, Barber writes, hope to "rekindle in grown-ups the tastes and habits of children so that they can sell globally the relatively useless cornucopia of games, gadgets, and myriad consumer goods for which there is no discernible 'need market' other than the one created by capitalism's own frantic imperative to sell" (2007:7).

Work-and-Spend   Related to the new consumerism is the emergence of a "work and spend" cycle. When given the choice between shorter hours and longer hours with more pay, workers almost always opt for more pay. That increase in income is usually spent on more material goods, but those goods are unable to provide long-term satisfaction, leading to further spending and, consequently, the need to continue working longer hours. To pay for the material goods that are increasingly seen as essential, major breadwinners have often lengthened their workdays and families have required a second income earner. The typical American family worked eleven more hours a week in 2006 than in 1979 (Williams and Boushey, 2010). Moreover, Americans work considerably more hours than Europeans and even more than Japanese workers (Mishel et al., 2009; Greenhouse, 2009). Americans, then, continue to acquire more material possessions but find themselves with insufficient time and, therefore, less opportunity to enjoy them.

To Schor, Barber, and others who share their view, the paradox of the current American economy—arguably the most prosperous in history—is that its major beneficiaries remain unfulfilled. People are caught on a "positional treadmill," continually pressured to maintain consumer parity with others. They must work harder and longer and often go into debt simply to keep pace, despite the fact that they consume more and more. As Schor argues, "We should be articulating an alternative vision of a quality of life, rather than a quantity of stuff" (2000:29).[5]

Consumer Debt

With upscale competitive consumption has come a steep rise in consumer borrowing. In the last decade, families have run up debt in record proportions. Starting in 2000, in less than ten years consumer credit had grown by $1 trillion, or about $4,400 for every adult (Sullivan, 2009). Moreover, the largest increases in debt occurred not only among low-income families, but also among those in the middle classes. More than three-quarters of American families now own debt in some form: home mortgage, credit card balance, or installment loan. The mortgage boom of the 1990s and early 2000s allowed more families to build wealth by buying homes, but this, of course, led to increasing debt. When the housing bubble burst in the late 2000s, the value of those homes declined, leaving many families with mortgage payments that exceeded what their home was actually worth or forced them into foreclosure. An increasing number of middle-class families expressed real anxiety about their ability to sustain a lifestyle to which they had become accustomed (Pew, 2008b; Weller and Lynch, 2009).

---

[5]A counter argument is that Schor and Barber are implicitly imposing their ideas of what is socially desirable consumer behavior on others, who may actually find meaning and pleasure in continual consumption. James Twitchell (1996) maintains that the consumption ethic is nothing new, but merely the latest expression of a human desire to amass things.

The competitive consumption described by Schor, Barber, and others is particularly evident in the accumulation of credit card debt. Almost 40 percent of all American families carry a credit card balance, the median of which in 2010 was $2,600 (Bricker et al., 2012). In their study of personal bankruptcy, Teresa Sullivan and her research associates concluded that "consumer debt has lowered many middle-class families' threshold for financial collapse" (Sullivan et al., 2000:22). If, for example, such families maintain high balances on credit cards, all other aspects of their financial status are profoundly affected. An extended period of unemployment or a serious illness can therefore be a disaster for those with high personal debt.

The Two-Income Trap   Elizabeth Warren and Amelia Warren Tyagi (2003) challenge the commonly held assumption that the financial plight of middle-class families is a product of out-of-control spending, addicted as those families are to consumerism. Rather, middle-class families are at risk of going into serious debt because of expenses incurred in consuming items that have become staple elements of the middle-class standard of living: good housing and quality schools for their children. Housing and education, they explain, are not unrelated. Middle-class parents today understand that education is the single most important factor in upward mobility. They are therefore determined to provide the best possible education for their children. To do this, they must live in those communities with the best quality schools. Because all families with children seek the same objective, this drives up the price of housing in such communities. It is mostly high mortgage payments and tuition for schools from prekindergarten to college, therefore, not expensive food, electronics, travel, and entertainment, that drain family budgets and lead to an ever more precarious financial state.

Curiously, Warren and Tyagi explain, it is the now-common dual-earner family that is most negatively affected by this bidding war for the best neighborhoods and schools. The conventional wisdom would assume that having two breadwinners instead of one—as was most common in the past—would provide more financial security for families. However, with two incomes, families are inclined to take on more expensive fixed expenses, specifically homes in better areas, medical insurance, more spacious automobiles, better quality day care for their young children, and tuition for older ones. But these financial obligations leave them with less discretionary income than in the past and more vulnerable to a financial disaster that may arise when a job is lost or a medical emergency arises. Before middle-class women began to enter the labor market in large numbers, the stay-at-home wife served as a safety valve, able to enter the job market when and if needed or to act as a backup caregiver. Because both she and her husband are now working, however, that is no longer possible. So, many such families find themselves going deeper into debt in their efforts to support their home, children's schooling, and other components of their lifestyle. Hence, "the two-income trap."

Warren and Tyagi document a ballooning rate of bankruptcy in recent years and, surprisingly, find that most families that file for bankruptcy are "solidly middle class." Again, they conclude that this is the result not of overconsumption, but of efforts to meet the demands of the middle-class lifestyle in the face of a job loss, a medical problem, a family breakup, or a combination of these. The ease with which consumer loans can be acquired—second mortgages, credit cards, and the like—merely exacerbates the problem. As noted earlier, over three-quarters of U.S. households have debt, most commonly home mortgages and home equity loans, installment loans (such as for automobiles), and credit card balances.

The End of the New Consumerism?

The easy access to credit (and its attendant debt) that has characterized the American capitalist economy in recent decades has contributed mightily to the character of its consumer culture. Are we now entering an era marking the end of the dominance of the consumption ethic in the United States (and much of the rest of the developed world)? Some maintain that the severe economic crisis that began in 2007, fueled by collapsing credit markets, will ultimately lead to a down-scaled commercial culture in which indiscriminate buying and selling will be modified into a more rational system based on real rather than created needs. The loss of income and wealth that fell on the middle classes as a result of the severe recession of the late 2000s would seem to compel this change. Families in the middle 60 percent sustained greater losses than those in the top and bottom 20 percent, largely as a result of the sharp drop in housing values. Most of middle class wealth is held in the form of home equity, which dropped in 2010 to a median of $75,000 from $110,000 in 2007 (Bricker et al., 2012).

In this view, families—particularly those of the intermediate classes—will become more conscious of spending patterns and begin to conserve and scale back consumption. Paco Underhill, a marketing consultant who has written extensively on consumer behavior, asserts that excessive consumerism based on debt that had characterized the past three or so decades will not return (2009). This will impact the middle classes more than either the rich or those at the bottom of the class hierarchy, both of whose consumption patterns have been only minimally affected. Those who are downwardly mobile are apt to be most profoundly impacted in their consumption patterns by the economic downturn, but others are also likely to consume more cautiously and with less concern for matching the spending of their peers (Cave, 2010; Frank, 2009; Goodman, 2009).

Summary

The middle, or intermediate, classes comprise three fairly distinct components: the upper-middle, lower-middle, and working classes. Each differs in income, occupation, education, and lifestyle, but together they are far apart from those at either the upper or the lower extreme of the American class hierarchy.

The emergence of the middle classes is a relatively recent historical phenomenon, but nowhere did they develop as thoroughly and early as in the United States. The American middle classes have experienced significant changes during the last two hundred years. Until the mid-nineteenth century, the majority of Americans were farmers and small business owners. The industrial revolution gave rise to a blue-collar workforce, which remained numerically dominant until the 1970s, when white-collar workers predominated. In the current postindustrial economy, most workers are providing services, not producing things, but the service sector comprises a wide range of occupations, extending from high-status to low-status.

The upper-middle class is made up of those who occupy high-status jobs with much power and authority that set them apart from the other classes in the middle. The lower-middle class is a diverse stratum, consisting mainly of small business owners and white-collar workers such as middle-level managers, clerks, and bureaucrats. The working class are blue-collar workers who occupy jobs with a range of skills. Increasingly, the blue-collar/white-collar distinction is less meaningful as the character of work becomes similar for many of the occupations in these two sectors.

The 1950s and 1960s marked a period in which the classes in the middle expanded greatly. Rising wages and general prosperity led to the fulfillment of the American dream for many. Starting in the 1970s, however, a deep fissure began to emerge between the upper-middle class and the lower-middle and working classes. For the latter, millions of jobs in the manufacturing sector were eliminated and replaced by poorer-paying jobs in the service sector. The former paid well, whereas most of the latter, by comparison, paid little. This shift was brought about by a combination of the emergence of a global economy in which American workers now had to compete with foreign workers, new technologies that facilitated the replacement of workers with machines and computers, and the decline in numbers and power of labor unions. By comparison, the upper-middle class thrived in the new economy. The protracted economic recession that began in 2007 has negatively affected each of the intermediate classes, though obviously the working and lower-middle classes have been more severely impacted.

One of the curious aspects of the intermediate classes is that despite rising family prosperity, particularly for the upper-middle class, many families find themselves in a precarious economic situation. This is a result of what has been called the "new consumerism," in which people's material standards and aspirations continually rise as they observe the lifestyles—mainly through television—of those more affluent than themselves. This, in turn, produces pressures to consume ever more.

6

Poverty and the Poor

People who are much too sensitive to demand of cripples that they run races ask of the poor that they get up and act just like everyone else in the society.
Michael Harrington

Lack of money is the root of all evil.
George Bernard Shaw

Hurricane Katrina, which struck the coastal areas of Louisiana and Mississippi in 2005, was one of the great tragedies of modern American history. Ghastly pictures of people in New Orleans stranded on rooftops, of thousands crammed into a fetid and noxious Superdome, and of bodies floating in debris-filled and polluted waters were shocking to Americans. The majority of Katrina's victims were black, but whether black or white, almost all were, by U.S. standards, poor. Many could not flee the city in advance of the storm because they lacked cars or money. In addition to the more than two thousand who perished, tens of thousands lost their jobs, their homes, and their personal belongings. Though their physical lives were preserved, their social and economic lives were shattered.

For a few weeks, media coverage of the aftermath of Hurricane Katrina provided a rare opportunity for Americans to catch a glimpse of the poor in their midst. For Americans in the middle class and above, the poor seem safely tucked away in low-income urban neighborhoods or hidden in outlying rural areas, out of sight and therefore out of mind. When they do think about the poor, Americans usually employ stereotypical images that are shaped in large measure by the mass media: unemployed, dependent on public assistance, homeless, drug-addicted, living out of wedlock, and so on, or in the case of Katrina, unfortunate victims of natural disasters. In fact, however, the poor are a diverse element of the population in terms of race and ethnicity, occupation, family makeup, residence, and other social characteristics. Moreover, studies have shown that a significant percentage of Americans—perhaps most—will experience poverty at some point in their lives, if only for a brief period.

Oddly, whereas the poor are the element of the American class structure that most laypersons give the least thought to, they are the stratum to which sociologists devote greater attention than any other. In part this is a result of the fact that the lives of the poor are the most easily exposed, in comparison with members of the upper or even middle classes, who have the ability to avoid the prying eyes of researchers. It is also the case because poverty seems an anomaly in the United States, which so often proclaims itself the wealthiest and most opportunity-rich society in the modern world.

In this chapter, we explore two basic questions: Who are the poor? and Why are they poor?

Defining Poverty

Defining those at the bottom would seem to be easier than trying to divide the various parts of the middle or to distinguish those at the top, but this is not the case. In large part, the imprecision of delineating the poor stems from the fact that there is much debate about what actually constitutes poverty. Those who see great injustices in the class hierarchy are apt to draw a broader, more inclusive boundary around those classified as poor, whereas those who defend the basic fairness of the class system enumerate the poor in less sweeping terms. Moreover, explanations of why people are poor and how best to address their problems are the basis of intense political debate.

To help clarify the issue, poverty can be conceptualized in three different ways: absolute, relative, and official.

Absolute Poverty

The least complicated way of defining poverty is to conceptualize it in absolute terms. This means that there are certain measures of poverty about which there are no disagreements. It is generally accepted that the poor in society are those who are unable to acquire the necessities of life. No one would argue that a basic diet, shelter from the elements, access to minimal health care, and a few articles of personal property such as clothing are essential, that anything less constitutes a state of poverty. Moreover, from society to society this formula for defining poverty would hold up. Those whose incomes caused them to fall beneath this absolute standard would comprise the poor, and the same criteria would apply to all countries. In an absolute sense, then, poverty is simply a socioeconomic condition in which people are unable, for whatever reason, to meet their fundamental human needs: "Subsistence or absolute poverty implies that there is a fixed basic minimum income below which physiological efficiency cannot be maintained" (Walker and Walker, 1995:655).

Relative Poverty

Defining poverty as an absolute standard, however, is not so simple. What constitutes "necessity"? In a modern society like the United States, is a telephone a necessity or a luxury? What about an automobile? Or a high-speed

"No, those people aren't anorexic. Those people are starving."

computer? Moreover, what constitutes a "minimal" level of health care or a "basic" diet? Arguments can be made on all these points.

Poverty, therefore, is more rationally defined in relative terms—relative, that is, to the standards and expectations of people in a particular society at a particular time. A basic diet in the United States, for example, would not be the same as a basic diet in Bangladesh or Bolivia. In the United States or a society of comparable economic development, a telephone and an automobile have become necessities, though in the past these were luxury items enjoyed by only a select few. Similarly, a computer has become a necessity merely to keep pace, let alone to advance, in the educational and occupational worlds and to supply vital information regarding all facets of social, economic, and political life.

Poverty, then, is contextual, subject to changing standards as situations change. Poverty is not the same everywhere, and it is not the same in any society from one historical period to another. Thus, we cannot easily impose our standards on other societies, nor can we impose past standards on current times.

Official Poverty

Unfortunately, neither absolute nor relative definitions permit us to actually make a count of the poor or to measure poverty. Even if, using either of these conceptions, there were no disagreement regarding what the general state of poverty is, there is no way of implementing that standard and enumerating the poor without imposing some measurable criteria. Government, in a sense, settles the argument about who is poor and what conditions actually constitute poverty by applying a uniform yardstick for counting the poor and measuring poverty. This is the official definition of poverty.

In 1964, as part of President Lyndon B. Johnson's War on Poverty, the Social Security Administration was asked to create a standard of living that would serve as a threshold of poverty. That standard would then constitute the poverty line, with those falling beneath it labeled by the federal government as "the poor" and thus eligible for various public assistance programs. It was determined that families spent about one-third of their income on food. The poverty line, therefore, was set at three times the cost of a nutritionally adequate diet. The initial formula for determining the official poverty count has not been altered.[1]

In 2010, the official poverty line was $22,113 for a family of four including two children. The poverty line, however, is a sliding scale, which changes with the number of people constituting a family. For a larger family the threshold is higher, and for a smaller family it is lower. Thus, for a family of five (with two children), the poverty line was set at $26,675; for a family of three, at $17,658; and so on. Also, the official poverty threshold is adjusted each year to account for increases in the cost of living.

Obviously, the official poverty line is somewhat arbitrary. If a four-person family earned $23,000 in 2010, would it be "safely" above poverty? Moreover, people live at different standards, regardless of what they earn. A family of very modest tastes that spent little on anything but basics might survive on an income below the official line. Similarly, one accustomed to a higher standard might find itself unable to function below a figure well above the official poverty line. Also, the cost of living varies from region to region, from city to city, and between rural and urban areas. Families in U.S. cities on the east or west coast would find it difficult to live at a level comparable to that of families with similar incomes in southern or midwestern cities. Finally, an official poverty standard accounts only for money income and neglects consideration of other aspects of poverty such as poor schools, health care, and the like. For example, income statistics alone would fail to reveal that the poor are far more likely than the nonpoor to be victims of violent crimes (Federman et al., 1996). We can easily see how the line is a convenient cutoff point, but it is hardly one that corresponds to the realities and vagaries of economic life.

Moreover, counting the poor by establishing an official poverty line is a highly political issue. Policymakers can choose to measure the extent of

---

[1]Although the original poverty indices are still in place, economic conditions have changed since the mid-1960s, making them, in effect, obsolete. Families now spend only one-eighth, not one-third, of their income on food, but they spend more on housing, child care, and health care than in 1964 (Levinson, 2012). In 2011, the Obama administration issued a new index of poverty, the Supplementary Poverty Measure, which did not replace the official measure but took into consideration additional expenses as well as in-kind aid such as food stamps and subsidized housing. Using this measure, the rate of U.S. poverty was several percentage points higher than the official rate.

poverty from a number of competing definitions of poverty, depending on their policy objectives. Those who approach the issue of poverty with a conservative political perspective point to the fact that the value of some welfare payments, such as food stamps, is not included in creating the poverty line, and that therefore the size of the poverty class is overstated. They argue that if these benefits were added, the number of poor would decline—that is, some would simply be "defined out" of poverty by being pushed over the official poverty cutoff point.

On the other side of the issue, those who subscribe to a more liberal view of poverty argue that the number of poor people is actually understated when the official definition is applied. The poverty line, they point out, is determined on the basis of pre-tax income. Since taxes on wages reduce income available for consumption, using after-tax income as the standard would increase the number calculated as poor. Also, they note that often poor people must spend a greater share of their income on housing and other needs. In this view, then, the official poverty line is not high enough. If, for example, poverty were defined as 125 percent of the current thresholds, the number of poor families would increase significantly. If the poverty line were set at one-half the median family income (as is done in most European Union countries), it would raise the number even more substantially.

Who Are the Poor?

Given the relative nature of poverty and the politics of actually counting the poor, the dividing line between the poor and the rest of the class hierarchy will always be subject to debate. In examining the dimensions of poverty in the United States, however, we need a working definition and so must use the official standard. Moreover, the data that government agencies collect, based on that standard, are the most complete and reliable available to us.

The Poor and Those at Risk

In 2010, 15.1 percent of the U.S. population were living below the official poverty line. This translated into almost 44 million people. Table 6-1 presents a more precise look at the U.S. poverty population. It shows that most of the poor (almost one-half) are white, not black or Hispanic, as is often assumed. The poor are also disproportionately children, with more than one-third below the age of eighteen and a large number in single-parent, female-headed families.

Merely enumerating the poor in absolute figures yields a somewhat distorted picture. It does not reveal what the risks, or chances, of being in poverty are. From which social groups are the poor most apt to come? That is, what are the probabilities of being in poverty? A truer portrait of the

Table 6-1 ▪ Number of Americans in Poverty, 2010

Category	Number (millions)
All Persons	46.2
Race/Ethnicity	
White, non-Hispanic	19.6
Black	10.7
Hispanic	13.2
Asian	1.7
American Indian	0.7
Age	
Children (under 18 years)	16.4
Adults (18 to 64)	26.3
Elderly (65 and over)	3.5
All Families	9.2
Family Structure	
Married couple	3.6
Female householder, no husband	4.7
Male householder, no wife	0.9

Source: U.S. Census Bureau, 2011a, 2012a.

poverty population is provided in Table 6-2, which shows the percentage of each social category that falls below the poverty line. Looking at poverty among different racial and ethnic groups, for example, we see immediately that although there are many more whites in poverty, the poor are disproportionately black and Hispanic. Whereas 9.9 percent of whites are in poverty, more than one-quarter of blacks and Hispanics are in this stratum. Thus blacks and Hispanics are almost three times as likely as whites to be in poverty. Table 6-2 also reveals that children are far more likely to be in poverty than either adults (between 18 and 64) or the elderly (those over 65); 22 percent of children are poor, compared to 13.7 percent of adults and 9 percent of the elderly. Also noticeable in Table 6-2 is that the at-risk poverty population is more concentrated in the central cities of metropolitan areas than in the suburbs.

Another common feature of the at-risk poverty population is a truncated family structure. Where families are dual-headed, that is, with two parents present, the incidence of poverty is far lower than in families with only one parent. The latter are almost always headed by females. Since women generally earn less than men, this exacerbates the rate of poverty among single-parent families. In 2010 the median income of married-couple families was more than

Table 6-2 ▪ Percentage of Each Category of Americans in Poverty, 2010

Category	Percentage
Total Population	15.1
Race/Ethnicity	
White, non-Hispanic	9.9
Black	27.4
Hispanic	26.6
Asian	12.1
American Indian	28.4
Family Structure	
Married-couple families	6.2
Families with male householder, no wife present	15.8
Families with female householder, no husband present	31.6
Age	
Children (under 18 years old)	22.0
Adults (18 to 64 years old)	13.7
Elderly (65 years old and over)	9.0
Nativity	
Native-born	14.4
Foreign-born	19.9
Residence	
Reside in metropolitan areas	14.9
Inside central cities	19.7
Outside central cities	11.8
Reside outside metropolitan areas	16.5
Region	
Northeast	12.8
Midwest	13.9
South	16.9
West	15.3

Source: U.S. Census Bureau, 2011a, 2012a.

twice that of female-headed families with no husband present (U.S. Census Bureau, 2011a). When family structure is combined with race and ethnicity, black and Hispanic female-headed families display the highest incidence of poverty. The continuing rise in the number of single mothers has created a trend referred to as the **feminization of poverty.**

The social characteristics with the strongest relation to poverty, then, are ethnicity, age, gender, and family structure. The profile of poverty that emerges is a population disproportionately made up of racial and ethnic minorities, females, young people, and those living as part of female-headed families.

Poverty Trends

How has the incidence of poverty in the United States changed in recent times? Have the number and proportion of the poor increased or declined, and have the characteristics of the at-risk population varied or stayed the same?

Figure 6.1 shows the trend of poverty over the last five decades. Several dips and rises are evident. The poverty rate dropped quite significantly in the 1960s and early 1970s. What had been a poverty population of over 22 percent in 1959 was reduced to 11.6 percent by 1973. The rate began to climb again in the 1980s, however, and appeared to stabilize at around 14 percent by the mid-1990s. In 2000 it dropped to 11.3 percent but rose steadily afterward, reaching over 15 percent by the end of the decade.

How can these peaks and valleys in the poverty rate be explained? Some understanding of these fluctuations can be captured by considering the general economic condition of the society during the past six or so decades and the introduction of particular public policies aimed at addressing poverty.

The Rediscovery of Poverty   As a result of what seemed like a continuing rise in prosperity, poverty in the years immediately after the end of World War II

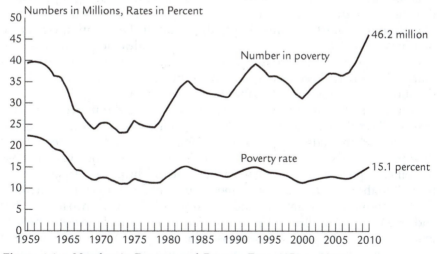

Figure 6-1 ▪ Number in Poverty and Poverty Rate: 1959 to 2010
Note: The data points are placed at the midpoints of the respective years.
Source: U.S. Census Bureau, 2011a.

was viewed as a receding problem that would soon disappear entirely. However, the poor in America were "rediscovered" in the early 1960s. A significant book of that time, which, many maintain, was largely responsible for alerting policymakers to the fact that poverty was not disappearing, was Michael Harrington's *The Other America* (1962). In it Harrington showed that poverty was a continuing phenomenon in American society but had become more difficult to discern because of its obscured nature. The poor, he explained, were now more concentrated in urban and rural ghettos where they were less visible to the nonpoor. They were, in a sense, out of sight and out of mind.

Poverty's rediscovery, in conjunction with the black civil rights movement, set off an ambitious government effort to address the issues of the lingering poor and to put an end to what seemed like an anomaly in the context of a robust economy and an expanding middle class. President Johnson announced an "unconditional war on poverty," prompting the creation of new antipoverty programs and agencies. These efforts were continued during the early years of the 1970s despite the more conservative political perspective of Johnson's successor, Richard Nixon. The impact of those expanded welfare programs was a general reduction in the number of poor, but the effect was especially great on reducing the elderly poor. Many who had previously faced old age with financial insecurity were lifted above poverty by the expansion of Social Security and the creation of Medicare, a health insurance system for the elderly. By 1973 poverty was at its lowest rate since such statistics had been collected.

The New Poverty   In 1984, two decades after *The Other America* had sparked the War on Poverty, Michael Harrington wrote a sequel called *The New American Poverty*. In it he explained that despite encouraging statistics, little had actually changed in the intervening years. Much of the decline of poverty in the late 1960s was simply the result of the booming U.S. economy, providing jobs and raising wages. Moreover, despite the enactment of many new government programs aimed at alleviating poverty, Johnson's War on Poverty had been feebly supported by comparison with the other—shooting—war being waged at that time in Vietnam.

The 1980s brought a new category of the poor to the public consciousness: the homeless. Although homeless people had always been part of the American urban landscape, in the early 1980s their numbers increased and their presence was magnified. Today, rare is the city, large or small, that has no homeless population. During the daylight hours these people may visually blend into the surrounding environment, but at night they can be seen sleeping in doorways, bus stations, and abandoned buildings, on park benches and even on sidewalks. Others, less visible, sleep in homeless shelters. Jennifer Toth (1993) studied homeless people in New York and found that at least five thousand were living in abandoned underground tunnels throughout the city. Rising costs of housing increase the number of so-called mobile homeless, those who don't earn enough to rent an apartment and must live in their cars. These are most often people who have lost their jobs or have fallen on hard times and remain homeless for shorter periods than do those who are street dwellers (Urbina, 2006).

The poverty that reemerged in the 1980s seemed even more intractable than in earlier decades, given the structural changes that had occurred in the American economy. Many of the low-skill jobs that had previously been occupied by the poor had been phased out of existence or had been moved abroad to countries with more pliant and docile workers prepared to work for wages that, to Americans, were unthinkably low. Thus, a new class of the poor had emerged, made up of those whose jobs had been eliminated or exported.

In addition to these structural changes, the 1980s brought to power an administration with a sharply divergent view of the poor and of how they should be dealt with. Ronald Reagan espoused a strong market-oriented approach to public policy and sought to reduce the role of government in all spheres of social and economic life. As a result, measures enacted in the 1960s and 1970s that were designed to benefit the poor were viewed skeptically, even disdainfully, and were seen not as solutions to poverty but as problems themselves that had created a culture of welfare dependency (Magnet, 1993; Murray, 1984). Many public assistance programs were slashed as the poor were seen in a new light: "deserving" or "undeserving." The latter were thought to be beneficiaries of a welfare system that was far too generous and easy to exploit. Reagan, in his 1980 campaign, spoke frequently of "welfare queens who drive Cadillacs."

The Persistence of American Poverty   During most of the 1990s, policies were revised in such a way as to adjust some of the extreme inequalities in income and in the tax burden that had been imposed by the Reagan and George H. W. Bush administrations. The poverty rate dipped to below 12 percent in 1999, marking a twenty-year low. Poverty seemed to be on a downward trajectory. During the 2000s, however, that movement was reversed, with official poverty again rising to more than 15 percent (Figure 6-1). Moreover, it became clear that greater distance was being established between the poor and the middle classes. Whereas in 1960 the poverty line had been about half of median family income, by the late 2000s it was less than a third (Mishel et al., 2009). And, many maintained that if nonofficial measures were used, the number of poor families would increase substantially. Thus, despite narrow fluctuations, the poverty rate in America has seemed to remain relatively steady.

What is baffling is that poverty has not dropped significantly over the past four decades despite a growing rate of economic productivity. How can the steadfast nature of the poverty rate be explained?

Structural factors account in major part for this continued pattern. As we saw in Chapter 5, the labor market in the United States and other advanced capitalist societies has undergone fundamental changes in the last three decades and in the process has eliminated many of the manufacturing-sector jobs that had been held by those on the lower rungs of the class hierarchy. These were jobs that enabled workers with limited skills and education to earn a livable wage. As those jobs are terminated or moved to areas or countries with cheaper labor, the remaining manufacturing jobs require higher skills which most of the poor do not have. Hence, no longer can those with a low level of education expect to find a decent-paying entry-level job, as was the case in the past.

To make matters worse, low-level jobs in the expanding service sector for which the poor might qualify rarely pay a wage that can vault them above the poverty line. For example, workers in the bottom tenth percentile of wage earners earned little more than $8.00 an hour in 2011. Workers in the fiftieth percentile, by comparison, earned at least $16.00 and those in the ninetieth percentile earned at least $38.00. Moreover, there were significant differences between men and women workers, with the latter earning less at each level (Mishel et al., 2012).

In sum, as those on the higher rungs of the occupational hierarchy thrive in an expanding economy, the ranks of the poor are increasingly filled by those who cannot find work or who can only find work that does not pay a viable wage. As sociologist William J. Wilson has put it, "economic growth today does not necessarily produce good jobs" (1996:153). Government policies designed to alleviate poverty are mostly ineffective since it is in the private sector—businesses large and small—that most jobs are created. (Government strategies that address the plight of the poor are discussed later in this chapter.)

Another factor in accounting for the obdurate nature of poverty is income inequality itself. As we saw in Chapter 3, starting in the mid-1970s, the income gap between top and bottom (as well as middle) strata has steadily widened. Economist Lawrence Mishel and his associates have shown that as income inequality grows, poverty rates are less affected by overall economic growth "because too little of that growth reaches the lower end of the income scale" (2009:319). Until the mid-1970s, the fruits of a continually growing economy were more widely shared and the poverty rate dropped accordingly (see Figure 6-1).

The Working Poor and the Underclass

The poor are not a homogeneous category in terms of either economic class or lifestyle. The most important division among them is between those who have been referred to as the *working poor* and those who have been called an *underclass*.

The Working Poor

Many workers in American society are caught in an economic vise. On the one hand, they are poor to the extent that their economic status is extremely precarious. They literally live from paycheck to paycheck. These are workers who commonly work on a part-time or temporary basis, rarely employed at any one job long enough to establish themselves solidly and build some economic security, unlike those in classes above them. Their wages are usually low, and therefore even if they do work regularly, they have difficulty making financial ends meet, let alone saving a portion of their income.

But at the same time that they are sufficiently stressed economically to qualify as poor by almost any definition, they are usually not poor enough to be eligible for public assistance. That is, their income, though low, may be adequate enough to push them above the official poverty line. Failing to qualify for welfare programs such as Medicaid makes their economic status especially unstable, perhaps even more so than that of the abject poor below them, who are chronically un- or underemployed and who therefore qualify for government benefits. Since they do not work enough hours to qualify for medical insurance or they work in a job that does not provide such benefits, a serious illness among working-poor families can be catastrophic.

The **working poor** (or, as some have referred to them, the "near poor") are those who occupy the bottom rungs on the occupational ladder, filling jobs that are lowest not only in wages but in prestige and power as well. Kitchen workers, unskilled factory operatives, migrant farm laborers, and laundry workers are typical of this category. These are jobs that pay at or close to the minimum wage. In 2012, at the federal minimum wage rate ($7.25 an hour), even if they had worked a full workweek (forty hours), their pay would have been only $290. Assuming that they worked fifty weeks during the year, their annual income would have been $14,500, about $2,500 below the official poverty threshold for a family of three and $8,000 for a family of four. This is a hypothetical case, of course, since most of the working poor do not work a full forty-hour week nor do they work for the entire year.[2]

Two Cases   To illustrate the working poor, consider two cases. Diana K. is a thirty-four-year-old single parent of three children. Her run-down apartment is sparsely furnished; its plumbing is in serious disrepair; and when it rains, the ceiling leaks. Diana works as a nurse's aide and is paid on an hourly basis, just above the minimum wage. At one time she was dependent on welfare, but now that she is working, she is no longer eligible for cash assistance. She does continue to receive food stamps, however, and is trying to move into a government-subsidized house that will cost her about the same as her apartment rent. Interestingly, Diana lives not in the inner city of Chicago or Philadelphia or in an impoverished rural area of the South— environments that are commonly believed to breed poverty. Rather, she and her family live in a midsize city in Iowa, where the population is virtually entirely white and non-Hispanic (Kilborn, 1992).

---

[2]Although the federal minimum wage in 2012 was $7.25, its real value was about the same as what it was in 1991 and actually less than its real value in 1967.

Carolyn P., despite her two-year associate's degree, wanders from job to job, never able to achieve financial security. A single parent with a teenage daughter, she earned almost as much twenty years ago as she does now stocking shelves and working cash registers at a Walmart superstore. Family disruptions and poor health have handicapped her throughout her adult life. The odds weighing against her are so great, it is unlikely she will ever rise higher than her present status (Shipler, 2004).

There are some common features of the working poor in these two cases. Most important, both Diana and Carolyn are raising their children alone. As shown in the previous section, family composition is a critical element of poverty. Single-parent, female-headed families are more likely than any others to be poor. Furthermore, both women lack the skills that would enable them to qualify for a better-paying job. Diana would like to become a registered nurse, which would more than triple her wages. But to do that would require a couple of years of full-time schooling. This would mean giving up her present job, which would be financially impossible. Thus, she is caught in a dilemma.

Living on the Edge   Another common feature of the working poor is their relentless struggle to make ends meet on bottom-level wages. In this condition workers can never be certain that their rent can be paid from one month or week to the next and that other life needs can be afforded. One unpredictable event—a sick child, a suddenly lost job, a marital rift—may abruptly thrust these families into the distresses of poverty from which many escaped only a short time ago.

Barbara Ehrenreich (2001), in a fascinating experiment, set out to explore this predicament faced by the working poor. Rather than studying economic statistics on wages, work hours, and family budgets, Ehrenreich—comfortably middle-class herself—worked at several entry-level, low-skill, low-paying jobs, living in housing comparable to that of her workmates, all the time recording her experiences. Knowing that she would return to her financially secure world after a few months, she was under no illusion, of course, that she actually would experience what it is like to live inescapably on the edge. Her aim, as she explains, was "just to see whether I could match income to expenses, as the truly poor attempt to do every day" (6).

Ehrenreich's chronicles provide a poignant look at the "low-wage way of life." She worked as a waitress, a cleaning person, a nursing home aide, and a retail clerk at Walmart. In her waitressing job she earned a bit more than $1,000 a month and spent half of it on food, gas, utilities, and other daily expenses. Her rent took up the rest of her earnings, however, and she discovered that only by working two physically demanding jobs would she be able to survive economically. Moreover, this did not provide for any unforeseen expenses such as medical or dental care, drugs, or car repairs. She faced a similarly perilous situation while working at Walmart. As a cleaning lady earning $6.65 an hour she came closest to balancing income and expenses, but only because she worked seven days a week after taking an additional weekend job in a nursing home as a "dietary aide" (serving meals and cleaning up afterward) at $7.00 an hour.

The conditions on these jobs are, as Ehrenreich describes them, dirty and demeaning, the kind of work that people will do only because they have no options. They also present workers with a conundrum: These are physically taxing jobs, invariably leading to premature health problems that cannot be attended to without jeopardizing one's job. This, in turn, leads to further ill health, pushing workers into a deeper occupational abyss.

Often the working poor are those who are temporarily in a poverty condition, either between jobs or experiencing a cut in wages. Workers whose jobs may be lost as a result of corporate downsizing, for example, and who are for a time unable to find work may suffer a sharp drop in income and in their standard of living, throwing them into the ranks of the poor. Changes in their employment or education may boost them out of poverty, just as sudden or unforeseen circumstances may push them back down. Thus, they should not be thought of as a permanent class of poor people.

Anthropologist Katherine Newman refers to another category of families who are living on the edge of poverty, "too prosperous to be the 'working poor,' too insecure to be 'middle income'" (2007:2). This so-called "missing class" illustrates the fine line between the working class and the working poor. Because they do not clearly fall into one class or the other, they fail to come to the attention of policy makers, journalists, or even sociologists. They do not live in blighted inner-city areas and they are solidly part of the labor force, working as bus drivers, day-care providers, hospital attendants, clerical assistants, and the like. But they suffer many of the same problems as those more clearly-defined as the working poor. Their hourly wages simply do not permit them to escape continual debt in their efforts to enjoy a more comfortable and secure life. They are too prosperous to qualify for public assistance, like Medicaid or day care, but they lack the financial ability to buy their own medical insurance or pay for child care. These are families that have suffered a loss of whatever financial security they had achieved prior to the economic downturn of the late 2000s.

Invisible Poverty The working poor are in some ways a hidden element of poverty. Because they are part of the mainstream labor force, their impoverishment does not easily come to the attention of the general public. Workers like those Ehrenreich describes serve our food and bus our dishes, pick up our garbage, tend to our elderly relatives in nursing homes, and make our beds and clean our bathrooms when we stay at a hotel. In brief, for the nonpoor they make life easier and more comfortable, providing services that are taken for granted. But they are such an expected part of the commercial landscape that in a sense they become invisible. Moreover, because their poverty is less severe than that of the chronically poor (discussed in the next section), their problems rarely are addressed by government policies.

Alluringly, socioeconomic security for working poor families is within sight but never quite reachable. During times when labor markets are tight and wages are rising, they can get a taste of middle-class stability. But without the human capital (education and job skills) that might give them protection during economic downturns, the working poor are first to suffer the effects of rising unemployment and sinking wages, as occurred in the severe recession of the late 2000s. As noted earlier, in recent years an increasing number of working- and lower-middle class families have teetered on the abstract poverty line, often jumping back and forth between poverty and a more secure economic condition as their employment status fluctuates.

The Underclass

In recent years, Americans have become accustomed to viewing the poor not as people who may drift in and out of poverty because of changes in their jobs or other personal or societal circumstances but rather as a population that remains more or less permanently impoverished. The majority of the poor do not correspond to this popular view; they are working but simply do not always earn enough to boost them over the poverty threshold. However, there is a segment of the poverty population that does seem to fit the popular description: They have few occupational skills, are undereducated, are rarely employed, and are ordinarily dependent on some form of public assistance. Sociologists and others have referred to this element of the poor as an **underclass.** Two essential characteristics define this stratum: poverty that is chronic, not temporary or short-term, and social and economic isolation. Perhaps more than anything else, it is the fact that they are largely cut off from the mainstream society and its major institutions that makes the plight of this part of the poverty population so intractable.

The Makeup of the Underclass   The dividing line between those who drift in and out of poverty and those who remain mired permanently in that condition is by no means clear-cut. What seems to be the key differentiating factor, however, is the loose connection of the underclass to the mainstream labor force. The working poor often live below the official poverty line, but they are usually employed, at least for a portion of the year. They are in a precarious situation, of course, and are always in danger of falling further into poverty. Unlike the working poor, the underclass, for the most part, do not participate in the general labor force. Most depend to some degree on government welfare, and some may engage in illegal activities. Others are among those referred to by Ken Auletta (credited with popularizing the term "underclass") as "the traumatized," troubled individuals who, for various reasons, drift or live on city streets.

Much of the economic activity among the underclass is part of what is called the **underground economy.** This covers a wide range of economic activities that occur outside the mainstream economy where activities are regulated through licensing and other requirements and where earned income is taxed. Activities within the underground economy are ordinarily "off the books"—that is, exchanges are made only in cash with no record of transfer of money. Hence, earnings are not reported to the government, and no taxes are paid on them. Many activities in the underground economy are legitimate, such as selling goods on the street or bartering services, but many are illegal, like drug dealing and prostitution.

Trying to enumerate the underclass is difficult. More than other classes, those who constitute this stratum are apt to slip through the cracks of census counts. The underclass resides mostly in inner-city ghettos that characterize almost all large U.S. cities. This, by itself, serves as an effective isolating mechanism. Some of these areas are treated as "no-go zones" by all but those who have obligations to enter them, like police or social workers. People living in concentrated ghettos are not likely to talk to census takers or to fill out census forms. Also, since they are not active in the mainstream labor market, they do not earn enough to pay income taxes; hence, there are no IRS statistics on this group, as there are for other classes. Their numbers, to all intents and purposes, can only be guessed at.

Because the underclass is confined mainly to inner-city neighborhoods of urban areas, it has been seen as essentially a black and Latino population, though its racial and ethnic composition is varied. Nonetheless, it is true that the underclass in American society today is made up disproportionately of racial-ethnic minorities. "Poverty most definitely cuts across racial lines," notes Peter Edelman, "but it doesn't cut evenly" (2012:13).

The urban ghettos in which the underclass is found have been chronicled widely by social scientists and journalists (Kotlowitz, 1991; Kozol, 1995; Wilson, 1987, 1996). In a real sense, those who make up this part of the poverty population constitute "a separate America" in that they are virtually detached from the remainder of the U.S. population. Moreover, the conditions of life in these areas are so alien to the more affluent neighborhoods and suburbs that surround them that they could just as well exist on another continent. Consider Wards 8 and 3, two areas of Washington, D.C., only a few miles apart, shown in Table 6-3. Ward 8, in the city's southeast section, is a largely black area where the median household income is a little more than $22,000. More than a third of the people are living below the poverty line (almost half of all children), and over a third of adults lack even a high school diploma. In Ward 3, a largely white area in the northwest corner of the city, the median household income is almost four times greater than in Ward 8. Here, less than 8 percent are below the poverty level, and almost all adults are at least high school graduates. But the differences in income and education are only part of the story, for these class differences translate into shockingly contrasting social conditions. In Ward 8, over 30 percent of children are in single-parent families, compared to 2 percent in Ward 3, and almost 37 percent rely on food stamps. Security

Table 6-3 ▪ Two Areas of Washington, D.C.

	Ward 3	Ward 8
Population (2005)	72,000	75,000
Median household income (2000)	$84,609	$22,410
Percent persons below poverty (2000)	7.5	36.0
Percent children below poverty (2000)	2.9	47.1
Percent persons receiving food stamps (2007)	<1	36.8
Percent unemployed (2008)	9.6	22.0
Percent single parents with children (2000)	2.1	31.4
Percent adults without a high school diploma (2000)	4.0	34.0
Violent crimes per 1,000 population (2007)	1.8	19.3

Source: Reproduced by permission of Urban Institute Press

is hardly a concern in Ward 3, unlike Ward 8, where the rate of violent crime is more than ten times higher. Nothing better illustrates the growing bifurcation of the class system in the United States today than comparisons such as these, juxtaposing those in urban areas who are relatively well off with those who are in a constant struggle for survival.

The Underclass Debate   Since the term "underclass" was introduced in the 1960s, social scientists have debated ideas concerning this element of the poverty population. Some contend that the chronically poor are behaviorally flawed, maintaining a degraded and dysfunctional lifestyle, and that this is the major cause of their condition. Lawrence Mead, for example, defines the underclass as "a disorganized group unable to get ahead because of a lack not so much of opportunity as of personal organization" (1992:29). Only by adopting mainstream norms and values, therefore, can they hope to alter their predicament.

Others hold that the condition of the underclass is the result of structural forces outside their control. The most critical of these is the basically restructured urban economy, creating an exodus of jobs and industry from inner cities (Wilson, 1987, 1996). This has left the urban underclass a redundant population whose labor is no longer needed. Without jobs, a panoply of attendant social problems—drugs, crime, welfare dependency, and so on—has arisen. In this view, only through the restoration of jobs with livable wages can the underclass be expected to advance out of its current state.

The debate, then, boils down to a view of the underclass as either cultural or structural in its formation and continuation. In the cultural view, underclass people are not only economically deprived but culturally deficient, their lifestyle and general values antithetical to the mainstream society.

In the structural view, members of the underclass are ill equipped in skills and education and thus unable to enter the mainstream workforce; they are victims of a restructured economy. The very term *underclass*, in this view, is pejorative (Gans, 1996).[3]

Sociologist Christopher Jencks (1993) points out that much of the controversy swirling around the notion of an underclass stems from the fact that, like most class terms, this one is ambiguous. He suggests that there are at least four ranking schemes, each of which implies a different definition of the underclass: an impoverished underclass, a jobless underclass, an educational underclass, and an underclass that violates middle-class values. Hence, there are significant differences among people within the so-called underclass.

The underclass debate is part of a larger theoretical clash that consists of contrasting views of the causes of poverty in general, which are discussed in more detail in the next section.

Why Are the Poor Poor?

Explanations of poverty, like explanations of inequality in general, differ in several ways. They may focus on individuals or on social structures. They may interpret poverty as inevitable—perhaps even necessary—or as the product of the efforts of the powerful and wealthy to protect their own interests. Let's look at some of these explanations, keeping in mind that despite their differences, each may contain elements of validity and therefore may offer at least a partial answer to the question of why some people are poor.

Individual-Focused Explanations

In explaining poverty, individual-focused theories stress the personal responsibility of people in determining their place in the social hierarchy. These theories fall closely in line with the popular thinking about the poor in America. This is because they complement well the dominant ideology of individualism. The essential idea is that if people are poor, it is mainly because of their own actions or inaction, as well as their personal traits. The source of poverty, in other words, lies with the poor themselves. The two major individual-focused theories emphasize either biological traits or cultural traits.

Biological Explanations A theory once widely held maintains that people are poor because of inherent deficiencies in their character or mental makeup—that is, they are biologically less "fit" than others. Because they are genetically handicapped, they are bound to be poor.

---

[3]Some favor dispensing with the term *underclass*, given its pejorative connotations. Substitute terms, however, like *ghetto poor* suggested by Wilson (1991), seem hardly more flattering. As Morris (1996) has pointed out, the real issue is not terminological but rather whether the underclass is cultural or structural in nature.

This biological deterministic explanation was popular early in the last century and was a basic part of the notion of **social Darwinism.** Some social scientists and commentators held that one's wealth or poverty was a demonstration of one's inherent capabilities. This idea was put forth by those such as British social scientist Herbert Spencer, who asserted that the emergence of the poor, as well as the emergence of an elite at the top of the social hierarchy, was a natural development. Spencer drew an analogy to Darwin's notion of survival of the fittest among animal species. Applying the idea to human societies, Spencer maintained that through a process of free and natural competition, the most able would rise to the top and the least able would sink to the bottom. In this way the social Darwinists rationalized the extreme inequality that typified the newly industrialized societies at the turn of the twentieth century, like Britain and the United States.

If the poor were a natural development, so the theory went, there was nothing that could be done to alleviate their condition. Giving assistance to the poor would only extend their inevitable decline. Indeed, the most desirable occurrence would be the rapid extinction of this element of the society. Calls for social welfare programs of one kind or another to help lift the poor from their condition were therefore met with the argument that these were fruitless and wasteful efforts.

Social Darwinism in its most crude form is an idea that no longer holds much weight among social scientists or even the general public. Yet there are remnants of a genetic explanation for poverty that occasionally surface. In 1994 psychologist Richard J. Herrnstein and sociologist Charles Murray authored a controversial book, *The Bell Curve,* in which they proffered a theory of poverty that is well within the tradition of social Darwinism. The essence of their position is that IQ is the most significant factor in determining people's place in the social hierarchy. Herrnstein and Murray posit that intelligence, as measured by IQ, is in large part genetic. They see strong relationships between IQ and various social pathologies. Those with lower IQs have a greater proclivity toward poverty, crime, illegitimacy, poor educational performance, and other social ills. Because IQ is mostly genetic, they argue, there is no way to change the condition of those with low intelligence through educational reforms or welfare programs. Because lower-intelligence people are reproducing much faster than are higher-intelligence people, the society is faced with the possibility of a growing underclass increasingly dependent on the more intelligent and productive classes. Herrnstein and Murray hold that such an underclass is apt to remain in a state of dependency on the nonpoor and continue to engage in antisocial activities. Thus, they question the value of welfare payments, remedial educational programs, affirmative action, and other efforts designed to raise the social and economic levels of the poor.

Herrnstein and Murray's arguments were countered by most mainstream sociologists, who claimed that their methods were flawed and their reasoning specious (Fischer et al., 1996; Fraser, 1995; Jacoby and Glauberman,

1995). Moreover, many considered *The Bell Curve* as much a statement of the political leanings of the authors as a work of social science. Specifically, Herrnstein and Murray were challenged on a number of points: For one, IQ has been shown to measure only certain kinds of intelligence. Furthermore, IQ is not fixed but is subject to variation within one's lifetime and, for groups, subject to change over generations. Perhaps most important, the authors failed to place sufficient weight on the environmental factors that enable people, regardless of IQ, to express their intelligence.

Certainly *individuals* differ in terms of their natural abilities, and these differences will affect their socioeconomic positions. But that does not mean that there are differences among *groups* that ultimately determine their position in the social hierarchy. Theoretical views like Herrnstein and Murray's have appeared periodically, but the understanding that environment, not inheritance, is the key influence in shaping social behavior remains the dominant perspective in social science, as it has for many decades.

Public policies often reflect the philosophies and ideologies of those in power at any particular time. The policies of the Reagan administration in the 1980s regarding social welfare and inequality were put forth much in the tradition of social Darwinism. Administration officials believed that the public assistance programs of the 1960s and 1970s were self-defeating and had actually exacerbated poverty. It was suggested that the poor were discouraged from taking responsibility for their condition by welfare that was too generous. The seemingly chronic condition of the underclass was interpreted as the result of government policies that had disinclined people from seeking work and rewarded them for idleness (Danziger and Danziger, 2005). In 1984, Charles Murray (coauthor of *The Bell Curve*) authored *Losing Ground*, a book that became a primer, of sorts, for Reaganites and conservatives in general on why the poor were poor and why they seemed to stay that way. Murray suggested that programs of the Great Society, begun by the Johnson administration in the 1960s, were responsible for creating the urban underclass. The AFDC (Aid to Families with Dependent Children) program was a prime example, according to Murray. He argued that giving welfare payments to poor mothers only in cases where a male was not residing with the family was a way of encouraging the breakup of poor families and perpetuating their poverty. More recently Murray has argued that the causes of poverty continue to lie in a combination of fatherless families (and moral decline generally) and differences in cognitive abilities (Murray, 2008; 2012).

The Culture of Poverty   Few today subscribe to biological theories like social Darwinism. A more compelling individual-focused theory, however, is what has been called the **culture of poverty.** Essentially the idea is this: Poverty is the result of a set of norms and values—a culture—that is characteristic of the poor. Because those norms and values are not compatible with the society's dominant culture, its practitioners are unable to function in and adapt to the mainstream. The poor, then, are attuned to a dysfunctional culture. Although poverty is not seen as biologically based, it is nonetheless attributable, in this view, to personal characteristics of the poor.

The idea of a culture of poverty was first put forth in the early 1960s by anthropologist Oscar Lewis, who studied poor families in Mexico City, San Juan, Puerto Rico, and New York City. Lewis lived among those families and concluded that there were basic behavioral traits and attitudes that typified the poor everywhere, which together constituted a coherent "culture of poverty." Some of the key features of that culture, Lewis explained, were a present orientation (rather than the future orientation typical of the middle class), a fatalistic view of the world and one's place in it, a tendency toward female-headed families, authoritarianism within the family, a high rate of abandonment of wives and children, frequent use of violence in settling disputes and in disciplining children, a high rate of alcoholism, a belief in male superiority, and a martyr complex among women (Lewis, 1961, 1965, 1966).

Lewis maintained that these values and behaviors are responses to the conditions of poverty but that in the process they become well-entrenched cultural traits that are passed on from one generation to the next. "By the time slum children are age six or seven," Lewis wrote, "they have usually absorbed the basic values and attitudes of their subculture and are not psychologically geared to take full advantage of changing conditions or increased opportunities which may occur in their lifetime" (1965:xlv). Lewis explained, however, that not all poor people necessarily live in or develop a culture of poverty.

A related view of poverty and the poor is suggested in the work of political scientist Edward Banfield (1968, 1974). Banfield asserted that the plight of the urban poor was a result of their failure to adopt conforming, specifically middle-class, social values. He focused primarily on the urban black poor, claiming that their situation and their behaviors must be seen not as a product of racial discrimination but as class behavior. European immigrants of earlier decades, he pointed out, were also mostly poor and manifested high crime rates, unstable families, and low school performance, but they eventually assimilated to the dominant culture and improved their economic standing. Poor blacks are therefore simply experiencing the same process of transition to a higher class position. The problems of the urban black poor, in this view, will abate once they are solidly part of the middle class and have embraced middle-class values and lifestyles.

As part of the culture-of-poverty thesis, structural factors and the "accident of birth" may be acknowledged, but these are not seen as unconquerable obstacles. People may not choose to be poor, but through their personal efforts, the road out of poverty is open to them. They need only subscribe to the mainstream culture.

Critics of this cultural explanation of poverty have pointed out that the basic argument blames the poor themselves for being poor. That is, their condition is essentially a product of their failure to adopt middle-class norms and values rather than of a restructured economy or ethnic discrimination (or both) that makes escape from poverty, for most, difficult at best (Ryan, 1975; Valentine, 1971). Moreover, much debate has centered on the culture-of-poverty concept itself. Some sociologists and anthropologists took issue with Lewis's conceptualization of the poor as a "culture." Are the behaviors and values of the poor a culture in the sense of a way of life consciously passed on from one generation to the next, or are these traits simply adaptive mechanisms that would be discarded once the material conditions of poverty were removed (Gans, 1968; Lewis, 1967)? Critics of the culture-of-poverty thesis suggest the latter and contend that its exponents confuse cause and effect.

Even if poor families could somehow be transformed culturally into some middle-class ideal (both parents present, working, religious), this would have very limited impact on preventing future poverty. Researchers Jens Ludwig and Susan Mayer (2006) explain that there is a dearth of evidence to support the idea that parents who choose to marry, work, and regularly attend church are more likely to produce children who will experience long-term economic success. Moreover, they show that a majority of poor adults have grown up in just such "pro-social" households.

Structure-Focused Explanations

In contrast to individual-focused theories, structure-focused theories stress factors that lie outside the realm of individual behavior. In this view, it is structural forces stemming from the workings of the major societal institutions that have an impact on people and contribute to their poverty. Through the accident of birth or through social and economic circumstances over which they have little control, individuals are thrust into poverty with few resources to disengage from that situation. The explanation for poverty, therefore, is found in how the society's institutions, especially the economy and the government, operate so as either to create opportunities or to lodge people in deprived conditions. Structural explanations hold sway among sociologists on issues of poverty.

The Cycle of Poverty The idea of a **cycle of poverty** is that an array of societal institutions sustains a poverty class through a kind of circular process. When individuals find themselves enveloped by this institutional web, they face daunting obstacles to overcoming their circumstances.

It is primarily within the society's economic institutions that the cycle is most compelling, but the effect extends well beyond the economy into other institutional realms. By definition, the poor are those at the bottom of the class hierarchy. This means that their income, their occupational opportunities, and their educational achievement are all at the lowest levels. These factors have devastating effects on all aspects of social life. And the effects of low income, occupation, and education operate in a kind of circuit, making it improbable that individuals can break the cycle and either move out of poverty themselves or enable their children to do so.

If we start with education, it is obvious that those with the fewest years and the poorest quality of schooling will take their place at the end of the job queue. As a result of their low educational level, they will have the fewest skills. Thus, they will qualify only for jobs that are the least challenging and that offer no opportunities for advancement. In a word, they are dead-end jobs. Many, of course, will be unable to find even these low-level jobs. Thus, just as low education assures a correspondingly low level of work, poor jobs assure a low income since these are the jobs that pay minimally. Low income forces people to live in the poorest neighborhoods, where schools are ill equipped and where few highly educated people who might serve as positive role models live. The result is a disincentive for children to value education and a tendency to drop out of school. The cycle, then, is complete: Low education leads to low occupational level, which leads to low income, which leads, in the succeeding generation, back to low education.

This is a cycle that operates perpetually. Unless a breakout can occur at some point by having a family member acquire more and better education or earn a more substantial income, nothing will change. It is a kind of catch-22: Without more income, one cannot acquire more education, but without more education, one cannot acquire more income. Moreover, the same cycle will ensnare the children. Unless they can be afforded more education, the likelihood that family poverty will be sustained in their generation is very great.

At various points in this cycle, other aspects of social life, such as health care, housing, and criminal justice, are affected, reinforcing the negative effects of low income and education. Take housing, for example. Where people live, that is, their neighborhood or community, usually determines the quality of schooling they receive. Suburban communities in which middle- or upper-middle-class families reside will be able to support their schools more amply than poor inner-city neighborhoods. Thus, moving poor families to more affluent areas might result in breaking the cycle of poverty for many. But poor families are prevented from moving to these areas mainly because they cannot afford the price of housing.

The effects of racial and class discrimination further reduce the opportunities to move out of impoverished neighborhoods with inferior schools. Efforts to build public housing—occupied mainly by the poor—in suburban communities are almost always resisted strongly by the residents of those communities and by the politicians who represent them, for fear of the infestation of crime, drugs, and other social pathologies that, they assume, will follow. The poor, then, are confined to self-contained communities not only by their place in the economic structure but also by political action and by social discrimination.

Adding to the difficulty of breaking the cycle of poverty is the fact that the cost of living is proportionately higher for the poor than it is for other classes. In purchasing basic necessities—rent, food, transportation—the poor are presented with fewer choices and higher prices. A study of major

U.S. metropolitan areas (Fellowes, 2006) revealed that lower-income families pay more for financial services (such as check cashing and short-term loans), cars and car insurance, furniture and appliances, home loans and home insurance, and groceries. This is accounted for by the fact that companies face higher risks in doing business in low-income areas, by unscrupulous business practices, and by poor people's lack of access to market information.

The Political Economy of Capitalism   A second structural theory focuses on the uneven economic development that results from capitalism. As a capitalist system works, business enterprises seek to maximize their profits. This is true whether the enterprise is as massive as General Electric or as diminutive as Harry's Hot Dog Stand. In the United States and other industrialized societies, it is large corporations that are the major capitalist enterprises. It is they that control the rate of economic development in communities because it is they that create jobs and generate economic activity generally. Through their decisions, the fate of workers is largely determined. Given the capitalist principle of profit maximization, these firms will move their capital, and thus employment opportunities, from location to location as their interests dictate. If a manufacturing firm located in community X can secure its labor more cheaply in community Y, it will be inclined to move its production facilities to community Y. In the process of such corporate decisions, some communities win and others lose. As we saw in Chapter 5, this capitalist rationale is not limited to local communities within a particular country but extends beyond national borders.

Deindustrialization is a term that has been used to describe the flight of capital and industrial jobs from communities where they had been traditionally located. Many cities in the U.S. Northeast and Midwest have been especially impacted by this shift in recent decades (Bluestone and Harrison, 1982). As a result, many communities have been left with few, if any, jobs for workers who are unskilled and poorly educated. Between 1967 and 1987, Philadelphia, for example, lost 64 percent of all its manufacturing jobs (Kasarda, 1995). Similar losses were experienced by other industrial cities like Chicago and Detroit. Shrinking employment in the manufacturing sector continued unabated throughout the 2000s as millions of blue-collar jobs were eliminated. Neighborhoods and communities dependent on those jobs are transformed into blighted areas, where much of the population is unemployed and welfare-dependent. As businesses and middle-class residents leave, they take with them their wealth and the taxes they pay to support public services, such as police, transportation, and schools. Those left behind are the poor who are not economically capable of moving but who now live in a community that is deteriorating. The lack of jobs, and thus income, leads to an even lower tax base and further deterioration.

Sociologist William J. Wilson (1987, 1996) has been the most influential exponent of this explanation of the poor in America, specifically the urban poor who are trapped in inner-city ghettos. As he explains, changes in the society's economic structure have made lower-class, unskilled people an excess labor force that is becoming a permanent underclass. The labor market today calls for jobs requiring technical and educational skills, for which such persons cannot qualify. Moreover, industry has moved to areas on the urban fringe so that those low-level jobs still available are outside the range of central-city residents. The result is a semipermanent state of unemployment. The lack of job opportunities creates a vicious circle in which the poor are forced to remain concentrated in the inner city, attending inferior schools and thereby reinforcing their disadvantaged position in the labor market. Wilson further explains that the problems of the urban underclass—high rates of joblessness, school dropouts, crime, teenage motherhood, and so on—have been exacerbated by the exodus of middle- and working-class families from inner-city neighborhoods, removing vital role models and a support system of basic institutions.

Poverty as "Functional" Sociologist Herbert Gans has suggested that poverty can be explained as a social phenomenon that serves certain societal functions. That is, it is beneficial to some elements of the society, namely, the nonpoor, and thus it endures so long as it serves those purposes.

Gans explains that it is particularly those who are labeled the **undeserving poor** who are used by the nonpoor. The "undeserving poor" are those who appear to be able-bodied but who are unemployed and who are receiving welfare benefits of one kind or another. Gans explains that labeling some of the poor "undeserving" creates a number of positive functions for those who are not poor or, at least, for some groups and institutions. These functions are unintended and unrecognized, but nonetheless they serve to benefit the nonpoor in some fashion.[4]

The undeserving poor, for example, can be used as ideal scapegoats and thus "blamed for virtually any shortcoming of everyday life which can be credibly ascribed to them" (Gans, 1994:274). The undeserving poor also serve as suppliers of illegal goods—drugs, for example—to the nonpoor. They create jobs for many in the better-off population, such as social workers who attend to them, police and others in the criminal justice system who deal with them, and even social scientists who study them. Moreover, the undeserving poor contribute to the reinforcement of mainstream norms and values: "If the undeserving poor can be imagined to be lazy, they help to reaffirm the Protestant work ethic; if poor single-parent families are publicly condemned, the two-parent family is once more legitimated as ideal" (276).

---

[4]Gans is among those who feel that the term underclass has been used pejoratively to describe the undeserving poor. He sees it as a term applied not simply to those who are chronically poor and unemployed but also to those who choose not to work or to engage in crime and thus do not deserve public aid.

What can be seen in this explanation is a focus away from individuals themselves and upon the social institutions that give support to poverty and, in some ways, are actually dependent on it. Eliminating poverty, in this view, would require that poverty become dysfunctional for the people who most benefit from it: the nonpoor (Gans, 1971).

Popular Views of Poverty

Although few laypersons think of poverty in systematic and formal terms as sociologists do, almost all have some explanation, simple though it may be, for why people are poor and why so few seem to rise from that position. In general, the prevailing public view of poverty is that it is largely self-imposed—that is, it is mostly the fault of the poor themselves. In terms of the theories we have considered, it is the individual-focused explanations that seem most persuasive to the American public. Structural factors—the changing economy, lack of jobs, poor educational opportunities, and so on—are not discounted, but they are secondary to individual shortcomings. This stress on individualism has basically shaped government policies toward the poor. There is little disagreement regarding the belief that the needy should be helped. However, the belief is equally strong that if they are able, they must first make efforts to help themselves. Surveys have confirmed repeatedly this individualistic view of poverty in America (Davis and Smith, 1994; Kluegel and Smith, 1986; McClosky and Zaller, 1984).

Surprisingly, even the poor themselves are not in sharp disagreement with the dominant view. Wilson, in his study of Chicago's inner-city poor, found that a substantial majority agreed with the idea that opportunities are plentiful and that people are rewarded on the basis of their efforts. Typical were the observations of one poverty-area resident: "Life is what you make it. . . . If you want something from life you have to go for it. Everybody can go for it, you see, but there's nobody that's gonna give you somethin' for nothin': you gotta work for what you want" (1996:180).

A basic premise of the dominant American ideology is that opportunities are unlimited. If people want to work, they can work. No individuals need be in a situation of helplessness and dependency if they simply make the effort to better themselves. So, as the ideology explains it, people get what they deserve, and in the case of the poor, they merit their poverty. More precisely, however, Americans tend to separate what they see as the **deserving poor** from the "undeserving" poor. The former are those who are poor through no apparent fault of their own: the disabled, the elderly, widows, children, and those who work steadily but do not earn enough. The undeserving, in contrast, are people who lack ambition, are irresponsible, are morally weak, and so on. These are men and women who "should" work regularly but don't, and who are poor as a result (Jencks, 1993).

Public Policies and Poverty

All societies in the modern world acknowledge that poverty is a public issue and that efforts should be made to ameliorate the plight of the poor. But as to the strategies for attaining the agreed-upon societal objective of minimizing poverty, there is wide disagreement among policymakers, social scientists, and the general public.

As a public issue, poverty is also a political issue. Thus, people of varying political persuasions will respond to poverty and the poor in different ways. At one extreme are those who would leave the plight of the poor to the market, essentially removing government entirely from the picture. This is almost always a minority view, however. Even those who are political conservatives recognize that the existence of poverty impedes the smooth functioning of the society and its economy. It is beneficial to aid the poor in some fashion, therefore, if only to assure that the poor do not upset the peace and security of the nonpoor. Conservatives, however, do not look kindly on ambitious assistance programs, given their stress on individual-focused explanations of poverty.

At the other end of the political spectrum are those who see the desirability of government playing a major role. For them, an advanced welfare state offering the indigent maximum assistance is the proper objective. This, too, appears to be a minority view among citizens of most industrialized societies. Even those who strongly favor public assistance recognize its limits and insist that the poor make at least some effort to help themselves.

Public policy issues regarding poverty evoke the societal values of liberty and equity and the balance between them. Those favoring the liberty side of the equation contend that people should be free to rise or fall on their own efforts. For them, the market naturally and fairly sifts out society's winners and losers. On the other side, those who favor equity insist that all members of society are part of a community, and as such, it is the social obligation of the "haves" to make sure that the "have-nots" receive their share of the society's wealth. In this view, there should not be gaping disparities between rich and poor; rather, economic differences, ideally, should be minimized. The difference in the two views, then, boils down to a vision of the good society as one in which either equality of *opportunity* or equality of *condition* is the proper goal. The problem, then, is finding the acceptable equation between these two ideals.

Welfare Programs

Social welfare in the United States consists of a broad variety of programs designed to assist people in need. Some are basically **social insurance programs,** like Social Security and Medicare, and are financed through payroll taxes. All people in the society regardless of their economic status are the beneficiaries of these programs. Others are what are called **public assistance programs** and are financed through general government revenues. They are "means-tested," requiring that recipients demonstrate a need in order to qualify for them. It is the public assistance programs that constitute what most people think of as "welfare."[5] Until 1996, four programs made up the bulk of public assistance: AFDC (Aid to Families with Dependent Children), SSI (Supplemental Security Income), Food Stamps, and Medicaid.

AFDC had been the most expensive of these programs and also the most controversial. Indeed, few government programs have been as thoroughly vilified. For several decades, this had been the primary family assistance program of the federal government. Originally enacted during the Great Depression of the 1930s, it was designed to provide temporary assistance to families that had suffered the loss of a parent, particularly through death or incapacitation of a father or mother. By the 1960s, however, its recipients had become mostly young unmarried women with children; in 1993, it was helping to support 5 million single-parent families. As a result, AFDC became the special target of those who strongly opposed the welfare system as it had traditionally functioned. It was a symbol for all of the negative assumptions made about public assistance programs and had come to represent "welfare" in the minds of Americans.

Opponents of AFDC assumed that the program was the cause of high rates of illegitimacy. Young mothers were having children, they believed, in order to collect more welfare. AFDC, then, perfectly represented the cause of the "culture of dependency" that had formed around welfare recipients. Another common belief regarding welfare was that most of its recipients were permanently welfare-dependent, unable or unwilling to ever assume financial responsibility for themselves. Welfare was also seen in racial terms, the assumption being that it was benefiting primarily African Americans. Finally, popular views of welfare assumed that payments were generous, providing recipients with luxuries at taxpayers' expense.

In fact, most of the assumptions regarding AFDC and welfare programs generally were faulty. Studies found that most teenage pregnancies were unintended and that families receiving welfare were, on average, no larger than most. Sociologists pointed out the lack of evidence to support the belief that welfare causes illegitimacy and single parenthood, noting that the rate of single motherhood in western European countries was lower than in the United States despite their far more generous welfare programs (Sandefur, 1996; Sidel, 1996). Also, single motherhood had increased throughout the 1980s and early 1990s despite the fact that AFDC benefits had declined. Furthermore, single motherhood had grown among *all* social classes, not only the poor. Regarding the permanency of welfare, research showed that most recipients did not stay dependent but drifted in and out of welfare as they drifted in and out of the workforce (Wilson, 1996). As to the racial

---

[5]In Chapter 9 we return to the issue of welfare and examine its different forms. Here the focus is specifically on public assistance programs designed to ameliorate poverty.

connotations of welfare, more whites than blacks were the recipients of public assistance (including AFDC), though blacks did represent a disproportionately large percentage. Less than 10 percent of whites were receiving some form of welfare, compared to one-third of blacks. Finally, to assume that families could live comfortably on welfare was a gross exaggeration. AFDC payments varied from state to state, but in 1993 the average monthly payment was $377. Even with the addition of other forms of public assistance, total payments were hardly sufficient to push recipients above the poverty line. Furthermore, until AFDC was abolished in 1996, the benefits it provided had dropped consistently for the previous twenty years.

Welfare Reform   Despite misunderstandings of welfare and misperceptions of its recipients, the federal welfare changes enacted in 1996 seemed motivated primarily by these popular assumptions. The welfare system had come to be seen as a giant bureaucracy providing assistance but not demonstrating the capacity to actually lift people into a productive life in the mainstream economy. Recipients, therefore, were portrayed as welfare-dependent and the system as broken and ineffective. The prevailing view had come to be that simply being poor should not automatically entitle an individual or family to public assistance. In the 1990s, the political environment had become conducive to, as it was popularly expressed, "change welfare as we know it." These changes in the welfare system represented a fundamental shift in government policy.

Chief among the basic changes in the welfare system contained in the 1996 legislation was a mandate that welfare recipients must work if they are able-bodied. Failure to work within two years after the start of receiving welfare would result in a loss of benefits. In no case, however, were families to receive welfare benefits for longer than five years. Under the legislation, in which AFDC was replaced by TANF (Temporary Assistance to Needy Families), the federal government agreed to give to individual states block grants that they could then use to shape their own welfare programs. Thus, each state now had the power to tailor its welfare program as it saw fit, providing state-specific requirements for people to qualify and varying levels of benefits.

The revised welfare rules evoked mixed reactions from policymakers and social scientists. Although some believed that they would vault the chronically poor into the mainstream labor market and impose more personal responsibility, others contended that they would impose even further hardship on needy families. What do we know of the results of the 1996 welfare reform measures over the past almost two decades?

A few trends have become clear. First, there is no debate about the fact that the number of people on welfare declined sharply. This can be seen in Figure 6-2. By 2000 the number of families receiving TANF had been cut in half, and by 2005 fewer were receiving aid under this program than had received AFDC forty years earlier. Second, as the reform measures

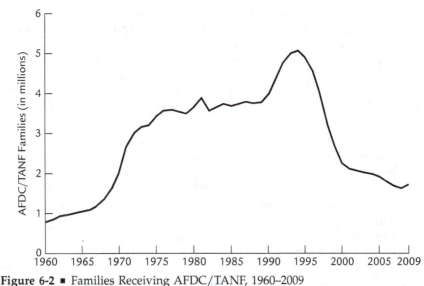

Figure 6-2 ▪ Families Receiving AFDC/TANF, 1960–2009
Source: U.S. Department of Health and Human Services, 2012.

intended, many former recipients were placed in the workforce. In fact, the employment of poor single mothers increased dramatically. Third, welfare reform did not lead to a significant increase in child poverty, as many had feared (Haskins, 2006).

Despite these apparent successes, a number of problems were brought to light by the new system, leaving some basic issues in dispute. The key question is whether welfare reform led to a decline in poverty, not simply a reduction of the welfare rolls. Although millions of former welfare recipients found work, it appears that most were unable to earn wages sufficient to boost them above the poverty level (Cancian et al., 2003; *Congressional Digest,* 2002). Jencks et al. (2006) show that living standards for low-income single mothers did not change much between 1996 and 2003. They explain that a sharp increase in poverty failed to materialize not so much because of the pressure placed on poor people to enter the workforce but as a result of a combination of rising wages and measures such as Medicaid and the Earned Income Tax Credit (EITC), whose purpose is to raise the income of poor workers. Also, state governments were able to transfer the unemployable into other support programs.

Studies that have followed welfare recipients show that getting people into the labor market and keeping them there are not the same (Boushey, 2002; 2003; McMillan, 2008). Because they are mostly single mothers, the most critical need for such persons to function successfully over a long period is the provision of affordable child care. This is in short supply in many communities, however, and where it is available it absorbs a huge portion of those families' earnings. It is important to consider that the United States provides less in the way of public support for child care than most comparable societies. These studies also found that single women parents understood well that training and education were key to finding and retaining good jobs. The approach to welfare after the reform of 1996, however, was to get people into the workforce as quickly as possible. The haste to reduce the welfare rolls often meant disregarding training and education, thus moving people into low-paying, dead-end jobs, which did not promise long-term stability and wage growth. Moreover, the work requirement made it more difficult to go to school and care for children at the same time. One study found that welfare reform significantly reduced the probability of both high school and college enrollment among adult women at risk for reliance on welfare (Dave et al., 2008).

Another problem stems from the fact that not all who have been taken off the welfare rolls have blended into the mainstream labor force. Some stripped of welfare may simply have been left adrift, thrust into an even more desperate and helpless state, as many critics of the new welfare measures feared. In New York City, for example, fewer than 10 percent of welfare recipients find and keep a job for six months (McMillan, 2008). Nationally, it is estimated that there are over 1 million poor single mothers who are without jobs and are not receiving any public assistance, TANF or other (Loprest and Nichols, 2011). Other former welfare recipients may be working only part-time or may have found employment in the underground economy.

In sum, welfare reform may have succeeded in reducing the welfare rolls, but it is not evident that it has reduced poverty (Edelman, 2012; Jencks et al., 2006; Lerman, 1999; Rainwater and Smeeding, 2003; Trisi and Pavetti, 2012). The responsibility for welfare has been shifted largely to the states, which have handled reform in a variety of ways. Some have set up programs such as child care, wage supplements, and tuition for job training and education. The emphasis in most, however, has been on reducing case loads, not on placing people in jobs that pay a living wage and offer long-range opportunities. Accomplishing that goal entails providing the poor with hard skills as well as a combination of other forms of assistance like child care, expanded income tax credits, and a higher minimum wage (Valletta, 2006). Moreover, addressing the issue of poverty must take into account the fact that the poor are not a homogeneous collectivity. Some are in need of only a slight push to boost them into the ranks of the working class or even the lower-middle class. Others need more assistance, and still others may be incapable of ever competing independently in the job market. For those in the latter group, it is questionable whether they can overcome a lack of social skills (what sociologists sometimes refer to as "cultural capital") and prolonged separation from the worlds of education and work to make a successful transition into the mainstream labor force (Havemann, 1996).

The debate continues regarding which approach to welfare reform is likely to be most effective. Some emphasize that getting people into the occupational world, regardless of the type of job or its pay, is more important than providing education and job training (Mead, 1996). "Forcing welfare parents to get even modest jobs can contribute to giving new hope and motivation to their children," notes economist Gary Becker (1996:22). Others, however, stress that without developing skills, it is unlikely that people can earn enough to significantly affect their economic status and enable them to escape the conditions of dependency. As sociologist Christopher Jencks has put it, the essence of the welfare trap is not that it makes people pathologically dependent but that "although welfare pays badly, low-wage jobs pay even worse" (1993:225).

The arguments on either side of this debate hinge on the creation of jobs. Unless there are decent-paying long-term jobs into which those who have been receiving welfare can be placed, the debate about how to get them into the workforce is not meaningful. As noted earlier, this is an issue on which government policymakers can have only a limited impact, since it is within the private sector that the creation of most jobs occurs. In the robust economy of the late 1990s, placing many former welfare recipients in low-level jobs seemed relatively easy because of high labor demand. It was not at all certain, however, whether many of these jobs would survive a severe economic downturn, as occurred in the late 2000s. Even the apparent successes of the welfare reform measure of 1996 remain debatable as to whether they were the result of the policy change per se or simply the result of a favorable economic climate (Blank, 2006; Edelman, 2012). The great test of welfare reform, therefore, will continue to play out as the U.S. economy experiences a longer, deeper recession and the labor market shrinks.

Public Views of Welfare   Welfare for the poor has always been controversial in the United States. Moreover, in a society more thoroughly committed to a laissez-faire style of capitalism, welfare has seemed to be at odds with individualistic values. Given the American ideology's emphasis on self-reliance, those who are able-bodied but who are not employed are seen not as the victims of structural economic and social changes but as individual failures. The same is true of those who find themselves as single mothers. Their plight, in this view, is their own doing, and therefore they do not merit taxpayers' assistance.

To portray Americans as stridently opposed to public welfare of any sort, however, is too simplistic. Rather, it appears that Americans are generally sympathetic to such programs so long as they are designed to aid those who were earlier described as the "deserving poor." It is primarily the willingness to work that, in the public mind, separates the "deserving" from the "nondeserving" poor (Mead, 1992). This is wholly in line with the individualistic American ideology. Welfare programs that encourage people to better themselves (like job training) or provide aid to people who are unable to support themselves (such as day care or medical care for the elderly), therefore, are supported, at least in principle (Cook and Barrett, 1992; McClosky and Zaller, 1984; Page and Jacobs, 2009). It is the negative image of traditional welfare recipients (the "*un*deserving poor") that elicits the strong antiwelfare bias. This image, notes political scientist Martin Gilens, is in large measure driven by mass media portrayals of welfare recipients as irresponsible and disinclined to work even though they appear capable (Gilens, 1999, 2004). Moreover, as Gilens explains, the undeserving character of welfare recipients, in the minds of many white Americans, has come to be associated specifically with African Americans. Historically well-worn racial stereotypes of blacks—as lazy and irresponsible—were first projected by the mass media in the mid-1960s, when many welfare programs were created or expanded. These negative images continue to influence the view of white Americans of the typical beneficiary of welfare.

Although welfare has been the focus of most public policies in attempting to deal with the issues of poverty, alternative strategies have been suggested. One is the expansion of EITC, which reduces taxes for people who work at low wages. This program, in effect since 1975, has been acceptable even to those who take a hard line on welfare since it emphasizes work over cash assistance (Berlin, 2009; Edelman, 2012). Another that has been put forth in recent years is the idea of reestablishing a public works program, similar to the Works Projects Administration (WPA) and the Civilian Conservation Corps (CCC) introduced by President Franklin D. Roosevelt in the 1930s, when almost a quarter of the entire workforce was unemployed. The WPA put people to work building thousands of projects, such as roads, bridges, schools, post offices, and other public facilities. Those who have proposed bringing back something like the WPA contend that such a program would get people out of socially isolated environments, would instill a work ethic, and would possibly give them some occupational skills. At the same time, the entire society would benefit from the improvements such an agency would make on an American infrastructure in serious disrepair (Kaus, 1995; Wilson, 1996). Calls for the establishment of such public works programs have become stronger as the American economy continues to recover from a severe recession and more working families fall into the ranks of the poor.

Poverty in Comparative Perspective

How does the United States stand in comparison with other societies in its rate of poverty and in the level of living of its poor?[6] Using an absolute definition, it is clear that there are fewer poor in the United States than in most other societies. There is a destitute population of homeless people that can be found in almost all large American cities, and the conditions of the underclass are indisputably wretched. But such groups represent only a relatively small proportion of the general population. In short, the percentage of Americans

---

[6]Here it should be reemphasized that comparing class systems, especially particular parts of those systems—such as the poor—is not without problems. Standards of living are not the same from one society to another, and cultural systems dictate different ways of dealing with inequality. Moreover, definitions of poverty may vary from society to society.

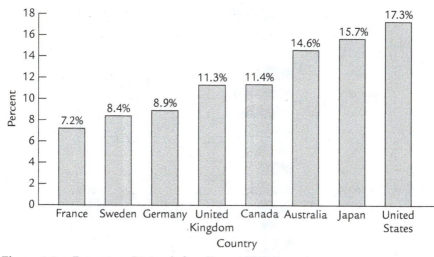

Figure 6-3 ▪ Percentage Living below Poverty Line*
*Because poverty is defined somewhat differently from one society to another, a uniform poverty line for these societies was set at 50 percent of equivalent median disposable household income.
Source: Data taken from Percentage Living below Poverty Line. © OECD, 2011. Reprinted by permission.

who lack sufficient food and shelter to maintain their lives is smaller than that of citizens in much of the rest of the world. Consider the conditions of life in Zambia, for example, a country of 10 million in east central Africa. A widowed mother of five describes her daily plight, waking up each morning not knowing if she will be able to feed herself and her children. In her town's market she sells tomatoes and explains, "If I sell my tomatoes, we will eat today. If I don't, we don't eat" (Jeter, 2002). Her predicament is not atypical, however; eight of every ten of her fellow citizens live on less than $1 a day. Not surprisingly, life expectancy in Zambia is less than forty years.[7]

Defining poverty in a relative fashion, however, gives us a different perspective. Comparing American poverty with poverty in a developing society like Zambia is hardly meaningful in light of the very different social and economic resources of the two countries. As with income, a more valid comparison, therefore, would be the United States with other societies of approximately similar economic and social development, that is, other highly advanced societies. As noted in Chapter 3, the United States today exhibits the most unequal distribution of income and wealth among advanced industrial societies. The rate of American poverty is consistent with that finding. Comparative rates of poverty are shown in Figure 6-3.

---

[7]In the developing world today, about 1.4 billion people (one in four) live in extreme poverty—on less than $1.25 a day. This actually represents a significant reduction of the world's poor since the 1980s, when more than half lived in this condition (World Bank, 2009).

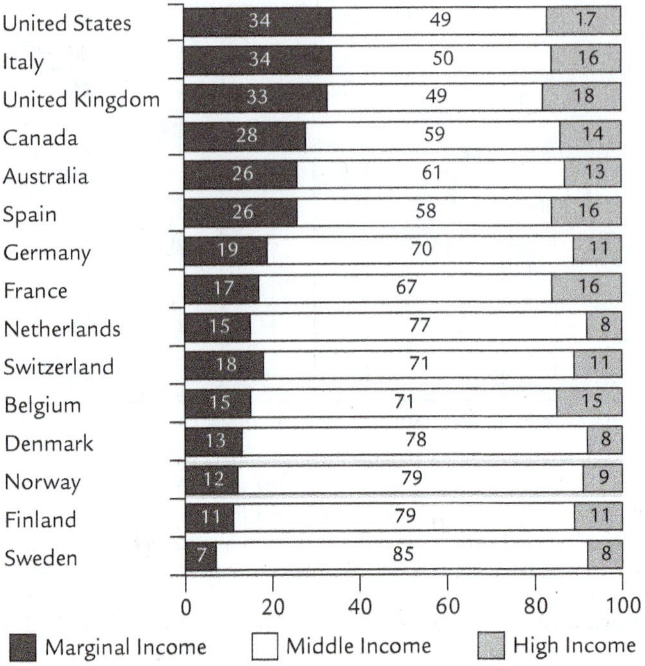

Country	Marginal Income	Middle Income	High Income
United States	34	49	17
Italy	34	50	16
United Kingdom	33	49	18
Canada	28	59	14
Australia	26	61	13
Spain	26	58	16
Germany	19	70	11
France	17	67	16
Netherlands	15	77	8
Switzerland	18	71	11
Belgium	15	71	15
Denmark	13	78	8
Norway	12	79	9
Finland	11	79	11
Sweden	7	85	8

■ Marginal Income   ☐ Middle Income   ■ High Income

Figure 6-4 ■ Marginal-, Middle-, and High-Income Children in Fifteen Countries in the 1990s
Source: "Rainwater, Lee, and Timothy M. Smeeding. 2003." "Marginal-, Middle-, and HighIncome Children in Fifteen Countries in the 1990s," "Figure 2.1 from Poor Kids in a Rich Country: America's Children in Comparative Perspective. New York: Russell Sage Foundation. © 2003 Russell Sage Foundation, 112 East 641h Street, New York, NY 10065. Reprinted with permission."

Not only is the rate of poverty higher than in other advanced industrial societies, but the extent of poverty is more severe. In their study of comparative poverty in fifteen highly developed countries, Lee Rainwater and Timothy Smeeding (2003) showed that, compared to the other societies, a lower percentage of American children lived in middle-income families and a higher percentage lived in low-income families (Figure 6-4). Moreover, among those fifteen societies, the United States, along with Italy, was distinctive in that about 10 percent of the children in the poor category were not just poor but extremely poor. The researchers also found that whether children lived in no-earner, one-earner, or two-earner families, American child poverty rates in each case were considerably higher. For example, the poverty rates for children in families with one earner were 35 percent in the United States, 28 percent in Italy, 19 percent in Canada, and 13 percent in Spain. These findings belie the notion that the poor in the United States are better off than the poor in other countries. While that assumption may be true in comparison with developing societies, it is plainly not the case when the United States is placed beside countries with comparable standards of living.

The approach to solving problems of poverty also is markedly different in most western European countries and Canada from that in the United States. The welfare states of those countries are far more comprehensive and generous and thus provide a much broader and deeper safety net for those who are economically in need. For example, among advanced industrial societies, only the United States has no universal preschool, child-support, or parental-leave programs. This places poor children in the United States at an almost automatic disadvantage in their educational quest and puts onerous burdens on single mothers who must work while raising their families.

Economist Lester Thurow (1999) has explained that for the United States to eradicate poverty would be an accomplishment that most other advanced societies in the world have already achieved. Americans have simply failed to adopt public policies that would lead to a similar outcome.[8] The effects of the low level of public spending on efforts to reduce poverty in the United States compared to spending levels in other advanced industrial societies will be explored again in Chapter 9, where we examine more broadly the impact of public policies on economic inequality.

Comparing the problem of poverty in the United States with that of other industrialized countries is important, for it broadens our perspective and forces us to dismiss assumptions of well-being that are often based more on ideology than on reality. Those assumptions often blind us to the number of poor in our midst and to the severity of their condition. If we ourselves are not among the poor, in many ways we can lose sight of their presence or simply choose to ignore them, going about our daily lives confined to our immediate social environments. Moreover, poverty is more than an economic condition. For the poor it is also a social condition that creates a stigma and a psychological state that erect further barriers separating them from the remainder of the population. Paradoxically, then, only by looking at American poverty in comparison with that in other societies can we begin to more fully perceive and, ultimately, understand its character and dimensions.

Summary

Poverty may be conceptualized in three ways. In absolute terms, it is a condition in which people are unable, for whatever reason, to meet their fundamental human needs. Relative poverty means that poverty is contextual, subject to different standards as societal conditions change. Official poverty is the government-defined measure delineating the poor.

Over 15 percent of the U.S. population falls below the official poverty line. Disproportionately, the American poor are found among racial and

---

[8]Mayer (1995), however, suggests that the American poor may not be worse off compared to the poor of other advanced industrial societies if living conditions, rather than income, are used as a measuring rod.

ethnic minorities, females, young people, and those living as part of female-headed families. The poverty rate has fluctuated over the last four decades, dropping in the late 1960s and early 1970s, climbing in the 1980s with no significant decline until the late 1990s, then climbing again in the 2000s.

The poor may be divided into two relatively distinct components: the working poor and the underclass. The former ordinarily work but do not earn sufficient wages to lift them over the poverty line; the latter are chronically unemployed and socially isolated. Much debate has centered on those who constitute the underclass. Some see them as culturally deficient and, in large measure, victims of their own behavior; others view them as the victims of structural changes in the economy.

Individual-focused and structure-focused theories offer varying explanations of why the poor are poor. Among the former are biological theories, such as social Darwinism, and the culture of poverty. These theories attribute poverty to the actions and values of the poor themselves. Structure-focused theories include the cycle of poverty, the political economy of capitalism, and the functions of poverty. These posit the workings of the economy and other institutions as the sources of poverty.

Measures aimed at alleviating poverty have been standard public policies in all modern societies. There is wide disagreement, however, regarding the strategies for dealing with issues of the poor. In the United States, public assistance programs have traditionally constituted what most people think of as "welfare" for those in poverty. Though never as extensive as popularly believed, most of the major public assistance programs have been radically reformed in recent years, resulting in major cutbacks.

Comparisons with other advanced industrial societies reveal that in the United States the poverty rate is higher and the gap between rich and poor is wider. Other countries also provide a broader and deeper safety net for those who are economically in need.

7

Stratification Systems and Social Mobility

The idea that you get a lifetime supply of food stamps based on coming out of the right womb strikes at my idea of fairness.
WARREN BUFFETT

For years, opinion leaders have told us that it's all about family values. And it is—but it will take a while before most people realize that they meant the value of coming from the right family.
PAUL KRUGMAN

For Americans, to aspire to a higher social position is looked upon as natural and expected. Indeed, striving to improve one's social status is, in American society, recognized as a very positive personal characteristic. It is a basic part of the socialization process, and as a result, most young people believe that they will improve their social standing as they move through their careers. Most of them also believe that they will exceed their parents in acquiring income and wealth.

As common as the belief in and expectation of changing one's social status may be in the United States and other modern societies, it is a relatively recent phenomenon in the longer span of human development. In most societies throughout history, the presumption was that people would stay in the social position into which they were born. To aspire to a higher place not only was seen as unrealistic but was disapproved and perhaps even considered heretical.

This chapter looks at the phenomenon of **social mobility**, that is, the movement of people up and down the society's various hierarchies. How much mobility is there in the United States and similar societies, and what are the factors that promote or repel it? As noted in Chapter 1, although patterns of social inequality are structured and endure for long periods, they are not unchangeable either for individuals or for social groups. The accident of birth is a powerful force in determining people's social standing, but some do overcome economic and social disadvantages to rise in the class system and some born into families of high status may drop despite their relative advantages.

Whatever mobility occurs is dependent on the limitations presented by the society—specifically, the manner in which stratification is arranged. Depending on the society, stratification systems are structured to either impede or facilitate movement from one stratum to another. In some societies, like the United States, Canada, and western Europe, the class system is open and provides opportunities for mobility; in others the stratification system may make mobility rare or limited at best. Before examining the forms and extent of social mobility in American society, we look at different systems of stratification and how they both induce and obstruct movement.

Systems of Stratification

The extent to which people move up or down the society's hierarchies always rests most basically on the opportunities presented by the stratification system. Stratification systems are either rigid, with strata relatively sealed, making it difficult for people to change their status, or porous, providing for free and perhaps even frequent movement between strata.

Closed societies are those where mobility is uncommon and where political and cultural norms and values dictate against it. People are assigned a status at birth, which ordinarily does not change during their lifetime. Individuals may have the ambition and skills to move upward, but they are locked into their hereditarily acquired position. Similarly, people do not move downward regardless of their failures.

In traditional societies, where closed stratification systems prevail, custom rules the social order. People look to the past to solve current problems and do not believe that they are capable of changing their circumstances. They rarely question their status since the prevailing social and religious institutions validate social inequality. The predominant view is that inequality is a product of deities, not humans, and therefore it is not within human capacity to change that system or anyone's place in it. As Philip Mason has described such societies, "Everywhere, the top classes made some kind of alliance with the belief that the world was divinely ordained and persuaded their subjects that it was by divine intention that they must work so hard for so little" (1970:7).

Open societies, by contrast, ideally present few impediments to mobility. People move up and down the class hierarchy on the basis of desire, merit, and talent. This form of stratification typifies the class systems of modern societies. Individuals compete for positions in the social hierarchy and gather resources that enable them to move upward. Downward movement can occur as well, of course, as people fail for lack of skills or because of circumstances over which they may have little control.

Stratification systems, whether open or closed, are never perfectly fluid on the one hand or rigid on the other. Some degree of competition for social positions is always evident, as is some degree of ascription. Thus, the systems of inequality found among different societies are mixed, with both open and closed features. Societies, however, may be much closer to one side or the other of this scale. Let's look at the different types of stratification systems that have characterized human societies.

Slavery

Slavery has been a persistent form of inequality throughout most of recorded human history and even remains in evidence today. Moreover, it has existed in all regions of the world. In some societies, slaves were captured in war; in others, slavery was the result of unpaid debts; and in others, enslavement was a form of punishment for crimes (Patterson, 1982). In the southern United States, Brazil, and the West Indies, Africans were captured and sold into slavery through a thriving slave trade that started in the fifteenth century (Rawley, 1981).

Slavery in the United States   When blacks first entered American society in 1619, their status as servants was not essentially different from that of many others, including some Europeans. Various forms of bondage had been prevalent in all the colonies almost from the founding of the society (Handlin, 1957). Perhaps the most common was voluntary, or indentured, servitude, in which a person was bound by contract to serve a master for a certain length of time, usually four to seven years (Jordan, 1969). In exchange, the servant's passage to the colonies was paid. A great number of people, particularly those from Scotland and Ireland, entered the country in this manner. By the 1660s, however, most southern states had enacted laws defining blacks as slaves rather than as indentured servants.

The evolution of slavery in the United States was primarily a consequence of economic rationality, prompted above all by the demand for cheap labor in the underpopulated colonies. "The use of slaves in southern agriculture," explains historian Kenneth Stampp, "was a deliberate choice (among several alternatives) made by men who sought greater returns than they could obtain from their own labor alone, and who found other types of labor more expensive" (1956:5).

The American brand of slavery operated as a system of paternalistic domination, resembling, in a way, a parent-child relationship between master and slave (Elkins, 1976). The slaves' lives on American plantations were controlled totally by the master, his power legitimized by the slave codes of the various slaveholding states. Slaves lacked almost all legal rights. They could not own property, testify in court, inherit property, hire themselves out, or make contracts. Moreover, slave laws held that marriage between slaves carried none of the legal rights of marriage between free people. As a result, families could be broken up in trade, with no consideration given to keeping husband, wife, and children together. Since slave laws prohibited slaves from learning to read and write, their dependence on their masters was virtually total.

Because slaves represented a significant financial investment, their treatment, though cruel and inhumane in the extreme, would ordinarily not extend to the point of rendering them unable to perform their work. Historians Robert Fogel and Stanley Engerman (1974) explain, for example, that although slave marriages were not legally recognized, masters still encouraged their slaves to marry and establish families in order to ensure an atmosphere of stability. Hence, slave families were kept intact if possible.

During the 1830s, slavery came under serious attack from abolitionists, who argued that blacks should be free to develop their capacities to the fullest. In response, pro-slavery advocates developed a racist belief system that held that fundamental physiological differences existed between blacks and whites, thereby rendering blacks mentally and physically inferior. Also stressed in these new racist theories was the failure of blacks to develop what Westerners considered a "civilized" life in Africa and the dangers of miscegenation, leading to racial degeneracy. After the 1830s, almost all whites of whatever persuasion agreed that blacks were inferior to whites in certain fundamental qualities, especially intelligence and initiative, and that those differences were essentially unchangeable. Because of those presumed differences, subordination of blacks was deemed natural and necessary (Fredrickson, 1971).

In a paternalistic system like American slavery, strict segregation of masters and slaves is not required. Rather, it is the *social* distance between them that is of greatest importance. Everyone knows his or her place in the social arrangement and sticks to it. In the South, to enforce this stratification, a well-understood racial etiquette developed in which physical contact was not uncommon but the social places of whites and blacks were not violated. Social intimacy might often be seen in the form of black women serving as mistresses to white slave masters or of the raising of white children by black "mammies." Such intimate personal contacts in a paternalistic system, however, are always relationships between unequals.

Slavery in the United States ended in 1865, but not long after, a new stratification system emerged that reinstalled the subordinate status of blacks and their economic dependence on whites. The new system, called "Jim Crow," is discussed later in this chapter.

Slavery in Brazil   The slave system in Brazil exceeded U.S. slavery both in numbers and in duration. The Portuguese began importing African slaves into their Brazilian colony as early as the late sixteenth century, after the indigenous population, used as slave laborers, was decimated. Slavery in Brazil was not abolished until 1888, over two decades after it ended in the United States. As in the American system, it was designed to supply an agricultural labor force, mainly for Brazil's sugar plantations, but in its actual administration, Brazilian slavery differed in a number of ways from its American counterpart.

Some have argued that the Brazilian form of slavery was typified by less brutal treatment of slaves. The Brazilian historian Gilberto Freyre maintained that the Anglo-Saxon and Portuguese cultures differed sufficiently to produce divergent patterns of master-slave relations. Freyre held that the Portuguese came to Brazil with a more tolerant attitude toward people of color. Portugal had experienced contact with Africans in its colonial ventures as early as the fifteenth century and had endured a long period of rule by the Moors even earlier. The Portuguese sense of racial difference, therefore, was not as absolute as that of the Anglo-Saxons, who had had little contact with nonwhites. As a result, sexual relations between Portuguese slave masters and their slaves were far more commonplace and socially accepted than in the American system. This, Freyre contended, was evidence of a more compassionate and essentially altruistic master-slave relationship (1956, 1963).

Historian Frank Tannenbaum (1947) argued that the Brazilian slave system was more humane as a result of the difference between the Portuguese and Anglo-Saxon legal and religious concepts of slavery. The Portuguese did not perceive Africans as nonhuman, but simply as unfortunate people who wound up as slaves by an accident of fate. Slavery was understood as a necessary evil and therefore was not defended on the basis of religious or biological notions of racial inferiority and superiority, as in the United States.

Brazilian slaves also retained certain legal rights and were not considered simply chattel. They could own property, marry freely, seek out another master, and even buy their freedom. Thus, there were greater opportunities for manumission (release from slavery) than in the U.S. system. This in itself, Tannenbaum held, was evidence of a milder form of slavery. Also, once slaves were freed, they were afforded full and equal rights in Brazilian society. In the United States, by contrast, even if slaves gained their freedom, they did not acquire full citizenship but continued to suffer the economic, social, and legal handicaps that attached to their racial status.

Although certain differences from the U.S. and Caribbean patterns of slavery are indisputable, later historical accounts of Brazilian slavery have questioned whether it was in fact a more humane system. Humane slave owners may have been the exception, not the rule (Davis, 1966; Graham, 1970). Historian Charles Boxer (1962), for example, has described the brutish and often sadistic cruelty the Portuguese planters used to keep slaves in line. To tie a slave to a cart; flog him; rub his wounds with salt, lemon juice, and urine; and then place him in chains for a number of days was not considered excessive. Runaways were dealt with by branding for the first offense; cutting off an ear for the second; and, usually, death for the third. That such punishments did not prevent slaves from continuing to run away on a large scale would seem to indicate the desperation to which they were driven.

Although slavery in both Brazil and the United States was a tightly closed system of stratification, there was always some movement of people upward into a higher rank, exceptional though such cases may have been. As noted, slaves could occasionally attain freedom (more commonly in Brazil) and thus change their status. The freeing of some slaves has typified slavery in most societies where it has been practiced (Meltzer, 1971).

Slavery in Modern Form   Slavery is not simply a historical peculiarity that has no modern counterpart. Rather, it exists today as a viable system of inequality but in mostly new and unique forms. Estimates range from 21 to

27 million people in the world today who can be accurately described as slaves. Kevin Bales (2012) has researched modern slavery in detail and explains that today's slavery involves not legal ownership, as in systems of the past, but *control* over persons for the purpose of economic exploitation. Whereas slavery in the antebellum U.S. South or Brazil involved a substantial financial investment for the slave owner, today slave labor can be purchased quite cheaply and yields much higher and quicker profits. Moreover, in its modern forms there is no long-term relationship of slave to slave owner, nor is there an obligation of the latter to protect his investment. Although slavery today can be found in virtually all countries, it is most evident in the Indian subcontinent and the Far East (Figure 7-1).

One form of modern-day slavery is the trafficking of people, mainly women and children, for forced labor in the sex industry, as sweatshop workers, and as domestic servants. This is a flourishing international activity carried out mainly by organized crime rings (ILO, 2012). In Asia, impoverished young girls are lured into the sex trade by strangers, kidnapped off the street, or sold by their families to pay off debts. In eastern Europe, women are seduced by promises of legitimate jobs in Germany, Belgium, and the Netherlands but are then forced to work as prostitutes. This trade is prevalent in the United States as well. Thousands of women and children, mostly from Southeast Asia and Latin America but increasingly from eastern Europe as well, are trafficked each year to all regions of the country (ILO, 2012; Miko and Park, 2002).

Reports of slavery in Mauritania and Sudan, poor Arab-dominated countries in Africa, bear a striking resemblance to the older, classic form of slavery. Black Africans are bought and sold as property, to be used by their owners as servants or laborers. In Mauritania, slaves are estimated to number

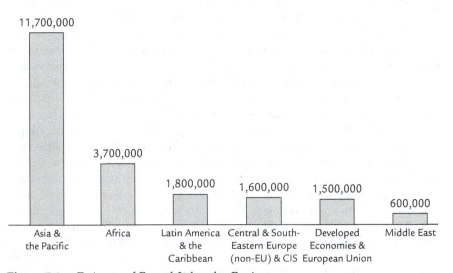

Figure 7-1 ▪ Estimate of Forced Labor, by Region
Source: Copyright © International Labour Organization 2012.

in the tens of thousands in a country whose population is between 2 and 3 million. Although slavery has been technically abolished several times, no legal framework has been established to actually put an end to the practice. Moreover, in underdeveloped societies, secular law often takes second place to custom, which in the case of Mauritania has upheld the property rights of slaveholders (Bales, 2012; Finnegan, 2000; Jacobs and Athie, 1994).

Debt bondage is another modern-day form of slavery. Here, laborers may be lured by promises of good-paying jobs, only later to find themselves in wretched work conditions, entrapped by debts imposed by the employer that can never be paid off. Bales studied the production of charcoal in the interior of Brazil and returned with a gruesome picture of an industry thoroughly dependent on workers enslaved in debt bondage for months or years. Men, desperate for work, are recruited from the slums of cities and towns of the state of Minas Gerais. Driven deep into the *cerrado*, or rain forest, they are dumped into camps, their work papers are confiscated—thereby denying them any legal protection—and they are forced to load and then unload wood packed into charcoal ovens. Bales was able to observe a charcoal camp and recounted the grim scene he witnessed:

> All the charcoal workers cough constantly, hacking and spitting and trying to clear lungs that are always full of smoke, ash, heat, and charcoal dust. If they live long enough most will suffer from black lung disease. . . . For the workers who have to climb inside the still-burning ovens to empty charcoal the heat is unimaginable. . . . The workers hover on the edge of heatstroke and dehydration. Sometimes in their conversation they were confused as if their brains had been baked. The workers who empty the ovens stay almost naked, but this exposes their skin to burns. Sometimes standing on the piles of charcoals they will stumble or the charcoals will give way and they will fall into red-hot coals. All of the charcoal workers I met had hands, arms, and legs crisscrossed with ugly burn scars, some still swollen and festering. (1999:130–131)

The camps are so isolated that there is no escape. As Bales depicts it, "Since no police ever come out here, and the workers' families have no idea where they are, it is easy to see how a troublesome worker can just be killed and dumped in the forest" (134).

Other instances of debt peonage may have long historical roots as, for example, the plight of brick makers in Pakistan or agricultural slaves in India. There the bondage of entire families is not short-term, as in the Brazilian charcoal industry, but may be lifelong, with debts passed on to children. These systems involve millions of persons.

Unlike past forms of slavery, these modern-day examples are not legitimized. To hold people against their will to be used as laborers or prostitutes is today universally recognized as morally reprehensible. The slave trade, therefore, is always conducted surreptitiously. Even in Mauritania and Sudan, where slavery takes on features of the past, it is officially denied. Slavery in the Americas, by contrast, was rationalized, justified, and socially approved.

Much of slavery in its modern forms is integrally related to the global economy. The overarching objective of transnational corporations, as we saw in Chapter 5, is to lower their cost of production and, in the process, maximize their return on investment. This impels them to move across borders as they seek out cheaper labor. This, in turn, often leads them to employ subcontractors, some of whom use slave workers, thereby reducing labor costs to the utmost. Ultimately, then, investors and consumers in the wealthy, developed countries (like the United States) may unwittingly support slavery while earning handsome dividends on their corporate investments or enjoying the privilege of purchasing goods more cheaply than they otherwise would be able to do.

Modern slavery is abetted as well by corrupt governments. To sustain all forms of slavery requires violence, or its threat, in some degree. As Bales explains, "For slaveholders to use violence freely, the enforcement of law must be perverted and its protection denied to slaves" (1999:245). This requires that government officials, in their approach to slavery, either look the other way or become part of the trade themselves. Even governments that are not directly involved in sustaining slavery—and may even loudly denounce it—do not employ effective tools to end it.

Caste

Caste is the purest type of social stratification in which mobility is severely constrained. The term **caste** has been commonly used to describe any system in which the different strata are rigidly fixed. The caste system of India is the most noted example, but the pre-1960s segregated American South and the apartheid system of South Africa are also instances of caste. In the Indian case, strata are divided not by physical distinctions between groups but by people's social descent (Béteille, 1969). As it is used in non-Indian settings, the idea of caste more generally refers to "a major dichotomous division in society between pariahs and the rest of the members of the society" (Berreman, 1966:292). Pariahs are those who are stigmatized on the basis of some physical or cultural characteristic.

All caste systems display certain common features. Perhaps the most basic is the hereditary nature of a person's position in the social hierarchy. Membership in a caste is inherited and thus fixed for life; the individual is unable to change his or her social position through achievement. Second, castes are endogamous, with marriage restricted to other members of the caste. Segregation between castes in various areas of social life is also evident, particularly as it pertains to residence and other forms of social intercourse. Finally, a caste system of inequality is ordinarily based on either civil or religious law.

Caste in India   Caste has prevailed in India for centuries, well predating the Christian era (Kolenda, 1985). Members of each caste are guided in their social lives by a set of regulations that pertain to marriage, work, recreation, and most other social spheres. Each caste is assigned different rights and obligations, and the system is undergirded by a rigid set of rules governing social interaction, based on the Hindu principle of purity-impurity. The lower castes are considered unclean, and higher castes avoid physical contact with them (Lannoy, 1971).

The ancient classification of the Indian caste system consisted of a structure of four *varnas* (or castes), each occupying a specialized occupational role: *Brahmans* (priests), *Kshatriya* (princes), *Vaishya* (merchants), and *Shudra* (ordinary people). All of those not part of the castes were considered polluted outsiders, referred to as "untouchables." The top three *varnas* were the privileged, and it was from among them that those with education and political and economic power came. These were referred to as the "twice-born" (Leach, 1967). *Shudras* comprised a peasantry whose members could not hope to better their position. Untouchables (*Harijans*), outside the *varna* system, performed jobs that were deemed unclean in Hindu principles, such as collecting garbage and working with leather. The four traditional *varnas* were actually overlaid by virtually thousands of distinct subcastes (*jatis*) in different regions and communities (Mayer, 1955).

The stability of this extreme system of inequality stems from the idea of reincarnation. The most essential moral duty is to accept one's place and fulfill one's tasks according to caste principles. The rewards for virtue come in the next life. With the idea of reincarnation, one's place in the current caste system reflects one's past life. To have been born an untouchable signifies a more sinful previous life than to have been born a *Brahman* (Kolenda, 1985).

Although traditional caste in India appears to be an extremely closed stratification system, its inflexibility is an ideal picture and cannot be taken literally. Some mobility and social change in the system have always been evident (Rudolph and Rudolph, 1967). Moreover, entire castes might raise their collective position in the hierarchy over several generations through control of power or land and the purification of ritual symbols (Sinha, 1967).

Today, caste in India has been officially repudiated and with industrialization is giving way to a more class-based system of stratification. Barriers to mobility for the untouchables (who sometimes refer to themselves as *Dalit*, meaning "oppressed") have been eliminated, and government measures have been put in place to help improve their occupational and educational status. It is now possible, therefore, to attain different economic and political positions despite one's birth into a particular caste (Béteille, 1996; Sengupta, 2008).

It is foolish, however, to think that a stratification scheme in operation for several thousand years could be eliminated so quickly and easily. Caste remains in evidence in rural and traditional parts of the country and, in subtle ways, even in urban areas. The specialization of occupations by caste has declined, but caste still sets limits on occupational choice (Béteille, 1996; Deliège, 1999). In 1999, after a devastating cyclone struck eastern India, hundreds of thousands of animal carcasses were left rotting. Since handling the dead is considered one of the most demeaning tasks in the traditional Hindu caste system, not even poor people could be induced to gather and dispose of them. As a result, government officials had to fly in several hundred scavengers of the sweeper caste from New Delhi to do the job (*Globe and Mail*, 1999). Moreover, political factions may form around caste on particular issues (Béteille, 2012; Patel, 2012). And caste attitudes continue to influence people's views of each other, thus affecting to some degree the distribution of life chances.

Caste in South Africa   Another illustration of caste is the former apartheid system of South Africa. In no other modern multiethnic society has stratification been so clear-cut, and in no other so fixed and rigidly enforced. As recently as twenty years ago, the boundaries between strata were, by law, relatively impermeable.

The South African system of inequality was essentially "whites at the top and nonwhites at the bottom." More accurately, however, the society was divided into four officially designated categories, based on perceptions of racial difference: whites, Coloreds, Asians (mostly Indians), and Africans. The allocation of justice, health care, jobs, education, living quarters, and so on, all depended, to some degree, on one's racial classification. Whites received the bulk of the society's resources; Africans, the least. The distance between the whites and the other three racial categories was so great, however, that the hierarchy was in effect a dichotomy—whites over nonwhites.

The South African caste system, called **apartheid,** was maintained by an elaborate arrangement of law and custom ensuring white dominance. Apartheid provided specific legislation mandating the social separation of the racial groups, the maintenance of separate social institutions for each, and, as it was envisioned, the eventual formal division of South Africa into separate and independent white and black nations. Indeed, so blatant and uncompromising was the South African system that the very term *apartheid* has, in recent times, come to be applied commonly outside the South African context, signifying any rigid and durable aspect of ethnic separation and inequality.

Under apartheid, each person in South Africa was classified by race and placed into one of the four official racial categories. Africans, Asians, and Coloreds were required to carry passbooks, identifying them by their official classification. Physical contact between nonwhites and whites was minimized through a system of petty apartheid, consisting of dozens of laws and mandates created to maintain racial separation in almost every conceivable area of social relations (van den Berghe, 1967, 1978).

As in other caste systems, the extreme inequality of apartheid was legitimized by an ideology that claimed the superiority of the dominant caste. South African whites, particularly Afrikaners (those whose ancestors had been among the first European settlers), believed themselves to be natural overseers of primitive Africans. The view that it was necessary to maintain white rule, based on the understood cultural superiority of whites, was thoroughly incorporated into all institutions.

The apartheid system was dismantled starting in the 1980s and was officially abolished in 1994. Blacks voted in a national election for the first time in 1994 and elected a black-dominated government led by Nelson

Mandela, the most revered leader of the anti-apartheid movement, who had been imprisoned for twenty-six years. The end product of the radical changes that have occurred in South Africa as part of the abolition of the racially based caste system is still uncertain. Though the official system of racial inequality has been abandoned and blacks now dominate the political system, the major components of white economic domination remain in place (Leibbrandt et al., 2010). Moreover, in residence and social interaction, the society remains strongly segregated along racial lines (Durrheim and Dixon, 2010; Vincent 2008). The key issues of South Africa's immediate future, therefore, concern the manner in which the tremendous economic and social gaps separating whites and blacks will be reduced.

Caste in the United States   Not long after the American slave system was abolished, a system of white control reemerged in the southern states. The system was called **Jim Crow,** and it essentially consisted of a set of relations between blacks and whites that constituted a caste-like form of stratification. Although blacks were no longer held in slavery, their dependence on their former slave masters was reestablished by the denial of their voting rights and by the adoption of the sharecropping system.

Unlike slavery, the Jim Crow system called for the segregation of blacks and whites in almost all areas of social life: housing, work, education, health care, transportation, leisure, and religion. Most important, this social segregation was based in law. Although the presumption was that facilities for the two races would be equal, in fact they were inherently unequal; those reserved for blacks were grossly inferior or inadequate, usually by design (Woodward, 1974).

In addition to physical separation, there was the need for a system of racial etiquette, for blacks and whites obviously could not be totally isolated from each other. The etiquette was intended to make clear the caste positions of dominant and subordinate groups. Whites could not shake hands with blacks, for example, nor would blacks be addressed as "mister" but rather as "boy" or by the person's first name. And most important, racial endogamy was strictly enforced. Indeed, the prohibition of interracial marriage was one of the first formal measures enacted by southern states in the formation of the Jim Crow system.

The racial caste system was abetted by a racist ideology. Popular ideas of racial superiority and inferiority were given additional credence by scientific thought of the time. That blacks were innately inferior to whites was, as noted earlier, a belief that most people did not question (Fredrickson, 1971).

Some sociologists have equated the color bar between whites and blacks in the Jim Crow era with aspects of the Indian caste system. Berreman (1961), for example, points out that in both situations caste membership was inherited and membership was unalterable. Those of the lowest caste were deemed inferior and relegated to the least desirable occupational positions. Moreover, as in the Indian system, rigorous rules of avoidance between castes existed, and certain types of contact were defined as contaminating.

The similarities of the Jim Crow system to South African apartheid, however, seem even more compelling.

Caste in Japan   An interesting case of caste exists in Japan, where those called Burakumin experience extreme discrimination based on beliefs that portray them as a separate race. Although the Burakumin are physically indistinguishable from the rest of the population, a commonly shared social myth claims they "are descendants of a less human 'race' than the stock that fathered the Japanese nation as a whole" (De Vos and Wagatsuma, 1966:xx). The Burakumin are considered mentally inferior, basically immoral, and unclean.

In the past, Burakumin were required to wear unique identifying garb, were strictly segregated residentially, and were limited to low-status occupations (Aoyagi and Dore, 1964). Although today they are not as stigmatized as in the past, their social and economic standing remains low (Lie, 2001; Onishi, 2009; Saito and Farkas, 2004; UNESCO, 2006). Legal measures have been enacted to discourage discrimination against the Burakumin and affirmative action policies have been in effect for several decades. Nonetheless their outcast status remains evident. Although intermarriage has become more common, many Japanese still take care to avoid marriage with a Buraku individual. A family may research in great depth the background of a potential mate to assure that there is no trace of Burakumin ancestry.

Estate

Another closed type of stratification is feudalism, sometimes referred to as the **estate system.** Although feudalism typified European societies in the Middle Ages prior to the ascendancy of capitalism in the eighteenth century, it has also existed in other areas of the world, including Asia and Latin America. Indeed, most agrarian societies have experienced some form of feudalism. This is a system of stratification that is linked closely to land and is therefore more typical of agriculturally based societies. The owners of land, the most critical economic resource in such societies, are the dominant stratum, or "estate."

In the European system, the nobility were referred to as "lords," and although they constituted only a tiny portion of the population, they controlled not only most of the society's productive land but other resources, including, of greatest importance, an army. A peasantry, or "serfs," who were thoroughly dependent on the landowners for their livelihood, made up the bulk of the society's population. The lord offered protection to serfs in return for their labor and for a portion of what they produced on his land. As in a caste system, marriage was usually endogamous among those in the same social position. Moreover, people could not remove themselves from their assigned position without violating mutually understood rights and duties. The inequalities inherent in this system were based essentially on custom, but as the many feudal states began to consolidate, legal justifications became more important.

The nobility, though clearly the most privileged and powerful stratum, was in itself varied on the basis of land and wealth. Most often, the noble was a vassal, who held his land as a grant from the king or from another noble in return for military service or other obligations. Gradually, however, nobles began to assume their position as a hereditary right (Mayer, 1955).

At the bottom of the feudal hierarchy, serfs, or peasants, worked the land and served as soldiers when needed. In all cases, serfs were obligated to pay a substantial portion (not uncommonly as much as half) of what they produced to those who owned the land. In almost all agrarian societies, living conditions for the peasantry were extremely primitive, "at, or close to, the subsistence level" (Lenski, 1966:271). The serfs were not slaves, but as Robert Heilbroner has described them, they were in many respects "as much the property of the lord as were his (or their) houses, flocks, or crops" (1993:28).[1]

As with other systems of stratification, an ideology explained and justified the feudal system. The Catholic Church, which endorsed social inequality and deemed it divinely ordained, supplied the ideology in this case. The church's role gave rise to a third major estate, the clergy or priestly class. Like the nobility, it enjoyed opportunities to accumulate wealth, especially in the form of land. The clergy was internally stratified, however, with those at the top of the clerical order constituting a kind of nobility in its own right (Mayer, 1955). The priestly class was important to rulers because, as religious leaders, priests were able to confer legitimacy on a system that generated such enormous inequalities. Since no ruling group was able to rule by force alone, the priestly class served to induce acceptance of the regime among those who least benefited by its actions (Lenski, 1966).

The stratification system of agrarian societies was made up of more than simply nobility, clergy, and peasants, however.[2] A governing class, the small number who shared the responsibilities of government, also enjoyed the right to share in the economic surplus that the peasant masses and the urban artisans produced. A retainer class, made up of officials, professional soldiers, household servants, and others who were basically in service to the ruler and governing class, served as a kind of mediator between the top stratum and the common people. A merchant class, though low-ranking on the social hierarchy, nonetheless often managed to acquire a significant portion of the society's wealth. Small populations fell even below the peasantry in social status. These included artisans, usually working for the merchant class; unclean or pariah classes; and those who were expendable, such as petty criminals, beggars, and prostitutes. Figure 7-2 shows the relationship among strata in agrarian societies.

As with caste systems, feudal or estate systems dictate that people do not move from their ascribed position in the social hierarchy. Lenski (1966), however, has suggested that mobility in agrarian societies was not as uncommon as is usually believed. Downward mobility was far more common than upward mobility, though, due to the surplus of manpower. More

---

[1]Despite their commonly servile conditions, there were differences among the peasantry of medieval Europe, with some enjoying greater privileges than others (Bennett, 1969).
[2]The following description is based on Lenski (1966).

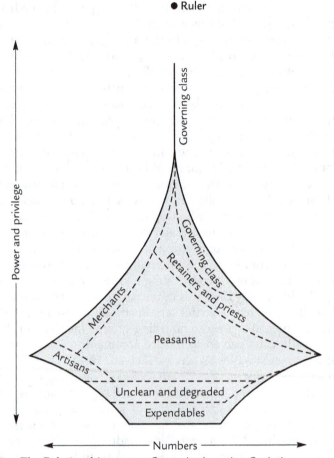

Figure 7-2 ■ The Relationship among Strata in Agrarian Societies
Source: From *Power and Privilege: A Theory of Social Stratification* by Gerhard Emmanuel Lenski, Jr.
Copyright © 1984 by the University of North Carolina Press. Used by permission of the publisher.

offspring were produced, in all stratification groups, than available positions existed for them. But even upward mobility was, if not commonplace, certainly possible. For example, an ambitious and talented serf might rise to a position in the clergy, or a warrior might attain a position of nobility. In addition, serfs in medieval Europe who escaped and evaded capture for more than a year could be declared "free." Sometimes people filled new positions, as in the rising merchant class, as trade and commerce expanded. More frequent, however, were cases in which positions were vacated by the death of men who left no heirs or where people vacated their positions because they lacked the skills needed to hold them.

The merchant class, or bourgeoisie, increasingly assumed a greater importance in the economies of medieval societies, and as their influence grew, they were recognized as a major estate, beside the nobility and the clergy.

With urbanization and the expansion of trade and commerce, the interests of the bourgeoisie came into conflict with those of the landed nobility. The die was cast for the emergence of capitalism and the end of feudalism in Europe.

Class Systems

By comparison with other forms of structured social inequality, class systems are the most open, affording individuals opportunities to earn their social place rather than having it assigned at birth. Class systems emerged in Europe with industrialization, beginning in the eighteenth century. A more fluid form of stratification was required by the new industrial system of production, which called for a mobile workforce. With skills needed in a variety of occupations, social placement could no longer be left primarily to ascription.

Class systems characterize most societies of the modern world. People are not formally blocked from rising in social class, nor are they guaranteed that they will not drop from a high social standing. An individual born into a poor or working-class family can, with talent, ambition, and luck, rise in the class hierarchy, just as upper- or upper-middle-class individuals may lose their wealth and status and drop to a lower rank. Laws or customs do not preclude such movement in either case. The divisions between classes, then, are quite permeable, with no one permanently locked into a social position. Indeed, most people expect upward mobility and are encouraged to do better than their predecessors. Consider how American society judges those who do not maintain or exceed the status of their parents—such persons are seen, to some degree, as failures.

The description of stratification systems as open or closed should not be taken literally. As discussed earlier, no system, even caste in India, ever completely constrains mobility on the one hand or provides unhindered mobility on the other. In all cases, there are at least some opportunities for changing one's status. And similarly, in class systems where mobility is theoretically unhindered, in fact people are not completely free to move up or down. Where people ultimately end up in the class system is never simply a product of their individual achievement but is very much a function of the accident of birth.

Descriptions of societies as open or closed merely point out the most egregious differences among them. What is unmistakable, however, is that modern industrial societies are more open than developing or traditional societies, where agrarianism still predominates. In the latter, the clash between open and closed systems is often starkly evident. As these societies industrialize and urbanize, there is a push toward social placement by achievement; at the same time, traditional forces remain strong, and people's occupational and social status is therefore determined to some extent by their family of birth.

Patterns of Social Mobility in Modern Societies

With industrialization, a large proportion of the population of a society finds itself in occupations that are different from those of their parents. "These changes in the distribution of occupations from generation to generation," write sociologists Seymour Martin Lipset and Reinhard Bendix, "mean that no industrial society can be viewed as closed or static" (1959:11).

Measurements of Mobility

Although social mobility seems to be a constant feature of industrial societies, its dimensions (how much, in which direction, and so on) may differ both within and between societies.

Generation   Social mobility may be observed and measured either from one generation to another or within one's own lifetime. In the first form, **intergenerational mobility,** a person's class position is compared to his or her parents' position. A son, for example, may be a middle-level manager, whereas his father had been an unskilled factory worker. This indicates upward mobility for the son, occupying, as he does, a higher occupational position than his father.

The second form is **intragenerational mobility,** in which a person's movement is observed and measured during his or her lifetime. A woman, for example, begins her working career as a hamburger flipper at a fast-food restaurant, and by age forty, she owns several fast-food franchises. She has experienced upward mobility, then, as measured by her markedly improved socioeconomic status.

Direction   The movement of people up or down the class hierarchy is **vertical mobility.** Although this needs little explanation, remember that not all mobility is upward in direction. So focused are we on upward mobility and so common is it assumed to be in American society, we sometimes forget that in class systems it is possible for people to lose their socioeconomic status and move downward. During the Great Depression of the 1930s, for example, many people did just that, suffering not only economic losses but psychological deprivation as well. This was an experience that would forever frame their social perspectives. Anthropologist Katherine Newman (1993) describes this generation:

> As the depression passed from view, to be replaced by the war and the good times that followed, it never faded from the consciousness of the generation that lived through it. It remained their leitmotif and continues to be the central, defining experience of their lives. (63)

As noted in Chapter 5, during the last two decades, many within the working and middle classes have experienced downward mobility as industries have internationalized and downsized their workforces and as the society has experienced its worst economic recession since the 1930s. Lillian Rubin (1994) relates the experience of downward mobility of one working-class family in which the husband had been laid off:

> [My husband] was out of work so long that even he finally got it that he didn't have a choice. So he took this job as a dishwasher in this

restaurant. It's one of those new kind of places with an open kitchen, so there he was, standing there washing dishes in front of everybody. I mean, we used to go there to eat sometimes, and now he's washing the dishes and the whole town sees him doing it. He felt so ashamed, like it was such a comedown, that he'd come home even worse than when he wasn't working. (219)

Horizontal, or **lateral, mobility** is movement sideways, involving a change of position that, in terms of socioeconomic status, is neither better nor worse than the previous position. A person might move, for example, from one company to another, maintaining the same occupational position. Corporate managers often engage in this kind of lateral movement, looking for new challenges or for a more compatible work environment. Or a person might change occupations resulting in little or no difference in socioeconomic status. A lawyer, for example, might become a corporate manager; an electrician, a plumber; or a teacher, an educational consultant. None of these occupational switches entails much change in income, prestige, or power.

Mobility Trends

On the basis of empirical studies conducted by sociologists over the last five decades, several observations can be made regarding individual mobility trends in the United States and other contemporary societies.

The Rate of Mobility First, as earlier noted, upward mobility becomes more common as societies industrialize. A number of factors seem to account for this. Education becomes more accessible to greater numbers of people. As this occurs, more people acquire the qualifications to enter higher-status jobs. Job qualifications have also been standardized, and this, in combination with greater accessibility to education, has made it possible for people to rise despite the handicaps of birth into a less-well-to-do family. Most important, however, are the greater opportunities brought about by structural changes that occur with the movement from agrarianism to industrialism. Shifts in the occupational structure create more well-paying and high-skilled jobs and eliminate more low-level jobs.

Sociologists Peter Blau and Otis Dudley Duncan, in one of the most comprehensive studies of mobility ever conducted in the United States (1967), showed that mobility is in fact quite common in American society. They found that from one-third to one-half of all people achieve an occupational status at least one level higher than that of their fathers. Blau and Duncan's findings were subsequently confirmed by other studies in the United States as well as in other industrialized countries (Hauser et al., 1975; Lipset and Bendix, 1959; McClendon, 1977; Grusky and Hauser, 1984; Slomczyński and Krauze, 1987). It is important to remember, however, that even though these studies confirm much mobility, they indicate that more than half the population does *not* experience upward mobility. Most people, then, do not change their place on the class hierarchy throughout their lifetime, and some may even experience downward mobility.

Table 7-1 ■ Intergenerational Income Mobility

Parent's Quintile	Children's Quintile				
	Poorest	Second	Middle	Fourth	Richest
Poorest	42	23	19	11	6
Second	25	23	24	18	10
Middle	17	24	23	17	19
Fourth	8	15	19	32	26
Richest	9	15	14	23	39

Source: From Getting Ahead or Losing Ground: Economic Mobility in America. 2008 by Julia B. Isaacs et al. Reprinted by permission of the Brookings Institution.

This basic finding has been confirmed by many studies (Gottschalk and Danziger, 1998; Hertz, 2006; Isaacs et al., 2008; Nasar, 1992; Thurow, 1999).

Tables 7-1 and 7-2 show patterns of intergenerational mobility in the United States, measured by both income and wealth. In Table 7-1 we can see the probability of children reaching an income ranking higher than that of their parents. For example, 42 percent of children born into families of the bottom income quintile remained there as adults, 23 percent entered the second income quintile, 19 percent the third, and so on. At the other end of the class hierarchy, 39 percent of those born into the richest 20 percent of families ended up there in adulthood. Obviously, in terms of income, although some do experience broad leaps in class position from their parents, most remain within or near their class of origin.

A similar persistence from one generation to the next is evident when looking at wealth. As we saw in Chapter 3, wealth, as distinguished from income, is extremely important in establishing and maintaining one's class position. Table 7-2 shows that, like income, children's wealth is strongly correlated with their parents' wealth. Although there is a good deal of movement, 45 percent born into low-wealth families (the poorest wealth quintile) end up in the same position in adulthood, just as 55 percent of those born

Table 7-2 ■ Intergenerational Wealth Mobility*

Childhood Quintile	Adult Quintile				
	Poorest	Second	Middle	Fourth	Richest
Poorest	45	27	11	9	8
Second	24	35	20	14	7
Middle	11	20	35	21	13
Fourth	7	11	23	33	25
Richest	5	6	9	25	55

*1979–2000.
Source: Keister, 2005.

into high-wealth families (the richest quintile) do. And, for those who do move, mobility is short-range. Moreover, the parental influence on wealth accumulation of children is long-lasting, extending for four or five generations (Isaacs et al., 2008). Not surprisingly, income and wealth mobility are strongly related. It is parents' income more than any other factor that explains the persistence of wealth across generations (Charles and Hurst, 2003).

Mobility may also be measured in terms of occupation. Do children tend to work in jobs that are similar to those of their parents in prestige, skill, and pay? Emily Beller and Michael Hout grouped men in a rank order of six general occupational categories (Table 7-3) and found that, as with income and wealth, most men stay in or near the class where they began.

Direction of Mobility   A second conclusion that can be made about mobility in the United States and other comparable societies regards direction: Clearly, most social mobility is upward. One of the reasons for this is, again, the provision of higher levels of education to more and more people. But structural factors are of even greater significance. More skilled jobs have been created at the same time that jobs requiring fewer skills have declined. The most significant increases in the occupational system over the last several decades have occurred in the professional-managerial categories—doctors and other medical personnel, lawyers, engineers, teachers, and managers. At the same time, unskilled blue-collar jobs—factory production workers, for example—are gradually being phased out. Each generation has thus

Table 7-3 ■ Intergenerational Occupational Mobility*

Father's Occupation	Son's Occupation					
	Upper pro'al	Lower pro'al and clerical	Self-employed	Technical and skilled	Farm sector	Unskilled and service
Upper professional	42	24	7	12	0	15
Lower professional and clerical	29	27	7	17	0	20
Self-employed	29	18	16	19	0	18
Technical and skilled	17	19	6	30	1	26
Farm sector	14	11	8	17	13	37
Unskilled and service	16	17	6	22	1	38

*Men born between 1950 and 1979.

Source: "From The Future of Children, a collaboration of the Woodrow Wilson School of Public and International Affairs at Princeton University and the Brookings Institution."

entered a labor market in which there are more high-status jobs than there were when the previous generation entered.

Trends of the last three decades, however, indicate that the traditional optimism regarding upward mobility in American society may be illusory. Recall the "middle-class squeeze" discussed in Chapter 5. We only need to reiterate that this pattern reflects increasing downward mobility for many Americans. Some occupying what seemed to be secure places in the middle classes have, in recent years, found themselves struggling to keep pace, let alone move upward. An extensive analysis of mobility in the United States concludes that for the most recent generations, that is, those born after 1970, "economic growth has had less impact on the average family and absolute mobility has declined" (Isaacs et al., 2008:8).

Range of Mobility   When upward mobility does occur, the distance most people move is only marginal. This means that intergenerational mobility involves movement incrementally, that is, in short steps (Blau and Duncan, 1967; Gottschalk, 1997). Broad leaps from one class to another are not common. Moving from the working class into the lower-middle class is more typical than movement from the working class into the upper class or even the upper-middle class. The rags-to-riches cases about which we so often hear are relatively rare; thus, the Horatio Alger notion remains more a myth than a reflection of reality. Certainly, some do experience spectacular leaps in mobility, moving from poverty into the ranks of the truly wealthy. But such cases are exceptional and do not represent the span of mobility for most people.

Also, in general, the lowest levels of mobility are found in the highest and lowest classes, whereas the highest levels of mobility are found in the middle classes. In a sense, the rich stay rich and the poor stay poor while most mobility occurs within the middle, or intermediate, classes. Moreover, as noted earlier, the tendency for the poor to stay poor and the affluent to stay affluent appears to have become stronger in the last two decades (Duncan et al., 1996; Mazumder, 2005; Mishel et al., 2009, 2012; Pew Charitable Trusts, 2012).

Comparative Mobility   Is there greater mobility in the United States than in other comparable societies? The simple answer is "no." In fact, studies find that the United States is a relatively low-mobility country (Alderson and Nielsen, 2002; Beller and Hout, 2006; Corak, 2006, 2009; Corcoran, 2001; d'Addio, 2007; Ferrie, 2005; Hertz, 2006; Jäntti et al., 2006; Smeeding, 1998, 2005). That is, the likelihood of parents passing their class position on to their children is higher than in Canada and most western European societies. This is shown in Figure 7-3. Moreover, these studies find that those starting at the bottom of the income hierarchy in the United States have more difficulty in moving upward than low-income starters in other rich nations. This, of course, belies the often held assumption of Americans that there are greater opportunities for and fewer impediments to upward movement in the United States

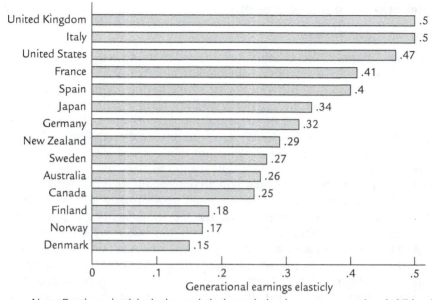

Note: Earnings elasticity is the statistical correlation between parents' and children's economic status. The higher the generational elasticity, the lower the rate of mobility

Figure 7-3 ■ Mobility among Rich Countries
Source: Miles Corak (2013), "Inequality from Generation to Generation: The United States in Comparison," in Robert Rycroft (editor), The Economics of Inequality, Poverty, and Discrimination in the 21st Century, ABC-CLIO. Reproduced by permission.

than in other countries. It also refutes popular beliefs about the commonality of rags-to-riches cases. What is abundantly clear is that such cases are highly exceptional.

Mobility in Historical Perspective

In studying mobility, we need to carefully consider how the parameters of social classes and occupations change over time. For example, the conceptualization of the "rich" in American society may be quite different today from what it was forty or fifty years ago. In the 1950s, having a million dollars was the defining mark of great wealth; today, as mentioned in Chapter 4, millionaires number in the hundreds of thousands. Being rich has changed meaning. The same changing standards apply to occupational titles. Being a sales clerk or a mechanic, for example, carried greater prestige in past times than it does today. Even the extremely high status of doctors may be undergoing change as they increasingly become paid employees of health care companies or practice as part of HMOs rather than independently (Lau and Ferguson, 1998).

Furthermore, class lines themselves may blur over time. Chapter 5 noted the hazy distinction, for example, between those who constitute the lower-middle class and those who are part of the upper levels of the working class.

Determinants of Social Mobility

Structural Mobility

Although Americans like to think that upward mobility is the result primarily of people's individual efforts—their talent, ambition, and perseverance—in fact, most mobility is the result of structural factors, namely, changes in the society's labor force and economy and innovations in technology.

The most critical aspect of structural mobility involves changes in the number and types of occupations relative to the number and qualifications of workers available to fill them. We might think of this as the **opportunity structure.** For individuals to move upward in the class system necessitates the presence of opportunities that will accommodate such movement. This means that the opportunity structure must provide new jobs into which people can move. At different times, the labor market has expanded or contracted, thereby affecting the rate, extent, and frequency of mobility.

As societies have industrialized, greater opportunities for improved occupational status have arisen naturally. The technological changes that came with industrialization created new occupations, many of them calling for a labor force more skilled than was needed in an agrarian economy. These were jobs, therefore, not available to previous generations. Also, as jobs requiring more skills emerged, increased educational opportunities were made available to more people. This further stimulated upward mobility. At the same time, some elements of the labor market suffered job losses as a result of industrialization. New techniques for growing crops and the mechanization of farm implements, for example, reduced the need for farmworkers. Technological changes, then, rendered a dual effect, both closing and opening new occupational opportunities.

A similar process appears to be occurring today as computer technology ushers in the "information society." Dozens of new job categories related to computers and satellite industries have developed as computers play an increasingly basic role in the production and distribution of goods and services. At the same time, of course, computers have displaced many workers from their traditional jobs.

Only if and when opportunities present themselves can people move into jobs that represent an improvement in their socioeconomic status. As mentioned in Chapter 5, during the two decades following World War II, for example, the American economy expanded enormously, creating millions of jobs that enabled people to move into the middle classes. By contrast, during the Great Depression of the 1930s, the labor market contracted and millions of jobs were eliminated, driving people downward. In a similar way, in the last two decades, especially during the severe economic recession of the late 2000s, many companies have cut their workforces or outsourced jobs, causing a shrinkage in certain segments of the labor market.

Another factor that may affect the opportunity structure is immigration. Currently and in the past, a large proportion of immigrants to the United States and other industrialized countries have been unskilled workers. The effect of such a population inflow is to push native workers upward into higher-status jobs as immigrants fill low-status jobs. In the short term, however, workers in low-status jobs may be displaced by immigrants prepared to work for lower wages.

Individual Mobility

Knowing that changes in the society's economy and other structural forces create the opportunities (or lack of opportunities) for people to change their class position does not tell us which individuals are more likely to actually make the most of those opportunities. Certainly, the desire to rise in status is basic to those lower in the social hierarchy; individuals will therefore seek to improve their status when they have the opportunity to do so (Lipset and Bendix, 1959).

If the American ideology were translated into reality, we could assume that those who work hardest, have the most ambition and perseverance, and possess the most talent will eventually rise in the class hierarchy regardless of the circumstances into which they are born. Research has shown, however, that certain social and economic factors outside the control of individuals are most critical in affecting the process of upward mobility. What are the factors that influence individual mobility?

The Accident of Birth: Family Background Perhaps the most significant single factor in raising the probability of upward mobility is the class position of one's family of birth. Quite simply, it is a combination of the occupational and educational levels of one's parents and the extent of their wealth that is the best predictor of mobility (Bowles and Gintis, 2002; Rytina, 2000). Those born into well-to-do families automatically possess resources that give them opportunities to rise in social class. The accident of birth sets in motion a kind of vicious circle in which life chances reinforce each other. Those born into affluent families receive good educations, which lead to good jobs, which, in turn, provide good incomes. The same applies in reverse for those born into less affluent families. Moreover, those life chances are passed on from one generation to the next.

The influence of family of birth is most direct in the upper class, where wealth and prestige are passed down from generation to generation. For those in other classes, inheritance is more indirect, resulting from different opportunities in education and occupation. In any case, the influence of family cannot be underestimated. Consider, for example, the advantages enjoyed by those whose parents and grandparents contribute to their homes, cars, college expenses, and so on. This support constitutes a form of inheritance, which in the long run may be even more valuable than what is transferred at the parents' or grandparents' death. In a study that compared the variation of economic status among brothers to its variation among all men, John Brittain (1977) found that the degree of inequality among brothers was substantially less than that among all men. He concluded that from one-third to two-thirds of the overall variance of economic status was accounted for by family inheritance. Moreover, Brittain found that much of the remainder of the explanation of inequality was accounted for by unmeasured parental influences, as well as by luck and other random factors. He concluded that the remarkable stability of economic inequality over many decades in various countries is in large measure the result of the tendency for economic status to be transferred from parents to children.

One's family of birth contributes to success or failure in other ways. Families that provide children with intellectual stimulation and a rich cultural environment—for example, eccouraging reading and problem solving at an early age or exposing them to travel, the arts, and interaction with diverse groups—increase the odds that the children will succeed in school and will be able to function well in a variety of social situations. Obviously, providing these advantages is to a great extent dependent on a family's material resources. Family structure also can help lead to different outcomes for children. Having both parents present, for example, may prove advantageous for children compared with those who are raised in single-parent homes (McMurrer and Sawhill, 1998).

We should also note the role of genetic inheritance, particularly cognitive skills, in patterns of economic success or failure. As the researchers Daniel McMurrer and Isabel Sawhill bluntly put it, "Genes clearly matter" (1998:13). The question is, how *much* do they matter? Parents unavoidably pass their genes on to their children. The mistake often made, however, is to attribute more significance to this inheritance than is warranted. Most researchers seem to agree that genes account for some part—still difficult to calculate—of the explanation for where one winds up on the social hierarchy. But as noted in Chapter 6, what is beyond doubt is that those genes interact with and are outweighed by other, environmental, influences (Björklund et al., 2005; Corcoran, 2001; Fischer et al., 1996).

Education   The second most critical factor (some would argue, the *most* critical factor) in individual mobility is education (Featherman and Hauser, 1978; McMurrer and Sawhill, 1998; Pew Charitable Trusts, 2012). The relationship is quite simple: The higher the number of years of education, the greater the probability of upward mobility. A higher credential translates into higher earnings over one's lifetime. Those with four-year college degrees therefore will usually earn more than those with only high school diplomas but not as much as those with graduate degrees. This is illustrated clearly in Figure 7-4. Furthermore, the payoff for education has risen in the last few decades. In 1975, workers with a bachelor's degree had 1.5 times the annual earnings of workers with only a high school diploma. This ratio had risen to 1.9 by 2005. In 1975, workers with degrees beyond the bachelor's level had 2.1 times the annual earnings of high school graduates, but 2.7 times by 2005. Going in the opposite direction, not having a high school diploma became more costly; whereas in 1975 those lacking a high school diploma had 0.9 times the earnings of high school graduates, by 2005 they earned only 0.7 times as much. When looked at in simple dollar terms, the difference between a bachelor's

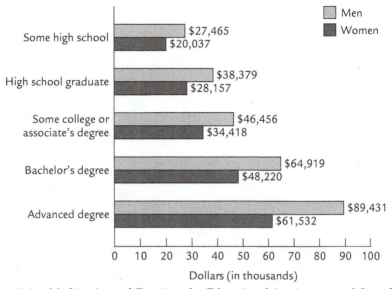

Figure 7-4 ■ Median Annual Earnings, by Educational Attainment and Sex of Full-time Workers Aged Twenty-five and Over, 2009
Source: U.S. Census Bureau, 2012b.

degree and a high school diploma is staggering. In 2009, workers with a bachelor's degree earned an average of $56,000 compared to $33,000 for high school graduates, and over one's lifetime, the added value of a four-year degree over a high school diploma was well over $1 million. Wealth is also very much a function of education, as shown in Figure 7-5.

Because a college degree is so critical to upward mobility, the question is, who goes to college? That is, what are the class backgrounds of those who enter colleges and universities and who ultimately graduate? Nothing could better illustrate the close relationship between education and social class than college attendance. Most simply, as family income rises, college attendance (and, perhaps more important, college graduation) rises. This means that upper- and upper-middle-class high school graduates are most apt to go to college and, beyond the bachelor's degree, to graduate and professional schools. Even when low-income students demonstrate the ability to go on to college, they lack the same access as high-income students. Studies show that a low-income student with high test scores has a lower probability of completing college than a low-scoring, high-income student (Bailey and Dynarski, 2011; Gould, 2012). This is shown in Figure 7-6.

The severe economic recession beginning in 2007 widened the educational gap between students from well-to-do families and those lower in the class hierarchy. State universities and colleges, which rely primarily on public funding, were forced to slash budgets and raise tuition fees. Private institutions, heavily dependent on tuition, were compelled to do the same. Students from middle-class families, as a result, were faced with a heavier financial burden and

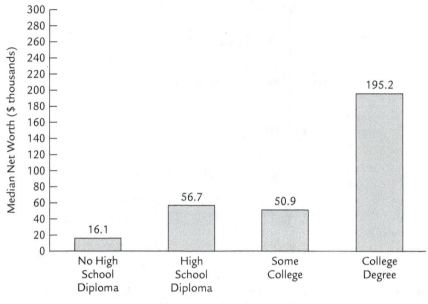

Figure 7-5 ▪ Education and Net Worth, 2010
Source: Bricker et al., 2012.

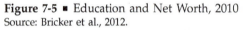

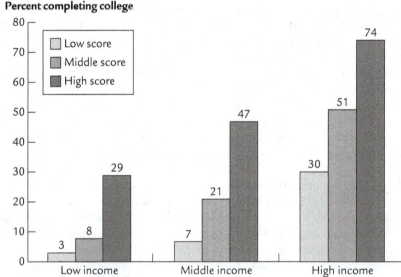

Figure 7-6 ▪ College Completion by Income Status and 8th Grade Test Scores*
*Low income is defined as the bottom 25 percent, middle income middle 50 percent, and high income is top 25 percent.
Source: From "High Scoring, Low-Income Students No More Likely to Complete College Than Low-Scoring, Rich Students." by Elise Gould. Economic Policy Institute Blog, March 9. Reprinted by permission of The Economic Policy Institute.

the prospect of delaying or even foregoing college. For students of working-class or poor families, attending college became even more uncertain (Kirp, 2009).

In an era in which many attend and graduate from college, however, merely having a bachelor's or even a master's degree is, in itself, no guarantee of upward mobility. It is not only a college degree per se, therefore, but also the perceived *quality* of one's college education that counts. There is a tiered prestige structure in the American university system, with highly selective private universities and colleges ranked highest, followed by top state universities and then by regional state universities. Given these perceived differences, a degree from a more prestigious university usually means higher earnings. After examining the annual earnings of graduates of different types of colleges at various stages of the life cycle, economist Dominic Brewer and his colleagues found "a large premium to attending an elite private institution" (1999:119).[3]

The critical question, then, is who gets admitted to the best-regarded, most prestigious universities—that is, Ivy League schools and other elite private and public institutions? In the past, entrance to these schools was heavily influenced by one's family. Those from the upper class, many of whom attended elite prep schools, dominated the student bodies. Today, the selection process is more competitive and merit based. Also, scholarships and loans make it possible for qualified students from less affluent families to attend those schools, where costs are exorbitant. Almost all of the most selective colleges and universities have made themselves more accessible to a broader class range of qualified students in recent years by reducing or, for low-income families, entirely eliminating tuition (Glater, 2008; Leonhardt, 2008). Nonetheless, despite their greater social diversity, the selection process at these institutions continues to favor those higher on the class hierarchy, albeit more indirectly than in the past (Carnevale and Rose, 2003; Golden, 2007; Pallais and Turner, 2007; Symonds, 2006). Given the rigorous academic entrance requirements, those who have received the best training at the secondary school level will, not unexpectedly, receive preference. And the secondary schools that best prepare students for the most prestigious universities are overwhelmingly private—and costly. One nationwide study, for example, found that private schools have a far better record than public schools in placing students at Harvard, Yale, and Princeton (Yaqub, 2002). But even at elite public universities, the student mix is heavily skewed toward the higher classes. At the University of Michigan, for example, more entering freshmen in 2003 came from families earning at least $200,000 than were from the entire bottom half of the income distribution (Wilson, 2012).

Economic forces at times trump purely academic ones in determining who is admitted to top-ranked schools, and it is here that the wealthy may

---

[3]Some maintain that the value of attendance at elite colleges is exaggerated or is not as great today as it once was (Dale and Krueger, 2002; Easterbrook, 2004). What is indisputable, however, is the return on investment of higher education.

exert their influence. Ivy League and other prestigious institutions reserve so-called legacy preferences or development admits for applicants whose families are able to give a generous donation to the school. "Billionaires' children," as *Wall Street Journal* education writer Daniel Golden characterizes them, "are like top quarterbacks: they go anywhere they want, displacing students with more potential but smaller bankrolls" (2007:61).

Because education is so critical to social mobility, it is discussed in more detail later in this chapter.

Ethnicity   Although blatant forms of discrimination no longer typify the workplace and the job market, indirect institutional forms of discrimination continue to have an impact on the mobility paths of members of ethnic minority groups, such as African Americans, Hispanic Americans, and Native Americans. Many of the disadvantages in the labor market suffered by these groups are the result of lower educational and job skills, which, to some degree, can be traced to continued negative stereotyping and, in some cases, residential segregation.

Gender   Gender continues to have an impact on the mobility paths of women. Much has been accomplished in the last three decades in creating a more equitable opportunity structure for women, yet, as we will see in Chapter 11, structural impediments remain in place, making it difficult for women to enter certain occupations, particularly those that are high in status.

For married women, the class position and prestige of their husbands have an impact on their own ultimate class position. This does not seem to work in reverse—that is, married men are not affected by the class and prestige of their wives.

Social Networks   Having skills, talent, education, and all the other requirements for upward mobility may be outweighed by one's ability to access key social networks. Consider, for example, how people acquire their jobs. Ideally, many apply and one or a few are chosen through a relatively objective, blind process. But more often than not, jobs are obtained through more informal processes such as word-of-mouth, knowing the "right" people, or knowing those who know the "right" people. Having access to influential social networks, then, is a decisive factor in accounting for why some rise and others do not despite comparable qualifications (Granovetter, 1995).

Often, making connections vital to one's career occurs during one's college years. Reich (2001) describes the process:

> The real value of a college education to one's job prospects has less to do with what is learned than with who is met. The parents of one's classmates, and the friends of their parents, provide connections to summer jobs and first jobs, then later to clients and business customers. Loyal alumni offer further leads. The more prestigious the university, the more valuable such connections are likely to be. To the extent that an Ivy League education has superior value, that value has less to do with the grandeur of its libraries or the cleverness of its professoriat than with the superiority of its connections. (134)

Enhancing one's career often depends on being able to demonstrate one's talents and skills for those who control the selection process. To illustrate, think of the thousands of extremely talented and well-trained people in the performing arts—music, acting, dance—who seek to rise in their profession. There is usually only a nuance of difference among them in terms of talent, yet only a few are ever able to attain huge success in the music world, the theater, or the movies. Being seen or heard by those who are able to steer their careers in the right direction becomes key. This often means knowing who the selectors are and where and when such staging opportunities occur. A similar kind of network access operates in the careers of people in the business world and in academia. Understanding the selection process and having connections to those who regulate it become critical.

Luck   One might scoff at the idea that luck plays some part in the mobility process, but it cannot be so easily dismissed. All of us are familiar with the expression "being in the right place at the right time." Many Texas oil millionaires made their fortunes as wildcatters, gambling by drilling for oil in areas not known to be oil rich. They were successful because they were lucky enough to sink their drills at precisely those places where oil did in fact lie beneath the earth. We do not hear about the thousands who were unsuccessful because they had the misfortune to drill in unproductive sites. In addition, consider those who strike it rich in the stock market, subject to highly unpredictable trends (Sherden, 1998).[4]

As noted in Chapter 4, luck always plays a huge role in the formation of great fortunes. Those who find themselves in a position to capitalize on opportunities that arise out of technological or social change have the greatest chance to enter the tiny ranks of the fabulously rich. In addition to possessing the requisite skills, they are in the right place at the right time. The idea that one can rise to great wealth through personal savings or through diligence and hard work (à la Horatio Alger) is pure fiction. Thurow characterizes the sudden acquisition of great wealth as a "conditional lottery," where luck is critical. "Ability by itself," he notes, "is not enough" (1999:205). Many people may have the entrepreneurial skills and talents to excel in the business world—to "enter the lottery"—but few will become instantaneously wealthy.

Sometimes individuals find themselves in fortuitous situations through no design of their own. In 1935, an influential Hollywood publisher spotted an attractive fifteen-year-old girl in the drugstore across the street from her

---

[4]Winning a lottery is obviously one way in which luck is the path to upward mobility, but sometimes simply being in the right place at the right time yields a tremendous payoff. Consider Dan Jones, a salesman who in 1996 happened to be in a particular seat in Camden Yards Stadium, watching the Baltimore Orioles play. He caught Eddie Murray's five-hundredth home run and was paid a half million dollars for the ball. Eleven years later, Matt Murphy, a twenty-two-year-old tourist visiting San Francisco, found himself a similar beneficiary of good fortune. At AT&T Park, he caught Barry Bonds's historic 756th home run ball, which was later auctioned off for $750,000.

high school. When he asked her the hackneyed question "How would you like to be in pictures?" in this case, it was more than a glib line. The publisher introduced her to an agent who subsequently took her to one of Hollywood's top directors. Without a day's experience as an actor, Lana Turner was signed to a movie contract and went on to become one of the top stars of her time (*Current Biography*, 1943).

Those who are wealthy or highly successful in their careers like to think that their accomplishments are the product of their own endeavors, that they are "self-made" men and women who have succeeded on their own talents, skills, wits, and intelligence, enabling them to rise above others. But every society is replete with people of exceptional talent, high IQs, and extraordinary skills in various fields; not all rise to riches or fame. Malcolm Gladwell (2008) refers to eminently successful people as "outliers," explaining that they are not necessarily smarter, more talented, or better biologically endowed than others, but are simply the fortunate beneficiaries of a set of opportunities and circumstances that present themselves at critical junctures in their lives. What was earlier explained as the "accident of birth," specifically the class of one's family, as well as ethnicity and gender, shape virtually everything that follows. But even within that social framework, some things are simply the result of good fortune. The year (or even month) of one's birth, the nature of the society during one's formative years, the state of the job market when one enters the world of work—any one or a combination of these, for example, might help propel an individual along a trajectory of success in the business world, in science, in athletics, or in any area of human endeavor, or, by the same token, confine one to a life of minimal monetary or status rewards.

As an example of simple good (or bad) fortune, consider the impact on people's careers of the severe economic recession beginning in 2007. Most economic analysts expected this downturn to be a long-lasting one, affecting the job market for many years. Those having the misfortune of having graduated from college and entering the labor force at this time may find themselves at a disadvantage throughout the remainder of their working lives. One's first job has been shown to be critical to subsequent upward mobility and most of the unlucky graduates of the late 2000s may never catch up in earnings and occupational status with those who had entered the job market in more economically auspicious times (Kahn, 2009; Peck, 2010). The impact on those without college degrees will, of course, be even more disastrous.

Education and the Process of Mobility

In the United States and other societies with open systems of stratification, education becomes the primary means by which individuals equip themselves to move upward in the social hierarchy. Moreover, education, in the modern ideal, creates equality of opportunity. Regardless of where people start out in the quest for the society's rewards, educational opportunities presumably create a common starting line. Given its focal place in the mobility process, let's look more carefully at the functions and effects of education.

Education: The Key Life Chance

Schools perform a variety of functions in modern societies. Some of these functions are manifest, or intended, whereas others are latent, that is, not intended, designed, or even acknowledged. Among their manifest functions, schools traditionally have been responsible for contributing to the development of students as workers and citizens by communicating social, political, and occupational skills. Another intended function of schools is to foster upward mobility.

In American society, there is an especially strong egalitarian attitude and approach to education. Beginning in the early nineteenth century, public education was recognized as a necessary component in a society that was founded so fundamentally on ideas of equality. Education, including higher education, was, in this view, not for an elite class only, but to be made available to all. The notion of "equal educational opportunity" has historically supported the commitment to an open society. It is the popular belief, therefore, that the effects of class of origin (or of ethnicity or gender) are canceled out by education.

Despite their role in fostering upward mobility and creating a more equal opportunity structure, schools, ironically, play a major role in sustaining the structure of *in*equality. The relationship between education and socioeconomic status operates in a cycle that is perpetuated from one generation to the next: The higher the income and occupational status of the parents, the greater the amount and quality of the children's education. In turn, the greater the amount and quality of the children's education, the higher will be their income and occupational status as adults. Several factors operate to assure the continuity of this relationship.

Access to Quality Education   If access to quality education were the same for all students, regardless of their families' socioeconomic status, the school would in fact serve as a kind of leveling mechanism. All students would be able to start at the same point, and the competition among them would be relatively equal. However, this is not the case. There are vast differences in the quality of education from community to community and from neighborhood to neighborhood. In the United States, this is a result primarily of the way in which public schools are financed: mainly by property taxes. This creates a system in which school districts where property values are high will have more money available to support their schools, and school districts with low property values will have less. Upper- and upper-middle-class communities therefore have greater resources to invest in their schools—more money to pay teachers' salaries, finance buildings and laboratories, and supply educational materials. In Lake County, Illinois, for example, a suburban area of Chicago, an affluent school district spent almost three times more per pupil than a neighboring district where property values were much lower (Rado, 2007).

Jonathan Kozol, who has studied and written widely about American schools, argues that educational inequality created by the reliance on property taxes to finance public schools has produced a kind of caste system. The quality of a child's education locks that child into a place in the social hierarchy that cannot be easily rearranged at a later point in life:

> We are children only once; and after those few years are gone, there is no second chance to make amends. In this respect, the consequences of unequal education have a terrible finality. Those who are denied cannot be "made whole" by a later act of government. Those who get the unfair edge cannot be later stripped of what they've won. (Kozol, 1991:180)

This educational inequality is abetted by the fact that people with high levels of education are more likely to support higher property taxes to support schools. Thus, communities with the best-educated populations will generally have the best schools. This is another reflection of the class-education relationship: The best educated are ordinarily those of the upper and upper-middle classes. As Sidney Verba and Garry Orren (1985) explain, in the United States,

> people who are better educated, more affluent, and higher in occupational status are more likely to participate in politics. The politically active are more concerned about education, as both a personal and a community need, than are the less active or the inactive citizens, whose highest priority is immediate economic problems. Consequently, public officials, attuned to the concerns of politically active Americans, perceive far more public support for educational programs than for other social policies. As the government responds to this support by strengthening education, the cycle of inequality begins anew. (17–18)

In addition to the fact that public schools are better financed in more prosperous communities, those communities can augment state and local tax funds with moneys they can raise independently through parent groups and foundations. In a well-publicized case, parents at New York's Public School 41, in a relatively affluent Manhattan neighborhood, raised $46,000 in a few weeks. Their objective was to offer to pay the salary of a teacher who was to be reassigned to another school. Losing the teacher would have raised the number of fourth graders in each class from twenty-six to thirty-two, a change that the parents saw as detrimental to the school's quality (Hammonds, 1997).[5] Another advantage held by more affluent families is that, in the end, they have the option of sending their children to private schools if they are dissatisfied with the public system.

The issue of school financing reflects clearly the ideological conflict between liberty and equity. Conservatives, concerned with liberty, argue that parents

---

[5]The city did not accept the parents' offer, but the teacher was retained.

should be free to use whatever resources they possess or can marshal to assure their children the best education. In this view, the most affluent school districts are perfectly justified in raising as much money as they can and in using their tax money as they see fit. This, of course, perpetuates the discrepancy between rich school districts and poor ones. Liberals, by contrast, are most concerned with creating equity among different class groups. Regarding school financing, this means distributing tax revenue more equally among both rich and poor school districts. In the process, however, this option infringes on the liberty of local school districts to spend their money as they choose.

It should be noted that the gap between high-income and low-income school districts, though still very apparent, has been narrowing gradually. In response to court orders, equalization formulas have been put in place in many states, requiring more uniformity in per-student spending. Also, state governments now play a larger role in financing schools, counteracting some of the inequalities created by class differences among local school districts (Corcoran et al., 2004). These measures have helped reduce the disparities that Kozol and others have described. Nonetheless, the fact remains that children from high-income families attend schools that on all measures are superior to those of poorer families.[6] The result, as researchers Cecilia Elena Rouse and Lisa Barrow conclude, is that "rather than encouraging upward mobility, U.S. public schools tend to reinforce the transmission of low socio-economic status from parents to children" (2006:116).

Computer Technology As the Internet (and computer technology in general) becomes a more basic component of education, those who have easy access to computers will extend their advantage over those who do not. And as with other aspects of education, the relationship between computer technology and social class is very evident (Lee and Burkam, 2002; Hoffman and Novak, 1998). This can be seen clearly in Figure 7-7. Whereas 89 percent of households earning more than $75,000 have broadband (high-speed) Internet access, only 41 percent of those earning below $30,000 do. As long as the information technology gap—the "digital divide," as it has been called—remains wide, the children of more well-to-do families will automatically have a step up on others. "The great divide, in the coming age," writes Jeremy Rifkin, "is between those whose lives are increasingly taken up in cyberspace and those who will never have access to this powerful new realm of human existence" (2000:14).[7]

---

[6]One researcher has shown that much of the variation in per-pupil spending occurs *within* school districts. This can be seen in teachers' salaries. In the same district, new teachers often begin in low-income schools, earning comparatively low salaries, while veteran, higher-paid teachers are likely to be found in richer neighborhood schools with few minority students (Spatig-Amerikaner, 2012).

[7]Sociologist Paul DiMaggio and his colleagues (2004), however, have pointed out that, as the Internet is a relatively new form of technology, we don't yet know very much about the long-term effects of Internet access on educational attainment and success in the labor market.

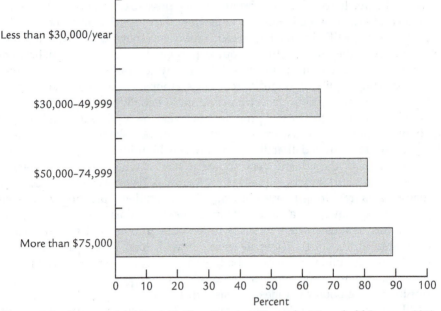

Figure 7-7 ▪ Percent of Adults with Broadband at Home, by Household Income, 2011
Source: Pew Research Center's Internet & American Life Project Please see our citation
guidelines here: http://www.pewinternet.org/About-Us/Our-Research/Use-Policy.aspx

Student Placement   Another way in which schools perpetuate class inequality is by the use of tests and tracking. IQ and other placement tests geared to middle-class children are critical devices that schools use to sort students by cognitive ability. Often this results in a self-fulfilling prophecy. Those who, as a result of scores on placement examinations, are labeled "smarter" or "more talented" may be tracked into particular programs, apart from others who do not score as high. At all levels, teachers and administrators deal with the presumed superior students differently, creating for those students a better quality of education. Thus, the initial evaluation becomes a reality (Jessim and Harber, 2005). Again, however, there is a clear relationship between placement examinations and social class—those from families of higher socioeconomic status tend to perform better than those from poorer families.

Teachers also have higher expectations of students from more affluent families than of those coming from low-income families. This, too, often creates a self-fulfilling prophecy. Expecting that students they identify as high achievers will perform better than others, teachers are apt to devote more personal time and effort to present these students with greater intellectual challenges. Conversely, teachers will expend less effort on students they identify as underachievers. The result is higher academic achievement by those initially classified as "better" students and lower achievement by those classified as "poorer" students (Figlio, 2005; Rosenthal and Jacobson, 1968).

Source: Reprinted by permission of The Permissions Group, Inc. on behalf of TMS/MCT Reprints.

Tracking students is another means by which schools perpetuate the class system. In American society, high schools commonly channel students into different academic programs, depending on their past performance as well as the evaluations of advisers and teachers. Some are placed into college preparatory curricula, and others are tracked into vocational programs. Social class is often a criterion in deciding where students will be placed. Low-income students, for reasons explained earlier, probably will have already demonstrated less academic promise and will be placed in vocational tracks. Once placement is made, the direction students will follow after high school is a foregone conclusion: College prep students will go to college, and vocational students will look for jobs.

Family Environment and Educational Inequality   The family environment of students provides another clue to explaining the relationship between social class and education. Generally, the higher the social class of the parents, the higher will be their expectations for their children's education. This means they will provide them with more psychological and material support in their school efforts and activities. They will stress the importance of education and instill in their children values that are compatible with achievement. Throughout their schooling, children in higher-income families will be prepared for college—assumed from the outset—with the necessary social support and encouragement (Carnevale and Rose, 2003; Lareau, 2003). Poorer families, in contrast, may undervalue education and fail to convey to children the long-range worth of investing time and effort into educational pursuits. They may encourage children to enter the workforce rather than spend time and money on higher education.

Sociologist Annette Lareau has shown how different outcomes in education are determined in large part by parental behavior and what she calls "cultural repertoires" practiced by families of different social classes:

> Middle class child-rearing . . . generally conforms to the logic of *concerted cultivation,* according to which parents view it as their duty to actively foster the development of their children's potential skills and talents. By contrast . . . working class and poor child-rearing conforms to a logic of the *accomplishment of natural growth,* according to which parents assume that if they provide their children with love, feed and clothe them, and keep them safe, the children will grow and thrive spontaneously" (Lareau and Weininger, 2008:123).

As noted earlier, families higher in class are also apt to create an environment for their children that subtly and indirectly instills educational values. At an early age, these children are likely to be introduced to books and educational toys, for example, and exposed to cultural events such as concerts, plays, and museum exhibits. This equips the child with what Bourdieu called "cultural capital," providing valuable preparation for formal schooling.

All of this cultural training is reinforced by the child's peers. Children grow up with others who are generally of the same social class. Thus, peer pressure further stimulates middle- and upper-class children to do well in school. Children of lower-income families, by contrast, often find themselves pressured to perform poorly in school (Fordham and Ogbu, 1986; McWhorter, 2000).

These factors, it must be remembered, are external to the school itself. The material and instructional quality of the school may therefore have less influence on student success than is generally believed (Cheadle, 2008; Coleman, 1966; Goldthorpe and Jackson, 2008).

In sum, there are significant class differences in access to quality education and in the educational process itself. Regarding social mobility, this creates an irony: Since the educational system in American society has been the main channel for upward mobility, "it is a source of economic inequality rather than equality" (Verba and Orren, 1985:12).

Summary

Social mobility is movement upward or downward in the stratification system. Different types of stratification systems either limit or encourage mobility. In closed systems, cultural norms dictate against mobility, making it relatively uncommon, whereas open systems allow people to move up and down the class hierarchy on the basis of desire, merit, and talent.

In reality, closed systems are never entirely rigid and open systems are never perfectly fluid.

Slavery has been a historically persistent form of inequality throughout most of human history. In the United States, Brazil, and the Caribbean, slavery was a vital component of plantation economies. Slavery remains evident today in different forms. Caste is a type of social stratification in which people acquire their social position at birth and remain in that status for life. The caste system of India is the most noted example, but the pre-1960s American South and the apartheid system of South Africa are also cases of caste. The estate system, or feudalism, typified European societies of the Middle Ages but has been a common form of stratification in all agrarian societies. Class systems, in which the opportunities for mobility are greatest, emerged with industrialization in the eighteenth century and have been prevalent in modern industrial societies.

Intergenerational mobility is movement up or down from one generation to another; intragenerational mobility is movement within one's lifetime. Mobility may be vertical or lateral. Mobility in the United States has been frequent and mostly of an upward nature; however, the distance moved is usually quite limited. Mobility trends indicate that people, for the most part, remain at or close to their class of origin and whatever mobility does occur is ordinarily of short range. Horatio Alger success stories are exceptional. Furthermore, despite the common assumption of America as a unique land of opportunity, it presently lags behind most other postindustrial societies in rate of upward class mobility.

Social mobility in industrial societies is determined to a large degree by structural changes such as shifting labor markets and occupational trends, accessibility to higher education, and changing demographic patterns. These factors operate in such a way as to push people up or down the class hierarchy from generation to generation as well as within their own lifetimes. The determinants of individual mobility include family of birth, educational attainment, ethnicity, gender, situational opportunities, and luck.

Modern societies are open in some regards but relatively closed in others. On the one hand, socioeconomic status is, to a significant degree, self-perpetuating. A cumulation of advantages or disadvantages makes it difficult for individuals to modify their status: Birth into a high-income family leads to quality education, which leads to a better job, which leads to a high income. On the other hand, despite the existence of this vicious circle, a significant minority in all contemporary societies does move upward or downward in the class structure, albeit usually in small increments.

Education is an extremely critical aspect of the mobility process. Access to higher education is the primary means by which individuals equip themselves to move upward. There are vast differences, however, in the quality of education from one local community to another, in the educational process, and in the family environment, guaranteeing that those from more affluent families receive more and better education; this assures the continuity of social inequality.

8

Ideology and the Legitimation of Inequality

Man's ability to interpret facts and turn them to his advantage is as well known as his ability to forget and repress facts that conflict with his convictions or stereotypes. Facts have never convinced anyone or modified anyone's view of the world.
JACQUES ELLUL

A well-established ideology perpetuates itself with little planned propaganda by those whom it benefits most. . . . Systems of life which confer special benefits on the other fellow need no plots or conspiracies when the masses are moved by faith and the elites are inspired by self-confidence.
HAROLD LASSWELL

As we have discovered, inequality of income and wealth is a basic characteristic of the United States and of all societies, past and present. Moreover, access to the resources of power is hardly the same for all groups and individuals, and power elites do not, in the main, resemble the general populace in their class origin and other sociological traits. And as will be shown in Chapter 12, the democratic character of the American sociopolitical system is in many ways questionable. Given these facts, one might logically ask, How is a system in which privilege and power are so unequally distributed given legitimacy? Why, in other words, do those lacking great wealth and political influence—a decided majority—accept a system that remains so apparently inequitable?

What is perhaps even more puzzling is the fact that those with little wealth and power not only tolerate the prevailing socioeconomic system but, for the most part, consider it just and beneficial. In short, few ever question any of the basic assumptions of the society's major economic, political, and social institutions. People may recognize certain societal shortcomings from time to time and may acknowledge the realities of inequality, but the system as a whole is seen as fundamentally fair and the best that humans have yet devised.

The acceptance of inequality is not a recent occurrence; indeed, it is as old as human societies. And the extremes of inequality in societies of past ages were much greater than those found in the modern world. Recall the feudal system that characterized Europe during the Middle Ages. Here was a socioeconomic arrangement that nicely illustrated Marx's notion of a two-part division of society into those who owned the means of production and those who were forced to work for the owners. The most puzzling aspect of feudalism was not its injustice and the degree of inequality it produced, however, but its duration. Until it was replaced by capitalism, feudalism in Europe lasted for several centuries. How could a system so unjust and unequal be sustained for such a long period?

Other systems of production in human societies have yielded as much or even more inequality than feudalism. And they, too, proved to be quite enduring and stable. The very idea of "equality" is a relatively new and unusual notion. It is essentially an idea that stems from the eighteenth-century philosophic movement known as the Enlightenment, or Age of Reason, which held that humankind, through the application of reason and science, could achieve increasing material and moral progress. Until relatively recently, the thought that people were to be seen as equals and that they were deserving of an equal share of the society's product was a radical idea. Even in the contemporary world, social inequality has not often been challenged by mass movements. Whereas political revolutions, in which one ruling group replaces another, have been numerous, social revolutions, in which the entire stratification system is radically reconfigured, have been rare. Put simply, most people at all times have accepted the system of inequality in the societies in which they live. The willing acceptance of the prevailing institutional system and its attendant social inequality by most members of the society is called **legitimacy,** and the process by which it is brought about is **legitimation.**

Legitimation

How is the enigma of mass acceptance of inequality to be explained? Might it be that support for the prevailing institutions is produced by force? Do the powerful and wealthy few induce the masses to obey on the basis of fear? Coercion is, in fact, always at the root of obedience to authority, and all states use force when the need arises. Coercive techniques are most common in societies in which the dominant system is not accepted by a significant part of the populace. In modern autocratic societies such as China and North Korea, the powerful must often enforce their will through blatant forms of repression.

The stability of sociopolitical systems that rely primarily on coercion is, however, always precarious. Indeed, the use of raw force alone cannot be effective in prompting compliance over long periods. For government and related institutions to establish and sustain a system of inequality that is popularly supported over many generations requires that power be enforced in less repressive and direct ways. In protecting their privileges, dominant groups try to engender loyalty and respect in subordinates, not fear. Force and the threat of force, therefore, are to be avoided as much as possible (Jackman, 1994). People must come to see the exercise of power by the few as natural and socially beneficial. Only then does power become authority, that is, *legitimate* power. When this is accomplished, ruling groups need no longer resort to force as the principal means of assuring their will. Without creating legitimacy, the powerful in society would be continually faced with a rebellious population questioning the dominant institutions and the inequality they produce.

It is only when a society's economic, political, and social institutions are supported reflexively—almost unconsciously—by the masses that long-range stability is evident, as in the United States. "The surest method of social control," writes sociologist Mary Jackman, "is to induce subordinates to regulate themselves" (1994:59). Occasionally, there are signs of discontent and even mild rebellion (the urban riots of the 1960s, for example), but those unusual instances are generally squelched with a display of force or through minor concessions. The widespread and consistent support of the society's institutional system is not often seriously challenged. To assure legitimacy and thus to sustain the system's long-range stability requires the development of an effective ideology and its communication through the process of socialization. People must come to *believe* that the system is fair and deserving of their allegiance. Dominant groups, explains Jackman, therefore "work to engage subordinates in a common view of the world that rationalizes the current order" (1994:59). The answer to the perplexing question of why the feudal system endured so long is, in great measure, that the serfs believed in the system; they accepted it as legitimate. Their view of the system as just and acceptable was founded on an ideology that explained that feudalism was divinely ordained. It was God who shaped society, and thus society was not to be questioned. If a serf were asked why he must toil in the fields each day, forever indebted to the lord of the manor, his answer would be simple: "Because God intended for me to be a serf." This belief, widespread and accepted by virtually all, contributed heavily to the legitimizing of the system, enabling it to endure for more than five centuries.

In the following section, we examine how ideology plays a major role in legitimizing inequality.

The Nature of Ideology

An **ideology** is a set of beliefs and values that rationalizes a society's structure of power and privilege.[1] Most simply, it is both an explanation of how and why a society's major institutions work as they do and a justification for the outcomes produced by those institutions. "Sets of beliefs or theories that are ideological," notes John Plamenatz, "purport to tell us how things are or

---

[1]As with other sociological concepts, ideology has been applied in a variety of ways. Some have used the term broadly to denote a society's entire belief system, and others have used it very narrowly to describe a specific program of action of a particular group or party. My use of the term is less extreme than either of these two. On varying definitions of ideology, see Shils (1968), Lane (1962), and Plamenatz (1971).

were, and how they come or came to be so" (1971:75). Ideologies can be propounded not only for the purposes of stabilizing and defending a prevailing system but also for changing it.[2] Ideology can therefore be an instrument for ruling groups or for those who oppose them. Ideologies are also used to provide support for specific forms of inequality; for example, racism and sexism are particular sets of beliefs that have provided a rationale for racial/ethnic and gender inequality. This chapter discusses ideology as a force for stabilizing and perpetuating the general structure of power and privilege.

Dominant Ideologies

An ideology that explains and justifies the prevailing power and reward structures is called the **dominant ideology.** Since power and wealth are never distributed equally in any society, some justification and explanation must be provided not only for those at the top who gain the most from the way the system works but for those lower on the social ladder who get progressively less. As sociologists Joan Huber and William Form have put it, "Dominant ideologies function to comfort those whom the system rewards and to justify the system to those who fail" (1973:79). A society's dominant ideology, then, explains and rationalizes the great discrepancies in power and wealth.

It is not surprising that those at the top of the society's power and wealth hierarchies should believe in the justness of their position. But people across the entire class range pay allegiance to the ideology, including even those in the lowest social positions. Sociological theorists have offered several explanations for this paradox.

Marx and Ideology   As explained in Chapter 2, Marx was one of the first sociological theorists to deal with the issue of ideology. As he saw it, ideology was an important tool for assuring the interests of the few over the many. It was not so much the deliberate creation of a ruling class as the natural product of the society's productive forces. Recall that in the Marxian scheme, those who control the means of production are the ruling class. This class controls not only the means of economic production but also the means of *mental* production. This assures that the ideas of the ruling class regarding all aspects of social life—government, religion, family, and so on—become those of the entire society. Institutions such as the school and the media, which impart ideas about politics and economics, quite naturally disseminate ideas that reflect the interests of the ruling class.

This predominance of ruling class ideas is often referred to in Marxist writings as **ideological hegemony.** Hegemony is a term that refers to

---

[2]In a classic work, Karl Mannheim (1936) termed ideologies that seek to change a social system "utopias" and those that seek to keep them as they are "ideologies" per se.

dominance; ideological hegemony is therefore the prevalence of one group's ideology over all others. Antonio Gramsci, an Italian Marxist writing in the 1920s, described this phenomenon as

> the "spontaneous" consent given by the great masses of the population to the general direction imposed on social life by the dominant fundamental group; this consent is "historically" caused by the prestige (and consequent confidence) which the dominant group enjoys because of its position and function in the world of production. (1971:12)

Ideological hegemony is, in other words, a legitimation of the status quo wherein those values that favor the interests of the ruling group become the acceptable standards of subordinate groups as well. The predominance of the ruling group's standards is dependent on the development and maintenance of false consciousness. As explained in Chapter 2, false consciousness is a belief on the part of nonruling groups that the prevailing political and economic systems work in their interests, when in fact they work primarily in the interests of the ruling class. The power of the capitalist class, then, is enforced and perpetuated so long as the workers remain in a state of ignorance of where their true interests lie.

The Elitist View of Ideology Some social scientists explain that ideology consists of ideas produced by elites themselves to justify their dominance. In this view, elites use ideology to support their power, similar to the Marxian idea, but they may claim their right to power through various rationales. The divine right of kings, the assertion that kings were rulers chosen by God, was an effective ideology during the Middle Ages in Europe. European colonialists of the nineteenth century claimed their right to power over indigenous peoples on the basis of biological and moral superiority, a rationale also employed by Euro-Americans in their dealings with African Americans and Native Americans. A common modern-day elitist justification for the maldistribution of power and wealth is the possession of skill or expertise in a particular field. A few believe those at the top are entitled to their positions because of a biologically based superiority in the form of high IQ (Herrnstein and Murray, 1994). In short, those at the top are thought to merit their positions because they have exceptional qualifications, talents, or abilities.

Some elite theorists see the use of ideology by the wealthy and powerful as conscious manipulation of the masses. In this view, elites are fully aware of what they are doing and seek to enhance and protect their power through propaganda. Other elite theorists explain that elites believe in the ideology and see themselves as naturally taking their places at the top and being rewarded accordingly. In this sense, ideologies differ from propaganda, which, as Alvin Gouldner explains, "is not believed in—at least at first—by those spreading it." Ideologies, by contrast, "are intended to be believed in by those affirming them publicly and by all men, because they are 'true' and they thus have a universal character" (1976:33).

Functionalist Theory and Ideology A third explanation of how and why people come to accept the dominant ideology rests on the functional theorists' notion of societal need. Unlike the Marxian and elite theories, this perspective does not postulate that ruling groups have the capacity to impose their version of social reality on the remainder of the society. Acceptance of the ideology, therefore, is based neither on false consciousness nor on elite manipulation. Rather, it arises from a general consensus of values among the society's people. The idea is that people abide by the prevailing system because they share the basic values on which the system rests (Parsons, 1953). There is, in this view, a fundamental consensus of values among a society's populace that creates stability and order. Without that consensus, society could not function and would exist in a constant state of turmoil and uncertainty.

The stress, then, is on the role that ideology plays in maintaining societal balance. Like the debate between functional and conflict theorists regarding the cause and inevitability of stratification, a similar disagreement is evident here. Functionalists maintain that people recognize the need for a common set of values, whereas conflict theorists hold that those values are created and imposed by the powerful in society.

Ideology: Beliefs and Reality

Although the beliefs that constitute ideology are held by the bulk of a society's population, people's *beliefs* about society do not always coincide with the conditions of social *reality*. Thus, the dominant explanation of how social, economic, and political institutions work is never entirely or even in large part accurate. Much of ideology is oversimplification, distortion, and even myth. It comprises beliefs that, through constant articulation, become accepted as accurate descriptions of how and why things work as they do.

People may accept much or perhaps all of the ideology in the abstract, but when faced with their own situation, they may interpret it selectively, picking and choosing parts, often in an inconsistent or contradictory manner (Kluegel and Smith, 1986). "[E]veryone makes sense of his or her environment partly by applying beliefs about distributive justice to specific circumstances" (Hochschild, 1981:44). In addition, people's class position and racial identity commonly affect the degree of commitment to the ideology. In the United States, for example, not surprisingly, those higher in the class and racial/ethnic stratification systems more fervently subscribe to the dominant ideology (Huber and Form, 1973; Kluegel and Smith, 1986; Ladd, 1994; Mann, 1970; Swidler, 1992).

So although the dominant ideology may be hegemonic in the sense that it pervades all societal institutions, it is neither accepted in total by all people at all times nor universally interpreted. In short, the dominant ideology is not a set of beliefs that everyone accepts in the same way and in the same degree.

The Dominant American Ideology

Although it hardly resembles feudal societies of medieval Europe or contemporary developing societies, the United States is acutely unequal in power and privilege, more so, in fact, than most Western industrialized societies. Nonetheless, for its entire history the United States has never faced a serious challenge to its basic economic and social institutions. Even during the Great Depression of the 1930s, when as many as a quarter of the total workforce was unemployed, the capitalist socioeconomic framework was altered but not overthrown. What is perhaps most puzzling is that even the poor have not strongly supported political efforts aimed at redistributing income and wealth (Hochschild, 1981; Ladd, 1994; Ladd and Bowman, 1998).

What beliefs and values have contributed to the stabilization of this system? What is the societal rationale for the obvious facts that some get more than others and that the system of stratification has not changed substantially for most of American history? What, in other words, is the dominant American ideology regarding inequality, and why do most people subscribe to its basic components?

Because of the discrepancy between beliefs and reality, describing the dominant American ideology, as Huber and Form write, can be both simple and difficult:

> On the one hand, the stuff of the dominant ideology is embedded in political campaign literature, newspaper editorials, TV shows, civics textbooks, stories about Dick, Jane, and Sally, and Chamber of Commerce brochures. It is the sum and substance of what every child has learned about the way the American system works. It is what everybody *knows*. . . . On the other hand, what everybody knows sometimes turns out to be wrong. (1973:3)

Despite the facts that ideology and reality do not always coincide and that the dominant ideology is neither supported unquestioningly by all people nor interpreted in the same way, there is a recognizable body of interrelated beliefs and values that strongly guides most Americans' thoughts about inequality. Among the most essential of these are *individualism, equality of opportunity, meritocracy, the work ethic,* and *liberal capitalism.*

Individual Achievement

Perhaps the most basic component of the dominant American ideology, individual achievement is the belief that each member of society is responsible for his or her fate and that one's social position is a product of personal efforts and talents. The place of individualism as the most basic component of the American creed and its pervasiveness throughout American culture have been recognized almost since the country's founding. Scholars and social commentators have repeatedly shown this aspect of American society to be truly exceptional in comparison with other societies (de Tocqueville, 1966 [1840]; Bryce, 1959 [1912]; Lipset, 1996; McClosky and Zaller, 1984).

With the stress on individual achievement, the effect of structural factors, over which the individual has little or no control, is seen as less critical. As we have seen, the accident of birth and the society's opportunity structure mostly account for social inequality, but those factors are given short shrift by most people. This shows how ideology may mask reality. In extensive surveys, political scientists James Kluegel and Eliot Smith found that "Americans consistently strongly endorse individual reasons for economic position, particularly for poverty, and reject liberal and (especially) radical explanations emphasizing structural causes" (1986:100–101). In her research, sociologist Mary Jackman (1994) found a similar absence of support for income equality among people of all social classes, stemming from a belief in the principle of individualistic achievement: In the end, it is individuals themselves who control their economic and social destinies. And, in this view, it is individuals themselves who therefore are responsible for their class position.

The basic idea is that anyone can succeed with enough effort, whatever one's social and economic handicaps at birth. It all depends on personal effort, ambition, and talent. Differences in wealth and power are not denied, but they are seen as the product of individual factors rather than as the workings of a class system that favors success for the wellborn and failure for the poor.

Self-Reliance   As a corollary of individual achievement, self-reliance is the notion that people should pursue their objectives of success through their own efforts rather than rely on others. Social rewards, in this view, are earned by personal effort. "The 'success story' and the respect accorded to the self-made man," notes sociologist Robin Williams, "are distinctly American, if anything is" (1970:417).

Consider how fundamental this idea is in almost all areas of American social life. Children are taught from their earliest moments of life to be as self-reliant as possible. As they grow older and enter school, they are instructed in the correctness of doing their own work and of not relying on others. And they learn that their rewards are contingent on their individual efforts. Group or communal efforts in the school are sometimes encouraged but are usually limited to extracurricular events. The distribution of really meaningful rewards, namely, grades and honors, is dependent on a student's own efforts, not on how much or how well he or she has contributed to the class's performance.

The idea of self-reliance remains powerful throughout one's working career and extends even into old age. A national survey in 1997 asked people what they feared most about growing old. Sixty-four percent were "very worried" about spending their last years in a nursing home, and 48 percent about becoming a financial burden on their families. Only 28 percent were worried about death (Morin, 1997). So potent is the self-reliance value that people who find themselves in dire economic straits will commonly balk at the idea of accepting welfare or handouts of any kind.

The power of this value accounts in large measure for the strong antiwelfare bias in American society. Those recognized as genuinely needy are viewed

Table 8-1 ▪ Percentage Saying the State Should Guarantee that Nobody Is In Need

Country	Percentage
United States	35
Britain	55
Germany	62
France	64
Spain	67

Source: © 2011 Pew Research Center, Social & Demographic Trends Project. Wealth Gaps Rise to Record Highs Between Whites, Blacks and Hispanics http://www.pewsocialtrends.org/2011/07/26/wealth-gaps-rise-to-record-highs-between-whites-blacks-hispanics/

sympathetically. Thus Americans, as noted in Chapter 6, are willing to support measures like job training and education, but such compassion does not extend to those who seem unwilling to make the effort to support themselves and their families. It is the latter who are seen as undeserving welfare recipients (Gilens, 1999; Ladd, 1994). Despite their acceptance of the notion that some of the poor are in need of help, there is a far weaker commitment to government assistance in this regard than in other industrialized nations (Table 8-1).[3]

It is interesting to consider how persistent the belief in individual responsibility for one's social place seems to remain in American thought. In their classic study of a midwestern community in the 1920s, Robert and Helen Lynd (1929) asked high school students whether they agreed with the statement "It is entirely the fault of a man himself if he does not succeed." Forty-seven percent answered yes. In a replication of this study almost fifty years later, Caplow and Bahr (1979) asked the same question and got the same 47 percent yes response.

The individual responsibility model is adopted by a wide variety of class groups (Coleman and Rainwater, 1978; Lane, 1962; Page and Jacobs, 2009; Pew Economic Mobility Project, 2009; Sennett and Cobb, 1973). It would not be surprising to learn that people of higher social standing would subscribe to this notion. In her study of downwardly mobile middle-class workers, anthropologist Katherine Newman describes managers who, having been imbued with the notion of meritocratic individualism, blame themselves for their dismissal or demotion, even when these things are the result of structural factors, not of their making:

> One's occupation, or more precisely one's career or trajectory within an occupation, are viewed as a test of commitment, and the product of hard

---

[3] Americans' views on the role of government vis-à-vis the poor can be influenced by current events. In the wake of Hurricane Katrina, for example, a majority felt that government wasn't doing enough to help ameliorate poverty. However, political partisanship and race helped shape people's opinion in this case: A substantially higher percentage of Democrats and African Americans as opposed to Republicans and whites saw government efforts as inadequate (Raksha, 2005).

work and self-sacrifice. Cast this way, success is not a matter of luck, good contacts, credentials, or technical skill but is a measure of one's moral worth, one's willingness and ability to drive beyond the limitations of self-indulgence and sloth. It is this equation of occupational success and inner or moral qualities that rebounds on the unemployed manager's self-image, making him or her feel not just unsuccessful but worthless. . . . If the market rewards the competent and casts out the inefficient, unemployment is perforce a judgment of one's abilities. (1999:76–77)

More curiously, even those lower in the social hierarchy accept it to some degree. In a national survey conducted in the 1960s, Free and Cantril (1968) found that whereas most affluent people attributed poverty simply to "lack of effort," a majority of the poor also agreed that they were at least partially to blame for their own condition.[4]

A recent national survey (Pew Economic Mobility Project, 2009) revealed the continuing strength of the individual responsibility model in American society. When asked which factor is more important in achieving economic mobility, "the individual person and things like hard work and drive," or "outside factors and things like the economy and their economic circumstances growing up," almost three-quarters of respondents answered "the individual person."

Even when individuals themselves are not totally faulted for their social disadvantages, their problems are seen not as deep-seated and widespread but rather as marginal and amenable to relatively quick and easy solution. Poverty, after its rediscovery in the 1960s, was seen not as a creation of the normal workings of a capitalist socioeconomic order but as a minor imperfection of an otherwise healthy system. Government leaders saw alleviation of poverty as requiring only a "mopping-up" effort, not basic institutional change. Today, efforts at addressing poverty continue to focus on changing the poor themselves, not on changing the institutional structure within which the poor must function.

Although the belief that individual achievement and initiative are most important in getting ahead in life is particularly strong in the United States, it is also evident to some degree in other Western societies. Whereas in the United States and Canada "ambition" is viewed as critical, in Britain "hard work" is seen as the key to success, and in Germany it is "having a good education" (Pammett, 1996). Common to all these views, however, is the belief that people attain success mostly on the basis of their own ability. Other factors, like "luck" and "knowing the right people," are acknowledged as helpful, but they are not seen as primary. Sociodemographic factors like race or gender are believed to play only a minor role in handicapping individuals in pursuit of their goals.

---

[4]Most of the poor, however, combined "lack of effort" with "circumstances" in explaining poverty, unlike the affluent, who explained it more exclusively as a result of "lack of effort."

Equality of Opportunity

If people earn their position and wealth through their own talents and efforts, the resultant inequality is fully justified. But this justification for inequality hinges on the condition that all people are given the same opportunities to display their individual talents and fulfill their capacities. The competition must be unobstructed. Thus Americans are firmly committed to the principle of equality of opportunity (Citrin, 2008; Ladd, 1994; Ladd and Bowman, 1998; Lipset, 1963; Page and Jacobs, 2009; Williams, 1970). The society's opportunity structure is pictured as open, providing equal chances for all to achieve material success or political power regardless of their social origin. This being the case, each individual controls his or her social destiny. Political scientist Jennifer Hochschild (1995) has described the dominant American ideology as pursuit of the "American dream." A basic tenet of that dream is that everyone can pursue it.

Studies have repeatedly confirmed the acceptance of this principle among Americans of different social classes (Coleman and Rainwater, 1978; Jackman and Jackman, 1983; Ladd, 1994; Ladd and Bowman, 1998). This does not mean, however, that Americans do not recognize the advantages enjoyed by the wealthy. Kluegel and Smith, for example, concluded that "the American public has little illusion that the rich share the same opportunity for economic advancement as the rest of society." They found that 83 percent believe that the children of the rich have "a better or much better chance to get ahead than the average person" (1986:48).

The emphasis on equality of opportunity accounts for why Americans seem more prepared to invest public dollars in education than in most other areas. Overwhelmingly, Americans see education as the key to economic advancement (Hochschild and Scovronick, 2003; Kluegel and Smith, 1986). Providing individuals with opportunities through education is quite different from providing aid to the poor. Education, in this view, equips people with skills and enables them to compete on their own. Welfare assistance, in contrast, is designed to improve people's actual living conditions. The contrast with western European societies (and, to some extent, Canada) in this regard is noteworthy. The United States spends proportionately more on education at all levels, whereas the Europeans devote far more public funds to welfare services (Lipset, 1996). This is perfectly in line with the contrasting social philosophies of the United States and most European societies: equality of opportunity, stressed in the United States, and equality of condition, stressed by Europeans.

Meritocracy and Universalism

As a corollary of the principle of equality of opportunity, **meritocracy** is a system in which rewards are yielded on the basis of performance and qualification. That is, people are expected to earn their social standing and

"Meritocracy worked for my grandfather, it worked for my father, and it's working for me."

property. These things are not to be acquired through inheritance or through the influence of family and friends. So long as people are perceived to have the same chances to succeed or fail, those in the upper rungs of the social hierarchy deserve their positions (Turner, 1960).

Meritocracy is consonant as well with both individualism and the work ethic. We are told that in the competition for society's rewards, after taking into consideration individual ambition and hard work, those who succeed do so on their merits. They have demonstrated their superior skills and talents through performance. Ascribed factors like family of birth, race, ethnicity, and gender are not seen as critical.

The meritocratic idea assumes **universalism,** the notion that everyone should be treated the same regardless of ascribed personal characteristics. This social egalitarianism demands that there be a denial of social rank and any claim to precedence. As Everett Ladd describes this aspect of the American ideology, "Having a lot of money, for example, is O.K. But it's not O.K. to act as though you think you are better than someone else" (1994:9–10). More than a hundred years earlier, James Bryce, an Englishman who wrote a classic description of American society, made a similar observation:

> In America men hold others to be at bottom exactly the same as themselves. If a man is enormously rich . . . or if he is a great orator . . . or a great soldier . . . or a great writer . . . so much the better for him. He is an object of interest, perhaps of admiration, possibly even of reverence. But he is deemed to be still of the same flesh and blood as other men. (1959 [1912]:520)

The stress on egalitarianism explains in some part the tendency for Americans to deny the importance of social class or, as discussed in Chapter 3, to fail even to recognize the strong class divisions in their society.

Lowered Class Consciousness   Placing emphasis on the availability of opportunities, in combination with individual achievement and meritocracy, stabilizes the system by discouraging collective efforts that may turn into sociopolitical movements seeking to alter the society's major institutions (Ossowski, 1963). This accounts for the fact that there is not much sympathy among Americans for divesting the rich of their wealth. Anti-rich sentiment is diffused in large measure because Americans see the possibility that they themselves have a chance to be wealthy. In a 1990 Gallup survey, for example, over half said that people have a good chance to become rich if they are "willing to work hard." In a more recent survey, Page and Jacobs (2009) found that three-quarters of Americans continue to feel that way. Here, for example, is the view of Arthur Ford Jr., a produce department employee at a high-end gourmet food market: "When I step out and see those people in nice cars and nice suits, I think that maybe in five years I'll be one of them. One day I'll be owning my own business. I don't look at them with envy" (Daniel, 2008).

Moreover, antipathy toward the wealthy is not as strong in the United States as in many other countries because Americans are more likely to perceive the rich as having earned their wealth. Consider the view of Maria, one of Hochschild's interviewees, who lives in poverty and cleans other people's homes for a living. Does she feel that her wealthy employers are undeserving of their wealth? Although she resents them, she respects their right to be wealthy: "You work for it, it's fair. If I got a good education and I'm doing a different job [than you] and a harder job, I deserve more. But if you deserve it, you deserve it. I don't believe in this equal, all equal" (Hochschild, 1981:28). As economist Robert J. Samuelson has put it,

> Getting rich is the end point of economic opportunity, and faith in the self-made person is a central part of the national folklore. Americans

believe in ambition and don't reject those who fulfill their ambitions. If the victors in the economic struggle were all suspect, then the ideals of hard work, risk-taking and self-improvement would be illegitimate. (1997:24)

Americans also do not see the rich as naturally antagonistic to their interests. In the Gallup survey cited above, over half indicated their belief that the United States had the "right number of rich," and two-thirds said that the country "benefits from having a wealthy class." The fact that conservative politicians can sometimes win election in districts where the poor or working classes predominate demonstrates this low level of class consciousness.

In line with this view of the wealthy and the belief in an open opportunity structure, few in the United States see government's proper role as equalizing income (Hochschild, 1981; Ladd, 1994; Ladd and Bowman, 1998; Lipset, 1996; Page and Jacobs, 2009). In their analysis of Americans' attitudes toward government policy over the last half century, political scientists Benjamin Page and Robert Shapiro found limited enthusiasm for the idea of income redistribution. Most Americans, they conclude, "are content with the distributional effects of private markets" (1992:127–128). This is in sharp contrast to citizens' views in other advanced societies (Table 8-2).

Recall the difference between liberty and equity. In American society, liberty, in the sense of individual freedom to pursue one's objectives and reap the profits of those efforts, is stressed over equity, the notion of a fair distribution of societal resources. As Ladd and Bowman explain,

Table 8-2 ▪ Percentage Agreeing That "It Is the Responsibility of the Government to Reduce the Differences in Income between People with High Incomes and Those with Low Incomes"

Country	Percentage
United States	32
Canada	44
Japan	48
Australia	48
Sweden	57
France	62
United Kingdom	64
Austria	70
Israel	81
Russia	82

Source: Reprinted by permission of the Secretary of The International Social Survey Program.

In general . . . while many Americans are ambivalent about great wealth, few are hostile to it. This goes far to explain why disparities in wealth in this country have generated so little political heat. (1998:13)

The belief in an open class system in which people can rise without limit on the basis of their own effort is strengthened by the few who actually do make spectacular leaps in class position. In fact, rising from poverty to great wealth is, and always has been, very exceptional in American society. But the handful who, for whatever reasons, break out of poverty and rise to the top are widely heralded, whereas the vast majority of those who remain poor are ignored. These few exceptional cases "confirm" the reality of the American Dream, "proving" that success is mainly dependent on individual effort.

The Work Ethic

The **work ethic** is the notion that hard work is the key to success and is the most noble of human activities. Social and economic success, in this view, is the result of one's willingness to work hard; failure is the result of lack of ambition or desire to improve oneself. Through sufficient effort, anything can be accomplished. The work ethic obviously overlaps with the tenets of individual achievement and self-reliance. It basically defines *how* one is to accomplish upward mobility or measurably change one's material condition.

There is much empirical evidence that demonstrates the continued belief in the Horatio Alger formula for improving oneself. Consider that in 1952, 88 percent of Americans agreed with the statement that "there is plenty of opportunity and anyone who works hard can go as far as he wants." Almost thirty years later, 70 percent still agreed with that statement (Kluegel and Smith, 1986). In 1993, when given a choice of which factors they felt were important to success, 94 percent of Americans felt that "hard work" was the most crucial (Marsden and Swingle, 1994). And in 2005, 80 percent expressed the belief that "it's still possible to start out poor in this country, work hard, and become rich" (*New York Times*, 2005). The contrast between the United States and other developed societies on this point is indicated in Table 8-3. Americans clearly believe that hard work is the route to success and, moreover, believe that the chances favor their own upward mobility (Kohut and Stokes, 2006; Ladd, 1994; Ladd and Bowman, 1998; Lipset, 1996).

Coleman and Rainwater (1978) asked their respondents what they thought was the most effective way for individuals to improve their social standing in America. They found that "ambition, energy, and application" were seen as the prime virtues; "dereliction" was the prime defect. In this view, victory in the quest for success goes to the vigorous, while defeat goes to the lazy. Coleman and Rainwater suggested that the most fitting name for this perceived system is "effortocracy":

Table 8-3 ▪ Percentage Agreeing That "In [COUNTRY] People Get Rewarded for Their Effort"

Country	Percentage
United States	61
Australia	58
Canada	49
Japan	41
Spain	38
Israel	35
Sweden	34
United Kingdom	33
France	22
Russia	8

Source: Reprinted by permission of the Secretary of The International Social Survey Program.

The people who rise in this system—in our respondents' idealized view—are those who have been the most determined to do so, who have put out the greatest efforts toward that end. The people who fall—again in this idealized view—are those who have lacked the character, the will, and the enterprise even to maintain the social position they inherited. (241)

This is a strongly held belief that cuts across class lines. "People can make money if they put their minds to it and get off their little rear ends. People get lazy, but I have no doubt that I will make out well. Because I'm very ambitious, so if there's something I want, I'll do it." We would naturally assume that this is the view of someone occupationally successful and economically secure. But these are the words of an unemployed secretary living below the poverty line (Hochschild, 1981:29).

Liberal Capitalism

As components of the dominant American ideology, individual achievement, equality of opportunity, meritocracy, and the work ethic are woven together with the fundamental premises of **liberal capitalism,** that is, a democratic political system combined with a capitalist socioeconomic system. As the framework around the tenets of the American ideology, liberal capitalism is a reflection of the philosophy of classical liberalism.

As it emerged in Western thought, classical liberalism stems mainly from the writings of seventeenth-, eighteenth-, and nineteenth-century philosophers, including Adam Smith, John Locke, Voltaire, Jean Jacques Rousseau, Thomas Jefferson, and John Stuart Mill. All extolled the worth of individuals and their right to control their destiny. Liberalism challenged the notions of hereditary rights and privileges that had been part of the feudal system. In this view, humans are rational beings who, if left to their own efforts, will naturally pursue their self-interest. Indeed, self-interest is seen as the primary human dynamic. Liberty, therefore, is the most critical right of individuals in society. Government should be as limited as possible; its singular role should be the protection of individual rights, particularly property rights. *Classical* liberalism should not be confused with *modern* liberalism. Today, liberalism is associated with the philosophy that government should play an active economic role in assuring equitable social and economic opportunities. Paradoxically, many of the tenets of classical liberalism are today most consistent with modern conservatism.

Personal property and liberty, in the classical liberal view, are sacrosanct, and the two are not unrelated. These are natural rights, not to be violated by government. Locke, whose central ideas form the basis of most theories of democracy, proclaimed that property (broadly defined as life, liberty, and estate) was the chief motivation for people to establish governments and laws. Consequently, no government has the right to "take from any man any part of his property without his own consent" (Locke, 1960 [1690]:408).

Classical liberalism converges logically with capitalism in its advocacy of individual responsibility and the rational pursuit of self-interest. Through competition, individuals will succeed or fail on their own initiative and ambition. The free market, it is believed, provides a neutral competitive setting. Government, therefore, is not to interfere with natural market processes. Its role in economic affairs is reluctantly accepted as long as it remains minimal. Individuals must be assured unhindered movement in the labor market and absolute freedom to buy and sell what they choose. Such competition is bound to create inequality, of course, but what is of utmost importance is not true equality—which, in this view, is a chimera— but equal opportunity for all to compete in the marketplace.

In the political realm, the economic freedoms inherent in the capitalist market are related to the political liberties of democracy. In a sense, the free market is replicated in the competitive electoral system. The people as a whole must be free to choose and hold accountable their leaders through democratic elections. Hereditary monarchies and aristocracies, characteristic of feudalism, are contrary to liberal notions. In the political realm, inequality is not as readily accepted as it is in the economic. Americans, note political scientists Sidney Verba and Gary Orren, "have a stronger taste for political than for economic equality" (1985:2). The tolerance for economic inequality alongside the ideal of political democracy is indeed a curious paradox of the American ideology.

Both economic and political processes, in the classical liberal view, are seen as "free markets" in which the individual can choose from among competing products and businesses in the economic sphere and from among competing candidates and parties in the political.

Ancillary Beliefs

A set of ancillary beliefs undergirds the dominant American ideology. These are general ideas that complement and reinforce its basic components, that dispel contrary beliefs and strengthen people's commitment to dominant institutions. They are basic to the legitimation process.

Unchanging Human Nature   The prevailing stratification system is not likely to be questioned when people view it as founded on unchangeable human traits. For example, the political and economic relations of a capitalist system are based on avarice and competition. These can be explained and justified by declaring such behavior merely "human nature." Expressions such as "keeping up with the Joneses" are commonly voiced. Most Americans tend to believe that competition and the pursuit of personal interests are simply basic human qualities. They are, in this view, "natural." This, in turn, further deflates any ideas of change. If competition and the pursuit of individual interests are merely "human nature," the resultant inequality is, similarly, only natural. Efforts to bring about radical change are therefore futile. "What can you do? It's always been that way and always will be."

The Neutrality of Societal Institutions   Another way in which inequality is given legitimacy is by the depiction of societal institutions as neutral, serving the interests not of particular groups but of the society as a whole. Americans are inclined to see major institutions—school, government, criminal justice, the media, and business—as functioning in a neutral fashion, not favoring the interests of any particular class, ethnic group, or gender. Government agencies or legislatures, for example, are not pictured as representatives of special economic or regional interests but as objective public institutions. That certain interest groups are far more resourceful than others in fashioning and benefiting from these public institutions is not stressed. Each political party may decry the influence of "special interests" on the other, but rarely do these exhortations move beyond political rhetoric.

Similarly, law enforcement agencies are seen as disinterested crime-fighting organizations, not as politicized groups that enforce laws more or less vigorously depending on who the criminal is or what the crime may be. "Crime" is ordinarily understood as acts that are clearly visible and blatantly offensive, like street muggings and homicides, committed mostly by the poor. The criminal justice system and the media focus most of their attention on these types of crime. Indeed, in the popular mind, crime and poverty are closely associated (Reiman, 2005). But crimes committed by those of higher social classes (such as embezzlement) or by powerful corporations (such as price fixing and the dumping of pollutants into the environment) are more silent and invisible. Hence, they are not treated with the urgency of crimes committed by lower-income groups and rarely engage the attention of the media. As a result, only in the most egregious cases—the accounting fraud of the Enron Corporation in 2001, or the reckless manipulations of banks and investment companies in the financial meltdown of 2008, for example—do they become the concern of the general public.

Giant corporations are similarly portrayed as neutral organizations that provide people with goods and services they want and need. Corporate advertising and public relations are aimed at strengthening a belief in the naturalness and goodness of the prevailing economic system, of which the corporation is, of course, the chief element. That corporations are profit-seeking entities whose purposes are primarily to enrich those who own them is rarely brought to public consciousness. Occasionally, when corporations are seen as profiteering at public expense, there still remains little question that no realistic alternative to the corporate economy exists. Moreover, calls for fundamental reform or tighter government regulation of these institutions are typically portrayed as threats to the American capitalist system and are generally met with resistance or, at best, minor changes that have little impact on the way the system functions.

The mass media are also generally understood to be objective in their presentations of news and entertainment. In the case of news, the media become reporters of events "as they occur"; in the case of entertainment, the public is given "only what it wants." That media elites select news events from among countless events of social significance and present them in a predesigned manner is not often considered. Nor is much thought given to the fact that the U.S. media are private business enterprises that rely for their revenue on commercial advertisers, who may have much to say about what will or will not be printed or broadcast.

Finally, schools, from primary to graduate levels, picture themselves and are generally seen by the public as nonideological institutions that train students in practical skills and impart a curriculum that is objective and fair. The curriculum is supposedly designed to enable students to think independently. Schools are not seen as "political" in function despite the constant enunciation and glorification of dominant political and economic values. Also, the popular picture of the educational system in the United States is one in which no particular class or ethnic group is favored over others. This neutral image prevails despite the fact that, as seen in Chapter 7, schools function in some ways as social placement agencies, assuring top places for those of higher class origins and making upward mobility for those at the opposite end of the social hierarchy difficult at best.

Fear and Doubt of Other Systems   A compelling aspect of the society's dominant ideology is that, as it is propagated, other systems based on different ideologies are seen as neither viable nor credible. Thus, even if there is doubt about prevailing values and the institutions built upon them, there are no workable alternatives. "The American system may have its short-comings," leaders admit, "but the shortcomings of other systems are much greater." Such an admission, along with its implicit warning of the uncertainties and insufficiencies of other systems, serves to defuse efforts at mobilizing people around counterideologies. Fear of other systems additionally serves to affirm and strengthen the belief in the American system despite its inequalities. Communism, for many decades, served as an effective countersystem to American capitalism. Here was an alternative, it was held, whose economic failures and political repression demonstrated the superiority of American economic and political institutions. Today, suggestions of even minor changes in the capitalist political economy are commonly depicted by opponents as attempts to impose "socialism."

In addition, when there is a recognition of institutional deficiencies in meeting social ideals, violence and serious social disturbances are averted by calling up the larger ideological principle that only within the prevailing political framework can changes eventually be realized. Groups calling for change are advised to "work within the system." The black civil rights movement of the 1950s and 1960s serves as an example. As white people became collectively conscious of the plight of blacks in all areas of social life, the movement was recognized as legitimate and justifiable. But only traditional methods of the political process—voting, lobbying, and so on—were deemed acceptable as part of the movement. Violence was not recognized as either legitimate or effective. Civil rights groups and leaders calling for direct and sometimes violent confrontations with the white power structure were denounced as radicals, and their tactics were labeled counterproductive.

Persistence and Change in the American Ideology

Previous chapters have shown the very clear trend of an ever-widening gap between those at the top and the remainder of the U.S. class structure during the last three decades. Has this trend diminished the strength and effectiveness of traditional American beliefs regarding inequality and mobility?

Research conducted by the Pew Economic Mobility Project in the late 2000s reveals that the dominant American ideology remains a powerful force in molding people's ideas about how and why class inequalities are shaped and sustained. Most Americans are steadfast in their beliefs in individual achievement, equality of opportunity, meritocracy, the work ethic, and liberal capitalism.

Through focus groups and surveys, the Pew research confirmed that Americans continue to subscribe to the notion that personal attributes outweigh structural factors as determinants of social inequality. The unwavering belief in individual effort as the major influence on one's place in the social hierarchy and one's ability to move upward is revealed in Figure 8-1. Here we see that the overwhelming majority of Americans, regardless of social class, level of education, or race/ethnicity, feel that they themselves are in control of their economic destiny. When asked

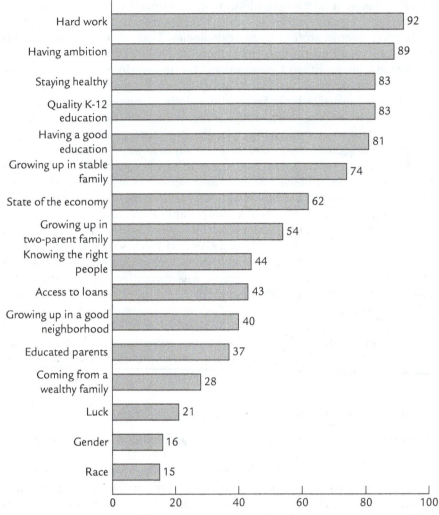

Figure 8-1 ▪ Percentage Answering "Essential" or "Very Important" When Asked
If This Factor Is "Essential, Very Important, Not Very Important or Not Important
at All to Economic Mobility"
Source: Reproduced by permission of the Pew Charitable Trusts.

specifically which factors are essential or very important to economic
mobility, 92 percent ascribe most importance to hard work and 89 percent
to ambition. In contrast, only 28 percent attribute importance to having
come from a wealthy family and 21 percent to luck. Gender and race are
seen as even less important.

The Pew research revealed as well the commitment of Americans to
equality of opportunity rather than equality of condition. Figure 8-2

What do you think is more important for this country: to reduce inequality in America or to ensure everyone has a fair chance of improving their economic standing?

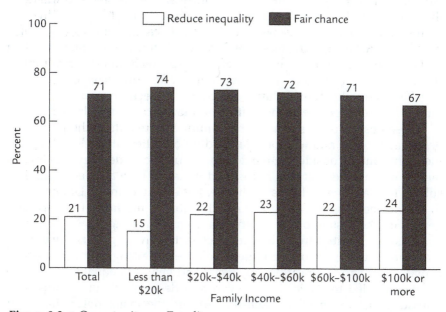

Figure 8-2 ▪ Opportunity vs. Equality
Source: Reproduced by permission of the Pew Charitable Trusts.

shows that more than 70 percent thought it more important to give people "a fair chance to succeed" than to "reduce inequality in this country." Notice that there is hardly any difference among different class groups. Moreover, when they were informed of some facts regarding the reality of income mobility in the United States, less than 20 percent of Americans believed that the low rate of mobility among those at the top of the class structure was a major social problem.

The tenacity of prevailing beliefs among Americans regarding social inequality and opportunities for mobility is even more remarkable in light of the very clear trend of an ever-widening gap between those at the top and the remainder of the class structure during the past three decades. The Pew research revealed that in 2009, in the midst of the most severe economic crisis since the Great Depression of the 1930s, Americans remained optimistic about the possibility of themselves or their children getting ahead even under such dismal circumstances. Moreover, this view was consistent across the entire class range, even among lower-income, less-educated, and unemployed persons.

Tolerance of increasing inequality and an enduring belief in the openness of the opportunity structure might be understood more readily if upward mobility were widespread and common. But, as we saw in Chapter 7, that is not the case. Moreover, the persistence of these beliefs among most Americans is striking given the fact that inequality in income and wealth in the United States is higher and intergenerational mobility lower than in other economically advanced societies. Nor have political movements of any significance aimed at arresting these trends arisen. Americans remain unyielding in their commitment to relatively unfettered capitalism, wherein government is seen as an intrusive, not supportive, force in fostering economic mobility. The Pew research showed that more people believe government hinders rather than helps people in their efforts to move up the class ladder.[5]

These observations speak to the continued strength of the prevailing beliefs about how and why people wind up on different levels of the class hierarchy. But in considering the dominant American ideology, it is important to understand that it is not etched in stone. Like all ideologies, it is subject to challenge and thus to change. For example, in the United States in recent decades, a much greater realization of the impact of race and gender on the system of inequality has emerged among the general public. This has resulted from the successes of the civil rights and women's movements that put forth counterideologies, challenging the long-held explanations and justifications for racial and gender inequality. Although this has not led to a rejection or even to a de-emphasis of the idea that individual achievement and self-reliance are the major determinants of social position, it has brought about an acknowledgment that inequality can be explained in some part as a result of ascribed factors. Similarly, although the classical liberal notion of liberty remains paramount, most Americans today, as we will see in the next chapter, expect government to regulate the market to some degree in order to reduce the gross inequalities produced by unfettered, laissez-faire capitalism.

Legitimation, Ideology, and Socialization

Having now looked at ideology and how it helps to legitimize inequality, we turn our attention to how the dominant ideology is transmitted and how loyalty to the system is infused. How do ideas about social inequality unfold? And what is the process by which people come to accept them?

Socialization

Socialization is the process through which people learn their society's culture. This involves not simply learning the rules and beliefs of the society but internalizing them, making them an integral part of one's way of seeing

---

[5]This view differed slightly among different racial/ethnic and age groups. Also, it should be remembered that these are expressions of how people see and believe the American system to be working. Their responses to specific government policies that have a direct effect upon them might be quite different.

and making judgments about the world. Most simply, socialization consists of learning and accepting the socially defined rights and wrongs of thought and action. If they are successfully imparted by socializing agents such as the school, the family, and the media, the correctness of those beliefs is henceforth seldom questioned or even given much conscious thought.

In American society, for example, there is rarely any question regarding the desirability of applying democratic principles to power conflicts in all areas of social life. From choosing members of a neighborhood softball team to selecting members of Congress, the same basic notions of fairness and equality are assumed. From the time children begin to interact with peers, and particularly when the school begins socializing them, they learn the "rightness" of democratic practices in social relations.

Such beliefs and preferences are, like all other cultural values, imparted through various learning experiences. They are no more natural to the individual than is riding a bicycle or having a preference for chocolate rather than vanilla ice cream. People of different societies are exposed to different ideologies and thus learn different norms and values. What few people ever recognize, however, is that this learning process is aimed at acceptance of the dominant sociopolitical and economic systems. It is the subtle and essentially unconscious nature of the process that makes it so effective. The given system is accepted as seemingly natural; other systems become, in our minds, deviant or inadequate. As already noted, the effectiveness of socialization to the dominant ideology and to the system of inequality is revealed by the fact that even those who are severely disadvantaged by the prevailing institutional arrangement come to accept, at least in the abstract, most elements of it.

Let's look at the major transmitters of the dominant ideology and see how they function in the socialization process and in legitimizing the system of inequality. In examining the way these institutions work, remember that the extent of their effectiveness will differ from person to person. As explained earlier, ideology is not interpreted and accepted in the same manner or degree by all people. Some will accept the system almost blindly, whereas others will question some of its most fundamental features. Most fall at neither of these extremes. In any case, our focus here is on the socializing agents rather than the individual being socialized.

Legitimation, Socialization, and the School

Socialization takes place through the workings of many institutions, beginning with the family. But it is in the school that the process is most deliberate and systematic. Social critic Ivan Illich described the school in modern society as serving a purpose similar to that of powerful churches in past eras: "It is simultaneously the repository of society's myth, the institutionalization of that myth's contradictions, and the locus of the ritual which reproduces and veils the disparities between myth and reality" (1971:37). Schools do not turn out loyal and unquestioning citizens who act more like robots than humans; the educational system is never totally effective in perfectly reproducing a social consciousness in each new generation. But as one of the key agents of socialization in modern societies, the school must be viewed "as an instrument of power" (Spring, 1972:23). Socialization in the school occurs in deliberate as well as indirect ways.

Deliberate Socialization   The school creates legitimacy and imparts the dominant ideology in a variety of ways, some of which are quite straight-forward. Although educators proclaim a spirit of objectivity in the content and methods of their teaching efforts, it is apparent that at all levels of instruction, from kindergarten to college, there is little real competition of ideas. This is particularly the case in the social sciences and history, where course content is heavily biased in favor of the prevailing political and economic institutions; alternative systems or counterinterpretations of events are rarely considered, much less studied intensively.

Some have pointed out that a distinction must be made between the political, or civic, education provided by the school and outright indoctrination (Coleman, 1965). The difference between these two concepts, however, is highly subjective and often difficult to discern. For example, teaching students principles of capitalism while ignoring disparate ways of organizing an economy is viewed as "educational" despite its indoctrinating character. In effect, education, no matter how seemingly neutral, is always political in nature. As the political scientist V. O. Key observed, "In the American setting the schools are not so obviously seen as arms of governance; yet in the large they play a significant role in the perpetuation of the values of the culture, including those habits, patterns of action, norms, and outlooks that are fundamental to the political order" (1964:316).

Despite the common application of such direct techniques, research is inconclusive regarding their impact (Langton, 1969; Litt, 1963; Niemi and Sobieszek, 1977). Several studies indicate that their effects may not be very great in actually molding attitudes. High school civics courses, for example, appear to do little more than reinforce an already well-accepted ritual of the democratic creed (Dawson et al., 1977; Ehman, 1980; Zeigler and Peak, 1970). In any case, however, these educational efforts complement those of other institutions in solidifying the legitimacy of the prevailing system in the minds of students (Hess and Torney, 1967).

What students are *not* exposed to may be as important as what they are exposed to. For example, students at the primary or secondary level are rarely given a realistic picture of the acute economic and political stratification of the society. Serious socioeconomic differences among class and ethnic groups and conflict among them are minimized. "The categories of exploitation, dominance, structure, repression, class, and socialist perspectives," notes Murray Levin, "are not only not transmitted to the young, they are presented as antitruth, intellectually shallow, irrelevant, or utopian" (1971:267).

Efforts to assure that only dominant values will be taught in the schools have led at times to very explicit policing measures. For example, during the hysteria of the "Red scare" following World War I and during the McCarthy period of the early 1950s, teachers were often required to sign loyalty oaths; those suspected of espousing "un-American" ideas were admonished and in some cases even dismissed (Caute, 1978; Murray, 1955). Such blatant tactics to assure educational conformity, however, are usually unnecessary. In most cases, teachers, school board members, and others who determine the content and direction of schooling conform naturally to acceptable standards since they, too, are products of the same socialization process.

Freer expression of ideas occurs at the college level, where the boundaries of tolerance imposed by authorities are much wider than in the public schools. Some, in fact, maintain that the content of higher education in the United States has a natural tendency to undercut rather than reinforce traditional ideologies, unlike that in primary and secondary schools (Milner, 1972). Yet colleges and universities, though less constrained, also operate in a cultural, political, and economic milieu that dictates their conformity to dominant ideas. Most U.S. institutions of higher education are heavily dependent on federal and state governments for operating funds and on corporations for developmental and research programs. Therefore, they cannot stray too far from acceptable political and economic values and objectives.

Incidental Socialization   Direct forms of instruction may be less important than indirect ones in the school's socialization role. Sociologists refer to this as a *hidden curriculum*. Schools at all levels teach fundamentally individualist, capitalist values in a largely unintentional manner. Competition, for example, is an important incidentally imparted value of the classroom. From the first day of school to the conclusion of one's educational experience, competitive incentives are the chief tools used by the educational system—grades, promotion, awards, and so on. With few exceptions, these are individualized competitive situations in which the person rather than the group is held responsible for his or her success or failure. Collective efforts, particularly in academic matters, are not encouraged. This solidly reinforces the principle of individual responsibility, so basic a part of the dominant ideology.

Another theme emphasized by the American educational system is the practical usefulness of education as opposed to its intellectual or abstract value (Williams, 1970). Education is seen as training, leading to economic improvement. Students attend college mainly to acquire a better job rather than to raise their political awareness or to ponder social issues such as inequality. As a result, utilitarian curricula stressing technical skills are more highly valued than are philosophy, the humanities, or the social sciences—fields of study that often force students to consider alternative systems of thought and social action. Preparing people for careers thus acts as an important mechanism in maintaining the status quo.

The Mass Media in the Legitimation Process

In modern societies, the mass media—television, radio, newspapers, magazines, books, motion pictures, and increasingly the Internet—serve a critical role in the legitimation process. First, they are the major sources of information, supplying citizens with knowledge about the society and especially about the political economy. Second, they function as propaganda mechanisms through which powerful units of the government and economy seek to persuade the public either to support their policies, as with government, or to buy their consumer products, in the case of corporations. Third, they are primary agents of socialization, instructing people in the norms and values of their society. All of these functions contribute to the process of legitimation, generating mass belief in and acceptance of dominant political and economic institutions and acceptance of the system of inequality. In examining the role of the mass media in the legitimation process, we need to consider their economic context, their content, and their effects.

The Economic Context of the Media: Control and Accessibility   As they are organized in the United States and, to some extent, in other modern societies, the mass media are mostly capitalist institutions. Today, the mass media are dominated by television and, to a lesser degree, newspapers, both of which are organized within a few giant media corporations (Bagdikian, 2004; McChesney, 1999). Disney, for example, one of the largest of these conglomerates, earned revenues of $41 billion in 2011. Among its vast holdings are the ABC television network, numerous cable networks (including ESPN, the Disney Channel, A&E, and the History Channel), film companies, television production companies, publishing houses, magazines, and radio networks. The intent of these media corporations is to sell news and entertainment to advertisers, which in turn use them to sell products and services to the audiences they attract. This places constraints on the media and forces them to reflect the interests of those who support them—advertisers.

Today, publicly communicating views or ideas requires using the media. A critical concern, therefore, is not only who owns or controls the media but also who has access to them. In modern societies, only government and big business have the resources—money, authority, and influence—to employ the media regularly and effectively.

As privately owned enterprises, the major objective of the various media is to generate revenue. This objective requires that the media cater primarily to those who can pay to put their views on the air or into print: the major corporations, which use the media primarily to create demand for their products and services through advertising. Consider that a thirty-second television commercial on Super Bowl Sunday costs $3.5 million; or that a full-page color ad in *People* magazine costs $300,000; or that Procter and Gamble spends $10 billion each year on media advertising. Advertising not only serves to generate consumer demand but also provides corporations with a means of creating a positive public image. For many years, General Electric, for example, used as an advertising slogan "we bring good things to life." Most corporations convey similar messages in which they are portrayed not as profit-seeking enterprises but as compassionate, publicly responsible citizens.

The economic constraints of the media affect their accessibility. If you feel strongly about a social or political issue, how can you make it known? You can talk to your friends and relatives. You might even go so far as to write a letter to the editor of your local newspaper and have it printed. But how many ears or eyes will those efforts reach? Obviously, very few. Those who are able to communicate their messages to the society as a whole or to large segments of it are those who have the economic resources to buy the use of the media or who possess the authority and influence to command them. This means the corporate wealthy and the politically powerful.

Government access to the media is founded not on financial power but on the fact that the media are closely interwoven with government, particularly at the national level. Put simply, the relationship between government and media is symbiotic; neither can function effectively without the other. As a regulated industry in the United States, the media must take into account the interests of government elites. More important, however, the media are heavily dependent on government elites as their major source of political information, which is the core of news. Studies have indicated that not only are government officials the source of most news but most news stories are drawn from situations over which newsmakers have substantial control (Gans, 1979, 2003; McChesney, 1999). On the opposite side of this relationship, political elites need the media to communicate their views and actions to the citizenry and to maintain their public images. They can easily gain access to the mass media not only because they are the primary newsmakers but also because they possess credibility among the public as well as among the media elite. Accounts of events and policies given by political elites are more likely to be accepted and thus become part of the news format than are accounts and interpretations provided by other sources.

In sum, given the way in which the media are organized in the United States and most other modern societies as well, it is the wealthy and powerful who have maximum access to them. It is those at the top of the power and wealth hierarchies, therefore, who can convey their messages to the public and help shape public opinion. Their views, objectives, and interpretations become those that most people see or read.

It has been suggested that the increased influence of the Internet as a means of political communication may lead to a greater degree of media democracy. The Internet is a two-way medium, unlike other mass media, and thus presents unique possibilities. Also, its easy accessibility reduces considerably the costs of gathering political information, thereby potentially engaging many otherwise politically inactive people. To date, however, there is little evidence of these effects; the Internet seems to be mainly complementing, not replacing, more traditional media. As Paul DiMaggio and colleagues have explained, "Those who seek political information online are generally well informed to begin with, politically oriented, and heavy users of other media" (2001:320). Also, as the battle for control of the Internet intensifies, large commercial enterprises may ultimately prevail as they have done in all other mass media. "Corporate dominance and commercialization of the Internet," writes communications researcher Robert McChesney, "have become the undebated, undebatable, and thoroughly internalized truths of our cyber-times" (1999:136).

Media Content   Think for a moment about where you get your information about what is happening outside the confines of your immediate social world, that is, your family, friends, school, workplace, and neighborhood. To find out what is occurring in the larger society, or in the world, you rely on the mass media—specifically radio, newspapers, television, the Internet, and various forms of social media, like Twitter and Facebook. For the average American, television remains the most popular news source, though its predominance is increasingly challenged by the Internet, especially among young persons (Pew Research Center, 2012d). Newspapers and radio are also popular suppliers of news. These mass media, then, act as gatekeepers of political, economic, and social information—what is ordinarily termed "news." As information gatekeepers, the media are your window on the world, and it is through them that you learn about key events and personalities. Since they define what is news and what is socially significant, the media, in a sense, have become a source of reality itself. As media expert Ben Bagdikian has put it, "For most of the people of the world, for most of the events of the world, what the news systems do not transmit did not happen. To that extent, the world and its inhabitants are what the news media say they are" (1971:xii–xiii).

Given the media's strong influence on the molding of political, economic, and social reality, a key issue concerns the decision-making process of news selection and presentation. Like major decisions of government and the economy, this process is essentially an elite function. Events become newsworthy, and thus of importance to the society, only after they have been selected by the communications elite—editors, journalists, and media executives (Cohen and Young, 1973; Epstein, 1974; Gans, 1979, 2003; Tuchman, 1978).[6] It is the media elite, therefore, who are largely responsible for molding the public's conception of political, economic, and social events and conditions.

In a sense the media act as a filter between political actors and the general public. What powerful elites do and say matters less than the way their actions and words are interpreted and reported by the media. The key to

---

[6]Even though the Internet may increasingly be a public source of news and information, what is reported and commented on in that newest major medium is still framed and informed primarily by what is chosen by the journalistic elite of the more traditional media, namely, television and newspapers.

political success, therefore, lies in creating and sustaining favorable images, especially those that are televised. This is where the powers of the media are so profound. An incident can take on enormous public significance or can fade into obscurity, depending on how it is reported or whether it is reported at all. The Whitewater scandal of the Clinton administration is an example. Essentially the affair emanated from legal questions regarding an Arkansas land deal entered into years earlier by Clinton and his wife, but its scope eventually encompassed an inquiry into the president's personal life. Though it later was seen to be an organized attempt by right-wing partisans to discredit Clinton's presidency (Brock, 2002; Conason and Lyons, 2000), the mass media devoted sustained attention to it, defined its significance, and confirmed its importance for the public. No acts of wrongdoing on the part of the Clintons were ever uncovered despite a three-year investigation that cost the U.S. government $73 million. If the media had chosen to cover this story differently, giving it limited exposure and examining it as a partisan campaign, it could not have emerged as a critical public issue.

Given this concentration of control over the "shaping of reality," what is most critical is gaining access to or influence on the media elite. Because the major media operate as business enterprises, the media elite, when making decisions about what to present, must take into account the interests of dominant economic groups—the large corporations—that supply them with revenue. Second, in light of their symbiotic relationship with government, these decisions must be weighed against the interests of political elites. The result is that ideas of groups and individuals outside the political and economic mainstream receive little attention. In U.S. elections, for example, the mass media generally treat minor parties and candidates as curiosities, not as legitimate contenders, and thus they are rarely taken seriously. So political debate is narrowly limited to the two major parties in the mainstream political arena. In short, parties, organizations, and individuals who advocate serious economic or political change but lack financial and political resources have a very difficult time communicating their messages through the mass media. Ruling business and political elites are best situated to exercise influence over media content.

The emphasis on official perspectives results in limited public understanding of the nature of political, economic, and social problems and how they might be resolved. Rarely do the mass media subject the dominant political economy and the system of inequality to serious scrutiny and criticism. Moreover, even when attention is drawn to societal shortcomings by public affairs or news programs (*60 Minutes*, for example) or by investigative journalists, it is done in the spirit of the dominant ideology. That is, problems are presented as the products of deviant individuals or groups within the context of an otherwise healthy social system. The *systemic* origins of chronic problems—like poverty—are rarely explained or even acknowledged. As David Paletz and Robert Entman have observed, "The mass media have never given powerless Americans the necessary information to link the ubiquitous rotten apples to the structure of the barrel" (1981:167). Questioning the structure and functioning of the dominant political and economic institutions is clearly beyond the capabilities of the mass media as they are organized and operate in the American political economy (Gans, 1979; Gitlin, 1980; McChesney, 1999; Parenti, 1986).

The bias of mass media content toward the dominant system should not be seen, however, as the result of government and economic elites conspiring with media editors, journalists, and executives or of efforts to infiltrate and directly control the media. At times this may occur. Numerous incidents of direct media manipulation were brought to light during the eight years of the George W. Bush administration. For example, representatives of the administration were found to be posing as "reporters," journalists were paid to write favorable or demonstrably false information, and propaganda segments produced by the administration were distributed to local television stations for presentation as regular "news" (Derber, 2005). For the most part, however, there need be no guile, cajolery, or collusion to shape reportage in ways that reflect dominant values. The media elite express dominant values largely unconsciously: They see themselves as objective journalists, not bearers of opinion. As Herbert Gans has noted, "The values in the news are rarely explicit and must be found between the lines—in what actors and activities are reported or ignored, and in how they are described" (1979:39–40). Political objectivity, therefore, is not political neutrality. Critical information presented by the media in the form of news and public affairs is framed by dominant values and shaped by power elites, no matter how seemingly indifferent the presentation may be (Iyengar and Kinder, 1987).

The inability of the mass media to present issues to the public in a thorough and critical manner is largely a result of their commercial imperatives. News, like other aspects of mass media, must be sold as a consumer product. This requires that it be presented in an entertainment format and, as political scientist Lance Bennett (2003) has explained, be personalized, dramatized, fragmented, and reported in a way that stresses the efforts of authorities to bring order to chaotic or crisis situations. It is personalized in the sense that it tends to "downplay the big social, economic, or political picture in favor of the human trials, tragedies, and triumphs that sit at the surface of events" (45). Similarly, the media seek out dramatic incidents and personalities in a story-like form to which viewers and readers can easily relate rather than those that may be more politically significant though less glamorous and fascinating. The entertainment format of news forces it to be presented in unrelated bits and pieces rather than as a meaningful whole. As a result, news becomes a series of what Neil Postman (1985) called "decontextualized facts," comparable to background music. Finally, information presented as news is filtered through a dramatic theme in which officials are constantly dealing with threats, large and small, to social order. The picture that emerges is one in which "the forces of good" (public authorities) are fighting "the forces of evil"—crime, corruption, foreign menaces, and the like.

In short, although they may engage in social criticism, the mass media frame their presentations in a way that legitimizes the prevailing political economy and the attendant structured social inequality. Although there is no blatant censorship of media content in the United States, as there is in a totalitarian society, an implicit understanding exists on the part of the media elite regarding their role in upholding the status quo. Self-censorship by the media is reinforced when they anticipate the reactions of political and economic elites and alter their presentations in advance. At times, of course, more blatant attempts at censorship may arise, as when corporate advertisers exert direct pressure to influence the content of the media or when government elites pressure the media to "toe the line" (Gans, 1979). Although the media elite may resist those pressures, more often their ideological perspectives are fully compatible with those of political and economic elites, and they therefore have little inclination to follow a path not basically in line with those views. Moreover, although the media commonly present opposing sides of social and political issues, the two perspectives are only narrowly divergent, and the issues are presented in ideologically safe stereotypes. The irony of modern communications systems is that despite the profusion of messages with which the citizenry is bombarded daily, the absence of a thorough exploration of issues by the mass media results in an increasingly uninformed public.

Media Effects   Given the immense power of and limited access to the traditional mass media in the United States and other modern societies, are we to conclude that they are simply propaganda tools for the wealthy and powerful? More than fifty years ago C. Wright Mills explained that there is a growing tendency for mass media to be manipulative devices rather than channels for the interchange of opinion: ". . . in the mass society of media markets, competition, if any, goes on between the manipulators with their mass media on the one hand, and the people receiving their propaganda on the other" (1956:305). But concentrated media power does not necessarily guarantee that the media are always effective in molding public opinion and in shaping people's versions of political and social reality.

Although sociologists and communications experts are not certain about the precise effects of the mass media on socialization or how the media modify the influences of other socializing agents such as the family and the school (Comstock, 1980; Thompson, 1995), it appears that the media are becoming the chief means through which people construct their versions of social reality. Well before the advent of television, Walter Lippmann (1922) explained how the mass media, by selectively reporting and interpreting events and personalities, determine the pictures in our heads (stereotypes, as he referred to them) that shape our social worlds. With the predominance of television, this "reality-shaping" function of the mass media has become much more complete. Television serves increasingly in this capacity because few can escape its influence. Only sleep and work occupy more of Americans' time than television viewing, though the

Internet has rapidly established itself as a rival attention-absorbing medium. Most important, the mass media serve as the primary organs of political communication, setting the framework of public discourse, solidifying the legitimacy of powerful institutions and elites, and transmitting the society's dominant ideology.

Early research led communications theorists to conclude that mass media had a direct and significant influence on public attitudes and beliefs. Further research, however, concluded that such direct media power had been exaggerated. People's interpretations of media presentations, it was explained, were modified by social class, ethnicity, religion, and other social variables (Lazarsfeld et al., 1948). The same message, therefore, was unlikely to have the same effects on the shaping of attitudes among all people. Moreover, media messages might simply reaffirm people's prior beliefs and views (Gollin, 1988).

Later communications research pointed out that the emphasis on what media were doing to shape attitudes overlooked the more significant impact of mass media on creating a public *awareness* of issues (McCombs and Shaw, 1972). The idea is that although television and other mass media may not be overly effective in telling us *what* to think, they are extremely effective in telling us what and whom to think *about* (McCombs, 2004; Shaw and McCombs, 1977; Iyengar and Kinder, 1987). Issues the media emphasize become the issues viewers and readers regard as significant. As the media shift their emphasis to new issues, public perceptions change correspondingly.

In setting the framework of social discourse and describing events and personalities, the traditional mass media convey the society's dominant ideology. It is in this sense that they are agents of social control, used by power elites not only to communicate and legitimize their policies and actions but to stabilize the political and economic systems by generating allegiance among the public. As the sociologist Todd Gitlin has explained,

> The media bring a manufactured public world into private space. From within their private crevices, people find themselves relying on the media for concepts, for images of their heroes, for guiding information, for emotional charges, for a recognition of public values, for symbols in general, even for language. Of all the institutions of daily life, the media specialize in orchestrating everyday consciousness—by virtue of their pervasiveness, their accessibility, their centralized symbolic capacity. They name the world's parts, they certify reality *as* reality—and when their certifications are doubted and opposed, as they surely are, it is those same certifications that limit the terms of effective opposition. To put it simply: the mass media have become core systems for the distribution of ideology. (1980:1–2)

We should not assume that the presentation of news is the mass media's only way of creating support for the society's dominant ideology and institutions. In modern societies, news and public affairs represent only a small portion of all media fare, particularly of television. The remaining entertainment, and especially the advertising that constantly accompanies it, is no less reflective and supportive of the society's prevailing value system (Bagdikian, 2004; Goldsen, 1977; Parenti, 1986).

In recognizing the enormous power of mass media in modern societies to portray a particular version of reality, it should be understood that this is not consummate power. The ability of the media to propagate dominant values and shape political reality is by no means absolute. The messages transmitted by the mass media, notes sociologist Herbert Gans, "can neither produce a single and homogeneous audience nor create a single effect on people" (2003:70). Moreover, the increasing influence of the Internet may produce radical changes in how political thought and action are shaped and sustained, though the nature and scope of its influence await future analysis.

Acknowledging the less-than-total power of mass media to influence people's social and political worlds, however, should not lead to an underestimation of the power of this institution. In all modern societies, control of information is critical: Whoever controls the means of communication has great power. Marx posited that those who control the society's means of material production are the most powerful. It might be claimed that in modern societies great power hinges on control of the means of information— the media. This is the reason that political and economic elites make great efforts to dominate them and to control the flow of information. Those who exert significant control over the media or who can freely gain access to them are able to exercise great influence in determining the views, images, and ideas that will become part of the public consciousness.

Summary

Legitimation is the process by which people come to accept the stratification system. As part of this process, ideology is a set of beliefs and values that support the major societal institutions and the unequal outcomes they produce. The dominant ideology in a society explains and justifies the prevailing power and reward structures.

Several explanations have been offered as to why most people in the society, including even those in the lowest social positions, give allegiance to the dominant ideology. Marxists explain it in terms of ideological hegemony and false consciousness. The ideas and values of the ruling (capitalist) class become those of the entire society, despite the fact that they work only in the interests of the ruling class. Elitist theorists explain ideology as ideas produced by elites themselves to justify their dominance. Functionalist theorists explain that people accept the dominant ideology because they share the basic values represented by the ideology; this consensus assures social stability.

The dominant American ideology consists of a number of basic beliefs and values that strongly guide most Americans' thoughts about inequality.

The most essential of these are individual achievement and self-reliance, equality of opportunity, the work ethic, and meritocracy. These beliefs are framed within the context of liberal capitalism. Several ancillary beliefs give additional support to the ideology. These include the ideas that competition and inequality are natural and unchangeable human traits; that societal institutions operate in a neutral, objective fashion; and that there are no viable alternatives to the prevailing political and economic systems.

Legitimation occurs as part of the socialization process. The dominant ideology is transmitted primarily through the workings of two institutions: the school and the mass media. The school imparts dominant beliefs and values both deliberately and indirectly. School curricula that support the prevailing social, political, and economic systems are stressed overwhelmingly, with little attention paid to alternatives.

In modern societies the mass media are the chief sources of information for the public, and they strongly influence the molding of political, economic, and social reality. Ownership of the media is highly concentrated in a few major corporations, giving their owners, editors, and producers great power to determine their content. Because the mass media are profit-generating firms, they are dependent on corporate advertisers for their revenue. Also, through regulation and mutual dependence, they are strongly linked to political elites. Hence, regular access to the media is limited primarily to the wealthy and the politically powerful. This results in what is generally a media defense of the status quo, including the system of stratification. New, alternative forms of communication, particularly the Internet, may give rise to greater media democracy in the form of more widespread access and use, though their impact is still uncertain.

9

Public Policy and
the Class System

*Much of the inequality that exists today is a result of government policy, both what the
government does and what it does not do. Government has the power to move money
from the top to the bottom and the middle, or vice versa.*
JOSEPH E. STIGLITZ
CHUCK COLLINS

Only the little people pay taxes.
LEONA HELMSLEY

Although inequality is characteristic of all societies, the nature and extent
of inequality are not fixed. They vary from society to society, and they
change within societies. In modern societies, such changes take place
primarily through public policies carried out by the state, or government.[1]

This chapter examines how public policies help determine the distribution of societal resources. What, in other words, does government do that
helps shape social stratification? The state is not a neutral observer of the
class system, and almost all of its actions affect the distribution of income
and wealth, prestige, and power, whether intended or not. The political
scientist Harold Lasswell (1936) described this relationship in his classic
definition of politics as "who gets what, when, how."

The Political Economy

To understand how public policies affect the class system, we need to consider the central role of government in the economy. The study of how
government relates to and affects the economy is called **political economy.**
Government can affect the economy in various ways, helping to stimulate
economic development in one area or another, thereby creating (or abolish-
ing) jobs and revenue and thus affecting the general level of prosperity.

---

[1]Although *the state* and *government* are technically not synonymous, in this chapter the terms
are used interchangeably.

The opportunity structures within which people must operate, therefore, are fundamentally shaped by public policies. If the differential between the top and bottom income fifths in Germany, for example, is less discrepant than it is in the United States, that difference is in large measure the result of different public policy choices. Both are capitalist societies, but in Germany the state is more actively involved in assuring a more equitable distribution of the society's resources.

Throughout American history, government has enacted measures that have benefited one class or another. As discussed in Chapter 5, most people identify with the middle classes, and the classes in the middle do in fact represent the vast majority of the American populace. What is often overlooked, however, is the role of government in promoting the growth and expansion of the middle classes during the course of U.S. history. This has occurred as a result of policies that at different times created new economic opportunities and distributed resources in ways that improved the condition of workers and other previously deprived groups, bringing them into the socioeconomic mainstream.

- The creation of compulsory public schools, starting in the early nineteenth century, is the first and, some would argue, the most important of these policies. Those who are not born into fortunate economic circumstances can nonetheless improve their position by acquiring, through public education, skills that qualify them for better jobs and improve their market capabilities.

- In the mid-nineteenth century, the federal government went further in providing economic opportunities for those who were not privileged by legislating a system of land-grant colleges and universities. The Morrill Act of 1854 provided for the establishment of colleges and universities in all states, offering higher education to the children of farmers and workers, who before then had been effectively denied this opportunity.

- The Homestead Act of 1862 opened the West to settlers by giving land to those who promised to farm it. As a result, thousands became property owners through the largess of the federal government.

- At the turn of the nineteenth century, giant corporations, led by the so-called robber barons, attempted to extend their power by creating great trusts and huge industries that maintained inordinate control over their markets. In response, the federal government enacted anti-trust legislation that provided for the regulation of railroads, oil, steel, and other major industries. The intent was to check the power of a few over the many in a capitalist economy.

- In 1913 the United States instituted an income tax for the first time. Most important, it was a *progressive* income tax, which promised to tax people on the basis of their ability to pay. The mechanism was now in place to make a direct impact on the distribution of income and wealth.

- The 1930s brought forth a spate of social legislation spurred by the disastrous economic circumstances of that decade and designed to provide people with economic security. Among the most significant was the Social Security system, which mandated a safety net for those who were beyond their working years and no longer capable of earning a living. Unemployment insurance was another such measure giving workers some security against injury and incapacity.

- The Wagner Labor Relations Act of 1935 fundamentally changed the place of workers in American capitalism. This legislation made it possible for industrial workers to organize into labor unions. Prior to 1935, employers could fire workers for promoting unions. Now industrial workers were given some countervailing power.

- Following World War II, the federal government enacted important new measures that greatly contributed to the expansion of the middle classes in the 1950s and 1960s. One was the G.I. Bill of Rights. Through this measure, returning veterans were given the opportunity to attend colleges and universities, with the federal government picking up the cost of tuition and books. As a result, thousands who otherwise would never have seen the inside of a college classroom availed themselves of higher education.

- Home ownership was also made affordable to hundreds of thousands of families as a result of the G.I. Bill. The federal government guaranteed mortgages for returning veterans, stimulating the housing industry and marking the advent of the great movement of families from the cities to the suburbs.

- When President Lyndon Johnson announced his Great Society in 1964, many public assistance measures were introduced for the first time and others, established earlier, were expanded. The elderly poor were among the key beneficiaries. Social Security was strengthened, and Medicare, a health care system for the elderly, was instituted. Largely as a result of these policies, poverty plummeted among the elderly.

- Johnson's War on Poverty instituted many welfare programs aimed at giving the poor greater competitive opportunities. Medicaid, for example, now provided health care for the very poor. These measures in total lowered the rate of poverty substantially in just a few years.

- The passage of civil rights and voting rights legislation in the 1960s gave many African Americans the opening they needed to establish themselves solidly within the middle classes. Before that time, blatant discrimination had prevented them from entering into better-paying occupations and had held them out of positions of political importance. As a result of protection now provided by the federal government, a huge segment of the African American population was able to move upward in the class system.

- Affirmative action, starting in the 1960s, gave first to African Americans and then to other minorities and women access to jobs and educational opportunities that they had previously lacked. Although these groups were already beginning to make inroads into jobs at the higher levels and were entering institutions of higher education, their progress was accelerated by affirmative action measures.

All of these policies can be seen as stimuli for the reduction of inequality and the expansion of the middle classes. Groups that had been previously excluded or had been disadvantaged in the quest for the society's rewards were now given a boost in life chances. Keep in mind that these measures were aimed not at creating equality of results but rather at creating equality of opportunity.

Of course, government can also act in ways that perpetuate or even enhance *in*equality. For example, it can tax in a way that will benefit the wealthy at the expense of those in the middle and working classes. Or it can provide benefits to those groups and individuals who are already powerful, thus creating an even wider gap between classes. As the economist Joseph Stiglitz has put it, ". . . inequality is, to a very large extent, the result of government policies that shape and direct the forces of technology and markets and broader societal forces" (2012:82).

Capitalism, Democracy, and Inequality

American society is both capitalist and democratic. These two features, however, create a dilemma: How can capitalism, an economic system that generates and assures inequality, coexist with democracy, a political system that encourages equality? Let's look more closely at how the political economies of democratic capitalist societies deal with this dilemma.

The Capitalist Framework   To understand how capitalism as an economic system creates and assures inequality, we need to consider the capitalist framework. The two most basic characteristics that shape economic activity in capitalist society are the competitive pursuit of profit and the private ownership of property.

That profit maximization is the motivational underpinning of capitalism needs little discussion. Most simply, people seek to enhance their wealth by competing with one another for the society's products and services within a free and open market. Business owners try to sell their goods at the highest price, while consumers try to buy them at the lowest price. Capitalists, big or small, try to contain the cost of labor while, on the other side, workers try to maximize their wages.

Pursuing self-interest is certainly common in all societies, but in capitalist societies such activity is considered socially beneficial and morally correct. Moreover, wealth and the means by which it is produced are primarily private. This means that profits generated are private profits. Most basically, capitalism is driven by liberty, the idea that people should be free to pursue their self-interests as they wish and to possess the fruits of their efforts. But individual liberty generates inequality—it can be no other way. In a capitalist system, then, there are winners, but there are also losers. Capitalism is a competitive system, remember, which means that not all can win. Quite simply, in the competition of the market, some are bound to get more than others.

The United States as a Political Democracy   Along with capitalism, the United States is defined most basically as a political democracy. Indeed, Americans commonly think of the United States as the quintessential democracy, emulated but rarely equaled by other societies of the world. The essential components of political democracy have been debated as far back as the Greek city-states over two thousand years ago. But there is widespread agreement that the fundamental objective of a democratic system is to maximize the power of each individual citizen. People are to be afforded equal political rights in their pursuit of the good life; all are given the vote, and all can participate in the political process. Unlike capitalism, democracy generates equality: the more democracy, the more equality.

The Contradiction of Democracy and Capitalism   The confluence of capitalism and democracy thus seems to create a contradiction. Capitalism is founded on *liberty,* which creates inequality; democracy is founded on *equity,* that is, fairness for all.[2] In an ideal capitalist system, a truly equal opportunity structure would exist, wherein all citizens have the same life chances to acquire the society's rewards. As we have now seen, of course, that is not the case in the United States or in any other capitalist society. In all capitalist democracies, however, the state intervenes in the market with a variety of programs that are intended to promote greater equality; in other words, the state attends to the needs of those who do not win in the capitalist competition and provides public goods and services used by all citizens.

Consider what we expect government to do: to assist those who cannot work or who cannot adequately care for themselves and their families; to protect people against foreign threats and control crime domestically; to maintain public schools, from kindergarten to graduate schools; to build and maintain an infrastructure—roads, airports, water lines, and the like. All these activities, along with thousands more, have economic implications that bear on who gets what.

---

[2]Thurow (1975) points out that Americans often use the words *equity* and *equality* as if they were synonymous, though they are not. Equity has to do with the just distribution of economic resources. Justice may or may not require equality, however.

In addition to providing these goods and services to their citizens, all national governments today recognize that certain economic problems and issues cannot be left entirely to the market. We expect government to help assure as low a rate of unemployment as possible and to contain the rate of inflation. We also assume that government will regulate trade and commerce both at home and within the global economy. A capitalist economy, based as it is on the fluctuations of the market, experiences swings, upward and downward. Government is expected to play a major part in minimizing the negative effects of those business cycles. In the last half century, these economic functions of government have grown enormously.

Macroeconomic Policy

The role of government in managing the national economy is called **macroeconomic policy.** Government acts in three ways to influence the society's economy and thus affect the distribution of income and wealth: It *taxes*, it *spends*, and it *regulates*. Each of these processes is subject to intense debate among competing political interests. Each also affects the balance between liberty and equity, and it is the contest between these two that constitutes the essence of national politics in America and other modern societies.

Taxation: How Much, from Whom

Through taxes, government finances all of its activities. Nothing that government does, whether building roads or missiles, operating universities, or providing police and fire protection, is done without cost. To finance these things requires that government raise revenue. This is done primarily through taxation. Government may also borrow to pay its bills, but borrowed moneys must be paid back, along with interest—and they are paid back, of course, with tax dollars. Although few cheerily make their tax payments, in the end, this is the only way that government can function. Often people take for granted what government provides, but it is tax dollars that pay for those public goods and services. We sometimes need to be reminded that, as the jurist Oliver Wendell Holmes put it, "taxes are what we pay for civilized society."

In the early nineteenth century, people paid taxes mainly locally and then only minimally. Gradually, however, government, especially at the federal level, expanded enormously. In the twentieth century, it became the supplier of goods and services that the market could not or would not provide. As people came to expect more from government, the need for more revenue grew correspondingly. Two things occurred in the United States and in other advanced industrial societies that especially propelled the emergence of an active government requiring massive revenues: wars and the development of a welfare state.

The two world wars created a need for armed forces that had been unprecedented. After World War II, with the onset of the so-called Cold War, the U.S. defense establishment grew enormously and became one of the major areas of public spending. Although the military portion of the federal budget has been reduced since the 1960s, it remains a major government expenditure, about 20 percent.

More than military spending, however, the emergence of a welfare state changed the role of government fundamentally. The **welfare state** refers to government insurance, public assistance, education, and medical programs designed to maximize the economic and social welfare of the society's population (Greenberg and Page, 1995). In the United States, Social Security, Medicare, family allowances, unemployment insurance, and support to educational and other related institutions are all part of the welfare state. Thus, the entire range of the citizenry is covered in one form or another. Although, by comparison with some western European societies, the welfare state was relatively late in coming to the United States, Americans of all social classes have come to expect the benefits of its programs.

Fiscal Policy and the Distribution of Income and Wealth   The rate at which people are taxed determines, in some measure, how much disposable income they will have. In effect, taxation has a redistributive influence, and policymakers can affect the distribution of income and wealth by deciding who is taxed at what rate. How government spends the tax dollars it collects has a similar effect. Taxation and public expenditures are together referred to as **fiscal policy.**

How Government Collects Taxes   There are different ways of taxing people, and, depending on the method, different effects may be created. Essentially there are three types of taxes: progressive, regressive, and proportional.

Progressive taxes require that as one's income rises, one's tax payment rises proportionately. This means that those with higher incomes will pay a greater percentage. The federal income tax is the best example of a progressive tax. The effect is to redistribute wealth downward, that is, from the richer classes to the poorer. As the economist John Kenneth Galbraith put it, "The only effective design for diminishing the income inequality inherent in capitalism is the progressive income tax" (1992:179).

Regressive taxes impose a heavier relative burden on the lowest income earners. As income rises, the proportion one pays in taxes declines. This causes an upward redistribution of income, increasing the level of inequality. Social Security taxes, for example, are regressive. In 2013 the Social Security tax was 6.2 percent of income up to a ceiling amount. That ceiling was $110,100. Thus, if you earned, for example, $40,000, you paid 6.2 percent of that amount, or $2,480. If you made $150,000, you paid only on the first $110,100, that is, $6,826, and so your effective Social Security tax rate was not 6.2 percent but about 4.5 percent. If you earned a half million dollars, your effective rate was little more than 1 percent.

Proportional, or flat, **taxes** levy the same percentage rate on all income earners and leave income distribution unaffected. Sales taxes, for instance, are proportional. Everyone pays at the same rate regardless of income. In practice, however, sales taxes have a regressive effect. Wealthier people need to spend less of their income on consumer items and so a lesser proportion is paid in taxes. Someone earning $100,000 may need to spend only $50,000 (50 percent) on living expenses. A person earning $25,000 will have to spend much more of his or her personal income, perhaps as much as 75 percent, and thus will pay proportionately more in sales taxes. Governments usually try to modify this effect by exempting fundamental needs, like groceries or drugs, from taxation.

The impact of tax policies on the distribution of income and wealth can be seen during the post–World War II decades. In the 1950s and 1960s, the tax code was steeply graduated, with high income tax rates imposed on the top income earners. During those years, the bottom half of taxpayers paid less than 10 percent of their total income in taxes while the top bracket was 91 percent (Kuttner, 1996).[3] The gap between top and bottom of the class hierarchy, as a result, began to close.

Changes in the tax code in the early 1980s resulted in a reversal of that trend, contributing to substantial redistribution of income upward. During the 1980s, taxes paid by workers on their wages and salaries rose while the tax obligation of the wealthy and the corporations was reduced. The result was a sharp rise in after-tax income for the top classes and a concomitant loss for the middle and working classes. From 1977 to 1989, the average after-tax income of the top fifth of families grew by 28.1 percent. But the most dramatic growth occurred among the top 1 percent, the families at the very apex of the class system, whose average income grew by 102.2 percent. By contrast, the after-tax income of families in the bottom 80 percent fell by 2.3 percent, with the largest declines occurring among the poorest (Mishel and Bernstein, 1993). These changes in income distribution were not the result only of changes in the tax structure, of course, but those changes contributed significantly.

The regressive changes in the federal income tax that began in the early 1980s were arrested somewhat with modifications to the tax code in 1993, as well as the expansion of the Earned Income Tax Credit (EITC), a program that enabled low-income workers to retain more of their wages. Nonetheless, the continued decline in corporate income taxes and an increasing dependence on state and local taxes precluded the tax system from contributing to a significant closing of the income gap. The massive federal tax cuts of the 2000s enacted by the Bush administration and the Republican-controlled Congress created additional regressive effects (Piketty and Saez, 2006). Indeed, the impact of lowered income tax rates for the wealthiest households

---

[3]Very few wealthy taxpayers actually paid at the rate of 91 percent, however. Abundant loopholes in the tax code made it possible for most to pay at a substantially lower rate.

was extraordinary. A detailed study showed that the average tax cut received by people making over $1 million amounted to more than $110,000 in each year between 2004 and 2012 (Huang and Frentz, 2012).

Who Pays What in Taxes?   Everyone is familiar with the saying that the only sure things in life are death and taxes. No one completely escapes the tax burden. Even if one were to pay no income tax (the poor not earning enough, for example, or the rich employing tax attorneys to find tax loopholes), state governments impose sales taxes on most consumer goods and services. Also, excise taxes must be paid on such things as gasoline, liquor, and cigarettes. Most important, workers pay wage taxes, which finance social insurance programs (like Social Security) and other entitlements. At the federal level, the income tax is the major source of government revenue. Most state governments also impose income taxes of their own. Put simply, individuals as well as corporations must pay taxes on their earnings, but it is individual taxpayers who bear the major income tax burden.

Focusing on the income tax shows how changing policies can create a greater or lesser burden for both corporations and individuals. In the 1980s, corporations paid less, and individuals made up the difference. The corporate share of total U.S. income taxes collected in the 1950s was 39 percent, but during the 1980s that share had been reduced to only 17 percent. Hence, from the 1950s to the 1980s, taxes paid by corporations increased 264 percent, but during the same period, taxes paid by individuals rose by over 1,000 percent (Barlett and Steele, 1992). Today, 8 percent of the federal budget is financed through corporate taxes, with most of the remainder coming from income and payroll taxes paid by individuals (Figure 9-1).

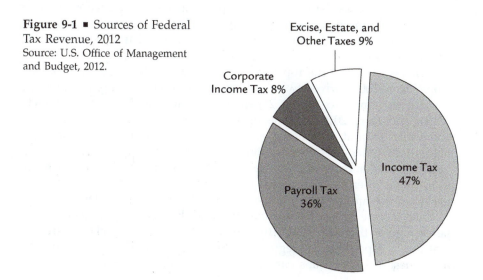

Figure 9-1 ▪ Sources of Federal Tax Revenue, 2012
Source: U.S. Office of Management and Budget, 2012.

Excise, Estate, and Other Taxes 9%

Corporate Income Tax 8%

Income Tax 47%

Payroll Tax 36%

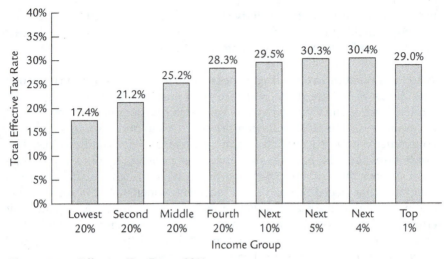

Figure 9-2 ▪ Effective Tax Rates, 2011
Source: From "Who Pays Taxes in America?," The Institute on Taxation and Economic Policy.

In addition to *how* governments tax, the distribution of income and wealth is affected by *what* is taxed. In the United States, there is a capital gains tax, for example, that is applied to earnings from the sale of assets. Sales of stocks and bonds that result in a profit are subject to capital gains tax, as would be profits earned through the sale of a house or any other asset. Because most assets are held by those at the top of the class hierarchy, this tax falls most heavily upon them. Taxes on wages and salaries (like Social Security), however, impact most heavily on the middle and working classes, whose income derives mainly from their jobs.

Huge tax breaks to the super-rich, specifically sharp reductions in taxes on various forms of unearned income such as capital gains, during the 2000s have increasingly shifted the tax burden to the middle classes. The top marginal tax rate on capital gains and dividends today is 15 percent; this is less than half the top rate on wages and salaries. The richest 400 taxpayers in 2007 derived two-thirds of their income from capital gains and dividends, compared to just 2 percent for those making under $50,000 (Feller and Marr, 2010). The result is that, when all forms of taxation are taken into account, the wealthiest Americans pay at a rate not markedly higher than other class groups (Figure 9-2). David Cay Johnston, investigative journalist and former tax reporter for the *New York Times*, concludes, in fact, that when the unreported income and economic benefits that go to the super-rich are factored into the equation, "they pay a smaller percentage of their income in taxes than does the middle class and about the same percentage as the poor" (2005:167). At the very top of the class hierarchy, that is, the super-rich, the regressive effect is stunningly apparent. In 2009 the richest 400 Americans earned $81 billion—more than 1 percent of all income in the United States—yet paid an average tax rate of less than 20 percent (Stewart, 2012).

In looking at the society's tax burden it is also important to recognize that the United States has very mild inheritance taxes, unlike some other societies. Remember that it is through the inheritance of wealth that the wealthy are able to maintain their status from one generation to the next, thus assuring the stability of the class system. Consider how a 100 percent inheritance tax would change the system. It would assure that everyone did in fact begin their lives at the same point, at least in terms of wealth. Differences in social and cultural capital (recall from Chapter 2, Bourdieu's different forms of capital), of course, might still divide the population, but the equal opportunity ethic would be far more viable.

The United States and Other Societies: A Comparison   Most Americans, if asked their feelings about taxes, would claim that they pay too much. And few politicians voice a contrary opinion. But this view, popular as it is, does not reflect what is actually the case. Not only are Americans not overtaxed, their overall tax burden is markedly lower than that of citizens of almost all other developed societies. This can be seen in Figure 9-3. Furthermore, in recent decades an anti-tax ideology has developed in the United States, to the point at which opposition to raising income taxes has become the most fundamental element of the Republican Party's policy

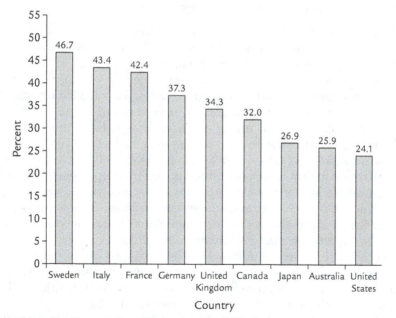

Figure 9-3 ▪ Tax Revenue as a Percentage of GDP
Source: Data taken from Tax Revenue as a Percentage of GDP. © OECD, 2011. Reprinted by permission.

platform. The political scientist Thomas Byrd Edsall has described the pledge to never raise taxes on the affluent as the party's Berlin Wall which no member "can cross over without risking sanctions" (2012:131). But neither have political leaders of the Democratic Party seemed eager to suggest higher tax rates (except on top income earners), despite huge budget deficits. Some social scientists have even suggested that Americans, by comparison with citizens of other postindustrial societies, are simply more averse to paying taxes, given their stronger commitment to individualistic values (Alesina and Glaeser, 2004).

Government Spending: On What, for Whom

Governments do not collect revenue and then stash it away. Nor do tax dollars fall into a bottomless pit, as many taxpayers cynically claim. What governments collect in tax revenue, they spend on goods and services that are returned, in some form, to citizens. As the largest consumer of everything from paper clips to airplanes, the federal government has an automatic impact on the entire economy. State and local governments also spend tax dollars and have a similar, though less widespread, economic impact. Beyond their general economic impact, government spending policies affect specific parts of the class structure. As it turns out, all social classes, from top to bottom, are beneficiaries of government spending in some form.

Categories of Government Spending

There are three general areas in which government spends. First, it supplies public goods, such as defense and highways. These are goods that everyone in the society derives some benefit from, either directly or indirectly. Here, there are no intended class biases. In constructing highways, for example, the government does not build special superexpressways for the wealthy, two-lane highways for the middle classes, and unpaved roads for the poor. People of all classes make use of public highways. Government also provides institutions, like the public school system, that serve everyone, regardless of class position. These public goods theoretically have the effect of maximizing equality of opportunity, but some groups benefit more than others from them. For instance, upper-middle-class commuters who drive from their suburban homes to the inner city and back each day make much greater use of expressways than do inner-city residents, who rely more on public transportation than on private automobiles.

Second, government provides services of various kinds and distributes transfer payments to people. There are virtually thousands of such programs provided by federal, state, and local governments. Some, like public assistance ("welfare"), provide minimal resources to those who do not prosper in the market system. Others, like Social Security and Medicare, focus on the elderly. Still others, such as home mortgage insurance and low-cost loans for college students, benefit working- and middle-class families.

Figure 9-4 ■ The Federal
Budget, 2012
Source: U.S. Office of Management
and Budget, 2012.

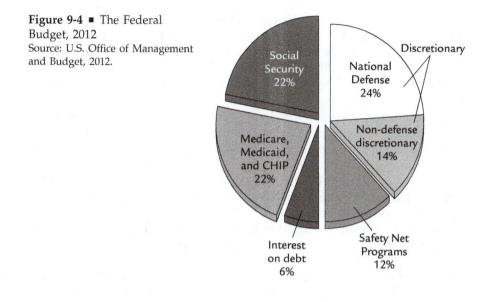

Third, government pays interest on the debt it accumulates. When the federal government cannot pay for its purchases with tax revenues, it borrows, just as a family might borrow money to purchase a house or a car. The interest paid on those accumulated debts amounts to a significant part of the federal budget (Figure 9-4), currently around 6 percent.

It is the second part of government spending—payments and services to individuals and groups—that has the greatest direct impact on the class system. Obviously, *who* government spends its revenue on and *what* it spends it on will benefit different groups in different ways. Let's look in more detail at this part of government spending.

Welfare for the Poor, the Middle, and the Wealthy

Welfare supplied by government takes several forms. First, there is welfare in the popular sense—*public assistance*—means-tested programs designed mainly for the indigent. A second form is *social insurance*, payments in cash or kind to all eligible citizens. A third form of welfare is not easily recognized or even acknowledged—welfare for the well-off and the corporations, referred to by some as "upside-down welfare" or "corporate welfare" (Huff, 1992; Stiglitz, 2012). The implication is that these are welfare programs designed to benefit those who would seem to need them least.

Welfare for the Poor: Public Assistance   Welfare for the poverty classes was discussed in Chapter 6, but we need to review it briefly and place it in the context of the overall tax system. A number of myths have surrounded public assistance. Never has it been as widely applied or as generous as is commonly believed. At no time has public assistance to the poor been a major component of the federal budget. Indeed, efforts to alleviate poverty through government benefits have been and remain less substantial in the United States than in any other advanced nation (Alesina and Glaeser, 2004; Corak, 2005; Freeman, 2007; Noble, 1997).

Welfare for the poor reached a peak in the late 1960s with the Great Society programs of the Johnson administration. The average annual AFDC (Aid to Families with Dependent Children) payment in 1996, when the program was abolished, was around 40 percent of the official poverty line. Adding in noncash programs like food stamps and Medicaid still did not enable families to rise above the poverty line. What's more, even before the radical welfare reform measures of 1996, the most costly public assistance programs—AFDC, food stamps, and Medicaid—had been declining as part of the federal budget. Even during their peak years of the 1960s, these traditional welfare programs constituted a relatively small part of the federal budget. Today, many of them have been either abolished or reduced in scope and content.

Welfare for the Middle Classes: Entitlements and Tax Expenditures   The classes in the middle of the stratification system, not the poor, are the major recipients of government welfare. This takes the form of programs that are often referred to as **entitlements.** Unlike public assistance, these are not means-tested programs wherein recipients must prove their need. So long as one has reached a particular age, as in the case of Social Security, or otherwise qualifies under the law, one is "entitled" to a benefit.

The two largest entitlement programs are Social Security and Medicare, both social insurance programs that benefit primarily the elderly middle classes. Social Security is a program originally instituted in the 1930s that provides old-age insurance. Wealthy individuals and families are usually able to provide for their long-term security through the accumulation of assets, but this is not the case for the working- and lower-middle classes and even for many of the upper-middle class. Hence, it is the intermediate classes that are most dependent on Social Security, and they are its chief beneficiaries. The same is true of Medicare, the government-funded health insurance program for the elderly. Unemployment benefits constitute another entitlement. All these programs are of aid primarily to working people who are dependent mainly on wages and salaries.

A public benefit afforded mostly middle-class families, though rarely seen as a form of welfare, is state-supported higher education. Although students and their families may often grouse about the rising costs of tuition, in no public university does students' tuition pay the full costs of operating the institution. The balance is financed through taxes paid by all citizens, not only those who attend or send their children to state universities.

Those in the middle and upper income brackets receive a number of "hidden" welfare benefits, referred to as **tax expenditures.** These are tax breaks that are, in effect, large subsidies. One of the largest and certainly the most popular of these tax breaks is the deduction that families are allowed to take for interest paid on their home mortgages. This has been of significant benefit to homeowners of all classes and has encouraged home ownership. The poor, however, are less likely to be homeowners than are those in the intermediate classes. Obviously, the more expensive the home, the more substantial the tax break. Thus, the wealthy get an even larger benefit than do those in the middle.

It is not difficult to see how such hidden welfare has a redistributive effect. When people, or corporations, are relieved of some of their tax burden, this provides them with more disposable income. Moreover, tax dollars not collected as a result of tax breaks must be collected from another source. The deduction allowed for mortgage interest for homeowners, for example, cost the government over $110 billion in 2013 (U.S. Census Bureau, 2012c). To finance these benefits, then, may require cuts in other forms of social welfare for other groups. The recipients of these hidden welfare benefits, of course, rarely see them as tax breaks, that is, that their tax obligations are being reduced (Howard, 1997; Mettler, 2007).

Corporate Welfare   Perhaps the least obvious form of welfare is that which goes to the giant corporations in the American economy. This has sometimes been facetiously referred to as "wealthfare." How does this work?

First, large corporations have been particularly adroit at avoiding taxes on income through a complex system of corporate tax laws enacted over many decades. Some of the more striking inequities are reflected in the extremely low or, for some, nonexistent tax bills incurred by the largest and most profitable firms. A government study revealed that in 2004 almost one-third of large U.S. corporations paid taxes on their domestic income at a rate of less than 5 percent (GAO, 2008).

Other corporate tax loopholes are enormous. The Corporate Foreign Tax Credit, for example, lets U.S.-based transnational corporations reduce their U.S. taxes dollar for dollar for foreign tax obligations, saving them billions. Many companies simply move their headquarters offshore to avoid paying taxes on their profits. When Tyco International, a huge conglomerate of electronics, health care products, and industrial equipment firms, claimed Bermuda as its nominal headquarters (it was, in effect, a mailbox), the company saved $500 million annually in U.S. taxes (Johnston, 2003).

In addition to tax breaks, much corporate welfare comes in the form of subsidies and loans. Subsidies are payments made for the support of the economic health of certain industries or companies. Among the more highly subsidized industries over the years have been airlines, defense contractors, and commercial agriculture. As to the last, the bulk of agricultural subsidies such as price support payments are paid not to small farmers but to large corporate farm operations (Moore and Stansel, 1995). The sugar industry, for example, receives $1.4 billion in subsidies each year. The oil and gas industries, among the most profitable of corporations, receive tax credits from the federal government for depletion of reserves.

Source: JIMMY MARGULIES © 2012 NORTH AMERICA SYNDICATE, INC.

Another subsidy is the exploitation of public property by private corporations. A classic example is the 1872 Mining Act—still in effect—that permits mining on federal land for the nominal charge of $5 an acre. This means that mining companies (as well as the timber industry, which cuts trees on federal land) earn profits by mining what belongs to the public. Many of the items produced and sold by large corporations are initially developed largely at public expense. The computer industry is a good example. Much of the early work done by scientists in developing computer technology was related to military projects financed by the Defense Department. The same is true of the aviation industry. The Boeing 707, for example, one of the most successful commercial airplanes, was originally developed at government expense as a military aircraft, the KC-135, for the U.S. Air Force. Boeing took the design and used it to produce the 707, from which it derived billions of dollars in profit. Recently the federal government established a $25 billion loan program for American automakers that will enable them to retool their factories and develop new technologies in order to produce more fuel-efficient vehicles (Bunkley, 2009). All these programs reflect the socialization of investment and costs of production. At the same time that government subsidizes capital investment of large corporate enterprises, profits earned on that investment remain private.

State and local governments routinely induce companies to locate facilities in their states or communities by helping to finance their projects or by awarding them tax abatements. In 1993 the state of Alabama, for example, gave $253 million in economic incentives to Mercedes-Benz to build an automobile assembly plant near Tuscaloosa that would employ 1,500 workers. This amounted to a subsidy of $169,000 for each job (Barlett and Steele, 1998). Nine years later, it gave Hyundai almost $200 million in incentives to locate a production facility in the state (Reeves, 2002). Similar economic gifts are given to the owners of professional sports franchises when state and local governments help finance stadiums and arenas for their teams at public expense. Hundreds of millions in taxpayer funds in the form of various subsidies were used in the construction of the new Yankee Stadium, for example, opened in 2009, though most New York residents would be unable to afford the price of admission for the majority of seats (let alone the luxury suites) in the stadium (New York State Assembly, 2008).

Indirect forms of subsidization to corporations are of even greater significance. The trucking industry, for example, is subsidized by highway construction, as are airlines and shipping companies by the building of airports and harbors. Many of the costs of cleaning up environmental damage created by industry, such as oil spills and water pollution, are borne by consumers and ordinary taxpayers, not only through higher prices of goods but also through government environmental programs. Most industries also benefit from state-supported education, particularly colleges and universities, which train their workers at public expense.

Trade restrictions are another indirect subsidy to corporations. Some industries have been successful in getting the federal government to enact protections against foreign imports through tariffs. This enables U.S. corporations to keep the prices of their products artificially high. The sugar industry, for example, has for decades effectively limited sugar imports through a system of price supports, quotas, and marketing rules, thereby keeping the price of sugar (which is found in almost all processed foods) for American consumers at more than twice that of the estimated world price (Norton, 2005).

Another form of corporate welfare is the protection government provides to especially large corporations or industries when they face financial difficulties. Several times in the last four decades, the federal government has come to the rescue of a large corporation when it was threatened with bankruptcy (Kraar, 1977). The failure of the savings and loan industry in the late 1980s, brought about in large measure by mismanagement and a failure of government oversight, resulted in what, at that time, was the most costly case of corporate welfare, a public bailout that eventually amounted to $300 billion (Waldman and Thomas, 1990).

The financial meltdown of the late 2000s, however, prompted the most massive and far-reaching government bailout of private sector institutions in U.S. history. With the collapse of several giant Wall Street investment firms, it was feared that the entire financial system, and thus the larger economy, was in jeopardy. The response of the Bush and, later, Obama administrations was to infuse threatened banks, investment houses, and insurance companies with hundreds of billions of dollars in government loans and purchases of assets, in hopes of averting what appeared to be an economic catastrophe. AIG, the country's largest insurance company, alone received $173 billion. Huge federal loans and investments were also extended to General Motors and Chrysler in an effort to save these firms from almost certain demise, taking with them tens of thousands of jobs. By mid-2009, it was estimated that more than $10 trillion in public funds had been committed to rescue programs of one sort or another in hopes of staving off a global financial tsunami and stimulating an economic recovery.

The U.S. Welfare State in Comparative Perspective

As noted at the outset of this chapter, no capitalist democracy fails to ameliorate in some degree the inequalities that are naturally created by a capitalist economy. The welfare state provides a safety net—that is, a minimal standard of living that no one is expected to fall below. But societies differ in the extent of their welfare systems; some are more comprehensive and generous than others. Where does the United States stand in this regard?

As with levels of poverty and wealth, the United States must be compared with societies in which the standard of living is not significantly different—the societies of western Europe, Canada, and Japan.

The Scope and Impact of the U.S. Welfare State

We can make comparisons of public assistance on three bases: (1) How much is provided? (2) How broadly is it allocated? (3) What effect does it have on the distribution of income and wealth?

Scope and Size   On most measures, the American welfare state is *less comprehensive* and *less generous*. Despite common public complaints about its size and cost, in reality it is, by comparison, a rather limited and stingy system, particularly as it affects the poor (Fischer et al., 1996; Gautié and Schmitt, 2009; Schmitt, 2009). "For all its potent imagery," notes political scientist Jacob Hacker, "welfare has always been a financially modest component of U.S. social policy" (2002:317). Compared to other developed societies, the U.S. welfare state appears minuscule. Consider maternity leave, for example. In the United States, there is no societywide provision for paid leave. The best that women having children can hope for is to work for a company that offers its workers such benefits. By comparison, Norwegian women automatically receive forty-six weeks of fully paid maternity leave, as well as virtually full reimbursement for all medical costs. The UK gives thirty-nine weeks of paid maternity leave, Canada gives twenty-nine weeks, and Japan, twenty-six weeks (Ray et al., 2009; Social Security Administration, 2012).

Perhaps the most noticeable shortcoming of the American welfare state is its lack of a universal health care component. Medical care, except for Medicare and Medicaid, is a primarily privatized system. Those who can afford to purchase medical insurance or who work for employers who provide it have most of their medical expenses covered. But today almost 50 million persons have no medical insurance. Moreover, 15 percent of the uninsured are actually full-time workers. Even those workers who do have coverage through their employer must pay an increasingly substantial part of their insurance premium. Remember that health care is among the basic life chances.

Range of Coverage   In addition to its less comprehensive form, the American welfare system *covers fewer people* than others. The most highly developed systems blanket their entire populations with benefits. Family allowances in Austria, the Netherlands, and Canada, for example, go to all families with children regardless of their economic status. Medical coverage, as already noted, is universal in most. The U.S. system, by contrast, is a patchwork in which many of those in actual need are not covered. The Affordable Care Act, passed in 2012, mandates that many families and individuals previously not covered will be afforded health care insurance. But unlike programs in other postindustrial countries, medical care in the United States remains uniquely a profit-driven system dominated by private insurance companies.

Distributive Effects   The U.S. welfare state is *less redistributive* than others. This is one of the major factors that contributes to the wider gap between top and bottom income earners in the United States. A key function of the welfare state in other countries is to redistribute wealth so that the extremes of the class system are reduced. Where there is a more advanced welfare state, there is a less acute class hierarchy. Certainly, there are rich and poor in these societies, but the gap between them is narrower than in the United States. Thus the poor are less poor and the rich are less rich. It is, in large measure, the provision of public benefits that narrows the differential. Studies show that although levels of income inequality are not radically higher in the United States before taxes and transfers, once those government measures are factored into the equation, the redistributive effect is much greater in other countries, narrowing the gap between classes (Hacker et al., 2005; Meyer and Wallace, 2009; Smeeding, 2006; Smeeding et al., 2001).

The limited effect of government policies on the reduction of poverty—both relative and absolute—is especially apparent. Although median income is higher in the United States than in most other developed societies, a much

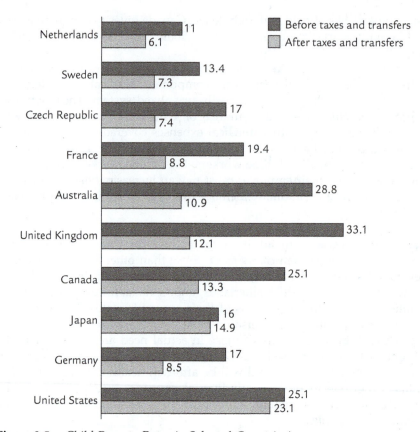

Figure 9-5 ▪ Child Poverty Rates in Selected Countries*
*Poverty line at 50% of median income.
Source: "Bradshaw, Jonathan, Yekaterina Chzhen, Gill Main, Bruno Martorano, Leonardo Menchini, and Chris de Neubourg (2012), 'Relative Income Poverty among Children in Rich Countries', Innocenti Working PaperNo. 2012-01, UNICEF Innocenti Research Centre, Florence."

higher percentage of families are poor relative to that median. Moreover, as was shown in Chapter 6, absolute poverty is also significantly higher. Yet U.S. efforts fall far short of those of economically similar nations in addressing this greater incidence and level of poverty. In his analysis of the impact of public policy on economic inequality in eight affluent nations, the economist Timothy Smeeding (2004) shows that taxes, transfers, and social assistance programs reduced U.S. poverty by 28 percent compared to the average reduction of 62 percent. In some countries, such as Sweden and Germany, the reduction was over 70 percent. Although the antipoverty programs in those nations are not "universally generous and common," concludes Smeeding, "they all are more effective than the United States" (11).

The contrast in the effectiveness of public policies is shown in Figure 9-5. In the United States child poverty is reduced only marginally from 25 to 23 percent as a result of taxes and social programs, a reduction rate far lower than in any European country. Notice in particular that the U.S. rate of child poverty before the impact of taxes and social assistance is not inordinately higher than in many of these countries and is actually lower than in Australia and the United Kingdom. But in the latter countries, a more generous welfare state sharply reduces child poverty. Also noteworthy is the fact that the child poverty rate in the U.S. before taxes and transfers is exactly the same as that in Canada, a country closer culturally and geographically, but the aftereffect of public policies is to cut the Canadian rate almost in half.

Accounting for the Difference

Several factors seem evident in accounting for the difference between the United States and other postindustrial societies in their welfare states, including the American traditions of individualism and self-reliance, American-style capitalism, a basic distrust of government, the power of business, and the weakness of labor.

Individualism First, as we saw in Chapter 8, individualism and its correlate values are in no other society as overarching as they are in the United States. As a result, people are not overly sympathetic to those who are not able to succeed in the capitalist system by their own efforts. Self-reliance is a slavishly adhered-to principle. Thus, welfare in the traditional sense is viewed as appropriate only for those who are physically unable to earn a living or care for themselves. As long as one is able-bodied, no matter the social circumstances, one is expected to be able to support oneself and one's family. Americans are simply less inclined to see government as responsible for caring for the presumably "undeserving" poor. Europeans and Canadians, by comparison, have come to expect major welfare benefits from government.

Capitalism American-Style Second, capitalism in the United States is more unfettered than it is in other contemporary capitalist societies. This, too, is in large measure an outgrowth of the primacy of individualism. The United States provides greater opportunities than do most societies to rise as far as one can go on individual efforts. But it also provides the same kind of individualistic freedom to fail. And in a capitalist system, there are winners and losers—people may be able to climb higher in the United States, but they are also free to fall lower, with no guarantee of a social safety net to catch them. In other countries where capitalism is not so unencumbered, there is a higher limit below which people cannot fall, and by the same token, of course, there are lower limits to what people can earn. Thus, democratic societies make choices in public policies that result in greater or less inequality.

Also as part of the firmer commitment to a more free-wheeling, laissez-faire style of capitalism, Americans seem more willing to accept a higher degree of risk than other societies. While Americans commonly live beyond their means, building up large debts, Europeans seem less prone to gamble in this fashion. They do not carry much consumer debt, do not invest in the stock market as commonly as do Americans, and even buy homes with less mortgage debt (Geoghegan, 2010; Nash, 1995).

Distrust of Government   Third, Americans traditionally have expressed a basic distrust of government. As the economists Robert Heilbroner and Lester Thurow have put it, "Americans have always been disposed to regard government as an interloper, not as an integral part of a society" (1981:57). And in recent years, this antigovernment bias has grown stronger. Ronald Reagan rode to the presidency in 1980 with the message that the best government is the least government. The belief that "government is the problem, not the solution" became a mantra of the Reaganites, and it continues to characterize the major philosophical position not only of Republicans but of many Democrats as well. That idea has seemed to resonate strongly with the U.S. public in the last three decades. There is, however, a long history of suspicion of government that derives from the purer form of capitalism that has always guided the American political economy.

In other societies, although government may be viewed with some suspicion, there is a perception of the state as a necessary and beneficent institution. It is, if not the "solution," at least that institution responsible for finding solutions. Consider the Canadian case in this regard. As political commentator Richard Gwyn has written, "Canadians don't lobby and fight for their rights against government, because, in the collective perception, their government is *theirs*. They assume it is working for them. And it is enough of the time to continue being trusted" (1985:194).

Americans' attitude toward taxes is also noticeably more negative despite the lower rates they pay in comparison with those in other societies. The welfare state in European societies, by contrast, is understood as a necessary component of government that can be financed only with taxes. A German worker, for example, explains that Germans feel secure knowing that if they or their parents become ill, they will be cared for and that their children will receive a good education. "To Americans, these can be financially disastrous," he states. "But we don't fear them. That is why we keep paying. That is why we say we don't like it but the taxes are necessary." He says this despite the fact that his own tax rate is approaching 60 percent! (Nash, 1995:A4).

The commitment of the Scandinavian countries (Norway, Sweden, Denmark, and Finland) to egalitarianism through the tax system would seem utterly astonishing to most Americans. Consider that a typical working-class family in Denmark pays more than one-third of its adjusted income in national and local income taxes. A typical upper-middle-class family might pay almost 50 percent of its income in income taxes (Einhorn and Logue, 2003). Moreover, a 25 percent value-added tax (VAT) is levied on all consumer goods, including groceries, and there are even higher taxes on items such as gasoline and alcohol. Scandinavians, however, seem prepared to tolerate this situation as the price of having a stratification system in which there are comparatively only slight differentials between top and bottom classes. American values simply do not seem to support such a public attitude. Americans, in short, are more firmly committed to equalizing the opportunity structure rather than assuring greater equality of condition, and that is reflected in their attitude toward taxes (Page and Jacobs, 2009).

Business Power and Labor Weakness   Business power is another factor that accounts for the more limited American version of the welfare state. Business in the United States has historically opposed the creation of a larger and more comprehensive welfare state along European or Canadian lines. It has, instead, been a voice for lower taxes, limited benefits, individual effort over government support, and limited responsibility on the part of private enterprise (Noble, 1997). In a striking comparison, the strength of the Norwegian commitment to greater social equality is attested to by the lack of resistance, even from business owners, to that society's extremely generous welfare state. The chief executive of Norway's largest supermarket chain, for example, declares, "We are a very social democratic society, and we don't know another system. It may be costly, but there is social peace. There are no poor people in Norway and I don't want to see any. There are no strikes, and no high demand for salary increases. I want to adjust the system, but only to preserve it" (Ibrahim, 1996).

Along with the resistance of big business, the weakness of labor has been another contributing factor to the reduced size and scope of the U.S. welfare state. Labor unions in the United States have never had the kind of power and influence they have had in Europe or even in Canada, but the decline of American union power has been especially evident since the 1970s (Krugman, 2007; Kuttner, 2007; Lipset, 1996). Neither of the two major political parties identifies itself with labor unions or identifies itself as a working-class party, though Democrats, to some extent, did this in the 1950s and 1960s. In countries with strong welfare states, there has always been a socialist or social democratic political party committed to creating greater economic equality and redistributing societal wealth. There have been no effective American counterparts.

Public Perceptions of Government Spending

The welfare state in the United States, despite its comparatively limited form and content, is grossly misconceived by much of the American public. Most people wildly overestimate what government currently spends and has spent in the past on welfare for the poor, a consistently unpopular government expenditure. By contrast, Americans seriously underestimate spending on hidden or indirect welfare that goes mainly to the middle and upper classes. A national survey conducted in 1996 asked respondents whether more of the federal budget was being spent on Medicare or on foreign aid; 58 percent answered "foreign aid," 27 percent answered "Medicare" (Morin, 1996). In fact, almost twelve times as much was spent on Medicare.[4]

Government Regulation

The state regulates the capitalist market by setting and enforcing the rules by which it operates. It does this through regulation of the monetary system and through various government regulatory agencies. As with taxation and spending, regulatory policies affect the class system.

Regulatory Agencies

Government regulates almost all industries in some fashion, either directly or indirectly. Virtually every business activity in the United States is linked to some government agency. The intent is to assure a more competitive and fair market system. To the extent that powerful industries are able to influence those agencies, however, this objective is sacrificed, and power and wealth continue to flow to the top.

Particularly important government-business ties are found in the independent regulatory commissions. Beginning with the Interstate Commerce Commission in 1887, a succession of agencies has been created by Congress to regulate various parts of the society's commercial life. For example, new foods and drugs that are marketed must meet standards established by the Food and Drug Administration (FDA); the broadcasting industries are regulated by the Federal Communications Commission (FCC), which grants new licenses and maintains broadcast standards; and so on. Even those industries that do not come under the purview of a specific regulatory agency are covered by general-purpose agencies such as the Federal Trade Commission (FTC). The regulatory bodies, then, serve as a key bridge between government and business.

In theory, these agencies have the potential to play a powerful controlling role over big business. It is therefore not surprising that they have become prime targets of corporate influence in government. Moreover, their ability to accomplish real control is often frustrated by the fact that the personnel who occupy the decision-making positions in the regulatory agencies commonly come from the very industries that they are regulating or are sympathetic to their interests. Hence, those charged with regulation often become spokespersons for the industry rather than its critics or enforcers. Over a dozen high-ranking appointees of President George W. Bush to the U.S. Department of Agriculture, for example, came directly from the

---

[4]Respondents were asked how much of the federal budget went to foreign aid. The median estimate was 15 percent; in actuality, foreign aid accounted for less than 1 percent.

meat industry, and his choice to head the Mine Safety and Health Administration had actually lobbied to ease government regulations of coal-dust levels prior to his appointment.

The regulatory function of government in the political economy is further undermined by continual efforts on the part of giant corporations and the business sector in general to maximize *de*regulation or to *self*-regulate. The near-collapse of the U.S. financial system in 2008 was attributed in large measure to the failure of federal agencies to monitor the investment practices of banks and other large financial firms. Efforts to reduce government controls on the corporation are channeled through lobbying and campaign financing, as we will see in Chapter 12. But they are also abetted by the simple lack of adequate resources of government at all levels to effectively challenge corporate influence.

Antitrust laws are another theoretical means of controlling excessive corporate power, but their ineffectiveness and lack of enforcement are well understood. The continued concentration of market power in almost every industry in the American economy affirms this. Hundreds of mergers of industrial corporations occur each year in the United States, but only a few are ever seriously challenged by the government.

In sum, government regulation, in theory, holds powerful economic institutions under control and forces them to act in the public interest. In effect, however, the very opposite is often glaringly evident. In such cases, government regulation of big business acts to solidify the power of large economic enterprises by stifling competition and providing the corporate elite steady access to government policymakers. This leads not to a fairer distribution of societal resources but to a reinforcement of the stratification system.

Efforts to Influence the Business Cycle

A capitalist system operates, in theory, through the dynamics of the market. The laws of supply and demand dictate prices, costs, and other key decisions, all of which are decided by the natural workings of the market. Individual responsibility and the rational pursuit of self-interest, curiously, are balanced, making it impossible for any one firm to dominate the system. Adam Smith, in his famous treatise on capitalism, *The Wealth of Nations*, written in 1776, called this the "invisible hand." In this classic view, the success of capitalism is contingent on the market operating in a condition of laissez-faire—without interference by government. Through competition, individuals will advance or fall back on their own initiative and ambition. The free market, it is believed, provides a neutral competitive setting. Government, therefore, is not to interfere with these natural market processes. Individuals must be assured unhindered movement in the labor market and absolute freedom to buy and sell what they choose. Such competition is bound to create inequality, of course, but what is of utmost importance is not true equality—which, in this view, is a chimera—but equal opportunity for all to compete in the marketplace.

This classical view of the way the market works has never reflected reality. In fact, the state always plays a significant role in the capitalist economy. In the United States over the last hundred or so years, efforts to influence the market through state intervention have occurred in various ways.

Industrial Growth   Although the laissez-faire conception of business-government relations was never more than a figment of capitalist ideology, in the United States an unregulated market was most fully realized during the period of industrial growth following the Civil War. Big business strongly resisted attempts at government control or regulation, successfully in most cases. Furthermore, the industrial expansion that marked the Age of Enterprise was characterized by the unrelenting efforts of big business to assure the enactment of favorable government policies and to maximize its exploitation of government-controlled resources such as land, mining, and timber. Business involvement in government in the 1880s often featured the active role of corporate leaders themselves in politics. The U.S. Senate in 1889 was known as the "Millionaire's Club," since it included numerous industrial magnates of the day (Epstein, 1969:26).

The early part of the twentieth century, known as the Progressive Era, saw the emergence of a reform movement that was based in large part on the belief that the giant corporations had amassed enormous and potentially dangerous powers. As a result, government regulatory agencies were established and antitrust legislation was enacted. Efforts to restrain corporate power and influence, however, were limited (Kolko, 1967; Weinstein, 1968).

The Emergence of Keynesian Principles   The 1930s marked a major change in the relationship of government and business. The most serious economic depression in American history gave rise to the active role of government in shaping as well as influencing economic trends. Government controls became more direct in nature, and the fiction of laissez-faire was finally put to rest. Influenced most strongly by the economic theories of John Maynard Keynes, the federal government under the administration of Franklin D. Roosevelt instituted a sweeping series of measures, the basic purpose of which was to stabilize the business cycle.

Economists had traditionally argued that each economic recession or depression would reverse itself naturally, and this had generally been the case until the 1930s. The depression of that era, however, simply did not turn about, and the economy continued to stagnate. Keynes argued that during periods when private industry was unable to generate consumer demand, there was no necessary upswing, and the level of production and employment might continue to remain low indefinitely. Keynes's solution was for the government to step in and stimulate demand through its own spending programs and through tax cuts. In the same manner, if consumer demand were excessive and inflation were threatening economic stability, government could reverse its policies by cutting its expenditures and raising taxes. With these policies, government assumed unprecedented responsibility for monitoring the economic system.

Despite the more active role of government in the economy, the basic capitalist system was upheld. But the fear of another depression of the severity of the 1930s created a general acceptance of the idea that government had at least some role to play in managing the capitalist economy.

Managed Capitalism The most forceful convergence of state and corporation took place in the era after World War II. Big business viewed the rise of big government and its intervention in the economic process not as a countervailing threat but as a guarantor of a stable economy as well as a vital customer for its products and services. Likewise, government came to accept the inevitability, and indeed the necessity, of the large corporate enterprise as the dominant form of business in the society (Barber, 1970; Kuttner, 2007; Reich, 2007).

This era, from 1946 to 1973, has sometimes been called the "Golden Age" of the American economy.[5] An unprecedented period of economic prosperity ensued, brought about largely through public policies supported by both major political parties. Despite fundamental differences in philosophy, Republicans now went along with Democrats and accepted a political economy characterized as "managed capitalism," underwritten by Keynesian economic principles. Business, labor, and government entered into a kind of pact in which each implicitly understood that their mutual cooperation in this system would continue to foster a well-functioning and increasingly productive economy. Workers gained economic security and rising wages as productivity soared and a more equitable distribution of income and wealth began to emerge. As we saw in Chapters 3 and 5, it was during this period that the modern American middle class was created.

Partisan Differences in Public Policy in the Modern Era

Both major American political parties in the modern period have aimed for economic growth and prosperity, but their strategies for assuring those conditions have been radically different. For the past three decades their policy positions have deviated sharply from the largely bipartisan and relatively cooperative mood that characterized relations among political and corporate elites during the twenty-five years after World War II.

---

[5]Robert Reich (2007) refers to this period as "The Not Quite Golden Age" since a poverty class was still present (if largely hidden from most of the nation), African Americans were still second-class citizens economically, socially, and politically, and women had yet to begin their entrance into all segments of the labor force.

Competing Approaches to the Political Economy

The most essential differences in their approach to public policy lie in what the parties and their followers view as the proper role of government in the political economy. During the past three decades, these differences have been greatly accentuated.

Republicans, despite their acquiescence in Keynesian policies during the age of managed capitalism, have traditionally advocated a less active state. Solutions to economic problems, they believe, lie in the workings of the market. Thus, the public sector—government—is to play only a minimal economic role. This view stems from the basic belief that markets are self-correcting and function best when left to their own dynamics. But it is founded as well in the ideological position of American conservativism: in a free-market system, people are rewarded on the basis of their efforts; rewarding people solely on the basis of need through government assistance, therefore, hinders incentives for work and innovation. Inequality as an outcome of this system is inevitable and acceptable.

Although Democrats, like Republicans, also see solutions in the market, they advocate more state intervention. Inequality may be unavoidable under any circumstances, but it can be reduced through the use of macroeconomic policies and specific government programs. This approach rests on the ideological notion that government is a necessary actor in areas in which the free market cannot or will not meet basic human needs.

Demand-Side Policies: The Democratic Approach   Democrats have favored economic policies that derive basically from Keynesian ideas. The problem of the economy, in this view, is that producers try to limit supply in order to maximize their profits and reduce inflation. In limiting supply, however, people lose their jobs; unemployment, therefore, is the major demand-side problem (Froman, 1984). The solution is to put money in the pockets of workers—consumers—who will spend it and thus generate economic activity, creating demand and keeping people employed. To accomplish this, policies are favored that give workers tax breaks and pass more of the tax burden to the rich and the corporations. Similarly, social assistance programs are expanded, leaving more money for workers to spend in the consumer market.

This approach was employed during the Great Depression of the 1930s, when government became the employer of last resort, putting people to work on public projects in its efforts to create consumer demand and lift the economy out of the doldrums. Since that time, Democratic administrations—and even Republican ones until 1980—have adopted some form of the Keynesian strategy, acknowledging the important role of government in minimizing unemployment and assuring economic growth. These policies tend to shift wealth downward as the rich receive less of a return on their tax dollars and the middle, working, and poverty classes receive more.

Supply-Side Policies: The Republican Approach Starting in the late 1970s but building greatest momentum during the Reagan era of the 1980s, the Republican Party veered sharply to the right, adopting a new economic philosophy that rejected Keynesian principles and the managed capitalism model that had prevailed during the previous three decades. In its place Republicans now took a more purely laissez-faire approach to the political economy: Government, it is maintained, is an intrusive institution whose influence is overbearing and whose economic role, therefore, should be minimized so that market forces can operate relatively unfettered. From this view emerged what came to be known as supply-side or "trickle down" policies.

The supply-side strategy for stimulating economic growth, minimizing unemployment and keeping inflation in check, begins from the direction opposite to that of Keynesian or demand-side policies. Supply-siders maintain that it is suppliers (that is, producers) who must be given incentives to produce more, which, in turn, will eventually create demand. In this view, normal investment activities of the private sector can generate sufficient demand that, in turn, can generate economic growth without having the government intervene (Heilbroner and Thurow, 1994). Rather than putting more money into the pockets of workers, therefore, more money is made available to the wealthy and to the corporations, who, it is assumed, will invest it in productive projects—corporations will purchase new machinery, build new factories, and so on—and in the process create employment. Hence, the presumed "trickle down" effect.

To accomplish this, the tax burden is shifted downward from those at the top to those in the intermediate classes. Tax breaks and lower marginal income tax rates are enacted, placing a higher burden on taxes on workers' wages. A reduction of corporate taxes and taxes that impact most heavily on the wealthy, like capital gains, is also employed. With the same objective in mind, welfare is shifted from the bottom of the social hierarchy to the top. This is what has been characterized as "upside-down welfare." The short-term redistributive effect, as a result, is the converse of demand-side policies. Rather than lifting those in the middle and lower income groups, more wealth flows to those at the top.

The Reagan Revolution The supply-side strategy was adopted zealously by the Reagan administration in the 1980s. Much of the mixed-economy, or managed capitalism of the post–World War II era was henceforth dismantled. Marginal tax rates for corporations and the wealthy were lowered, while taxes on wages rose. Regulation of banks and other financial institutions as well as of key industries was rolled back. Labor unions, as noted in Chapter 5, were largely disempowered as their membership dwindled.

The outcome of these policies was not the trickle down that had been theorized, but creation of the widest discrepancy between the top and the bottom of the class hierarchy since the 1920s (Phillips, 1990, 1994). Recall the statistics in Chapter 3 regarding the expansion of inequality during this decade, a reversal of the trend in the 1950s and 1960s. Average wages declined even though new jobs were created. The expected investment in productive projects, moreover, did not materialize, and rapid and substantial industrial growth did not occur (Atkinson, 2006; Ettlinger and Linden, 2012). Also, because of the reduction in federal revenue resulting from lowered income taxes, government had to borrow to pay for a huge increase in military spending. This produced a tripling of the national debt. Some suggest that the creation of great national debt was purposeful: to "starve" the federal government so that it would be forced to reduce the welfare state, to which the Reaganites were philosophically opposed. In any case, the deficit became a force in its own right in reducing social welfare expenditures (Galbraith, 1994).

The Clinton Years   Although Bill Clinton and his advisors were not devout Keynesians and for six of his eight years he faced a contentious Republican-controlled Congress, the impact of Reagan-era policies was reduced somewhat during his administration. Top income tax rates were raised, the Earned Income Tax Credit (EITC) was expanded, and the minimum wage was increased. These measures were more closely in line with the traditional Democratic approach to the political economy, that is, efforts aimed at raising the income of families in the intermediate classes rather than wealthy families and large corporations. The economy did expand greatly, creating more than 20 million new jobs, and poverty rates dropped (see Figure 6-1). Moreover, the huge federal debt that had been run up by the Reagan administration was sharply reduced, actually creating a budget surplus for the first time in decades.

Despite its greater adherence to the demand-side model, however, the Clinton administration was not immune to the rightward shift that had so fundamentally defined the Reagan years. Clinton himself famously declared in 1996 that "the era of big government is over." In fact, what is perhaps the most enduring public policy legacy of his presidency is the radical reform of the welfare system, as we saw in Chapter 6. Most important, the income and wealth gap between the rich and the remainder of the class hierarchy that had so greatly expanded during the previous decade was not reduced.

The Bush Years and the Great Recession   The administration of George W. Bush, aided by a submissive Republican Congress, revitalized the supply-side approach with even greater fervor than had been applied during the Reagan years. Massive tax cuts were enacted that benefited mostly the very top income earners (Andrews, 2007; Johnston, 2006). Deregulation of financial institutions and the business sector generally created an era of laissez-faire that was unprecedented since the 1920s. The result was an even greater expansion of the gap between those at the top of the class system and the remainder of the population than had been produced by Reagan policies in the 1980s. The very wealthiest families thrived enormously while workers' wages were basically stagnant and the poverty rate again climbed upward.

Declining tax revenues, along with continued large budgets, produced a massive federal debt. The federal budget surplus of $236 billion that Bush had inherited in 2001 had turned into a $420 billion deficit by 2006. And, the long-term effect of those policies was expected to create huge government deficits far into the future (Atkinson, 2006; Leonhardt, 2009). Once again questions were raised as to the ulterior motive of tax cuts that contributed to the accumulation of huge government debt. Was the real intention to purposely reduce the ability of the federal government to fund social welfare programs to which the administration and the Republican-dominated Congress were ideologically averse? In any case, the tax burden, now even more dependent on regressive taxes, was shifted further downward in the class hierarchy (Beatty, 2003; Johnston, 2006; Mishel et al., 2009).

Political writer Naomi Klein (2008) gives credence to the view that the underlying purpose of the creation of huge debts was an implicit strategy to reduce the size of the federal government. A guiding principle of the Bush administration, with roots in the Reagan era, she writes, was the privatization of government, that is, "huge transfers of public wealth to private hands." Thus, outside contractors were given tasks ordinarily carried out by public agencies. The use of private security firms and suppliers performing duties in Iraq ordinarily the responsibility of the military is, perhaps, the most obvious example, but many other traditional government functions were outsourced to private contractors. Privatization accomplished two objectives of the Republican philosophy: strengthening the government-corporation nexus and helping to downsize—ultimately emasculate—the federal government, with the vision of creating a virtually unfettered capitalist market.[6]

In 2008, the United States entered into an economic crisis that few had imagined possible. The near-collapse of the financial system was followed by the decompression of the entire economy. The ensuing recession, subsequently referred to as the "Great Recession," was the deepest since the Great Depression of the 1930s, affecting all sectors of the U.S. economy.

The Obama Ascendancy   The presidency of Barack Obama, along with a Democratic-controlled Congress, starting in 2009 promised to reverse the direction of public policies of the previous three decades and to begin to

---

[6]Privatization not only benefited large corporate donors but enabled public officials to enrich themselves after their government service by selling their inside expertise to those same interest groups. As Klein writes, "stay in government just long enough to get an impressive title in a department handing out big contracts and to collect insider information on what will sell, then quit and sell access to your former colleagues" (2008:379).

move the political economy in a new direction. Those policies had enabled the winners in the American economic system to use their political power "to expand their winnings" (Levy and Temin, 2007:41). The new administration acknowledged the enormity of the income and wealth gap that had been created and gave indications of its intention to arrest and reverse that trend.

The alarming failure of the financial system was attributed in large measure to the cycle of deregulation and general lack of government oversight of banking and industry that had been in effect since the late 1970s; that cycle now seemed clearly at an end. Keynesian principles, dismissed by Reagan and Bush, were once again embraced. As the first decade of the twenty-first century came to an end, many anticipated that new public policies, defined by a proactive government in the political economy, would begin to address the deep inequalities in income and wealth that had come to define so basically the American class system. However, the depth of the recession, in combination with extraordinarily bitter political conflict between the President and his Republican opponents, who regained ascendancy in the House of Representatives in 2010, precluded the introduction of such measures (Edsall, 2012; Mann and Ornstein, 2012). The administration's single policy success, the passage of an act intended to provide health insurance to a broader range of Americans, was met with intense Republican resistance and was validated only as a result of a five to four Supreme Court decision.

More or Less Inequality? Policy Choices

When and where public investment in education, health care, housing, and other key life chances is great, inequalities are ameliorated; when and where it is low, inequalities are sustained and even intensified. Class differences, then, are in large measure the product of public policies. But these differences in public investment from society to society, and within societies from one historical period to another, are the result of decisions made by governments, at least in some measure in accordance with public opinion. The level of investment will vacillate: In the United States, at times, like the 1950s and 1960s, it was substantial and resulted in inducing greater equality. At other times, like the 1980s and 2000s, it was constricted and resulted in greater inequality. In any case, however, public investment has always been lower in the United States than in other advanced industrial nations (Alderson and Nielsen, 2002; Smeeding, 2004; Fischer et al., 1996).

What distinguishes American society from other contemporary capitalist societies is not the domination of its economy by a small number of giant corporations—that is characteristic of western Europe, Canada, and Japan as well. What *is* strikingly different is the distribution of resources and power among government, business, and labor. The United States stands out clearly as the society most thoroughly dominated by private power—the business sector—with relatively underdeveloped public institutions and a historically weak labor movement. This influences all parts of the American political economy, especially the distribution of income and wealth and the public policies aimed at altering that distribution.

Summary

All contemporary capitalist societies make attempts to ameliorate the inequalities that are naturally generated by a capitalist economy. To affect the distribution of income and wealth, government acts in three ways: It taxes, it spends, and it regulates. The first two functions are called fiscal policy.

Progressive taxes have the effect of redistributing income downward. Regressive taxes have the opposite effect. Proportional taxes leave income distribution unaffected. The income tax is the major source of government revenue. Although individuals as well as corporations pay taxes on their earnings, the bulk of income taxes is paid by individuals. Despite popular beliefs to the contrary, Americans pay less in taxes than do citizens of other Western industrial societies.

Government spends its revenue in three general areas: It supplies public goods, which benefit everyone regardless of social class; it provides services of various kinds and distributes transfer payments to people; and it pays interest on the national debt. The first two, especially the provision of various benefits, directly affect the class system.

Various government welfare policies benefit different classes. Public assistance is welfare for the poverty classes. This is what the general public commonly understands as "welfare." Welfare for the middle classes—namely, entitlements and tax expenditures—constitutes a much greater percentage of government spending; Social Security and Medicare are the two major entitlement programs. Corporate welfare takes several forms, including tax avoidance, direct and indirect subsidies by government, and government assistance to corporations in financial difficulty.

In the United States, public spending policies of the 1950s and 1960s had equalizing effects. Social Security and Medicare, for example, made it possible for millions of elderly Americans to escape poverty and avoid the insecurity of old age. The federal government provided relatively inexpensive home loans, enabling millions to own their homes for the first time. Government subsidies to education like the G.I. Bill made it possible for millions to earn a college degree who would never have had the opportunity without such assistance. And the War on Poverty, comprising numerous public assistance programs, helped reduce the poverty class. These spending policies were reversed beginning in the 1980s as assistance programs were slashed and government spending was redirected to defense industries and other activities that benefited higher social classes.

The U.S. welfare state is less comprehensive and generous than that of other Western industrial societies. It is also less redistributive than others. These differences are accounted for by a stronger American belief in individualism, a more unfettered form of capitalism, a public distrust of government, and stronger business power combined with a weaker labor movement. Most Americans seriously overestimate the dimensions of the welfare state, particularly as it affects the poor.

Through regulation of the economy, the state tries to maximize fairness and equity in the distribution of societal resources. It does this through regulatory agencies that, in theory, have the potential to play a strong role in checking the power of big business. In reality, however, regulation often functions as a means of solidifying the power of large corporate enterprises by stifling competition and providing the corporate elite steady access to government policymakers.

Government also seeks to keep the economic system functioning smoothly by influencing the business cycle. Starting in the 1930s, all federal administrations adopted Keynesian policies in some degree, in which consumer demand is influenced by fiscal and monetary policies. With political control passing to a radically conservative Republican Party in the 1980s, however, public policy for almost three decades turned back to a laissez-faire approach, minimizing government influence in the political economy. Deregulation of business and industry prevailed and tax policies were enacted that widened the gap between the super-rich and the rest of the class system. That approach seemed at an end with the economic collapse of the late 2000s, but hyper-partisanship and ideological conflict at all levels of government frustrated efforts at change.

10

Racial/Ethnic Stratification

If put in sufficiently general terms, the essence of the good society can be easily stated. It is that every member, regardless of gender, race or ethnic origin, should have access to a rewarding life.
JOHN KENNETH GALBRAITH

In 1963 we were un-free; today we are unequal.
REV. JESSE JACKSON

To point out that the United States is a **multiethnic society,** one that has incorporated a variety of racial and ethnic groups throughout its history, is to state the obvious. Indeed, it is not exaggerating the matter to declare that no society today or in the past has attempted to accommodate as great a mix of peoples as has the United States. In that sense, it remains one of the great social experiments of human development. Throughout American history, however, race and ethnicity have served as critical sources of social and economic division. And they continue to do so today. The major purpose of this chapter is to examine how America's racial/ethnic diversity translates into a hierarchical arrangement.

As a prerequisite to understanding the American system of racial/ethnic stratification, we need to examine a few terms and concepts that are basic to a study of ethnic relations and ethnic inequality generally. These terms and concepts are used commonly but inconsistently, and they often are seriously misunderstood. A second prerequisite is a brief look at the actual racial/ethnic composition of American society and how it is changing. It is surprising how misinformed most Americans are about the actual ethnic makeup of their society. Despite the virtually unparalleled heterogeneity within which they live, the majority of Americans cannot describe the actual size of various ethnic groups with anything approaching accuracy.

Ethnicity and Race

We begin with two concepts that are among the most misunderstood and controversial in all of the social sciences: ethnicity and race.

Ethnicity

Ethnicity is the easier concept to deal with and the one less debatable. **Ethnic groups** are groups within a larger society that to some degree are set off from others by displaying a unique set of cultural traits: language, religion, diet, and so on. Members of an ethnic group perceive themselves as a community, in a broad sense, and thus maintain feelings of "we" (group members) as opposed to "they" (those who are outside the group). They share what they believe to be common historical roots and experiences and are therefore apt to feel a stronger affinity for each other than for those of other ethnic origins (Blauner, 1992).

Not all members of an ethnic group, of course, feel as strongly as others about their ethnicity. Some are very conscious of their ethnic ties and make efforts to sustain them by choosing coethnics as friends, neighbors, and marital partners. Others may de-emphasize ethnicity to the point where it is no longer a significant part of their personal identity and affects little of their social life. In immigrant societies, like the United States, ethnicity is commonly diluted with each successive generation. Ethnic identity and association progressively fade as people are more thoroughly assimilated into the larger society and its culture. Ethnicity declines in importance for many as they marry across ethnic lines and maintain social relationships devoid of ethnic content.

Nonetheless, ethnicity remains a fundamental source of identity and determines much of how a person thinks, acts, and is treated by others. Ethnic conflicts in many contemporary societies demonstrate the intractability of group boundaries and the power of ethnicity as a mobilizing force. Other social categories in modern society—social class, gender, age, occupation, and so on—provide a source of identification for people and, like ethnic groups, become bases of solidarity, social cleavage, and social hierarchies. But in multiethnic societies, ethnicity is an especially strong base of loyalty and consciousness for most people and thus serves as a catalyst for competition and conflict. In addition, ethnicity is usually interrelated and overlaps with these other sources of group identification and attachment. Most important, ethnicity is a basis of ranking, in which one is treated according to the status of one's ethnic group. In this sense, ethnicity is a dominant force in people's lives whether or not they are strongly conscious of their ethnic identity and regardless of the degree to which ethnicity shapes their social relations.

In the United States several ethnic groups are often lumped together into more inclusive categories ("**panethnic groups**"), usually based on their world region of origin: Asian Americans, Hispanic Americans, Euro-Americans, and so on. Each of these broad ethnic categories actually consists of different specific ethnic groups whose only similarity may be the continent from which they originally came. Japanese Americans, Vietnamese Americans, and Indian Americans, for example, are all considered part of the Asian American category, even though in terms of language, religion, and even physical appearance they exhibit few commonalities. Even America's black population is emerging as an ethnically varied category. African Americans whose origins reach back to the seventeenth century are being joined by recent black immigrants from Caribbean countries like Haiti and Jamaica and from African countries such as Somalia and Nigeria, creating a more culturally diverse panethnic category.

Race

A case can be made that the concept of race is the most highly charged and contentious in the entire lexicon of social science. Without question, it is one of the most misconceived and misused ideas of the modern world, and rarely is it used dispassionately.

To begin with, "race" is not applied consistently and thus may mean different things to different people. In popular usage it has been applied to a wide variety of human categories, including people with roughly similar physical features (the white race), religion (the Jewish race), nationality (the English race), and even the entire human species (the human race). None of these applications is accurate and meaningful from a social scientific standpoint.

The best that can be said is that **race** crudely describes people who share a set of similar genetic characteristics or, as biologists refer to them, gene frequencies. Racial categories, however, must be understood as entirely arbitrary. Physical differences among people obviously exist, and these differences are statistically clear among groups. It is true that, through a high degree of inbreeding over many generations and as adaptations to different physical environments, groups with distinctive gene frequencies and phenotypic traits (i.e., observable physical features) are produced. There are evident differences, for example, between a "typical" black person and a "typical" white person in the United States. People therefore may be said to fall into statistical categories by physical type.

These statistical categories, however, should not be mistaken for actual human groupings founded on unmistakable hereditary traits. Because all human types are capable of interbreeding, there are no clear-cut divisions between groups. Moreover, differences among individuals of the same group (or "racial type") are greater than the differences found between groups (Marks, 1995). Even the most inattentive person can see that the skin color of many people in the United States who are considered "black" is as light as that of those considered "white," and vice versa. Popular and uncomplicated racial divisions of the human population are thus overly simplified and essentially discretionary.

Races, then, are social creations. This can be seen easily when we compare different societies, each with numerous physical types. The same individual categorized as "black" in the United States, for example, might be categorized as "white" in Brazil. Brazilians do not see or define races in exactly the same way as Americans, nor do they necessarily use the same physical characteristics as standards with which to categorize people (Harris, 1964; Marger, 2012; van den Berghe, 1978). Each heterogeneous society takes whatever are perceived as important physical differences among people and builds a set of racial categories into which people are placed. Different societies will use different criteria with which to assign people racially, thereby creating classification systems that may have little or no correspondence from one society to the next.

Even *within* societies, the definition of races has never been consistent. Consider the United States, where many Euro-American ethnic groups— Italians, Jews, Poles, for example—were classified by the U.S. Census as "races" as late as 1900. Also, "mulatto," "quadroon," and "octoroon" categories (neither "black" nor "white") existed in the 1800s but were later discarded. Today people's racial identity is essentially a combination of *self*-identification, wherein they declare their "race," just as they declare their religion, and *social* identification, in which commonly ascribed physical characteristics are used by others to informally assign people to racial categories. Why is Barack Obama America's first "African American" president? His heredity is as much white as black, being the son of a black Kenyan father and a white American mother from Kansas. Obama has described himself as African American and his physical characteristics are sufficiently reflective of most African Americans that this description is affirmed.

Racial-Ethnic Categories

Given the complicated, inconsistent, and dubious meaning of "race," some social scientists have suggested doing away entirely with it, using "ethnicity" instead to describe and subdivide the population of a multiethnic society (Montagu, 1974; Patterson, 1997). But the notion of race is so venerable and commonly used that we are forced to recognize it and deal with it. Familiar racial and ethnic categories currently in vogue in the United States have become so ingrained in our thinking and our social observations that we evoke them almost automatically. Again, it is important to remember that these categories are purely abstract and arbitrary.

In 1977, the U.S. federal government, as a means of monitoring and enforcing civil rights legislation and affirmative action programs, adopted a set of racial and ethnic categories by which people could be classified and counted (Wright, 1994). These categories were subsequently adopted by virtually all government agencies, including the U.S. Census Bureau, as well as by educational institutions, corporations, and the mass media. Five major categories were established, which have been changed only in minor form since then: white, black, Hispanic, Asian/Pacific Islander, and American Indian/Alaskan Native. These have become familiar categories, appearing, as they do, on educational and employment applications, census forms, and surveys of one sort or another. Unfortunately, rather than clarifying the conceptual morass of race and ethnicity in American society, these categories have further confounded the issue and contributed to even greater confusion.

Let's start with "white" and "black." Obviously, as a basis for classifying people, white and black no more accurately describe people physically than do green and blue. And even if they did, what would those divisions really mean? As noted earlier, the very idea of "race" is scientifically questionable, at best. Yet here we have a classification system—endorsed by the U.S. government and other major societal institutions—that obligates people to identify themselves "racially" and thus subdivides the population into so-called racial categories. I prefer to conceptualize these as ethnic groups or, in some cases, panethnic groups. In the remainder of this chapter, for the most part, I use the terms African American and Euro-American in place of black and white.

Next, let's consider the category *Hispanic*. The first two classifications, black and white, are "racial" designations, but here, alongside them, is an ethnic designation. Hispanic[1] refers to anyone whose ancestral origins are Mexico, Central and South America, Spanish-speaking islands of the Caribbean, and Spain. Hispanics can therefore be of any "race." More confusion! Increasingly, the Hispanic category is being conceptualized and used as a racial, not ethnic category (Rumbaut, 2011; Taylor et al., 2012). Though people of Latin American origin run the entire gamut of physical characteristics (and prefer to identify themselves mostly by their specific country of origin), one commonly hears reference to people who "look Hispanic." The Asian/Pacific islander category might seem more straightforward than the others, but it too contains numerous inconsistencies and conceptual problems. Not only are a myriad of cultures combined into this single "racial" category, it encompasses a broad range of physical types, extending from Middle Eastern people (who are virtually indistinguishable from Europeans), to East Indians (who have European features with generally darker skin), to Chinese, Japanese, Koreans, Filipinos, and other East Asians who resemble not at all the first two. Even Native Americans constitute neither a physically distinct group (given their widespread intermarriage, most are hardly distinguishable from Euro-Americans) nor even a culturally demarcated group, since they derive from literally dozens of different tribal cultures.

What the current U.S. classification system represents, then, is a crude and bewildering attempt to count the population by ethnicity. It also demonstrates the arbitrariness of racial and ethnic classification. Remember, race and ethnicity are social constructs, not biologically fixed divisions of

---

[1]*Latino* is sometimes preferred to *Hispanic,* and I use these terms interchangeably.

the human population or of the population of any particular society. The ways that societies choose to subdivide and classify their populations can and do change. Until social scientists can collaborate with policymakers to construct a more rational and meaningful way of conceptualizing ethnic boundaries, we are constrained to use the categories currently in place in gauging the ethnic makeup of the society.

The American Ethnic Configuration

Table 10-1 shows the current U.S. ethnic breakdown and how it has changed since 1980. It also shows probable future trends. Projections into the years 2030 and 2050 reveal the rapidly advancing ethnic heterogeneity of the society. America is being transformed into what some have called a "majority-minority" society. Euro-Americans, the dominant group, are declining as a percentage and may constitute less than half the total population by midcentury.

Table 10-1 ▪ Racial/Ethnic Makeup of the United States

Racial/Ethnic Group	1980	2010[†]	2030	2050
Euro-American	80.0%	63.7%	55.5%	46.3%
African American	11.5	12.2	13.0	13.0
Hispanic American	6.4	16.3	23.0	30.2
Asian American*	1.5	4.7	6.5	8.1
Native American	0.6	0.7	1.2	1.2

*Includes Native Hawaiians and Pacific Islanders.
[†]Does not include those who declared more than one race.
Source: U.S. Census Bureau, 2003b, 2011c.

Such demographic probes into the future, however, must be looked at with some caution. To begin with, these are projections, which means they are merely estimates demographers construct based on current and, what they assume to be, future population trends. But demographers have no way of predicting what kind of fertility and mortality rates might be unleashed by economic and social forces. Nor can they know what immigration rates will be in the future, since these are determined mostly by federal legislation, making them a key political issue subject to the influence of all kinds of interest groups.

Even if demographers were capable of making accurate predictions, these estimates do not take into consideration that the categories currently being used to classify the population by race and ethnicity are likely to change in the future. There is much intermarriage occurring across racial and ethnic lines, the effect of which is to further blur these already fuzzy and politically-influenced categories (Pew Research Center, 2012a). The result is that the familiar racial/ethnic categories—white, black, Hispanic, Asian—no longer make much sense (if they ever did) in classifying people and simply no longer work in accurately describing American society. What is unmistakable, however, is that the United States continues to evolve into a more ethnically heterogeneous society.[2]

Racial-Ethnic Stratification: Majority and Minority

In no multiethnic society are ethnic groups unranked and rewarded equitably. The historical development of ethnic inequality in the United States, therefore, has a counterpart in all multiethnic societies. A hierarchical arrangement of ethnic groups emerges in which one establishes itself as the dominant group, with maximum power and prestige. Other, subordinate, ethnic groups exert less power and receive less of the society's rewards, corresponding to their place in the hierarchy, extending down to the lowest-ranking groups, which may wield little power and receive little in the way of rewards.

Group rank is determined mainly on the basis of distance from the dominant ethnic group in culture and in physical appearance. Those most like the dominant group are more highly ranked, and those markedly different are ranked lower. A system of **ethnic stratification** is a rank order of groups, each made up of people with presumed common cultural or physical characteristics, interacting in patterns of dominance and subordination. This chapter looks specifically at the American ethnic hierarchy and the way in which class stratification intersects with ethnic stratification.

Minority Groups

Ethnic stratification systems are made up of a dominant group (or groups) and minority groups. **Minority groups** are groups that, on the basis of their physical or cultural traits, exert less power and receive fewer of the society's rewards than does the dominant group. In a classic definition, the sociologist Louis Wirth defined a minority group as "a group of people who, because of their physical or cultural characteristics, are singled out from the others in the society in which they live for differential and unequal treatment, and who therefore regard themselves as objects of collective discrimination" (1945:347). Members of minority groups more commonly occupy poorer jobs, earn less income, live in less desirable areas, receive an inferior education, exercise less political influence, and are subjected to various social indignities. These inequalities are, to some degree, the result

---

[2]The idea of a "mixed race" category does nothing to clarify or make more meaningful the classification system. It only creates yet another category into which people are conveniently pigeon-holed. Moreover, to speak of "mixed racial" or "multiracial" groups implies, erroneously, that there are "pure" races to begin with.

of their social mark, that is, the physical or cultural features that distinguish them. And, as Wirth pointed out, minority group members are conscious of the fact that they are differentially treated.

It is important to understand that the sociological meaning of minority is not the same as the mathematical definition. Numbers have no necessary relation to a group's minority status. As mentioned in Chapter 7, for example, nonwhites in South Africa, though over 85 percent of the population, traditionally constituted a sociological minority. Essentially, minority groups are afforded unequal treatment because they lack the power to negate or counteract discriminatory treatment. Dominant or minority status is most clearly a result of differences in societal power.

Types of Minorities   In its sociological meaning, the term *minority* can be applied to a variety of social groups. In addition to ethnic traits, many other physical or behavioral characteristics are sufficient to set off groups from the society's mainstream, resulting in differential treatment. To equate minority groups only with highly visible ethnic groups fails to account for the many other types of minorities found in complex societies.

Sex, for example, is a distinguishable physical characteristic that in most societies serves to single out one group—ordinarily, women—for unequal treatment. Women throughout the world have rarely occupied positions of great political or economic power, have been barred from entrance into many occupations, and have been excluded from various areas of social life. As we will see in the next chapter, only in recent decades have these deeply rooted patterns of sex discrimination begun to change.

Physically challenged people—the blind, the deaf, those confined to wheelchairs, and so on—are another evident minority. Age, too, constitutes a physical feature that serves to set groups apart for differential and unequal tretment. In all societies, of course, certain limitations necessarily are placed on people according to their age; but in some cases, this differentiation and unequal treatment exceeds any rational explanation. Some workers are forced into retirement at age sixty-five even if they remain capable of carrying out their occupational duties and wish to do so. Or certain occupations are denied to those who exceed an arbitrarily selected age requirement. These are examples of age discrimination.

Groups might be singled out for differential treatment not on the basis of physical distinctions but on the basis of their past or current behavior. Gays and lesbians are obvious examples, as are the mentally ill and ex-convicts. Those acknowledging homosexuality, past treatment for mental illness, or a prison record risk social exclusion and discrimination by employers, landlords, and law enforcement agencies.

For each of these groups, a belief system, or ideology, explains and justifies their differential treatment; each is deemed to be "inferior" in some way. These beliefs serve as devices to sustain unequal treatment.

Ethnic Minorities   Ethnic minorities are those groups singled out and treated unequally on the basis of their cultural or physical differences from the dominant group. In multiethnic societies, ethnic minority status is most significant because, more than any other minority status, it intersects most sharply with class. In the United States today, the groups that are especially prominent in terms of cultural and, in many cases, physical differences are African Americans, American Indians, Asian Americans, and Hispanic Americans. These are the groups that have historically experienced the most serious forms of discriminatory treatment and about whom mythical belief systems have been created to justify such treatment.

For much of American history the belief system, or ideology, that has rationalized racial/ethnic inequality has been **racism.** This is essentially the belief that races are real (not social constructs) and that there are innate behavioral differences among members of each racial category. Groups can thus be ranked as superior or inferior (Nash, 1962; Montagu, 1972). The presumed superiority of some groups and the inferiority of others is subsequently used to legitimate the unequal distribution of rewards.

Although applied most vehemently to African Americans, some variant of this ideology has been applied to other minority ethnic groups as well. Southern and eastern European groups (such as Poles, Jews, and Italians) who entered the society in large numbers during the late nineteenth and early twentieth centuries, for example, were commonly perceived as "races," and their innate inferiority was commonly assumed, often by social scientists.

Today, few in the academic world accept such beliefs, and they have waned significantly among laypersons as well (National Conference, 1995; Sniderman and Piazza, 1993). Most now view discrepancies in social achievement among ethnic groups more as cultural differences, not as biogenetic ones (Banton, 1970; Schuman et al., 1998). Nonetheless, racist ideology has proved tenacious, though modifiable in form and content, in multiethnic societies.

Although African Americans, Hispanic Americans, Asian Americans, and American Indians are the most noticeable ethnic minorities, remember that the treatment of minorities is relative and thus will vary from group to group and from time to time. Some groups may be consistently singled out and deprived of social rewards, whereas others experience only minimal discriminatory treatment. Moreover, members of a particular group may encounter rejection and denial in some areas of social life but not in others.

Dominant Groups

The existence of minority groups logically implies a majority group. Most simply, the **dominant,** or majority, ethnic group is the group at the top of the ethnic hierarchy, with maximal access to the society's power resources, particularly political authority and control of the means of economic production.[3] This does not mean, of course, that all those classified as part of the dominant ethnic group enjoy equally great wealth and power advantages. It means only that members of the dominant ethnic group occupy *disproportionately* such positions. Consider American society, where Anglo Americans historically have been and, to a great extent, remain the dominant ethnic group. Obviously, not all members of this category are high-ranking officials of government or corporation executives. Nor are they all wealthy and holders of university degrees. They do, however, *disproportionately* occupy the most important positions in government and the economy and, compared with other ethnic groups, attain more of the society's valued resources.

In addition to its greater economic and political power, the dominant group has much cultural power: Its norms and values prevail in the society as a whole and become the society's standards. Minority groups are expected to acculturate to the dominant group's customs and ideals. In American society, it is assumed that all groups will speak English, maintain Judeo-Christian ethics, abide by democratic principles, and accept capitalist values. Although specific facets of these cultural standards are transformed over the long run, such changes are slow, deliberate, and usually accompanied by controversy and open conflict. For example, the use of languages other than English in schools, businesses, and government is a hotly debated national issue.

The Relativity of Dominant Status and Minority Status

Group membership in a modern, complex society is rarely a simple matter of either-or but instead takes the form of combinations that often yield confusing and ambiguous statuses. Whether a person is part of the dominant group or a minority group depends in all cases on the social context. In some instances, people will be part of one, and in other instances, they may find themselves part of another. For example, Jews in American society are ordinarily designated a minority group. Yet from the standpoint of African Americans, who generally rank lower in economic class and prestige, Jews are part of the dominant Euro-American group.

The Origins of Ethnic Stratification

Patterns of dominance and subordination among ethnic groups characterize all multiethnic societies in the modern world. How does ethnic stratification arise, and why does it seem so inescapable?

---

[3]I prefer the term *dominant* rather than *majority* since this avoids the tendency to think in numerical terms, especially in cases where the dominant group may be a numerical minority.

Forms of Contact   Ethnic stratification systems are created by the movement of people across national boundaries, bringing with them different languages and cultural systems, or by the establishment of new political boundaries. What may have been a relatively homogeneous society thus becomes more diverse. This can take place through several processes.

One group may establish dominance over others through *conquest*. European colonialism of the eighteenth and nineteenth centuries illustrates this pattern. Through greater military technology, the British, French, Spanish, Dutch, Belgians, and Portuguese conquered peoples in Asia, Africa, Australia, North America, and South America. Indigenous groups were brought under colonial rule and became economic appendages of the mother country. The ruling colonists became the dominant group, and the natives, the minority. The case of European settlers and North American Indians is an example of such contact and the subsequent establishment of dominant-minority relations.

Another means by which ethnic stratification can occur is *annexation*, a political occurrence in which a part or perhaps all of one society is incorporated into another. For example, after the transfer of territory at the conclusion of the war with Mexico in 1846, Mexicans living in those annexed areas became a minority, subject to the dominance of Anglo cultural and political institutions.

Voluntary immigration is the most common pattern by which ethnic groups come into contact with each other. This has traditionally been and remains the chief source of ethnic heterogeneity in all contemporary societies, including the United States and Canada. Each entering group finds its place in the ethnic hierarchy, with those further culturally from the dominant group starting at a lower level.

A parallel case of the emergence of dominant-subordinate relations as a result of voluntary immigration can be seen in western Europe. Following World War II, workers from southern European countries such as Italy, Portugal, Greece, Spain, Turkey, and Yugoslavia or from newly independent former colonies such as Algeria and Indonesia migrated to Germany, France, Switzerland, the Netherlands, and Belgium as those nations experienced their postwar industrial expansion. A similar voluntary immigration occurred in Britain with the entry of thousands of people from the newly independent countries of the British Commonwealth—India, Pakistan, Jamaica, and others (Castles et al., 1984). This population movement accelerated in the 1960s, leaving previously homogeneous western European societies with substantial ethnic communities made up of immigrants of vastly different cultures and physical characteristics. The upshot of the creation of these multiethnic societies has been the emergence of conflict and competition among ethnic groups and the development of dominant-minority relations. In Germany, for example, the foreign-born are 13 percent of the population, with those from Turkey constituting the largest single group. Various forms of discrimination, not uncommonly involving violence, have been aimed at these groups, and obstacles to citizenship are daunting (Castles and Miller, 2009; OECD, 2001; Seifert, 1998).

Involuntary immigration involves the forced transfer of people from one society to another. The prime example is the slave trade starting in the seventeenth century that brought millions from Africa to work the cotton and sugar plantations of the United States, Brazil, and the West Indies.

Consequences of Contact   The way in which diverse ethnic groups initially come into contact has been shown to be a critical factor in the patterns of ethnic stratification that subsequently emerge.

Stanley Lieberson (1961) suggests two major types of contact situations. One involves the subordination of a native population by a more powerful migrant group. Here, long-term conflict is very likely. Native groups less powerful than the arriving colonials are left with few options other than resistance to the new social order imposed on them. The arrival of Europeans in North America, for example, ignited a continuous struggle between the indigenous Indian tribes and the more powerful settlers.

A second situation involves the subordination of a migrant population by an indigenous ethnic group. This typifies most voluntary and involuntary immigrations like those to North America; in such cases, the arriving groups are initially made subordinate to a resident dominant group. The arriving immigrants who followed the Anglo Americans were obligated to assimilate to that group's culture and accede to its political and economic power.

Donald Noel (1968) has pointed out that there are additional factors following intergroup contact that give rise to and shape the eventual system of ethnic stratification. When they initially meet, divergent groups judge each other ethnocentrically, that is, in terms of their own culture. These judgments are usually negative, particularly if the groups are quite distant culturally or, perhaps, physically. *Ethnocentrism*, while a necessary precondition, is not by itself sufficient to bring about ethnic stratification. Groups may view one another negatively without dominant-subordinate relations emerging among them. What is further required is *competition* among the groups for the same scarce resources, like jobs and land. The more intense such competition, Noel points out, the greater the likelihood of ethnic stratification. Those with greater resources wind up higher on the ethnic hierarchy. The final prerequisite for the development of ethnic stratification is *differential power*. Unless one group can overpower another, there is no basis for a stable rank order of ethnic groups, even if there is competition and ethnocentrism among them. When there is a particularly wide power gap between competing and ethnocentric groups, the emergent stratification system is likely to be quite durable. Power breeds more power, and once established, the dominant group uses its power to obstruct the competition of other groups and to solidify its dominance.

In sum, Noel's theory postulates that competition for scarce resources provides the motivation for stratification, that ethnocentrism channels this competition along ethnic lines, and that differential power determines whether one group will be able to subordinate others (Barth and Noel, 1972).

The Intersection of Class and Ethnicity

Although ethnicity and class are distinct dimensions of stratification, they are closely interrelated. In virtually all multiethnic societies, people's ethnic classification becomes an important factor in the distribution of societal rewards and, hence, in their economic and political class positions. Put simply, power, wealth, and prestige are in some part a function of ethnicity. The ethnic and class hierarchies are largely parallel and interwoven. In all multiethnic societies, where people begin their quest for the society's rewards and what they ultimately achieve depend to a significant extent on their ethnicity.

If a person is a member of the dominant ethnic group, his or her way will not necessarily be unimpeded; being part of the dominant ethnic group as a result of the accident of birth does not, in itself, assure success. As noted earlier, obviously not all Anglo Americans, for example, are doctors, lawyers, corporate executives, and high-ranking politicians. Many people living in the hills of rural Appalachia who are Anglo Americans and whose ancestors extend back to the eighteenth century are among the poorest in the United States. What is important, however, is that for members of the dominant group, the ethnic factor is removed as an impediment to upward mobility; other factors, both individual and structural, will affect their fortunes, but ethnicity will not.

In the same way, of course, minority status does not mean that a person is automatically relegated to the bottom rungs of the class hierarchy. The election of Barack Obama as U.S. president is a dramatic illustration of this fact. But the chances of winding up at the bottom are much greater for minorities. As we proceed down the ethnic hierarchy, we find increasing political powerlessness, lack of economic opportunity, and social discrimination and exclusion. The closer to the bottom of the hierarchy, the more difficult the path to social success in whatever form, regardless of other nonethnic social traits.

In short, the effect of ethnicity is that minority ethnic group members encounter barriers to the attainment of the various rewards of their society that dominant ethnic group members do not face.

This does not mean, however, that all minorities are affected to the same extent. For those who are members of low-ranking groups with high ethnic visibility—African Americans, for example—minority status may be the overriding determinant of their economic class. For other minorities more highly ranked and less visible—for example, Polish Americans or Irish Americans—ethnicity will be of little consequence. It is important to remember that there are *degrees* of minority status. The ethnic hierarchy in any society is rarely a simple two-part structure with a dominant group at the top and subordinate groups at the bottom. Minority groups occupy places on a continuum, and the impact of ethnicity varies among them. The question for minority group members is, then, "To what extent does ethnicity become a factor in the allocation of jobs, education, wealth, political influence, and all other life chances?"

Minority status does not necessarily indicate where in the class hierarchy a group's members *enter* the society but rather where they *remain* long after they have entered (Gans, 1967). Indeed, most groups, even those that immigrate voluntarily, enter collectively at or near the bottom. Some may rise very quickly, whereas others remain trapped at the bottom generation after generation.

The American Ethnic Hierarchy

The American ethnic hierarchy today is broadly divided into three comprehensive tiers:

1. The top tier comprises Euro-American Protestants, for whom ethnicity has no real significance except to distinguish them from the remainder of the ethnic hierarchy.

2. Tier two, the intermediate tier, consists of Euro-American Catholics and Jews of various national origins and many Asians, for all of whom ethnicity continues to play a role in the distribution of the society's rewards and continues to influence social life, but in both instances, decreasingly so.

3. The bottom tier is made up of ethnic groups, often defined in racial terms, for whom ethnicity today has the greatest consequences and for whom it continues to shape many of the basic aspects of social and economic life. This includes African Americans, Latinos, Native Americans, and some Asian Americans.

This ethnic hierarchy has remained essentially unchanged for the last century and a half. Although the distance between many of the groups has been reduced, their rank order has, with few exceptions, not been basically altered.

Perhaps the most important aspect of this three-part American ethnic hierarchy is that the gap between the bottom tier of groups and the other two is much greater than the gap between the top and intermediate tiers. In terms of socioeconomic status, prestige, and access to power, the division between tier one and tier two is fading. Differences in wealth, prestige, and power are far more steadfast, however, between tier three and the other two (Figure 10-1). The overriding issues of American ethnic relations, therefore, remain focused on the economic, political, and social disparities between these ethnic categories and the policies intended to reduce them. Some of these issues are addressed later in this chapter.

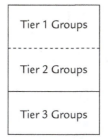

Figure 10-1 ▪ The American Ethnic Hierarchy

The Bases of the Hierarchy   Arranging ethnic groups in such a rank order, of course, masks the more specific class and cultural differences among them as well as the internal differences within each. But in a very general sense, each of the society's ethnic groups can be placed on this hierarchy on the basis of a combination of several factors:

- The place of the group on the society's economic hierarchy.
- The place of the group in the society's political power structure.
- The extent to which prejudice and discrimination remain significant for the group.
- The extent to which group members have entered into full social participation with those of the dominant group.[4]

Let's look at each of these factors.

Ethnicity and the Economic Hierarchy

Individual members of various American ethnic minorities will be found at all points on the occupation, income and wealth, and education hierarchies. Looking specifically at occupation, we find, for example, African American doctors, Jewish American construction workers, Mexican American engineers, and Anglo American kitchen workers. But these combinations of ethnicity and occupation are not typical. It would be more common to find Jewish American doctors, Mexican American construction workers, Anglo American engineers, and African American kitchen workers. Ethnic groups tend to concentrate in particular areas of work, especially as they enter the society, and these patterns may remain evident for several generations. In the

---

[4]Using a combination of these factors means that some will offset others. For example, although Jews and Asians rank higher than northwestern Europeans in their aggregate economic class position, they still do not fully interact at the primary level with those groups, and the extent of prejudice and discrimination directed against them is much greater. Hence, when all these factors are considered, Jews and Asians are part of the intermediate tier of groups rather than the top.

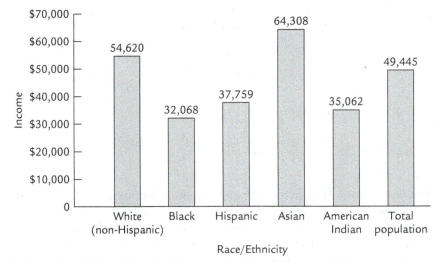

Figure 10-2 ▪ Median Household Income by Race/Ethnicity, 2010
Source: U.S. Census Bureau, 2011a.

United States in the 1830s and 1840s, Irish workers built the canal system. In the second half of the nineteenth century and the early twentieth century, Italians were heavily represented in building construction, Jews in the garment trades, and Slavs in the steel industry. Racially defined ethnic groups such as African Americans remained overwhelmingly in the least advanced sectors of the economy, as agricultural and service workers. Though ethnic groups today are far more occupationally dispersed, the remnants of these earlier patterns are still evident. In the same way, newer ethnic groups display much occupational concentration (Portes and Rumbaut, 2006; Wilson, 2003).

In addition to occupation, other aspects of economic class—education, income, and wealth—are closely linked to ethnicity. Those most highly educated, those earning the highest incomes, and those possessing the greatest wealth are statistically more likely to be members of the dominant ethnic group or members of ethnic groups closest to the dominant group in culture and physical appearance.

Figures 10-2 through 10-5 show this relationship. They also demonstrate the economic gap referred to earlier regarding the place of the third-tier groups relative to others. Figure 10-2 shows that median household income for African Americans is about 60 percent of white income, and for Hispanic Americans, about 70 percent. Figure 10-3 shows that on average, black wealth and Hispanic wealth are each about 5 percent of white wealth.[5]

---

[5]In this chapter, the terms *black* and *white*, rather than "African American" and "Euro-American" are sometimes used, simply because those are the descriptive terms used by the U.S. Census Bureau in reporting socioeconomic differences among racial and ethnic groups.

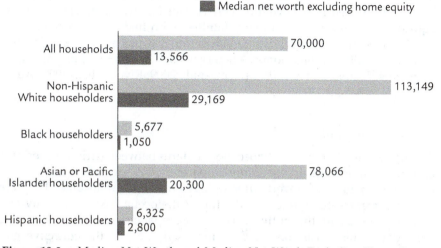

■ Median net worth
■ Median net worth excluding home equity

All households — 70,000 / 13,566

Non-Hispanic White householders — 113,149 / 29,169

Black householders — 5,677 / 1,050

Asian or Pacific Islander householders — 78,066 / 20,300

Hispanic householders — 6,325 / 2,800

Figure 10-3 ■ Median Net Worth and Median Net Worth Excluding Home Equity of Households by Race and Hispanic Origin of Householder: 2009 (2009 Dollars) Source: © 2011 Pew Research Center, Social & Demographic Trends Project. Wealth Gaps Rise to Record Highs Between Whites, Blacks and Hispanics http://www.pewsocialtrends.org/ 2011/07/26/wealth-gaps-rise-to-record-highs-between-whites-blacks-hispanics/

Recall that wealth is even more important as a key to upward mobility than is income. The possession of wealth, regardless of income, relieves families of dependence on others and furthermore can be passed on from parents to children. Thus, even if aggregate income between dominant and minority groups were not sharply different, white families would be at a significant advantage for they start with considerably more in assets (Landry, 1987; Oliver and Shapiro, 1995; Shapiro, 2004). This also means that black and Latino middle-class families are in a more precarious financial state than are white middle-class families. Whereas the latter may be able to withstand a loss of job or a temporary layoff, given their assets, black and Latino families in a similar situation are apt to lose quickly much of what they have gained.

This is evident when looking at home ownership. To own one's home is by all accounts the most fundamental part of the American dream and, except for the very wealthy, is the most substantial form of family wealth. It is also a symbolic measure of economic stability and of middle-class status. There are sharp differences among racial/ethnic groups on this dimension of wealth, however, with three-quarters of whites owning their homes, compared to three-fifths of Asians and slightly less than half of African Americans and Latinos (Kochhar et al., 2009). Although the gap in home ownership rates had begun to close in the ten years after 1995, with the housing bust of the late 2000s, rates fell more steeply for African Americans and Latinos than for whites. Compared to whites, much more of the wealth of African American and Latino families is in the form of home equity and, as a result, they are more susceptible to losing what they have accumulated in the event of a crisis. This heavy dependence on home equity proved disastrous to many families who had assumed costly sub-prime loans (twice as likely to be blacks and Latinos as whites or Asians) and, as a result, lost their homes when they could no longer make mortgage payments (Hinojosa et al., 2009; Lopez et al., 2009; Rivera et al., 2009; Weller et al., 2012; Wright, 2009).

African Americans

The aggregate difference in socioeconomic status between African Americans and Euro-Americans is especially apparent: African Americans exhibit much higher rates of poverty, unemployment, and low income. They are also underrepresented in jobs at the top of the occupational hierarchy and overrepresented at the bottom. These discrepancies, however, must be viewed in a historical context. In some ways, despite the collective gap between whites and blacks, there has been a significant movement in the direction of greater equity over the last several decades. One must remember that until well into the 1960s, a system of direct and intentional discrimina-tion effectively thwarted efforts of African Americans to compete with Euro-Americans for jobs and wealth. When considered in that light, there are grounds for both positive and negative views regarding the socioeconomic status of African Americans.

Regarding income, it is clear that the status of black families has improved markedly during the last five decades. And the enormous expansion of the black middle class is undeniable. The negative view arises, however, in con-sidering the gap between median black income and median white income: It has narrowed only marginally since 1950. In 2010 median black household income was 59 percent of median white (non-Hispanic) household income; in 1950 it was 54 percent. Similarly, the percentage of blacks below the poverty line remains almost three times greater than the percentage of whites (Figure 10-4). Moreover, the rate of upward mobility out of poverty for blacks remains many times lower than the rate for whites (Corcoran, 2001; Hertz, 2005; Isaacs et al., 2008). Indeed, African Americans make up the bulk of the long-term poor in America. The Great Recession, starting in 2007, had an especially severe impact on African American families. Although almost all population groups experienced an income loss, the African American decrease was considerably greater (Austin, 2012). In addition, the wealth gap between whites and blacks, already extremely wide, expanded even more (Weller et al., 2012; Pew Research Center, 2011).

Studies have found that many middle- and upper-middle-class black families are beginning to experience downward intergenerational mobility. The children of these families actually show a lower income status than their parents, with some falling out of the middle class completely. One study concludes that "For every parental income group, white children are

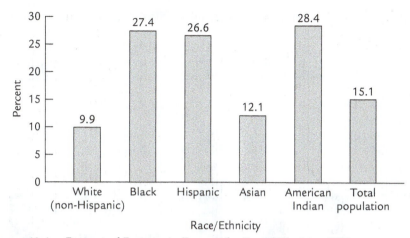

Figure 10-4 ▪ Percent of Persons in Poverty by Race/Ethnicity, 2010
Source: U.S. Census Bureau, 2011a.

more likely than black children to move ahead of their parents' economic rank, while black children are more likely than white children to fall behind." (Isaacs et al., 2008:75–76).

Education, as discussed in Chapter 7, is a key life chance, arguably the most critical. Blacks have almost reached parity with whites in median years of schooling completed, and substantial gains have been made in black college attendance and graduation. In 1980, 8 percent of adult blacks had earned at least a bachelor's degree; by 2010, almost 20 percent had done so. On the negative side, however, the quantity of education is not necessarily commensurate with its quality. Despite the narrowing differential in years of schooling, black achievement continues to lag behind white achievement at all school levels and regardless of social class (Dillon, 2006, 2009; Kane, 2004; Massey et al., 2003; Schmidt, 2007). The educational gap separating African Americans and other tier-three groups from the rest of the ethnic hierarchy is very apparent in Figure 10-5.

These aggregate figures should not obscure the fact that comparisons between black income and white income are subject to a number of factors, including region and urban location. More important, the African American population is polarized between relatively stable middle- and working-class families on the one hand and those in poverty on the other. The substantially greater percentage of blacks over whites below the poverty line accounts in large measure for the general differences in income patterns between the two populations. The gap between whites and blacks with higher education has diminished considerably, and for black women it has virtually disappeared.

Another important factor accounting for the income disparity between blacks and whites is changes in the African American family structure. Families that have experienced income stability or increases have been dual-breadwinner families, among which only slight differences exist between

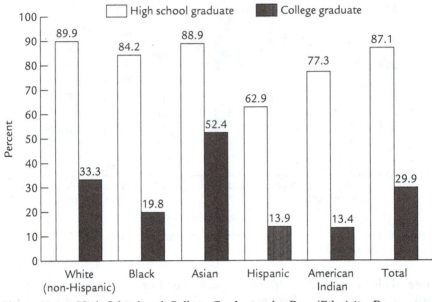

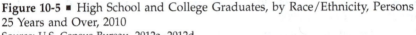

Figure 10-5 ▪ High School and College Graduates, by Race/Ethnicity, Persons 25 Years and Over, 2010
Source: U.S. Census Bureau, 2012a, 2012d.

blacks and whites. But the number of single-parent, female-headed families (which, as noted in Chapter 3, earn considerably less than husband-wife families) among African Americans remains three times the number among whites (U.S. Census Bureau, 2012a).

An often overlooked factor in explaining the lingering black–white economic gap is the much higher rate of imprisonment in the United States compared to other advanced societies. The effects of this uniquely American phenomenon have been felt most acutely by poor, undereducated African Americans (Bobo and Thompson, 2010; Western, 2006; Western and Pettit, 2005; Western and Wildeman, 2009). In 2000, 20 percent of young non-college-educated African American men were incarcerated, compared to 5.5 percent of Hispanics and 3.2 percent of whites (Guetzkow and Western, 2007). Since unemployment figures do not include jail inmates, black unemployment is understated and median black family income is obviously pulled down as well. The higher rate of black incarceration (and the sharp rise in U.S. imprisonment rates generally) is accounted for in large measure by the harsh drug laws enacted beginning in the 1970s. Orlando Patterson (2008) points out that higher crime and incarceration rates among African Americans are also strongly related to family instability and isolation: lower rates of marriage, higher divorce rates, and a much higher proportion of single-parent families.

Debating the Economic Gap between Whites and Blacks   The lingering economic gap between whites and blacks (and, to some extent, between whites and Latinos) has prompted debate among sociologists: Is this persistent gap attributable to lingering racism; is there something unique about the African American experience that contributes to the group's continued plight; or are there deeper structural forces that impede the attainment of economic equality?

In considering this issue, remember that the black population is by no means homogeneous in terms of economic status. Indeed, some have suggested that there are really "two black Americas"—one that has established itself solidly within the middle and working classes and one that is isolated and not fully part of the mainstream workforce.[6] The latter is the black underclass, or ghetto poor, and constitutes perhaps one-third of the total black population (Hochschild, 1995; Smith, 2001; Wilson, 1980). What is really being analyzed, then, is the persistence of a much larger low-income proportion of the African American population, compared to the Euro-American population.

Some see the economic gap between whites and blacks as the result of *continued discrimination in labor and housing markets* (Hacker, 1995; Pager and Karafin, 2009; Steinberg, 1995). Andrew Hacker, for example, takes this position: "To be black in America is to know that you remain last in line for so basic a requisite as the means of supporting yourself and your family. More than that, you have much less choice among jobs than workers who are white" (1995:110). The idea is that whites still harbor negative stereotypes of blacks, which prevents full acceptance of blacks into the workforce. Employers, for example, often see blacks as less dependable and less trustworthy than members of other ethnic groups and, even for low-skill jobs, prefer to hire immigrants (Wilson, 1996).

In a related argument, Douglas Massey and Nancy Denton (1993) point to the continuation of residential segregation as preventing the movement of blacks out of inner-city areas where decent jobs are scarce or where there is no accessible transportation to areas where jobs do exist. Residential segregation is sustained, they argue, by the continued refusal of whites to accept more than a token representation of blacks in primarily white suburban neighborhoods. As a result, poor blacks remain trapped in neighborhoods that are resistant to racial change, perpetuating a cycle of poverty (Sampson, 2009).

A family's residential environment affects not only poor families, but those that are near or part of the middle class as well. A recent study shows that only a small percentage of white children live in high-poverty

---

[6]Some have suggested that the black middle class itself is subdivided into a "fragile" lower middle class that continues to lag behind the white middle class on most measures of socioeconomic status, and a "stable" middle class, virtually the same as its white counterpart in occupation, income, education, and housing (Lacy, 2007; Pattillo, 1999).

neighborhoods throughout childhood, but a majority of black children do. This is found to be a critical factor in accounting for the lower rate of upward economic mobility for blacks and their considerably greater chance of experiencing downward mobility. Living in a socially disadvantaged environment makes it difficult for black families that have achieved middle-class status to retain the advantages of their class position and to pass them on to their children (Sharkey, 2009).

Others see the continued high proportion of poor blacks as the product of a *dysfunctional culture*. This is a variant of the culture-of-poverty thesis discussed in Chapter 6. The essential idea is that blacks living in a ghetto subculture find it difficult to thrust themselves out of that environment and to take advantage of available opportunities. The environment to which observers refer is one in which there are mostly families without fathers, neighborhoods infested with drugs and crime, and residents heavily dependent on welfare. Perhaps most important, the work ethic has disappeared. The underclass—not entirely, but primarily, black—therefore lacks the attitudes that lead to meaningful employment in the mainstream workforce (Kaus, 1995). The solution, in this view, is to instill a work ethic and a sense of personal responsibility and initiative among the underclass, suggesting a kind of self-help approach (McWhorter, 2000; Puddington, 1992).

Still others see the lag of poor blacks economically as more *structural* than the result of either white racism or cultural failures. William Julius Wilson has addressed the issue most directly in this way. His position is that although discrimination based on race accounted for the denial of necessary economic resources to African Americans in earlier times, the traditional patterns of black-white interaction have been fundamentally altered so that class factors are today the dominant influence on African American life chances (1980, 1987, 1996, 2009). It is the poverty population, of which African Americans make up a disproportionate percentage, that has borne the negative consequences of economic restructuring. As explained in Chapter 5, the American economy has changed radically, tossing aside those who lack the skills necessary to compete in an increasingly high-tech workforce or forcing them permanently into dead-end, low-paying jobs. Thus, lower-class, unskilled African Americans have become a redundant labor force that is becoming a permanent underclass. The labor market today calls for jobs requiring technical and educational skills, for which such persons cannot qualify. Moreover, industry and commerce have moved to areas on the urban fringe so that any available entry-level jobs are outside the range of the central city where most low-income African Americans live. The result is a semipermanent state of unemployment (Sharkey, 2009; Stoll, 2006, 2008; Wilson, 1999). African American men were particularly hard hit by the deep recession of the late 2000s as unemployment rates rose sharply (Cawthorne, 2009; Weller et al., 2012).

The lack of job opportunities creates a vicious cycle in which blacks are forced to remain in inner-city areas, attending inferior schools and thereby reinforcing their disadvantaged position in the labor market (Haskins, 2009). Moreover, high rates of joblessness, Wilson explains, "trigger other neighborhood problems that undermine social organization, ranging from crime, gang violence, and drug trafficking to family breakups and problems in the organization of family life" (1996:21). Recent studies support this view (Haskins, 2009; Holzer, 2009). The development of a ghetto culture, then, is a product of larger structural forces. Wilson describes this relationship: "Structural conditions provide the context within which cultural responses to chronic economic and racial subordination are developed" (2009:61).

Hispanic Americans

As part of the third tier of groups in the American ethnic hierarchy, Hispanic Americans rank well below average on all measures of class: income, occupation, and education. Keep in mind, however, that there are important differences among the three major Latino groups: Cubans are highest in socioeconomic status, followed by Mexicans in the middle, and Puerto Ricans at the bottom.

As seen in Figure 10-4, almost 27 percent of Latinos fall below the official poverty line, more than two and a half times the percentage for non-Hispanic whites. As with income, however, there is a range among the major Latino groups: One in four Puerto Ricans, Dominicans, and Mexicans were in poverty in 2010, compared to 15 percent of Cubans (U.S. Census Bureau, 2012a).

The low income and high poverty rates of Latinos, particularly Mexicans and Puerto Ricans, reflect their generally lower occupational levels. Except for Cubans, Latinos are underrepresented in the higher-status occupational categories and overrepresented in the lower ones. They also exhibit high unemployment rates.

Although employment discrimination has historically been a factor for particular groups, especially Mexicans in the Southwest and Puerto Ricans in New York, today their low levels of education and relatively recent entry into the labor force seem most critical in accounting for the generally low levels of income and occupation of Latinos. Large proportions of all Latino groups have immigrated to the United States since 1950. As latecomers to the American postindustrial economy, they have necessarily taken the least-skilled and lowest-paying jobs. Like African Americans, Latinos have become a disproportionately large part of the most expendable element of the workforce: those lacking the requirements for positions above the semiskilled or unskilled levels. Moreover, as an unusually young population, Mexican Americans and Puerto Ricans are most likely to lack marketable skills and work experience.

Education, however, appears to be an even more important factor in explaining the lower income and occupational positions of the Hispanic population. As the gap grows between those with higher education and those without, Latinos have been especially hard hit, given their relatively lower educational levels in general and the group's low proportion of members with a college education in particular (Bean and Stevens, 2003; Carnoy et al., 1993). Language, too, is a critical barrier to upward mobility for Latinos, many of whom are first-generation immigrants (Moll and Ruiz, 2002).

Despite their low aggregate economic standing, some see Latinos following a path toward upward mobility more in line with the past experience of Euro-Americans, particularly those of the second wave of immigration, the southern and eastern Europeans (Chavez, 1991). Especially noteworthy is the recent surge in Hispanic college enrollment (Pew Hispanic Center, 2011). Moreover, evidence indicates that when human capital, especially education and English language proficiency, is controlled, there is not much difference between Hispanics and whites in occupational status and earnings (Duncan et al., 2006).

Asian Americans

One of the most striking features of Figures 10-2 through 10-5 is the high ranking of Asian Americans compared to the other ethnic categories. Put simply, Asian Americans rank higher than most ethnic groups in family income, occupational prestige, and level of education. As is seen in Figure 10-2, Asian median household income is substantially in excess of household income of other ethnic categories, even Euro-Americans. Asian Americans are more heavily represented in white-collar occupations and less represented in blue-collar occupations than are non-Hispanic white men. Especially noteworthy is the fact that 48 percent of Asian Americans are managers or professionals, compared to 40 percent of non-Hispanic whites (U.S. Census Bureau, 2012a).

Perhaps the most astonishing statistic regarding the socioeconomic status of Asian Americans is level of education. Not only are they significantly higher in number of years of education (Figure 10-5), but in terms of academic achievement, Asian American students are above average on almost every measure. For example, Asian American high school students score higher than students from any other ethnic category in mathematics scholastic aptitude tests and are second only to whites on verbal aptitude tests (Toppo, 2003; U.S. Department of Education, 1992). Predictably, Asian students enter top universities far out of proportion to their numbers.

In looking at the comparatively high class position of Asian Americans, two caveats are in order. First, there are wide discrepancies within this diverse panethnic category. As with Latinos, there are differences among specific groups as well as among members of the same group. For example, while Asian American families are more likely than non-Hispanic white families to have incomes of $75,000 or more, they are also more likely to have incomes of less than $25,000. Likewise, Asian Americans are more likely than non-Hispanic whites to have earned a college degree (Figure 10-5), but they are also more likely to have less than a ninth-grade education (U.S. Census Bureau,

2006). It is the Southeast Asian groups (Cambodians, Vietnamese, Hmong) who make up a disproportionate share of those in the lowest socioeconomic categories. The Asian-American population, then, appears in a kind of bipolar distribution on the class hierarchy, well above average or well below.

Second, the Asian American population consists of two historical components: those who immigrated as early as the mid-nineteenth century and those who have come since 1965. Many of the more recent Asian Americans have come with class and educational backgrounds considerably higher than those of earlier times. They have therefore raised the collective level of the entire Asian American category. Still, the contemporary Asian American experience has been marked by an unusual degree of high achievement.

Explaining High Asian American Achievement   Attempts to explain the extraordinarily high rates of Asian American mobility, educational attainment, and social adaptation take several different lines of thought. Some sociologists and psychologists point to cultural factors. Stressed in this explanation are values that emphasize the importance of education and the cohesiveness of the family. Studies that have taken this approach seem to converge on one point: Asian Americans are prepared to work arduously and, in turn, are able to instill in their children a great motivation to work hard (Kim, 1981; Light and Bonacich, 1988; Nisbett, 2009; Stevenson and Stigler, 1992).

That cultural factors are of key importance in explaining Asian American educational and economic success is suggested by a study conducted by University of Michigan researchers investigating the social and economic adaptation of Vietnamese refugees. At the time of their arrival in the United States, most of the subjects of this study had completed little formal education, few had any marketable skills, and only one in a hundred spoke fluent English. The researchers found that despite those handicaps, many had achieved economic independence after only a few years. Furthermore, whatever success they had realized was almost entirely a product of their own efforts; the assistance of outside agencies had played a very limited role. The academic achievement of school-age children from these families was even more remarkable. Despite their severe language deficiencies and family poverty, after an average of only three years, they were experiencing success in American schools. This rapid educational success was found to be closely linked to a cluster of core values deriving from the Confucian and Buddhist traditions of East and Southeast Asia: education and achievement, a cohesive family, and hard work. These, the researchers found, were highly congruent with mainstream American values regarding the role of education in getting ahead (Caplan et al., 1989; Caplan et al., 1991).[7]

---

[7]Some contend that Asians are innately superior to other ethnic groups (Lynn and Vanhanen, 2002). Few social scientists acknowledge the validity of such biological arguments, however, whether applied to seemingly high-achieving or to low-achieving groups.

A second explanation for high Asian American achievement recognizes the fortuitous fit between the opportunity structure of contemporary American society and the class background of the new Asian immigrants. A disproportionate number of highly skilled and educated individuals make up the Asian immigrant population. Hence, the existence of many doctors, engineers, and highly trained professionals among them is largely a function of their preimmigration class position. In some ways, then, today's Asian immigrants represent a select subset of the population of their origin societies. Such people recognize the more abundant opportunities to employ their skills and training in the United States and also the possibility of earning substantially more income. Many are not poor, underprivileged immigrants but are already imbued with achievement-oriented values and possess the class qualifications to implement those values. Structural opportunities, therefore, in addition to a cultural heritage compatible with American achievement values, are critical in accounting for the relatively rapid success of so many Asian Americans.

The consistent evidence of Asian-American economic and educational integration into American society sometimes masks disadvantages that are also part of the Asian-American experience. The discrepancies among specific Asian-American groups have already been noted. Racial bias, however, continues to contribute to some overall group patterns. For example, Asian Americans in general have higher long-term unemployment rates than white workers at nearly every educational level, and racial bias to some degree appears to account for this pattern (Kim, 2012). And, the higher household income of Asian Americans is often explained as a result of the fact that there are more breadwinners in these families and that they work longer hours. Also, Asian Americans, like other groups, suffered severe declines in both income and wealth as a result of the Great Recession (Pew Research Center, 2011; Weller et al., 2012).

Native Americans

Wherever Native Americans reside, on reservations or in urban areas, they are below the national average on most socioeconomic measures. Median household income is well below average, and the percentage of families in poverty is three times greater than for non-Hispanic whites. The social and economic conditions on reservations are especially harsh and remain resistant to significant change.

Of particular consequence is the serious Native American unemployment rate. Inadequate educational preparation and, on reservations, geographical isolation have contributed to extremely severe employment problems. Native Americans commonly find themselves without the skills and qualifications to secure steady jobs. Thus the impoverished status of many Native Americans continues from one generation to the next.

Regarding education, Native American students have a relatively high dropout rate compared to other ethnic groups, and their achievement levels are among the lowest (U.S. Census Bureau, 2003c, 2003d). More than any other factor, the low level of human capital among Native Americans, primarily in the form of education, accounts for the socioeconomic discrepancy between Indian and white populations (Waters and Eschbach, 1995).

Economic insecurity and low educational achievement translate into other forms of deprivation and long-term problems, including low health standards, high rates of alcoholism and suicide, and high crime rates (Indian Health Service, 2006; Josephy et al., 1999; Nieves, 2007; U.S. Commission on Civil Rights, 2004).

Although the differences between Native Americans and the remainder of the population are wide, progress has been made in recent years in closing the gap, particularly in improving health and educational standards. The numbers of Native American students attending college and pursuing graduate and other professional degrees, for example, have steadily risen (Thornton, 2001). Nonetheless, there remains a glaring socioeconomic discrepancy between Native Americans and the larger society. One reason for this continued gap is that government policies and favorable court decisions aimed at improving the quality of life of Native Americans have mainly affected those living on reservations, leaving unaddressed problems faced by two-thirds of all Native Americans, who live off reservations in urban areas.

Ethnicity and Power

The power dimension of stratification entails the extent to which people are able to affect others through their actions in positions of authority. This kind of power ordinarily occurs within two realms: government and the corporation. In considering the relationship of power and ethnicity, then, we need to look at the extent to which members of different ethnic groups occupy top decision-making positions in those institutions.

Government   There is a lengthy U.S. history of resistance to the efforts of minority ethnic groups to attain political equality. Through immigration quotas and exclusionary measures, Indian-removal acts, slave laws, institutionalized segregation, antilabor regulations, voting restrictions, and an array of other measures, dominant interests have traditionally been protected. Throughout American history, of course, these policies have all generated great controversy and conflict, and minority challenges have often met with success. But concessions wrested from the dominant group have always been slow, costly, and incremental.

To observe that Euro-Americans have dominated American political institutions in the past and continue to do so today overlooks the sharp differences within this panethnic category and the different pace at which members of its various groups have penetrated the highest levels of political power. Southern and eastern European groups, for example, mostly Catholic and Jewish, began to enter high governmental positions in significant numbers only in the years after World War II. Consider that a Catholic was not elected president of the United States until 1960. Indeed, until recent decades, Catholics traditionally were underrepresented in all the highest offices of the three branches of American government (Alba and Moore, 1982; Davidson et al., 1995; Mills, 1956; Stanley et al., 1967). Today, Catholics are represented in Congress approximately in proportion to their share of the total population and experience no evident impediments to their entrance into top positions in any sphere of government.

Jewish Americans were also denied full entrance into the political world in past eras, but in their case too, this situation has been rectified in recent decades. Indeed, in some spheres, Jews are actually overrepresented, considering their minor proportion of the general populace. In the U.S. Congress, for example, Jews make up 11 percent of the Senate and 5 percent of the House despite the fact that Jewish Americans constitute no more than 2 percent of the total population. The acceptance of Jews in higher politics is demonstrated as well by the fact that Jewish candidates are today commonly elected by overwhelmingly non-Jewish constituencies.

Asian Americans, another tier-two ethnic category, have been slower to penetrate the world of political power. This is due in largest part to the fact that most of the Asian American population has entered the society only since 1965. Thus, they have not had sufficient time to build a power base within the American political system. Second, their numbers have not been as large as those of other ethnic categories, and furthermore, they are highly concentrated in just a few large states. Nonetheless, as their population base widens and as the newer immigrants experience progressive assimilation, Asian Americans are likely to play a more active political role, especially where they constitute a sizable proportion of the population or where they are a significant minority.

Among the tier-three groups, the substantial increase in the number of African American elected officials in the last three decades is an indication of expanding political power. This is particularly so when compared with the virtual absence of African Americans in national politics during the early part of the twentieth century. By the mid-1990s, over forty African Americans were serving in the U.S. Congress. At the local level, the election of African American mayors in cities throughout the United States had become commonplace. What's more, an increasing number had won election from majority white districts or communities. In addition to a growing presence in Congress, in recent decades African Americans have served in powerful positions, both elected and appointed, at all levels of federal and state governments. Most significant, of course, a self-identified African American was elected U.S. president for the first time in 2008, an event considered highly improbable only a few years earlier.

Hispanic Americans have not yet seemed to mobilize as effectively as African Americans, and their political power is still in its primary stages. As with Asian Americans, many are immigrants who are not naturalized citizens and thus cannot vote. Nonetheless, Latinos are a growing political force, especially in cities and states where they constitute a large proportion of the population. In California, Texas, and Florida, Latinos have already established a very strong political influence, winning elective offices at all levels of government. With a rapidly expanding population base, the long-range outlook for Hispanic political power is bright (DeSipio, 2006; Taylor et al., 2012). Moreover, continued assimilation will stimulate increased activism in both national and local politics.

The Corporate World   Power in American society is certainly not limited to the governmental sphere. In the economic realm, key societal decisions regarding jobs, incomes, the standard of living, and the society's general economic condition are made by executives of the giant corporations. Here the dominance of Euro-Americans is much more thorough than in the political world. Moreover, the ethnic origins of American business leaders have been and remain primarily those of the tier-one groups (Alba and Moore, 1982).

In recent years, however, tier-two groups have begun to penetrate corporate elites in significant numbers. Jewish Americans, for example, were historically limited to high positions in the corporate world only through the growth of their own companies rather than by climbing the organizational ladder of well-established firms. Cearly this has changed significantly, with Jews increasingly entering the top executive positions of major corporations (Klausner, 1988; Christopher, 1989; Zweigenhaft, 1984, 1987; Zweigenhaft and Domhoff, 2006).

For third-tier groups, entrance into corporate executive positions has been more limited. Few African Americans serve on the boards of directors or in top-level executive posts of the largest corporations, and these few are often token rather than bona fide decision-making appointments (Collins, 1997). Despite these limitations, African Americans continue to increase their presence in executive and managerial positions, small though their numbers are (Meeks, 2005; Stodghill, 2007).

The role of Latinos in the corporate world has also been limited. Fewer than one hundred Latinos sit on boards of Fortune 500 companies, and appointments to executive positions are fewer still (*Hispanic Business,* 2009). Despite their underrepresentation an increasing number of Latinos are moving through the corporate elite pipeline (Zweigenhaft and Domhoff, 2006). Although Hispanic-owned firms are growing in number and economic significance, most of those owned by Mexican Americans or Puerto Ricans are small, family-operated businesses. Cuban Americans, by contrast, play a very significant role in the Miami business world, where they have helped to develop trade and banking ties to Latin American countries (Illa, 2010; Whitefield, 2000). Their economic power, however, remains primarily local and does not translate into national influence within the corporate economy.

Asian Americans are underrepresented in corporate managerial positions despite their comparatively large numbers in professional and technical positions. And at the very top of the corporate ladder, their numbers are as small as for African Americans and Hispanic Americans. Despite their tiny numbers at the executive level, Asian Americans are rising faster in the corporate world than any other minority group and are increasingly occupying high-powered jobs in finance and advertising (Sakamoto et al., 1998). Furthermore, as the number of Asian Americans in the general population grows, corporations will find it in their competitive interest to seek out and place more Asian Americans into higher-ranking positions, much as they have done with African Americans and Hispanic Americans.[8]

Richard Zweigenhaft and G. William Domhoff (2006) have studied the socioeconomic backgrounds of top political and corporate leaders and conclude that executive positions in the corporate world and high-ranking political positions are in fact occupied today by a more ethnically diverse group than in the past. Nonetheless, regardless of ethnicity, the class requirements for membership in the power elite remain much the same: at least middle-class in origin and well above average in education, usually with a degree from a prestigious university.

Prejudice and Discrimination

Another basis of the ethnic hierarchy is the extent to which ethnic group members continue to be the targets of prejudice and discrimination. Widely held beliefs regarding the character and capacities of particular groups are necessary to assure the long-range maintenance of ethnic inequality. These beliefs and values take the form of **prejudices,** that is, negative ideas regarding subordinate ethnic groups and ideas expressing the superiority of the dominant group. These beliefs may come together in a cohesive ideology of racism, as was the case in the nineteenth and early twentieth centuries. At other times, however, they are applied to groups in a somewhat disparate, unsystematic fashion.

Perhaps more important than beliefs, the dominant group in an ethnic hierarchy applies actions against minority ethnic groups that create disadvantages for them in various areas of social, economic, and political life. These actions are collectively termed **discrimination.** Whereas prejudice is the attitudinal element in enforcing ethnic stratification, discrimination is the active, or behavioral, element. Although there is ordinarily a

---

[8]Although they are underrepresented in the corporate elite, Asian Americans play a disproportionately prominent role in the small business world; 30 percent of all minority-owned firms and over half of all sales of such firms are Asian (U.S. Census Bureau, 2001).

tendency for prejudicial attitudes to accompany discriminatory behavior, there is no necessary relation between the two (Merton, 1949).

The discriminatory actions that create disadvantages for minority group members may vary widely in both form and degree. Verbal discrimination, that is, using ethnic slurs or derogatory labels, is a relatively minor form. More serious forms with much greater consequences involve the denial of access to various life chances such as jobs, housing, health, education, justice, and political participation. The most severe forms of discrimination involve acts of aggression against ethnic minorities, ranging from isolated incidents of violence to genocide, the deliberate destruction of an entire group.

Individual and Institutional Discrimination   Discrimination is not always overt, nor does it always entail intentional actions of denial or aggression. Moreover, there is a vast difference between the isolated actions of individuals and the deliberate policies of institutions that create and sustain patterns of discrimination. The behavior of an apartment-building owner in refusing to rent to members of a particular ethnic group, for example, is hardly the equivalent of a corporation's policy of not hiring that group's members or of a government policy requiring separate public facilities for them. The first example is **individual discrimination**—actions carried out by individuals or small groups, usually in violation of the society's laws or norms. The latter examples illustrate **institutional discrimination,** which is the result of the policies and structures of organizations and institutions.

Individual discriminatory actions obviously continue to occur, particularly as they involve third-tier ethnic groups. In 1997, for example, skinheads in Denver, Colorado, beat to death a black person whom they encountered on the street, because, as they explained it, "he didn't belong there" (Murr, 1997). In the past, individual discriminatory actions against particular ethnic groups were commonly sanctioned by the society's normative code. To taunt with ethnic slurs, to harass, to threaten, or to commit violence against minority ethnic group members was simply a well-understood feature of the society. Today, however, such actions are no longer normative and those who carry them out are seen as deviants. Moreover, antidiscrimination laws are further disincentives to individual forms of discrimination.

Institutional (or "structural") discrimination occurs in more complicated and less easily understood forms. Such actions may be legal or customary, in which case they are not socially unexpected or disapproved but are legitimized. The Jim Crow system of the pre-1960s American South and the South African apartheid system, for example, were fully supported in law. The forced removal of Native Americans to lands west of the Mississippi in the nineteenth century and the internment of Japanese Americans in the 1940s are other historical illustrations of a consciously constructed policy designed to keep a minority in its subordinate place.

Sometimes institutional discrimination is unintentional and not the result of prejudicial beliefs or the deliberate establishment of rules seeking to withhold privileges or injure members of particular ethnic groups. Rather, it exists as a product of the normal functioning of the society's institutions. Because of past discrimination of an overt, intentional nature or because of the spillover effect of intentional discrimination in one institutional area into another, certain groups find themselves perpetually at a disadvantage in the society's opportunity and reward structures (Feagin and Feagin, 1978). A large proportion of the African American population, for example, is confined to inner-city areas. Because most new jobs are in the outlying suburbs and because of a lack of public transportation, those people find themselves at a disadvantage in the labor market. Note what has occurred here: No person and no organization has directly discriminated against inner-city African Americans, but residential segregation has produced a powerful discriminatory effect.

The most evident, persistent, and consequential form of institutional discrimination in American society occurs in the area of housing, and it affects groups of the third tier, particularly African Americans, more than others. What's more, the patterns of discrimination here are often deliberate, whereas in the areas of work and education de facto discrimination occurs indirectly as a result of spatial arrangements and demographic trends. It is well recognized that less progress in breaking down ethnic barriers has been made in housing than in other spheres of social life (Massey, 2001; Massey and Denton, 1993; Brown et al., 2003). Although the level of black-white residential segregation in the largest U.S. metropolitan areas has declined somewhat in recent years, the simple fact is that most African Americans, regardless of their social class or the geographic area in which they live, continue to reside in predominantly black neighborhoods (Iceland, 2009; Logan et al., 2004; Wilkes and Iceland, 2004). Although this pattern is partly the result of voluntary action, it has been well documented that much of it is the result of discrimination, both individual and institutional (Massey and Denton, 1993). In turn, residential discrimination produces, often unintentionally, institutional discrimination in other areas, like schools and jobs.

It is important to point out that the United States holds no monopoly on ethnic prejudice and discrimination. Comparable actions typify the history, current and past, of most multiethnic societies. Indeed, when looked at in historical and global perspective, the American experience at times seems mild. The nineteenth and twentieth centuries witnessed occurrences of horrific ethnic violence and destruction in almost all world areas, including, among many other events, the annihilation of native peoples in Australia and South Africa, the slaughter of over a million Armenians by Turks, the systematic murder by Nazi Germany of 6 million Jews, and, more recently, massacres of entire populations in Rwanda and Bosnia.

Social Integration

A final indicator of placement on the ethnic hierarchy concerns the extent to which groups remain socially segregated. Sociologists use the terms **assimilation** and **pluralism** to describe how completely members of particular ethnic groups interrelate with others in various spheres of social life. There are two dimensions of assimilation and pluralism: cultural and structural. **Cultural assimilation** refers to the adoption by the minority ethnic group of the dominant group's norms and values. **Cultural pluralism,** in contrast, refers to the retention of ethnic ways. **Structural assimilation** is the gradual integration of the minority group into the societal mainstream: entering into the workforce at all levels, occupying positions of political power, living in dominant-group neighborhoods, and, ultimately, intermarrying with the dominant group. The converse of structural assimilation is **structural pluralism,** in which minority ethnic group members remain socially apart from the dominant group. Assimilation and pluralism must be understood not as absolute conditions but as relative processes; that is, they occur in degrees and will vary from group to group and from individual to individual.

All American ethnic groups except Native Americans entered U.S. society as immigrants, voluntarily or involuntarily. Most commonly, immigrants, following their arrival, begin to interact with out-group members and to adopt the ways of the dominant culture.[9] Obviously, groups and individuals experience this process at different rates. Some assimilate relatively quickly and without much difficulty, whereas others may remain apart from the societal mainstream for generations. Crucial to understanding assimilation are the cultural and physical differences between the minority ethnic group and the dominant group. Those groups more similar physically and culturally to the dominant group will be integrated into the mainstream more readily.

The key measures of social integration are residence and intermarriage. In this aspect of the ethnic hierarchy, as in others, it is third-tier groups that are most negatively affected. As mentioned earlier, residential segregation remains persistent in American society, particularly the black-white pattern. For other groups, this phenomenon is evident but not nearly as tenacious (Alba, 2009; Charles, 2003; Iceland, 2009; Logan et al., 2004). As to marriage across ethnic lines, for Euro-American groups it has become so common as to be almost the norm (Alba, 1995; Alba and Nee, 2003; Sherkat, 2004; Waters, 1990). Hispanic Americans and Asian Americans are intermarrying at lower, though increasing, rates. The intermarriage rate for African Americans is below that for all other ethnic groups, although it, too, is on the increase (Lee and Edmonston, 2005; Pew Research Center, 2012a; Qian and Lichter, 2007).

---

[9]Cultural assimilation is not a unilateral process but actually entails, to some degree, an exchange of cultural traits between dominant and minority ethnic groups.

Stability and Change in the American Ethnic Hierarchy

As we have now seen, the American ethnic hierarchy consists of three tiers, with groups arranged according to where they stand in aggregate income and wealth, occupation, and political power; the degree to which they are the targets of prejudice and discrimination; and the extent to which they have been socially integrated into the mainstream society.

Clearly, the division between tier-one and tier-two groups is gradually evaporating, but the third tier of groups continues to maintain a markedly lower aggregate economic and social status. In a number of ways, the status of ethnic minorities, especially African Americans, can be seen as a glass half full or a glass half empty.

Regarding the collective status of African Americans as well as other tier-three groups, it can be argued that greater progress has occurred in the last four decades than at any time in the society's history (Patterson, 1997). Stephan and Abigail Thernstrom (1997, 1998) explain that the persisting stereotype of African Americans as mostly being part of the economic underclass has contributed mightily to a failure to recognize the enormous changes that have taken place over the last five or so decades, especially the burgeoning of the African American middle class. In addition, studies have shown that whites are now less resistant to blacks in most areas of social and political life, and it is only in residence that resistance to black-white interaction remains strongly evident. The same trends are apparent for other ethnic minorities as well. This view of the hierarchy reflects a glass half full.

The glass half-empty view is equally compelling, however. Along with great progress, there is no denying that members of the third-tier groups remain disproportionately among the poor and the powerless. Comparisons presented earlier in this chapter demonstrate clearly the disadvantaged socioeconomic status of these groups. Moreover, in addition to economic disparities, the social boundaries separating the third tier from the first and second tiers, particularly within personal or informal settings, are dissolving only very slowly. Members of third-tier groups continue to encounter higher levels of prejudice and discrimination, and the extent to which they have been afforded entry into the full range of societal institutions remains lower than that afforded tier-one and tier-two groups. There are, then, significant economic and social gaps that persist between Euro-Americans and America's ethnic minorities.

Efforts at Changing the Hierarchy

The recognition of these economic and social gaps has given rise in recent decades to a number of highly controversial public policies. Recall (from Chapters 8 and 9) the ongoing societal debate in the United States between liberty and equity regarding the size and scope of the welfare state. American society, it was noted, is constantly engaged in a kind of battle between the forces of individual freedom and social equality. Those who feel that liberty should take precedence over equity argue that people must be left alone to lead their lives as they choose and to succeed or fail on their own efforts. This is to be done within the context of the free market. As was explained, however, the vagaries of the market unavoidably give rise to inequalities; as a result, there arises a counterforce in all modern capitalist societies that compels the state to intervene to some degree in the market in order to give people more opportunities to compete fairly. The end product of individualistic competition—inequality—is thus acceptable so long as there is assurance that the competition is fair and that everyone has an equal opportunity to win. It is the provision of those equal opportunities that therefore becomes critical.

Starting in the 1960s, it was recognized that the success of the civil rights movement, securing equal political and legal rights for African Americans, did not necessarily affect African American economic status. President Johnson, in announcing the federal government's intention to address this issue, put it this way: "You do not take a person hobbled by chains and liberate him, bring him up to the starting line of a race and then say, 'you are free to compete with all the others,' and still justly believe that you have been completely fair" (quoted in Skrentny, 1996:153).

It was acknowledged that African Americans had been systematically excluded from the mainstream society economically, politically, and socially and thus had been handicapped as a result of direct policies and customs. Other minority ethnic groups as well as women were subsequently added as target groups, the argument being that they, too, had been the victims of long-standing exclusion. Given generations of denied opportunities, was it fair to expect African Americans and other minorities to compete on an equal basis with the white—and essentially male—majority? How could these groups ever hope to catch up if they entered the competition burdened by decades of imposed disabilities and discrimination?

Affirmative Action

In response to the handicap imposed by past systematic discrimination, the federal government undertook sweeping measures to help bring about the economic improvement of African Americans and, later, that of other minority groups. These measures became known as **affirmative action.** As these policies evolved in the 1960s, they stipulated that those doing business with the federal government (universities as well as businesses) were required to take steps to increase their minority representation and establish goals and timetables to meet that objective.

As with other aspects of affirmative action, there is disagreement about the effects these policies have had during the last five decades. One point about which most seem to agree is that affirmative action opened opportunities to qualified minorities to a degree and at a pace that would not have otherwise occurred. In particular, it is claimed, expansion of the African

American middle class was stimulated. Even here, however, there is argument. Stephan and Abigail Thernstrom (1997) contend that economic opportunities for African Americans were opening quite rapidly even before the advent of affirmative action and in some ways actually slowed down once those policies were in place.

With more widespread and stringent application in the next two decades, affirmative action grew increasingly controversial, and by the 1990s antipathy to these policies seemed to grow more popular and shrill (Skrentny, 1996, 2002; Sniderman and Piazza, 1993). Quite simply, most Euro-Americans had come to see such measures as "reverse racism" and in violation of the American creed. The lack of political support for affirmative action was abetted by the courts in a number of relevant decisions as well as by the passage of referendums in several states that called for the abolition of the use of affirmative action in all state hiring and university admissions.

The issue of affirmative action has continued to fuel heated and politically volatile public debates in recent years, pitting those who favor the continuation of such policies against those who feel they should be abandoned. Let's examine the major points made by proponents and opponents of these policies.

Pro–Affirmative Action   Those who favor affirmative action build their case on a few critical points, namely, that these policies have accomplished what they were intended to do and that their need is still evident. Advancing the position of minorities through the use of goals and preferential hiring practices is necessary if the victims of past discrimination are eventually to attain equity with the majority (Kennedy, 1994; Taylor, 1997). Even if direct forms of discrimination no longer prevail, proponents point out, the indirect and institutional forms continue to perpetuate nonwhite (and female) disadvantages in the labor market and in higher education (Bergmann, 1996). Simply protecting minority individuals against ethnic or sex discrimination is therefore inadequate by itself. Hiring workers or admitting students without regard to ethnicity or sex will automatically preserve the disproportionate representation of white males because they enter the competition with background advantages accumulated over many generations. Artificial incentives for minorities are needed temporarily until the opportunity structure is made more truly equitable. Most important, proponents of affirmative action argue that without such policies, there is a risk of returning to an ethnic (and gender) norm of discrimination.

Some maintain that the critical importance of affirmative action lies in providing access for minorities to social networks that aid in securing better jobs and educational opportunities (Patterson, 1997). In this view, having education and skills is important, but even more important is being enmeshed in key networks through which individuals find jobs, meet influential people, and learn bargaining skills (essentially much like the idea, explained in Chapter 7, of having social connections, and the idea, discussed in Chapter 2, of what Bourdieu calls "social capital"). Individuals may possess formal qualifications, but unless they are able to move into the inner circles of the educational and work worlds, their chances of moving into elite positions and top jobs are diminished. African Americans have lacked the connections, ordinarily developed through ties made in universities, in the corporate world, or through intermarriage, that Euro-Americans have been able to avail themselves of more easily. Here is where affirmative action can play a role, casting African Americans and other minorities into networks that they otherwise would have little chance of penetrating (Loury, 1997; Patterson, 1998).

Anti–Affirmative Action   Those who oppose affirmative action programs or who strongly criticize the way they have been carried out argue that, in effect, these programs have become a kind of reverse discrimination in which those previously discriminated against are given preference over others merely on the basis of ethnicity (Glazer, 1975; Yates, 1994). Hence, opponents maintain, the very objective intended—reducing ethnic discrimination—has been undermined, the victims now being white males. Government is seen as re-creating racial and ethnic categories that had rightfully been abandoned. The effect of affirmative action in many cases has been to create quotas favoring minorities.

Another charge against affirmative action policies has been that they shift emphasis from equality of opportunity to equality of result, thus distributing social benefits on the basis of group membership, not individual merit. Less-qualified minority persons, as a consequence, may be promoted over better-qualified majority persons. Moreover, the targeted groups of affirmative action, it is argued, are stigmatized because of their special treatment, thus producing negative social and psychological effects on those who are supposedly the beneficiaries of these programs (Sowell, 1990). Shelby Steele (1991), for example, has suggested that affirmative action programs create a kind of implied inferiority. Whites commonly view blacks as having acquired their positions on the basis of special preference and, thus, as less than qualified or less than competent. This not only fuels negative stereotypes by whites, argues Steele, but also creates self-doubt among African Americans and other minorities.

In addition to charges of reverse discrimination and negative effects on employment and educational qualifications, affirmative action programs have been criticized as too sweeping in application and therefore unable to select out from among the various targeted minorities those who are in fact the past or present victims of discrimination (Schrag, 1995). For instance, although Latinos are covered under the principles of affirmative action, this broad panethnic category, as shown earlier, comprises several disparate components, each with different American experiences. Should Cuban Americans, who have not been discriminated against in work and education, be entitled to the benefits of these programs in the same way as Mexican Americans in the Southwest, who have been past victims of discrimination? Such problems suggest that minority group membership is no longer unambiguous. Moreover, many have pointed out that the major recipients of affirmative action benefits have been middle-class ethnic and gender minorities, not the "truly needy," that is, those in disadvantaged class positions. Filtering out those truly deserving of compensatory benefits has therefore become more complicated not only between various groups but within them as well.

Advocates of affirmative action have countered their detractors on these points. As to the lack of qualifications of those employed or admitted through preferential policies, proponents argue that "qualifications" can be variously interpreted, no matter how seemingly objective and valid tests or other sorting mechanisms may seem. They also point out that merit has never really been the sole criterion used in filling occupational and educational positions. Athletes have been given preference in university admission for decades, for example, as have veterans in applying for jobs. On the matter of quotas, it is argued that the objective of affirmative action is to facilitate the entrance of minorities into various institutions, not to keep them out, as was the purpose of earlier discriminatory quotas. And while opponents see ethnic minorities as being stigmatized by affirmative action, defenders argue that their absence in jobs and schools would create an even greater stigma (Kennedy, 1994).

Affirmative Action and Societal Values   To see the issue of affirmative action as a fundamental split between Euro-Americans on the one hand and ethnic minorities on the other hand is too simple. Although ethnic minorities are generally more supportive of such programs, national surveys have consistently indicated that a majority of Americans, regardless of ethnicity, support compensatory policies *in principle* if those policies are not perceived as special preferences or quotas (Sniderman and Piazza, 1993; Pew, 2009b; Plous, 1996). Whether they are prepared to support the idea in practice, however, is debatable (Bobo and Charles, 2009).

Opposition to affirmative action, then, must be seen as stemming not simply from prejudicial attitudes but from a number of factors. People may oppose or feel resentment toward these policies not because they are anti-minority or wish to keep things as they are (surely many *do* oppose these policies for such reasons) but because they see them as fundamentally in violation of the value of fairness (Sniderman and Carmines, 1997). In a number of ways, affirmative action is incompatible with some basic tenets of the dominant American ideology, individual achievement in particular. It creates a system in which rewards are distributed on the basis of group membership, not individual merit, and substitutes group rights for individual rights. It also contradicts the popular belief in personal effort as the key to upward mobility. Finally, as they have been implemented, affirmative action policies have at times seemed to violate the belief in equality of opportunity, substituting instead equality of result.

The Future of Compensatory Policies Just as the implementation of affirmative action has stimulated much controversy, the future of these policies has been subject to political debate. Again, to think of the issue as either a clear and simple "favor" or "disfavor" is too simple. Much of the debate revolves around whether these policies can, or should, be made more fair.

Some maintain that social class—not race or ethnicity—should be the major criterion by which people are deemed eligible for compensatory advantages (Kahlenberg, 1996, 2004; Michaels, 2006; Schrag, 1995) or that policies should be applied in a "race neutral" fashion (Wilson, 1994). Others maintain that such measures bring with them the same kinds of inherent problems as those based on race and ethnicity, that is, issues of determining who should be eligible and how they are to be chosen (Hacker, 1994; Kinsley, 1991).

Another confounding aspect of affirmative action concerns the very objective of such policies. They were originally intended to provide a temporary advantage to those ethnic minorities who had been the historical victims of systematic discrimination. As they evolved, however, their purpose was transformed into an effort to create schools and workplaces that resembled proportionately the ethnic makeup of the society, state, or community. So, is their purpose to help bring about greater equity among the society's diverse groups or is it to create more ethnic diversity within the society's major institutions? Efforts at attaining one of these objectives do not necessarily correspond to attainment of the other.

In light of political and social pressures, the content and implementation of affirmative action policies will continue to be debated and reshaped. Supreme Court decisions and state referendums in recent years have reduced the force and limited the scope of these policies in schools and the workplace (Fulwood, 2012). But it is unlikely that compensatory measures will be totally abandoned in the near future. Educators, particularly at the university level, deem the creation of a diverse student body necessary in establishing a positive learning environment and will likely employ other policies to assure that outcome (Pérez-Peña, 2012). And employers recognize that recruiting more minority managers and workers is simply good business in an increasingly ethnically diverse society and in the context of a global economy. As the nature and scope of affirmative action evolve, what is likely to emerge are compensatory policies based more on social class than on race and ethnicity, thus assuring greater economic (i.e., class) diversity. This is especially pertinent to universities and colleges, which already seem to be moving in that direction (Kahlenberg, 2012).

Affirmative action, in sum, remains one of the most vexing issues of ethnicity in America. Yet it is important to consider the widespread use of such measures in other multiethnic societies. Preferential policies designed to bring about more equity among diverse groups have been adopted in countries as divergent as Australia, India, Brazil, and Malaysia (Jenkins, 1998; Marger, 2012; Parikh, 2001). The problems revolving around this issue are not unique to the United States. As countries everywhere are transformed into multiethnic societies, ameliorating the inequitable distribution of societal resources among various ethnic groups has become an inescapable predicament.

Summary

Ethnic stratification systems are made up of dominant and minority groups. Minority groups receive fewer of the society's rewards on the basis of their physical or cultural traits. The dominant group is the group at the top of the ethnic hierarchy that disproportionately holds elite positions in government and the economy and generally possesses more of the society's valued resources. Also, the dominant group's norms and values become the society's standards.

Ethnic stratification is the product of contact between previously separate groups. The manner in which ethnic groups meet—through conquest, annexation, voluntary or involuntary immigration—is a critical factor in explaining the shape of the system of ethnic inequality that ordinarily ensues.

Ethnicity and social class are closely interrelated. In multiethnic societies, ethnicity becomes an important factor in the distribution of societal rewards and thus in the determination of people's class position. Members of minority ethnic groups are never randomly scattered throughout the economic and political class hierarchies but tend to cluster at specific points.

The American ethnic hierarchy can be viewed as being divided into three comprehensive tiers: Euro-American Protestants constitute tier one; Euro-American Catholics and Jews of various national origins and many Asians make up tier two; and groups often defined in racial terms—African Americans, Native Americans, some Asians—as well as Latinos make up tier three. Ethnicity is not a critical factor in social or economic life for those of tier one, but it remains evident for those of tier two (though decreasingly so), and it has great social and economic consequences for those of tier three. The hierarchy is based on aggregate income and wealth, political power, extent to which prejudice and discrimination remain significant, and extent of participation in all societal institutions.

There is a wide gap between aggregate income and wealth of African Americans and Euro-Americans, for which there are several competing explanations. Hispanic Americans also generally lag behind Euro-Americans, but Asian Americans exceed Euro-Americans on most measures of social class. None of the three non–Euro-American panethnic categories have entered into political and corporate elites in proportion to their population.

Prejudice and discrimination are most consequential for tier-three groups. Discrimination may take individual and institutional forms. The most persistent form of institutional discrimination today in the United States occurs in housing and affects groups of the third tier, particularly African Americans, more than others. Similarly, on key measures of social integration, third-tier groups are most affected, experiencing more persistent residential segregation and lower intermarriage rates.

Efforts to change the prevailing patterns of American ethnic inequality have centered on closing the economic gap between third-tier groups, particularly African Americans, and the larger society. Affirmative action measures have been the major public policy tool in addressing this issue. Proponents of affirmative action argue that such measures are necessary and productive and that there is much historical precedent for them. Opponents argue that they constitute a form of reverse discrimination, are too sweeping in application, stigmatize targeted groups, do not benefit those who most need help, and promote group rights over individual rights. Affirmative action policies appear to conflict with some basic elements of the American ideology, especially individual achievement. Nonetheless, these policies—in some form—are likely to remain in effect for the foreseeable future.

11

Gender Inequality

The true Republic: men, their rights and nothing more; women, their rights and nothing less.
SUSAN B. ANTHONY

Real equality is going to come not when a female Einstein is recognized as quickly as a male Einstein, but when a female schlemiel is promoted as quickly as a male schlemiel.
BELLA ABZUG

Lee Un Kee lives in a tiny farming village in South Korea named Punsooilri, thirty miles from Seoul, the capital city. He has been married for twenty-four years. When asked if he has beaten his wife, he indignantly replies, "How could I have been married all these years and not beaten my wife? Of course, you have to apologize afterward," he adds. "Otherwise, you can have bad feelings in your relationship with your wife." Chong Chin Suk, a fifty-six-year-old woman who runs Punsooilri's village store, admits, "Of course my husband beats me. But it was my fault because I scolded him." She explains, "Maybe there are some cases where it's just the man's fault. But ultimately the woman is to blame, because if she won't argue with her husband, he probably won't beat her." Speaking with other women in the village, it is apparent that wife-beating is quite commonplace in Punsooilri (Kristof, 1996b).

In 1996, a reactionary Islamic movement called the Taliban gained power in Afghanistan and ruled the country until 2001. Imposing what it interpreted as strict Islamic principles, the Taliban placed women into a state of virtual imprisonment. In Kabul, the country's major city, women were forbidden to work or go to school. If they left their homes, they were ordered to wear garments that completely covered their bodies and concealed their eyes behind cloth mesh. If they did leave their homes, they ran the risk of being assaulted by militiamen who might deem their attire not sufficiently modest. "I'm very afraid to go out on the street," said a female surgeon. "It's terrible for a woman to be hit by a strange man" (Cooper, 1996).

Late one night in Lima, Peru, a group of drunken men in their twenties raped María Elena, a seventeen-year-old girl who was on her way home from work. At the time of the incident, in Peru the law exonerated a rapist if he offered to marry the victim and she accepted. This created a situation in which relatives of rape victims would put pressure on the girl to accept the rapist's offer, believing this would restore honor to the victim and her family. María Elena's family, though incensed by the attack, encouraged her to accept when one of the rapists offered to marry her. When she first declined, the attacker's two accomplices threatened to slash her face. Yielding to the threat and to her family's urging, she finally relented. "What choice did I have?" she asked. "Everyone insisted that the way to solve the problem was for me to get married." Three months after the wedding, her husband abandoned her (Sims, 1997). Not long after this occurrence, the Peruvian law allowing rapists to avoid punishment if they agreed to marry their victims was repealed. But similar statutes pertaining to rape remain part of the legal code in a number of other Latin American countries.

In several countries in the Middle East and South Asia, women or girls who have committed adultery or have had premarital sex are in some cases killed by their husbands, brothers, or fathers. These so-called honor killings are a means of restoring the family's status and dignity, which, in the eyes of the community, have been severely tarnished by the woman's or girl's sexual behavior. The slayings are usually condoned by the society or punished only lightly. In Jordan, a man who is prosecuted and found guilty can be sentenced to as little as a few months in prison. The mother of one victim who was shot dead by her brother justified the killing: "We were the most prominent family, with the best reputation. Then we were disgraced. Even my brother and his family stopped talking to us. No one would even visit us. They would say only, 'You have to kill.'" Afterward, the slain woman's sister declared, "Now we can walk with our heads held high" (Beyer, 1999; Jehl, 1999; Mitchell, 2001).

To most Americans these are shocking instances of discrimination against women. But such incidents are commonplace in much of the world. Most discrimination is not as blatant and abusive as these cases demonstrate, but male dominance is virtually universal in the contemporary world. The systematic dominance of males over females is referred to as **patriarchy**.

This chapter looks at the nature of gender inequality and explores the ways in which men and women are treated differently in society. Examining gender inequality reveals an equivocal picture of both change and inertia. On the one hand, men everywhere outrank women and receive more of the society's rewards. The United Nations reports that women, though one-half the world's population, do two-thirds of the world's work, earn one-tenth of the world's income, and own one-hundredth of the world's property. Clearly, social, economic, and political inequality between men and women is a ubiquitous phenomenon. However, changes in women's subordinate status during the last four decades in the majority of the world's societies are equally obvious. In some cases the gap between men and women has narrowed dramatically in a relatively brief time. Both of these realities must be recognized.

Gender Differentiation

Sex and Gender

What is "gender"? And how does it differ from "sex"? These are commonly used terms, often without consideration for the important difference between them. Let's consider *sex* first. At birth, we are biologically male or female. Our sexual organs are different, our hormones and other aspects of body chemistry are different, and our biological functions are different: Women give birth; men do not. These relatively fixed physiological and biological differences are what define **sex.**

But the differences do not end here. Men and women differ as well as a result of cultural, social, and psychological factors. These are differences acquired not through birth but through the socialization process. Every society establishes a set of accepted behaviors to which males and females are expected to conform. How are women expected to act, *qua* women? And how are men expected to act, *qua* men? These are standards of femininity and masculinity and, as learned patterns of behavior, vary from society to society; they are not fixed or constant. These socially and culturally deter-mined differences are what constitute **gender.** In a very real sense, then, we are born male or female, but we must learn to be men and women.

Whether gender identity and gender roles stem from biological differ-ences or are the product of historical, social, environmental, and techno-logical circumstances is a matter of intense debate among anthropologists and sociologists (Chafetz, 1978; Lorber, 1994; Pinker, 2008; Rivers and Barnett, 2011; Walsh, 1997). Although few hold that gender roles are entirely either biologically or socially determined, the prevailing social science position is that culture is the key to understanding most differences in male and female behavior. In this view, there is nothing "natural" about women playing nurturing occupational roles (like nurse or schoolteacher) or men playing more assertive and peremptory roles (like soldier or doctor). Gender differences are primarily a product of socialization, discrimination, and other forms of social control (Bem, 1993; Epstein, 1988).

Proof of this position is found in the fact that women do not fill the same roles (spouse, mother, and so on) the same way from one society to another. Moreover, the "correct" or expected behavior for males and females, that is, the standards that define masculinity and femininity, constantly undergo change. As social conditions change, gender roles change accordingly. Anthropologist Marvin Harris points out that evidence from primate studies indicates that there is no hormonal barrier "that would prevent women from learning to be more aggressive than men if the exigencies of social life were to call for women to assume aggressive gender roles and for men to be more passive" (1989:266). This is already beginning to occur in modern societies as men take on more child-rearing responsibilities, calling for more nur-turant behavior, and as women enter into highly competitive professional occupations.

Nonetheless, few would deny that biology imposes limits on the social roles that men and women play. The anthropologist Lionel Tiger (1969), for example, explains that human gender roles evolved naturally as males were physically equipped to be hunters and women were the bearers of children.

Biology and culture should not be seen as mutually exclusive in any case. What is generally understood is that the two are inextricably linked in determining male and female roles and behavior. Biologically derived characteristics are always processed by cultural influences. For example, recent research has shown that there are at least some sex differences in brain functions that are not the result of cultural influences or hormonal changes but are present at birth (Cahill, 2005). But it has also been shown that the gender gap in math achievement is smallest in countries where women experience greater status equality in politics and leadership positions, demonstrating that there are no innate differences that are not subject to cultural alteration (Penner, 2008). As Alice Rossi explains, men and women are biologically predisposed to certain roles, but those roles are subsequently refined by and fitted into various cultures (1977, 1984). Thus, social processes, in combination with biological influences, shape patterns of gender differences and inequalities (Ridgeway, 2011).

Gender Stratification

Whatever the basis of gender roles, it is quite evident that they are not evaluated or rewarded equally; in virtually all societies, women are subordinate to men (Brown, 1991; Chafetz, 1978; Friedl, 1978). There is, then, in all societies a gender hierarchy, just as there is a class hierarchy, an ethnic hierarchy, and so on. And as the subordinate stratum in this hierarchy, women have less access to wealth, power, and prestige. The gender hierarchy, however, is less complex and variegated than the others, simply because most societies have constructed only two genders.[1]

Why Gender Inequality?

Explanations of why men and women have, throughout human history, played different roles and why those roles have been unequally rewarded have been the focus of much social science research and remain strongly debated issues. The intention of this chapter is not to engage the debate but simply to explore the various forms of gender inequality in the United States and other contemporary societies. In brief, however, as with explanations

---

[1]As Judith Lorber points out, however, neither gender nor sex is a pure category. "Combinations of incongruous genes, genitalia, and hormonal input are ignored in sex categorization, just as combinations of incongruous physiology, identity, sexuality, appearance, and behavior are ignored in the social construction of gender statuses" (Lorber, 1995:34). Alternative, or third, genders have been recognized in some societies (Lacey, 2008; Nanda, 1990).

for class inequality (Chapter 2), gender inequality has been explained from various theoretical perspectives, each offering a somewhat different account for the virtually universal feature of male dominance in human societies. These different perspectives have given rise to several factions of the contemporary feminist movement and have become the basis of different views on how gender inequality can be attenuated. What follows represents a small sample of theoretical attempts at explaining gender inequality.

Functional theories posit that gender differentiation and stratification contribute in some fashion to accomplishing critical tasks (Nielsen, 1990). These theories focus on the different roles that men and women play and the way each contributes to the society's survival. Gender inequality is seen not as the outgrowth of differential power but rather as functionally necessary.

In preindustrial societies, the role differentiation of men and women can be seen clearly. In hunting-and-gathering societies, which typified the economic structure of societies for most of human history, hunting was almost universally a male activity whereas foraging was mostly done by women. Ernestine Friedl (1978) suggests that one of the major reasons for this specialization was that women were usually either pregnant or caring for young children. The particular skills required for hunting precluded women's participation since they could not be performed by a woman carrying a child, either in pregnancy or in her arms.

With the emergence of agrarian societies, preparing the soil and planting crops became mostly a male function, and tending and harvesting were assigned to women (Murdock, 1937). Although in industrial societies these role assignments no longer seem functionally necessary, certain roles, in the functionalist view, remain gender-specific. Women continue to fulfill roles like child rearing that require expressive qualities such as affection and compassion. Men, by contrast, fulfill instrumental roles as major breadwinners (Parsons and Bales, 1955).

Theorists using a conflict perspective see gender differentiation not as functionally necessary but as attributable to some form of power that one gender—almost always men—derives from its social role. This power differential generates gender inequality.

Some theorists in this camp stress control over the distribution of material goods. Friedl (1978) explains that in a few technologically simple societies, there is relative equality between men and women because both sexes work side by side in food production and what is produced is distributed equitably among workers. Gender inequality begins to emerge as societies become more productive and as women play a reduced economic role. In modern societies, so long as women do not exercise control over the investment of money—the key societal resource—they will have little power and social recognition. Within the home, too, women who work not in the labor force but as housewives, providing services to husbands and children without pay, are especially vulnerable to male dominance. Progress toward true gender equality is stimulated by women's acquisition of positions of power in the economy and political system, as in the United States and other advanced societies.

A somewhat related theory suggests that gender inequality stems from the childbearing role of women. The essential argument is that women are encumbered for lengthy periods by pregnancy, nursing, and related activities. Logically, then, as human societies evolved, women assumed domestic roles, those that revolved around child care and household duties, and men assumed hunting and related activities that occasionally took them away from the family or community (Huber, 1990). The resources of knowledge, weaponry, and technology that derived from these activities provided men with economic power and prestige. Women's activities, in contrast, were seen as routine and mundane.

Randall Collins (1971) theorizes that innate physical differences are the key to understanding the origins of gender inequality. He explains that since humans have a strong drive for sexual gratification and males are, on average, bigger and stronger than females, men can force themselves on the weaker sex. This element of coercion has thus shaped the fundamental features of the woman's role.

Sexism and Sexist Stereotypes

As with other forms of social inequality, an ideology has served to rationalize and stabilize male dominance. This ideology, **sexism,** is essentially the belief that women and men are innately different and that those innate differences translate into female inferiority. With sexism, sex differences are assumed to produce differences in social behavior. Women or men can be no other way because they are born that way. "Biology is destiny," as the expression goes.[2]

Over many generations, the sexist ideology has created a self-fulfilling prophecy. Male dominance in various spheres of social life led to the assumption that their superiority was natural. This, in turn, shaped people's expectations. One did not expect to see a woman military leader or a woman business executive or a woman politician. These were assumed to be "naturally" male-occupied positions, requiring skills and talents that women, by nature, did not possess. Hence, women were not trained to take such positions, which, as a result, continued to be filled primarily by men.

Sexist Stereotypes   A set of stereotypes has developed historically that has served as the basis of the ideology of sexism. As with racism, members of the categories "male" and "female" are assumed to carry with them certain innate characteristics. Women are "ruled by emotion," they are "less intelligent" than

---

[2]Sexism has been variously defined. Some see it as any form of prejudice or discrimination against people based on their sex (Benokraitis, 1997). Others have defined it as "the subordination of women by men" (Rothenberg, 1998:132), and others as a synonym for gender stratification (Nielsen, 1990). The term as it is used here implies a belief in the biological grounding of social and behavioral differences between men and women.

men, and so on.[3] Women are commonly portrayed as being more compassionate, sensitive, and dependent than men, who are seen as mentally tough, decisive, and independent. These stereotypes are supported by various types of gendered language: sex-linked adjectives (for example, a "beautiful" woman but a "handsome" man), occupational titles and forms of address, slang phrases, and so on (Chafetz, 1978). Even if the biological origins of gender differences are thrown into dispute, what remains are thoroughly embedded cultural beliefs—stereotypes—about what are assumed to be fundamental behavioral differences between men and women, leading to "naturally" gendered social roles, with men occupying those most powerful and prestigious (Ridgeway, 2011).

Surprisingly, despite recent changes in gender relations and in women's family and occupational roles, many of these stereotypes remain widespread. A national survey in 2008, for example, found that an overwhelming majority of Americans believed women to be more compassionate, creative, and emotional than men, and more than half characterized women as more manipulative (Pew, 2008c).

Sexist stereotypes continue to serve as justifications for gender inequality in different spheres of social life. Thus, if women are assumed to be more compassionate and sensitive, it is only logical that they continue to play occupational roles that complement those traits. And by the same token, if they are not confident and decisive, they are not as capable as men of assuming important positions in key institutions. These stereotypes have begun to lose their effectiveness, however, as women increasingly move into social roles previously dominated by males. A paradox of the survey referred to above is that a majority of respondents, despite offering many of the standard gender stereotypes, believed women to be equal to or better than men on most of the traits deemed necessary for political leadership.

Gender Inequality in the Workforce: Continuity and Change

The gender division of labor in the workforce is a critical factor in understanding the more general system of gender stratification. As noted in earlier chapters, power is very much dependent on control of economic resources. Thus, to the extent that women do not play a role in the economy that would enable them to control or direct the distribution of those resources, their subordinate place is sustained (Friedl, 1978). A comparative study of 111 societies concluded that women's roles are less traditional where their economic power, as indicated by their labor force participation rate, is high (South, 1988).

---

[3]Nineteenth-century scientists assumed that since women's brains were smaller than men's, the superior male intellect was a given. We know today, however, that brain size differs with body weight and that when average disparity in body weight is taken into account, women's brains are actually a bit larger than men's.

Table 11-1 ▪ Percentage of Women and Men in the U.S. Labor Force

Year	Women in Labor Force as % of All Women	Men in Labor Force as % of All Men	Women as % of Total Labor Force
1900	20.0	85.7	18.1
1930	23.6	82.1	21.9
1950	33.9	86.4	29.6
1970	43.3	79.7	38.1
1990	57.5	76.1	45.2
2010	58.6	71.2	47.0
2018*	58.7	70.6	47.0

*Projected.
Source: U.S. Census Bureau, 1975, 2012c.

Labor Force Participation

A powerful trend of the last several decades has been the vastly increasing number and percentage of women who have entered the workforce. This is especially evident in the United States, where a remarkable transformation has occurred within one generation in the occupational expectations of and for women (Bianchi and Spain, 1996; Boushey and O'Leary, 2009). As Table 11-1 shows, women have steadily become a larger portion of the workforce over the last hundred years. Figure 11-1 shows the dramatic change in labor force

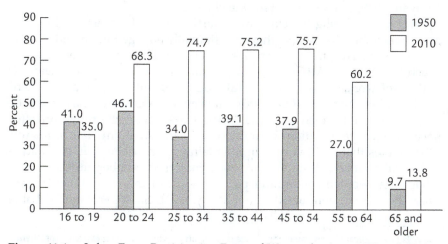

Figure 11-1 ▪ Labor Force Participation Rates of Women by Age, 1950 and 2010
Source: Bureau of Labor Statistics, 2011; Fullerton, 1999.

participation by women in almost all age groups since 1950. In light of the job losses brought about by the severe economic recession of the late 2000s, particularly in manufacturing and construction, women were poised to surpass men as a percentage of the American workforce.

Today, women from families of all social classes and ethnic groups are workers. To be sure, women in the past were also part of the labor force, particularly working-class, immigrant, and minority women, whose economic situation required that they contribute to their family's livelihood. In recent decades, however, women from the entire social spectrum have increasingly entered the mainstream labor force as full- or part-time workers. They also work a substantial number of hours while raising families. Almost three-quarters of women with dependent children (a majority of whom are under six years of age) work in the paid labor force, most of them full-time workers (Bureau of Labor Statistics, 2011). Unlike in past generations, the expectation of most women is no longer that they will stay at home attending to domestic chores. Although they may see themselves in this traditional family role for a period of time, they fully expect to be working in the mainstream labor force at some point in their lives.[4]

The rate of labor force participation is not the same in all societies of the modern world. In less-developed societies and in societies where religion dictates most societal norms (particularly Muslim countries), there is less female participation than in Western industrialized countries. However, in recent decades, economic globalization has drawn many women in the developing world into the unskilled labor force. In those settings, multinational corporations manufacturing electronic products, shoes, clothing, and other consumer goods employ mainly women in their assembly plants. The low wages and often oppressive work conditions of these women have been well documented (Klein, 1999; Peterson and Runyan, 1999; Fuentes and Ehrenreich, 1983).

When considering the expanding participation of women in the workforce, remember that women have traditionally engaged in unpaid, or nonmarket, work. And the performance of such work by women remains very much in evidence. A United Nations study reported that worldwide, 66 percent of women's work is unpaid, compared with 34 percent of men's work (United Nations, ILO, 1996). Housework and child rearing are the major forms of women's unpaid labor. Think about the time and effort spent in meal preparation, cleaning, child care, shopping, and numerous other chores that are involved in maintaining a household. Even today in industrial societies, despite their vastly increased numbers in the general labor force, women continue to perform most of this work. *The American Time Use Survey*, conducted annually by the U.S. Department of Labor,

---

[4]Surveys have indicated growing ambivalence on the part of women in their expectations of entering the workforce. In one poll (Moore, 2005), a slight majority of women said they would choose the traditional female role of staying at home. This view was stronger among younger women.

reports that in households with children where both parents are working, mothers spend an average of 2.1 hours a day doing household activities, compared to about 1.4 hours for fathers (Bureau of Labor Statistics, 2008b). In her interviews of working couples, the sociologist Arlie Hochschild (1989) asked about how they juggled work and family responsibilities. One woman described her duties as homemaker with the metaphor of the "second shift": "You're on duty at work. You come home, and you're on duty. Then you go back to work and you're on duty" (7).

In addition to their sharply increased numbers, there are three outstanding trends in analyzing the place of women in the labor force: They are occupationally concentrated, they are likely to be paid less than men, and they are less likely to occupy positions of authority and prestige. Let's look more carefully at each of these trends.

Occupational Concentration

In virtually all societies, work is divided along sexual lines: Some roles are assigned to men, and others to women. In the 1930s, the anthropologist George Murdock surveyed over three hundred technologically simple societies around the world and found in all of them a gendered division of labor. In none did men and women share work roles (Murdock, 1937). Which particular roles are typically male and which are typically female, however, may differ from society to society. That is, occupations ordinarily reserved for women in one society may be reserved for men in another. For example, in the United States, the overwhelming majority of physicians have typically been men; only in recent years have women begun to enter the medical profession in large numbers. In Russia, however, most physicians have been—and continue to be—women (Knaus, 1981; Ramer, 1990). In the United States, women have traditionally been clustered in certain occupations, such as nurse, schoolteacher, retail salesperson, and domestic service worker. Table 11-2 shows the extent of occupational concentration in some selected cases. Note how jobs with the highest percentage of women are those that involve interpersonal skills assumed to be natural to women. Likewise, those with the fewest women involve more physically active duties, assumed to be natural to men.

Much of the occupational segregation based on gender in the United States is evident in other societies. A United Nations study of twenty-four countries indicated that over 90 percent of typists and nurses were women, closely in line with U.S. patterns (United Nations, 1991). And at least three-quarters of all primary school teachers in virtually every European and North American society are women (ILO, 2004). Indeed, one comparative study concludes that gender segregation in the labor market "seems to be a universal and persistent phenomenon" (Kreimer, 2004:229).

Gender stereotypes sustain and reinforce occupational clustering. If it is assumed that men are more aggressive and daring by nature, police officer and

Table 11-2 ▪ Percentage of Women in Selected Occupations

Occupation	1983	2010
Secretaries	99.0	96.1
Dental hygienists	98.6	95.1
Preschool and kindergarten teachers	98.2	97.0
Registered nurses	95.8	91.1
Data entry keyers	93.6	80.5
Bank tellers	91.0	88.0
Hairdressers and cosmetologists	88.7	91.9
Waiters and waitresses	87.8	71.1
Elementary and middle school teachers	83.3	81.8
Social workers	64.3	80.8
High school teachers	51.8	57.0
Real estate agents	48.9	54.0
Bartenders	48.4	55.2
College and university teachers	36.3	45.9
Lawyers	15.8	31.5
Physicians	15.8	32.3
Police officers	9.4	13.0
Clergy	5.6	17.5
Truck drivers	3.1	4.6
Airplane pilots	2.1	5.2
Carpenters	1.4	1.4
Firefighters	1.0	3.6
Automotive mechanics	0.5	1.6

Source: U.S. Census Bureau, 2002b; Bureau of Labor Statistics, 2011.

firefighter become "natural" male occupations. If women are assumed to be more compassionate and nurturing, nurse and schoolteacher become "natural" female occupations. These stereotypes often lead to self-fulfilling prophecies. If women are believed to be less adept at math and science, they are apt to be counseled along those lines in high school, leaving them ill prepared for a rigorous engineering curriculum, for example, when they enter college. Women students themselves may see engineering as a male dominion and not as a field that they would find comfortable or appropriate. The overwhelming majority of engineers thus continue to be men, and engineering schools continue to struggle to attract female students (Burke and Mattis, 2007).

Examples abound of the ways in which gender stereotypes influence occupational selection. Consider automobile sales. Not only are automobile salespersons—mostly men—expected to be aggressive (a "naturally" male trait), but as men they are assumed to be more familiar with automobiles and things mechanical and thus can be more effective in dealing with customers. Real estate sales, by contrast, is a relatively gender-neutral field, with virtually no obstacles to women. Again, consider the gender stereotypes that might account for this. Women are presumably no less "naturally" knowledgeable about homes and things that relate to them than men. In both cases, there is no validity to presumed natural gender differences, but stereotypes, reinforced in all spheres of social life, continue to influence our assumptions about who should fill these positions. This **gender essentialism**—the idea that there are unique male and female traits that make men and women naturally suited to different occupational roles—continues to drive women into the nonmanual sector of the labor force and, conversely, men into the manual sector (Charles and Grusky, 2004). A glance back at Table 11-2 confirms this.

Although it usually is seen as negatively affecting women, gender segregation is a two-way street. Just as common gender stereotypes help channel women into particular fields, they do the same thing for men. As a result, men face barriers—subtle and informal, though well understood—to entrance into certain occupations held primarily by women. Whereas women entering traditionally male-dominated fields enhance their status, men entering primarily women-dominated fields risk a loss of status. As Christine Williams (1995) suggests, "'My daughter the physician' resonates far more favorably in most people's ears than 'my son, the nurse'" (262).

Although in the United States and other modern societies men and women remain concentrated in particular occupational roles, the sexual division of labor is not as rigidly enforced as in the past, and in some cases dramatic change has occurred in recent decades. Certain fields remain overwhelmingly female and the manual-nonmanual divide persists, but occupational gender segregation has steadily declined since the 1970s (Bowler, 1999; Reskin and Padavic, 2002; Wootton, 1997). Women can now be found in the entire range of occupations and are the majority in some fields (e.g., pharmacology, editing, insurance adjustment) that were formerly male dominated. Particularly striking change is evident in the two most prestigious professions: medicine and law. In 1961, 95 percent of degrees in medicine and 97 percent in law were awarded to men; forty years later, almost half of medical and law school graduates were women.

Although gender segregation still characterizes the labor force, changes are taking place not only because more women are stepping into jobs that had typically been male-dominated; the converse is also occurring. An increasing number of men are moving into occupational areas that had always been overwhelmingly female, such as dental hygienists, kindergarten teachers, and nurses. A combination of factors is at work here, including the tighter job market for men as a result of the Great Recession, issues of job satisfaction, and the breakdown of traditional gender stereotypes (Dewan and Gebeloff, 2012).

Most important, American women are progressively moving into occupational areas involving managerial and professional roles that were previously difficult, at best, to enter. These are precisely the kinds of positions—those involving control of valued resources and decisions regarding their distribution—that contribute to increased societal power. Women in 1970 were 18 percent of all managers; ten years later they were 30 percent, and twenty years later, 40 percent (Reskin and Padavic, 2002). This is a continuing trend (Bowler, 1999; Glater, 2001). At the very top of the managerial ladder, however, women have not experienced a comparable degree of mobility (Creswell, 2006; Leonhardt, 2006). This point is addressed later in this chapter.

Earnings

As with occupational concentration, a mixed picture is evident regarding men's and women's earnings: Changes are occurring, but significant discrepancies remain. Over the last twenty years, women's earnings have increased as those of men have declined. Thus, the ratio of women's to men's earnings has narrowed considerably. Figure 11-2 shows that trend very clearly. Among the college-educated in particular, the growth in women's earnings far outpaced that in men's. Still, women's wages, on average, are about 77 percent of men's wages. This disparity is evident whether comparisons are made by education, occupation, age, or race/ethnicity.

In regard to education, while the earnings of college-educated women rose during the last three decades, those with no college advanced only marginally. Women with some college but no degree earn only two-thirds

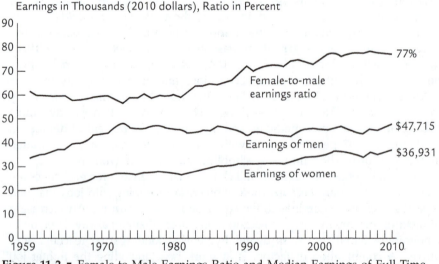

Figure 11-2 ■ Female-to-Male Earnings Ratio and Median Earnings of Full-Time, Year-Round Workers 15 Years and Older by Sex: 1960 to 2010
Source: U.S. Census Bureau, 2011a.

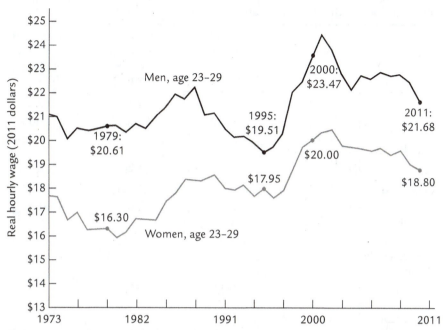

Figure 11-3 ▪ Entry-Level Wages of College Graduates, by Gender, 1973–2011
Note: Entry-level wages are for workers with one to seven years of potential experience.
Source: From "The State of Working America, 12 ed." by Lawrence Mishel et al. Reprinted by permission of The Economic Policy Institute.

of what women with a four-year degree earn; those with only a high school diploma earn little more than half the income of college graduates (Mishel et al., 2009). In the next section, we will see that women no longer trail men in the rate of college graduation. In fact, more women than men today earn college degrees, both undergraduate and graduate. Yet, as can be seen in Figure 11-3, the entry-level wage gap (that is, beginning wages following graduation) has basically remained unchanged since 1973.

Women's wages lag men's in almost all occupational areas, even those in which women predominate. Table 11-3 shows, for example, that women social workers, registered nurses, and secretaries earn less, on average, than their male counterparts. Not surprisingly, in occupations traditionally held by men, women's wages are lower, particularly at the higher status levels, such as chief executives and managers. Also, women are more likely to be earning poverty-level wages than men. In 2011, almost one-third of women earned poverty-level wages or less, compared to one quarter of men (Mishel, 2012d).

In the past, discrepancies in pay between men and women were the result largely of direct discrimination. Employers would routinely pay women less than men for doing the same job. Their rationale was that women were not breadwinners and therefore did not require the same

Table 11-3 ▪ The Gender Wage Gap in Selected Occupations

	Women's Median Weekly Earnings	Men's Median Weekly Earnings	Women's Earnings as % of Men's
Chief executives	$1,464	$2,122	69.0%
First-line supervisors/ managers of office and administrative workers	$741	$833	89.0%
Managers, all other	$1,047	$1,406	74.5%
Registered nurses	$1,034	$1,081	95.7%
Secondary school teachers	$989	$1,049	94.3%
Elementary and middle school teachers	$933	$1,022	91.3%
Secretaries and administrative assistants	$651	$757	86.0%
Stock clerks and order fillers	$501	$488	102.7%
Retail salespersons	$466	$620	75.2%
Waiters and waitresses	$389	$466	83.5%

Source: Reproduced by permission of the Institute for Women's Policy Research.

salary as men. Moreover, it was assumed that women were working only as a temporary measure and were not reliant on their jobs for a living, as were men. Two measures destroyed the legal basis for gender discrimination in the workforce: the Equal Pay Act of 1963 and Title VII of the Civil Rights Act, passed in 1964. The former prohibited employers from paying women less than men for doing essentially the same job. Title VII prohibited discrimination in hiring or in wages on the basis of race or sex.

What, then, accounts for the continued gender discrepancy in pay? Economists today explain that the differentials in pay between men and women are mostly the result of the particular occupational areas in which women find themselves concentrated (Reskin and Padavic, 2002). More are in unskilled, poor-paying jobs, particularly at the low end of the service sector. This includes restaurant workers, retail salespersons, and domestic service workers. Because of child-rearing responsibilities, women have often chosen less demanding or part-time jobs in order to assure flexibility. These jobs pay less and provide little in the way of training or skills acquisition that would lead to more challenging and better-paying jobs. Women must also take time away from work after childbirth, causing a further loss of opportunity to improve skills and wages (Bianchi and Spain, 1996; Boushey and O'Leary, 2009; Glass, 2004). As women increase their investment in human capital (education, skills, and experience) and also delay childbirth, they should, in this view, increase their productivity and earnings vis-à-vis men. To the extent that women continue to perform the major tasks of raising children and attending to other family needs, however, a gender gap is likely to persist. "The top jobs in industry are largely filled by people who invest heavily in their careers," note sociologists Eva Meyersson Milgrom and Trond Petersen, "and such investments are diminished by home-care responsibilities" (2006:205).

Another explanation for the wage gap between men and women is the **cohort effect.** This describes the process in which successive generations of women catch up to men in fields in which they previously had been only marginally present. In her study of engineers, Laurie Morgan (1998) found that women who entered the profession more recently faced fewer career obstacles than those who had entered it earlier. Thus, the lower earnings of women versus men and their failure to win promotions as rapidly were the result of a cohort effect rather than a glass ceiling effect. That is, the gap in earnings between male and female engineers was more a matter of when an individual entered the profession than of how long that individual had been in it. For younger women engineers, the earnings gap with men was essentially nonexistent. Women in each successive cohort, therefore, should face fewer career obstacles and should earn increasingly comparable wages; where a **glass ceiling** is in effect, women (or racial/ethnic minorities) improve their status on a par with men only up to a point where their progress is blocked.

Some sociologists, however, point to continuing discrimination, albeit in more subtle, institutional forms than in the past, as a factor in accounting for the wage gap between men and women (Correll et al., 2007; Gorman, 2005). They emphasize that the increasing convergence of men's and women's wages is the result primarily of changes in societal views of women's abilities, as well as affirmative action and other legal measures, that have forced employers to hire more women. Also, they explain the narrowing gender gap in some part as simply a result of the decline in men's earnings. Sociologists also stress the power advantages that men continue to hold in gaining access to elite positions, enabling them to define how jobs are to be categorized and rewarded (Bianchi and Spain, 1996; Corbett and Hill, 2012).

Comparable worth is an issue that emerged in the 1980s and is seen by some as a principal means of closing the pay gap between men and women. **Comparable worth** refers to the proposition that men and women should be paid the same for jobs of equal or comparable value. This idea extends the notion of "equal pay for equal work," which merely holds that women and men should be paid the same wage for doing the same jobs (Goldin, 1990). Not only should male and female nurses, for example, be paid the same, but the pay of nurses should be comparable to the pay of workers in occupations that require a similar level of skills (airline pilots, perhaps). The question of how jobs are assessed in terms of skill and merit, of course, is highly problematic and has created wide disagreements about measurement and about whether the concept of comparable worth has any real meaning (Barko, 2000; England, 1992; Hutner, 1986). Presumably, implementing comparable worth would serve to increase the earnings of workers in occupations that are heavily dominated by women, which are currently undervalued.

Another consistent occupational pattern among societies is that traditional female roles are accorded less prestige than traditional male roles (Linton, 1936). As Friedl has explained, "Evidence of a society . . . in which women's activities are the most prestigious has never been found" (1978:69). Moreover, the kind of work done by women is usually considered less valuable and is rewarded accordingly (England, 1992). It is generally the case that the more women who work in an occupation, the less both its female and male workers earn (Reskin and Padavic, 2002).

It is of note that the earnings gap between men and women is not unique to the United States. Multinational firms in developing countries routinely pay women employees far less than they pay men. Indeed, this is one reason women employees are preferred (Safa, 1990). In a number of countries, mostly in the industrialized world, the earnings gap is narrower than in the United States, but this is ordinarily not the case. Although women make up a large part of the European workforce, on average they continue to earn considerably less than men in both the manufacturing and service sectors. Conditions vary regionally and from country to country, of course, and, as in the United States, women have entered occupations at various levels of skill and compensation. But in all cases the tendency for working women to earn less than their male counterparts is most common, whether in the developing or industrialized worlds (UNICEF, 2007).

Authority

It is obvious that women in all areas of the labor force work not only in jobs that pay less than men's jobs but also in those in which authority is limited. In the same occupational fields, women tend to be in less authoritative positions than men. What is more striking is the finding that women are underrepresented in power positions even in fields that they numerically dominate, like nursing and librarianship (Reskin and Padavic, 2002; Williams, 1995).

Moreover, even where they have entered previously male-dominated fields, women often are relegated to specific positions that are lower in prestige and income. Women in the legal profession, for example, have advanced markedly in the last three decades. In the early 1970s, only one of every thirty-three lawyers was a woman; today one of every three lawyers and nearly half of all law students are women. Yet women lawyers continue to average less in salaries than their male counterparts, and they lag in attaining partnerships in large firms (Epstein, 1996; O'Brien, 2006). In medicine, too, the gender gap is obvious. Women physicians are clustered in less prestigious specialties such as pediatrics and family medicine. The more prestigious and higher-paying specialties, like surgery and cardiology, remain male-dominated (Steinhauer, 1999; Leonhardt, 2006).[5]

Opportunities for women to reach authoritative positions differ from industry to industry. A study of the United States and three other industrial societies found that women were more inclined to rise to managerial positions in service industries, such as publishing, and were less likely to do so in heavy industries, such as automobile manufacturing (Clement and Myles, 1994). Industries in which women did have easier access to the top were those in which women made up the bulk of the workforce.

Work and the Family

Traditionally, women have been expected to perform household duties centering on child rearing and domestic functions. Men, in contrast, have been expected to leave the home to work, with primary responsibility for supporting the family economically and protecting its members. This traditional arrangement has been brought into question by the entrance of women in significant numbers into the mainstream workforce in recent decades, often as primary breadwinners.

Despite the changed work role of women, the gender breakdown of traditional family roles has not changed radically. Indeed, "the household division of labor," as sociologist Cecilia Ridgeway describes it, "has been one of the most obdurate features of the gender structure of contemporary America" (2011:194). Today, although a majority of all adult women are in the labor force, women continue to do the bulk of child care and household tasks. Indeed, the actual number of hours they work in the home is not much different from what it was in the early part of the twentieth century (Schor, 1992). Although a majority of Americans believe that women today should work even if they are raising families, the prevailing view of "normal" gender roles still conforms to that of an earlier time. Consider how odd, even in the early twenty-first century, we find a family in which the wife is the major breadwinner while the husband remains at home caring for the children and attending to household chores. Even when men and women both work full-time and provide equal income, women tend to do more housework than men (Bittman et al., 2003). A Canadian study showed that men

---

[5]A recent study has shown that male physician researchers earn more than their female counterparts, even when adjustments are made for differences in specialty and other factors (Jagsi et al., 2012).

were spending somewhat more time on housework than they did in the past (1.4 hours a day in 2005 compared to 1 hour a day in 1986), but clearly the division of labor within the home persists (Marshall, 2006).

The unequal gender arrangement of the family directly impacts gender inequality in other social realms. The frequent conflicts women encounter between their family and work roles account in large part for the extent to which they lag behind in higher-status and higher-paying occupational positions. This is evident in medicine, for example, where, as noted earlier, women earn less than men and are concentrated in less prestigious specialties. Aside from lingering sexism in the profession, women cite the difficulties of combining family obligations (especially child care) with professional demands as the major hindrance to promotion in their fields. Trying to balance work and family, many young female doctors choose specialties that require less training, since most of that training coincides with their prime childbearing years. Others may work part-time or take positions that offer a less demanding and more flexible schedule. Their earnings and prestige suffer as a result (Steinhauer, 1999; Leonhardt, 2006).

Sociologist Pamela Stone (2009) has found an increasing number of working women, particularly in high-status, professional occupations, choosing to drop out of the labor force. This growing phenomenon, she explains, is accounted for not by sexist discrimination on the job or even a newly found desire to pursue a more traditional domestic role, but by a "motherhood" penalty. These women find that having children forces them to devote time to child care, thereby reducing their ability to work regular hours or devote full attention to their careers. The conflicting demands of a high-powered professional job with the demands of motherhood create a time bind. Much of this predicament is a product of inadequate public policies that fail to provide support for child care or paid leave and of inflexible job requirements. All of these factors, however, work in tandem with the continuing traditional division of labor in the family, that is, the "gendered nature of care." With husbands who have similar job demands, these women find themselves assuming most of the responsibilities of child care. "We'll know we have achieved true gender parity," notes Stone, "when men and women participate equally and fully in market-based work and the unpaid work of the family, when women are not only just as likely as men to be CEOs, but men are just as likely as women to stay at home" (7).

Patterns of Gender Inequality: Politics, the Corporation, and Education

The picture of women in the labor force reveals clearly that inequality in the world of work continues to prevail, but it reveals equally clearly that traditional patterns have undergone fundamental change. In almost every other area of social, political, and economic life, the place of women in American society is decidedly different from what it was little more than three decades in the past. This section examines patterns of gender inequality in three major institutional realms: the political world, the corporate world, and education.

Gender Inequality in the Political World

It is extremely important to examine the extent of gender inequality and its patterns of change in the political realm because it is here that power is most evident and that many critical decisions are made regarding fundamental changes in the structure of social inequality.

Political Participation   The United States and other modern societies moved toward gender equality in politics only in the twentieth century. So taken for granted are equal political rights for men and women today that we often forget how thoroughly excluded women were from political participation just a short historical time ago. Not until ratification of the Nineteenth Amendment to the U.S. Constitution in 1920 were women nationwide able to vote. A few European countries, as well as Australia and New Zealand, had provided women's suffrage before that time, but many, such as France, Italy, and Japan, did not give women the vote until the 1940s. Women's suffrage is by no means universal even today. In some Arab countries, women are still denied political participation.

Political Leadership   Voting in elections is only a small part of effective political participation. Occupying leadership positions is infinitely more critical. To what extent have women begun to play significant political roles in the United States and other modern societies?

At the top levels of government, women have made some significant inroads, far more than in the corporate world. Looking first at elective offices, we can see clearly that women office holders have increased their numbers substantially over the last few decades. Whereas in 1979 women were no more than 3 percent of the U.S. Congress, in 2013 they held 19 percent of seats, including 20 in the Senate and 81 in the House of Representatives. Included among the latter was the Minority Leader, who had formerly served as Speaker of the House. One must consider these accomplishments, of course, in light of the fact that women constitute over half the total population. Moreover, in a few countries, the contrast with the United States is sharp. For example, more than 45 percent of national parliamentary seats are held by women in Sweden, the top-ranked country in women's political representation (UNDP, 2011).

At lower levels of government, American women have made even more significant gains in numbers and in leadership posts since the 1970s. Women today occupy over 24 percent of the nation's state legislative seats, three times their proportion in 1975. Moreover, an increasing number of women are winning election to governorships and other statewide executive offices, as well as mayorships, city councils, and county boards. In other spheres of government, the role of women has also begun to change significantly. Currently, three women serve on the U.S. Supreme Court (there were none before 1981), and women are being appointed to federal and state judgeships in unprecedented numbers.

The presence of women in the president's cabinet is today commonplace, and the appointment of a woman to a powerful cabinet office prompts little media attention. Three of the past five appointees as secretary of state, the government's top foreign policy post, have been women. This holds particular symbolic importance since in most countries, not only in the United States, women in legislative or ministerial positions of high rank have rarely held office in the most "masculine" areas, such as defense, foreign policy, and finance (Peterson and Runyan, 1999). Nonetheless, one must consider how relatively recently in U.S. history have women been appointed to *any* cabinet positions: Almost all have occurred in the last thirty years.

Finally, a female American president is no longer the improbable case it had seemed in the not-so-distant past. Indeed, Hillary Clinton's nearly successful bid for the Democratic presidential nomination in 2008 indicated clearly that a woman occupying the highest political office is inevitable. As Clinton herself put it during her campaign, from now on it will be "unremarkable to think that a woman can be President of the United States" (Hertzberg, 2008). Little more than sixty years earlier, only one-third of Americans had declared that they would vote for a qualified woman for president (Jones, 2005). In other parts of the world women have already achieved the most powerful offices of government. In fact, in thirty-four countries, both developed and developing, the president or prime minister for some period of time during the 1990s was a woman (United Nations, 2000).[6]

Gender Inequality in the Corporate World

In the sphere of work, women generally occupy fewer positions of authority, but their specific place in the corporate world, especially in posts at the top, presents a mixed picture. On the one hand, women, as already noted, continue to be severely underrepresented in top managerial positions. Moreover, the wage gap is more evident here than in the general workforce. On the other hand, when looked at in historical perspective, women have made substantial gains in recent decades, and they continue to advance into power positions at an increasing rate.

Until relatively recently, women were virtually absent from top-ranking posts of the corporate world. In the mid-1970s women as a proportion of the boards of directors of the 250 largest corporations constituted only 1.8 percent

---

[6]Peterson and Runyan (1999) note, however, that women who have held the highest-ranking office of government have been typically perceived as exceptional women, who act "like men."

(Herman, 1981; Robertson, 1973). Little change was evident by 1980, when only 36 of the 1,499 top positions in the 100 largest corporations were filled by women (Dye and Strickland, 1982). In addition, most of those few women were recruited from outside the corporate world, leading to speculation that they were serving as "window dressing." Ten percent of the most senior jobs at the 500 largest U.S. companies in 1996 were held by women, and at the very highest levels—CEO, president, executive vice president—2.4 percent were women (Himelstein, 1996). Today 14 percent of the top officers of those firms are women, as are 16 percent of their boards of directors. Despite these increases, however, women undeniably still play a diminutive role at the highest corporate levels; fewer than 4 percent of the CEOs of those corporations are women (Catalyst, 2012; Creswell, 2006).

The question of why women continue to lag in achieving top corporate posts is not easily answered. As with the wage gap, some point to a continuation of sexist attitudes and blatant discrimination. Others explain it as a more subtle reluctance of male executives to accept women or ethnic minorities into a clubby environment in which these men feel comfortable with each other. Zweigenhaft and Domhoff, in their analysis of diversity in power elites, note that in the corporate world, playing golf is a common bonding mechanism among executives that affords assimilation into this well-understood comfort zone: "Just as football is often identified as the classic competitive and aggressive team sport that prepares men for the rough-and-tumble (and hierarchical) world of the corporation, an individual sport, golf, is the more convivial, but still competitive, game that allows boys to play together, shoot the breeze, and do business" (2006:55). Women do not easily break through this social barrier.

In addition, the positions into which most women are initially placed at higher managerial levels within the corporation handicaps them in moving up the corporate hierarchy. Women executives are disproportionately found in corporate divisions that are traditionally "female," such as public affairs, human resources, and community relations. These are mostly non–decision-making areas that rarely lead to positions at the very top (GAO, 2002; ILO, 2004; Himelstein, 1996; Glass Ceiling Commission, 1995).

Finally, some maintain that the slower advancement of women in the corporate world is a function of family roles in conflict with work roles. Dye (1995), for example, suggests that because women must take time off if they are to have children, they fall further behind men in the competition for top positions. Some have described a "maternal wall," built on the assumption that women returning to work after having children will not be as committed to their jobs as they were before they left, thus resulting in less promising assignments and positions (O'Brien, 2006).

A survey of 461 women executives of Fortune 1000 companies found that male stereotyping and preconceptions of women continue to act as barriers to advancement at top corporate levels. The respondents in this study claimed that the most important factor in their own success was having

Source: Kirk Anderson/www.kirktoons.com.

consistently exceeded performance expectations—that is, they had to be not only good but exceptionally good. The second most important factor was adjusting their personal style so as not to appear threatening to male executives. This is quite different from the view of a majority of male executives who explained the low numbers for women at the top as a result of simply not having been on the executive trajectory long enough; eventually, in their view, women will catch up (Grimsley, 1996; Dobrzynski, 1996).

Despite social impediments to upward movement in the corporate world, the number of female executives is rising, and it seems safe to assume that in the not too distant future even women CEOs will be unremarkable. A study showed that from 1995 to 2000, for example, the number of Fortune 500 companies in which more than 25 percent of corporate officers were women doubled from 25 to 50. The study projected that women would constitute more than 27 percent of top corporate officers by 2020 (Catalyst, 2000). Companies are beginning to establish goals for placing more women in executive positions, with some even creating quotas mandating minimum numbers of women in the senior ranks (Himelstein, 1997).

As increasing numbers of women are playing decision-making roles in the corporate world, women's earnings in top positions are changing as well. A study that examined the compensation patterns of the top five executive officers of a large group of U.S. firms showed that the gender gap in pay virtually disappears once age and experience are accounted for. That is, female executives at the top level earn, on average, considerably less than their male counterparts, but this pay disparity is mostly a product of the fact that they are younger and have less seniority (Bertrand and Hallock, 2000).

Although American women are still severely underrepresented in the highest posts of the corporate world, their progress toward the top is no less rapid than that of women in most countries of the world. Even in Europe, the percentage of women on the boards of the largest and most powerful corporations is the same as in the United States, and only one in ten board members of these firms are women (European Commission, 2008).

Dye and Strickland concluded in 1982 that "the major institutions of U.S. society are managed and directed almost exclusively by men" (340). Clearly, that is no longer the case. Nonetheless, it remains equally apparent that women have far to go before they achieve parity with men in both the political and the corporate worlds.

Women and Education

Much of the explanation for the rapidly changing status of women in politics and the economy can be attributed to the changes in education that women have experienced over the last few decades. As discussed in Chapter 4, the key to entrance into the society's power elites today is access to higher education. And as women have secured more education, their political and economic status has changed concomitantly.

Consider the remarkable changes in the number and percentage of women in higher education that have taken place in a relatively short period of time. Whereas in 1960 almost twice as many males as females attended college, by 1980 females were a majority of college students. As seen in Table 11-4, more women than men now earn bachelor's and master's degrees, and they earn roughly the same number of doctoral and professional degrees.

Although the increase in higher education for women vis-à-vis men is clear and dramatic, the types of degrees they earn continue to be sex-typed. In the 2000s, while women were awarded almost 90 percent of undergraduate degrees in the health professions and almost 80 percent of undergraduate education degrees, they earned only 18 percent of undergraduate

Table 11-4 ▪ Degrees Earned, by Level and Sex (in thousands)

Degree	1970		1980		1990		2000		2009	
	M	F	M	F	M	F	M	F	M	F
Bachelor's	451	341	474	456	492	560	530	708	685	916
Master's	126	83	151	147	154	171	192	265	260	397
First professional	33	2	53	17	44	27	44	36	47	45
Doctorate	26	4	23	10	24	14	25	20	32	35

Source: U.S. Census Bureau, 2012c.

engineering degrees (U.S. Department of Education, 2009). Nonetheless, even here there have been marked changes. In 1970 women earned only one out of one hundred engineering degrees (Bianchi and Spain, 1996).

It is of note that the educational level of women in elite positions is even higher than their male counterparts' levels. Dye's study of top institutional leaders in the United States (2002) showed that nearly half of the women leaders had earned master's or doctorate degrees and another quarter held law degrees. As Dye explains, "This strongly suggests that women need more education than men to compete effectively for top posts" (2002:157).

The Status of Women in Global Perspective

Many of the changes in women's status and power that have occurred in the United States and other Western societies in the past several decades have taken on a global character. The traditional gender hierarchy, in place in some countries for centuries, has been subjected to question everywhere, leading to advancements for women in almost all societal institutions. Yet, gender differences remain very evident not only between developed and developing societies, but even within societies at similar levels of economic and social advancement. Let's look at some of these differences.

Discrimination

Despite the progress that women in the United States and other advanced societies have made in the last four decades in securing political rights and economic power, discrimination in the workplace is by no means a thing of the past. Moreover, in the realm of interpersonal relations, problems of harassment and physical abuse, sexual and otherwise, continue to be serious issues. Domestic violence and rape are frequent occurrences in the United States, particularly among young women and women in low-income families, and official statistics understate their numbers. Still, in looking at the status of women in a global context, the forms and degree of discrimination that North American and western European women face appear mild. In comparing their status with that of women in most of the remainder of the world, it could be argued that they are an extremely privileged female population.

Women in the Developing World   In many developing societies, female subordination is especially harsh. Women in these societies continue to be treated in a fashion that would bewilder—and anger—most North Americans. Bride burnings remain widespread today in India, for example, and rape is almost commonplace in South Africa (Kumar and Kanth, 2004; Wax, 2008). These are by no means extraordinary situations, as the vignettes at the outset of this chapter suggest. Much of the discrimination against women in these societies not only is based on tradition but is built into the legal structure.

For example, there are laws in some countries that prohibit women from traveling abroad without male permission. In other countries women are under the legal guardianship of their husbands and have no property rights (United Nations, 2000).

In much of Latin America and the Caribbean, wife beating and domestic violence in general have a lengthy tradition, solidified by a legal system that often tolerates these actions. In Brazil, because male police rarely treated wife beating as more than a domestic matter, in 1985 a number of women's police stations were established in the larger cities. Despite this measure, as well as laws that address the issue of discrimination and violence against women, in practice the penalties for such actions are relatively mild and ineffective (Robinson and Epstein, 1994). Moreover, police records reveal only a small proportion of violent acts against women (Lucas d'Oliveira and Schraiber, 2005). The anthropologist Richard Parker (1991) studied the Brazilian sexual culture and concluded, "The social, political, and economic institutions that work together to minimize the opportunities for choice and self-determination on the part of women from all walks of life in Brazil continue to function with ruthless efficiency" (169). The fact that some changes have begun to take place among the most privileged sectors of Brazilian society, Parker notes, should not be seen as indicative of a decline of oppression for the vast majority of Brazilian women. Brazil remains "a profoundly patriarchal social order" (170). As in Brazil, laws against gender-based violence have been enacted in most countries of the region, but enforcement remains a major concern. The value of "machismo," which evokes male dominance over women, is firmly embedded in these societies' major institutions, often making police and judicial responses to domestic violence slow and indifferent (Cole and Phillips, 2008; Creel, 2001; Hernandez, 2003). Ironically these patterns continue despite the fact that in the past decade, the presidents of the three most economically and socially advanced countries of Latin America—Brazil, Argentina, and Chile—have been women.

Similar circumstances are found in many Asian societies, where women are routinely excluded from access to justice. Despite widespread domestic violence against women, such incidents are rarely brought to the attention of authorities since there are different evidential requirements for men and women in corroborating sexual offenses. Moreover, in many of these countries there are no laws at all to deal with domestic abuse cases, and where laws do exist, they are not effectively enforced. Perhaps even more disturbing is the unusually low ratio of women to men in many Asian countries, brought about by practices that assure this population imbalance. Some occur early on, such as female infanticide, the neglect of female children, and son preferences. Others occur later—the mysterious disappearance of women, for example. A United Nations report estimates that almost 100 million women in Asia are "missing," having died because of discrimination in access to health and nutrition or through pure neglect, or because of abortion based on sex selection they were never born in the first place (UNDP, 2010).

The circumstances of women in some Muslim societies of the Middle East are particularly arresting (Brooks, 1995; Haddad and Esposito, 1998). Women have few political rights, they are not encouraged to enter the workforce but are expected to remain at home, and they remain strictly segregated from men in schools, mosques, and other social settings. Marriages are usually prearranged, and women may have no right to refuse the choice of a partner.[7]

Perhaps the most shocking aspect of women's subordination in the developing world is the widespread practice of female circumcision in at least twenty-eight African societies (Feldman-Jacobs and Clifton, 2008). This involves the ritual excision of some or all of the female external genitalia (the clitoris and small and large genital lips), resulting in diminished ability to experience sexual pleasure. The procedure is usually performed on girls in their teens or younger and is done to assure their virginity for their future husbands. The cutting is ordinarily done in a crude fashion with a knife, razor blade, or broken bottle, using no anesthetic, and often results in serious health problems, including hemorrhaging, infection, problems during childbirth, and even death.

Female circumcision, or genital mutilation, has come under attack in recent years from various sources, including governments and human rights groups. However, it is firmly entrenched in the culture of those societies, making change slow and difficult. Families insist on having female children circumcised since the honor of the girl and the family dictates it. Social pressures can be so great that some wives who have not been cut as children will choose to have the operation performed on them as adults (Abusharaf, 1998). Even when there is objection, cultural norms may prevail. In Ivory Coast, for example, the wife of a man who insists on having his daughter circumcised says that she despises the practice. Yet she admits, "It is up to my husband. We live in Africa. The man makes the decisions about the children" (Dugger, 1996). Many of the girls themselves look forward to the cutting, understanding that the rite represents an entry into adulthood and makes them desirable marriage partners. In Somalia, almost all women have been cut, and in Egypt, despite an official ban, the procedure remains widespread (Feldman-Jacobs and Clifton, 2008; OECD, 2009; Slackman, 2007; UNICEF, 2012).

Many of the societal norms of traditional societies that support what Americans would consider oppressive conditions for women are being challenged and changed. For example, in Qatar, a small Persian Gulf country strongly ruled by Islamic principles, an increasing number of women attend university—in fact, 70 percent of the country's university students are women—and go on to professional occupations, often working with men. Many drive cars of their own and defend their right to refuse a marriage

---

[7]It is important to note that there are major differences among predominantly Muslim societies regarding women's rights.

proposal, something that was not acceptable just a few years earlier. Of singular importance is the fact that women in most Arab states have been granted the right to vote and to run for political office, freedoms that had been denied until recently (Coleman, 2004; MacKinnon, 2006).

Nonetheless, change is coming piecemeal and only gradually. To the surprise of many Westerners, women themselves in these societies do not necessarily advocate quick and thorough change in their circumstances. This may reflect not only the perceived need to proceed slowly with what are radical social and political changes but also a commitment to traditional cultural ways. Recall the practice of female circumcision in Central Africa, which continues to be condoned and even desired by many women. In Qatar, much the same attitude toward change in women's roles is evident. "I think in our society we should cover our faces," says a twenty-six-year-old clerical worker who also wears a head scarf and a cloak that covers her entire body. She acknowledges that when she travels to Europe or the United States, she does not cover herself, but she believes there remain lines in Qatar that should not be crossed. Another working Qatari woman, a bank manager who was among the first women in the country to drive and to work with men, expresses the view that "It's part of our religion." Working and studying are accepted, she added, "but going to mixed parties and having contact with foreign men—these things cannot be done" (Jehl, 1997:A7).

Cultural insensitivity often leads Americans to make ethnocentric and simplistic assumptions about women in developing societies, who by U.S. standards suffer oppression. In 2005, a senior Bush administration official was sent to the Middle East with the objective of spreading the message of full social participation for women. In Saudi Arabia, where women's rights are perhaps more limited than in any society of the region, she herself was greeted with an unexpected message. Speaking before a group of students and professional women at a Saudi university, she was told by one audience member that, contrary to the image of Arab women as living in misery, "we're all pretty happy," a remark that elicited resounding applause. Others in the crowd voiced the view that Americans fail to understand that traditional Saudi ways are often embraced by men and women alike and that there is no natural desire to adopt all Western cultural norms (Weisman, 2005).

Japanese Society   Japan presents an interesting comparison with American society in gender stratification. It is not a developing society but rather one that rivals the United States in economic prosperity and productivity. Yet the place of women in Japan could not present a stronger contrast. "Japanese men are blatantly male chauvinists," wrote the noted Japan scholar Edwin Reischauer, "and women seem shamefully exploited and suppressed" (1988:175). In a number of ways, that observation still holds true.

In the realm of work, until recently Japanese women were not a significant portion of the labor force. Today, however, about half of all Japanese women are employed, and they make up 40 percent of workers (Pollack, 1997,

Ogasawara, 2004). Most important, Japan's sagging economy in the 1990s thrust more women into the workforce. As in the United States, many Japanese families now find it necessary to have two breadwinners in order to maintain their economic status. In the past, Japanese working women were rarely found in other than menial, often part-time, jobs, and they continue to be concentrated in low-status positions. The glass ceiling blocking the movement of women into managerial positions is far more implacable than in the United States (ILO, 2004; Sugimoto, 1997). The thirty-six-year-old female president of a small manufacturing firm that supplies parts to Nissan inherited her position after her father, the company owner, died. As the only woman executive among 160 Nissan suppliers, she recalls that the first time she attended the group's twice-annual meetings she was asked to wait in a room with secretaries. "I still have to prove all the time that a woman can be president," she admits (Fackler, 2007).

Sexual discrimination against women in Japan is, by American standards, blatant. In want ads, companies often specify the sex of employees they seek and set an age limit for women applicants. In the workplace, women are commonly relegated to subservient roles, such as pouring tea for male colleagues (Ogasawara, 2004; Pollack, 1996). Many Japanese women are hired in electronics assembly plants, where work is considered a more natural female setting. Very few women work in automobile factories, however. This contrasts with the workforce composition of Japanese firms in their U.S. plants. Not surprisingly, there is a wide earnings gap between Japanese men and Japanese women; women earn about 65 percent of men's income (recall that the comparable U.S. percentage is about 77).

Some of these conditions are undergoing slow but gradual change. Antidiscrimination laws have recently been enacted in Japan, requiring companies to provide equal opportunities for men and women. Also, the ban on women working at night has been lifted, opening up new job opportunities (Pollack, 1997). Moreover, as Japan's population continues to decline, the need to find managers has compelled Japanese firms to begin to recruit women as career-track employees, eventually qualifying for managerial positions (Fackler, 2007).

If the place of women in the workforce seems harsh by American standards, the family provides no haven. Japanese families have traditionally been notoriously patriarchal, with women playing a mainly perfunctory role. As one Japanese husband put it, referring to his wife, "She's like air or water. You couldn't live without it, but most of the time, you're not conscious of its existence" (Kristof, 1996a). Traditionally, women have had virtually no social life outside the family, in contrast to their husbands, who usually spend much time with their co-workers (Reischauer, 1988).

Another view of Japanese women, however, suggests that they are not as powerless as is often assumed. Although formally they may be subservient to their husbands, Japanese women are strongly influential within the family, though often in a behind-the-scenes manner (Kato, 1989). Moreover, their increasingly prominent place in the workforce has opened new worlds for Japanese wives who had previously been relegated to a stay-at-home role. As their responsibilities have increased, their influence in the family has risen accordingly (Goodman and Kashiwagi, 2002).

Even at work, Japanese women are not hopelessly compliant and oppressed. Yuko Ogasawara (2004), in her research on Japanese office workers, has shown that women do not necessarily envy men's status and responsibilities. Understanding, as they do, the overwhelming obstacles to advancement and thus relieved of career pressures, they do not suffer the onerous work schedules and sacrifices of family relations that typify the lives of Japanese men. They have more time and freedom, as Ogasawara explains, "to plan, organize, and carry out their lives in a way not possible for men whose life is confined and regimented to an extreme degree by corporate demands" (243). As a result, rather than feeling afflicted, these women workers seem content with their lives.

Japanese marriages are consummated not so much on the basis of love and high expectations as on the basis of duty and children. This, in combination with the social pressures on women to make adjustments to an unhappy relationship, has resulted in a comparatively low rate of divorce. Also, the severe economic and social hardship that women encounter following a marital breakup serves as an additional disincentive to divorce (Vogel, 1979). Nonetheless, divorce rates in Japan are on the rise, a trend that appears to be spurred by cultural shifts comparable to those experienced by the United States in the 1960s and 1970s (French, 2003). In total, these changes reflect a progressive breakdown of traditional female roles.

Political and Economic Power

The gender patterns in the United States with regard to political and economic elites are very much the same in other comparable societies: The number and percentage of women in positions of power are disproportionately small but increasing, albeit at a slow pace (Moore, 1988; Vianello and Moore, 2004; ILO, 2004).

Table 11-5 shows the role of women in political and economic life in a range of contemporary societies. It indicates the percentage of powerful and prestigious political and occupational positions held by women. A strong relation is evident between the degree of economic development of the country and the percentage of women in important roles. With few exceptions, women in highly developed, industrialized countries occupy comparatively significant percentages of parliamentary seats, managerial and administrative posts, and professional and technical jobs. These percentages taper off sharply as the level of development drops.

Intimately related to women's subordinate status in political and economic life in most developing societies is their deprived status in education. Two-thirds of the world's illiterates are women, and most of them are in

Table 11-5 ▪ Positions Held by Women (percentages)

Country*	Seats Held in Parliament	Legislators, Senior Officials, and Managers	Professional and Technical Workers
Sweden (1)	47	32	51
Denmark (4)	38	28	52
Australia (7)	30	37	57
Germany (9)	31	38	50
Canada (12)	25	37	56
United States (18)	17	43	56
Portugal (19)	28	32	51
Italy (21)	20	34	47
Israel (23)	18	30	52
Poland (38)	18	36	60
Mexico (39)	22	31	42
Panama (47)	17	44	52
Japan (57)	12	9	46
Botswana (65)	11	33	51
Bolivia (78)	15	36	40
Brazil (82)	9	35	53
Ukraine (86)	8	39	64
Pakistan (99)	21	3	25
Turkey (101)	9	8	33
Saudi Arabia (106)	0	10	29

*The countries are arranged in the order of their "gender empowerment measure," an index developed by the United Nations Development Programme to measure gender inequality in key areas of economic and political participation and decision making in countries at various stages of development. Each country's rank is shown in parentheses beside its name.
Source: 2009 Human Development Report, United Nations Development Programme. Reprinted by permission.

societies that are relatively underdeveloped economically and politically (United Nations, 2003). In these societies, it is often an economic decision to educate sons rather than daughters. It is not uncommon for girls to be taken out of school to work at home or to care for younger siblings. Usually there are more and better-paying jobs for men than for women. Early pregnancy, too, prevents many girls from staying in school.

Changes in women's educational status are occurring, however. The gender gap at the primary school level has narrowed significantly in developing countries as a whole, though it persists in sub-Saharan Africa, North Africa, and South Asia. Women are an increasing percentage of secondary and post-secondary students as well, though the differences between males and females are still extremely wide (United Nations, 2010).

Focusing on the education gender gap in the developing world should not discount the lag in women's participation in higher leadership positions and in nontraditional occupations in developed societies, despite the attainment of educational equity. In all, there remains a gender wage gap, and in all, occupational segregation along gender lines is still very obvious.

The Feminist Movement

In every society today there is an active movement seeking to change the structure of gender stratification. And it is quite obvious that everywhere change is, in fact, occurring, albeit at noticeably different rates. Consider again the incidents described at the outset of this chapter, for example, in light of the changes that have been prompted by a global feminist movement. The routine abuse of women, as in Punsooilri, is no longer accepted as the norm, even in rural South Korea. Before the regime's overthrow by U.S. forces in 2001, the restrictions imposed on women by the Taliban in Afghanistan had been recognized as exceedingly repressive even in the Muslim world. And laws pertaining to rape and other forms of violence against women in Peru and other Latin American countries have been challenged by advocates of women's rights.

In the United States and in other Western industrial societies, women as a collectivity start from a more advanced position, and thus the focus of the feminist movement in these countries has fallen on securing equal political and economic opportunities rather than on preventing women's physical and mental abuse. But in all cases the objective in a broad sense is the same: the advancement of the status of women.

Feminism

The set of beliefs and actions that center on assuring the equality of men and women in various areas of social life is referred to as **feminism.** It is important to consider in the context of human social development how radically new is the idea of gender equality. Although sexist ideology has been successfully challenged in the last several decades, for most of human history the notion that men are intellectually as well as physically superior to women was taken for granted. Thus, thoughts of gender equality were always outside the mainstream. Until the last few decades, sexist ideology, like beliefs regarding racial superiority, was the accepted view among the overwhelming majority of people.

The Feminist Movement in the United States Although the contemporary phase of the U.S. feminist movement stems from around 1960, an earlier movement began in the mid-nineteenth century and continued for over seven decades. The Seneca Falls Convention of 1848 marked a point at which women began to mobilize against discrimination in education and politics. The most important objective was the franchise, which was finally secured in 1920 with passage of the Nineteenth Amendment to the U.S. Constitution. After the attainment of its major goal, the early feminist movement receded and did not experience a revival until the 1960s.

During that decade, a number of factors came together to give momentum to a resurgent feminist movement, often referred to as "Second Wave Feminism." First, a book of seminal importance was published, Betty Friedan's *The Feminine Mystique* (1963), with a message that instilled a new consciousness among many women. Friedan spoke of an inchoate problem in which women of the post–World War II generation, despite their increasing prosperity, felt unfulfilled. As she put it, "We can no longer ignore that voice within women that says: 'I want something more than my husband and my children and my home'" (32).

Second, women piggybacked onto the civil rights movement of the 1960s, calling attention to the fact that, as a collectivity, they too were targets of blatant as well as subtle forms of discrimination. The civil rights movement provided a model for organizing and political action, and it was at this point that women were increasingly acknowledged as a sociological minority (Freeman, 1975; Skrentny, 2002).

A third factor concerns changes in women's reproductive rights. These changes took two forms. One was the introduction of birth control pills, which provided women with greater options regarding issues of childbearing. The other was the legalization of abortion in 1973, which provided further control over reproductive issues. Before that time, unwanted pregnancies were either carried to term or aborted surreptitiously. These medical and legal innovations led to monumental changes in the role of women in the family and ultimately in the workforce.

Varieties of Feminism   The current feminist movement is a constantly evolving complex of organizations, individuals, and ideologies that is difficult to define with clarity. The very meaning of feminism today is subject to different definitions and interpretations propounded by a number of theoretical branches, within which are further divisions that maintain somewhat different agendas and perspectives (Ferree and Hess, 2000; Lorber, 2005). The fundamental rationale of all, however, is the challenge to gender inequality in its various dimensions.

A prevailing assumption of feminist thought today is that gender is not fixed but is flexible and interdependent with other spheres of inequality and forms of stratification. Hence there is no "female experience" as such. Using the idea of "multiple feminisms," women and men are acknowledged to be diverse categories, divided in modern societies along many lines, especially race/ethnicity, class, and age (Amott and Matthaei, 2006; Andersen and Collins, 1998). Thus, the notion that all women—*qua* women—experience social life in the same way and therefore can be studied using a single theoretical model is seen as naive. The intersections of gender with other social statuses produce particularly intricate and complex forms of differentiation and stratification for any particular individual. Consider, for example, the contrast between a working-class African American woman and an upper-middle-class Euro-American woman. Their common status as "woman" is played out in radically different ways as race/ethnicity, class, and gender converge.

The majority of American women today do not consider themselves part of an organized feminist movement, regardless of its branch, and some may even speak disparagingly of it; nonetheless, they favor unquestioningly the basic goals of the movement: equality for women in various facets of social, economic, and political life (Frey et al., 2001). In the sociologist Lillian Rubin's interviews of working-class women, she found such ambiguity in their responses to the notion of feminism. On the one hand, they saw feminists stereotypically as overly aggressive, demanding, and not sufficiently feminine. "I'd never be a feminist," explained a mother working as an insurance company claims adjuster, "because they want women to give up being feminine and soft." On the other hand, on specific issues, like pay equity, sexual harassment, and women in politics, they voiced decidedly feminist opinions. The same woman who earlier said she would never be a feminist recognizes the significance of the movement in opening up occupational opportunities for women that previously didn't exist. "Yeah, I'm glad it [the women's movement] happened because otherwise I wouldn't have my job. My company didn't used to hire women to be adjusters before that" (Rubin, 1994:73).

The continued relevance of a feminist movement has been brought to light in the last few years as attempts have been made to repeal what had seemed well-secured women's reproductive and health-related rights. Conservative-dominated legislatures in many states enacted measures that made access to abortion difficult or, in effect, impossible. And, at the federal level, access to birth-control and other female health care matters became hotly-debated political issues in the Congress and even as part of the 2012 presidential campaign.

Summary

Sex refers to the relatively fixed physiological and biological differences between men and women; gender refers to differences that are determined socially and culturally and that are manifest in the different roles men and women play in all societies. The question of whether gender identity and gender roles are biologically rooted or are socially determined is a debatable issue, but the prevailing social science position strongly favors the latter.

Gender stratification is evident in all societies. The gender hierarchy is almost always one in which women are the subordinate stratum. The ideology of sexism holds that male and female differences are biological in origin and not subject to change. This belief, reinforced by a set of stereotypes, has traditionally helped rationalize and stabilize male dominance.

Women have entered the workforce in unprecedented numbers in the last several decades, but they remain heavily concentrated in certain occupations, generally earn less than men, and do not often occupy positions of authority. Nevertheless, legal and traditional impediments to occupational mobility have been reduced enormously, and significant changes continue to occur in the status of women. In certain areas, namely, education and the professions, change has come quite rapidly. In politics and the corporate world, the rate has been slower but gradual nonetheless. Women have begun to enter lower and middle managerial positions in greater numbers, but at the uppermost echelons societal power remains overwhelmingly male.

Women in the developing world experience a level of subordination that is far more profound and consequential than in the United States and most other Western industrial societies. In all societies, an active feminist movement seeks changes in the structure of gender stratification.

The feminist movement in the United States experienced a resurgence beginning in the 1960s, stimulating the push for women's rights and socioeconomic equality. The feminist spectrum is broad, comprising numerous theoretical and political positions. Most women do not consider themselves part of an organized feminist movement, but they overwhelmingly endorse feminist goals of gender equality in various areas of social, economic, and political life.

12

Political Inequality

[The poor] have to labor in the face of the majestic equality of the law, which forbids the rich as well as the poor to sleep under bridges, to beg in the streets, and to steal bread.
ANATOLE FRANCE

We can have democracy in this country or we can have great wealth concentrated in the hands of a few, but we can't have both.
LOUIS D. BRANDEIS

The political philosopher Bertrand de Jouvenel described politics as "a systematic effort . . . to move other men in the pursuit of some design cherished by the mover" (1963:30). Max Weber defined power in much the same way Jouvenel defined politics: "the possibility of imposing one's will upon the behavior of other persons" (1954:323). *Politics*, then, is about *power*; to speak of the pursuit and exercise of power is to imply the pursuit and exercise of politics.

Most often we think of politics as the actions of politicians and government officials, the comings and goings of people in Washington or in one of the state capitals. But politics, in a broad sense, is the exchange of power resources, that is, people using money, material goods, knowledge, fame, information, influence, beauty, authority, and so on, in attempts to affect other people's behavior. As such, politics—and therefore power—is inherent in all human relations, from the family to the society as a whole. This chapter focuses on power in the societal realm. In the modern world, societal power is attached to decision-making positions in organizations, particularly those that are part of the state, the economy, and the media. It is in those organizations that people in positions of authority make decisions that have the broadest impact on the society.

Political Stratification

The Scope and Dimensions of Power

If power involves making decisions, we can begin to understand power inequality by thinking about the critical decisions that affect our lives and the extent to which we can influence those decisions. Essentially,

365

decision-making power can be seen at two social levels: the interpersonal and the societal.

Interpersonal Power   At the interpersonal level, most of us can pretty much shape our lives as we choose. Shall I go to work, or shall I stay home and watch television? Shall I dress casually today, or more formally? Shall I have pizza or tacos for lunch? These are the kinds of decisions that may be important to us at the moment, but they have little or no impact on anyone but ourselves. It is decisions at this level, however, over which we have utmost personal control.

If we move up the power scale a notch, we find that our ability to influence decisions begins to decline. This level of power is apparent in the relationships between husbands and wives, parents and children, employers and employees, and teachers and students. In these situations, people seek to exert their will over others, but in none of these cases do the consequences of the actions of anyone extend much beyond the immediate group. You might fail to convince your friends that the movie you wish to see will be more entertaining than the one they want to see, but no one outside the circle of friends will feel the effects of this power act. Similarly, a teacher may wield significant power over her students in the classroom, but only her students will be directly affected.

Societal Power   Once we move beyond the relatively narrow range of personal actions that we take on a day-to-day basis, most of us have very little say (Figure 12-1). On major issues that profoundly affect us, decisions are made by others who are not subject to our direct influence. How much

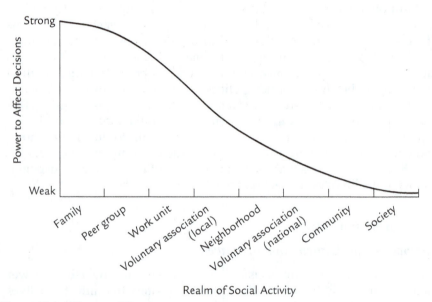

Realm of Social Activity

Figure 12-1 ▪ Range of Power

will we earn, and how much will we have to pay for the consumer goods we want and need? What will be the content of our formal education, and to what ends will we be able to apply it? What opportunities will the labor market offer? Will our society live in peace, or will it be at war with other nations? What will be the quality of the air we breathe or the water we drink? On these and other issues of the economy, government, education, international affairs, and the environment, most of us are simply observers, lacking the capacity to affect decisions directly in any meaningful way. However, a small number of people in the society—an elite—*do* have the power to decide these and other vital issues that fundamentally shape our lives. Thus, we can begin to see the outlines of political inequality.

Societal power is exercised when the effects of an organization's or an individual's decisions are felt, either directly or indirectly, by many—perhaps by all—people in the society. The actions of the state are the clearest example of such widespread power. Virtually no one is immune to the consequences of decisions made by government leaders. Issues of taxation, spending, welfare, war and peace, and a myriad of other vital concerns are decided by the political elite.

But societal power does not lie only within the sphere of government. Huge transnational corporations also exert a similar scope and depth of influence. The decision by one or a few oil companies to raise the price of oil, for example, will affect not only those who drive automobiles but the economy as a whole, given the importance of oil as a source of energy. Jobs, prices of consumer goods, and the fate of countless projects will be at stake. Or consider the societal power of the producers, editors, and owners of national television networks. As a source of information and entertainment, television in modern societies is predominant. Hence, the ability to choose what will be presented as news and other programming constitutes an enormous power. The policies and decisions of private organizations, like oil companies and TV networks, are therefore as public in their effect as the policies and decisions of government agencies.

Societal power ordinarily occurs only within institutions (like government, the corporation, and the mass media) within specifically large organizations that make up those institutions (such as the U.S. Congress, Exxon Mobil, and NBC). And it is exercised by key decision makers who occupy elite positions in those organizations.

Elites and Masses

In deciding the issues that affect all or great parts of the society, it is only the few at the top who are able to make their influence felt. As noted earlier, only on issues that affect limited and specific situations (mostly at the interpersonal level) do most people have any input. To simplify matters, then, we can divide the society into two main power strata: elites and masses.

Elites are tiny groups whose members occupy the society's top positions of power. They exercise authority, influence, and control of resources within the most important organizations (Marger, 1987). Elite members formulate the policies, guide the activities, and decide the significant issues of the government, the corporation, education, and other major societal institutions. Moreover, they possess the authority and credibility to transmit and defend the explanation and justification for the prevailing political and economic systems, that is, the dominant ideology.

Masses, or non-elites, are those who make up the vast majority of the society's populace, those whose power is limited. Obviously, there are great differences in power among non-elites. A middle-level bureaucrat working for a state government agency has less power than the governor but more power than lower-level agency workers. However, in deciding the fundamental issues of the political and economic systems—in political scientist Harold Lasswell's (1936) oft-quoted phrase, "who gets what, when, how?"—these differences shrink in significance. The important distinction is basically between the few at the very top—the elites—and the remaining populace.

The Inevitability of Elite Rule   In studying political inequality it is axiomatic that in every society a relatively small number of people—an elite—always rule. Here we might turn to the observations of Robert Michels, a contemporary of Max Weber, who offered one of the most cogent and compelling perspectives on the inequality of power in societies, which he described as "the iron law of oligarchy."

In his classic work *Political Parties* (1915), Michels explained that **oligarchy,** the rule of the many by the few, is inevitable, even in the most democratic groups and societies. This development is a product of the size and complexity of modern social organizations. It is simply not possible for large numbers of people to make decisions in an efficient manner as a unit. Hence, the only realistic alternative is to invest officers with power to make decisions on behalf of the collectivity. With such delegation of power, a stable—and eventually self-serving—leadership group is established. Thus Michels advanced his often-quoted dictum, "Who says organization, says oligarchy" (1962[1915]:365).

When collectivities reach a certain dimension, a division of labor emerges, even among the leadership group. Positions are created that are held by people with special expertise, who thereby become indispensable to the functioning of the organization:

> Just as the patient obeys the doctor, because the doctor knows better than the patient, having made a special study of the human body in health and disease, so must the political patient submit to the guidance of his party leaders, who possess a political competence impossible of attainment by the rank and file. (Michels, 1962[1915]:114).

Because of their specialized expertise, elites are further enabled to perpetuate themselves in high positions. In pointing to the masses' lack of knowledge in any particular area, elites can assert that they must therefore be given the power to make important decisions. Furthermore, elites can control the training and recruitment process of their successors, thereby creating a self-reproducing class. The gulf between elites and masses then becomes increasingly wide. Once in power, elites devote more and more of their energies to maintaining their positions.

It would seem that all these developments would ordinarily be met with strong resistance from the masses. On the contrary, however, the masses seem content to turn over the affairs of the state (or any other organization) to elites. Michels blames apathy, insufficient time, lack of expertise, and, in some cases, a predisposition to be led. The masses, then, are not only incapable of ruling themselves but are indifferent about relinquishing decision-making power to elites. As Michels put it, "Though it grumbles occasionally, the majority is really delighted to find persons who will take the trouble to look after its affairs" (1962[1915]:88).

This indifference and incapability, of course, considerably strengthen the positions of the leadership and make more unlikely the development of challenges to elite power among the masses. Such movements stand little likelihood of success even if they do materialize, explains Michels, since elites have all the power cards stacked in their favor: information the masses do not have, control of the flow of that information, the credibility and prestige that automatically accrue to incumbent officeholders, and, perhaps most important, cohesive organization. Through all of these power resources, the dominant leadership is able to carefully monitor the selection of new elites. This is a compelling explanation of why there are low rates of political participation in many democratic societies, including the United States.

We can see in Michels' theory an account of why "the people" never actually rule. This does not mean that masses are totally lacking in power, however. Particularly in democracies, citizens have opportunities to participate in the political process and to try to hold elites accountable. The key analytic questions, then, involve the relationship between elites and masses: how can masses hold elites accountable, and to what extent can they exert influence on elite decisions?

Political and Other Forms of Inequality   Political inequality should not be seen as unrelated to other forms of social inequality. As will become evident in the discussion that follows, there is a strong and ineluctable linkage of political inequality with other forms of inequality, particularly class inequality. Indeed, as noted in Chapter 1, power is at the base of all forms of stratification. In the end, those who have more wealth and prestige than others are usually able to convert that wealth and prestige into power. Whether power precedes wealth and prestige or vice versa is a chicken-and-egg question. In any case, they are closely interrelated. This linkage has been observed by many philosophers and social observers. Marx maintained that "political power, properly so called, is merely the organized power of one class for oppressing another" (Tucker, 1972:352). Coming from the opposite side of the political spectrum, the conservative philosopher Edmund Burke similarly observed, "As wealth is power, so all power will infallibly draw wealth to itself by some means or other" (Baker, 1992:245).

The following sections first examine the power structure in American society, along with some major theories of that structure. We then look at the extent of political inequality and how the power of elites may be checked by the democratic political process.

Three Models of Power in America

Social scientists' analyses of political power in the United States have boiled down to a debate among three major theoretical schools: class, elitist, and pluralist. As with any of the theories explored in previous chapters, it is important to keep in mind that there are no clear "rights" and "wrongs." Theoretical perspectives in the social sciences, remember, do not provide definitive answers; rather, they enable us to look at social structures and processes in different ways, each providing elements that together lead to a more informed view.

Sociological models of the American power structure present different scenarios of *who* has power, *how* they exercise it, and *in whose interests* they wield it. On one key point there seems to be general agreement among the three theories: In no modern society, regardless of how democratic its system may be, do masses actually rule in the sense that they themselves make critical political decisions. Instead, they rely on leaders to make those decisions. But on other details of elite rule there is a wide range of thought. Do elites use their power for the society's welfare or for personal gain? Are elites necessary, or might their functions be assumed by other forms of leadership? Are elites closed and cohesive units, or are they open and diverse? Is there only one ruling elite, or are there several? Also, the social characteristics of elites themselves have been subject to much investigation and debate. From what social classes, ethnic groups, and other social categories do elite members come? And how do patterns of elite circulation change, enabling those of different social origins to enter into positions of power and privilege?

Finally, and perhaps most important, how much power can masses exert against the power of elites? Is democracy real, or is it merely an illusion, even in societies like the United States that are considered thoroughly democratic in their politics?

The Class Model

The class model of the American power structure derives from the Marxian theory of inequality, discussed in Chapter 2. Power is seen as originating in the society's institutions of property and the class relations that derive from them. Political power, in this view, is exercised by those who control the means of production, that is, the capitalist class. Societal power, therefore, is concentrated in the hands of a few and is not subject to control by political institutions no matter how democratic they may seem to be. This obviously does not conform to the common perceptions of the structure of power and political behavior held by most Americans.

The Instrumentalist View   There are two ways of viewing the power structure using a Marxian, or class, perspective. One view holds that members of the capitalist class do not necessarily govern, in the sense of occupying political offices, but they *rule,* by controlling political officials and institutions (Gold et al., 1975). The critical question in this view is, Who are the people in strategic positions? Theorists using this perspective have investigated the relations between top corporate and political decision makers, usually finding them to be of similar social backgrounds with a strong understanding of common purpose. Corporate leaders and others of the capitalist class act in concert with political and other institutional leaders to protect capitalist interests and preserve the prevailing class system, from which, of course, they benefit the most.

In addition to the direct political influence of the corporate elite through exchange of strategic positions with government leaders, capitalist control is effected through campaign financing and lobbying. As discussed later in this chapter, the major contributors to the campaigns of political office seekers are corporations and the independently wealthy, that is, the capitalist class. Lobbying is another tool capitalist interests use to mold government policies in their favor. Through these means, then, the capitalist class is able to influence the decisions of politicians and their appointees in government agencies.

The Structuralist View   Another class, or Marxian-influenced, perspective on power contends that the interpersonal linkage between political and economic elites is of little importance in assuring the maintenance of capitalist class interests by the state. They argue that the structure of political and economic institutions in capitalist society makes it imperative that the state serve those interests regardless of whether capitalists directly or indirectly take part in state affairs. Attempts to influence government policymakers through campaign contributions, lobbying, and so on, are merely "icing on the cake." Plainly, the state cannot carry through anticapitalist policies because of mechanisms built into the modern capitalist political economy (Block, 1977; Poulantzas, 1973). Politicians, therefore, come naturally to view the interests of dominant economic groups as fundamental to a prosperous socioeconomic system and are prepared to accede to their needs more readily than to those of other interest groups. Recall from Chapter 9 the preparedness of the federal government to assist weak sectors of the corporate economy through subsidies and other aids or to rescue failing industries and banks.

In this view, social and strategic ties among corporate and government leaders are unimportant. Since the viability of the state is dependent on a healthy economy, state leaders *must* promote the interests of big business, that is, the large corporations, regardless of who they are or what their views may be. If the economy declines, tax revenues dry up, imperiling government programs and weakening public support for elected officials and other government leaders. The political scientist Charles Lindblom has neatly summarized this relationship:

> If business is not induced to perform, the result is economic distress. When the economy fails, the Government falls. . . . Hence, no category of persons is more attentive to the needs of business than the Government official. Businessmen consequently do not need to strain or conspire to win privileges already thrust on them by anxious legislators and administrators. (1978:A19)

In sum, whether because of influence on government leaders or because of the structural nature of the political economy, class theorists agree that the state sooner or later must weigh the interests of the capitalist class more heavily than others. Moreover, in modern capitalist societies the distinction between government leaders and corporate officials becomes less meaningful. With the active role of government in the making of economic policy, the various forms of public financial support given to private corporations, and the constant crossover of personnel from one sphere to the other, key economic and political decisions are often made by officials of government and corporations in concert.

The energy task force led by Vice President Dick Cheney in 2001 provides a vivid illustration of government and corporate elites' collaboration to further their mutual interests. The group was formed just nine days after the presidential inauguration, its purpose ostensibly to iron out the new administration's energy policy. Cheney refused to make public what had been discussed or how decisions had been made in meetings (or even the identity of the participants), but later accounts reported that that essentially secret body was composed, along with administration officials, almost exclusively of top corporate officers of the electricity, coal, natural gas, and nuclear power companies. Those corporate officers included executives of Enron, who later would be convicted of fraud in the wake of their company's demise, as well as Halliburton, the firm Cheney had run for five years before becoming vice president (Pasternak, 2001). Virtually all the corporate representatives were heavy financial contributors to the Bush-Cheney campaign. There were no representatives of environmental, labor, or other public sectors that would be affected by the decisions of this coterie of government and corporate elites. As might be expected, the group's final report called for measures that directly catered to the economic and political interests of the nation's major energy industries. Alternative energy sources, such as wind and solar power, were given short shrift, and the views of environmentalists were to all intents and purposes ignored.

The Power Elite Model

The power elite model begins with the premise that societal power is concentrated in elite groups that control the resources of key societal institutions. Moreover, masses, though not completely powerless, can exert little control over the decisions of elites. The presumption that societal power is concentrated in the hands of a few is, of course, also a fundamental premise of the class model. But the origins of societal power, in the power elite view, lie not in the institutions of property and the class relations that derive from them but in the control of social organizations, particularly the state and the corporation.

This perspective, like the class model, runs counter to the common American view of how leaders relate to citizens and how the power of the former is kept in check by the latter. But in this view, the dominant relationship of elites to masses is prevalent in *all* societies, democratic or not. The composition of the elites and the basis of their power may vary at different times, but the essential fact of elite rule remains unchanged.

Mills and the Power Elite   In Chapter 4, C. Wright Mills's theory of the power elite was introduced (Mills, 1956). To reiterate briefly, Mills held that a small group of leaders made up of top corporate executives, key government officials, and the highest-ranking military officers constitute an American power elite. These are the persons who actually have the capacity to make basic decisions in their institutions and thus to determine the society's key policy issues, both public and private.

Aside from the power elite, what is the actual structure of power in American society, according to Mills? Do the masses have a role to play at all, or is the power elite beyond the control of citizens? Mills conceptualized the hierarchy of power in the United States as a trilevel arrangement: the power elite at the top, the masses at the bottom, and a middle level of power wherein less consequential political decisions are made (Figure 12-2). This middle level consists essentially of Congress, important state and local political officials, organized labor, and various pressure

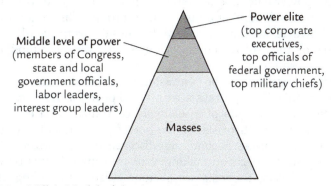

Figure 12-2 ■ Mills's Model of the American Power Structure

groups. There is a balance of power among the middle-level groups, but they are of little consequence in deciding the society's larger issues.

At the bottom, the bulk of the populace is relatively disorganized, inert, and in the process of becoming a "mass," that is, a society that responds with no countervoice to decisions made by a centralized power elite. The transformation of the American public into a mass society is due largely to the nature of mass communications, in which most people only receive but cannot respond to opinions voiced by organized authorities. Political ends are accomplished through successful manipulation of the populace, using such primary means as television. According to Mills, "The public is merely the collectivity of individuals each rather passively exposed to the mass media and rather helplessly opened up to the suggestions and manipulations that flow from these media" (1956:305).

The reaction among social scientists and other social observers to Mills's description of power in the United States was at first mainly negative. *The Power Elite* was published in 1956, and power in the United States during the 1950s was seen by most as a balanced plurality of various interest groups, none of which was dominant. The idea that a small and relatively cohesive group could determine the basic shape of political and economic life in the society did not sit well with those pluralist assumptions. Not until the late 1960s, after the society had experienced the reality of bitter and often violent domestic conflict, as well as the hubris of presidential power in Vietnam, was Mills's thesis reconsidered.

Perhaps the most important aspect of Mills's work is that it compelled political sociologists to rethink basic ideas about power in contemporary America. *The Power Elite* has become a classic work largely because of the controversy it initially aroused and still continues to provoke. Indeed, much of the research on power in the United States in the last several decades has been, by and large, a response to Mills's thesis.

The Pluralist Model

The class and power elite models coincide on the notion that societal power is held by a small, self-serving group—either a ruling class or a power elite. Americans, however, are reluctant to think of politics as the conflict between social classes or the covert actions of elites. The pluralist model breaks sharply from these ideas.

Specifically, pluralism can be contrasted with the class and elite models on two major points. First, pluralists see societal power as fragmented rather than as resting in the hands of a relatively centralized and cohesive few. Whereas elite and class theorists see the power pie as uncut, pluralists see it divided into many pieces. Second, pluralists see average citizens as having meaningful input into decision making, thus exerting effective power over leaders; elite and class theorists see average citizens as having little real control over leaders and thus having little or no say in the shaping and resolution of the most important and far-reaching societal issues.

It is clear, then, why pluralism is more palatable to the American political mind: It is based on the democratic image of the sociopolitical system into which Americans are socialized from their earliest school experience. The distrust of an all-powerful government is also a fundamental part of the American political tradition, and again pluralism complements this belief quite well. Most simply, pluralist systems are usually seen as democratic systems, and there is a tendency to equate the two. A well-functioning pluralist system is one in which no single group among many diverse groups is able to impose its will on the society as a whole. This is contrasted to an oligarchic system, in which a single group rules with minimal accountability to the citizenry.

Interest Groups Pluralists, unlike elite and class theorists, see a role for the masses in the power process. This is accomplished largely through the interest group system. The critical nature of interest groups as a democratizing force in politics was first suggested by Alexis de Tocqueville in the 1830s in his commentary on American society. Tocqueville pointed out that the ascendance of industrialization and the diffusion of democratic ideas in Europe in the late eighteenth and early nineteenth centuries caused the demise of a social aristocracy. This was a group that had traditionally served as an intermediary between the ruling monarch and the masses. In preindustrial societies an aristocracy stood as a stabilizing and generally benign force, acting as a filter of sorts through which the monarch's power was moderated as it passed down to the lower social levels. Tocqueville felt that without such an intermediate level of power, a society might easily be swept up by either an all-powerful tyrant or a "tyranny of the majority."

In modern democratic societies such as the United States, however, Tocqueville saw no aristocracy. What, then, substitutes for this important middle level of power? His answer: a network of well-organized voluntary associations, representing economic, political, and religious interests. Tocqueville was especially impressed with the American tendency to form innumerable autonomous and private organizations whose purposes were to further an almost endless variety of goals and activities. In Tocqueville's view this middle layer of organizations between rulers and masses serves a dual purpose. First, it prevents elites from exerting unmitigated power, and second, it provides the citizenry with a means of input into the power process. In other words, it is through these organizations that citizens are able to influence societal leaders and hold them accountable.

The existence of pluralism within government itself was also seen by Tocqueville as highly significant in the maintenance of political democracy. He was convinced that the American system of separation of powers and the proliferation of state and local units of government were additional safeguards against the growth of an all-powerful state. Thus, many competing power centers, he observed, typify the politics of American society both inside and outside its governmental institutions.

Modern Pluralism   Tocqueville's portrait of the American democratic system remains amazingly relevant to contemporary times and serves as the theoretical groundwork of modern pluralism. Following a similar line of thought, political scientists in the 1950s developed an updated theory that took as its central theme the interplay of many varied interest or pressure groups (Merelman, 2003; Truman, 1951). An **interest group** is made up of people who share a particular objective—an "interest"—and act collectively to persuade government decision makers to act toward the group's benefit. People may choose any number of associational ties, depending on their needs and desires. Labor unions, church groups, civic organizations, environmental groups, business and professional associations, and the like, all constitute interest groups. Through group efforts, people are more likely to be able to influence the political process than would be possible if they were to act alone. In the pluralist view, then, politics becomes a struggle of competing groups within an arena supervised by the state.

In sum, interest groups act as pressure groups on government, supporting issues and political actions of importance to their members. They serve as a means by which individuals with common interests can exert influence on decision makers through collective action. Voluntary associations are therefore vital to the functioning of the political system in enabling average citizens to exert at least some control over leaders. Interest groups, as one political scientist succinctly puts it, "link citizens to government" (Berry, 1999:15). Through interest group activities, in combination with elections, political officials are held accountable and cannot favor the interests of only one or a few groups on all issues. The system remains relatively balanced and tranquil through compromise among the competing groups and their leaders.

Strategic Elites   Modern pluralists concede that, necessarily, elites play a critical role in societal decision making even in democratic societies like the United States. What is important, however, is that elites are, in this view, not a single integrated unit. Rather, there are numerous elites that do not agree on all issues. It is the competition between and within elites that holds the power of leaders in check (Dahl, 1967; Rose, 1967). Elites oppose one another (Democrats versus Republicans, labor leaders versus business leaders, and so on), and differing views are held by different members of any one particular elite (liberal Democrats versus conservative Democrats, Republicans who support immigration reform versus Republicans who oppose it, and so on). Unavoidably, then, elites make the society's important decisions. But there are multiple elites, not the single, overriding power elite or governing class that Mills had portrayed.

The sociologist Suzanne Keller explained the role of a plurality of "strategic" elites in the power structure. She suggested that because of the complexity of modern societies, no single group of leaders can have the expertise or scope of influence to make critical decisions in every area of societal life. Numerous specialized or strategic elites therefore arise "whose judgments, decisions, and actions have important and determinable consequences for many members of society" (1963:20). Business leaders are competent to operate corporations but cannot run governments, which are the domain of political leaders; political leaders, in turn, know little about educational affairs, which is the specialty of an elite of professional educators; and so on. This view contrasts sharply with the notion of a relatively unified set of elites at the top of the power hierarchy that constitute a single "power elite" or "ruling class."

The American Power Structure: Unity and Division

The issue of whether a unified power elite or a diffuse power structure exists in the United States has absorbed the attention of sociologists and political scientists for several decades. Unfortunately, the issue is not easily resolved, because the actions of elites are never totally or even in large measure visible to non-elites. Rare are the occasions when the public actually gets a glimpse of what occurs behind the closed doors of congressional committees or corporate boards. The public speeches and pronouncements of politicians and business leaders are almost always scripted to create the most favorable image—they seldom reveal true motivations or objectives.

Another hindrance to a resolution of this long debate is the question of methodology. Using varying definitions of power as well as different strategies in discovering it, researchers have almost automatically been led to disparate findings. The picture of elite power in the United States or any other society as either totally unified or totally dispersed does not, of course, represent its true character. Realistically, the American power structure falls somewhere between these two extremes. Most class and elite theorists would not deny many elite divisions, nor would pluralists reject at least some degree of elite unity.

In addition, the shape of the elite structure and the nature of interrelations among its elements are not static. Pressures can bring elites of power together at certain times, and at other times separate them. Some of those pressures are found in the society's class system; others are the result of the structural nature of political and economic institutions.

Power in America: An Integrated Model

Drawing on all three theoretical perspectives, it is possible to pick out key features of the American power structure that together define its essential character. On the one hand, societal power is limited to a small number of individuals whose functional and social ties are unavoidably close. This relative integration of political and economic decision makers at the top of the power structure supports the basic point of the class and elitist views. On the other hand, there is also evidence to support a basic pluralist tenet, that is, the lack of consensus among elites on many critical issues.

Elite Integration   As G. William Domhoff (1971, 1998, 2010) has shown, corporate and political elites come together in various policy-planning groups, advisory councils, and lobbying situations. Through these points of interaction, they exchange views, come to know one another, and lay out long-range policy plans. Given these common sites of decision making, a natural confraternity of power emerges. Business and government leaders also frequently exchange positions, especially at the upper levels of national power. They move back and forth between the private and public sectors as top advisers, cabinet officials, and lobbyists. This constant interplay of functional power contributes to the development of a common frame of reference and a consensus regarding basic societal issues.

As Chapter 4 showed, those who dominate key societal institutions exhibit strikingly similar social backgrounds. Most important, their class origins are relatively narrow, with most coming from the upper or upper-middle classes. Even those who do move into power positions from lower social ranks will have been exposed to similar socialization experiences later in life, such as higher education and corporate affiliations. Indeed, these experiences may be more important than similar childhood experiences in molding common political interests (Putnam, 1976).

Predominance of the Corporate Elite   Resources of power are varied, but it is economic resources that are paramount in modern capitalist societies. Thus, economic leaders will generally, though not at all times, dominate the elite structure. Media coverage of news events leads one to assume that government leaders are the major decision makers who raise and settle issues. Power and politics, it seems, are limited to what occurs within the institutions of government: the presidency, the Congress, the bureaucracy, and so on. This view, however, seriously underestimates the ability of economic institutions and their leaders to influence the shaping of public policies.

The corporate elite may actually decide few public issues, but to a great extent they are able to set the agenda and boundaries of political debate. With control of the society's productive resources, economic leaders shape the framework within which political decision makers must operate. Political leaders are thus influenced by the long- and short-range interests of economically powerful institutions (i.e., corporations) more than any other factor. As Kenneth Dolbeare has described the American political economy:

> The policies of government and of business are so intertwined and mutually supportive that no citizen can tell where one ends and the other begins. . . . Thus the first priority that underlies the entire pattern of government activity, social welfare and regulatory measures included, is the furtherance of the growth and other needs of the economic system. (1974:26–27)

Politicians at all levels of government understand that political actions can never be completely divorced from economic consequences. Policies can be enacted only to the extent that economic circumstances permit. And those circumstances are very much determined by individuals who, through their organizations, control the society's productive resources—that is, by the corporate elite.[1]

Furthermore, no other societal institution can match the *political* resources of the giant corporation in efforts to shape public policies. On virtually every major political issue, whether it be tax policy, health care, energy, climate change, education, financial regulation, and dozens of others, giant corporations have an infinitely greater upper hand in influencing policy makers, possessing money, information, and communication tools that simply cannot be matched by competing interest groups.

The Commonality of Needs and Interests   Much interchange of personnel occurs among elites. Although there is no question that a certain degree of specialization makes it difficult for different elites to cross over from one institutional sphere to another (corporations, government bureaus, and universities all operate somewhat differently and have different objectives), the skills needed to manage corporations are increasingly the same as those needed to manage government bureaus and universities. When combined with similar socialization experiences stemming from relatively common class backgrounds, this makes for a natural coming together of elites.

There is also much interchangeability of government and corporate personnel. It is common for high corporate officials to leave the private sector and assume top positions in government, and the movement occurs in the opposite direction as well. When they finish their term of government service, most cabinet officers, for example, return to the corporate world or the legal profession, from which they came before their appointment to public office. With a mutual understanding of what constitutes a healthy and progressive society, and with an agreement that a stable corporate system is necessary to maintain that condition, corporate and political elites can interact with ease and can move back and forth between their two worlds with little difficulty. Few cabinet members of both Republican and Democratic administrations in recent decades have not had corporate connections prior to their political tenure, connections that usually were resumed and enhanced after they left government.

In addition to their back-and-forth movement between institutional sectors, top leaders commonly hold more than one position at a time. A corporate executive, for example, may also be a board member of other corporations, a member of a government commission, a trustee of a prestigious university, and a director of a civic or cultural organization. Thomas Dye, in his study of American institutional elites, found that approximately 15 percent of those

---

[1]One theoretical approach to power, however, holds that government (or "the state") is the ultimately powerful institution and thus it is the decisions of government leaders that, in the end, can supersede those of a corporate elite (Evans et al., 1985).

identified as the nation's elite held multiple top positions. He refers to this group as "interlockers," an inner group of top leaders who constitute a kind of "elite within the elite" (2002:140). Through their overlapping power positions, members of the inner group come to know one another socially, meeting not only in corporate boardrooms but at cultural and civic events, charitable functions, university trustee meetings, and alumni events. They are also members of the same exclusive social clubs. It is this inner group that links the corporate world with other major institutions, especially government, universities, and foundations (Dye, 2002; Useem, 1978).

Elite Divisions   Although elite integration is apparent, looking at the policy decisions of elites reveals that on many specific issues there are significant divisions among them. These policy differences are most evident among political elites, but even within the corporate world, decision makers are rarely unanimous in their views and actions. One need only glance at the front page of a daily newspaper or watch the national news on television to realize that there are deep and abiding disagreements on most issues, some of them quite basic. It is this lack of consensus on many issues to which pluralists point to support the view that elites are not socially cohesive, attitudinally unified, and dominated by business interests.

The fact that the power elites in American society come predominantly from the higher social classes does not assure that they will at all times act on behalf of the interests of those classes. That upper-class origins do not automatically guarantee sympathy for upper-class political values and interests is exemplified by political figures such as Franklin D. Roosevelt and, more recently, the Kennedys. Though possessing unquestionable aristocratic credentials, they often displayed concern for the interests of the working class and ethnic minorities, who were their major base of electoral support.

There are noticeable interest differences and ideological conflicts among elites that are recognized not only by pluralists but even, in part, by those who emphasize the cohesiveness of institutional leaders. Consider, as an illustration, the issue of free trade. Despite the fact that they are all capitalists, corporate elites may differ as to whether they think it is beneficial for the United States to open its markets—with no controls—to foreign economies. The automobile industry, for example, may lobby to limit imports from Asia and Europe. Corporations such as retail merchandisers may approach this issue quite differently, seeing the benefits of open markets. Politicians likewise view the issue with different perspectives, depending on their specific political interests and ideologies. Being strongly committed to laissez-faire principles, Republicans would be expected to adhere to the idea of free markets, with no tariffs or other controls on trade. But some Republicans may be fervent nationalists and thus oppose strong competition from other countries. Likewise, some Democrats support free trade, understanding that it will lower prices on consumer goods and therefore benefit middle- and working-class families. Other Democrats, however, oppose free trade, fearing that it will cost some American workers their jobs. These kinds of disagreements play themselves out constantly in the give-and-take of national and lower-level politics regarding trade issues, tax policies, environmental controls, and so on.

Consensus on Basic Issues The policy differences among elites are significant, but they do not represent basic disagreements on the most essential issues of the political economy and on the ways in which decisions are to be carried out. There is consensus on the fundamental shape of the capitalist political economy and its basic objectives. Above all, elites—from every institutional sector—are concerned with the maintenance of economic growth and political stability. Those who question or openly advocate systemic changes (introducing socialist elements, for example) are rarely taken seriously and are unlikely to enter the circle of political and economic power to begin with.

Consider, for example, the political response to the economic crisis of the late 2000s. None but the most ultra-right-wing elements of political and economic thought denied that the free-wheeling, largely unregulated style of capitalism that had predominated in the United States for three decades not only had contributed to a near-meltdown of the financial system but had given rise to the most unequal distribution of income and wealth since the Gilded Age of the late nineteenth century. Yet no interest group of any real influence on either side of the political spectrum, let alone members of either of the two major political parties, called for extensive changes in the fundamental workings of the U.S. political economy; even the "reforms" that were put forth, designed only to fine-tune some of the perceived flaws in the established system, were met apprehensively by most and strongly resisted by many.

The Role of Masses in the System of Power

If elites always rule, no matter what kind of political system prevails, where does this leave the rest of the populace? Are the masses simply pawns to be duped, deceived, and manipulated by self-serving elites? Is democracy merely a sham, more symbolic than real? These are particularly important questions in the United States since the system of governance is a democracy, wherein citizens are assumed to have some power in settling important societal issues and where elites are assumed to be held accountable. This section examines when and how citizens can apply power and thus reduce the inequality between themselves and the power elites.

Political Participation: A Key Life Chance

Like education and health care, the ability to influence the political system by having one's interests addressed is, in a democratic society, a critical life chance. This means having access to and being able to hold accountable those who make decisions—elites. The electoral process is seen as the key to mass input in selecting and holding accountable political leaders, and it is through this process that some degree of political equality is assured. "One person, one vote" is an axiom of electoral democracy, guaranteeing that everyone, regardless of wealth or social status, can exercise at least some political power on an equal basis. As Sam Rayburn, a Speaker of the U.S. House of Representatives, once earthily put it, "A whore's vote is just as good as a debutante's" (Baker, 1992).

Voting, however, is only one among a number of forms of political participation and is certainly not the most effective. The extent and scope of participation are strongly related to the class system. Those higher in income and wealth, occupation, and education are those who participate in the most meaningful and potent ways. The result is deep and abiding political inequality.

The Scale of Participation   The participation of citizens in the political process is assumed to be the most fundamental characteristic of democratic systems. Yet the level of participation by non-elites in *any* form of political activity is relatively low. This has been true of American society for most of its modern history despite the granting of voting rights and other political opportunities to previously disenfranchised groups such as women, African Americans, and other minorities.

The sociologist Marvin Olsen (1982) constructed a model of political roles that enables us to envision different forms and degrees of political participation. At one extreme are those who are maximally involved politically, whom Olsen calls *leaders*. They actually run for office or are government officials; they are a very small percentage. At the other extreme are the *isolates,* those who are politically unaware and apathetic and either acquiesce in or withdraw entirely from the political system; they constitute perhaps a fifth of the population. In between these two extremes are those who participate in varying degrees. Close to the leaders are *activists* who exercise influence on government through lobbying and contributing to political campaigns. They are important and effective participants in the political system. Below activists are *communicators,* who are informed and knowledgeable about politics and discuss it with others. *Citizens* are somewhat aware of current political issues and vote but do little else in the way of political participation. Although they constitute the power base of the political system, they exert influence only collectively, not individually. *Marginals* are potentially available for mobilization by parties and candidates and may respond from time to time to particular issues that directly affect their lives. But their exposure to issues is minimal and short-lived, and thus their political activity is never sustained.

What this hierarchy of political activity reveals is that most of the citizenry is, at best, involved at a very superficial level (Table 12-1). The important

Table 12-1 ▪ The Hierarchy of Political Participation

Leaders	Persons directly involved in government	3%
Activists	Persons engaged in organized political action within private organizations	14%
Communicators	Persons who receive and communicate political information	13%
Citizens	Persons who have knowledge of the political system, hold opinions on issues, have a party preference, and usually vote	30%
Marginals	Persons who have minimal contacts with the political system	18%
Isolates	Persons who rarely or never participate in politics in any way	22%

Source: Olsen, 1973.

players are the leaders and the activists. Accounting for less than 20 percent of the population, it is these two categories that exercise influence—the former through authority in the formal political system and the latter through lobbying, campaign financing, and the like.

Olsen's description is consistent with studies of political participation and with surveys of the American public (Brady et al., 2002; Davis and Smith, 1994; Schlozman et al., 2005; Verba et al., 1995). The level of citizen involvement in the political process is, in a word, low. Voting is the simplest and least expensive form of citizen participation. Yet even this act is usually performed by only a minority of the eligible population (Freeman, 2004). In no national U.S. election since 1932 have more than two-thirds of eligible voters actually cast their ballots. Only in presidential elections might the percentage of voters ever exceed 50 percent. In local elections, far less than half ever participate. In sum, most actions requiring time, energy, money, or information are engaged in by only a small fraction.

Low rates of citizen participation are not limited to the United States. Although voting percentages in most other democratic societies are considerably higher, the percentages involved in other forms of political activity in those societies resemble the U.S. pattern (López-Pintor et al., 2002; Milbrath and Goel, 1982; Olsen, 1982; Verba et al., 1995).

The Effective—and Costly—Forms of Participation

It is at the levels of leaders, activists, and, to a lesser degree, communicators that the effective forms of participation occur. These forms of participation are far more costly than others in terms of time, energy, and, especially, money. It is here that the most glaring evidence of political inequality occurs. A gulf separates those who can effectively make their interests known to the powerful and can expect them to respond and those who are relatively powerless. Two of the most important forms of participation are financial support of candidates for office and lobbying. In both cases, the connection between class inequality and political inequality is obvious. What is demonstrated is the inextricable link between money and political power. Quite simply, those with greater financial resources are far more able to exert their influence on decision makers.

In the contemporary American political economy, where money is the most crucial and effective power resource, large corporations have an automatic advantage over not only individual families, but other competing interest groups. All understand that public policies regarding efforts to regulate the financial system, control climate change, reform the health care system, introduce new sources of energy, and dozens of other critical issues will ultimately affect their economic destinies. Thus they engage in continual efforts to influence policy-makers. But in this political contest, giant corporations have an infinitely greater upper hand, with financial and information resources that simply cannot be matched by opposing interest groups. As Robert Reich has explained, competition among corporations has escalated in recent years as a result of globalization, new forms of communication, and the demands of investors and consumers. As this competition has intensified, corporations' efforts to influence public policy have grown accordingly. Hence the increased flow of political money in the form of lobbying and campaign funding, leading to what Reich describes as "the corporate takeover of politics" (2007:158).

Campaign Financing   Being elected to political office today generally requires a great deal of money. Campaign financing is, in itself, a major business. In 1952, the first year in which total political costs were calculated, $140 million was spent electing people to local, state, and federal offices (Alexander, 1992). By 1980 the figure had risen to $2 billion, and by 2004 it had increased to almost $5 billion (Rosenbaum, 1996; Center for Responsive Politics, 2006). By 2008, that figure had been surpassed for federal elections alone. The 2012 presidential and congressional elections were the most costly in U.S. history, estimated at $6 billion. Moreover, this does not include millions more contributed to candidates as "dark money," that is, anonymous and unreported cash donations. Consider the expense of running for a U.S. House or Senate seat. In 2012, congressional candidates of both Republican and Democratic parties spent about $1.82 billion. House campaign spending alone was more than $1 billion. The expenditures in some hotly contested races stand out even from these extraordinary total figures. Three months before the election, candidates in just four states had already spent more than $100 million (Center for Responsive Politics, 2012). Campaign financing for the presidency, of course, eclipsed all of these amounts, surpassing the $1 billion mark for the first time in 2008 and estimated to cost twice that amount in the 2012 presidential election (Figure 12-3).

Year		Total
2012		$2,500.0
2008		$1,324.7
2004		$717.9
2000		$343.1
1996		$239.9
1992		$192.2
1988		$210.7
1984		$103.6
1980		$92.3
1976		$66.9

Figure 12-3 ▪ Total Spending by Presidential Candidates ($ millions)
Source: Reprinted by permission of the Center for Responsive Politics-OpenSecrets.org.

Candidates who are independently wealthy can use personal funds to help finance their campaigns for political office. The number of wealthy candidates funding their own campaigns has risen dramatically in recent years. In 1998, fifteen House and Senate candidates spent more than $1 million in personal funds (Center for Responsive Politics, 2000). H. Ross Perot spent $63 million of his own money running for the presidency in 1992 and another $37.2 million four years later. Another multibillionaire, Steve Forbes, publisher of *Forbes* magazine (and son of the late Malcolm Forbes), spent $37 million of his fortune in his unsuccessful campaign for the Republican nomination for president in 1996 and millions more again in his 2000 quest for the nomination. In Illinois, a candidate for the Democratic nomination for the U.S. Senate in 2004 spent almost $29 million of his personal fortune in a losing cause. In the most ambitious expenditure of personal funds to date running for political office (other than the presidency), Linda McMahon spent $100 million of her fortune in two unsuccessful U.S. Senate campaigns in 2010 and 2012 (Applebome, 2012).

Given the costs of running for office, candidates who are not independently wealthy must turn to those who can provide them the financial aid they need. This is particularly true of positions at the federal level, where campaigns are of a broader scope than local ones, requiring costly television and other media advertising. So critical have campaign funds become to politicians that while in office they spend as much of their time raising money as attending to constituent and legislative matters. This is particularly the case for politicians who represent strongly contested districts. One member of Congress described his fund-raising activities as a constant chore:

> When I was here in Washington I would go over to the NRCC [National Republican Campaign Committee] or the Senatorial Committee offices to make telephone calls [for] an hour, two hours every day. When I was home in Florida, which was a good portion of the time, that's the bulk of what I did. It's a very time-consuming process, on the telephone mostly, organizing fundraisers or getting individual people to contribute (quoted in Makinson, 2003:36–37).

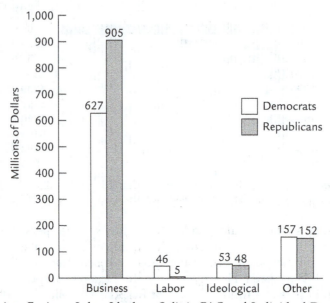

Figure 12-4 ▪ Business-Labor-Ideology Split in PAC and Individual Donations to Candidates and Parties, 2012 Election Cycle (in $ millions)
Source: Reprinted by permission of the Center for Responsive Politics-OpenSecrets.org.

Although labor unions and other organizations contribute to political campaigns, the two major sources of wealth are the giant corporations and wealthy individuals and families of the capitalist class. Figure 12-4 shows the total amounts given by business, labor, and ideological groups to candidates in federal elections in 2012. The dominance of the business sector is obvious.

One of the major forms of campaign contributions to candidates, particularly those running for Congress, is the PAC system. **Political action committees** (PACs) are organizations outside the official political parties that are designed to raise and distribute money to candidates. They are organized by particular interest groups, such as corporations, professional associations, and labor unions, or by groups that are concerned with a particular issue, such as abortion rights or gun control. The vast majority, however, are organized by big business, either by individual corporations or by trade and industry groups. Labor unions, ideological groups, and organizations that promote special issues, while also heavily contributing to PACs, run a distant second to the corporate sector.

In 2010, the U.S. Supreme Court, in a controversial 5 to 4 decision in the case of *Citizens United*, ruled that the government could not impose any limits on the amount of money corporations and other interest groups could contribute to political campaigns. The feared effect of this ruling was that it would enhance enormously the power of those already dominating the system of electoral financing, in effect, altering fundamentally the American political landscape. Such fears were confirmed in the 2012 election cycle, as wealthy donors and interest groups poured hundreds of millions of dollars into campaigns. A cascade of money flowed into so-called "super-PACs," independent political committees ostensibly not in direct coordination with the candidates themselves, in amounts never before realized. For example, Sheldon Adelson, a billionaire casino owner, and his wife gave $10 million to a super-PAC backing presidential candidate Mitt Romney; they had previously given Newt Gingrich $20 million in the Republican primary. Adelson had stated that he intended to spend $100 million of his own money by the end of the election (*New York Times*, 2012). Because many put their money into advocacy groups rather than directly into candidates' campaigns, they were not required to disclose their identities to the Federal Elections Commission, leaving unknown the true scale of their contributions.

In campaign financing, the gap between the political "haves" and "have-nots" could not be clearer. In 2008, less than one-half of 1 percent of Americans made a political contribution greater than $200 (Center for Responsive Politics, 2009). This means that the electoral system, so tied to money, is overly supported and influenced by very wealthy individuals and families and corporate executives. Mitt Romney, the Republican presidential nominee in 2012, for example, raised $3 million at a single event at the estate of Ronald O. Perelman, the billionaire financier and Revlon chairman, where tickets ranged from $5,000 for lunch to $25,000 for a V.I.P. photo reception (Rutenberg, 2012). Similar fund-raising events were held by President Obama. Several years ago, former Senate majority leader Trent Lott held a private luncheon with two hundred of his party's biggest patrons at a Palm Beach luxury resort. When asked about changing the way campaigns are financed, Lott defended unlimited donations as "the American way" (Seelye, 1997). As the political system is driven by money, the majority of the population is left on the margins of the process.

Those who contribute campaign moneys obviously do so with the expectation that they will realize a return on their investment. That is, they understand that there is a quid pro quo in which the recipient will remember them and will act in their interests on issues that affect them (Clawson et al., 1992). Money does not "buy" politicians; it buys access and influence. Who can phone his or her representative in Congress regarding a pressing issue and expect to speak directly with that person? Few constituents would expect, much less actually receive, such a personal response. Big campaign donors, however, regularly communicate and establish close relationships with elected officials who are expected to defend them when issues arise that are relevant to their interests. The money basis of the electoral system helps explain why, for example, the numerous tax bills enacted by Congress during the 1980s and 2000s resulted in huge tax cuts to corporations and families at the top of the income hierarchy while middle- and working-class families experienced a rise in their federal tax burden (Barlett and Steele, 1992; Jencks, 2004; Johnston, 2003). As the journalist William Greider

Source: Reprinted by permission of Universal U-Click.

describes it, "Behind all the confusion and complexity of the tax debate, democracy's natural inclinations were literally thrown into reverse—rewarding the few at the expense of the many" (1992:80).

Campaign spending has become a major political issue in recent years and, like other issues of social inequality, evokes the confrontation of liberty and equity. Conservatives often defend the system as providing an opportunity for people to express themselves and to support their candidates as they choose. In this view, to limit campaign contributions would violate a basic liberty: free speech. Liberals, on the equity side, see excessive campaign spending as unfair to those on the lower rungs of the class hierarchy by skewing the political system toward the wealthy, who are the major campaign contributors.[2]

---

[2]Barack Obama's presidential campaign in 2008 deviated somewhat from the usual financing path, drawing most of its contributions through the Internet, especially from millions of small donors in addition to the usual super-rich sources. Some believed that Obama's success might transform campaign funding, creating a more democratic process (Green, 2008). The changes brought about by the *Citizens United* Supreme Court ruling, however, seemed to cede campaign financing power back to the corporate sector and the super-wealthy.

Lobbying   Lobbying is an important means by which individuals and organizations, through their interest groups, seek access to public officials. As with the system of campaign financing, however, this is a part of the political process that is heavily biased in favor of those with great economic resources. Trying to persuade legislators and other government officials through direct efforts is a well-institutionalized practice in American politics. Indeed, the term "lobbyist" derives from the past, when representatives of interest groups would collar legislators in the lobby of the Capitol. But today lobbying efforts have become tools for groups whose wealth enables them to retain permanent staffs of lobbyists in Washington and in state capitals, constantly working to further their political interests. More than $3 billion is spent each year by organizations lobbying the U.S. Congress (Center for Responsive Politics, 2012). Table 12-2 shows the annual lobbying expenses of some of the largest U.S. corporations and interest groups.

Although lobbyists represent a diverse spectrum of social, political, and economic interests, it is the latter that dominate the system. As might be

Table 12-2 ▪ Spending by Top Lobbyists, 2011

Lobbying Client	Total
US Chamber of Commerce	$66,370,000
General Electric	$26,340,000
National Assn of Realtors	$22,355,463
Blue Cross/Blue Shield	$21,585,802
American Medical Assn	$21,500,000
ConocoPhillips	$20,557,043
American Hospital Assn	$20,482,147
AT&T Inc	$20,230,000
Comcast Corp	$19,615,000
Pharmaceutical Rsrch & Mfrs of America	$18,910,000
National Cable & Telecommunications Assn	$18,530,000
Boeing Co	$16,060,000
Verizon Communications	$15,470,000
AARP	$15,170,000
Lockheed Martin	$15,166,845
Royal Dutch Shell	$14,790,000
United Technologies	$14,270,000
National Assn of Broadcasters	$13,960,000
FedEx Corp	$13,161,784
Pfizer Inc	$12,890,000

Source: Reprinted by permission of the Center for Responsive Politics-OpenSecrets.org.

expected, corporations, given their immense financial capacities, are predominant lobbying forces. They support industrial and trade associations, which lobby for particular industries or business groups collectively. The American Petroleum Institute, for example, will lobby for the entire oil industry; the American Insurance Association, for the insurance industry. One of the most powerful lobbies in Washington is the Business Roundtable, made up of chief executive officers of the very largest U.S. corporations. Rather than rely on paid lobbyists, these corporate CEOs themselves lobby members of Congress as well as meet with the president and cabinet members (Domhoff, 1998). Also, and perhaps more significant, individual firms have their own lobbying staffs. Public-interest groups, labor unions, and professional groups such as doctors, lawyers, and educators also actively lobby, but their efforts do not match those of the corporate sector.

As the system works, lobbyists bestow monetary and material benefits on legislators and other government officials in hopes of favorable treatment on particular issues. In 1997, for example, Atlantic Richfield, one of the largest U.S.–based oil companies, paid for a five-day trip to London for then House Speaker Newt Gingrich, his wife, and two aides. During the trip, Gingrich spoke at the company's annual dinner. The group stayed at one of London's most upscale hotels, where the room alone for Gingrich and his wife cost over $12,000. The full cost of the excursion was $42,000. Upon his return, Gingrich was quoted as saying that "every American should make this trip" (Kamen, 1998). In the same year, the Tobacco Institute, representing cigarette companies, flew eleven Congress members to an exclusive Scottsdale, Arizona, resort for a "legislative conference" at a cost of $63,000 (Carlson, 1998).

The defense industry exemplifies the return on investment of the millions that huge corporations spend lobbying. In 2003, Lockheed Martin, the nation's largest defense contractor, paid out $3.3 million for lobbying, aimed in particular at members of Congress who sit on the influential Defense Appropriations Subcommittee. Lockheed had earned over $26 billion in the previous year, with about 80 percent of its revenue coming from U.S. government contracts. Other defense corporations, of course, maintained similar lobbying budgets.

In addition to such material benefits, lobbyists influence government in another and perhaps more important way. They constitute a key source of information for legislators and other policymakers on general as well as specific issues. Speaking to a meeting of lobbyists, former Senator Alan Cranston put the matter bluntly: "Lobbyists are in fact an extension of our congressional staffs, providing information and ideas that are vital to the molding of legislation" (quoted in Green, 1984:61). Given this understanding of their role, lobbyists are able to supply input into the shaping of government policies that affect their interests. When legislation arises concerning, for example, the pharmaceutical industry or the trucking industry, necessary information is supplied by the companies themselves, usually through their lobbyists. Such information will, of course, be presented in a way that reflects the interests of the lobbying group. Government officials, however, come to see such efforts as helpful and even vital to their decision-making functions.

The lobbying process illustrates well the idea of elite integration, discussed earlier in this chapter. What is evident is a kind of revolving door movement of top personnel between government and the corporate world. In the Lockheed case described above, for example, the company's vice president of legislative affairs was formerly minority staff director of the House Defense Appropriations Committee (Fred, 2003). After serving in the political world, Congress members and governors often move into the corporate world as consultants or executives or, more commonly, lobbyists. Their knowledge of the inner workings of the legislative process as well as their key political connections make former political officials valuable to corporations and trade groups as lobbyists or representatives. After retiring as House Speaker, Dennis Hastert, for example, joined a blue-chip lobbying firm at an annual salary estimated at more than $500,000. Daniel Glickman, former congressman from Kansas and Secretary of Agriculture in the Clinton administration, assumed the head of the Motion Picture Association of America, earning more than $1.3 million (Gilchrist, 2008). In 2009, firms in the financial services sector (banks, and investment, insurance, and real estate companies) had almost 1,500 former federal employees working as lobbyists, many of whom were former members of Congress themselves or had close connections to Congress (Center for Responsive Politics, 2010). Kevin Phillips describes the lucrative nature of this government-corporation pipeline, especially for Congress members turned lobbyist:

> Some people in Congress get tired after three terms and go home. They just don't want to bother with it. But most understand that it is the ticket to making real money. You can hang around Washington and be a lobbyist. Even if you're a jerk, you'll still make $300,000 a year, which is twice what a congressman makes (2008:39).

The process, of course, also works in reverse, with corporate executives regularly assuming key government posts; hence the "revolving door."

Other Factors in the Policymaking Process   Money, in the form of campaign contributions, and lobbying are not always decisive in the policymaking process. Indeed, some maintain that their impact is overrated (Burstein, 2003; Burstein and Linton, 2002). Paul Burstein (2003) contends that influences on policy creation and change are multifarious and that money and lobbying may not be among the most important. Party loyalty on the part of political decision makers, their ideological leanings, and public opinion, in his estimation, outweigh them. In most cases a politician will support or oppose an issue on the basis of where his or her party stands, personal ideology, and, most important, a reading of public opinion. Few would deny that these factors often come into play, particularly the latter. Despite occasional denials that they are not swayed by them, political leaders pay close attention to public opinion polls and constantly try to gauge their constituents' views on various issues.

Stressing the importance of public opinion, however, fails to take into account the ability of key interest groups to shape or, at minimum, influence public opinion itself. People's views on issues of the day do not arise in a vacuum.[3] This is why political leaders and well-funded organized interest groups devote such substantial resources to advertising and public relations campaigns, undertakings whose costs are prohibitive for most groups and individuals. Hence, even if policymakers respond dutifully to public opinion, the systemic inequality of the political process may work in favor of the interests of the wealthy and powerful. The political scientists Kay Schlozman and her colleagues (2005) describe this effect:

> If public opinion can be manipulated, and if the tools of opinion manipulation are most available to the wealthy and powerful—who tend to occupy "bully pulpits" and to have the rhetorical skills or money needed to persuade others—the result may be a subtle, indirect, but pervasive kind of inequality in political influence. (27)

Political Participation and Social Class

In a very broad sense, the political system is an open one in which equality of opportunity prevails: Everyone can follow the issues, become informed, and vote. All can participate. However, as was pointed out, the political process entails a great deal more than voting. The issue, then, is not *whether* people can participate, but *in what ways* they can participate. There is clearly a class bias in the political system, one in which those with substantial economic resources have tremendous advantages over others. In effect, they are the serious participants (the "activists" in the participation hierarchy) who can exert influence on political elites. Most of the remainder of the populace are minimally involved or are merely spectators. Even the most conscientious citizens, as William Greider describes them, become disillusioned: "They have become 'citizens' of a purified form—free to speak frankly on the public issues they value, but utterly disconnected from the power structure where those issues are decided" (1992:202).

In terms of social class, the serious players in this system are a distinct subset of the general populace. They are higher than average in income, occupation, and education. The relationship between social class and political participation extends over the entire spectrum of participation. Even voting, the simplest form of participation, is class related; the higher the social class, the more likely one is to vote (Verba and Nie, 1972; Schlozman et al., 2005;

---

[3]Of course, as Burstein points out, on a myriad of issues that come before policymakers, the public has no opinion at all because most people are unaware of or are not interested in them.

Wolfinger and Rosenstone, 1980). As seen in Table 12-3, the voting rate rises as family income rises. More important, of course, is the relationship between social class and campaign donations. Campaign contributions are the most significant form of political participation, but the participants are almost entirely from the top strata of the class system. Consider that 95 percent of the households that made substantial political contributions in 2000 were from the 12 percent of households with incomes of more than $100,000 (Schlozman et al., 2005). In the 2008 elections, about one-tenth of 1 percent of the adult population actually made a political contribution of more than $2,300 (Center for Responsive Politics, 2009).

This would not pose serious problems if the needs and wishes of these upper- and upper-middle-class citizens coincided with those of subordinate classes. But as the political scientists Sidney Verba and Norman Nie explain, "the participants differ substantially from the nonparticipants in the problems they consider salient and in the solutions they prefer" (1972:15). Those who participate most extensively bring their class outlooks and biases to the electoral process. As a result, to the extent that political leaders do respond to the electorate, they respond to the perceived needs of these classes rather than to the needs of the working and lower classes. During the last half century, the majority of Americans beneath the upper-middle class indicated consistently that they favored government efforts to establish social welfare programs including universal health care and guaranteed incomes. Yet throughout this period, legislators

Table 12-3 ▪ Voting and Family Income

Family Income	Percent Reported Voted 2008	Percent Reported Voted 2010*
Total	65.5	47.7
Under $10,000	49.0	26.7
$10,000–$14,999	51.2	29.8
$15,000–$19,999	55.9	33.4
$20,000–$29,999	56.3	40.4
$30,000–$39,999	62.2	44.3
$40,000–$49,999	64.7	49.0
$50,000–$74,999	70.9	51.9
$75,000–$99,999	76.4	57.8
$100,000–$149,999	78.4	61.0
$150,000 and over	81.6	61.6
Income not reported	49.0	38.5

*2010 was not a presidential election year.
Source: US Census Bureau, 2009, 2011.

responded carefully with conservative policies that did not basically threaten the status quo (Hamilton, 1972; Pew Research Center, 2005). In his sweeping analysis of the impact of public policies on changes in economic inequality over the past half-century, political scientist Larry Bartels concludes quite simply that "affluent people have considerable clout, while the preferences of people in the bottom third of the income distribution have *no* apparent impact on the behavior of their elected officials" (2008:285). Another political scientist, Martin Gilens, after examining government responsiveness to citizen preferences, reaches a similar conclusion: "Whether or not elected officials and other decision makers 'care' about middle-class Americans, influence over actual policy outcomes appears to be reserved almost exclusively for those at the top of the income distribution" (2005:794).

In any case, most legislators at the national level are from upper or upper-middle-class backgrounds—almost half of members of Congress in the 2010–2012 session were millionaires—and are thus not likely to hold views that reflect the needs of groups lower in the class hierarchy. Their perceptions of social and economic problems, therefore, will be consonant with those of the significant participants in the electoral process. The result, as the American Political Science Association's Task Force on Inequality and American Democracy concluded, is that in the political realm, "ordinary Americans speak in a whisper while the most advantaged roar" (2004:11).

That corporations and the wealthy are more apt to have their interests protected by government policies does not mean that other groups and interests do not benefit from government functions; obviously they do. And it is equally clear that noncorporate sectors of the society often successfully pressure political decision makers much as do the affluent and the corporations. Labor unions, for example, were an extraordinarily effective interest group during much of the last half century, and government has gradually responded to the demands of other groups, such as African Americans and women, as well. Nonetheless, the basic structure of the political economy remains intact. And as the nucleus of that system, the giant corporations and the wealthy can apply resources that will, if not assure, certainly strongly influence political action that addresses their interests and concerns.

In addition, giant corporations and the wealthy have the resources to persevere in the political system. Consider tax policies. The passage of a tax bill, whether favorable to corporate or upper class interests or not, does not end the matter. These groups continue to fight the battle with money and lobbyists, either protecting the privileges they have won or seeking those they desire. "Thus," as Greider notes, "the monied interests are always mobilized and working toward better results, knowing that the continuum of legislative action does not stop with one victory or one setback. Citizens may grow weary and move on to something else, but for obvious reasons, the wealthy are always on the case" (1992:81).

Participation and Elite Accountability

We have now seen that electoral activities—the primary form of non-elite political participation—may be limited in actually holding elites responsive to public needs and desires. Focusing only on electoral politics, however, may cause us to overlook other ways in which elites elude public accountability.

The classical view of democracy rests on the assumption that participation is equated with citizen power. Political leaders are ultimately required by the electorate to answer for their actions and must therefore respond to its general will. This assumption seems ill founded, however, for several reasons. One is simply the class bias of the system. As already noted, the serious participants do not represent a broad spectrum of the class hierarchy; rather, they are concentrated at the upper levels. The connection between participation and control of political elites, however, is frayed for several additional reasons. These relate to the roles of interest groups, economic elites, and the mass media in the policymaking process.

Interest Groups   Pluralists have considered interest group activity one of the most important instruments of citizen input into the policymaking process. If elections are not always effective in communicating the needs and desires of the people to the political elite, interest groups, serving as intermediaries between people and government, may do so. This assumes, of course, that most of the populace will be active members of one or several interest groups. Studies have shown, however, that this is not ordinarily the case (Almond and Verba, 1963; Putnam, 2000; Verba et al., 1995).

As with participation in the electoral process, there is a definite link between the scope and intensity of activism in interest groups and one's class position. Most simply, the higher one's class, the greater the number of memberships and the greater the extent of participation in such organizations. Thus, like the electoral process, the interest group system is heavily class biased. Furthermore, the most effective interest groups are those that are firmly part of the lobbying system, that do not come and go with changing issues. These mainly represent dominant economic interests.

Power without Participation   Focusing attention on electoral behavior may cause us to mistakenly accept this as the most significant wellspring of power. Electoral decisions, however, are only secondary to the establishment of the political agenda itself. Rather than deciding *who* will argue and act on particular issues, deciding *which* issues will become part of the political debate is a more primary act of power. The political scientists Robert Alford and Roger Friedland (1975) point out that the traditional pluralist perception of the political process assumes that the most important decisions are made at the point where legislation is proposed and debated. But this overlooks the more important preemptive development of policy options by dominant—principally economic—interest groups. In these decisions, non-elites do not participate.

In any case, since the policymaking process is, in more cases than not, reliant on the cooperation of government and dominant economic groups, the latter are in a position to greatly influence the structure of political action no matter what role they may play in participatory politics. Whatever government does is dependent on tax revenues, and the ability of government at all levels to raise revenues is, in turn, dependent on the production and investment decisions of dominant economic groups, specifically major corporations. Alford and Friedland (1975) call this "power without participation."

The Unaccountability of Economic Elites   Let's assume for the moment that elections do serve their intended purpose: to give citizens some input into the decisions of political leaders and to hold the latter accountable. At best they can only help control the actions of political officials. The capacity of the corporate elite to make public policy, however, through its interaction with government officials and through its own decision-making power is enormous. Indeed, when considered in total, the decisions made by corporate leaders in regard to investment of capital, location of factories and equipment, employment levels, and so on, are often of greater public consequence than those made by public officials.

Despite these far-reaching public consequences, non-elites have virtually no control over the decision-making processes of corporations. Representatives of interest groups or of the general public neither sit on corporate boards nor participate in the selection of those boards. Corporate leaders do not seek input from the electorate; they are not required to maintain even the nominal public responsibility of elected or appointed government officials. The multifarious powers of the corporate elite are simply not publicly controlled. Even if we accept the most favorable picture of the role of the participatory process in democratic politics, it can affect only a part—and perhaps not the most critical part—of the mosaic of power in the United States and other advanced democracies.

The Unaccountability of Media Elites   Although not formally a part of either government or the economy, the mass media are integrally tied to both, and both rely on the mass media to function as they do. Moreover, the mass media have substantial independent resources that make them a formidable institution of power in their own right. Perhaps most important, the mass media, as explained in Chapter 8, are, for most people, the major sources of information regarding politics and public policy. Despite their great power and major influence on the shape of politics, the media are private institutions that operate largely free of citizen input into their content and direction. Decisions regarding what to print or televise are made unilaterally by the media elite, who are not publicly accountable through the electoral process and only minimally accountable through government regulation.

Not only do the media elite determine the content of the information the public receives, they monitor access to the media and thus are able to decide who will communicate their views to the society. Only those who are able to pay can send their messages to the widest audience through the mass media. This, again, means the largest corporations.

Might the Internet be a force for reducing the political influence of traditional media and their sponsors and introducing more democracy into the participatory system? As was discussed in Chapter 8, it appears that the Internet has not significantly altered inequalities in accessing political information. The same seems to be the case for exercising political voice (Mossberger et al., 2008; Prior, 2007). A recent national survey (Pew, 2009c) indicates that, as income rises, online participation in the political process (such as emailing a political official or signing a petition) goes up as well. Hence, the most frequent users of this newest channel of political participation are, as before, those highest in income and education. Although this is a result, in part, of unequal Internet access, the correlation between social class and online political activity is evident even within the online population. The study concludes quite simply that "the Internet is not changing the socioeconomic character of civic engagement in America."

Mass Participation and the Class Structure

What impact can non-elite participation, particularly the electoral process, have on the distribution of the society's rewards? Can it, in Lasswell's terms, affect "who gets what, when, and how"? In short, can it change the shape of the society's class and status hierarchies?

As shown in earlier chapters, the class structure in the United States has remained amazingly stable during the last century. The distribution of wealth and power has not been fundamentally affected by the techniques of procedural democracy. Indeed, in some ways mass participation may actually serve to stabilize the system of inequality and assure the status quo by giving the illusion of power. The political scientist Murray Edelman has described the symbolic functions of participatory politics:

> To quiet resentments and doubts about particular political acts, reaffirm belief in the fundamental rationality and democratic character of the system, and thus fix conforming habits of future behavior is demonstrably a key function of our persisting political institutions: elections, political discussions, legislatures, courts, and administration. Each of them involves motor activity (in which the mass public participates or which it observes from a distance) that reinforces the impression of a political system designed to translate individual wants into public policy. (1964:17)

If the electoral process has the effect of stabilizing the opportunity and reward structures of the society, it is not surprising that those of higher social class and status should be its main participants. Indeed, if participation through normal channels has little effect on government responses to the needs of subordinate groups, and if the party system and other aspects of electoral politics frustrate these groups' effective mobilization, low rates of participation by those at the lower end of the class and status hierarchies are, in Alford and Friedland's words, "neither analytically surprising nor politically irrational" (1975:448). Verba and Nie (1972) contend that the upper-class bias of participatory politics is not easily overcome, even by lower-class citizens who do choose to become politically active; their numbers are too small and their organizational resources too limited for them to be an effective voice.

Political participation by non-elites, then, is simply not the same for all class groups since each has access to different resources that affect the ultimate payoff for participating. Participation is meaningful for those groups that bring to the political arena sufficient political and economic resources to make themselves heard. Those with the time, skills, organization, and, especially, money to participate convincingly—not simply by voting or joining an activist group—are likely to see the system as working effectively, and indeed for them it *is* working effectively. It is to these groups that government leaders respond, thereby preserving the basic political economy and its attendant structure of inequality.

Political scientist Sidney Verba (2006) writes that politics is analogous to a "game," the fairness of which depends on an equal opportunity to take part. Thus, "equal voice" is the key feature of any fair political system: "The fair game has rules and procedures that give each player (citizen) and each team (group or category of citizens) an equal chance of winning" (505). To the extent that there are wide differentials in income (that is, great inequality in the economic realm), however, equality in the political realm is undercut. Clearly those with the most substantial economic resources are the important and effective players in the American game of democracy, whether through electoral or interest group activities.

Noninstitutional Forms of Participation

What has been discussed to this point are institutional means by which masses can try to influence elites. These are legitimate ways in which, presumably, people can make their views known and pursue their interests through the prevailing political system. This is a system, however, that seems to work most effectively in the interests of the wealthy and powerful, giving ordinary citizens very limited ability to hold elites accountable or gain access to institutions of power.

When people find that their political objectives cannot be met by using the conventional institutions, that is, the electoral system with its attendant parties and interest groups, they may act outside the established political framework. Such nontraditional political behavior can be quite diverse, ranging from petitions, peaceful meetings, demonstrations, sit-ins, marches, and rallies to acts of civil disobedience, strikes, violent protests, and even armed confrontations with government authorities. Most actions are short-lived and have minimal subsequent impact on the political system, but others evolve into organized and prolonged sociopolitical movements that ultimately affect the society's dominant institutions.

Sociopolitical Movements   Sociopolitical movements may involve various class or minority groups seeking concessions from ruling elites, or they may involve groups seeking more fundamental changes in the society's institutional arrangement. In all cases they represent a challenge, to some degree, to the political or economic status quo. At certain moments, large numbers of people choose to use unconventional political tactics. They may also question the legitimacy of leaders and no longer feel that prevailing institutions are entirely just or unchangeable. In short, at such times people's political behavior and consciousness change (Piven and Cloward, 1978).

These collective attempts to alter the society's institutions of inequality differ, depending on the scope of change sought (sweeping or limited), the direction of change desired (progressive or regressive), and the methods used (persuasive and legitimate or coercive and unlawful). On the basis of these features, three general types of sociopolitical movements can be distinguished: reform, revolutionary, and reactionary.

Reform movements, the most common of the three, are relatively limited in terms of scope, direction of change, and methods. Their intent is the acquisition of social and political rights and economic benefits for certain disenfranchised or subordinate groups (workers, African Americans, gays, women) or the resolution of a certain issue to the benefit of some group (voting rights, welfare, health care). The objective is thus limited to making the prevailing system more responsive to the needs of such groups. Proposed changes are progressive in direction, and actions are taken, for the most part, within the existing political framework. In a sense, the idea is for aggrieved groups to secure a piece of the action. The industrial labor movement of the 1930s is a good example. Traditionally, leaders of heavy industries with many unskilled workers had resisted efforts at collective bargaining. When automobile and steel workers, along with coal miners, challenged big industrial employers to recognize their labor unions, the workers eventually won by engaging in strikes, sit-downs, and at times violent confrontations with both company and public police. The industrial labor movement did not aim for a complete dismantling of the capitalist system but only for a greater role for workers within that system.

Whereas reform movements focus on specific issues or groups and do not seek to basically alter the society's institutional system, **revolutionary movements** are sweeping in scope and aim for a restructuring of societal institutions and, ultimately, the class system itself. Franz Schurman (1971:20) has defined a revolution as "an overturning of fundamental hierarchical relationships in a society—what is below displaces what is above." Simply put, following revolution, those previously at the top of the social hierarchy may be at the bottom.

Since a revolution's aim is basically to replace the existing social order, its adherents, of course, operate outside the established political framework. And their methods are bound to be coercive rather than persuasive; indeed, violence is usually assumed to be an integral element of revolution. Turning the social structure upside down obviously does not occur without the use of coercion by those seeking change and forceful retaliation by those resisting it. Ruling groups do not voluntarily relinquish their power. As Michels (1962[1915]:245) observed, "A class considered as a whole never spontaneously surrenders its position of advantage. It never recognizes any moral reason sufficiently powerful to compel it to abdicate in favor of its 'poorer brethren.' "

Given the scope and intensity of such change, it is not surprising that we have witnessed so few truly revolutionary movements in modern times. The first, and perhaps prototypical, social revolution occurred in France in 1789. There the traditional ruling class, made up of the landowning aristocracy, was ultimately replaced by a new ruling class, the bourgeoisie, whose economic base was commerce and industry. An entirely new social order emerged based on the ideology of this now-dominant class. Other total revolutions that have basically altered class relations occurred in Russia in 1917, China in 1949, and Cuba in 1959.

Whereas both reform and revolutionary movements seek to establish new societal institutions and relations, **reactionary movements** are regressive, designed to resist progressive changes in the structure of inequality or perhaps even to re-create social hierarchies that existed in earlier times. The scope of change sought may be limited, as in reform movements, or quite broad, as in revolutionary ones. To explain and justify these goals, reactionary ideologies are often predicated on claims of the cultural, physical, or moral superiority of some social groups and the inferiority of others. Racist, sexist, and homophobic movements are founded on such beliefs and thus aim to deny rights and privileges to their targeted groups. Such movements may also be built upon the fear of privileged classes of losing their economic and political advantages.

Beginning in the late 1950s and early 1960s, a number of sociopolitical movements aimed at bringing about changes in the class, racial/ethnic, and gender hierarchies arose in the United States. Most were nonviolent and reformist in nature, but some were marked by violence, and a few even had revolutionary overtones. These movements focused on a diversity of groups and issues, including black civil rights, the Vietnam War, student rights, women's liberation, gay rights, consumerism, the environment, nuclear power, and the proliferation of nuclear weapons. Some of these movements had a strong impact that led to profound societal changes. Then, in the late 1970s and 1980s, a number of conservative and reactionary sociopolitical movements emerged whose focus included a range of social, political, and moral issues such as abortion, prayer in public schools, educational curricula, and pornography. Led by rightist elements of the Republican Party and by Christian fundamentalists, these movements seemed to coalesce around a broad ideology whose theme called for the reversal of what was perceived as the political and social liberalization of American society during the previous two decades. These movements sought to impose a strict version of morality on the society and return it to more traditional values.

In the second decade of the twenty-first century, American society seemed intensely polarized around issues of inequality. Class divisions and expanding differences in income and wealth had become a part of the national consciousness and a critical point of political debate to an extent unmatched since the Great Depression of the 1930s. On the political right, groups and organizations seemed to coalesce around resistance to efforts on the part of government to actively address the society's huge, and increasingly evident, economic disparities. Their ideology was dominated by the notion of laissez-faire, in which a severely constrained state would provide minimal assistance to individuals and families. Indeed, government itself was portrayed as an oppressive and invasive institution that, ideally, would be reduced in size and scope, leaving people to fend for themselves. This extreme individualism was complemented by the somewhat contradictory vision of a strong state imposing more rigid and traditional cultural values. The Tea Party Movement best reflected that part of the societal divide (Skocpol and Williamson, 2012).

On the political left, a more inchoate movement seemed to take form, spurred by the increasing awareness of the growing gap between the very wealthy and the remainder of the class system. In late 2011, a protest movement calling itself "Occupy Wall Street" sprung up in Lower Manhatten in New York and spread to numerous cities across the United States. Its immediate purpose was to call attention to the economic abyss that had opened between the wealthiest 1 percent and the remaining 99 percent of American families (Gitlin, 2012; Ketcham, 2012). But its specific political goals and strategies were not clearly enunciated, and its potency seemed to ebb a year later. Nonetheless, it had helped to bring about a sharper societal awareness of the extent of income and wealth inequality and had become a symbol of resistance to an institutional system that seemed to be working primarily in the interests of those at the top of the class hierarchy.

Out of the broad array of sociopolitical movements of the last several decades, then, has emerged a somewhat ambiguous picture. Undeniably, class, racial/ethnic, and gender hierarchies have been altered, in some cases quite significantly. Nonetheless, social inequality in numerous forms remains a fundamental societal feature. Those at the top of the society's hierarchies have great resources with which to resist mass challenges and thus to ensure stability and order in the stratification system: Most of the society's wealth and productive resources are owned and controlled by a relatively small number of persons and organizations; the dominant ideology, as we saw in Chapter 8, works in an invidious fashion to instill support of the stratification system among most people, regardless of their class position; and, as explained in this chapter, the institutional means available to masses to influence political elites are in large part only symbolic. The result is that those with wealth, power, and status retain their privileges without serious challenge from below. It is revealing that in 2012, survey data showed both a growing public perception of social and economic inequality in American society, along with little change in attitudes toward support for government measures to actually reduce those inequalities (Pew Research Center, 2012b, 2012c). Systems of inequality do undergo some alteration, but the changes are ordinarily slow, deliberate, and mild rather than radical and profound. Sociopolitical movements that do not pose a threat to dominant institutions and to the prevailing class system are likely to be more successful than those calling for sweeping and fundamental changes.

Summary

Political inequality essentially entails a hierarchy of decision-making power. On the significant societal issues, a few at the top—an elite—are able to make their influence felt. Elites are tiny groups whose members occupy the society's top positions of power, exercising authority and control of resources within the government, the corporation, and other major societal institutions. Masses, or non-elites, are those who make up the vast majority of the society's populace, whose power is limited.

Since it is elites that actually rule in any society, one of the key questions of sociology concerns the nature of leadership: Are leaders unified in thought and action, or are they sufficiently divided to assure at least some degree of mass control? Three general groups of theories have clustered around this issue, particularly as it pertains to the United States. Class theorists and elite theorists posit a unified elite structure whose members have common social backgrounds and common ruling interests. Pluralist theorists, in contrast, see power at the top as diffuse, with no single group able to dominate.

There is some evidence to support each of these general views of the power structure. Elites are integrated through the interweaving of their organizations (the corporation and the federal government, in particular), their interchange of positions, and their common social background. At the same time, there is no absolute unity of purpose and belief among them. Political and economic elites do not always see eye to eye on issues, and there are splits even within each of these two power groups.

An integrated model of power in America, combining elements of the three major theories, recognizes discord among elites but not basic disagreements on essential issues of the political economy. Within the power elite, corporate leaders, though not actually deciding most public issues, are best able to set the agenda and boundaries of political debate.

There is a hierarchy of participation in the political system in which only a relative few participate in any significant way; these few tend to be mainly from the society's top class and status groups. The relationship between social class and participation is very strong: the higher one's social class, the higher the level and significance of participation. The most effective forms of participation are campaign financing and lobbying, both dominated by large corporations and wealthy individuals.

Electoral politics has a limited impact on the policy decisions of political elites. In any case, elections can seek to hold accountable only those who are part of the political elite. Elections have no bearing on the selection or actions of decision makers of nongovernmental institutions, especially the corporation and the media. Thus, the electoral process represents only a limited aspect of the panorama of societal power in the United States and in other advanced democracies.

Sociopolitical movements are forms of participation in which masses seek change in the distribution of economic and political power outside the conventional electoral system. They can range from reform movements, with limited objectives and tactics, to revolutions that seek complete transformation of the class hierarchy. Reactionary movements are aimed at resisting progressive changes in the system of inequality or reinstalling earlier forms of inequality.

Glossary

absolute poverty A socioeconomic condition in which people are unable, for whatever reason, to obtain the fundamental necessities of life.

accident of birth Placement into a family of a particular class and ethnic status through birth.

affirmative action Public policies designed to provide, through preferential measures, wider opportunities in work and education for ethnic minorities and women.

apartheid The former system of caste in South Africa based on racial categorization.

assimilation The integration of a minority ethnic group into the societal mainstream. *See* **cultural assimilation; structural assimilation.**

authority Legitimate power.

blue-collar workers Those who work in manual occupations.

bourgeoisie The merchant class or, in Marxian theory, the capitalist class.

bureaucracy A type of social organization, typical of modern societies, that enables large numbers of people playing specialized roles to operate as a cohesive unit.

capitalism A system of economic production based on market principles and guided by the private ownership of property and the competitive pursuit of profit.

capitalist class The class at the pinnacle of the stratification system, whose members derive most of their income from investments and assets. In Marxian theory, the class that owns the means of production.

caste A type of social stratification in which status is acquired by heredity and in which mobility is severely constrained by law and custom.

charismatic authority As described by Weber, authority that derives from a leader's personal appeal.

class consciousness Awareness among members of a social class of their common economic and political interests vis-à-vis other classes.

closed societies Societies in which social mobility is uncommon and where political and cultural norms and values dictate against it.

cohort effect The process in which each successive generation of women, previously only marginally present in an occupational field, catches up to men in earnings.

comparable worth The idea that women and men should be paid equal wages for jobs that require comparable skill levels; sometimes referred to as *pay equity*.

corporate welfare Tax breaks, subsidies, and other government measures designed to benefit large corporations.

cultural assimilation The adoption by a minority ethnic group of the dominant group's norms and values.

cultural pluralism The maintenance of many varied ethnic cultural systems within the framework of a common economic and political system.

culture of poverty A theory that explains poverty as the result of a set of norms and values—a culture—that is uniquely characteristic of the poor.

cycle of poverty The idea that poverty is sustained by the entrapment of people in an array of social circumstances—low income, poor education, poor housing, poor health, and the like—that together operate in a circular process, making it improbable for individuals to break the cycle.

deindustrialization The departure of capital and industrial jobs from communities where they traditionally had been located.

demand-side policies Government efforts to reduce unemployment and stimulate economic demand by increasing public spending and imposing a greater tax burden on the wealthy.

deserving poor An element of the poor who are seen as being poor through no apparent fault of their own.

discrimination Actions against minority ethnic groups that create disadvantages in various areas of social, economic, and political life. *See* **individual discrimination; institutional discrimination.**

distributive justice The determination of how a society's valued resources should be apportioned: "Who should get what?"

dominant group In a multiethnic society, the group that exerts predominant economic, social, and political power and that has the greatest influence on shaping the society's cultural system.

dominant ideology An ideology that explains and justifies the prevailing power and reward structures.

downsizing The tendency for large corporations to reduce their workforce, with the objective of greater efficiency and profitability.

economic restructuring The radical shift in the last several decades from what had been a manufacturing-based economy to a service-based economy, eliminating, in the process, many traditional blue-collar jobs; related to the emergence of new technologies and the development of a global economy.

elite The tiny percentage of the population who occupy the society's top positions of power.

entitlement A government benefit that is automatically given to all who have reached a particular age (e.g., Social Security) or who otherwise qualify under the law for the benefit.

equity The distribution of the society's rewards in a just manner.

estate system A closed type of stratification, sometimes referred to as feudalism, based on land ownership; typical of agrarian societies.

ethnic group A group within a larger society that to some degree is set off from others by unique cultural traits.

ethnic minority A group singled out and treated differentially on the basis of its cultural or physical differences from the dominant group.

ethnic stratification A rank order of groups, each made up of people with presumed common cultural and/or physical characteristics, interacting in a system of dominance and subordination.

false consciousness A Marxian notion that refers to a belief on the part of nonruling groups that the prevailing political and economic systems work in their interests, when in fact they work primarily in the interests of the ruling class.

family As it pertains to income and wealth data, two or more persons related by blood or marriage who are living together.

feminism A set of beliefs and actions that center on assuring the equality of men and women in various areas of social life.

feminization of poverty A tendency for women to constitute an increasingly large proportion of the poverty population, due in large measure to single parenthood.

fiscal policy Government measures involving taxation and public spending that influence the economy.

flat tax *See* **proportional tax.**

gender The socially and culturally defined roles of males and females.

gender essentialism The idea that there are unique male and female traits that make men and women naturally suited to different occupational roles.

gender stratification The hierarchical order of men and women in society.

glass ceiling A reference to the failure of women and racial/ethnic minorities to advance beyond a certain point in the managerial ranks.

global economy The interconnection of the economies of politically independent countries in trade, transfers of capital, labor, production, and distribution.

Horatio Alger myth The idea that anyone, regardless of social standing, can become wealthy and successful through hard work and perseverance.

horizontal mobility *See* **lateral mobility.**

household As it pertains to income and wealth data, all persons occupying a housing unit, that is, separate living quarters.

ideological hegemony A Marxian notion referring to the predominance of ruling class ideas.

ideology A set of beliefs and values that rationalizes a society's structure of power and privilege.

income Money received over a period of time.

individual achievement A term reflecting the belief that each member of society is responsible for his or her fate and that one's social position is a product of personal efforts and talents.

individual discrimination Actions against minorities carried out by individuals or small groups, usually in violation of the society's laws or norms.

inequality of condition Differences in people's living standards or life conditions.

inequality of opportunity Differences in people's opportunities to acquire the rewards offered by their society.

influence A form of power that entails the ability of some people to get other people to do what they want them to do voluntarily, without coercion.

institutional discrimination Actions, often unintentional, against minorities that are the result of the policies and structures of organizations and institutions.

interest group People who share a particular objective or policy position and act collectively to persuade government officials to make decisions toward that end.

intergenerational mobility Change of position in the class hierarchy from one generation to the next (e.g., father to son).

intragenerational mobility Change of position in the class hierarchy during an individual's lifetime.

Jim Crow The system of black-white segregation maintained in the U.S. southern states until the 1960s that constituted a caste-like form of stratification.

lateral mobility A change of position that in terms of socioeconomic status is neither better nor worse than the previous position.

legal-rational authority As described by Weber, authority that derives from specific duties and obligations assigned to a particular position in an organization.

legitimacy The willing acceptance of the prevailing institutional and stratification systems by most members of the society.

legitimation The process by which people come to accept willingly the society's institutional system and its attendant social inequality.

liberal capitalism A democratic political system in combination with a capitalist socioeconomic system.

liberalism, classical The philosophy that extols the worth of individuals and their right to control their destiny.

liberty Freedom to pursue one's interests as one desires and to reap the benefits of one's efforts.

life chances Opportunities that people have to acquire those things that are valued and desirable in their society.

lifestyle The behaviors and values common to the members of a social class.

lobbying Efforts by individuals and organizations to access and influence public officials, usually through interest groups.

lower-middle class An occupationally diverse class composed of middle managers, semiprofessionals, craftspersons, and many service workers.

macroeconomic policy The role of government in managing the national economy.

masses Non-elites, those who make up the vast majority of the society's populace and whose power is limited.

means of production In Marxian theory, productive resources, i.e., things that are necessary to supply the society's economic needs.

meritocracy A system in which rewards are given on the basis of performance and qualification.

middle-class squeeze The tendency for those of the middle, or intermediate, classes to be pushed either upward or, more commonly, downward in terms of wages, salaries, and family income.

minority group A group that, on the basis of members' physical or cultural traits, exerts less power and receives fewer of the society's rewards. *See also* **ethnic minority.**

mode of production In Marxian theory, the economic base, including the forces and relations of production; a society's system of economic production (e.g., feudalism, capitalism).

multiethnic society A society made up of various ethnic groups.

multinational corporation *See* **transnational corporation.**

official poverty Poverty as defined by government-imposed standards of measure.

offshoring A type of outsourcing in which U.S. companies use workers in other countries, where wages are lower, to perform business and technical services.

oligarchy A form of rule in which the few, an elite, rule the many.

open societies Societies in which there are ideally few impediments to social mobility.

opportunity structure The number and types of occupations relative to the number and qualifications of workers available to fill them.

outsourcing An arrangement in which a large corporation subcontracts a business or production function to another company.

panethnic group Several distinct ethnic groups lumped together into an inclusive category, usually based on the groups' world region of origin (e.g., Asian Americans).

patriarchy The systematic dominance of men over women, especially within the family.

pluralism (1) The retention of ethnic cultures within the larger society; *see* **cultural pluralism; structural pluralism.** (2) A political system in which there are numerous competing centers of power, none capable of dominating at all times.

political action committees (PACs) Political organizations established by interest groups, which raise and distribute money for political candidates.

political economy The interrelationship of government and the economy.

postindustrial society A society characterized by the production mainly of services and information rather than finished goods, as in a traditional industrial society.

poverty *See* **absolute poverty, relative poverty,** and **official poverty.**

power The ability to realize one's will despite the resistance of others. *See also* **societal power.**

power elite Those who occupy positions of great importance in key institutions, especially the economy and government, and whose decisions have a profound impact on the society.

power structure The relatively fixed distribution of power among groups and organizations that set the agenda of public policy.

prejudice Negative ideas regarding subordinate ethnic groups.

prestige The deference that people are given by others; social esteem.

progressive tax A tax in which those with higher incomes pay a higher percentage.

proletariat In Marxian theory, the industrial working class.

proportional tax A tax that levies the same percentage rate on all income earners; also called *flat tax.*

public assistance programs Social welfare programs that are means-tested, requiring that recipients demonstrate a need in order to qualify for them, and that are financed through general government revenues.

race A socially created category of people who share a set of roughly similar genetic characteristics, or gene frequencies.

racism A belief system that avers the reality of races and the inherent behavioral differences between members of racial groups.

reactionary movement A sociopolitical movement designed to re-create conditions and institutions that prevailed in an earlier time.

reform movement A sociopolitical movement whose objectives are to obtain a greater share of power within the existing sociopolitical system and whose tactics are usually part of the legitimate system of rule.

regressive tax A tax that imposes a heavier relative burden as income declines.

relative poverty Poverty that is relative to the standards and expectations of people in a particular society at a particular time.

revolutionary movement A sociopolitical movement whose objective is to change radically the system of stratification.

ruling class In Marxian theory, the class that controls the means of production and, thereby, the political system as well.

sex The relatively fixed physiological and biological differences between men and women.

sexism A belief in the biological grounding of social and behavioral differences between men and women; implicit is the notion of male superiority.

social class A category of people with approximately similar incomes and occupations who have similar lifestyles.

social Darwinism A theory, based on the notion of "survival of the fittest," holding that one's wealth or poverty is the product of one's inherent capabilities.

social differentiation The division of the society into different roles; the horizontal dimension of social structure, implying no rank order.

social insurance programs Social welfare, primarily Social Security and Medicare, financed through payroll taxes.

social mobility The ability of individuals or groups to change their position on a social hierarchy. *See also* **intergenerational mobility** and **intragenerational mobility.**

social resources What is valued and scarce, for which people in society compete.

social stratification The ranking of persons and groups on the basis of various social, and sometimes physical, characteristics; the vertical dimension of social structure, implying inequality.

socialization The process through which people learn their society's culture.

societal power Power exercised by individuals and organizations, public and private, whose scope of activity is broad enough to affect many, if not all, elements of the society.

socioeconomic status (SES) A combination of income and wealth, occupation, and education.

status As described by Weber, differences in prestige that derive from a particular lifestyle, not from purely economic factors.

status communities As described by Weber, groupings of people who have similar cultural and social interests and common consumer patterns.

structural assimilation An increasing degree of social interaction among different ethnic groups of a multiethnic society.

structural mobility Changes in class position that are the result of changes in the society's labor force and economy as well as innovations in technology.

structural pluralism The continued social separation of minority ethnic groups from the dominant group.

structured inequality Stratification that is not random but is sustained by the society's institutional arrangement.

supply-side policies Government measures designed to stimulate economic production by giving tax breaks to corporations and the wealthy, who, it is assumed, will subsequently increase investment in productive projects such as factories and machines.

tax expenditures Tax breaks that benefit mostly middle- and upper-income families.

traditional authority As described by Weber, authority that derives from custom or tradition.

transnational corporation A corporation that manufactures and sells products and services in numerous countries.

underclass That element of the poor who are chronically unemployed, largely dependent on social welfare, and socially isolated from the mainstream society.

underground economy Economic activities that occur outside the mainstream economy, untaxed and unregulated.

undeserving poor An element of the poor who are seen as able-bodied but who are unemployed and therefore not considered to merit public assistance.

universalism The notion that everyone should be treated the same regardless of ascribed personal characteristics.

upper class That class at the top of the society's stratification system, whose members earn the most income and own the most wealth.

upper-middle class That class whose members have above-average income and wealth and occupy critical managerial, professional, and technical positions.

vertical mobility The movement of people up or down the class hierarchy.

wealth One's assets, in particular those that are income-producing.

welfare state Government insurance, public assistance, education, and medical programs designed to maximize the economic and social welfare of the society's population.

white-collar workers Those who work in nonmanual occupations, ranging from low-skilled and low-status to highly skilled and high-status.

work ethic The notion that hard work is the key to success.

working class That class whose members occupy manual laboring jobs or work at low-status white-collar jobs.

working poor Those who occupy the lowest paying, least prestigious and powerful jobs, usually not poor enough to qualify for public assistance.

References

Abusharaf, Rogaia Mustafa. 1998. "Unmasking Tradition." *The Sciences* 38 (March/April):22–27.

Alba, Richard D. 1995. "Assimilation's Quiet Tide." *The Public Interest* (Spring):3–18.

———. 2009. *Blurring the Color Line: The New Chance for a More Integrated America.* Cambridge, MA: Harvard University Press.

Alba, Richard D., and Gwen Moore. 1982. "Ethnicity in the American Elite." *American Sociological Review* 47:373–383.

Alba, Richard, and Victor Nee. 2003. *Remaking the American Mainstream: Assimilation and Contemporary Immigration.* Cambridge, MA: Harvard University Press.

Alderson, Arthur S., and François Nielsen. 2002. "Globalization and the Great U-Turn: Income Inequality Trends in 16 OECD Countries." *American Journal of Sociology* 107:1244–1299.

Alesina, Alberto, and Edward L. Glaeser. 2004. *Fighting Poverty in the US and Europe: A World of Difference.* Oxford: Oxford University Press.

Alexander, Herbert E. 1992. *Financing Politics: Money, Elections, & Political Reform.* 4th ed. Washington, DC: CQ Press.

Alford, Robert R., and Roger Friedland. 1975. "Political Participation and Public Policy." In *Annual Review of Sociology*, vol. 1, edited by A. Inkeles, 429–479. Palo Alto, CA: Annual Reviews.

Allegretto, Sylvia A. 2011. "The State of Working America's Wealth, 2011." EPI Briefing Paper #292 (March 23).

Allen, Charles F., and Jonathan Portis. 1992. *The Comeback Kid: The Life and Career of Bill Clinton.* New York: Carol Publishing Group.

Allen, Michael Patrick. 1987. *The Founding Fortunes: A New Anatomy of the Super-Rich Families in America.* New York: E. P. Dutton.

Almond, Gabriel, and Sidney Verba. 1963. *The Civic Culture.* Princeton, NJ: Princeton University Press.

Alperovitz, Gar, and Lew Daly. 2008. *Unjust Deserts: How the Rich Are Taking Our Common Inheritance.* New York: New Press.

Amer, Mildred, and Jennifer E. Manning. 2008. "Membership of the 111th Congress: A Profile." Washington, DC: Congressional Research Service.

American Experience, The. 1997. "The Richest Man in the World" (January 20). http://www.pbs.org/wgbh/pages/amex/carnegie.

American Political Science Association. 2004. *American Democracy in an Age of Rising Inequality.* Task Force on Inequality and American Democracy. www .apsanet.org.

Amott, Teresa L., and Julie A. Matthaei. 2006. "Race, Class, Gender, and Women's Works: A Conceptual Framework." In *Workplace/Women's Place: An Anthology,* 3d ed., edited by Paula J. Dubeck and Dana Dunn, 184–193. Los Angeles: Roxbury.

Andersen, Margaret L., and Patricia Hill Collins (eds.). 1998. *Race, Class, and Gender: An Anthology.* 3d ed. Belmont, CA: Wadsworth.

Anderson, Sarah, John Cavanagh, Chuck Collins, Sam Pizzigati, and Mike Lapham. 2008. *Executive Excess 2008: How Average Taxpayers Subsidize Runaway Pay. 15th Annual CEO Compensation Survey.* Washington, DC and Boston: Institute for Policy Studies and United for a Fair Economy.

Andrews, Edmund L. 2007. "Bush Tax Cuts Offer Most For Very Rich, Study Finds." *New York Times* (January 8):A16.

Aoyagi, Kiyotaka, and Ronald P. Dore. 1964. "The Buraku Minority in Urban Japan." In *Transactions of the Fifth World Congress of Sociology,* vol. 3, 95–107. Louvain: International Sociological Association.

Applebome, Peter. 2012. "Personal Cost for 2 Senate Bids: $100 Million." *New York Times* (November 3):A16.

Aron, Raymond. 1968. *Main Currents in Sociological Thought,* vol. 1. Garden City, NY: Anchor.

Atkinson, A. T. 1975. *The Economics of Inequality.* Oxford: Clarendon Press.

Atkinson, Robert D. 2006. *Supply-Side Follies: Why Conservative Economics Fails, Liberal Economics Falters, and Innovation Economics Is the Answer.* Lanham, MD: Rowman & Littlefield.

Auletta, Ken. 1999. *The Underclass.* Updated and revised ed. Woodstock: Overlook Press.

Austin, Algernon. 2012. "Reversal of Fortune: Economic Gains of 1990s Overturned for African Americans from 2000–07." Washington, DC: Economic Policy Institute.

Bagdikian, Ben. 1971. *The Information Machines.* New York: Harper & Row.

———. 2004. *The New Media Monopoly.* Boston: Beacon Press.

Bailey, Jeff, and Eric Dash. 2006. "How Does Warren Buffett Get Married? Frugally, It Turns Out." *New York Times* (September 1):B1, B6.

Bailey, Martha J., and Susan M. Dynarski. 2011. "Gains and Gaps: Changing Inequality in U.S. College Entry and Completion." National Bureau of Economic Research. http://www.nber.org/papers/w17633.

Baker, Daniel B. 1992. *Power Quotes.* Detroit: Visible Ink Press.

Bales, Kevin. 1999. *Disposable People: New Slavery in the Global Economy.* Berkeley: University of California Press.

———. 2012. *Disposable People: New Slavery in the Global Economy.* Updated ed. Berkeley: University of California Press.

Baltzell, E. Digby. 1958. *Philadelphia Gentlemen.* New York: Free Press.

———. 1964. *The Protestant Establishment: Aristocracy and Caste in America.* New York: Vintage.

Banfield, Edward. 1968. *The Unheavenly City.* Boston: Little, Brown.

———. 1974. *The Unheavenly City Revisited.* Boston: Little, Brown.

Banton, Michael. 1970. "The Concept of Racism." In *Race and Racialism,* edited by Sami Zubaida, 17–34. London: Tavistock.

Barber, Benjamin R. 2007. *Consumed: How Markets Corrupt Children, Infantilize Adults, and Swallow Citizens Whole.* New York: Norton.

Barber, Richard J. 1970. *The American Corporation.* New York: Dutton.

Baritz, Loren. 1982. *The Good Life: The Meaning of Success for the American Middle Class.* New York: Harper & Row.

Barko, Naomi. 2000. "The Other Gender Gap." *American Prospect* (June 19–July 3):61–63.

Barlett, Donald L., and James B. Steele. 1992. *America: What Went Wrong?* Kansas City, MO: Andrews and McMeel.

———. 1998. "Corporate Welfare." *Time* (November 9):36–54.

Bartels, Larry. 2008. *Unequal Democracy: The Political Economy of the New Gilded Age.* Princeton, NJ: Princeton University Press.

Barth, Ernest A. T., and Donald L. Noel. 1972. "Conceptual Frameworks for the Analysis of Race Relations." *Social Forces* 50:333–348.

Bean, Frank D., and Gillian Stevens. 2003. *America's Newcomers and the Dynamics of Diversity.* New York: Russell Sage Foundation.

Beard, Charles. 1913. *An Economic Interpretation of the Constitution.* New York: Macmillan.

Beatty, Jack. 2003. "Politics and Prose: When the Sun Never Sets." *The Atlantic Online* (June 6). http://www.theatlantic.com.

Becerra, Jorge, Peter Mamisch, Bruce Holley, Monish Kumar, Matthias Naumann, Tjun Tang, and Anna Zakrzewski. 2012. *The Battle to Regain Strength: Global Wealth 2012.* The Boston Consulting Group. https://www.bcgperspectives.com/Images/BCG_The_Battle_to_Regain_Strength_May_2012_tcm80-106998.pdf.

Becker, Gary S. 1996. "What Makes the Welfare Bill a Winner." *BusinessWeek* (September 23):22.

Bell, Daniel. 1973. *The Coming of Post-Industrial Society.* New York: Basic Books.

Beller, Emily, and Michael Hout. 2006. "Intergenerational Social Mobility: The United States in Comparative Perspective." *The Future of Children* 16(Fall):19–36.

Bem, Sandra Lipsitz. 1993. *The Lenses of Gender: Transforming the Debate on Sexual Inequality.* New Haven, CT: Yale University Press.

Bennett, H. S. 1969. *Life on the English Manor: A Study of Peasant Conditions, 1150–1400.* Cambridge: Cambridge University Press.

Bennett, W. Lance. 2003. *News: The Politics of Illusion.* 5th ed. New York: Longman.

Benokraitis, Nijole V. 1997. *Subtle Sexism: Current Practice and Prospects for Change.* Thousand Oaks, CA: Sage.

Berger, Peter. 1963. *Invitation to Sociology: A Humanistic Perspective.* New York: Anchor Doubleday.

Bergmann, Barbara R. 1996. *In Defense of Affirmative Action.* New York: Basic Books.

Berlin, Gordon. 2009. "Transforming the EITC to Reduce Poverty and Inequality." *Pathways* (Winter):28–32.

Bernstein, Jared, and Lawrence Mishel. 2000. "Income Picture" (September 26). Washington, DC: Economic Policy Institute.

———. 2004. "Weak Recovery Claims New Victim: Workers' Wages." *EPI Issue Brief #196* (February 5): Washington, DC: Economic Policy Institute.

Berreman, Gerald D. 1961. "Caste in India and the United States." *American Journal of Sociology* 66:510–512.

———. 1966. "Structure and Function of Caste Systems." In *Japan's Invisible Race: Caste in Culture and Personality,* edited by George De Vos and Hiroshi Wagatsuma, 277–307. Berkeley: University of California Press.

Berry, Jeffrey. 1999. *The New Liberalism: The Rising Power of Citizen Groups*. Washington, DC: Brookings Institution.

Bertrand, Marianne, and Kevin F. Hallock. 2000. "The Gender Gap in Top Corporate Jobs." NBER Working Paper No. W7931 (October). Cambridge, MA: National Bureau of Economic Research.

Béteille, André. 1969. *Castes Old and New: Essays in Social Structure and Social Stratification*. Bombay: Asian Publishing Home.

———. 1996. *Caste, Class and Power: Changing Patterns of Stratification in a Tanjore Village*. 2d ed. Delhi: Oxford University Press.

———. 2012. "India's Destiny Not Cast in Stone." *The Hindu* (February 21). http://www.thehindu.com/opinion/lead/article 2913662.ece.

Beyer, Lisa. 1999. "The Price of Honor." *Time* (January 18):55.

Bianchi, Suzanne M., and Daphne Spain. 1996. *Women, Work, and Family in America*. Washington, DC: Population Reference Bureau.

Bittman, Michael, Paula England, Nancy Folbre, Liana Sayer, and George Matheson. 2003. "When Does Gender Trump Money? Bargaining and Time in Household Work." *American Journal of Sociology* 109:186–214.

Bivens, Josh. 2012. "Inequality, Exhibit A: Walmart and the Wealth of American Families." Economic Policy Institute. http://www.epi.org/blog/inequality-exhibit-wal-mart-wealth-american/

Björklund, Anders, Markus Jäntti, and Gary Solon. 2005. "Influences of Nature and Nurture on Earnings Variation." In *Unequal Chances: Family Background and Economic Success*, edited by Samuel Bowles, Herbert Gintis, and Melissa Osborne Groves, 145–164. New York: Russell Sage Foundation.

Blank, Rebecca M. 2006. "What Did the 1990s Welfare Reforms Accomplish?" pp. 33–79 in Alan J. Auerbach, David Card, and John M. Quigley (eds.), *Public Policy and Income Distribution*. New York: Russell Sage Foundation.

Blau, Peter M., and Otis D. Duncan. 1967. *The American Occupational Structure*. New York: John Wiley & Sons.

Blauner, Bob. 1992. "Talking Past Each Other: Black and White Languages of Race." *American Prospect* 10(Summer):55–64.

Block, Fred. 1977. "The Ruling Class Does Not Rule: Notes on the Marxist Theory of the State." *Socialist Review* 7(May–June):6–28.

Bloom, David E., and Adi Brender. 1993. *Labor and the Emerging World Economy*. Washington, DC: Population Reference Bureau.

Bloomberg Businessweek. 2012. Who's Getting the Big Speaker's Fees?" http://images.businessweek.com/ss/08/06/0610_speakers/source/6.htm.

Bluestone, Barry, and Bennett Harrison. 1982. *The Deindustrialization of America*. New York: Basic Books.

———. 2000. *Growing Prosperity: The Battle for Growth with Equity in the Twenty-First Century*. Boston: Houghton Mifflin.

Bobo, Lawrence D., and Camille Z. Charles. 2009. "Race in the American Mind: From the Moynihan Report to the Obama Candidacy." *Annals of the American Academy of Political and Social Science* 621(1):243–259.

Bobo, Lawrence D., and Victor Thompson. 2010. "Racialized Mass Incarceration: Poverty, Prejudice, and Punishment." pp. 322–355 in Hazel R. Markus and Paula Moya (eds.), *Doing Race: 21 Essays for the 21st Century*. New York: Norton.

Borjas, George J. 2001. *Heaven's Door: Immigration Policy and the American Economy.* Princeton, NJ: Princeton University Press.

Bottomore, Tom, and Robert J. Brym (eds.). 1989. *The Capitalist Class: An International Study.* New York: Harvester Wheatsheaf.

Bourdieu, Pierre. 1977. "Cultural Reproduction and Social Reproduction." In *Power and Ideology in Education,* edited by Jerome Karabel and A. H. Halsey, 487–511. New York: Oxford University Press.

———. 1986. "The Forms of Capital." pp. 241–258 in John G. Richardson (ed.), *Handbook of Theory and Research for the Sociology of Education.* Westport, CT: Greenwood Press.

Boushey, Heather. 2002. "'This Country Is Not Woman-Friendly or Child-Friendly': Talking about the Challenge of Moving from Welfare-to-Work." *Journal of Poverty* 6(2):81–115.

———. 2003. "Staying Employed after Welfare." *EPI Briefing Paper.* Washington, DC: Economic Policy Institute.

———. 2011. "Family Time and the Middle Class." *The American Prospect* (March):A18.

Boushey, Heather, and Ann O'Leary (eds.). 2009. *The Shriver Report: A Woman's Nation Changes Everything.* Washington, DC: Center for American Progress.

Bowler, Mary. 1999. "Women's Earnings: An Overview." *Monthly Labor Review* (December):13–21.

Bowles, Samuel, and Herbert Gintis. 1976. *Schooling in Capitalist America: Educational Reform and the Contradictions of Economic Life.* New York: Basic Books.

———. 2002. "Schooling in Capitalist America Revisited." *Sociology of Education* 75:1–18.

Boxer, Charles R. 1962. *The Golden Age of Brazil.* Berkeley: University of California Press.

Brady, Henry E., Kay Lehman Schlozman, Sidney Verba, and Laurel Elms. 2002. "Who Bowls? The(Un) Changing Stratification of Participation." In *Understanding Public Opinion,* 2nd ed. edited by Barbara Norrander and Clyde Wilcox, 243–268. Washington, DC: CQ Press.

Braverman, Harry. 1974. *Labor and Monopoly Capital.* New York: Monthly Review Press.

Brewer, Dominic J., Eric R. Eide, and Ronald G. Ehrenberg. 1999. "Does It Pay to Attend an Elite Private College? Cross-Cohort Evidence on the Effects of College Type on Earnings." *Journal of Human Resources* 34:104–123.

Bricker, Jesse, Arthur B. Kennickell, Kevin B. Moore, and John Sabelhaus. 2012. "Changes in U.S. Family Finances from 2007 to 2010: Evidence from the Survey of Consumer Finances." *Federal Reserve Bulletin* 98 (June):1–80.

Brittain, John A. 1977. *The Inheritance of Economic Status.* Washington, DC: Brookings Institution.

———. 1978. *Inheritance and the Inequality of Material Wealth.* Washington, DC: Brookings Institution.

Brock, David. 2002. *Blinded by the Right: The Conscience of an Ex-Conservative.* New York: Crown Publishers.

Brooks, Geraldine. 1995. *Nine Parts of Desire: The Hidden World of Islamic Women.* New York: Anchor Hardcover.

Brown, Donald E. 1991. *Human Universals.* Philadelphia: Temple University Press.

Brown, Michael, Martin Carnoy, Elliott Currie, Troy Duster, David B. Oppenheimer, Marjorie M. Shultz, and David Wellman. 2003. *Whitewashing Race: The Myth of a Color-Blind Society.* Berkeley: University of California Press.

Bryce, James. 1959. *The American Commonwealth*, vol. II, edited by Louis Hacker. New York: G. P. Putnam's Sons.

Bryner, Sarah McKinnon. 2011. "From Hired Guns to Hired Hands: 'Reverse Revolvers' in the 111th and 112th Congresses." (July 12). Washington, DC: Center for Responsive Politics.

Bucks, Brian K., Arthur B. Kennickell, Traci L. Mach, and Kevin B. Moore. 2011. "Changes in U.S. Family Finances from 2004 to 2007: Evidence from the Survey of Consumer Finances." *Federal Reserve Bulletin* (February):A1–A56.

Bucks, Brian K., Arthur B. Kennickell, and Kevin B. Moore. 2006. "Recent Changes in U.S. Family Finances: Evidence from the 2001 and 2004 Survey of Consumer Finances." *Federal Reserve Bulletin*. (March 22):A1–A38.

Bunkley, Nick. 2009. "Ford among First to Get Loans for More Efficient Cars." *New York Times* (June 23):B3.

Burch, Philip H., Jr. 1980. *Elites in American History. Vol. 3: The New Deal to the Carter Administration*. New York: Holmes and Meier.

Bureau of Labor Statistics. 2008a. *Women in the Labor Force: A Databook*. http://www.bls.gov/cps/wlf-databook2008.htm.

———. 2008b. "Married Parents' Use of Time, 2003–2006." Washington, DC: U.S. Department of Labor.

———. 2011. *Women in the Labor Force: A Databook*. http://www.bls.gov/cps/wli-databook2011.htm.

———. 2012. "Union Members—2011." http://www.bls.gov/news.release/pdf/union2.pdf

Burke, Ronald J., and Mary C. Mattis. 2007. *Women and Minorities in Science, Technology, Engineering and Mathematics: Upping the Numbers*. Northampton, MA: Edward Elgar Publishing.

Burstein, Paul. 2003. "Is Congress Really for Sale?" *Contexts* 2 (Summer):19–25.

Burstein, Paul, and April Linton. 2002. "The Impact of Political Parties, Interest Groups, and Social Movement Organizations on Public Policy." *Social Forces* 81:380–408.

Burton, Lawrence, and Jack Wang. 1999. "How Much Does the U.S. Rely on Immigrant Engineers?" Arlington, VA: Division of Science Resources Studies, National Science Foundation.

Cahill, Larry. 2005. "His Brain, Her Brain." *Scientific American* (May):40–47.

Camarota, Steven A. 2007. "Immigrant Employment Gains and Native Losses, 2000–2004." In *Debating Immigration*, edited by Carol M. Swain, 139–156. New York: Cambridge University Press.

Cancian, Maria, and Sheldon Danziger. 2009. "Changing Poverty and Changing Antipoverty Policies." Institute for Research on Poverty, Discussion Paper no. 1364–09. http://www.irp.wisc.edu.

Cancian, Maria, Marieka M. Klawitter, Daniel R. Meyer, Anu Rangarajan, Geoffrey Wallace, and Robert G. Wood. 2003. "Income and Programs Participation among Early TANF Recipients: The Evidence from New Jersey, Washington, and Wisconsin." *Focus* 22 (Summer):2–10.

Caplan, Nathan, Marcella H. Choy, and John K. Whitmore. 1991. *Children of the Boat People: A Study of Educational Success*. Ann Arbor: University of Michigan Press.

Caplan, Nathan, John K. Whitmore, and Marcella H. Choy. 1989. *The Boat People and Achievement in America*. Ann Arbor: University of Michigan Press.

Caplow, Theodore, and Howard M. Bahr. 1979. "Half a Century of Change in Adolescent Attitudes: Replication of a Middletown Survey by the Lynds." *Public Opinion Quarterly* 43(Spring):1–17.

Card, David. 2009. "Immigration and Inequality." NBER Working Paper No. 14683. Cambridge, MA: National Bureau of Economic Research. http://www.nber.org/papers/w14683.

Carlson, Margaret. 1998. "The Gravy Train Never Stops." *Time* (January 19):14.

Carnevale, Anthony P., and Donna M. Desrochers. 2002. "The Missing Middle: Aligning Education and the Knowledge Economy." Washington, DC: Office of Vocational and Adult Education, U.S. Department of Education.

Carnevale, Anthony P., and Stephen J. Rose. 2003. *Socioeconomic Status, Race/Ethnicity, and Selective College Admissions.* New York: Century Foundation.

Carnoy, Martin, Hugh M. Daley, and Raul Hinajosa Ojeda. 1993. "The Changing Economic Position of Latinos in the U.S. Labor Market since 1939." In *Latinos in a Changing U.S. Economy,* edited by Rebecca Morales and Frank Bonilla, 28–54. Newbury Park, CA: Sage.

Carpiano, Richard M., Bruce G. Link, and Jo C. Phelan. 2008. "Social Inequality and Health: Future Directions for the Fundamental Cause Explanation." In *Social Class: How Does It Work?* Edited by Annette Lareau and Dalton Conley, 232–263. New York: Russell Sage Foundation.

Castles, Stephen, Heather Booth, and Tina Wallace. 1984. *Here for Good: Western Europe's New Ethnic Minorities.* London: Pluto Press.

Castles, Stephen, and Mark J. Miller. 2009. *The Age of Migration: International Population Movements in the Modern World.* 4th ed. New York: Guilford.

Catalyst. 2000. *2000 Catalyst Census of Women Corporate Officers and Top Earners of the Fortune 500.* New York: Catalyst.

———. 2012. "U.S. Women in Business." http://www.catalyst.org/publication/132/us-women-in-business.

Caute, David. 1978. *The Great Fear: The Anti-Communist Purge under Truman and Eisenhower.* New York: Simon & Schuster.

Cave, Damien. 2010. "In Recession, Americans Doing More, Buying Less." *New York Times* (January 3):A14.

Cawthorne, Alexandra. 2009. "Weathering the Storm: Black Men in the Recession." Washington, DC: Center for American Progress.

CBO (Congressional Budget Office). 2011. *Trends in the Distribution of Household Income Between 1979 and 2007.* Washington, DC: Congressional Budget Office.

Center for Responsive Politics. 2000. *Who's Paying for This Election?* Washington, DC: Center for Responsive Politics.

———. 2006. *Business-Labor-Ideology Split in PAC, Soft & Individual Donations to Candidates and Parties.* http://www.opensecrets.org/bigpicture/blio.asp?Cycle=2004&display=Total.

———. 2009. OpenSecrets.org. http://www.opensecrets.org.

———. 2010. "Banking on Connections." http://www.opensecrets.org/news/FinancialRevolvingDoors.pdf.

———. 2011. *OpenSecretsblog.* "Most Members of Congress Enjoy Robust Financial Status, Despite Nation's Sluggish Economic Recovery." (November 15). http://www.opensecrets.org/news/2011/11/congress-enjoys-robust-financial-status.html

———. 2012. *OpenSecrets.* http://www.opensecrets.org.

Chafetz, Janet Saltzman. 1978. *Masculine Feminine or Human?: An Overview of the Sociology of the Gender Roles.* 2d ed. Itasca, IL: F. E. Peacock.

Charles, Camille Z. 2003. "Dynamics of Racial Residential Segregation." *Annual Review of Sociology* 29:167–207.

Charles, Kerwin Kofi, and Erik Hurst. 2003. "The Correlation of Wealth across Generations." *Journal of Political Economy* 111:1155–1182.

Charles, Maria, and David B. Grusky. 2004. *Occupational Ghettos: The Worldwide Segregation of Women and Men.* Palo Alto, CA: Stanford University Press.

Charlson, May E., John P. Allegrante, and Laura Robbins. 1993. "Socioeconomic Differentials in Arthritis and Its Treatment." In *Medical Care and the Health of the Poor,* edited by David E. Rogers and Eli Ginzberg, 77–89. Boulder, CO: Westview.

Chavez, Linda. 1991. *Out of the Barrio: Toward a New Politics of Hispanic Assimilation.* New York: Basic Books.

Cheadle, Jacob E. 2008. "Educational Investment, Family Context, and Children's Math and Reading Growth from Kindergarten through Third Grade." *Sociology of Education* 81:1–31.

Christopher, Robert C. 1989. *Crashing the Gates: The De-WASPing of America's Power Elite.* New York: Simon & Schuster.

Citizens for Tax Justice. 2012. "Who Pays Taxes in America?" http://www.ctj.org

Citrin, Jack. 2008. "Political Culture." In *Understanding America: The Anatomy of an Exceptional Nation,* edited by Peter H. Schuck and James Q. Wilson, 147–180. New York: PublicAffairs.

Clawson, Dan, Alan Neustadtl, and Denise Scott. 1992. *Money Talks: Corporate PACs and Political Influence.* New York: Basic Books.

Clement, Wallace. 1975. *The Canadian Corporate Elite.* Toronto: McLelland & Stewart.

Clement, Wallace, and John Myles. 1994. *Relations of Ruling: Class and Gender in Postindustrial Societies.* Montreal: McGill-Queens University Press.

Coates, David. 1989. "Britain." In *The Capitalist Class: An International Study,* edited by Tom Bottomore and Robert J. Brym, 19–45. New York: Harvester Wheatsheaf.

Cohen, Stanley, and Jock Young, eds. 1973. *The Manufacture of News.* London: Constable.

Cole, Sally, and Lynne Phillips. 2008. "The Violence against Women Campaigns in Latin America: New Feminist Alliances." *Feminist Criminology* 3:145–168.

Coleman, Isobel. 2004. "The Payoff from Women's Rights." *Foreign Affairs* 83(May/June):80–95.

Coleman, James S. 1965. *Education and Political Development.* Princeton, NJ: Princeton University Press.

Coleman, James et al. 1966. *Equality of Educational Opportunity.* Washington, DC: U.S. Government Printing Office.

Coleman, Richard P., and Lee Rainwater. 1978. *Social Standing in America: New Dimensions of Class.* New York: Basic Books.

Collins, Randall. 1971. "A Conflict Theory of Sexual Stratification." *Social Problems* 19:3–21.

Collins, Sharon M. 1997. *Black Corporate Executives: The Making and Breaking of a Black Middle Class.* Philadelphia: Temple University Press.

Comstock, George. 1980. "The Impact of Television on American Institutions." In *Readings in Mass Communication: Concepts and Issues in the Mass Media*. 4th ed, edited by M. Emery and T. C. Smyth, 28–44. Dubuque, IA: Wm. C. Brown.

Conason, Joe, and Gene Lyons. 2000. *The Hunting of the President: The Ten-Year Campaign to Destroy Bill and Hillary Clinton*. New York: St. Martin's.

Congressional Budget Office. 2005. "The Role of Immigrants in the U.S. Labor Market." http://digitalcommons.ilr.cornell.edu/key_workplace/269/

Congressional Digest. 2002. "Welfare Reauthorization: The Debate over the 1995 Reform Continues." 81 (September):193–204.

Conley, Dalton. 2008. "Reading Class between the Lines (of This Volume): A Reflection on Why We Should Stick to Folk Concepts of Social Class." In *Social Class: How Does It Work?* Edited by Annette Lareau and Dalton Conley. 366–373. New York: Russell Sage Foundation.

Cook, Fay Lomax, and Edith J. Barrett. 1992. *Support for the American Welfare State: The Views of Congress and the Public*. New York: Columbia University Press.

Cooper, Kenneth J. 1996. "Women under Virtual House Arrest." *Washington Post* (October 7):A01.

Corak, Miles. 2005. "Principles and Practicalities for Measuring Child Poverty in Rich Countries." Luxembourg Income Study, Working Paper No. 506. http://www. lisproject.org/publications/liswps/406.pdf

———. 2006. "Do Poor Children Become Poor Adults? Lessons from a Cross Country Comparison of Generational Earnings Mobility." IZA Discussion Paper No. 1993. Bonn: Institute for the Study of Labor.

———. 2009. "Chasing the Same Dream, Climbing Different Ladders: Economic Mobility in the United States and Canada." Economic Mobility Project, Pew Charitable Trusts. http://www.economicmobility.org.

———. 2011. "Social Mobility and Social Institutions: Canada in International Perspective." Presentation for CSLS Subscription Series on Living Standards (September 20, 2012). Ottawa, ON. http://www.csls.ca/presentations/CorakPresentation.pdf

Corbett, Christianne, and Catherine Hill. 2012. *Graduating to a Pay Gap: the Earnings of Women and Men One Year after College Graduation*. Washington, DC: AAUW.

Corcoran, Mary. 2001. "Mobility, Persistence, and the Consequences of Poverty for Children: Child and Adult Outcomes." In *Understanding Poverty*, edited by Sheldon H. Danziger and Robert H. Haveman, 127–161. New York: Russell Sage Foundation.

Corcoran, Sean, William N. Evans, Jennifer Godwin, Sheila E. Murray, and Robert M. Schwab. 2004. "The Changing Distribution of Education Finance, 1972 to 1997." In *Social Inequality*, edited by Kathryn M. Neckerman, 433–465. New York: Russell Sage Foundation.

Correll, Shelley J., Stephen Benard, and In Paik. 2007. "Getting a Job: Is There a Motherhood Penalty?" *American Journal of Sociology* 112:1297–1338.

Creel, Liz. 2001. "Domestic Violence: An Ongoing Threat to Women in Latin America and the Caribbean." Population Reference Bureau (October). http://www.prb.org.

Creswell, Julie. 2006. "How Suite It Isn't: A Dearth of Female Bosses." *New York Times* (December 17):BU1, BU9, 10.

Croteau, David. 1995. *Politics and the Class Divide: Working People and the Middle-Class Left*. Philadelphia: Temple University Press.

Current Biography. 1943. "Lana Turner." 4(June):77–79.

D'Addio, Anna Cristina. 2007. "Intergenerational Transmission of Disadvantage: Mobility or Immobility across Generations? A Review of the Evidence for OECD Countries." OECD Social, Employment and Migration Working Papers No. 52. Paris: OECD.

Dahl, Robert A. 1967. *Pluralist Democracy in the U.S.: Conflict and Consensus.* Chicago: Rand McNally.

Dahrendorf, Ralf. 1959. *Class and Class Conflict in Industrial Society.* Stanford, CA: Stanford University Press.

Dale, Stacy Berg, and Alan B. Krueger. 2002. "Estimating the Payoff of Attending a More Selective College: An Application of Selection on Observables and Unobservables." *Quarterly Journal of Economics* 107:1491–1527.

Daniel, Trenton. 2008. "Income Disparity on Miami Beach Is Highest in Nation." *Miami Herald* (December 30). http://www.miamiherald.com/news/top-stories/v-print/story/830748.html.

Danziger, Sheldon, and Peter Gottschalk. 1993. "Introduction." In *Uneven Tides: Rising Inequality in America,* edited by Sheldon Danziger and Peter Gottschalk, 1–18. New York: Russell Sage Foundation.

———. 1995. *America Unequal.* New York: Russell Sage Foundation.

Danziger, Sheldon, and Sandra K. Danziger. 2005. "The U.S. Social Safety Net and Poverty: Lessons Learned and Promising Approaches." Paper presented at the Conference on "Poverty and Poverty Reduction Strategies: Mexican and International Experiences." Monterrey, Mexico.

Dave, Dhaval M., Nancy E. Reichman, and Hope Corman. 2008. "Effects of Welfare Reform on Educational Acquisition of Young Adult Women." NBER Working Paper No. 14466. Cambridge, MA: National Bureau of Economic Research. http://www.nber.org/papers/w14466.pdf.

Davidson, James D., Ralph E. Pyle, and David V. Reyes. 1995. "Persistence and Change in the Protestant Establishment, 1930–1992." *Social Forces* 74:157–175.

Davies, James B., Susanna Sandström, Anthony Shorrocks, and Edward N. Wolff. 2008. "The World Distribution of Household Wealth." Discussion Paper No. 2008/03. United Nations University—World Institute for Development Economics Research.

Davis, David Brion. 1966. *The Problem of Slavery in Western Culture.* Ithaca, NY: Cornell University Press.

Davis, James A., and Tom W. Smith. 1994. *The General Social Surveys: Cumulative Code Book, 1972–1994.* Chicago: National Opinion Research Center.

Davis, Kingsley, and Wilbert E. Moore. 1945. "Some Principles of Stratification." *American Sociological Review* 10:242–249.

Dawson, Richard E., Kenneth Prewitt, and Karen S. Dawson. 1977. *Political Socialization.* 2d ed. Boston: Little, Brown.

De Jouvenel, Bertrand. 1963. *The Pure Theory of Politics.* New Haven, CT: Yale University Press.

Deliège, Robert. 1999. *The Untouchables of India.* (Trans. Nora Scott.) Oxford: Berg.

Derber, Charles. 2005. *Hidden Power: What You Need to Know to Save Our Democracy.* San Francisco: Berrett-Koehler.

De Tocqueville, Alexis. 1966. *Democracy in America.* Edited by J. Mayer and M. Lerner. New York: Harper & Row. (original work published 1840)

DeSipio, Louis. 2006. "Latino Civic and Political Participation." In *Hispanics and the Future of America,* edited by Marta Tienda and Faith Mitchell, 447–479. Washington, DC: National Academies Press.

De Vos, George, and Hiroshi Wagatsuma. 1966. *Japan's Invisible Race: Caste in Culture and Personality.* Berkeley: University of California Press.

Dewan, Shaila, and Robert Gebeloff. 2012. "More Men Enter Fields Dominated by Women." *New York Times* (May 21).

Diamond, Robert S. 1970. "A Self-Portrait of the Chief Executive." *Fortune* 81(May):181, 320–323.

Dillon, Sam. 2006. "Schools Slow in Closing Gaps between Races." *New York Times* (November 20):A1, A21.

———. 2009. "'No Child' Law Is Not Closing a Racial Gap." *New York Times* (April 29):A1, A16.

DiMaggio, Paul, Eszter Hargittai, Coral Celeste, and Steven Shafer. 2004. "Digital Inequality: From Unequal Access to Differentiated Use." In *Social Inequality,* edited by Kathryn M. Neckerman, 355–400. New York: Russell Sage Foundation.

DiMaggio, Paul, Eszter Hargittai, W. Russell Neuman, and John P. Robinson. 2001. "Social Implications of the Internet." *Annual Review of Sociology* 27:307–336.

DiPrete, Thomas A. 2002. "Life Course Risks, Mobility Regimes, and Mobility Consequences: A Comparison of Sweden, Germany, and the United States." *American Journal of Sociology* 108:267–309.

Dobrzynski, Judith H. 1996. "Gaps and Barriers, and Women's Careers." *New York Times* (February 28):C2.

Dohm, Arlene, and Lynn Shniper. 2007. "Occupational Employment Projections to 2016." *Monthly Labor Review* (November):86–125.

Dolbeare, Kenneth. 1974. *Political Change in the U.S.* New York: McGraw-Hill.

Domhoff, G. William. 1967. *Who Rules America?* Englewood Cliffs, NJ: Prentice Hall.

———. 1971. *The Higher Circles.* New York: Vintage.

———. 1974. *The Bohemian Grove.* New York: Harper & Row.

———. 1979. *The Powers That Be.* New York: Vintage.

———. 1983. *Who Rules America Now? A View for the '80s.* Englewood Cliffs, NJ: Prentice Hall.

———. 1993. "The American Power Structure." In *Power in Modern Societies,* edited by Marvin E. Olsen and Martin N. Marger, 170–182. Boulder, CO: Westview.

———. 1998. *Who Rules America? Power and Politics in the Year 2000.* 3d ed. Mountain View, CA: Mayfield.

———. 2010. *Who Rules America? Challenges to Corporate and Class Dominance.* 6th ed. New York: McGraw-Hill.

Dowd, Douglas. 1993. *Of, by, and for Which People? U.S. Capitalist Development since 1776.* Armonk, NY: M. E. Sharpe.

Dugger, Celia W. 1996. "African Ritual Pain: Genital Cutting." *New York Times* (October 5):1, 4.

Duncan, Brian, V. Joseph Hotz, and Stephen J. Trejo. 2006. "Hispanics in the U.S. Labor Market." In *Hispanics and the Future of America,* edited by Marta Tienda and Faith Mitchell, 228–290. Washington, DC: National Academies Press.

Duncan, Greg J., Johanne Boisjoly, and Timothy Smeeding. 1996. "Economic Mobility of Young Workers in the 1970s and 1980s." *Demography* 33:497–509.

Duncan, Greg J., Timothy M. Smeeding, and Willard Rodgers. 1993. "W(h)ither the Middle Class? A Dynamic View." In *Poverty and Prosperity in the USA in the Late Twentieth Century,* edited by Dimitri B. Papadimitriou and Edward N. Wolff, 240–271. London: Macmillan.

Durrheim, Kevin, and John Dixon. 2010. "Racial Contact and Change in South Africa." *Journal of Social Issues* 66:273–288.

Dye, Thomas R. 1995. *Who's Running America: The Clinton Years.* 6th ed. Englewood Cliffs, NJ: Prentice Hall.

———. 2002. *Who's Running America: The Bush Restoration.* 7th ed. Englewood Cliffs, NJ: Prentice Hall.

Dye, Thomas R., and Julie Strickland. 1982. "Women at the Top: A Note on Institutional Leadership." *Social Science Quarterly* 63(June):333–341.

Easterbrook, Gregg. 2004. "Who Needs Harvard?" *The Atlantic* (October): http://www.theatlantic.com/magazine/archive/2004/10/who-needs-harvard/3521/

Economic Policy Institute. 2000. "Wage and Income Trends—Up the Down Escalator." Washington, DC: Economic Policy Institute.

———. 2006. "Economic Snapshots." (May 17). http://www. epi.org/content.cfm/webfeatures_snapshots_20060517.

Edelman, Murray. 1964. *The Symbolic Uses of Politics.* Urbana: University of Illinois Press.

Edelman, Peter. 2012. *So Rich, So Poor: Why It's So Hard to End Poverty in America.* New York: The New Press.

Edsall, Thomas Byrne. 2012. *The Age of Austerity: How Scarcity Will Remake American Politics.* New York: Doubleday.

Ehman, Lee H. 1980. "The American School in the Political Socialization Process." *Review of Educational Research* 50:99–119.

Ehrenreich, Barbara. 1989. *Fear of Falling: The Inner Life of the Middle Class.* New York: HarperPerennial.

———. 2001. *Nickel and Dimed: On (Not) Getting By in America.* New York: Metropolitan Books.

Einhorn, Eric S., and John Logue. 2003. *Modern Welfare States: Scandinavian Politics and Policy in the Global Age.* 2d ed. Westport, CT: Praeger.

Elkins, Stanley M. 1976. *Slavery: A Problem in American Institutional and Intellectual Life.* 3d ed. Chicago: University of Chicago Press.

Engardio, Pete. 2006. "The Future of Outsourcing." *BusinessWeek* (January 30):50–58.

England, Paula. 1992. *Comparable Worth: Theories and Evidence.* New York: Aldine de Gruyter.

Epstein, Aaron. 1996. "Female Lawyers Move Up, Still Face Glass Ceiling." *Detroit Free Press* (January 8):5A.

Epstein, Cynthia Fuchs. 1988. *Deceptive Distinctions: Sex, Gender, and the Social Order.* New Haven, CT: Yale University Press.

Epstein, Edwin Jay. 1974. *News from Nowhere.* New York: Vintage.

Epstein, Edwin M. 1969. *The Corporation in American Politics.* Englewood Cliffs, NJ: Prentice Hall.

Ettlinger, Michael, and Michael Linden. 2012. "The Failure of Supply-Side Economics." Center for American Progress. http://www.americanprogress.org/issues/2012/08/failure_supply_side_econ.html.

European Commission. 2008. Employment, Social Affairs and Equal Opportunities. "European Network Set to Boost Women in Power." (June 2). http://ec.europa.eu

Evans, Peter, Dietrich Rueschemeyer, and Theda Skocpol (eds.). 1985. *Bringing the State Back In.* Cambridge, MA: Cambridge University Press.

Fackler, Martin. 2007. "Career Women in Japan Find a Blocked Path." *New York Times* (August 6):A1, A6.

Farley, Reynolds. 1996. *The New American Reality: Who We Are, How We Got Here, Where We Are Going*. New York: Russell Sage Foundation.

Farrell, Christopher, Ann Therese Palmer, and Seanna Browder. 1998. "A Rising Tide." *BusinessWeek* (August 31):72–75.

Feagin, Joe R., and Clairece Booher Feagin. 1978. *Discrimination American Style: Institutional Racism and Sexism*. Englewood Cliffs, NJ: Prentice Hall.

Featherman, David L., and Robert M. Hauser. 1978. *Opportunity and Change*. New York: Academic Press.

Federman, Maya, Thesia I. Garner, Kathleen Short, W. Boman Cutter IV, John Kiely, David Levine, Duane McGough, and Marilyn McMillen. 1996. "What Does It Mean to Be Poor in America?" *Monthly Labor Review* 119(May):3–17.

Feldman-Jacobs, Charlotte, and Donna Clifton. 2008. *Female Genital Mutilation/Cutting: Data and Trends*. Washington, DC: Population Reference Bureau.

Feller, Avi, and Chuck Marr. 2010. "Tax Rate for Richest 400 Taxpayers Plummeted in Recent Decades, Even as Their Pre-Tax Incomes Skyrocketed." Washington, DC: Center on Budget and Policy Priorities.

Fellowes, Matt. 2006. *From Poverty, Opportunity: Putting the Market to Work for Lower Income Families*. Washington, DC: Brookings Institution.

Ferree, Myra Marx, and Beth B. Hess. 2000. *Controversy and Coalition: The New Feminist Movement across Four Decades of Change*, 3d ed. New York: Routledge.

Ferrie, Joseph P. 2005. "The End of American Exceptionalism? Mobility in the U.S. since 1850." *Journal of Economic Perspectives* 19:199–215.

Figlio, David N. 2005. "Names, Expectations and the Black-White Test Score Gap." NBER Working Paper No. W11195. Cambridge, MA: National Bureau of Economic Research.

Finnegan, William. 2000. "A Slave in New York." *New Yorker* (January 24):50–61.

Fischer, Claude S., Michael Hout, Martin Sanchez Jankowski, Samuel R. Lucas, Ann Swidler, and Kim Voss. 1996. *Inequality by Design: Cracking the Bell Curve Myth*. Princeton, NJ: Princeton University Press.

Fogel, Robert William, and Stanley L. Engerman. 1974. *Time on the Cross*. Boston: Little, Brown.

Forbes. 1988. "The 400 Richest People in America." (October 24):142–320.

———. 1992. "The Richest People in America." (October 19):90–254.

———. 1997. "The Forbes 400." (October 13):147–378.

———. 2009. "The Forbes 400." (October 19).

———. 2012a. "The World's Biggest Public Companies." http://www.forbes.com/global2000/

———. 2012b. "The Forbes 400: The Richest People in America." http://www.forbes.com/forbes-400/

———. 2012c. "The World's Most Powerful Celebrities." http://www.forbes.com/celebrities.

Fordham, Signithia, and John U. Ogbu. 1986. "Black Students' School Success: Coping with the "Burden of 'Acting White.'" *Urban Review* 18:176–206.

Frank, Robert. 2007. *Richistan: A Journey Through the American Wealth Boom and the Lives of the New Rich*. New York: Three Rivers Press.

———. 2011. *The High-Beta Rich: How the Manic Wealthy Will Take Us to the Next Boom, Bubble, and Bust*. New York: Crown.

Frank, Robert H. 2000. "Why Living in a Rich Society Makes Us Feel Poor." *New York Times Magazine* (October 15):62–64.

————. 2005. "How the Middle Class Is Injured by Gains at the Top." In *Inequality Matters: The Growing Economic Divide in America and Its Poisonous Consequences*, edited by James Lardner and David A. Smith, 138–149. New York: New Press.

————. 2009. "Post-Consumer Prosperity." *American Prospect* (April):12–15.

Fraser, Steven, ed. 1995. *The Bell Curve Wars: Race, Intelligence, and the Future of America*. New York: Basic Books.

Fred, Sheryl. 2003. "The Best Defense: A Guide to the Interests Driving the Defense Budget." (October 1). Washington, DC: Center for Responsive Politics.

Fredrickson, George M. 1971. *The Black Image in the White Mind*. New York: Harper & Row.

Free, Lloyd A., and Hadley Cantril. 1968. *The Political Beliefs of Americans*. New York: Simon & Schuster.

Freeman, Jo. 1975. *The Politics of Women's Liberation: A Case Study of an Emerging Social Movement and Its Relation to the Policy Process*. New York: David McKay.

Freeman, Richard B. 1994. "How Labor Fares in Advanced Economies." In *Working under Different Rules*, edited by Richard B. Freeman, 1–28. New York: Russell Sage Foundation.

————. 1999. *The New Inequality: Creating Solutions for Poor America*. Boston: Beacon Press.

————. 2004. "What, Me Vote?" In *Social Inequality*, edited by Kathryn Neckerman, 703–728. New York: Russell Sage Foundation.

————. 2007. *America Works: The Exceptional U.S. Labor Market*. New York: Russell Sage Foundation.

Freeman, Richard B., and Lawrence F. Katz. 1994. "Rising Wage Inequality: The United States vs. Other Advanced Countries." In *Working under Different Rules*, edited by Richard B. Freeman, 29–62. New York: Russell Sage Foundation.

French, Howard W. 2003. "As Japan's Women Move Up, Many Are Moving Out." *New York Times* (March 25):A3.

Frey, William H., Bill Abresch, and Jonathan Yeasting. 2001. *America by the Numbers: A Field Guide to the U.S. Population*. New York: New Press.

Freyre, Gilberto. 1956. *The Masters and the Slaves*. New York: Knopf.

————. 1963. *New World in the Tropics: The Culture of Modern Brazil*. New York: Vintage.

Friedan, Betty. 1963. *The Feminine Mystique*. New York: Norton.

Friedl, Ernestine. 1978. "Society and Sex Roles." *Human Nature* (April):68–75.

Froman, Creel. 1984. *The Two American Political Systems: Society, Economics, and Politics*. Englewood Cliffs, NJ: Prentice Hall.

Fuentes, Annette, and Barbara Ehrenreich. 1983. *Women in the Global Factory*. Boston: South End Press.

Fullerton, Howard N., Jr. 1999. "Labor Force Participation: 75 Years of Change, 1950–1998 and 1998–2025." *Monthly Labor Review* (December):3–12.

Fulwood, Sam, III. 2012. "Race and Beyond: the Death of Affirmative Action." Washington, DC: Center for American Progress (April 3).

Galbraith, John Kenneth. 1992. *The Culture of Contentment*. Boston: Houghton Mifflin.

————. 1994. *A Journey through Economic Time: A Firsthand View*. Boston: Houghton Mifflin.

————. 1996. *The Good Society: The Humane Agenda*. Boston: Houghton Mifflin.

Gans, Herbert J. 1967. "Some Comments on the History of Italian Migration and on the Nature of Historical Research." *International Migration Review* 1:5–9.

————. 1968. *People and Plans: Essays on Urban Problems and Solutions.* New York: Basic Books.

————. 1971. "The Uses of Poverty: The Poor Pay All." *Social Policy* 2:21–23.

————. 1979. *Deciding What's News.* New York: Pantheon.

————. 1988. *Middle American Individualism: The Future of Liberal Democracy.* New York: Free Press.

————. 1994. "Positive Functions of the Undeserving Poor: Uses of the Underclass in America." *Politics and Society* 22(September):270.

————. 1996. "The So-Called Underclass and the Future of Antipoverty Policy." In *Myths about the Powerless: Contesting Social Inequalities,* edited by M. Brinton Lykes et al., 87–101. Philadelphia: Temple University Press.

————. 2003. *Democracy and the News.* New York: Oxford University Press.

Garson, Barbara. 1988. *The Electronic Sweatshop: How Computers Are Transforming the Office of the Future into the Factory of the Past.* New York: Simon & Schuster.

Gautié, Jérôme, and John Schmitt (eds.). 2009. *Low-Wage Work in the Wealthy World.* New York: Russell Sage Foundation.

General Accounting Office (GAO). 2002. *A New Look Through the Glass Ceiling: Where Are the Women?: The Status of Women in Management in Ten Selected Industries* (January). Washington, DC: U.S. General Accounting Office.

————. 2008. *U.S. Multinational Corporations: Effective Tax Rates Are Correlated with Where Income Is Reported.* Report to the Committee on Finance, U.S. Senate. Washington, DC: U.S. Government Printing Office.

Geoghegan, Thomas. 2010. *Were You Born on the Wrong Continent? How the European Model Can Help You Get A Life.* New York: The New Press.

Gerth, Hans, and C. Wright Mills. 1946. *From Max Weber.* New York: Oxford University Press.

Giddens, Anthony. 1975. *The Class Structure of the Advanced Societies.* New York: Harper & Row.

Gilbert, Dennis, and Joseph A. Kahl. 1993. *The American Class Structure: A New Synthesis.* 4th ed. Belmont, CA: Wadsworth.

Gilchrist, Tavia Evans. 2008. "Star Search." *National Journal* (February 16):32–33.

Gilens, Martin. 1999. *Why Americans Hate Welfare: Race, Media, and the Politics of Antipoverty Policy.* Chicago: University of Chicago Press.

————. 2004. "Poor People in the News: Images from the Journalistic Subconscious." In *Class and News,* edited by Don Heider, 44–60. Lanham, MD: Rowman & Littlefield.

————. 2005. "Inequality and Democratic Responsiveness." *Public Opinion Quarterly* 69:778–796.

Gitlin, Todd. 1980. *The Whole World Is Watching.* Berkeley: University of California Press.

————. 2012. *Occupy Nation: The Roots, the Spirit, and the Promise of Occupy Wall Street.* New York: HarperCollins.

Gladwell, Malcolm. 2008. *Outliers: The Story of Success.* New York: Little, Brown.

Glass Ceiling Commission. 1995. *Good for Business: Making Full Use of the Nation's Human Capital.* Washington, DC: U.S. Government Printing Office.

Glass, Jennifer. 2004. "Blessing or Curse?: Work-Family Policies and Mother's Wage Growth Over Time." *Work and Occupations* 31:367–394.

Glater, Jonathan D. 2001. "Women Are Close to Being Majority of Law Students." *New York Times* (March 26):A1, A16.

———. 2008. "Stanford Set to Raise Aid for Students in Middle." *New York Times* (February 21):A12.

Glazer, Nathan. 1975. *Affirmative Discrimination: Ethnic Identity and Public Policy.* New York: Basic Books.

Glenn, Evelyn Nakano, and Roslyn L. Feldberg. 1977. "Degraded and Deskilled: The Proletarianization of Clerical Work." *Social Problems* 25:52–64.

Globe and Mail. 1999. "Only Lower Caste Hindus Clean Up after Cyclone." (November 12):A13.

———. 2002. "Levi's Closes Six U.S. Plants as Sales Continue to Sag." (April 9):B12.

Gold, David A., Clarence Y. H. Lo, and Erik Olin Wright. 1975. "Recent Developments in Marxist Theories of the Capitalist State." Parts 1 and 2. *Monthly Review* 27 (October/November):29–43, 35–51.

Golden, Daniel. 2007. *The Price of Admission: How America's Ruling Class Buys Its Way into Elite Colleges and Who Gets Left Outside the Gates.* New York: Three Rivers Press.

Goldin, Claudia. 1990. *Understanding the Gender Gap: An Economic History of American Women.* New York: Oxford University Press.

Goldsen, Rose K. 1977. *The Show and Tell Machine: How Television Works and Works You Over.* New York: Dell.

Goldthorpe, John. 2008. "Two Oppositions in Studies of Class: A Reflection." In *Social Class: How Does It Work?*, edited by Annette Lareau and Dalton Conley, 350–353. New York: Russell Sage Foundation.

Goldthorpe, John, and Michelle Jackson. 2008. "Education-based Meritocracy: The Barriers to Its Realization." In *Social Class: How Does It Work?*, edited by Annette Lareau and Dalton Conley, 93–117. New York: Russell Sage Foundation.

Gollin, Albert E. 1988. "Media Power: On Closer Inspection, It's Not That Threatening." In *Impacts of Mass Media*, 2d ed., edited by R. E. Hiebert and C. Reuss, 41–44. New York: Longman.

Goodman, Peter S. 2009. "Consumer Thrift in U.S. May Last after Recession." *New York Times* (August 29):A1, A13.

Goodman, Peter S., and Akiko Kashiwagi. 2002. "In Japan, Housewives No More." *Washington Post National Weekly Edition* (November 4–10):18–19.

Goozner, Merrill. 2004. "Higher Skills, Fewer Jobs." *American Prospect* (January): 42–45.

Gordon, Robert J., and Ian Dew-Becker. 2008. "Controversies about the Rise of American Inequality: A Survey." NBER Working Paper No. 13982. Cambridge, MA: National Bureau of Economic Research. http://www.nberworkingpaper13982.org.

Gorman, Elizabeth H. 2005. "Gender Stereotypes, Same Gender Preferences, and Organizational Variation in the Hiring of Women: Evidence from Law Firms." *American Sociological Review* 70:702–728.

Gottschalk, Peter. 1997. "Inequality, Income Growth, and Mobility: The Basic Facts." *Journal of Economic Perspectives* 11(Spring):21–40.

Gottschalk, Peter, and Sheldon Danziger. 1998. "Family Income Mobility—How Much Is There, and Has It Changed?" In *The Inequality Paradox: Growth of Income Disparity*, edited by James A. Auerbach and Richard S. Belous, 92–111. Washington, DC: National Policy Association.

Gould, Elise. 2012. "High-scoring, Low-income Students No More Likely to Complete College than Low-Scoring, Rich Students." *The Economic Policy Institute Blog,* March 9. http://www.epi.org/blog/college-graduation-scores-income-levels/.

Gouldner, Alvin. 1976. *The Dialectic of Ideology and Technology.* New York: Seabury.

Graham, Richard. 1970. "Brazilian Slavery Reexamined: A Review Article." *Journal of Social History* 3:431–453.

Gramsci, Antonio. 1971. *Selections from the Prison Notebooks.* New York: International.

Granovetter, Mark S. 1995 [1974]. *Getting a Job: A Study of Contacts and Careers.* Chicago: University of Chicago Press.

Green, Joshua. 2008. "The Amazing Money Machine." *The Atlantic Online* (June). http://www.theatlantic.com/doc/print/00806/obama-finance.

Green, Mark. 1984. *Who Runs Congress?* 4th ed. New York: Dell.

Greenberg, Edward S., and Benjamin I. Page. 1995. *The Struggle for Democracy.* 2d ed. New York: HarperCollins.

Greenhouse, Steven. 2009. *The Big Squeeze: Tough Times for the American Worker.* New York: Anchor.

Greider, William. 1992. *Who Will Tell the People: The Betrayal of American Democracy.* New York: Touchstone.

Grimes, Michael D. 1991. *Class in Twentieth-Century American Sociology: An Analysis of Theories and Measurement Strategies.* New York: Praeger.

Grimsley, Kirstin Downey. 1996. "No Easy Path to the Top." *Washington Post Weekly Edition* (March 4–10):37.

Groves, Martha. 2008. "Stars Sue over Who May Use A Gate." *Los Angeles Times* (November 20).

Grusky, David B., and Robert M. Hauser. 1984. "Comparative Social Mobility Revisited: Models of Convergence and Divergence in 16 Countries." *American Sociological Review* 49:19–38.

Guetzkow, Joshua, and Bruce Western. 2007. "The Political Consequences of Mass Imprisonment." In *Remaking America: Democracy and Public Policy in an Age of Inequality,* edited by Joe Soss, Jacob S. Hacker, and Suzanne Mettler, 228–242. New York: Russell Sage Foundation.

Gumbel, Peter. 2008. "Big Mac's Local Flavor." *Fortune* (May 5):114–121.

Gwyn, Richard. 1985. *The 49th Paradox: Canada in North America.* Toronto: McClelland and Stewart.

Hacker, Andrew. 1994. "Education: Ethnicity and Achievement." In *Debating Affirmative Action: Race, Gender, Ethnicity, and the Politics of Inclusion,* edited by Nicolaus Mills, 214–229. New York: Delta.

———. 1995. *Two Nations: Black and White, Separate, Hostile, Unequal.* Expanded and updated edition. New York: Ballantine.

Hacker, Jacob S. 2002. *The Divided Welfare State: The Battle over Public and Private Social Benefits in the United States.* Cambridge: Cambridge University Press.

———. 2006. *The Great Risk Shift: The Assault on American Jobs, Families, Health Care, and Retirement and How You Can Fight Back.* New York: Oxford University Press.

———. 2009. "Northern Exposure: Learning from Canada's Response to Winner-Take-All Inequality." *Pathways* (Spring):24–30.

Hacker, Jacob S., and Paul Pierson. 2010. *Winner-Take-All Politics: How Washington Made the Rich Richer—And Turned Its Back on the Middle Class.* New York: Simon & Schuster.

Hacker, Jacob S., Suzanne Mettler, and Dianne Pinderhughes. 2005. "Inequality and Public Policy." In *Inequality and American Democracy: What We Know and What We Need to Learn,* edited by Lawrence R. Jacobs and Theda Skocpol, 156–213. New York: Russell Sage Foundation.

Hacker, Jacob S., Suzanne Mettler, and Joe Soss. 2007. "The New Politics of Inequality: A Policy-Centered Perspective." In *Remaking America: Democracy and Public Policy in an Age of Inequality,* edited by Joe Soss, Jacob S. Hacker, and Suzanne Mettler, 3–23. New York: Russell Sage Foundation.

Haddad, Yvonne Yazbeck, and John L. Esposito (eds.). 1998. *Islam, Gender, and Social Change.* New York: Oxford University Press.

Hamilton, Richard. 1972. *Class and Politics in the U.S.* New York: Wiley.

Hammonds, Keith H. 1997. "Rich School, Poor School: Can We Level the Field?" *BusinessWeek* (October 13):42.

Harrington, Michael. 1962. *The Other America: Poverty in the United States.* New York: Macmillan.

———. 1973. *Socialism.* New York: Bantam.

———. 1976. *The Twilight of Capitalism.* New York: Simon & Schuster.

———. 1984. *The New American Poverty.* New York: Holt, Rinehart and Winston.

Harris, Marvin. 1964. *Patterns of Race in the Americas.* New York: Norton.

———. 1989. *Our Kind.* New York: HarperCollins.

Haskins, Ron. 2006. Testimony before the Committee on Ways and Means, U.S. House of Representatives, July 19.

———. 2009. "Moynihan Was Right: Now What?" *Annals of the American Academy of Political and Social Science* 621(1):281–314.

Hauser, Robert M., Peter J. Dickinson, Harry P. Travis, and John N. Koffel. 1975. "Structural Changes in Occupational Mobility among Men in the United States." *American Sociological Review* 40:585–598.

Hauser, Robert M., and David L. Featherman. 1978. *Opportunity and Change.* New York: Academic Press.

Haveman, Robert, and Timothy Smeeding. 2006. "The Role of Higher Education in Social Mobility." *The Future of Children* 16(Fall):125–150.

Havemann, Judith. 1996. "Aiming for Zero—but Falling Short." *Washington Post* (December 2–8):29–30.

Heath, Rebecca Piirto. 1998. "The New Working Class." *American Demographics* (January):7–15.

Heilbroner, Robert. 1993. *The Making of Economic Society.* 9th ed. Englewood Cliffs, NJ: Prentice Hall.

Heilbroner, Robert, and Lester Thurow. 1981. *Five Economic Challenges.* Englewood Cliffs, NJ: Prentice Hall.

———. 1994. *Economics Explained.* Rev. ed. New York: Touchstone.

Herman, Edward S. 1981. *Corporate Control, Corporate Power.* Cambridge: Cambridge University Press.

Hernandez, Patricia M. 2003. "The Myth of Machismo: An Everyday Reality for Latin American Women." *St. Thomas Law Review* 15:859–882.

Herrnstein, Richard J., and Charles Murray. 1994. *The Bell Curve: Intelligence and Class Structure in American Life.* New York: Free Press.

Hertz, Tom. 2005. "Rags, Riches, and Race: The Intergenerational Economic Mobility of Black and White Families in the United States." In *Unequal Chances: Family Background and Economic Success,* edited by Samuel Bowles,

Herbert Gintis, and Melissa Osborne Groves, 165–191. New York: Russell Sage Foundation.

_____. 2006. "Understanding Mobility in America." Washington, DC: Center for American Progress.

Hertzberg, Hendrik. 2008. "Exhillaration." *New Yorker* (June 23):21–22.

Hess, Robert D., and Judith V. Torney. 1967. *The Development of Political Attitudes in Children.* Chicago: Aldine.

Himelstein, Linda. 1996. "Shatterproof Glass Ceiling." *BusinessWeek* (October 28):55.

_____. 1997. "Breaking Through." *BusinessWeek* (February 17):64–69.

Hindman, Nathaniel Cahners. 2011. "The Highest-Paid Public Speakers." *Huffington Post* (May 25). http://www.huffingtonpost.com/2010/05/25/the-highest-paid-public-s_n_588816.html.

Hinojosa, Raul Ojeda, Albert Jacquez, and Paule Cruz Takash. 2009. "The End of the American Dream for Blacks and Latinos: How the Home Mortgage Crisis Is Destroying Black and Latino Wealth, Jeopardizing America's Future Prosperity and How to Fix It." William C. Velasquez Institute. http://www.wcvi.org/data/pub/ wcvi_whitepaper_housing_june2009.pdf.

Hispanic Business. 2009. "2009 Corporate Elite." (January 28). http://www. HispanicBusiness.com.

Hochschild, Arlie, with Anne Machung. 1989. *The Second Shift: Working Parents and the Revolution at Home.* New York: Viking.

Hochschild, Jennifer L. 1981. *What's Fair? American Beliefs about Distributive Justice.* Cambridge, MA: Harvard University Press.

_____. 1995. *Facing Up to the American Dream: Race, Class, and the Soul of the Nation.* Princeton, NJ: Princeton University Press.

Hochschild, Jennifer L., and Nathan Scovronick. 2003. *The American Dream and the Public Schools.* New York: Oxford University Press.

Hoffman, Donna L., and Thomas P. Novak. 1998. "Bridging the Racial Divide on the Internet." *Science* 280(April 17):390–391.

Holt, Douglas B. 2000. "Postmodern Markets." In *Do Americans Spend Too Much?* Edited by Juliet Schor, 69–74. Boston: Beacon Press.

Holzer, Harry J. 2009. "The Labor Market and Young Black Men: Updating Moynihan's Perspective." *Annals of the American Academy of Political and Social Science* 621 (1):47–69.

Hout, Michael. 2008. "How Class Works: Objective and Subjective Aspects of Class since the 1970s." In *Social Class: How Does It Work?* Edited by Annette Lareau and Dalton Conley, 25–64. New York: Russell Sage Foundation.

Howard, Christopher. 1997. *The Hidden Welfare State: Tax Expenditures and Social Policy in the United States.* Princeton, NJ: Princeton University Press.

Huang, Chye-Ching, and Nathaniel Frentz. 2012. "Bush Tax Cuts Have Provided Extremely Large Benefits to Wealthiest American Over Last Nine Years." Washington, DC: Center on Budget and Policy Priorities.

Huber, Joan. 1990. "Micro-Macro Links in Gender Stratification." *American Sociological Review* 55:1–10.

Huber, Joan, and William H. Form. 1973. *Income and Ideology.* New York: Free Press.

Huff, Daniel D. 1992. "Upside-Down Welfare." *Public Welfare* (Winter):36–40.

Hutner, Frances C. 1986. *Equal Pay for Comparable Worth: The Working Woman's Issue of the Eighties.* New York: Praeger.

Ibrahim, Youssef M. 1996. "Welfare's Snug Coat Cuts Norwegian Cold." *New York Times* (December 13):A1, A8.

Iceland, John. 2009. *Where We Live Now: Immigration and Race in the United States.* Berkeley: University of California Press.

Illa, Hernán Iglesias. 2010. *Miami: Turistas, Colonos y Aventureros En La Última Frontera de América Latina.* Buenos Aires: Planeta/Seix Barral.

Illich, Ivan. 1971. *Deschooling Society.* New York: Harper & Row.

ILO (International Labour Office). 2004. *Breaking through the Glass Ceiling: Women in Management* (Update 2004). Geneva: International Labour Office.

_____. 2012. *Global Estimate of Forced Labour 2012.* Geneva: International Labour Office.

Indian Health Service. 2006. *Facts on Indian Health Disparities.* http://info.ihs.gov/Files/DisparitiesFacts-Jan2006.pdf.

Inhaber, Herbert, and Sidney Carroll. 1992. *How Rich Is Too Rich? Income and Wealth in America.* New York: Praeger.

Institute for Women's Policy Research. 2012. "The Gender Wage Gap by Occupation." IWPR #C350a. http://www.iwpr.org.

Isaacs, Julia B., Isabel V. Sawhill, and Ron Haskins. 2008. *Getting Ahead or Losing Ground: Economic Mobility in America.* Washington, DC: Brookings Institution, Economic Mobility Project.

ISSP (International Social Survey Program). 1999. *ISSP 1999 Inequality Final Questionnaire.* http://www.library.carleton.ca/ssdata/surveys/issp.html.

Iyengar, Shanto, and Donald R. Kinder. 1987. *News That Matters: Television and American Opinion.* Chicago: University of Chicago Press.

Jackman, Mary R. 1994. *The Velvet Glove: Paternalism and Conflict in Gender, Class, and Race Relations.* Berkeley: University of California Press.

Jackman, Mary R., and Robert W. Jackman. 1983. *Class Awareness in the United States.* Berkeley: University of California Press.

Jacobs, Charles, and Mohamed Athie. 1994. "Bought and Sold." *New York Times* (July 13):19.

Jacoby, Russell, and Naomi Glauberman, eds. 1995. *The Bell Curve Debate: History, Documents, Opinions.* New York: Times Books.

Jagsi, Reshma, Kent A. Griffith, Abigail Stewart, Dana Sambuco, Rochelle DeCastro, and Peter A. Ubel. 2012. "Gender Differences in the Salaries of Physician Researchers." *Journal of the American Medical Association* 307:2410–2417.

Jäntti, Markus, Bernt Bratsberg, Knut Roed, Raaum Oddbjörn et al. 2006. "American Exceptionalism in a New Light: A Comparison of Intergenerational Earnings Mobility in the Nordic Countries, the United Kingdom and the United States." IZA Discussion Paper No. 1938. Bonn: Institute for the Study of Labor.

Jehl, Douglas. 1997. "In a Changing Islamic Land, Women Savor Options." *New York Times* (July 20):3.

_____. 1999. "Arab Honor's Price: A Woman's Blood." *New York Times* (June 20):1, 9.

Jencks, Christopher. 1993. *Rethinking Social Policy: Race, Poverty, and the Underclass.* New York: HarperPerennial.

_____. 2004. "Our Unequal Democracy." *American Prospect* (June):A2–A4.

Jencks, Christopher, Joe Swingle, and Scott Winship. 2006. "Welfare Redux." *American Prospect* 17(March):36–40.

Jenkins, Laura D. 1998. "Preferential Policies for Disadvantaged Ethnic Groups: Employment and Education." In *Ethnic Diversity and Public Policy: A Comparative Inquiry*, edited by Crawford Young, 192–235. New York: St. Martin's Press.

Jessim, Lee, and Kent D. Harber. 2005. "Teacher Expectations and Self-Fulfilling Prophecies: Knowns and Unknowns, Resolved and Unresolved Controversies." *Personality and Social Psychology Review* 9:131–155.

Jeter, Jon. 2002. "Struggling for a Meal." *Washington Post National Weekly Edition* (March 4–10):10–11.

Johnson, Dirk. 1994. "Family Struggles to Make Do after Fall from Middle Class." *New York Times* (March 11):A1, A9.

Johnston, David Cay. 2003. *Perfectly Legal: The Covert Campaign to Rig Our Tax System to Benefit the Super Rich—and Cheat Everybody Else*. New York: Portfolio.

———. 2005. "The Great Tax Shift." In *Inequality Matters: The Growing Economic Divide in America and Its Poisonous Consequences*, edited by James Lardner and David A. Smith, 165–177. New York: New Press.

———. 2006. "Tax Benefits to the Rich and Patient." *New York Times* (May 11): C1, C8.

Jones, Jeffrey M. 2005. "Nearly Half of Americans Think U.S. Will Soon Have a Woman President." *Gallup Poll Tuesday Briefing* (October 4):3–4.

Jordan, Winthrop. 1969. *White Over Black*. Baltimore: Penguin.

Josephy, Alvin M., Jr., Joane Nagel, and Troy Johnson. 1999. *Red Power: The American Indians' Fight for Freedom*. Lincoln: University of Nebraska Press.

Judis, John B. 1994. "Why Your Wages Keep Falling." *New Republic* (February 14): 26–29.

Kacapyr, Elia. 1996. "Are You Middle Class?" *American Demographics* (October):30–35.

Kahlenberg, Richard D. 1996. *The Remedy: Class, Race, and Affirmative Action*. New York: Basic Books.

———. 2004. "Toward Affirmative Action for Economic Diversity." *The Chronicle of Higher Education* (March 19). http://chronicle.com Section: The Chronicle Review volume 50, Issue 28, Page B11.

———. 2012. "A New Kind of Affirmative Action Can Ensure Diversity." *The Chronicle of Higher Education* (October 3). http://chronicle.com/article/A-New-Kind-of-Affirmative/134840/?cid=cr&utm_source=cr.

Kahn, Lisa B. 2009. "The Long-Term Labor Market Consequences of Graduating from College in a Bad Economy." http://mba.yale.edu/faculty/pdf/kahn_longtermlabor.pdf.

Kamen, Al. 1998. "A Ticket to Ride." *Washington Post National Weekly Edition* (January 12): 14.

Kane, Thomas J. 2004. "College-Going and Inequality." In *Social Inequality*, edited by Kathryn M. Neckerman, 319–353. New York: Russell Sage Foundation.

Kasarda, John. 1995. "Industrial Restructuring and the Changing Location of Jobs." In *State of the Union: America in the 1990s*, vol. 1, edited by Reynolds Farley, 215–267. New York: Russell Sage Foundation.

Kato, Ryoko. 1989. "Japanese Women: Subordination or Domination?" *International Journal of Sociology of the Family* 19:49–57.

Kaus, Mickey. 1995. *The End of Equality*. 2d ed. New York: Basic Books.

Keister, Lisa A. 2000. *Wealth in America: Trends in Wealth Inequality*. New York: Cambridge University Press.

———. 2005. *Getting Rich: America's New Rich and How They Got That Way*. New York: Cambridge University Press.

Keister, Lisa A., and Stephanie Moller. 2000. "Wealth Inequality in the United States." *Annual Review of Sociology* 26:63–81.

Keller, Suzanne. 1953. "The Social Origins and Career Lines of Three Generations of American Business Leaders." Ph.D. diss., Columbia University.

———. 1963. *Beyond the Ruling Class*. New York: Random House.

Kennedy, Randall. 1994. "Persuasion and Distrust: The Affirmative Action Debate." In *Debating Affirmative Action: Race, Gender, Ethnicity, and the Politics of Inclusion*, edited by Nicolaus Mills, 48–67. New York: Delta.

Kennickell, Arthur B. 2006. *Currents and Undercurrents: Changes in the Distribution of Wealth, 1989–2004*. Washington, DC: Federal Reserve Board. http://www. federalreserve.gov/pubs/feds/2006/200613pap.pdf.

Ketcham, Christopher. 2012. "The New Populists." *American Prospect* (January/ February):10–24.

Key, V. O. 1964. *Public Opinion and American Democracy*. New York: Knopf.

Kilborn, Peter T. 1992. "Lives of Unexpected Poverty in Center of a Land of Plenty." *New York Times* (July 7):A1, A14.

Kim, Illsoo. 1981. *New Urban Immigrants: The Korean Community in New York*. Princeton, NJ: Princeton University Press.

Kim, Marlene. 2012. "Unfairly Disadvantaged?: Asian Americans and Unemployment during and after the Great Recession (2007–10)." Economic Policy Institute Issue Brief #323. http://www.epi.org/publication/ib323-asian-american-unemployment.

Kinsley, Michael. 1991. "Class, Not Race." *The New Republic* (August 19–26):4.

Kirkpatrick, David D. 2007. "Reports Show Wealth as a Common Factor among 2008 Contenders." *New York Times* (May 17):A23.

Kirp, David L. 2009. "Our Two-Class System." *American Prospect* (November): A2–A4.

Klausner, Samuel Z. 1988. *Succeeding in Corporate America: The Experience of Jewish M.B.A.'s*. New York: American Jewish Committee.

Klein, Naomi. 1999. *No Logo: Taking Aim at the Brand Bullies*. New York: Picador.

———. 2008. *The Shock Doctrine: The Rise of Disaster Capitalism*. Toronto: Vintage Canada.

Kluegel, James R., and Eliot R. Smith. 1986. *Beliefs about Inequality: Americans' Views of What Is and What Ought to Be*. New York: Aldine de Gruyter.

Knaus, William A. 1981. *Inside Russian Medicine: An American Doctor's First-Hand Report*. New York: Everest House.

Kochhar, Rakesh, Ana Gonzalez-Barrera, and Daniel Dockterman. 2009. "Through Boom and Bust: Minorities, Immigrants and Homeownership." Washington, DC: Pew Hispanic Center.

Kohut, Andrew, and Bruce Stokes. 2006. *America against the World: How We Are Different and Why We Are Disliked*. New York: Times Books.

Kolenda, Pauline. 1985. *Caste in Contemporary India: Beyond Organic Solidarity*. Prospect Heights, IL: Waveland Press.

Kolko, Gabriel. 1967. *The Triumph of Conservatism*. Chicago: Quadrangle.

Konigsberg, Eric. 1993. "No Hassle." *New Republic* (March 1):21–23.

Koretz, Gene. 1997. "Big Payoffs from Layoffs: How the Largest Downsizers Fared." *BusinessWeek* (February 24):30.

Kotlowitz, Alex. 1991. *There Are No Children Here: The Story of Two Boys Growing Up in the Other America.* New York: Anchor Books.

Kozol, Jonathan. 1991. *Savage Inequalities: Children in America's Schools.* New York: HarperPerennial.

———. 1995. *Amazing Grace: The Lives of Children and the Conscience of a Nation.* New York: Crown.

Kraar, Louis. 1977. "How Lockheed Got Back Its Wings." *Fortune* 96(October):199–210.

Kreimer, Margareta. 2004. "Labour Market Segregation and the Gender-Based Division of Labour." *European Journal of Women's Studies* 11:223–246.

Kristof, Nicholas D. 1996a. "Welfare as Japan Knows It: A Family Affair." *New York Times* (September 10):A1, A10.

———. 1996b. "Do Korean Men Still Beat Their Wives? Definitely." *New York Times* (December 5):A4.

———. 2008. "Need a Job? $17,000 an Hour. No Success Required." *New York Times* (September 18):A33.

Kristof, Nicholas, and Frank Bruni. 2000. "A Son of Politics, George W. Bush, Is Making an Uncommon Rise." *New York Times* (August 3):1, 14.

Krugman, Paul. 2002. "For Richer." *New York Times Magazine* (October 20):62–67, 76, 141–142.

———. 2007. *The Conscience of a Liberal.* New York: Norton.

Kumar, Virendra, and Sarita Kanth. 2004. "Bride Burning." *Lancet* 364, Supplement 1:S18–S19.

Kuttner, Robert. 1996. "Tipping the Income Scales." *Washington Post* (July 1–7):5.

———. 2007. *The Squandering of America: How the Failure of Our Politics Undermines Our Prosperity.* New York: Knopf.

Lacey, Marc. 2008. "A Lifestyle Distinct: The Muxe of Mexico." *New York Times* (December 7) WK4.

Lacy, Karyn R. 2007. *Blue-Chip Black: Race, Class, and Status in the New Black Middle Class.* Berkeley: University of California Press.

Ladd, Everett Carll. 1994. *The American Ideology: An Exploration of the Origins, Meaning, and Role of American Political Ideas.* Storrs, CT: Roper Center for Public Opinion Research.

Ladd, Everett Carll, and Karlyn H. Bowman. 1998. *Attitudes toward Economic Inequality.* Washington, DC: AEI Press.

Landry, Bart. 1987. *The New Black Middle Class.* Berkeley: University of California Press.

Lane, Robert E. 1962. *Political Ideology.* New York: Free Press.

Langton, Kenneth P. 1969. *Political Socialization.* New York: Oxford University Press.

Lannoy, Richard. 1971. *The Speaking Tree: A Study of Indian Culture and Society.* New York: Oxford University Press.

Lareau, Annette. 2003. *Unequal Childhoods: Class, Race, and Family Life.* Berkeley: University of California Press.

Lareau, Annette, and Elliot B. Weininger. 2008. "Class and the Transition to Adulthood." In *Social Class: How Does It Work?* Edited by Annette Lareau and Dalton Conley, 118–151. New York: Russell Sage Foundation.

Lasswell, Harold. 1936. *Politics: Who Gets What, When, How?* New York: McGraw-Hill.

Lau, Gloria, and Tim W. Ferguson. 1998. "Doc's Just an Employee Now." *Forbes* (May 18):162–172.

Lazarsfeld, Paul, Bernard Berelson, and H. Gaudet. 1948. *The People's Choice.* New York: Columbia University Press.

Leach, Edmund. 1967. "Caste, Class and Slavery: The Taxonomic Problem." In *Caste and Race: Comparative Approaches,* edited by Anthony de Reuck and Julie Knight, 5–16. Boston: Little, Brown.

Lee, Sharon M., and Barry Edmonston. 2005. "New Marriages, New Families: U.S. Racial and Hispanic Intermarriage." *Population Bulletin* 60(June):1–36.

Lee, Valerie E., and David T. Burkam. 2002. *Inequality at the Starting Gate: Social Background Differences in Achievement as Children Begin School.* Washington, DC: Economic Policy Institute.

Leibbrandt, Murray, Ingrid Woolard, Arden Finn, and Jonathan Argent. 2010. "Trends in South African Income Distribution and Poverty Since the Fall of Apartheid." OECD Social, Employment and Migration Working Papers No. 101. http://www.oecd.org/els/workingpapers.

Lenski, Gerhard. 1966. *Power and Privilege.* New York: McGraw-Hill.

Leonhardt, David. 2006. "Scant Progress on Closing Gap In Women's Pay." *New York Times* (December 24):1, 18.

———. 2008. "College, What a Deal!" *New York Times Education Life* (April 20): 26–29.

———. 2009. "Sea of Red Ink: How It Spread from a Puddle." *New York Times* (June 10):A1, A18.

Leonhardt, David, and Geraldine Fabrikant. 2009. "After 30-Year Run, Rise of the Super-Rich Hits a Sobering Wall." *New York Times* (August 21):A1, A16.

Lerman, Robert I. 1999. *Retreat or Reform? New U.S. Strategies for Dealing with Poverty.* Washington, DC: Urban Institute.

Lerner, Robert, Althea Nagai, and Stanley Rothman. 1996. *American Elites.* New Haven, CT: Yale University Press.

Levin, Murray. 1971. *Political Hysteria in America.* New York: Basic Books.

Levine. Linda. 2012. "An Analysis of the Distribution of Wealth Across Households, 1989–2010." Washingtin, DC: Congressional Research Service.

Levinson, Mark. 2012. "Mismeasuring—and Its Consequences." *American Prospect* (July–August):42–43.

Levy, Frank. 1995. "Incomes and Income Inequality." In *State of the Union: America in the 1990s. Vol. One: Economic Trends,* edited by Reynolds Farley, 1–58. New York: Russell Sage Foundation.

———. 1998. *The New Dollars and Dreams: American Incomes and Economic Change.* New York: Russell Sage Foundation.

Levy, Frank, and Peter Temin. 2007. "Inequality and Institutions in 20th Century America." NBER Working Paper 13106. Cambridge, MA: National Bureau of Economic Research.

Lewis, Hylan. 1967. "The Family: Resources for Change." In *The Moynihan Report and the Politics of Controversy,* edited by Lee Rainwater and William L. Yancey, 314–343. Cambridge, MA: MIT Press.

Lewis, John. 1972. *The Marxism of Marx.* London: Lawrence and Wishart.

Lewis, Oscar. 1961. *The Children of Sanchez.* New York: Random House.

———. 1965. *La Vida.* New York: Random House.

———. 1966. "The Culture of Poverty." *Scientific American* 215(October): 19–25.

Lie, John. 2001. *Multiethnic Japan.* Cambridge, MA: Harvard University Press.

Lieberson, Stanley. 1961. "A Societal Theory of Race Relations." *American Sociological Review* 26:902–910.

Light, Ivan, and Edna Bonacich. 1988. *Immigrant Entrepreneurs: Koreans in Los Angeles, 1965–1982.* Berkeley: University of California Press.

Lin, Ann Chih, and David R. Harris, eds. 2008. *The Colors of Poverty: Why Racial and Ethnic Disparities Exist.* New York: Russell Sage Foundation.

Lindblom, Charles E. 1978. "The Business of America Is Still Business." *New York Times* (January 4):A19.

Linden, Michael. 2012. "The Federal Tax Code and Income Inequality: How Federal Tax Policy Changes Have Affected and Will Affect Income Inequality." Washington, DC: Center for American Progress.

Linton, Ralph. 1936. *The Study of Man.* New York: Appleton-Century-Crofts.

Lippmann, Walter. 1922. *Public Opinion.* New York: Macmillan.

Lipset, Seymour Martin. 1963. *The First New Nation: The United States in Historical and Comparative Perspective.* New York: Basic Books.

———. 1996. *American Exceptionalism: A Double-Edged Sword.* New York: Norton.

Lipset, Seymour Martin, and Reinhard Bendix. 1959. *Social Mobility in Industrial Society.* Berkeley: University of California Press.

Lipsyte, Robert. 1996. "Knight: Can a Logo Conquer All?" *New York Times* (February 7):B7.

Litt, Edgar. 1963. "Civic Education, Community Norms, and Political Indoctrination." *American Sociological Review* 28:69–75.

Locke, John. 1960 [1690]. "Two Treatises of Government." In *Great Political Thinkers.* 3d ed., edited by W. Ebenstein, 393–413. New York: Rinehart.

Logan, John, Brian Stults, and Reynolds Farley. 2004. "Segregation of Minorities in the Metropolis: Two Decades of Change." *Demography* 41:1–22.

Lohr, Steve. 2006. "Outsourcing Is Climbing Skills Ladder." *New York Times* (February 16): C1, C17.

Lopez, Mark Hugo, Gretchen Livingston, and Rakesh Kochhar. 2009. "Hispanics and the Economic Downturn: Housing Woes and Remittance Cuts." Washington, DC: Pew Hispanic Center.

López-Pintor, Rafael and Maria Gratschew. 2002. "Voter Turnout Rates from a Comparative Perspective." In *Voter Turnout since 1945: A Global Report,* 75–94. Stockholm: International Institute for Democracy and Electoral Assistance.

Lopez, Steve. 2005. "Demons Are Winning on Skid Row." *Los Angeles Times* (October 16):A1, A35.

Loprest, Pamela, and Austin Nichols. 2011. *Dynamics of Being Disconnected from Work and TANF.* Washington, DC: Urban Institute.

Lorber, Judith. 1994. *Paradoxes of Gender.* New Haven, CT: Yale University Press.

———. 1995. "The Social Construction of Gender." In *Race, Class, and Gender in the United States: An Integrated Study.* 3d ed., edited by Paula S. Rothenberg, 33–45. New York: St. Martin's.

———. 2005. *Gender Inequality: Feminist Theories and Politics.* 3d ed. Los Angeles: Roxbury.

Loury, Glenn. 1997. "How to Mend Affirmative Action." *Public Interest* (Spring): 33–43.

Lowenstein, Roger. 1995. *Buffett: The Making of an American Capitalist.* New York: Random House.

———. 2006. "The Immigration Equation." *New York Times Magazine* (July 9):18–24.

Lucas d'Oliveira, Ana Flávia Pires, and Lilia Blima Schraiber. 2005. "Violence against Women in Brazil: Overview, Gaps and Challenges." Paper presented at UN Division for the Advancement of Women, Geneva, Switzerland (April).

Ludwig, Jens, and Susan Mayer. 2006. "'Culture' and the Intergenerational Transmission of Poverty: The Prevention Paradox." *The Future of Children* 16(Fall): 175–196.

Lyman, Rick. 1998. "Scene One: A Fire Escape." *New York Times* (February 13):B1, B14.

Lynd, Robert, and Helen Lynd. 1929. *Middletown.* New York: Harcourt, Brace and Co.

Lynn, Richard, and Tatu Vanhanen. 2002. *IQ and the Wealth of Nations.* Westport, CT: Praeger.

MacKinnon, Mark. 2006. "For Kuwaiti Women, A Vote of Confidence." *Globe and Mail* (June 24):A19.

Magnet, Myron. 1993. *The Dream and the Nightmare: The Sixties Legacy to the Underclass.* New York: William Morrow.

Makinson, Larry. 2003. *Speaking Freely: Washington Insiders Talk about Money in Politics.* 2d ed. Washington, DC: Center for Responsive Politics.

Mann, Michael. 1970. "The Social Cohesion of Liberal Democracy." *American Sociological Review* 35:423–439.

Mann, Thomas E., and Norman J. Ornstein. 2012. *It's Even Worse than It Looks: How the American Constitutional System Collided with the New Politics of Extremism.* New York: Basic Books.

Mannheim, Karl. 1936. *Ideology and Utopia.* New York: Harcourt, Brace and World.

Manza, Jeff, and Clem Brooks. 2008. "Class and Politics." In *Social Class: How Does It Work?* Edited by Annette Lareau and Dalton Conley, 201–231. New York: Russell Sage Foundation.

Maraniss, David. 1995. *First in His Class: A Biography of Bill Clinton.* New York: Simon & Schuster.

Marger, Martin N. 1987. *Elites and Masses: An Introduction to Political Sociology.* 2nd ed. Belmont, CA: Wadsworth.

————. 1993. "The Mass Media as a Power Institution." In *Power in Modern Societies,* edited by Marvin E. Olsen and Martin N. Marger, 238–249. Boulder, CO: Westview.

————. 2012. *Race and Ethnic Relations: American and Global Perspectives.* 9th ed. Belmont, CA: Wadsworth.

Marks, Jonathan. 1995. *Human Biodiversity: Genes, Race, and History.* New York: Aldine de Gruyter.

Marsden, Peter, and Joseph Swingle. 1994. "Conceptualizing and Measuring Culture in Surveys." *Poetics* 22:269–289.

Marshall, Katherine. 2006. "Converging Gender Roles." *Perspectives on Labour and Income* 7(July):5–17.

Marx, Karl. 1920. *The Poverty of Philosophy.* Chicago: H. Kerr.

Marx, Karl, and Friedrich Engels. 1968. *Selected Works in One Volume.* New York: International.

Mason, Christopher. 1996. "West of Eden." *New York* (September 2):20–27.

Mason, Philip. 1970. *Patterns of Dominance.* London: Oxford University Press.

Massey, Douglas S. 2001. "Residential Segregation and Neighborhood Conditions in U.S. Metropolitan Areas." In *America Becoming: Racial Trends and Their Consequences*, vol. 1, edited by Neil J. Smelser, William Julius Wilson, and Faith Mitchell, 391–434. Washington, DC: National Academy Press.

———. 2007. *Categorically Unequal: The American Stratification System*. New York: Russell Sage Foundation.

Massey, Douglas S., Camille Z. Charles, Garvey F. Lundy, and Mary J. Fischer. 2003. *The Source of the River: The Social Origins of Freshmen at America's Selective Colleges and Universities*. Princeton, NJ: Princeton University Press.

Massey, Douglas S., and Nancy A. Denton. 1993. *American Apartheid: Segregation and the Making of the Underclass*. Cambridge, MA: Harvard University Press.

Matthews, Donald. 1954. *The Social Background of Political Decision-Makers*. New York: Doubleday.

———. 1973. *U.S. Senators and Their World*. New York: Norton.

Mayer, Kurt B. 1955. *Class and Society*. Rev. ed. New York: Random House.

Mayer, Susan. 1995. "A Comparison of Poverty and Living Conditions in the United States, Canada, Sweden, and Germany." In *Poverty, Inequality and the Future of Social Policy: Western States in the New World Order*, edited by Katherine McFate, Roger Lawson, and William Julius Wilson, 109–151. New York: Russell Sage Foundation.

Mazumder, Bhashkar. 2005. "The Apple Falls Even Closer to the Tree Than We Thought: New and Revised Estimates of the Intergenerational Inheritance of Earnings." In *Unequal Chances: Family Background and Economic Success*, edited by Samuel Bowles, Herbert Gintis, and Melissa Osborne Groves, 80–99. New York: Russell Sage Foundation.

McChesney, Robert W. 1999. *Rich Media, Poor Democracy: Communication Politics in Dubious Times*. New York: New Press.

McClendon, McKee J. 1977. "Structural and Exchange Components of Vertical Mobility." *American Sociological Review* 42:56–74.

McClosky, Herbert, and John Zaller. 1984. *The American Ethos: Public Attitudes toward Capitalism and Democracy*. Cambridge, MA: Harvard University Press.

McCombs, Maxwell. 2004. *Setting the Agenda: The Mass Media and Public Opinion*. Cambridge: Polity Press.

McCombs, Maxwell, and Donald Shaw. 1972. "The Agenda-Setting Function of Mass Media." *Public Opinion Quarterly* 36:176–187.

McConnell, Sheila. 1996. "The Role of Computers in Reshaping the Work Force." *Monthly Labor Review* 119(August):3–5.

McMillan, Tracie. 2008. "Looks Good on Paper: With Welfare-to-Work, Presentation Is Everything." *Harper's* (August):46–49.

McMurrer, Daniel P., and Isabel V. Sawhill. 1998. *Getting Ahead: Economic and Social Mobility in America*. Washington, DC: Urban Institute Press.

McNamee, Stephen J., and Robert K. Miller, Jr. 1998. "Inheritance and Stratification." In *Inheritance and Wealth in America*, edited by Robert K. Miller, Jr., and Stephen J. McNamee, 193–213. New York: Plenum Press.

McWhorter, John H. 2000. *Losing the Race: Self-Sabotage in Black America*. New York: Free Press.

Mead, Lawrence M. 1992. *The New Politics of Poverty: The Nonworking Poor in America*. New York: Basic Books.

———. 1996. "Work Requirements Can Transform the System." *Chronicle of Higher Education* (October 4):B6, B7.

Mead, Walter Russell. 1998. "The New Global Economy Takes Your Order." *Mother Jones* (March/April):32–41.

Meeks, Kenneth. 2005. "The Most Powerful African Americans in Corporate America." *Black Enterprise* (February):104–142.

Meltzer, Milton. 1971. *Slavery: From the Rise of Western Civilization to the Renaissance.* New York: Cowles.

Merelman, Richard M. 2003. *Pluralism at Yale: The Culture of Political Science in America.* Madison, WI: University of Wisconsin Press.

Merton, Robert K. 1949. "Discrimination and the American Creed." In *Discrimination and National Welfare,* edited by R. H. MacIver, 99–126. New York: Harper & Row.

Mettler, Suzanne. 2007. "The Transformed Welfare State and the Redistribution of Political Voice." In *The Transformation of American Politics: Activist Government and the Rise of Conservatism,* edited by Paul Pierson and Theda Skocpol, 191–222. Princeton, NJ: Princeton University Press.

Meyer, Daniel R., and Geoffrey L. Wallace. 2009. "Poverty Levels and Trends in Comparative Perspective." *Focus* 26(2):7–13.

Meyersson Milgrom, Eva M., and Trond Petersen. 2006. "The Glass Ceiling in the United States and Sweden: Lessons from the Family-Friendly Corner of the World, 1970 to 1990." In *The Declining Significance of Gender?* Edited by Francine D. Blau, Mary C. Brinton, and David B. Grusky, 156–211. New York: Russell Sage Foundation.

Michels, Robert. 1962 [1915]. *Political Parties.* Translated by Eden and Cedar Paul. New York: Free Press.

Michaels, Walter Benn. 2006. *The Trouble with Diversity: How We Learned to Love Identity and Ignore Inequality.* New York: Metropolitan Books.

Miezkowski, Katherine. 2003. "White-Collar Sweatshops." *Salon* (July 2). http://www.salon.com/tech/feature/2003/07/02/outsourcing

Migration Policy Institute. 2006. *Immigration and America's Future: A New Chapter. Report of the Independent Task Force on Immigration and America's Future.* Washington, DC: Migration Policy Institute.

Miko, Francis T., and Grace (Jea-Hyun) Park. 2002. "Trafficking in Women and Children: The U.S. and International Response." Washington, DC: Congressional Research Service.

Milbrath, Lester, and M. L. Goel. 1982. *Political Participation: How and Why Do People Get Involved in Politics.* Washington, DC: University Press of America.

Miliband, Ralph. 1969. *The State in Capitalist Society.* New York: Basic Books.

Mills, C. Wright. 1951. *White Collar.* New York: Oxford University Press.

———. 1956. *The Power Elite.* New York: Oxford University Press.

———. 1959. *The Sociological Imagination.* New York: Oxford University Press.

———. 1962. *The Marxists.* New York: Dell.

Milner, Murray, Jr. 1972. *The Illusion of Equality.* San Francisco: Jossey-Bass.

Mishel, Lawrence. 2012a. "The Wedges between Productivity and Median Compensation Growth." Washington, DC: Economic Policy Institute.

———. 2012b. "Confirming the Further Redistribution of Wealth Upward." Economic Policy Institute. http://www.epi.org/blog/confirming-redistribution-wealth-upward/

———. 2012c. "Unions, Inequality, and Faltering Middle-Class Wages." Economic Policy Institute. Issue Brief #342. Washington, DC: Economic Policy Institute.

———. 2012d. "Women Much More Likely to Earn Poverty-Level Wages." Economic Policy Institute. http://www.epi.org/publication/women-earn-poverty-level-wages/

Mishel, Lawrence, and Jared Bernstein. 1993. *The State of Working America, 1992–1993*. Armonk, NY: M. E. Sharpe.

Mishel, Lawrence, and Natalie Sabadish. 2012. "CEO Pay and the Top 1%." Washington, DC: Economic Policy Institute.

Mishel, Lawrence, Jared Bernstein, and Heidi Shierholz. 2009. *The State of Working America, 2008/2009*. Ithaca: Cornell University Press.

Mishel, Lawrence, Jared Bernstein, and Sylvia Allegretto. 2005. *The State of Working America, 2004/2005*. Ithaca, NY: Cornell University Press.

Mishel, Lawrence, Josh Bivens, Elise Gould, and Heidi Shierholz. 2012. *The State of Working America*. 12th ed. Washington, DC: Economic Policy Institute.

Mitchell, Alanna. 2001. "Girl's Murder a Turning Point." *Globe and Mail* (January 11):A4.

Moll, Luis C., and Richard Ruiz. 2002. "The Schooling of Latino Children." In *Latinos: Remaking America*, edited by Marcelo M. Suárez-Orozco and Mariela M. Páez, 362–372. Berkeley: University of California Press.

Moncarz, Roger J., Michael G. Wolf, and Benjamin Wright. 2008. "Service-Providing Occupations, Offshoring, and the Labor Market." *Monthly Labor Review* 131 (December):71–86.

Montagu, Ashley. 1972. *Statement on Race*. 3d ed. New York: Oxford University Press.

———. 1974. *Man's Most Dangerous Myth: The Fallacy of Race*. 5th ed. New York: Oxford University Press.

Moore, David W. 2005. "Gender Stereotypes Prevail on Working Outside the Home." *Gallup Poll Tuesday Briefing* (August 17):109–110.

Moore, Gwen. 1988. "Women in Elite Positions." *Sociological Forum* 3:566–585.

Moore, Stephen, and Dean Stansel. 1995. *Ending Corporate Welfare as We Know It*. Washington, DC: Cato Institute.

Morgan, Laurie A. 1998. "Glass Ceiling Effect or Cohort Effect? A Longitudinal Study of the Gender Earnings Gap for Engineers, 1982 to 1989." *American Sociological Review* 633:479–493.

Morin, Rich. 2012. "Rising Share of Americans See Conflict Between Rich and Poor." Washington, DC: Pew Research Center.

Morin, Richard. 1996. "Tuned Out, Turned Off." *Washington Post Weekly Edition* (February 5–11):6–8.

———. 1997. "Aging with an Attitude." *Washington Post* (June 9):35.

Morisi, Teresa L. 1996. "Commercial Banking Transformed by Computer Technology." *Monthly Labor Review* 119(August):30–36.

Morris, Michael. 1996. "Culture, Structure, and the Underclass." In *Myths about the Powerless: Contesting Social Inequalities*, edited by M. B. Lykes, A. Banuazizi, R. Liem, and M. Morris, 34–49. Philadelphia: Temple University Press.

Mossberger, Karen, Caroline J. Tolbert, and Ramona S. McNeal. 2008. *Digital Citizenship: The Internet, Society, and Participation*. Cambridge, MA: MIT Press.

Mullaby, John, Stephanie Robert, and Barbara Wolfe. 2004. "Health, Income, and Inequality." In *Social Inequality,* edited by Kathryn M. Neckerman, 523–544. New York: Russell Sage Foundation.

Muller, Thomas. 1993. *Immigrants and the American City.* New York: New York University Press.

Murdock, George Peter. 1937. "Comparative Data and the Division of Labor by Sex," *Social Forces* 15:551–555.

Murr, Andrew. 1997. "'Didn't Seem Like Much.'" *Newsweek* (December 1):37.

Murray, Charles. 1984. *Losing Ground: American Social Policy 1950–1980.* New York: Basic Books.

———. 2008. "Poverty and Marriage, Income Inequality and Brains." *Pathways* (Winter):21–24.

———. 2012. *Coming Apart: The State of White America, 1960–2010.* New York: Crown Forum.

Murray, Robert K. 1955. *Red Scare: A Study in National Hysteria, 1919–1920.* Minneapolis: University of Minnesota Press.

Nanda, Serena. 1990. *Neither Man nor Woman: The Hijras of India.* Belmont, CA: Wadsworth.

Nasar, Sylvia. 1992. "Those Born Wealthy or Poor Usually Stay So, Studies Say." *New York Times* (May 18):A1, C7.

Nash, Manning. 1962. "Race and the Ideology of Race." *Current Anthropology* 3: 285–288.

Nash, Nathaniel C. 1995. "Europeans Shrug as Taxes Go Up." *New York Times* (February 16):A4.

National Conference. 1995. *Taking America's Pulse: A Summary Report of the National Conference Survey on Inter-Group Relations.* New York: National Conference.

NCES (National Center for Education Statistics). 2011. *Digest of Education Statistics 2010.* Washington, DC: U.S. Department of Education.

Newcomer, Mabel. 1955. *The Big Business Executive.* New York: Columbia University Press.

Newman, Katherine. 1993. *Declining Fortunes: The Withering of the American Dream.* New York: Basic Books.

———. 1999. *Falling from Grace: Downward Mobility in the Age of Affluence.* Berkeley: University of California Press.

Newman, Katherine S., and Victor Tan Chen. 2007. *The Missing Class: Portraits of the Near Poor in America.* Boston: Beacon Press.

New York State Assembly. 2008. *"The House That You Built": An Interim Report into the Decision by New York City to Subsidize the New Yankee Stadium.* Albany.

New York Times. 2005. "The *New York Times* Poll on Class." In Correspondents of the *New York Times, Class Matters,* 244–267. New York: Times Books.

———. 2007. "Buffett Says the Estate Tax Would Be a Gift to the Rich." *New York Times* (November 15):C8.

———. 2012. "Campaign Finance (Super PACs)." (July 8). http://topics.nytimes.com/top/reference/timestopics/subjects/c/campaign_finance/index.html.

Nielsen, Joyce McCarl. 1990. *Sex and Gender in Society: Perspectives on Stratification.* 2d ed. Prospect Heights, IL: Waveland Press.

Niemi, Richard G., and Barbara I. Sobieszek. 1977. "Political Socialization." In *Annual Review of Sociology*, vol. 3, edited by A. Inkeles, 209–233. Palo Alto, CA: Annual Reviews.

Nieves, Evelyn. 2006. "Skid Row Makeover." *Salon.com* (August 8). http://www.salon.com/news/feature/2006/08/08/skid_row/print.html.

———. 2007. "Indian Reservation Reeling in Wave of Youth Suicides and Attempts." *New York Times* (June 9):A9.

Nisbett, Richard E. 2009. *Intelligence and How to Get It: Why Schools and Culture Count*. New York: Norton.

Noah, Timothy. 2012. *The Great Divergence: America's Growing Inequality Crisis and What We Can Do About It*. New York: Bloomsbury Press.

Noble, Charles. 1997. *Welfare as We Knew It: A Political History of the American Welfare State*. New York: Oxford University Press.

Noel, Donald L. 1968. "A Theory of the Origin of Ethnic Stratification." *Social Problems* 16:157–172.

Norton, Stephen J. 2005. "'Big Sugar' Finds CAFTA Too Bitter to Swallow." *CQ Weekly* (June 20):1624–1625.

Nozick, Robert. 1974. *Anarchy, State, and Utopia*. New York: Basic Books.

O'Brien, Timothy L. 2006. "Up the Down Staircase." *New York Times* (March 19): 1BU, 4BU.

OECD (Organization for Economic Cooperation and Development). 2001. *Trends in International Migration: Annual Report*. Paris: OECD.

———. 2009. *The OECD Social Institutions and Gender Index*. http://www.oecd.org/dev/gender/sigi.

———. 2011. *Society at a Glance: OECD Social Indicators*. Paris: OECD.

———. 2012. *OECD Tax Database*. Paris: OECD. http://www.oecd.org/ctp/taxdatabase.

Ogasawara, Yuko. 2004. "The Japanese Paradox: Women's Voices of Fulfillment in the Face of Inequalities." In *Social Inequalities in Comparative Perspective*, edited by Fiona Devine and Mary C. Waters, 237–256. Malden, MA: Blackwell.

Ogmundson, Rick. 1999. "Perspectives on the Class Origins of Canadian Elites: A Methodological Critique of the Porter/Clement Tradition." In *Debates on Social Inequality: Class, Gender, and Ethnicity in Canada*, edited by M. Reza Nakhaie, 89–97. Toronto: Harcourt Brace Canada.

Oliver, Melvin L., and Thomas M. Shapiro. 1995. *Black Wealth/White Wealth: A New Perspective on Racial Inequality*. New York: Routledge.

Olsen, Marvin E. 1973. "A Model of Political Participation Stratification." *Journal of Political and Military Sociology* 1:183–200.

———. 1982. *Participatory Pluralism*. Chicago: Nelson-Hall.

Onishi, Norimitsu. 2009. "Japan's Outcasts Still Wait for Acceptance." *New York Times* (January 16):A1, A6.

Orshansky, Mollie. 1969. "How Poverty Is Measured." *Monthly Labor Review* 92 (February):12–19.

Osberg, Lars, and Timothy Smeeding. 2006. "'Fair' Inequality? Attitudes toward Pay Differentials: The United States in Comparative Perspective." *American Sociological Review* 71:450–473.

Ossowski, Stanislaw. 1963. *Class Structure in the Social Consciousness*. New York: Free Press.

O'Toole, James, and Edward E. Lawler III. 2006. *The New American Workplace.* New York: Palgrave Macmillan.

Page, Benjamin I., and Lawrence R. Jacobs. 2009. *Class War? What Americans Really Think about Economic Inequality.* Chicago: University of Chicago Press.

Page, Benjamin I., and Robert Y. Shapiro. 1992. *The Rational Public: Fifty Years of Trends in Americans' Policy Preferences.* Chicago: University of Chicago Press.

Pager, Devah, and Diana Karafin. 2009. "Bayesian Bigot? Statistical Discrimination, Stereotypes, and Employer Decision Making." *Annals of the American Academy of Political and Social Science* 621:70–93.

Paletz, David L., and Robert M. Entman. 1981. *Media Power Politics.* New York: Free Press.

Pallais, Amanda, and Sarah E. Turner. 2007. "Access to Elites." In *Economic Inequality and Higher Education: Access, Persistence, and Success,* edited by Stacy Dickert-Conlin and Ross Rubenstein, 128–156. New York: Russell Sage Foundation.

Pammett, Jon H. 1996. "Getting Ahead around the World." In *Social Inequality in Canada,* edited by Alan Frizzell and Jon H. Pammett, 67–86. Ottawa: Carleton University Press.

Pappas, Ben. 1997. "Cathedrals to Sunglasses and Other Fantasies of the Very Rich." *Fortune* (October 13):53–57.

Parenti, Michael. 1986. *Inventing Reality: The Politics of the Mass Media.* New York: St. Martin's.

Parikh, Sunita. 2001. "Affirmative Action, Caste, and Party Politics in Contemporary India." In *Color Lines: Affirmative Action, Immigration, and Civil Rights Options for America,* edited by John D. Skrentny, 297–312. Chicago: University of Chicago Press.

Parker, Richard G. 1991. *Bodies, Pleasures, and Passions: Sexual Culture in Contemporary Brazil.* Boston: Beacon.

Parkin, Frank. 1971. *Class Inequality and Political Order.* New York: Praeger.

Parsons, Talcott. 1953. "A Revised Analytical Approach to the Theory of Social Stratification." In *Class, Status and Power,* edited by R. Bendix and S. M. Lipset, 92–128. Glencoe, IL: Free Press.

Parsons, Talcott, and Robert F. Bales. 1955. *Family Socialization and Interaction.* Glencoe, IL: Free Press.

Pasternak, Judy. 2001. "Bush's Energy Plan Bares Industry Clout." *Los Angeles Times* (August 26):A1, A22.

Patel, Aakar. 2012. "Why Caste Persists in Politics." *The Hindu* (February 28). http://www.thehindu.com/opinion/op-ed/why-caste-persists-in-politics/article2939240.ece

Patterson, Orlando. 1978. "Inequality, Freedom, and the Equal Opportunity Doctrine." In *Equality and Social Policy,* edited by Walter Feinberg, 15–41. Urbana: University of Illinois Press.

———. 1982. *Slavery and Social Death: A Comparative Study.* Cambridge, MA: Harvard University Press.

———. 1995. "The Paradox of Integration." *New Republic* (November 6):24–27.

———. 1997. *The Ordeal of Integration: Progress and Resentment in America's "Racial" Crisis.* Washington, DC: Civitas/Counterpoint.

———. 1998. "Affirmative Action: Opening Up Workplace Networks to Afro-Americans." *Brookings Review* (Spring):17–23.

_____. 2008. "Black Americans." In *Understanding America: The Anatomy of an Exceptional Nation*, edited by Peter H. Schuck and James Q. Wilson, 375–410. New York: Public Affairs.

Pattillo, Mary. 1999. *Black Picket Fences: Privilege and Peril among the Black Middle Class*. Chicago: University of Chicago Press.

Paxton, Pamela, Melanie M. Hughes, and Jennifer L. Green. 2006. "The International Women's Movement and Women's Political Representation, 1893–2003." *American Sociological Review* 71:898–920.

Pear, Robert. 1997. "Academy's Report Says Immigration Benefits the U.S." *New York Times* (May 18):1, 12.

Peck, Don. 2010. "How a New Jobless Era Will Transform America." *The Atlantic* 305 (March):42–56.

Penner, Andrew M. 2008. "Gender Differences in Extreme Mathematical Achievement: An International Perspective on Biological and Social Factors." *American Journal of Sociology* 114:S138–S170.

Pessen, Edward. 1984. *The Log Cabin Myth: The Social Backgrounds of the Presidents*. New Haven, CT: Yale University Press.

Peterson, V. Spike, and Anne Sisson Runyan. 1999. *Global Gender Issues*. 2d ed. Boulder, CO: Westview.

Pérez-Peña, Richard. 2012. "To Enroll More Minority Students, Colleges Work Around the Courts. *New York Times* (April 2):A9.

Pew Charitable Trusts. 2012. *Pursuing the American Dream: Economic Mobility Across Generations*. Washington, DC: Pew Charitable Trusts, Economic Mobility Project.

Pew Economic Mobility Project. 2007. "Economic Mobility: Is the American Dream Alive and Well?" Washington, DC: Economic Mobility Project.

_____. 2009. "Findings from a National Survey & Focus Groups on Economic Mobility." (March).

Pew Hispanic Center. 2011. "Hispanic College Enrollment Spikes, Narrowing Gaps with Other Groups." Washington, DC: Pew Hispanic Center.

Pew Research Center. 2005. *Mapping the Political Landscape 2005*. Washington, DC: Pew Research Center.

_____. 2008a. "Internet Overtakes Newspapers as News Outlet." (December 23). http://people-press.org/reports/pdf/479.pdf

_____. 2008b. "Inside the Middle Class: Bad Times Hit the Good Life." (April 9). http://pewsocialtrends.org/pubs/706/middle-class-poll.

_____. 2008c. "Men or Women? Who's the Better Leader? A Paradox in Public Attitudes." Washington, DC: Pew Research Center.

_____. 2009a. *Pew Economic Mobility Survey*. (February). http://www.economic.mobility.org/poll2009.

_____. 2009b. "Public Backs Affirmative Action, But Not Minority Preferences." (June 2). http://pewresearch.org/pubs/1240/.

_____. 2009c. "Civic Engagement Online: Politics as Usual." (September 1). http://pewresearch.org/pubs/1328/.

_____. 2011. "Wealth Gaps Rise to Record Highs Between Whites, Blacks and Hispanics." Washington, DC: Pew Research Center.

_____. 2012a. *The Rise of Intermarriage*. Washington, DC: Pew Research Center.

_____. 2012b. "Rising Share of Americans See Conflict Between Rich and Poor." (January 11). http://www.pewsocialtrends.org.

_____. 2012c. *Trends in American Values: 1987–2012.* (June 4). Washington, DC: Pew Research Center.

_____. 2012d. "Trends in News Consumption: 1991–2012" (September 27). Washington, DC: Pew Research Center.

Phillips, Kevin. 1990. *The Politics of Rich and Poor: Wealth and the American Electorate in the Reagan Aftermath.* New York: Random House.

_____. 1994. *Boiling Point: Democrats, Republicans and the Decline of Middle-Class Prosperity.* New York: HarperCollins.

_____. 1995. "Rich Transforming U.S. Playgrounds." *USA Today* (August 23):11A.

_____. 2002. *Wealth and Democracy: A Political History of the American Rich.* New York: Broadway Books.

_____. 2004. *American Dynasty: Aristocracy, Fortune, and the Politics of Deceit in the House of Bush.* New York: Penguin.

_____. 2008. "High Noon for the Republican Party." *Harper's Magazine* (July):33–40.

Piketty, Thomas, and Emmanuel Saez. 2006. "How Progressive Is the U.S. Federal Tax System? A Historical and International Perspective." Working Paper 12404. Cambridge, MA: National Bureau of Economic Research.

Pinker, Susan. 2008. *The Sexual Paradox: Men, Women, and the Real Gender Gap.* New York: Scribner.

Piven, Frances Fox, and Richard A. Cloward. 1978. *Poor People's Movements.* New York: Vintage.

Plamenatz, John. 1971. *Ideology.* London: Macmillan.

Plous, Scott. 1996. "Ten Myths about Affirmative Action." *Journal of Social Issues* 52(4):25–31.

Polivka, Anne E. 1996. "A Profile of Contingent Workers." *Monthly Labor Review* 119(October):10–21.

Pollack, Andrew. 1996. "Few Women on Japan's Assembly Lines." *New York Times* (April 26):A8.

_____. 1997. "Opportunity at a Price." *New York Times* (July 8):C1, C4.

Porter, John. 1965. *The Vertical Mosaic: An Analysis of Social Class and Power in Canada.* Toronto: University of Toronto Press.

Portes, Alejandro, and Rubén Rumbaut. 2006. *Immigrant America: A Portrait.* 3d ed. Berkeley: University of California Press.

Postman, Neil. 1985. *Amusing Ourselves to Death: Public Discourse in the Age of Show Business.* New York: Penguin.

Poulantzas, Nicos. 1973. *Political Power and Social Classes.* London: NLB and Sheed and Ward.

Prewitt, Kenneth, and Alan Stone. 1973. *The Ruling Elites.* New York: Harper & Row.

Prior, Markus. 2007. *Post-Broadcast Democracy: How Media Choice Increases Inequality in Political Involvement and Polarizes Elections.* New York: Cambridge University Press.

Puddington, Arch. 1992. "Is White Racism the Problem?" *Commentary* (July): 31–36.

Putnam, Robert D. 1976. *The Comparative Study of Political Elites.* Englewood Cliffs, NJ: Prentice Hall.

_____. 2000. *Bowling Alone: The Collapse and Revival of American Community.* New York: Simon & Schuster.

Qian, Zhenchao, and Daniel T. Lichter. 2007. "Social Boundaries and Marital Assimilation: Interpreting Trends in Racial and Ethnic Intermarriage." *American Sociological Review* 72:68–94.

Rado, Diane. 2007. "Rich School, Poor School." *Chicago Tribune* (February 4). http://articles.chicagotribune.com/2007-02-04/news/0702040055_1.

Rainwater, Lee, and Timothy M. Smeeding. 2003. *Poor Kids in a Rich Country: America's Children in Comparative Perspective*. New York: Russell Sage Foundation.

Raksha, Arora. 2005. "Americans Dissatisfied with Government's Efforts on Poverty." *Gallup Poll Tuesday Briefing* (October 25):60–61.

Ramer, Samuel C. 1990. "Feldshers and Rural Health Care in the Early Soviet Period." In *Health and Society in Revolutionary Russia*, edited by Susan Gross Solomon and John F. Hutchinson, 121–145. Bloomington: Indiana University Press.

Ratcliffe, R. G. 1998. "Governor Gets His Pot of Baseball Gold from Sale of Texas Rangers." *Houston Chronicle* (June 18):35.

Rawley, James A. 1981. *The Transatlantic Slave Trade: A History*. New York: North.

Rawls, John. 1971. *A Theory of Justice*. Cambridge, MA: Harvard University Press.

Ray, Rebecca, Janet C. Gornick, and John Schmitt. 2009. "Parental Leave Policies in 21 Countries: Assessing Generosity and Gender Equality." Washington, DC: Center for Economic and Policy Research.

Reeves, Jay. 2002. "Hyundai Is Latest to Choose Alabama." *Detroit Free Press* (April 3):1E, 4E.

Reich, Robert B. 1992. *The Work of Nations: Preparing Ourselves for 21st Century Capitalism*. New York: Vintage.

———. 1998. "Working Class Dogged." *Mother Jones* (March/April):40.

———. 1994. "Meet the Nimble New Middle Class." *Washington Post* (March 27):M5.

———. 2001. *The Future of Success*. New York: Alfred A. Knopf.

———. 2007. *Supercapitalism: The Transformation of Business, Democracy, and Everyday Life*. New York: Knopf.

———. 2010. *Aftershock: The Next Economy and America's Future*. New York: Knopf.

Reiman, Jeffrey G. 2005. *The Rich Get Richer, and the Poor Get Prison: Ideology, Class and Criminal Justice*. 7th ed. Boston: Allyn & Bacon.

Reischauer, Edwin O. 1988. *The Japanese Today: Change and Continuity*. Cambridge, MA: Harvard University Press.

Reskin, Barbara, and Irene Padavic. 2002. *Women and Men at Work*. 2d ed. Thousand Oaks, CA: Pine Forge Press.

Rich, Motoko. 2010. "For the Unemployed Over 50, Fears of Never Working Again." *New York Times* (September 19).

Ridgeway, Cecilia L. 2011. *Framed by Gender: How Gender Inequality Persists in the Modern World*. New York: Oxford University Press.

Rifkin, Jeremy. 2000. *The Age of Access: The New Culture of Hypercapitalism Where All of Life Is a Paid-for Experience*. New York: Tarcher/Putnam.

———. 2004. *The End of Work: The Decline of the Global Labor Force and the Dawn of the Post-Market Era*. Rev. Ed. New York: G. P. Putnam's Sons.

Rivera, Amaad, Jeannette Huezo, Christina Kasica, and Dedrick Muhammad. 2009. "State of the Dream 2009: The Silent Depression." Boston: United for a Fair Economy.

Rivers, Caryl, and Rosalind C. Barnett. 2011. *The Truth About Girls and Boys: Challenging Toxic Stereotypes About Our Children.* New York: Columbia University Press.

Robertson, Wyndham. 1973. "The Highest Ranking Women in Big Business." *Fortune* 90(April):81–89.

Robison, Jennifer. 2003. "Social Classes in U.S., Britain, and Canada." *Gallup Poll Tuesday Briefing* (August 5):102–103.

Robinson, Linda, and Jack Epstein. 1994. "Battered by the Myth of Machismo." *U.S. News & World Report* (April 4):41–42.

Rose, Arnold. 1967. *The Power Structure.* New York: Oxford University Press.

Rosenbaum, David E. 1996. "In Political Money Game, the Year of Big Loopholes." *New York Times* (December 26):A1, A10.

Rosenblatt, Roger. 1999. "Introduction." In *Consuming Desires: Consumption, Culture, and the Pursuit of Happiness,* edited by Roger Rosenblatt, 1–22. Washington, DC: Island Press.

Rosenthal, Robert, and Lenore Jacobson. 1968. *Pygmalion in the Classroom: Teacher Expectations and Pupils' Intellectual Development.* New York: Holt, Rinehart, and Winston.

Rosenthal, Neal H. 1995. "The Nature of Occupational Employment Growth: 1983–93." *Monthly Labor Review* (June):45–54.

Rossi, Alice. 1977. "A Biosocial Perspective on Parenting." *Daedalus* 106:1–31.

———. 1984. "Gender and Parenthood." *American Sociological Review* 49:1–18.

Rothenberg, Paula S. 1998. *Race, Class, and Gender in the United States: An Integrated Study.* 4th ed. New York: St. Martin's.

Rothkopf, David. 2008. *Superclass: The Global Power Elite and the World They Are Making.* New York: Farrar, Straus and Giroux.

Rouse, Cecilia Elena, and Lisa Barrow. 2006. "U.S. Elementary and Secondary Schools: Equalizing Opportunity or Replicating the Status Quo?" *The Future of Children* 16(Fall):99–123.

Rubin, Lillian B. 1994. *Families on the Fault Line: America's Working Class Speaks about the Family, the Economy, Race and Ethnicity.* New York: HarperPerennial.

Rudolph, Lloyd, and Susanne Hoeker Rudolph. 1967. *The Modernity of Tradition: Political Development in India.* Chicago: University of Chicago Press.

Rumbaut, Rubén G. 2011. "Pigments of Our Imagination: The Racialization of the Hispanic-Latino Category." Washington, DC: Migration Policy Institute.

Rutenberg, Jim. 2012. "The Republicans' $3 Million Weekend in the Hamptons." *New York Times* (July 7).

Ryan, William. 1975. *Blaming the Victim.* Rev. ed. New York: Vintage.

Ryscavage, Paul. 1999. *Income Inequality in America: An Analysis of Trends.* Armonk, NY: M. E. Sharpe.

Rytina, Steve. 2000. "Is Occupational Mobility Declining in the US?" *Social Forces* 78:1227–1276.

Safa, Helen I. 1990. "Women and Industrialization in the Caribbean." In *Women, Employment, and the Family in the International Division of Labour,* edited by Sharon Stichter and Jane L. Parpart, 72–97. Philadelphia: Temple University Press.

Saez, Emmanuel. 2012. "Striking It Richer: The Evolution of Top Incomes in the United States (Updated with 2009 and 2010 estimates)." http://elsa.berkeley.edu/~saez/TabFig2010.xls.

Saito, Yoshitaka, and George Farkas. 2004. "The *Burakumin:* An Updated Review." *International Journal of Contemporary Sociology* 41:232–250.

Sampson, Hannah. 2010. "Fisher Island, Haven of the Rich, Experiences Dose of Reality." *Miami Herald* (May 23).

Sampson, Robert J. 2009. "Racial Stratification and the Durable Tangle of Neighborhood Inequality." *Annals of the American Academy of Political and Social Science* 621:260–280.

Samuelson, Robert J. 1997. "The Rich and Deserving." *Washington Post National Weekly Edition* (August 18):24.

Sandefur, Gary. 1996. "Welfare Doesn't Cause Illegitimacy and Single Parenthood." *Chronicle of Higher Education* (October 4):B7–B8.

Saunders, Peter. 1990. *Social Class and Stratification.* London: Routledge.

Scheuch, Erwin K. 2003. "The Structure of the German Elites across Regime Changes." *Comparative Sociology* 2(1):92–133.

Schlozman, Kay Lehman, Benjamin I. Page, Sidney Verba, and Morris P. Fiorina. 2005. "Inequalities of Political Voice." In *Inequality and American Democracy: What We Know and What We Need to Learn,* edited by Lawrence R. Jacobs and Theda Skocpol, 19–87. New York: Russell Sage Foundation.

Schmidhauser, John R. 1960. *The Supreme Court: Its Politics, Personalities, and Procedures.* New York: Holt, Rinehart and Winston.

Schmidt, Peter. 2007. "What Color Is an A?" *Chronicle of Higher Education* (June 1): A24–A28.

Schmitt, John. 2009. "Inequality as Policy: The United States since 1979." Washington, DC: Center for Economic and Policy Research.

Schor, Juliet B. 1992. *The Overworked American: The Unexpected Decline of Leisure.* New York: Basic Books.

———. 1998. *The Overspent American: Upscaling, Downshifting, and the New Consumer.* New York: Basic Books.

———. 1999. "What's Wrong with Consumer Society?" In *Consuming Desires: Consumption, Culture, and the Pursuit of Happiness,* edited by Roger Rosenblatt, 37–50. Washington, DC: Island Press.

———. 2000. *Do Americans Shop Too Much?* Boston: Beacon Press.

Schrag, Peter. 1995. "So You Want to Be Color Blind: Alternative Principles for Affirmative Action." *American Prospect* (Summer):38–43.

Schuman, Howard, Charlotte Steeh, and Lawrence Bobo. 1998. *Racial Attitudes in America: Trends and Interpretations.* Rev. ed. Cambridge, MA: Harvard University Press.

Schurman, Franz. 1971. "System, Contradictions, and Revolution in America." In *The New American Revolution,* edited by R. Aya and N. Miller, 18–96. New York: Free Press.

Scott, Janny. 2008. "Reflection on 'Class Matters.'" In *Social Class: How Does It Work?* Edited by Annette Lareau and Dalton Conley, 354–358. New York: Russell Sage Foundation.

Seelye, Katharine Q. 1997. "Lott Calls Gifts the 'American Way.'" *New York Times* (February 21):A15.

Seifert, Wolfgang. 1998. "Social and Economic Integration of Foreigners in Germany." In *Paths to Inclusion: The Integration of Migrants in the United States and Germany,* edited by Peter H. Schuck and Rainer Münz, 83–114. New York: Berghahn Books.

Sen, Amartya. 1995. *Inequality Reexamined.* Cambridge, MA: Harvard University Press.

Sengupta, Somini. 2008. "Crusader Sees Wealth as Cure for Caste Bias." *New York Times* (August 30):A1, A7.

Sennett, Richard, and Jonathan Cobb. 1973. *The Hidden Injuries of Class.* New York: Vintage.

Shapiro, Isaac, and Joel Friedman. 2006. "New CBO Data Indicate Growth in Long-Term Income Inequality Continues." Washington, DC: Center on Budget and Policy Priorities.

Shapiro, Thomas M. 2004. *The Hidden Cost of Being African American: How Wealth Perpetuates Inequality.* New York: Oxford University Press.

Sharkey, Patrick. 2009. *Neighborhoods and the Black-White Mobility Gap.* Pew Economic Mobility Project. www.economicmobility.org. (July).

Shaw, Donald L., and Maxwell E. McCombs. 1977. *The Emergence of American Political Issues: The Agenda-Setting Function of the Press.* St. Paul, MN: West Publishers.

Sherden, William A. 1998. *The Fortune Sellers: The Big Business of Buying and Selling Predictions.* New York: Wiley.

Sherkat, Darren E. 2004. "Religious Intermarriage in the United States: Trends, Patterns, and Predictions." *Social Science Research* 33:606–625.

Sherman, Arloc, Robert Greenstein, and Kathy Ruffing. 2012. "Contrary to 'Entitlement Society' Rhetoric, Over Nine-Tenths of Entitlement Benefits Go to Elderly, Disabled, or Working Households." Washington, DC: Center on Budget and Policy Priorities.

Shierholz, Heidi. 2012. "The 'Democratization of the Stock Market' that Never Happened." Economic Policy Institute. http://www.epi.org/publication/wealth-stock-maket-holdings/?utm_source=Economic+Policy+Institute&utm_campaign=46f159e07d-EPI-News&utm_medium=email.

Shils, Edward. 1968. "The Concept and Functions of Ideology." In *The International Encyclopedia of the Social Sciences,* vol. 7, edited by D. Sills, 66–76. New York: Macmillan.

Shipler, David K. 2004. *The Working Poor: Invisible in America.* New York: Knopf.

Shostak, Arthur B. 1969. *Blue Collar Life.* New York: Random House.

Sidel, Ruth. 1996. *Keeping Women and Children Last: America's War on the Poor.* New York: Penguin.

Simpson, Glenn R. 1994. "Of the Rich, by the Rich, for the Rich: Are Congress's Millionaires Turning Our Democracy into a Plutocracy?" *Washington Post* (April 17):C4.

Sims, Calvin. 1997. "Justice in Peru: Rape Victim Is Pressed to Marry Attacker." *New York Times* (March 12):A1, A8.

Sinha, Surajit. 1967. "Caste in India: Its Essential Pattern of Socio-Cultural Integration." In *Caste and Race: Comparative Approaches,* edited by Anthony de Reuck and Julie Knight, 92–105. Boston: Little, Brown.

Skocpol, Theda. 1996. "Unravelling from Above." *American Prospect* 25 (March–April):20–25.

Skocpol, Theda, and Vanessa Williamson. 2012. *The Tea Party and the Remaking of Republican Conservatism.* New York: Oxford University Press.

Skrentny, John David. 1996. *The Ironies of Affirmative Action: Politics, Culture, and Justice in America.* Chicago: University of Chicago Press.

————. 2002. *The Minority Rights Revolution*. Cambridge, MA: Belknap Press of Harvard University.

Slackman, Michael. 2007. "Voices Rise in Egypt to Shield Girls from an Old Practice." *New York Times* (September 20):A1, A8.

Slomczynski, Kazimierz M., and Tadeusz K. Krauze. 1987. "Cross-National Similarity in Social Mobility Patterns: A Direct Test of the Featherman-Jones-Hauser Hypothesis." *American Sociological Review* 52:598–611.

Smeeding, Timothy M. 1998. "U.S. Income Inequality in a Cross-National Perspective: Why Are We So Different?" In *The Inequality Paradox: Growth of Income Disparity*, edited by James A. Auerbach and Richard S. Belous, 194–217. Washington, DC: National Policy Association.

————. 2004. "Public Policy and Economic Inequality: The United States in Comparative Perspective." Syracuse, NY: Campbell Public Affairs Institute, the Maxwell School of Syracuse University.

————. 2005. "Public Policy and Economic Inequality: The United States in Comparative Perspective." *Social Science Quarterly* 86:955–983.

————. 2006. "Poor People in Rich Nations: The United States in Comparative Perspective." *Journal of Economic Perspectives.* 20:69–90.

Smeeding, Timothy M., Lee Rainwater, and Gary Burtless. 2001. "U.S. Poverty in a Cross-National Context." In *Understanding Poverty*, edited by Sheldon H. Danzier and Robert H. Haveman, 162–189. New York: Russell Sage Foundation.

Smith, Adam. 1776. *Inquiry into the Nature and Causes of the Wealth of Nations*. London: W. Strahan.

Smith, David H. 1980. *Participation in Social and Political Activities: A Comprehensive Analysis of Political Involvement, Expressive Leisure Time, and Helping Behavior*. San Francisco: Jossey-Bass.

Smith, James P. 2001. "Race and Ethnicity in the Labor Market. Trends over the Short and Long Term." In *America Becoming: Racial Trends and Their Consequences.* vol. II, edited by Neil J. Smelser, William Julius Wilson, and Faith Mitchell, 52–97. Washington, DC: National Academy Press.

Sniderman, Paul M., and Edward G. Carmines. 1997. *Reaching beyond Race*. Cambridge, MA: Harvard University Press.

Sniderman, Paul M., and Thomas Piazza. 1993. *The Scar of Race*. Cambridge, MA: Belknap Press.

Soltow, Lee. 1984. "Wealth Inequality in the United States in 1798 and 1860." *Review of Economics and Statistics* 66:444–451.

South, Scott J. 1988. "Sex Ratios, Economic Power, and Women's Roles: A Theoretical Extension and Empirical Test." *Journal of Marriage and the Family* 50:19–31.

Sowell, Thomas. 1990. *Preferential Policies: An International Perspective*. New York: William Morrow.

Spatig-Amerikaner, Ary. 2012. "Unequal Education: Federal Loophole Enables Lower Spending on Students of Color." Center for American Progress (August 22). http://www.americanprogress.org/issues/education/report/2012/08/22/29002/.

Spring, Joel H. 1972. *Education and the Rise of the Corporate State*. Boston: Beacon.

Stampp, Kenneth M. 1956. *The Peculiar Institution: Slavery in the Ante-Bellum South*. New York: Knopf.

Stanley, David T., Dean E. Mann, and Jameson W. Doig. 1967. *Men Who Govern*. Washington, DC: Brookings Institution.

Steele, Shelby. 1991. *The Content of Our Character: A New Vision of Race in America.* New York: HarperPerennial.

Steinberg, Stephen. 1995. *Turning Back: The Retreat from Racial Justice in American Thought and Policy.* Boston: Beacon Press.

Steinhauer, Jennifer. 1999. "For Women in Medicine, a Road to Compromise, Not Perks." *New York Times* (March 1):A1, A21.

Stevenson, Harold W., and James W. Stigler. 1992. *The Learning Gap: Why Our Schools Are Failing and What We Can Learn from Japanese and Chinese Education.* New York: Simon & Schuster.

Stewart, James B. 2012. "In Superrich, Clues to What Might Be in Romney's Returns." *New York Times* (August 10):A1.

Stiglitz, Joseph E. 2012. *The Price of Inequality: How Today's Divided Society Endangers Our Future.* New York: Norton.

Stodghill, Ron. 2007. "Is There Room at the Top for Black Executives?" *New York Times* (November 1):C1, C11.

Stoll, Michael. 2006. "Job Sprawl, Spatial Mismatch and Black Employment Disadvantage." *Journal of Policy Analysis and Management* 25:827–854.

———. 2008. "Race, Place, and Poverty Revisited." In *The Colors of Poverty: Why Racial and Ethnic Disparities Exist,* edited by Ann Chih Lin and David R. Harris, 201–231. New York: Russell Sage Foundation.

Stone, Chad, Hannah Shaw, Danilo Trisi, and Arloc Sherman. 2012. "A Guide to Statistics on Historical Trends in Income Inequality." Washington, DC: Center on Budget and Policy Priorities.

Stone, Pamela. 2009. "Getting to Equal: Progress, Pitfalls, and Policy Solutions on the Road to Gender Parity in the Workplace." *Pathways* (Spring):3–7.

Sugimoto, Yoshio. 1997. *An Introduction to Japanese Society.* Cambridge: Cambridge University Press.

Sullivan, Teresa A. 2009. "Consumer Indebtedness and the Withering of the American Dream." *Pathways* (Winter):3–5.

Sullivan, Teresa A., Elizabeth Warren, and Jay Lawrence Westbrook. 2000. *The Fragile Middle Class: Americans in Debt.* New Haven, CT: Yale University Press.

Swain, Carol. 2007. "The Congressional Black Caucus and the Impact of Immigration on African American Unemployment." In *Debating Immigration,* edited by Carol M. Swain, 175–188. New York: Cambridge University Press.

Swartz, Mimi. 2007. "Shop Stewards on Fantasy Island?" *New York Times Magazine* (June 10):58–64.

Swidler, Ann. 1992. "Inequality and American Culture: The Persistence of Voluntarism." *American Behavioral Scientist* 35:606–629.

Syme, S. Leonard, and Lisa F. Berkman. 1997. "Social Class, Susceptibility, and Sickness." In *The Sociology of Health and Illness,* 5th ed., edited by Peter Conrad, 29–35. New York: St. Martin's.

Symonds, William C. 2006. "Campus Revolutionary." *BusinessWeek* (February 27):64–70.

Tannenbaum, Frank. 1947. *Slave and Citizen: The Negro in the Americas.* New York: Knopf.

Tatian, Peter A., G. Thomas Kingsley, Margery Austin Turner, Jennifer Comey, and Randy Rosso. 2008. *State of Washington, D.C.'s Neighborhoods.* Washington, DC: Urban Institute.

Taylor, Paul, Ana Gonzalez-Barrera, Jeffrey Passel, and Mark Hugo Lopez. 2012. "An Awakened Giant: The Hispanic Electorate Is Likely to Double by 2030." Washington, DC: Pew Hispanic Center.

Taylor, Paul, Mark Hugo Lopez, Jessica Hamar Martinez, and Gabriel Velasco. 2012. "When Labels Don't Fit: Hispanics and Their Views of Identity." Washington, DC: Pew Research Center.

Taylor, William L. 1997. "Affirmative Action: The Questions to Be Asked." In *Double Exposure: Poverty and Race in America,* edited by Chester Hartman, 171–173. Armonk, NY: M. E. Sharpe.

Thernstrom, Abigail, and Stephen Thernstrom. 1998. "Black Progress: How Far We've Come—and How Far We Have to Go." *Brookings Review* (Spring):12–16.

Thernstrom, Stephan, and Abigail Thernstrom. 1997. *America in Black and White: One Nation, Indivisible.* New York: Simon & Schuster.

Thomas, Jo. 1997. "Satisfaction in Job Well Done Is Only Reward for E-Mail Software Inventor." *New York Times* (January 21):A6.

Thompson, Craig J. 2000. "A New Puritanism?" In *Do Americans Spend Too Much?* Edited by Juliet Schor. 63–68. Boston: Beacon Press.

Thompson, John B. 1995. *The Media and Modernity: A Social Theory of the Media.* Cambridge: Polity.

Thornton, Russell. 2001. "Trends among American Indians in the United States." In *America Becoming: Racial Trends and Their Consequences,* vol. 1, edited by Neil J. Smelser, William Julius Wilson, and Faith Mitchell, 135–169. Washington, DC: National Academy Press.

Thurow, Lester C. 1975. *Generating Inequality: Mechanisms of Distribution in the U.S. Economy.* New York: Basic Books.

———. 1995. "Why Their World Might Crumble." *New York Times Magazine* (November 19):78–79.

———. 1996. *The Future of Capitalism: How Today's Economic Forces Shape Tomorrow's World.* New York: William Morrow.

———. 1999. *Building Wealth: The New Rules for Individuals, Companies, and Nations in a Knowledge-Based Economy.* New York: HarperCollins.

Tiger, Lionel. 1969. *Men in Groups.* London: Nelson.

Toossi, Mitra. 2006. "A New Look at Long-Term Labor Force Projections to 2050." *Monthly Labor Review* (November):19–39.

Toppo, Greg. 2003. "SAT Scores Continue to Rise, Record Set in Math Section." *USA Today* (August 26).

Toth, Jennifer. 1993. *Mole People: Life in the Tunnels Beneath New York City.* Chicago: Chicago Review Press.

Trisi, Danilo, and LaDonna Pavetti. 2012. "TANF Weakening as a Safety Net for Poor Families." Washington, DC: Center on Budget and Policy Priorities.

Truman, David B. 1951. *The Governmental Process.* New York: Random House.

Tuchman, Gaye. 1978. *Making News.* New York: Free Press.

Tucker, Robert C., ed. 1972. *The Marx-Engels Reader.* New York: Norton.

Tumin, Melvin M. 1953. "Some Principles of Stratification: A Critical Analysis." *American Sociological Review* 18:387–394.

Turner, Ralph. 1960. "Sponsored and Contest Mobility and the School System." *American Sociological Review* 25:855–867.

Twitchell, James B. 1996. *ADCULTusa: The Triumph of Advertising in American Culture.* New York: Columbia University Press.

———. 2005. "Globalization: It's Not Just Wages." *New York Times* (June 17):C1, C4.

Underhill, Paco. 2009. Interview, *Future Tense,* ABC Radio National (May 28). www.abc.net/au/rn/futuretense/stories/2009/2578395.htm.

UNDP (United Nations Development Programme). 1993. *Human Development Report 1993*. New York: Oxford University Press.

_____. 2005. *Human Development Report 2005*. New York: Oxford University Press.

_____. 2009. *Human Development Report 2009*. Basingstoke, Hampshire: Palgrave Macmillan.

_____. 2010. *Power, Voice and Rights: A Turning Point for Gender Equality in Asia and the Pacific*. Colombo, Sri Lanka: United Nations Development Programme.

_____. 2011. *Human Development Index 2011*.

UNICEF. 2007. *State of the World's Children 2007: Women and Children: The Double Dividend of Gender Equality*. New York: United Nations.

_____. 2012. "Childinfo: Monitoring the Situation of Children and Women." http://www.childinfo.org/fgmc_progress.html.

UNICEF Innocenti Research Centre. 2012. "Measuring Child Poverty: New League Tables of Child Poverty in the World's Rich Countries." *Innocenti Report Card 10*. Florence, Italy: UNICEF Innocenti Research Centre.

United Nations. 1991. *The World's Women, 1970–1990: Trends and Statistics*. New York: United Nations Publications.

_____. 2000. *The World's Women, 2000*. New York: United Nations.

_____. 2003. "Background Paper of the Task Force on Education and Gender Equality." Millennium Project. http://www.unmillenniumproject.org/documents/tf03edapr18.pdf.

_____. 2010. *The World's Women 2010: Trends and Statistics*. New York: United Nations Department of Economic and Social Affairs.

United Nations Economic and Social Council (UNESCO). 2006. *Racism, Racial Discrimination, Xenophobia and All Forms of Discrimination: Mission to Japan*. New York: United Nations.

United Nations, International Labor Organization. 1996. "More and Better Jobs for Women." Report issued July 29, 1996.

Urbina, Ian. 2006. "Keeping It Secret as the Family Car Becomes a Home." *New York Times* (April 2):1, 20.

U.S. Census Bureau. 1975. *Historical Statistics of the U.S.: Colonial Times to 1970. Part I*. Washington, DC: U.S. Government Printing Office.

_____. 2001. *Survey of Minority-Owned Business Enterprises: 1997. Economic Census*. Washington, DC: U.S. Government Printing Office.

_____. 2002a. *The American Indian and Alaska Native Population: 2000*. Washington, DC: U.S. Government Printing Office.

_____. 2002b. *Statistical Abstract of the United States: 2002*. Washington, DC: U.S. Government Printing Office.

_____. 2003a. *The Hispanic Population in the United States: March 2002*. CPR P20–545. Washington, DC: U.S. Government Printing Office.

_____. 2003b. *Statistical Abstract of the United States: 2003*. Washington, DC: U.S. Government Printing Office.

_____. 2003c. *Educational Attainment: 2000*. C2KBR-24. Washington, DC: U.S. Government Printing Office.

_____. 2003d. *School Enrollment: 2000*. C2KBR-26. Washington, DC: U.S. Government Printing Office.

_____. 2006. *The Asian and Pacific Islander Population in the United States: March 2004*. Washington, DC: U.S. Government Printing Office.

———. 2009. *Voting and Registration in the Election of November 2008—Detailed Tables.* Washington, DC: U.S. Government Printing Office.

———. 2011a. *Income, Poverty, and Health Insurance Coverage in the United States: 2010.* Washington, DC: U.S. Government Printing Office.

———. 2011b. *Voting and Registration in the Election of November 2010—Detailed Tables.* Washington, DC: U.S. Government Printing Office.

———. 2012a. *American Community Survey.* http://factfinder.census.gov.

———. 2012b. Educational Attainment in the United States: 2009. Washington, DC: U.S. Government Printing Office.

———. 2012c. *Statistical Abstract of the U.S. 2012. Washington,* DC: U.S. Government Printing Office.

———. 2012d. *Educational Attainment in the United States: 2010, Detailed Tables.* http://www.census.gov/hhes/socdemo/education/data/cps/2010/tables.html.

———. 2012e. *Voting and Registration in the Election of November 2010.* Washington, DC: U.S. Government Printing Office.

———. 2012f. *Income, Poverty, and Health Insurance Coverage in the United States: 2011.* Washington, DC: U.S. Government Printing Office.

U.S. Commission on Civil Rights. 2004. *Broken Promises: Evaluating the Native American Health Care System.* http://www.usccr.gov/pubs/nahealth/nabroken.pdf.

U.S. Department of Education. 1992. *Digest of Education Statistics.* Washington, DC: U.S. Government Printing Office.

———. 2009. *The Condition of Education 2009.* Washington, DC: U.S. Government Printing Office.

U.S. Department of Health and Human Services. 2012. *Temporary Assistance for Needy Families Program. Ninth Report to Congress.* Washington, DC: U.S. Government Printing Office.

U.S. Department of Labor, Bureau of Labor Statistics. 2006b. "Work Stoppage Data." http://data.bls.gov/cgi-bin/surveymost.

U.S. Department of State. 2012. *Trafficking in Persons Report* (June). Washington, DC: U.S. Department of State.

Useem, Michael. 1978. "The Inner Group of the American Capitalist Class." *Social Problems* 25:225–240.

U.S. Government Accountability Office (GAO). 2006. *Employment Arrangements: Improved Outreach Could Help Ensure Proper Worker Classification. Report to the Ranking Minority Member, Committee on Health, Education, Labor, and Pensions. U.S. Senate.* www.gao.gov/cgi-bin/getrpt?GAO-06-656

U.S. Office of Management and Budget. 2012. *The Budget of the United States Government.* http://www.gpo.gov.

U.S. Social Security Administration. 2012. *Social Security Programs Throughout the World: Europe 2012.* Washington, DC: U.S. Government Printing Office.

Valentine, Charles A. 1971. "The 'Culture of Poverty': Its Scientific Significance and Its Implications for Actions." In *The Culture of Poverty: A Critique,* edited by Eleanor Burke Leacock, 193–225. New York: Simon & Schuster.

Valletta, Robert G. 2006. "The Ins and Outs of Poverty in Advanced Economies: Government Policy and Poverty Dynamics in Canada, Germany, Great Britain, and the United States." *Review of Income and Wealth* 52:261–284.

van den Berghe, Pierre L. 1967. *South Africa: A Study in Conflict.* Berkeley: University of California Press.

———. 1978. *Race and Racism: A Comparative Perspective.* 2d ed. New York: Wiley.

Veblen, Thorstein. 1899. *The Theory of the Leisure Class.* New York: Macmillan.

Verba, Sidney. 2006. "Fairness, Equality, and Democracy: Three Big Words." *Social Research* 73:499–540.

Verba, Sidney, and Norman H. Nie. 1972. *Participation in America.* New York: Harper & Row.

Verba, Sidney, and Garry R. Orren. 1985. *Equality in America: The View from the Top.* Cambridge, MA: Harvard University Press.

Verba, Sidney, Kay Lehman Schlozman, and Henry E. Brady. 1995. *Voice and Equality: Civic Voluntarism in American Politics.* Cambridge, MA: Harvard University Press.

Vianello, Mino, and Gwen Moore. 2004. *Women and Men in Political and Business Elites: A Comparative Study in the Industrialized World.* London: Sage.

Vincent, Louise. 2008. "The Limitations of 'Inter-Racial Contact': Stories from Young South Africa." *Ethnic and Racial Studies* 31:1426–1451.

Visser, Jelle. 2006. "Union Membership Statistics in 24 Countries." *Monthly Labor Review* 129(January):38–49.

Vlasic, Bill, and Nick Bunkley. 2009. "Dead End in Detroit for White-Collar Workers." *New York Times* (February 17):B1, B5.

Vogel, Ezra F. 1979. *Japan as Number 1: Lessons for America.* Cambridge, MA: Harvard University Press.

Wacquant, Loic. 2008. "Pierre Bourdieu." pp. 261–277 in Rob Stones (ed.), *Key Sociological Thinkers.* 2nd ed. Houndmills, Basingstoke: Palgrave Macmillan.

Waldman, Steven, and Rich Thomas. 1990. "How Did It Happen?" *Newsweek* (May 21):27–28, 32.

Walker, Alan, and Carol Walker. 1995. "Poverty." In *The Social Science Encyclopedia,* 2d ed., edited by Adam Kuper and Jessica Kuper, 655–657. London: Routledge.

Wallace, James, and Jim Erickson. 1992. *Hard Drive: Bill Gates and the Making of the Microsoft Empire.* New York: Wiley.

Walsh, Mary Roth (ed.). 1997. *Women, Men, and Gender: Ongoing Debates.* New Haven, CT: Yale University Press.

Warner, W. Lloyd, and James Abegglen. 1963. *Big Business Leaders in America.* New York: Atheneum.

Warren, Elizabeth, and Amelia Warren Tyagi. 2003. *The Two-Income Trap: Why Middle-Class Mothers and Fathers Are Going Broke.* New York: Basic Books.

Washington Post. 2012. "Washington Post–ABC News Poll, April 5–8." http://www.washingtonpost.com/wo-srv/politics/polls/postabcpoll_04082012.htn. Accessed April 11, 2012.

Waters, Mary C. 1990. *Ethnic Options: Choosing Identities in America.* Berkeley: University of California Press.

Waters, Mary C., and Karl Eschbach. 1995. "Immigration and Ethnic and Racial Inequality in the United States." *Annual Review of Sociology* 21:419–446.

Wax, Emily. 2008. "In India, New Opportunities for Women Draw Anger and Abuse from Men." *Washington Post* (August 25):A11.

Waxman, Sharon. 2006. "Paradise Bought." *New York Times* (July 2):1, 6.

Weber, Max. 1954. *Max Weber on Law in Economy and Society.* Edited by Max Rheinstein. Cambridge, MA: Harvard University Press.

Weinstein, James. 1968. *The Corporate Ideal in the Liberal State: 1900–1918.* Boston: Beacon Press.

Weisman, Steven R. 2005. "Saudi Women Have Message for U.S. Envoy." *New York Times* (September 28):A1, A12.

Weller, Christian E., and Jessica Lynch. 2009. "Household Wealth in Freefall: Americans' Private Safety Net in Tatters." Washington, DC: Center for American Progress.

Weller, Christian E., Julie Ajinkya, and Jane Farrell. 2012. *The State of Communities of Color in the U.S. Economy.* Washington, DC: Center for American Progress.

Western, Bruce. 2006. *Punishment and Inequality.* New York: Russell Sage Foundation.

Western, Bruce, and Becky Pettit. 2005. "Black-White Wage Inequality, Employment Rates, and Incarceration." *American Journal of Sociology* 111:553–578.

Western, Bruce, and Jake Rosenfeld. 2011. "Unions, Norms, and the Rise in U.S. Wage Inequality." *American Sociological Review* 76:532–533.

Western, Bruce, and Christopher Wildeman. 2009. "The Black Family and Mass Incarceration." *Annals of the American Academy of Political and Social Science* 621(1):221–242.

Whitefield, Mimi. 2000. "Hispanic Firms: Global View Spurs Growth of Hispanic Companies." *Miami Herald* (October 7). http://www.herald.com.

Whoriskey, Peter. 2012. "U.S. Manufacturing Sees Shortage of Skilled Factory Workers." Washington Post (February 19). http://www.washingtonpost.com/business/economy/US-manufacturing-sees-shortage-of-skilled-factory-workers/2012/02/17/gIQAoOMLOR-story.html.

Wilkes, Rima, and John Iceland. 2004. "Hypersegregation in the Twenty-First Century." *Demography* 41:23–36.

Williams, Christine L. 1995. *Still a Man's World: Men Who Do "Women's Work."* Berkeley: University of California Press.

Williams, David R. 1990. "Socioeconomic Differentials in Health: A Review and Redirection." *Social Psychology Quarterly* 53:81–99.

Williams, David R., and James Lardner. 2005. "Cold Truths about Class, Race, and Health." In *Inequality Matters: The Growing Economic Divide in America and Its Poisonous Consequences,* edited by James Lardner and David A. Smith, 102–114. New York: New Press.

Williams, Joan C., and Heather Boushey. 2010. "The Three Faces of Work-Family Conflict: the Poor, the Professionals, and the Missing Middle." Washington, DC: Center for American Progress.

Williams, Robin, Jr. 1970. *American Society: A Sociological Interpretation.* 3d ed. New York: Knopf.

Williamson, Jeffrey, and Peter H. Lindert. 1980. *American Inequality: A Macroeconomic History.* New York: Academic Press.

Wilson, Franklin D. 2003. "Ethnic Niching and Metropolitan Labor Markets." *Social Science Research* 32:429–466.

Wilson, William Julius. 1980. *The Declining Significance of Race.* 2d ed. Chicago: University of Chicago Press.

———. 1987. *The Truly Disadvantaged: The Inner City, the Underclass, and Public Policy.* Chicago: University of Chicago Press.

———. 1991. "Studying Inner-City Social Dislocations: The Challenge of Public Agenda Research." *American Sociological Review* 56:1–14.

———. 1994. "Race Neutral Programs and the Democratic Coalition." In *Debating Affirmative Action: Race, Gender, Ethnicity, and the Politics of Inclusion,* edited by Nicolaus Mills, 159–173. New York: Delta.

———. 1996. *When Work Disappears: The World of the New Urban Poor.* New York: Knopf.

_____. 1999 "Jobless Poverty: A New Form of Social Dislocation in the Inner-City Ghetto." In *A Nation Divided: Diversity, Inequality, and Community in American Society,* edited by Phyllis Moen, Donna Dempster-McClain, and Henry A. Walker, 133–150. Ithaca, NY: Cornell University Press.

_____. 2009. *More than Just Race: Being Black and Poor in the Inner City.* New York: Norton.

_____. 2012. "The Role of Elite Institutions." *The Chronicle of Higher Education* (July 2). http://chronicle.com/article/The-Role-of-Elite-Institutions/132639.

Wirth, Louis. 1945. "The Problem of Minority Groups." In *The Science of Man in the World Crisis,* edited by Ralph Linton, 347–372. New York: Columbia University Press.

Wolff, Edward N. 1995a. "How the Pie Is Sliced: America's Growing Concentration of Wealth." *American Prospect* (Summer):58–64.

_____. 1995b. *Top Heavy: A Study of the Increasing Inequality of Wealth in America.* New York: Twentieth Century Fund Press.

_____. 2000. *Recent Trends in Wealth Ownership, 1983–1998.* Working Paper No. 300. Annandale-on-Hudson, NY: Levy Economic Institute.

_____. 2002. *Top Heavy: The Increasing Inequality of Wealth in America and What Can Be Done about It.* New York: New Press.

_____. 2007. "Recent Trends in Household Wealth in the United States: Rising Debt and the Middle-Class Squeeze." Working Paper No. 502. Annandale-on-Hudson, NY: Levy Economics Institute.

_____. 2010. "Recent Trends in Household Wealth in the United States: Rising Debt and the Middle-Class Squeeze—an Update to 2007." Levy Economics Institute, Working Paper No. 589. http://www.levyinstitute.org/pubs/wp_589.pdf.

Wolfinger, Raymond E., and Steven J. Rosenstone. 1980. *Who Votes?* New Haven, CT: Yale University Press.

Woodward, C. Vann. 1974. *The Strange Career of Jim Crow.* 3d ed. New York: Oxford University Press.

Wootton, Barbara H. 1997. "Gender Differences in Occupational Employment." *Monthly Labor Review* (April):15–24.

World Bank. 2009. *World Development Indicators, 2009.* Washington, DC: World Bank.

_____. 2012. *World Development Indicators 2012.* Washington, DC: World Bank.

Wright, Erik Olin. 1978. *Class, Crisis, and the State.* London: Verso.

_____. 1985. *Classes.* London: Verso.

_____. 1997. *Class Counts: Comparative Studies in Class Analysis.* Cambridge: Cambridge University Press.

Wright, Erik Olin, Karen Shire, Shu-Ling Hwang, Maureen Dolan, and Janeen Baxter. 1992. "The Non-Effects of Class on the Gender Division of Labor in the Home: A Comparative Study of Sweden and the United States." *Gender and Society* 6: 252–282.

Wright, Kai. 2009. "The Assault on the Black Middle Class." *American Prospect* (July/August):A7–A10.

Wright, Lawrence. 1994. "One Drop of Blood." *New Yorker* (July 25):46–50, 52–55.

Wulf, Willam A. 2005. *The Importance of Foreign-born Scientists and Engineers to the Security of the United States.* Statement before the Subcommittee on Immigration, Border Security, and Claims, Committee on the Judiciary, U.S. House of Representatives, 15 September.

Wyatt, Ian D., and Daniel E. Hecker. 2006. "Occupational Changes during the 20th Century." *Monthly Labor Review* 129(March):35–57.

Yaqub, Reshma Memon. 2002. "Getting Inside the Ivy Gates." *Worth* (September): 94–104.

Yates, Steven. 1994. *Civil Wrongs: What Went Wrong with Affirmative Action.* San Francisco: ICS Press.

Yellen, Janet L. 1998. "Trends in Income Inequality." In *The Inequality Paradox: Growth of Income Disparity,* edited by James A. Auerbach and Richard S. Belous, 7–17. Washington, DC: National Policy Association.

Zeigler, Harmon, and Wayne Peak. 1970. "The Political Functions of the Educational System." *Sociology of Education* 43:115–142.

Zickuhr, Kathryn, and Aaron Smith. 2012. "Digital Differences." Pew Research Center's Internet and American Life Project. http://pewinternet.org/Reports/2012/Digital-differences. aspx.

Zweigenhaft, Richard L. 1975. "Who Represents America?" *Insurgent Sociologist* 5(Spring):119–130.

———. 1984. *Who Gets to the Top? Executive Suite Discrimination in the Eighties.* New York: American Jewish Committee.

———. 1987. "Minorities and Women of the Corporation: Will They Attain Seats of Power?" In *Power Elites and Organizations,* edited by G. W. Domhoff and T. R. Dye, 37–62. Newbury Park, CA: Sage.

Zweigenhaft, Richard L., and G. William Domhoff. 2006. *Diversity in the Power Elite: How It Happened, Why It Matters.* Lanham, MD: Rowman & Littlefield.

Index